Developing Core Literacy Proficiencies

GRADE 9

Teacher Edition

GRADE 9

TEACHER EDITION

Developing Core Literacy Proficiencies

JOSSEY-BASS
A Wiley Brand

Published by Jossey-Bass

A Wiley Brand

One Montgomery Street, Suite 1000, San Francisco, CA 94104-4594—www.josseybass.com

Library of Congress Cataloging-in-Publication Data

Names: Odell Education, author.
Title: Developing core literacy proficiencies. Grade 9 / Odell Education.
Description: Teacher edition. | 1 | San Francisco, CA : Jossey-Bass, 2016.
Identifiers: LCCN 2016007131 (print) | LCCN 2016013800 (ebook) | ISBN
  9781119192879 (paperback) | ISBN 9781119192886 (pdf) | ISBN 9781119192862
  (epub)
Subjects: LCSH: Language arts (Secondary)—Curricula—United States. | Common
  Core State Standards (Education)
Classification: LCC LB1631 .O39 2016 (print) | LCC LB1631 (ebook) | DDC
  428.0071/2—dc23
LC record available at http://lccn.loc.gov/2016007131

Cover Design: Wiley
Cover Image: ©Alfredo Dagli Orti/The Art Archive/Corbis Images

Printed in the United States of America

FIRST EDITION

PB Printing   10 9 8 7 6 5 4 3 2 1

ABOUT ODELL EDUCATION

Odell Education (OE) is dedicated to fostering creativity and critical thinking in students and the education community. OE has developed nationally validated and acclaimed literacy curriculum. OE collaborates with schools, states, and organizations on assessment, curriculum, and professional development projects and is recognized as a leading expert in the CCSS.

ACKNOWLEDGMENTS

Project director: Stephanie Smythe

Primary program designers:

- Rick Dills, EdD
- Judson Odell
- Ioana Radoi
- Daniel Fennessy

Curriculum consultant: Nemeesha Brown

Unit developers—Texts, notes, and questions:

- Reading Closely for Textual Details: "Education is the new currency": Luke Bauer
- Making Evidence-Based Claims: "The unexamined life is not worth living.": Mary Catherine Youmell, PhD, and Judson Odell
- Making Evidence-Based Claims about Literary Technique: "Macomber laughed, a very natural hearty laugh.": Judson Odell
- Researching to Deepen Understanding: Music: What role does it play in our lives?: Facundo Gomez and Keeva Kase

- Building Evidence-Based Arguments: "What is the virtue of a proportional response?": Judson Odell and Daniel Fennessy

We are grateful for feedback we received on early versions of units from Achieve's EQuIP Review Process, under the direction of Christine Tell, Alissa Peltzman, and Cristina Marks.

We are also grateful for the students and teachers of the Bay Shore Schools who collaborated with us to pilot the curriculum. Thanks especially to LaQuita Outlaw, Elizabeth Galarza, Caitlin Moreira, and Jen Ritter (who personally renamed the Supporting Evidence-Based Claims Tool).

We are especially grateful for New York State and the Regents Research Fund for funding the development of the earlier Open Educational Resource version of this curriculum. Without the support we received from Kristen Huff, David Abel, and Kate Gerson, none of this work would have been possible.

CONTENTS

Unit 3: Making Evidence-Based Claims about Literary Technique: "Macomber laughed, a very natural hearty laugh." 223

Contents

Contents

All materials from the Literacy Toolbox are available as editable and printable PDFs at www.wiley .com/go/coreliteracy. Use the following password: odell2016.

≡ DEVELOPING CORE LITERACY PROFICIENCIES: ≡ USER GUIDE

≡ A PROFICIENCY-BASED APPROACH TO DEVELOPING ≡ LITERACY

The Odell Education Developing Core Literacy Proficiencies Program is an integrated set of instructional materials designed to develop students' literacy and prepare them to succeed in college, career, and civic life. The program consists of five units that focus on four essential proficiencies:

Unit 1: Reading Closely for Textual Details

Unit 2: Making Evidence-Based Claims

Unit 3: Making Evidence-Based Claims about Literary Technique

Unit 4: Researching to Deepen Understanding

Unit 5: Building Evidence-Based Arguments

The program approaches the development of literacy through the intertwined building of knowledge, Literacy Skills, and Academic Habits. Over the course of the program's activities, students develop their literacy in an integrated, engaging, and empowering way, as they deepen their knowledge, improve their skills, and acquire habits that will serve them throughout their academic and professional careers.

KNOWLEDGE

Literacy is a dynamic mix of the skills and habits students develop and the knowledge they acquire. The content knowledge students have learned in one setting is often what sets them up for success in many others. Students' expanding base of important and interconnected ideas, concepts, and vocabulary becomes the foundation for their facility with challenging texts, topics, and tasks they encounter in the future. The texts and topics students encounter in the Developing Core Literacy Proficiencies Program have therefore been carefully selected to expose them to rich and varied ideas and perspectives of cultural significance. These texts not only equip students with key ideas for participating knowledgeably in the important discussions of our time but also contain the complexity of expression necessary for developing appropriate Literacy Skills.

In addition to the knowledge of their world that students build throughout the curriculum, students also learn key conceptual knowledge and academic vocabulary associated with literacy itself. The Developing Core Literacy Proficiencies Program explicitly teaches students the disciplinary concepts and words associated with reading, writing, discussion, and creative and critical thinking. By working with these concepts in a meaningful environment, students are empowered to understand, manage, and discuss their own literacy development with their peers and teachers.

LITERACY SKILLS

The curriculum's complex texts and the important cultural knowledge they present set the stage for students to learn the necessary skills to succeed in the information-rich contexts of our time. As students read and discuss the texts, activities focus on their development of an essential set of Literacy Skills. The Developing Core Literacy Proficiencies Program targets twenty essential skills ranging from **Making Inferences** to **Reflecting Critically**. These skills are indicated by short descriptors that articulate learning targets for students to achieve and criteria for assessment of their progress, thus aligning instruction and assessment. Moreover, these twenty discrete skills are derived from and aligned to the Common Core Literacy Standards so that as students develop skill sets, they are directly achieving the expectations of the Standards.

Instruction progressively introduces students to these skills and gives them specific opportunities to develop, apply, deepen, and demonstrate their growing skill sets over the course of the Core Literacy Proficiencies sequence. Each of the program's five units integrates the skills into a coherent, Core Literacy Proficiency that is the focus for instruction (the table at the end of the next section lists the skills by unit). These four Core Literacy Proficiencies build and deepen student ability in a learning arc that stretches across an academic year and that aligns with parallel, but more sophisticated instruction in ensuing academic years.

As students progress along this instructional path, they continually apply and deepen their abilities with the twenty essential Literacy Skills. Instructional activities and materials are designed to support teachers as they closely track and evaluate student development in each of the skill and proficiency areas. Because they frame diagnostic, formative, and summative assessment, these sets of skills can also be used to customize and differentiate instruction to meet individual and class learning needs.

ACADEMIC HABITS

Along with knowledge and skills, key Academic Habits are central to a student's literacy development. The program articulates twelve habits for students to develop, apply, and extend as they progress through the sequence of instruction. The activities of the Developing Core Literacy Proficiencies Program are therefore designed to integrate the development of Academic Habits into student learning. Instructional notes enable teachers to introduce and discuss Academic Habits such as "preparing for" and "completing tasks" central to the students' work. Development of the Academic Habits is integrated into the program's independent and collaborative activities in a way that enables teachers to emphasize them to the extent suitable for their local educational context.

The following tables list the twenty Literacy Skills and twelve Academic Habits by unit.

LITERACY SKILLS AND ACADEMIC HABITS—TEACHER VERSIONS

LITERACY SKILLS	DESCRIPTORS
Attending to Details	Identifies relevant and important textual details, words, and ideas
Deciphering Words	Uses word elements, context, and vocabulary resources to determine the meaning of unfamiliar words, usages, and figures of speech
Comprehending Syntax	Recognizes and interprets sentence elements and structures to determine meaning
Interpreting Language	Identifies how words and phrases convey meaning and represent an author's or narrator's perspective
Identifying Relationships	Identifies important connections among key details and ideas within and across texts
Making Inferences	Demonstrates comprehension by using connections among details to make logical deductions about a text
Summarizing	Recounts the explicit meaning of texts, referring to key details, events, characters, language, and ideas
Questioning	Formulates and responds to questions and lines of inquiry that lead to the identification of important ideas and themes
Recognizing Perspective	Uses textual details to recognize an author's or narrator's relationship to and perspective on a text's topic
Evaluating Information	Assesses the relevance and credibility of information, ideas, evidence, and logic presented in texts
Delineating Argumentation	Identifies the claims, evidence, and reasoning in explanations and arguments
Forming Claims	Develops meaningful and defensible claims that clearly state valid, evidence-based analysis
Using Evidence	Supports all aspects of claims with sufficient textual evidence, using accurate quotations, paraphrases, and references
Using Logic	Establishes and supports a position through a logical sequence of valid claims and evidence

LITERACY SKILLS	DESCRIPTORS
Using Language	Selects and combines words that precisely communicate ideas, generate appropriate tone, and evoke intended responses from an audience
Presenting Details	Describes and explains important details that effectively develop a narrative, explanation, or argument
Organizing Ideas	Sequences sentences and paragraphs to establish coherent, logical, and unified narratives, explanations, and arguments
Using Conventions	Uses effective sentence structure, grammar, punctuation, and spelling to express ideas and achieve writing and speaking purposes
Publishing	Uses effective formatting and citations to present ideas for specific audiences and purposes
Reflecting Critically	Uses literacy terminology and concepts to reflect on, discuss, and evaluate personal and peer literacy development

ACADEMIC HABITS	DESCRIPTORS
Preparing	Reads the texts, researches the topics, and thinks about the questions being studied to prepare for tasks
Engaging Actively	Actively focuses attention on independent and collaborative tasks
Collaborating	Pays attention to, respects, and works productively in various roles with all other participants
Communicating Clearly	Uses appropriate language and relevant textual details to clearly present ideas and claims
Listening	Pays attention to, acknowledges, and considers thoughtfully new information and ideas from others
Generating Ideas	Generates and develops ideas, positions, products, and solutions to problems
Organizing Work	Maintains work and materials so that they can be used effectively and efficiently in current and future tasks
Completing Tasks	Finishes short and extended tasks by established deadlines
Revising	Rethinks and refines work based on teacher-, peer-, and self-review processes
Understanding Purpose and Process	Understands the purpose and uses the process and criteria that guide tasks
Remaining Open	Adopts a stance of inquiry—asking questions to learn more—rather than arguing for entrenched positions
Qualifying Views	Modifies and further justifies ideas in response to thinking from others

To support student understanding and facility in thinking and talking about the twenty Literacy Skills and twelve Academic Habits, the Developing Core Literacy Proficiencies Program includes student versions of the descriptors, which articulate the learning targets in student-friendly language. These descriptors appear in Student Checklists that accompany each unit, and can be used for self- and peer-assessment, and for providing informal teacher feedback about progress.

☰ LITERACY SKILLS AND ACADEMIC
☰ HABITS — STUDENT VERSIONS

LITERACY SKILLS	DESCRIPTORS
Attending to Details	Identifies words, details, or quotations that are important to understanding the text
Deciphering Words	Uses context and vocabulary to define unknown words and phrases
Comprehending Syntax	Recognizes and uses sentence structures to help understand the text
Interpreting Language	Understands how words are used to express ideas and perspectives
Identifying Relationships	Notices important connections among details, ideas, or texts
Making Inferences	Draws sound conclusions from reading and examining the text closely
Summarizing	Correctly explains what the text says about the topic
Questioning	Writes questions that help identify important ideas, connections, and perspectives in a text
Recognizing Perspective	Identifies and explains the author's view of the text's topic
Evaluating Information	Assesses the relevance and credibility of information in texts
Delineating Argumentation	Identifies and analyzes the claims, evidence, and reasoning in arguments
Forming Claims	States a meaningful conclusion that is well supported by evidence from the text
Using Evidence	Uses well-chosen details from the text to support explanations; accurately paraphrases or quotes
Using Logic	Supports a position through a logical sequence of related claims, premises, and supporting evidence
Using Language	Writes and speaks clearly so others can understand claims and ideas
Presenting Details	Inserts details and quotations effectively into written or spoken explanations
Organizing Ideas	Organizes claims, supporting ideas, and evidence in a logical order

LITERACY SKILLS	DESCRIPTORS
Using Conventions	Correctly uses sentence elements, punctuation, and spelling to produce clear writing
Publishing	Correctly uses, formats, and cites textual evidence to support claims
Reflecting Critically	Uses literacy concepts to discuss and evaluate personal and peer learning

ACADEMIC HABITS	DESCRIPTORS
Preparing	Reads the text(s) closely and thinks about the questions to prepare for tasks
Engaging Actively	Focuses attention on the task when working individually and with others
Collaborating	Works well with others while participating in text-centered discussions and group activities
Communicating Clearly	Presents ideas and supporting evidence so others can understand them
Listening	Pays attention to ideas from others and takes time to think about them
Generating Ideas	Generates and develops ideas, positions, products, and solutions to problems
Organizing Work	Maintains materials so that they can be used effectively and efficiently
Completing Tasks	Finishes short and extended tasks by established deadlines
Revising	Rethinks ideas and refines work based on feedback from others
Understanding Purpose and Process	Understands why and how a task should be accomplished
Remaining Open	Asks questions of others rather than arguing for a personal idea or opinion
Qualifying Views	Modifies and further justifies ideas in response to thinking from others

EMBEDDING AND SEQUENCING THE DEVELOPING CORE LITERACY PROFICIENCIES UNITS IN YEARLONG AND MULTIYEAR PROGRAM

The Developing Core Literacy Proficiencies Program articulates a core set of knowledge, skills, and habits key to literacy development. It establishes a framework to guide instruction and evaluation of those key components; learning activities are sequenced to promote their development. The program and materials have been designed to be flexibly integrated into the local curricular context specific to its teachers and schools. Within a grade-level year teachers are encouraged to sequence and supplement the units with work on additional texts of their choice. Approaches, activities, and supporting tools and handouts can be used with locally selected texts.

For example, a teacher might begin the year with the *Reading Closely* unit to establish an approach to close reading, focusing on informational texts. The teacher might then practice the close reading approaches with a set of poems or short works of fiction. Next, the teacher might teach the *Making Evidence-Based Claims* and *Making Evidence-Based Claims about Literary Technique* unit to deepen students' abilities to analyze informational and fictional texts. After this, students might apply their close reading and textual analysis skills to a full-length novel. In later parts of the school year, the teacher can return to the Developing Core Literacy Proficiencies Program and work with students on the *Researching to Deepen Understanding* and *Building Evidence-Based Arguments* units. Once students have completed the culminating task for *Building Evidence-Based Arguments*—an issue-based argumentative essay—they might end the year by studying a complex, grade-appropriate, full-length text, and write an interpretive argument in response to their reading and analysis. The evaluative criteria established throughout the Developing

Core Literacy Proficiencies program can then inform the teacher's assessment of students' literacy development over the entire year, as demonstrated both in a portfolio of previous assignments and a culminating interpretative essay on the final text or novel.

In addition to structuring yearlong instruction, the Developing Core Literacy Proficiencies Program establishes a vertical literacy framework for grades 6–12 instruction. Each grade level of the Program uses the same approaches, foci, and evaluative criteria for teaching and assessing. Student literacy development across years within the program thus progresses along consistent and coherent pathways. Students return each year to further develop the same skills, deepening and extending them in new and more sophisticated contexts appropriate for their grade level. Likewise, teachers across grade levels can collaborate and communicate using a common framework to help integrate their students' literacy development and align their assessment of student progress. Because it supports this aligned scope and sequence of instruction, the flexibility of the program also enables schools, departments, and teachers to incorporate locally selected texts and topics into the Developing Core Literacy Proficiencies Program framework.

The approaches and materials of the program have also been designed to develop literacy in content areas beyond English Language Arts. Teachers in fields such as the humanities, art, science, and social studies can use the processes and materials in their own curricular context to provide a coherent and powerful school-wide approach to literacy development across disciplines.

THE LITERACY TOOLBOX

A key component of the Developing Core Literacy Proficiencies Program is the Odell Education Literacy Toolbox. The Literacy Toolbox is a series of materials carefully designed to support student success throughout the learning progressions of the units. Each piece of the toolbox is designed for flexible use in varying instructional contexts.

The Literacy Toolbox contains three types of materials: handouts, tools, and checklists and rubrics.

Hardcopy Student Editions that contain the toolbox materials and texts are available for each unit. Teachers may still want to make additional photocopies of the texts, tools, and handouts to facilitate annotation and facility with the materials. See the following section, "Electronic Supports and Versions of Materials," for information on how to access the handouts, tools and checklists online.

HANDOUTS

Handouts provide essential background knowledge on key literacy concepts and processes. They are written in student-friendly language so students can internalize conceptual knowledge about their own literacy development. The handouts can be used throughout the year as students deepen and apply their abilities in new contexts. Handouts also provide teachers with rich information to be used in instruction.

TOOLS

Tools are graphic organizers that break down complex literacy processes into tangible steps so that students are better able to learn and practice the skills. The tools are not worksheets that channel student thinking into predetermined answers or analysis nor are they related only to specific content. Rather, the tools teach students a structured way to approach texts critically while also facilitating their own creative thinking.

Tools can be used with a variety of informational and literary texts across grade levels. The tools are also an important way for teachers to obtain diagnostic information about student thinking for formative assessment. Because they capture students' discoveries and analyses within the reading process, they provide direct evidence of skills, proficiencies, and standards that are often hard to measure.

Once students have internalized the conceptual and critical processes the tools scaffold, students can leave them behind. This design enables teachers to differentiate instruction easily by providing supports to some students for texts and tasks that others are able to read and accomplish without the tools. As the year progresses, some students may need these scaffolds to gain proficiency, others may choose to continue using them to deepen proficiency, and still others may not need them until they encounter more challenging texts.

CHECKLISTS AND RUBRICS

Odell Education student checklists and teacher rubrics provide students and teachers with clear criteria for evaluating the development of literacy proficiency. The checklists and rubrics describe the goals for instruction and support students and teachers in discussing and tracking their developing literacy proficiency. For more description of the rubrics and checklists see the section called "A Skills-Based Approach to Assessment and Evaluation" in this User Guide.

A QUESTION-BASED APPROACH TO READING: QUESTIONING PATHS

At the heart of the Odell Education approach to teaching close reading is an iterative process for questioning texts that frames students' initial reading and then guides them as they dig deeper to analyze and make meaning. This questioning process differs from traditional text questioning in that its goal is not to "find the answer" but rather to focus student attention on the author's ideas, supporting details, use of language, text structure, and perspective—to examine a text more closely and develop deeper understanding.

With this approach, the key to examining text closely is the strategic use—by teachers and students—of text-dependent questions. Students should learn not only to *respond* to text-dependent questions posed by others but also to *generate* and refine their *own* questions as they dig deeper into a text and expand their comprehension and their independence as close readers.

Each Developing Core Literacy Proficiencies unit develops students' abilities to respond to and extend text-dependent questions. Initially, students learn to use broad (but text-based) Guiding Questions to help them *approach* any given text, *question* it to note details and connections, then *analyze* those connections through more focused questioning. Students work from these foundational questions, and the text-questioning process they define, to more sophisticated and text-specific questions, which move them from *literal* comprehension of a text's explicit meaning to *interpretive, evaluative,* and extended readings.

This process for reading and rereading a text is represented in various Odell Education handouts and tools, all of which are integrated into instructional sequences and included in the Student Edition and Literacy Toolbox for each unit. The **Reading Closely Graphic** is a simple graphic model that depicts in flow chart form the iterative questioning process: (1) *approaching*

a text and considering reading purpose and text information; (2) initial *questioning* of the text using more literal Guiding Questions; (3) further *analyzing* the text with more interpretive Guiding Questions; (4) *deepening* understanding by attending to text-specific questions (posed by OE, the teacher, or students themselves); and (5) *extending* reading through additional questioning, reading, or research.

This same organization frames the **Guiding Questions Handout**, a collection of general Guiding Questions that can be applied to any text and that lead to closer reading and analysis, and to more text-specific questioning. Students first learn to use this handout as a resource in planning a reading strategy, or Questioning Path, with an eventual goal that they internalize the model and those questions they find useful—and thus develop their own process for approaching, reading, and analyzing a text. This handout clusters Guiding Questions into four areas often examined in reading a text (and also areas often addressed on reading tests), the author's use of *Language;* presentation of *Ideas* and supporting details; *Perspective* on the topic or theme; and decisions about the *Structure* of the text. This aspect of the framework can be referred to through the acronym *LIPS* (a mnemonic representation of the reading focus on *Language, Ideas, Perspective,* and *Structure*).

A model **Questioning Path Tool** is provided for most texts in the first two units of the Developing Core Literacy Proficiencies Program. These question sets are organized by the stages in the questioning process and include Guiding Questions and text-specific questions related to one or more of the *LIPS* domains—depending on the approach to reading suggested at the start of the Questioning Path. OE has carefully analyzed the texts used in the units, selecting Guiding Questions and generating text-specific questions that take students deeper into the text (from literal to interpretive and evaluative readings) and also encourage multiple ways of reading the text. Teachers, however, and students themselves (as they gain proficiency in the process), are encouraged to develop and use their own Questioning Paths, using the OE questions as models only. For this reason, blank **Questioning Path Tool**s are available in the toolboxes.

The strategic text-questioning process and the various questioning tools and handouts are fully integrated with the other tools students encounter to support their learning in the units, most notably those introduced in the first two units: the **Approaching the Text Tool**, the **Analyzing Details Tool**, and the **Forming Evidence-Based Claims Tool**.

Activities in the Developing Core Literacy Proficiencies units that help students develop text-questioning processes and skills progress from teacher modeling and think-alouds, to guided practice in small groups, to independent work with more sophisticated text-dependent questions. Students become skilled discussion leaders in reciprocal-teaching activities, for which they develop and compare their own text-specific questions. They also apply their questioning skills as they conduct independent research in later units. The end goal is that each student will ultimately develop an innate questioning approach applicable to any text encountered.

The text-centered questioning framework aligns directly with the CCSS and national assessments so that as students learn to use and develop text-based questions, they also become strategic responders to test questions in domains such as main ideas and supporting details, language use, author's or narrator's perspective, text structure, and so on. Students learn strategies for analyzing and responding to questions, initially working within one text analysis domain (e.g., language) and then moving fluidly between and among domains and questions.

Students' developing abilities to respond to and generate complex text-dependent questions are assessed throughout the Developing Core Literacy Proficiencies Program through informal observation of discussions and more formal speaking and writing tasks. The questioning framework aligns directly with Literacy Skills targeted for teaching and assessment, including **Questioning**, **Attending to Details**, **Interpreting Language**, **Recognizing Perspective**, and **Making Inferences**. The questioning framework also aligns with the following Academic Habits: **Listening**, **Communicating Clearly**, and **Understanding Purpose** and **Process**.

TEXT-CENTERED DISCUSSIONS

Integral to a student's success in becoming a literate person is his or her ability to successfully communicate ideas to others. Exchanging ideas provides a crucial venue to develop key Literacy Skills and achieve understanding of texts or academic processes. As students share ideas and analyses with one another, they deepen their own understanding of texts and topics by (1) listening to others' views and analyses and revising their original thinking accordingly and (2) articulating in spoken words their own reading and thinking, helping them to formalize a pattern or structure of thought. Discussions challenge students to form articulate statements, develop coherent lines of thought, and use relevant evidence to support their thinking. Central then to the Developing Core Literacy Proficiencies Program is the instructional practice of text-centered discussion.

Throughout the entire program, students participate in discussions almost daily. Because this instructional strategy is central to developing literacy, it is the culminating activity in the first unit of the sequence, *Reading Closely for Textual Details*. In this activity, students conduct a formal text-centered discussion in order to demonstrate their proficiency in targeted Literacy Skills and

Academic Habits related to reading closely, speaking, and listening. This intentional focus on discussion in the first unit equips students with the necessary skills and habits to engage in rich, productive, and coherent text-centered discussions over the course of the entire Developing Core Literacy Proficiencies Program. As a formative assessment, the culminating discussion in the *Reading Closely* unit also serves as a diagnostic tool teachers can use to gauge how well individuals and the class as a whole can share ideas and actively listen to each other. In the ensuing three units, text-centered discussions continue to be part of informal daily activities in which students discuss their claims, perspectives, and research paths and of more formal processes in which students engage in collaborative, peer reviews of one another's work.

TEXT-BASED WRITING

Communicating understanding effectively is an essential part of the close reading and literacy development process. Although the Developing Core Literacy Proficiencies units focus initially on reading proficiencies, writing from textual evidence plays an increasingly important role in the activities as the units progress. The nature of the writing instruction in the Developing Core Literacy Proficiencies Program is rooted in several fundamental principles. First, strong writing flows from deep comprehension of a text or topic. Many deficiencies in writing are the result of shallow or uninformed critical thinking. The writing activities in each unit are thus linked closely to students' reading in ways that help them develop and express their emerging understanding of textual evidence. Students are continually asked to explain their thinking about texts in their writing. Developing this ability is fundamental to supporting them as they craft extended pieces of writing in later contexts.

Within every Developing Core Literacy Proficiencies unit, students practice what is described in the CCSS as "writing (and speaking) from sources" (text-based writing). The mode of writing they practice, the process they use, and the sophistication and independence of writing and speaking activities varies based on the focus of the unit and students' ages, backgrounds, and skills. Initially, students use graphic organizers to develop short, informal written segments— sentences and short paragraphs—that focus on communicating their thinking as they read, question, and examine a given text. These sorts of writing activities, however, do not suggest that writing is limited in importance. The limited scope of the assignments intentionally enables teachers and students to focus on building the abilities to incorporate textual evidence into their communication and to use effective word choice, punctuation, and syntax appropriate to the audience and task.

As students develop the analytical skills that let them transition from text-based observations to evidence-based claims, their explanatory writing activities progress to more formal paragraphs and short expository essays, refining students' abilities to use textual evidence as a basis for their claims. When students can clearly explain and substantiate their claims, they are ready for more sophisticated writing assignments in which they break their claims into component premises and develop interpretive arguments. Finally, students plan, write, and publish thesis-driven academic arguments, making the case for a position related to texts and their content. See the following table for a brief overview of the writing components throughout the program.

DEVELOPING CORE LITERACY PROFICIENCIES UNIT	WRITING COMPONENTS
Reading Closely for Textual Details	Text annotations and tools Text-based written paragraph(s) explaining the students' understanding of the unit's topic
Making Evidence-Based Claims	Text annotations and tools Essay explaining and supporting the student's global claim about the unit's text(s)
Researching to Deepen Understanding	Text annotations and tools Written and multimedia products communicating the student's evidence-based perspective on the unit's topic
Building Evidence-Based Arguments	Text annotations and tools Culminating argumentative essay presenting evidence-based support for the student's position on the unit's issue

THE COLLABORATIVE WRITING WORKSHOP: A QUESTION-BASED APPROACH FOR DEVELOPING AND STRENGTHENING WRITING

As students work on writing assignments and progress from short, informal text-based explanations to longer, more formal evidence-based claims and arguments, they learn to use a process for generating, reviewing, and improving writing that is *collaborative, question-based,* and *criteria-driven.* Thus, this writing process is interconnected to the processes used throughout the unit for questioning texts and participating in text-centered discussions.

The Developing Core Literacy Proficiencies Collaborative Writing Workshop is grounded in the French roots of the word *essay*—a term that can guide the way students write as much as designate what they are expected to produce. The French word *essayer* means to "attempt" or "try." As a verb, it actually means the same thing in English. In this way of thinking, when we talk about an *essay*, we are actually talking about writing "an attempt."

This idea might influence how a teacher and her students think about writing. A piece of writing can be seen as never finished. This is not to say that it is acceptable to present an unpolished

and unrefined work but rather that ideas, theories, information, and one's understanding and perspective constantly change and evolve. An essay then is an ongoing attempt to clearly communicate something. That idea could result in a description, explanation, narrative, argument, speech, or other written product. The motivation, purpose, and audience can change; however, the ongoing attempt to gain and present a clear understanding of a specific subject never changes. A writer works to get progressively closer to an ideal final product, viewing writing, thinking, and understanding of a particular topic as a continual work in progress.

Thus, writing an essay benefits greatly from a collaborative, question-based process. To think of an essay as a process rather than a product suggests that conversation, contemplation, consideration, and revision are all part of the attempts to get one's thinking down on paper so that others can understand and respond to it.

The Developing Core Literacy Proficiencies Program's approach to developing and strengthening writing recognizes the iterative nature of an essay and also acknowledges the need to ground the writing process in clear criteria in order to produce a final, polished product. There are many such processes that have been well described in the literature on writing, and many teachers have their own, favored approach to teaching what has become known as *the writing process*. If so, teachers are encouraged to follow what works for them and their students, adding what makes sense from the approaches and activities described below and in each of the units.

LEARNING PRINCIPLES

Central to the Developing Core Literacy Proficiencies Program approach in facilitating the development of student writing are the following principles:

Independence

Students need to discover and adopt personally effective writing processes as they develop their own essays—to become reflective and independent writers who persevere and grow through their attempts rather than learning and following the writing process in a rote and mechanical way. Thus, the Developing Core Literacy Proficiencies Program approach to writing and revising is iterative, flexible, and student-driven.

Collaboration

Becoming an independent writer also entails learning to seek and use constructive feedback from others, such as peers, teachers, and audience members, so that students develop and value the skills of thoughtful collaboration. Thus, the Developing Core Literacy Proficiencies writing classroom relies on text-centered discussions of student essays.

Clear Criteria

Clear, commonly understood criteria that describe the essential characteristics of a desired writing product serve two purposes: (1) they help students understand what they are trying to accomplish and (2) they support their participation in focused, criterion-based reviews of their own and their peers' writing. Thus, the criteria that drive reflection and conversation in a Core Literacy Proficiencies Writing Classroom focus on Literacy Skills and the critical characteristics of a specific piece of writing (e.g., the nature of a central claim and its support within an argument) rather than merely on mechanical issues (e.g., the number of sources used to support the argument or the number of spelling errors).

Guiding Questions

In addition to being rooted in clear criteria, student processes for developing and reviewing their writing should connect to their evolving skills as readers. Students are expected to use guiding and text-based questions to promote close reading of their developing drafts. Thus, in a Developing Core Literacy Proficiencies writing classroom, students are expected to frame text-based review questions before asking a teacher or peer to read an emerging draft.

Evidence

Whether driven by criteria or questions, student conversations and reflections about their writing should be based on specific textual evidence, which they or their reviewers cite when they are discussing the writing's strengths and areas for improvement. Thus, the review process in a Developing Core Literacy Proficiencies writing classroom involves making evidence-based claims about a piece of writing, much as students learn to do when they are reading and analyzing texts.

LEARNING PROCESSES

To make these principles come alive, learning activities in a Developing Core Literacy Proficiencies writing classroom are designed and sequenced to provide time and support for the *essay* process. Therefore, each stage of the process includes the following components:

Teacher Modeling

Each writing activity includes a teacher demonstration lesson, in which the teacher focuses on and models a specific aspect of writing, specific criteria and guiding question(s), and an approach to writing and reviewing that will be emphasized in that phase of the process.

Guided and Supported Writing

The bulk of class time is dedicated for students to *essay*: to freewrite, experiment, draft, revise, and polish their writing, depending on where they are in the process and guided by what has been introduced and modeled in the demonstration lesson.

Text-Centered Discussion

As students write, they are also engaged in ongoing discussions about their writing—sometimes in formal or informal sessions with the teacher, sometimes in structured peer reviews, and sometimes in more spontaneous conversations with a partner. At the center of all discussions are the fundamental principles of (1) using guiding or text-based questions to examine the writing, (2) applying clear criteria when determining and discussing its strengths and weaknesses, and (3) citing specific evidence in response to questions and in support of claims about the writing.

Read-Alouds

Periodically, students have opportunities to publicly share their emerging writing, reading segments to the class (or a small group) and using questions, criteria, and evidence to discuss what they are noticing (and working on) in their own writing.

As practiced in conjunction with a Developing Core Literacy Proficiencies unit, such as *Building Evidence-Based Arguments,* the process is sequenced as a series of attempts that are intended to produce a specific written product (an argument, explanation, or narrative) that also represents evidence of a student's reading and research skills.

LEARNING PROGRESSION

Thus the collaborative approach to writing emphasizes the following:

- Criteria that describe an effective final product and the skills it should demonstrate
- Questions that are intended to improve the product
- A process of revision to progressively revise and refine a piece of writing

As such, the iterative writing process moves through an increasingly focused sequence of activities, including the following:

- **Getting Started:** A broad scanning of the writer's thinking in the initial stages of the essay—turning thinking into writing and writing one's way to thinking
- **Thinking:** An initial, wide-angle view and review of the big picture—the thinking behind the writing and the ideas and information it presents (with the idea that until the thinking is clear and well developed, other revisions are premature)
- **Organization:** A still broad but somewhat more focused emphasis on organizing, reorganizing, and resequencing into a logical progression of thinking
- **Evidence:** A closer look at the use and integration of supporting evidence, through references, quotations, or paraphrasing
- **Connecting Ideas:** An emphasis on linking ideas—on connecting and transitioning among sentences and paragraphs
- **Expression:** Close attention to how ideas are expressed—to the writer's choices regarding sentence structure, variety, and language use
- **Final Editing:** A final, careful reading for editing and proofing, with an emphasis on particular language conventions and formatting issues related to the specific writing product
- **Publication:** The production and publication of a finished piece of writing that effectively communicates to its specified audience and achieves its intended purpose

Teachers and students can follow this entire progression of writing activities or choose to emphasize those that are most appropriate for a particular writing assignment and group of students.

For any writing assignment, teachers can use any or all of these ways of viewing and reviewing a piece of writing within a sequence of writing process instruction as appropriate for the assignment and their students. In early units, students might only apply a few criteria and a few of these ways of examining their writing. In the final unit, in which students write a more formal argument, they will likely consider most of these processes.

☰ A SKILLS-BASED APPROACH TO ASSESSMENT AND EVALUATION

The Developing Core Literacy Proficiencies units have been developed on the principles that (1) learning targets should be clear for teachers and students, (2) assessment tasks should be fully aligned with instruction to produce observable evidence of targeted Literacy Skills, and (3) assessment activities and rubrics should be growth-focused, informing future instruction and student development as much as evaluation and grading within any of the instructional units.

At the center of the assessment system used within the Developing Core Literacy Proficiencies Program are the criteria for Literacy Skills and Academic Habits that are listed at the start of each unit and each of its parts. These criteria—and especially those for Literacy Skills—are identified as the targets for instruction and assessment within the unit, and all activities and materials have been designed in conjunction with this approach. Moreover, the criteria are directly derived from and aligned to the language of the Common Core State Standards in English Language Arts and Literacy so as to ensure that when students are learning and demonstrating the targeted skills, they are also addressing the standards. However, instruction and assessment target the Literacy Skills and Academic Habits because the descriptors for these learning targets are more focused and discrete, more easily communicated to students, and more distinguishable in assessment evidence. (See the alignment chart for the CCSS and OE skills and habits at the end of this section of the User Guide.)

STUDENT ASSESSMENT CHECKLISTS

To facilitate ongoing emphasis on, discussion of, and reflection about student progress relative to these instructional targets, student checklists are included with each unit. The checklists include student language descriptors of the skills or habits that are emphasized in the unit. These checklists can be used at any point in the unit to introduce the goals of instruction, to support student reflection and peer and self-assessment, or to provide informal feedback from the teacher. In addition to student-language descriptors, the checklists include spaces for indicating *if* evidence of the skill or habit can be seen in the student's work, and if so, *where*. In using the checklists, teachers and other reviewers thus develop their own reading and feedback processes. First, a reviewer studies a student's work to find evidence that the student has used or demonstrated the skill or habit (indicating with a check if evidence is discernible). Then, the reviewer adds comments about the location, nature, sufficiency, and quality of the evidence. Finally, the reviewer adds summary comments about the student's overall performance and demonstration of the skills and habits. Teachers first model these review processes through classroom examples and their own feedback to students, explaining their thinking and thus helping students become better at using the checklists for self- and peer assessment as they progress through the Developing Core Literacy Proficiencies Program.

If a more evaluative approach to reviewing student work is preferred, the checklists can also be adapted to use a leveled rating system. For example, a teacher might employ a simple three-level, symbol-based system to communicate to students whether they are still developing the skill or habit, are demonstrating grade-level proficiency, or are excelling (using, respectively, a minus [−], check [✓], or plus [+]). Employing this more evaluative approach, wherein the reviewer not only looks to find evidence of the skill or habit but also determines the student's demonstrated level of proficiency, can provide students with formative feedback about their progress that is not yet connected to a numerical rating or grade.

TEACHER RUBRICS

Each unit also includes a more formal teacher rubric, again organized by the Literacy Skills (and sometimes Academic Habits) that are to be demonstrated in final assignments and assessments. Each of these unit-specific rubrics includes descriptors for the general skills and habits criteria to be assessed and measured (in the upper sections of the rubric) as well as criteria specific to the assignment itself (in the lower section). (*Note:* Teachers are encouraged to add their own assignment criteria.)

DEVELOPMENTAL RATING SCALES

All of the teacher rubrics employ a four-point developmental scale, which teachers interpret relative to their grade-level CCSS and classroom learning expectations. The scales are designed to support rating (and potentially grading) but also to provide feedback to students about where they have demonstrated growth—or where they need to grow further. The levels of the scale and related rating areas are as follows:

NE: Not enough evidence to make a rating

1—**Emerging:** needs improvement

2—**Developing:** shows progress

3—**Becoming proficient:** demonstrates skills

4—**Excelling:** exceeds expectations

+—**Growth:** evidence of growth within the unit or task

This scale prompts teachers to first consider if there is *evidence* of the skill demonstrated in the student's work and if that evidence is *sufficient* to rate the student's performance and growth. If not, the NE rating is used. When sufficient evidence is present, the teacher can then indicate where the student is along the scale, from emerging (1) to excelling (4), with a goal that all students work at least toward becoming proficient (3) at their grade level within the school year. Because Odell Education believes that student growth—and feedback about student growth—is also important to assess, the + column of the rubric enables a teacher to indicate in which areas the student has demonstrated growth within the unit or the assignment.

These teacher rubrics are designed to track and communicate student development of proficiency across the five Developing Core Literacy Proficiencies units and the school year. The rating check system enables a teacher to do so, and enables students to compare their evaluations in early units and assignments with those in later units and assignments. Teachers can also use the rubrics as part of a classroom grading system in several ways:

1. **Equal-weight point system:** In this sort of system, students earn points based on their ratings for each of the criteria in the rubric, with a bonus point added in for each area in which a student has demonstrated growth. (Thus, a student who has received a "Developing" or "2" rating for a skill such as "Using Evidence" but also received a "+" for growth would earn three points.) Students' grades are thus based on the total points they receive in the teacher's evaluation of their work.

2. **Weighted point system:** A teacher may not see all of the criteria as equal in importance. In this sort of system, the teacher can weight specific criteria or sections of the rubric as more important than others (i.e., 2×, 3×, etc.). This weighting factor then becomes a multiplier for the ratings themselves, again, producing a point total that can be used to determine a student's grade.

3. **Summary evaluation:** A teacher may prefer to make a summary evaluation of what the pattern of checks in the rubric adds up to (rather than actually computing a point total). A separate row at the bottom of each rubric is provided for recording this summary evaluation. The summary evaluation can then be converted to a grade in whatever system a teacher uses.

≡ ALIGNMENT OF TARGETED CCSS WITH ≡ OE SKILLS AND HABITS

The following table lists the anchor Common Core State Standards that are targeted within the five Developing Core Literacy Proficiencies units and indicates the Literacy Skills and Academic Habits that are derived from or are components of those standards. This chart can be used to walk backward from the OE criteria used in assessments and rubrics to the CCSS, especially if teachers are also trying to track student performance specific to the standards.

CCSS ANCHOR STANDARDS TARGETED IN DEVELOPING CORE LITERACY PROFICIENCIES UNITS	ALIGNED LITERACY SKILLS AND ACADEMIC HABITS (AH)
R.1: Read closely to determine what the text says explicitly and to make logical inferences from it; cite specific textual evidence when writing or speaking to support conclusions drawn from the text.	Attending to Details Summarizing Making Inferences Using Evidence
R.2: Determine central ideas or themes of a text and analyze their development; summarize the key supporting details and ideas.	Questioning Summarizing Identifying Relationships Making Inferences
R.3: Analyze how and why individuals, events, and ideas develop and interact over the course of a text.	Identifying Relationships Making Inferences
R.4: Interpret words and phrases as they are used in a text, including determining technical, connotative, and figurative meanings, and analyze how specific word choices shape meaning or tone.	Deciphering Words Comprehending Syntax Interpreting Language Making Inferences
R.5: Analyze the structure of texts, including how specific sentences, paragraphs, and larger portions of the text relate to each other and the whole.	Comprehending Syntax Identifying Relationships Delineating Argumentation
R.6: Assess how point of view or purpose shapes the content and style of a text.	Interpreting Language Recognizing Perspective
R.7: Integrate and evaluate content presented in diverse media and formats, including visually and quantitatively, as well as in words.	Identifying Relationships Evaluating Information

CCSS ANCHOR STANDARDS TARGETED IN DEVELOPING CORE LITERACY PROFICIENCIES UNITS	ALIGNED LITERACY SKILLS AND ACADEMIC HABITS (AH)
R.8: Delineate and evaluate the argument and specific claims in a text, including the validity of the reasoning as well as the relevance and sufficiency of the evidence.	Delineating Argumentation Recognizing Perspective Evaluating Information
R.9: Analyze how two or more texts address similar themes or topics in order to build knowledge or to compare the approaches the authors take.	Identifying Relationships Recognizing Perspective
R.10: Read and comprehend complex literary and informational texts independently and proficiently.	All Literacy Skills and Academic Habits
W.1: Write arguments to support claims in an analysis of substantive topics or texts, using valid reasoning and relevant and sufficient evidence.	Delineating Argumentation Forming Claims Using Logic Using Evidence Organizing Ideas
W.2: Write informative/explanatory texts to examine and convey complex ideas and information clearly and accurately through the effective selection, organization, and analysis of content.	Summarizing Organizing Ideas Presenting Details
W.3: Write narratives to develop real or imagined experiences or events using effective technique, well-chosen details and well-structured event sequences.	Using Language Presenting Details Organizing Ideas Recognizing Perspective
W.4: Produce clear and coherent writing in which the development, organization, and style are appropriate to task, purpose, and audience.	Using Language Organizing Ideas Using Conventions
W.5: Develop and strengthen writing as needed by planning, revising, editing, rewriting, or trying a new approach.	Using Language Organizing Ideas Using Conventions Understanding Process (AH) Revising (AH)
W.6: Use technology, including the Internet, to produce and publish writing and to interact and collaborate with others.	Publishing Organizing Work (AH)
W.7: Conduct short as well as more sustained research projects based on focused questions, demonstrating understanding of the subject under investigation.	Questioning Summarizing Recognizing Perspective Evaluating Information Completing tasks (AH)

CCSS ANCHOR STANDARDS TARGETED IN DEVELOPING CORE LITERACY PROFICIENCIES UNITS	ALIGNED LITERACY SKILLS AND ACADEMIC HABITS (AH)
W.8: Gather relevant information from multiple print and digital sources, assess the credibility and accuracy of each source, and integrate the information while avoiding plagiarism.	Questioning Summarizing Recognizing Perspective Evaluating Information Using Evidence Understanding Process (AH) Organizing Work (AH)
W.9: Draw evidence from literary or informational texts to support analysis, reflection, and research.	Using Evidence Organizing Ideas
SL.1: Prepare for and participate effectively in a range of conversations and collaborations with diverse partners, building on others' ideas and expressing their own clearly and persuasively.	Questioning Preparing (AH) Collaborating (AH) Listening (AH) Communicating Clearly (AH) Remaining Open (AH) Qualifying Views (AH)

INSTRUCTIONAL SUPPORTS FOR ENGLISH LANGUAGE LEARNERS AND STUDENTS READING BELOW GRADE LEVEL

The Developing Core Literacy Proficiencies Program is intentionally designed so that all students engage directly with activities and texts at grade-level complexity. Scaffolding is built into the activities and tools to make instruction comprehensible to all students—including those who are English language learners or are reading below grade level—so that they directly experience the complexity of the texts. The program actively supports these students through explicit instruction of skills and strategies, the building of background knowledge, progressions of increasing text complexity, a focus on student-developed questions, and instructional strategies associated with modeling, grouping, and graphic organizers. Instruction in each unit follows a progression that moves from scaffolding and support to independent application.

The supports for English language learners and below-grade-level readers are integrated into the units as follows.

UNIT DESIGN AND INSTRUCTIONAL SEQUENCE

By design, students begin learning to read closely by first encountering visual images, which they scan for details, and then multimedia texts that reinforce the skills of identifying details and making text-based observations from those details. Thus, before they ever encounter print texts of grade-level complexity, students begin to develop skills and strategies through visual learning experiences. They then learn to transfer these skills to the reading of more complex texts. The text sequences are also set up as a *staircase of complexity*: in these sequences, students move from more accessible texts that help them build background knowledge to more challenging texts that they analyze for perspective and use of language.

SHORT TEXTS, FOCUSED READING

Many of the texts are relatively short in length, enabling students to focus on individual paragraphs and sentences as they learn to read closely and derive meaning. Text-dependent questions included in the instructional notes further focus student reading on important or more challenging sections of text.

READ-ALOUDS AND MODELING

At key parts in the instruction, teachers read text aloud so that students can listen to the cadence and structure of texts while also following along themselves. By listening to a proficient reader, students pick up on natural pauses and pronunciation of words. Teachers also model think-alouds, wherein they discuss what they visualize and think as they read. Thus, teachers model reading proficiently and also model using the skills and graphic organizer tools that help students learn to read closely. Students see the tools and skills modeled before they apply them, first in pairs or small groups, then independently.

GUIDING QUESTION FRAMEWORK

The units break the reading process down into manageable steps that are increasingly complex. These steps are organized and framed by sets of guiding and text-specific questions that scaffold students' thinking as they develop reading skills. For example, rather than simply asking students to paraphrase or explain what they have read, an instructional sequence asks students to start by annotating or writing down details they have found in the text related to a guiding question. Already equipped with details they have written down, students are then asked to discuss these details and note connections among them. Only after having had these opportunities to interact with the text and peers do students attempt to paraphrase, explain, or make a claim about what they have read.

GRAPHIC ORGANIZERS

The program's instructional tools provide students with precise and guided processes and scaffolds for interacting with texts. These tools help break down the complex reading processes—processes that proficient readers inherently use—into clear, visual organizers. Visually, the tools help students understand the relationships among concepts, processes, and observations they make from texts.

READING TEAMS

Students are given chances to read in groups and individually. Teachers can group students in various ways, sometimes by reading abilities, sometimes by interests or target text, sometimes heterogeneously to pair less-able readers with more advanced readers. By reading in teams, students practice talking about texts in a structured and supported context.

ACADEMIC VOCABULARY

Although leaving many decisions about the teaching of vocabulary to the teacher, the program provides opportunities for students to increase their vocabulary in areas related to specific content and fundamental to overall literacy. Activities and tools use vocabulary related to reading skills that students can apply while reading and discussing texts. These tools thus equip students with the vocabulary necessary to understand and deepen their own literacy development. Additionally, students use guiding and text-specific questions to identify and think about key words in the texts. Vocabulary in the *Reading Closely* and *Making Evidence-Based Claims* units' texts are highlighted and defined so that students and teachers can focus on them as needed, either before or while reading. Teachers of English language learners and below-grade-level readers are encouraged to use additional vocabulary building strategies such as Word Walls, whereby students in the classroom can visually reference the meaning of key words as they read and discuss texts.

MEDIA SUPPORTS

The curriculum includes suggested multimedia to support teaching and learning. The media supports and extensions serve a variety of purposes including language development and building knowledge about the text content. These supports give teachers and students the freedom to take the class in directions they desire. The various media (i.e., videos, audio, images, websites) can be assigned and explored at the student or group level to differentiate experiences for students based on their interests and abilities. These media sources are located in the Media Supports sections of the *Reading Closely* and *Making Evidence-Based Claims* units. The *Researching to Deepen Understanding* and *Building Evidence-Based Arguments* units incorporate media sources into the text lists. Both the media supports and text lists briefly describe the content of the media and provide searchable terms to help locate the sources on the Internet.

ELECTRONIC SUPPORTS AND VERSIONS OF MATERIALS

The Odell Education Literacy Toolbox files, including handouts, tools, and checklists, are available as digital files. These files have been created as editable PDF forms. With the free version of Adobe Reader, students and teachers are able to type in the forms and save their work for recording and e-mailing. This enables students and teachers to work either with paper and pencil or electronically according to their strengths and needs. It also enables teachers to collect and organize student work for evaluation and formative assessment. These editable PDF files can be found here: www.wiley.com/go/coreliteracy. Use the following password: odell2016.

Many texts used throughout the Developing Core Literacy Proficiencies Program, especially in the fourth and fifth units, are available only online. Because of the ever-changing nature of website addresses, specific links are not provided. Teachers and students can locate these texts using provided key words (e.g., article titles, authors, and publishers). Some units also contain directions on how to access specific media supports online to accompany identified texts and topics.

UNIT 1

READING CLOSELY
FOR TEXTUAL DETAILS

DEVELOPING CORE LITERACY
PROFICIENCIES

GRADE 9

"Education is the new currency"

UNIT OVERVIEW

Becoming literate involves developing habits and proficiencies associated with many reading purposes, from summer pleasure reading to preparing for high-stakes business meetings. This unit develops students' abilities to read closely for textual details—a proficiency essential for a variety of purposes and contexts. Attending to and analyzing details are skills that are essential for building knowledge, enabling texts to inform our understanding and enrich our lives.

Rather than simply *ask* students to read closely, this unit instructs them in a process for doing so. The activities lay out a process for approaching, questioning, and analyzing texts that helps readers focus on key textual characteristics and ideas. Just as experts in any field access deep understanding by knowing what to look for in their particular fields, proficient readers know the questions to ask of texts in order to guide them to deep meaning. The framework of questioning presented in this unit takes the invisible process proficient readers have internalized and makes it explicit—to support teachers and students as they develop proficiency in reading text closely.

Proficient readers can also explain and share the discoveries they have made through their reading. Developing evidence-based explanations is essential for clarifying and deepening one's own understanding as well as the foundation for participation in academic and civic life. This unit integrates the development of explanatory communication skills into the close-reading process. Students learn to explain their thinking and link it with textual evidence in discussion and writing. The unit culminates in a structured text-centered discussion in which students examine discoveries they have made about an important topic by explaining and comparing their textual analyses with those of their peers.

TOPIC AND TEXTS

The grade 9 *Reading Closely for Textual Details (RC)* unit, "Education is the new currency," presents students with a series of texts related to the changing dynamic of education in the United States. Students read a series of texts that explore and argue for various approaches to education as well as the role education plays in the United States. Students encounter texts ranging from the autobiography of Helen Keller, to multimedia sources, to contemporary arguments by former Secretary of State and four-star general Colin Powell and former Secretary of Education Arne Duncan. All texts are available in the unit texts section.

LEARNING PROGRESSION

The unit activities are organized into five parts, each associated with short texts. The parts build on each other and can each span a range of instructional time depending on scheduling and student ability.

Part 1 introduces students to the idea of reading closely for details through an examination of a range of text types—including a series of visual images, a video, and web-based text. Part 2 introduces students to a particular process for close reading that involves questioning the text—at first generally and then in text-specific ways—to help them focus on important textual ideas and characteristics. Part 3 develops student proficiency in analyzing textual details and making comparisons across texts. Parts 4 and 5 develop students' abilities to express their analyses, first through writing multiparagraph, text-based explanations in Part 4 and then, in Part 5, through facilitating and participating in text-centered discussions. This organization is designed to strengthen the precision of instruction and assessment as well as to give teachers flexibility in their use of the curriculum.

The final activities in Parts 1 through 4 are designed as independent student tasks that can be done either in class or as homework. Part 5 includes an **Optional Extended Assessment Activity** involving the compilation of a student portfolio of work and the writing of a reflective essay on their experiences throughout the unit.

☰ SEQUENCING LEARNING OVER TIME ☰ AND ACROSS GRADE LEVELS

The learning sequence for this unit and the instructional notes within it have been developed on the assumption that students may be learning the process of reading closely for textual details for the first time. Thus, terms are introduced and explained, graphic tools are overviewed and modeled, and lessons move relatively carefully from teacher modeling to guided practice to independent application. The Literacy Skills that are targeted and the Academic Habits that are developed are assumed to be in early stages of development for many students, and thus extensive scaffolding is provided.

However, students may come to this first unit in the Developing Core Literacy Proficiencies series having developed their Literacy Skills, Academic Habits, and Core Literacy Proficiencies in other contexts. They may have become very familiar with tools, handouts, terminology, skills, and habits addressed in this unit, if they have experienced the *Reading Closely* instructional sequence in a previous grade or school or with other text sets.

For this reason, teachers should use their professional judgment to plan their instruction for this unit considering not only *what* they are teaching (close reading and the curriculum designed to develop students' skills) but also *whom* they are teaching (their students' backgrounds, previous experiences, and readiness levels). Before teaching the unit, teachers are encouraged to determine what students have previously experienced, learned, or produced.

If students have more advanced skills or extensive previous experience in reading closely, instruction can move more rapidly through many sections of this unit, concentrate more on extended reading to deepen students' understanding, and emphasize more complex topics, texts, or writing and discussion activities.

OUTLINE

PART 1: UNDERSTANDING CLOSE READING

- Students learn what it means to read a text closely by attending to and analyzing textual details. Students analyze visual-based texts.

PART 2: QUESTIONING TEXTS

- Students use Questioning Paths to guide their approach to reading and deeper analysis of texts. Students read and analyze informational texts.

PART 3: ANALYZING DETAILS

- Students learn to analyze textual details as a key to discovering an author's perspective. Students read, analyze, and compare texts.

PART 4: EXPLAINING UNDERSTANDING

- Students learn how to summarize and explain what they have learned from their reading, questioning, and analysis of texts. Students read and analyze three related texts.

PART 5: DISCUSSING IDEAS

- Students learn the characteristics of an effective text-based discussion and demonstrate skills in leading and participating in one.

INTRODUCTION TO THE READING CLOSELY LITERACY TOOLBOX

In the *Reading Closely* (RC) unit, students learn a foundational approach to reading and analyzing complex texts. The approach centers on a Guiding Question framework, in which students learn how to question strategically and to use text-based questions in an iterative process of reading closely and analyzing texts. Students consider and frame provocative questions to drive multiple readings and discover deeper meaning. As they return to sections of text with more honed and precise questions, they discover layers of meaning they may not have initially recognized.

To support this inquiry-based approach to reading, the *Reading Closely* unit uses handouts and tools from the **Reading Closely Literacy Toolbox** to introduce students to the Odell Education strategic-questioning process. In this process, students use the framework presented in the ***Guiding Questions Handout*** to guide their own reading of text. As they progress through the handout's Questioning Framework, students first consider more general, text-dependent, Guiding Questions, and then more precise, text-specific questions. Ultimately, they craft their own text-specific questions to drive further analysis, inquiry, and understanding. This process is captured in the ***Reading Closely Graphic*** and ***Questioning Path Tool***, which teachers can use to assign specific questions, and students can use to guide close reading and annotating of a text. Additionally, the ***Approaching Texts*** and ***Analyzing Details Tools*** support students in the *Reading Closely* process as they begin their reading and analysis of textual details.

The **RC Literacy Toolbox** also houses detailed tables of Targeted Literacy Skills and Academic Habits Developed in the unit as well as the ***Reading Closely Literacy Skills and Discussion Habits Rubric*** and ***Student Reading Closely Literacy Skills and Discussion Habits Checklist***.

If students have previously completed the *Reading Closely* unit, they should already be familiar with these tools and handouts. As they gain independence in practicing the proficiency of attending to and analyzing textual details and internalize the concepts and processes detailed in the unit, students might rely less and less on the tools and handouts. Depending on students' ability and familiarity with the **RC Literacy Toolbox**, teachers might encourage students to use these materials when they encounter difficulties in understanding sections of texts, require assistance in communicating observations, or need to organize their ideas for their text-based explanation and discussion. Otherwise, students can proceed through the readings, annotating, taking notes, and analyzing details using their own, developing strategies. If students are ready to move through the unit without these scaffolds, it is still important that teachers continually verify that they are attending to and analyzing salient details and using evidence to communicate their importance and significance.

> **NOTE**
>
> All tools and handouts, including model ***Questioning Path Tools***, and ***Student RC Literacy Skills and Discussion Habits Checklist*** can also be found in the Student Edition.

LITERACY SKILLS AND ACADEMIC HABITS

TARGETED LITERACY SKILLS

In this unit, students learn about, practice, develop, and demonstrate foundational skills necessary to *read closely,* to participate actively in text-centered questioning and discussion, and to write text-based explanations. The following Literacy Skills are targeted with explicit instruction and assessment throughout the unit:

TARGETED LITERACY SKILLS	DESCRIPTORS
QUESTIONING	Formulates and responds to questions and lines of inquiry that lead to relevant and important ideas and themes within and across texts
ATTENDING TO DETAILS	Identifies relevant and important textual details, words, and ideas
IDENTIFYING RELATIONSHIPS	Identifies important connections among key details and ideas within and across texts
SUMMARIZING	Recounts the explicit meaning of texts, referring to key details, events, characters, language, and ideas

TARGETED LITERACY SKILLS	DESCRIPTORS
INTERPRETING LANGUAGE	Identifies how words and phrases convey meaning and represent an author's or narrator's perspective
RECOGNIZING PERSPECTIVE	Uses textual details to recognize an author's or narrator's relationship to and perspective on a text's topic

NOTE

Student language versions of these descriptors can be found in the *Student RC Literacy Skills and Discussion Habits Checklist* in the **RC Literacy Toolbox** and Student Edition.

APPLIED LITERACY SKILLS

In addition to these targeted skills, the unit provides opportunities for students to apply and develop the following Literacy Skills:

- **Deciphering Words**
- **Using Language**
- **Using Evidence**
- **Using Conventions**
- **Comprehending Syntax**

ACADEMIC HABITS

In this unit, students will be introduced to specific Academic Habits associated with preparing for and participating in productive text-centered discussions. Though instruction will not explicitly focus on the Academic Habits until Parts 4 and 5 of the unit, students can begin to think about them in Parts 1 through 3. The descriptors for these habits do not need to be introduced to students at this time—but if students are ready to think about them, student versions of the descriptors are presented in the *Student RC Literacy Skills and Discussion Habits Checklist* found in the **RC Literacy Toolbox** and Student Edition. The following Academic Habits are developed throughout the unit:

HABITS DEVELOPED	DESCRIPTORS
PREPARING	Reads the texts, researches the topics, and thinks about the questions being studied to prepare for tasks
COLLABORATING	Pays attention to, respects, and works productively in various roles with all other participants
COMMUNICATING CLEARLY	Uses appropriate language and relevant textual details to clearly present ideas and claims

Developing Core Literacy Proficiencies

☰ COMMON CORE STATE STANDARDS ☰ ALIGNMENT

The instructional focus of this unit is on learning to read text closely: attending to details, language, and perspective; posing and responding to text-dependent questions; and analyzing connections and relationships to deepen understanding. The unit also emphasizes informational text while incorporating literary nonfiction and other literary texts. Accordingly, the unit is aligned to the following targeted CCSS: **CCSS.ELA-LITERACY.RI.1, CCSS.ELA-LITERACY.RI.2,** and **CCSS.ELA-LITERACY.RI.6** (respectively, *read closely to determine literal and inferential meaning, determine central ideas and supporting details,* and *assess author's point of view—while attending to and citing specific textual evidence*). Students address these standards and develop related Literacy Skills within the unit through direct instruction and guided practice, and their learning is assessed continually through activities, tools, and written products.

As students develop these primary targeted reading skills, they are also practicing, and eventually demonstrating, their abilities to engage in text-centered discussions. Thus, **CCSS.ELA-LITERACY.SL.1** (*engage effectively in a range of collaborative discussions, building on others' ideas, and expressing their own clearly and persuasively*) is also an emerging targeted CCSS as the unit progresses, and it is directly assessed in the final, discussion-based activity of Part 5.

Students also practice and use related reading and writing skills from supporting CCSS. Thus, in Part 2, they begin to focus on **CCSS.ELA-LITERACY.RI.4** (*interpret words and phrases as they are used in a text*) and in Part 3 on **CCSS.ELA-LITERACY.RI.9** (*analyze how two or more texts address similar themes or topics*), with **CCSS.ELA-LITERACY.RI.9** formatively assessed in Part 5.

Students focus on crafting effective evidence-based writing, working from titles and paraphrases to summary sentences and explanatory paragraphs. Thus, **CCSS.ELA-LITERACY.W.2** (*write explanatory texts to convey ideas and information clearly and accurately*) and **CCSS.ELA-LITERACY.W.9** (*draw evidence from texts to support analysis*) are also introduced and practiced in the unit, as is **CCSS.ELA-LITERACY.W.4** (*produce clear and coherent writing*).

Finally, because students are expected to read and analyze a grade-level text somewhat independently in Parts 4 and 5, the unit provides initial evidence of how well students can meet the expectations of **CCSS.ELA-LITERACY.RI.10** (*read and comprehend complex texts independently and proficiently*).

PART 1

UNDERSTANDING CLOSE READING

"At the beginning I was only a little mass of possibilities."

OBJECTIVE:	Students learn what it means to read a text closely by attending to and analyzing textual details. Students analyze visual-based texts.

ESTIMATED TIME: 3 to 4 days

MATERIALS:

Texts 1 through 4
- *Guiding Questions Handout*
- *Reading Closely Graphic*
- *Questioning Path Tools*

⬛ LITERACY SKILLS

TARGETED SKILLS	DESCRIPTORS
QUESTIONING	Formulates and responds to questions and lines of inquiry that lead to relevant and important ideas and themes within and across texts
ATTENDING TO DETAILS	Identifies relevant and important textual details, words, and ideas

⬛ ACADEMIC HABITS

HABITS DEVELOPED	DESCRIPTORS
PREPARING	Reads the texts, researches the topics, and thinks about the questions being studied to prepare for tasks
COLLABORATING	Pays attention to, respects, and works productively in various roles with all other participants in a text-centered discussion

ALIGNMENT TO CCSS

TARGETED STANDARDS:

CCSS.ELA-LITERACY.RI.9-10.1: Cite strong and thorough textual evidence to support analysis of what the text says explicitly as well as inferences drawn from the text.

CCSS.ELA-LITERACY.RI.9-10.2: Determine a central idea of a text and analyze its development over the course of the text, including how it emerges and is shaped and refined by specific details; provide an objective summary of the text.

SUPPORTING STANDARD:

CCSS.ELA-LITERACY.RI.9-10.4: Determine the meaning of words and phrases as they are used in a text, including figurative, connotative, and technical meanings; analyze the cumulative impact of specific word choices on meaning and tone (e.g., how the language of a court opinion differs from that of a newspaper).

ACTIVITIES

1. INTRODUCTION TO THE UNIT
The teacher presents an overview of the unit, discussing the purposes and elements of close reading.

2. ATTENDING TO DETAILS
Students are oriented to the idea of attending to details through examining images.

3. READING CLOSELY FOR DETAILS
Students use Guiding Questions to look closely for details in a text.

4. ATTENDING TO DETAILS IN MULTIMEDIA
Students use Guiding Questions to look closely for details in a multimedia text and write a few sentences explaining something they have learned.

5. INDEPENDENT READING AND RESEARCHING ACTIVITY
Students use Guiding Questions to independently explore a multimedia website.

ACTIVITY 1: INTRODUCTION TO THE UNIT

The teacher presents an overview of the unit, discussing the purposes and elements of close reading.

INSTRUCTIONAL NOTES

Introduce the central purpose of the unit—to develop the skills and habits of a close reader:

1. Initially approaching and surveying a text
2. Using a path of questions to examine the text's language, ideas, perspective, and structure
3. Questioning further to investigate and analyze the text
4. Analyzing key details and language to note connections and develop understanding
5. Considering others' questions to deepen understanding
6. Explaining what one has come to understand as a reader
7. Extending one's reading through further questioning or reading and research

INTRODUCTORY ANALOGY

To introduce the unit and establish a link among questioning, close examination, and deepening understanding, use an analogy from another field that requires careful study and analysis. For example:

- Compare the process of *close reading* to the analytical processes used by experts in other fields, such as musicians, scientists, or detectives.
- Present a *CSI* video that demonstrates how a detective asks herself questions when first approaching a crime scene.

Use any of these analogies to illustrate how practitioners in various fields are able to analyze and understand situations, events, places, phenomena, or artistic works because their training focuses them on details that others outside of the field do not typically notice. This training often involves using questions to direct their attention to key elements of their fields of study.

A musician might ask herself, "How do the sounds of the various instruments work together?" A crime scene investigator might ask, "What evidence suggests how the perpetrator came and went from the scene?" These general questions lead the practitioners to then ask specific questions directly related to the object of investigation. For example, the general question concerning the perpetrator's coming and going might lead the investigator to notice a set of muddy footprints. She then might ask, "What are the size and type of the shoes that left these muddy footprints?" Experts ask these questions so that they clearly understand what they are studying and can clearly communicate their understanding to others.

NOTE

If students have previously completed the *Reading Closely* unit, it may be sufficient to carry out an abbreviated version of Activity 1 without using an analogy. Review how students will accomplish the following:

NOTE

1. Use a Questioning Path Framework to analyze a series of texts around a topic.
2. Use tools and handouts from the **RC Literacy Toolbox** to guide their reading, annotating, and analyzing of complex texts.
3. Write a multiparagraph explanation of a text.
4. Conduct a text-based discussion based off their own comparative questions about texts in the unit.

LINK THE ANALOGY TO QUESTIONING SKILLS

- Using the introductory analogy as a reference point, explain that effective readers also use Guiding Questions to help them look for evidence in texts.
- Introduce the *Reading Closely Graphic* and *Guiding Questions Handout* (in the **RC Literacy Toolbox**), orienting students to the reading process represented in the graphic and the questions listed in each row of the handout in relationship to that same process. Explain that the graphic shows them what they will be working on throughout the unit and that the handout includes an organized set of general Guiding Questions that can direct their attention to key evidence as they read.

READING CLOSELY GRAPHIC AND GUIDING QUESTIONS HANDOUT

Note first that the graphic and the handout—and the question-based reading process they organize—are divided into five phases. Have students read and discuss the guiding statements for each of the five phases:

1. APPROACHING
I determine my reading purposes and take note of important information about the text.

2. QUESTIONING
I use questions to help me investigate important aspects of the text.

3. ANALYZING
I question further to analyze the details I notice and determine their meaning or importance.

4. DEEPENING
I consider others' questions and develop initial observations or claims.
I explain why and cite my evidence.

5. EXTENDING
I pose new questions to extend my investigation of the text and topic.
I communicate my thinking to others.

Let students know that they will be using this question-driven process throughout the unit and that they will self-assess, and be assessed, on their use of the process as well as on their close-reading skills and textual understandings developed through the process.

Having noted and discussed this vertical progression of the graphic—and the reading process it suggests—examine the horizontal organization of the *Guiding Questions Handout* and discuss the four domains in which we often examine texts: *Language, Ideas, Perspective,* and *Structure.* This organization for questions (which can be referred to with the acronym *LIPS*) can be used to help students focus on specific aspects of any text they are reading and also to see the relationships among the domains, as when, for example, language is a key to understanding perspective.

- Emphasize the purpose of these Guiding Questions: to focus a reader on specific aspects of a text and guide the reading process—rather than to lead to a single answer. Contrast this use of questions with what students have typically experienced, where "getting the right answer" (quickly) is typically how they have thought about responding to questions.

- Help students see how a broad, discovery question (what?) from phase 2 (Questioning) can lead to a more specific analysis question (how?) in phase 3 (Analyzing).

  For example, from the language domain:

  1. Questioning: <u>What</u> words or phrases stand out to me as I read?

  2. Analyzing: <u>How</u> do specific words or phrases affect the meaning or tone of the text?

- Discuss how a sequence of questions such as this can lead to a *Questioning Path,* in which a reader moves from broad Guiding Questions into more specific, text-based questioning, using the questions to drive closer reading and lead to deeper understanding.

- As a final introduction to the handout, consider modeling its use with a text the class has read recently, doing a think-aloud about how you approached the text and what you as a reader discovered in response to a selected set of questions and the Questioning Path they set up.

PREVIEW THE TEXTS AND CULMINATING TASKS

- Show students the text set table in the section "Reading Closely for Textual Details Unit Texts," indicating that there are connections among the texts, but do not stipulate what those connections are.

- Let them know they will be reading and studying those texts with increasing independence and will be expected to write a text-based explanation and lead a group discussion about one of the final texts at the end of the unit.

Referring back to the *Guiding Questions Handout*, let students know that they will begin examining the texts by looking at the ideas (and information) they present. First, students will examine visual and video examples and then transition to increasingly detailed texts, deepening their understanding of the unit's topics: the various forms and purposes of education and pedagogical approaches in the United States.

With Texts 5 and 6, they will encounter varying perspectives and ideas about how to teach children and will shift to questions drawn from the Language section to gain a sense of the perspectives of Colin Powell and Maria Montessori.

Finally, they will examine and compare the perspectives presented in various texts, more specifically noting the similarities and differences among the views of various leaders and their views on the purpose of public education in the United States.

ACTIVITY 2: ATTENDING TO DETAILS

Students are oriented to the strategy of questioning texts and attending to details by first examining a set of visual images.

INSTRUCTIONAL NOTES

Text 1 (found in the unit texts) presents students with a set of visual images selected to build curiosity about the unit's topic, create context for reading the texts, and provide initial practice in looking closely or visual scanning. Introduce students to the set of images they will study but provide minimal contextual information. Have students scan the images, then assign specific images to groups or individuals for closer analysis.

NOTE

This activity can be done using a printed copy of the visual image(s), a projection in the room, or on computers, enabling students to zoom in closer and note specific details.

QUESTIONING PATH TOOL

The **Questioning Path Tool** is an editable version of the **Reading Closely Graphic** with which teachers can provide model Questioning Paths (provided throughout this unit) to students and where students can record their own Questioning Paths as they grow familiar with the process. Teachers might use the included model Questioning Paths or create their own depending on student and classroom needs. Students can use the tool to create their own Questioning Paths when ready to do so. They will formally have the opportunity to create their own Questioning Paths in the *Making Evidence-Based Claims* unit.

Included in the model **Questioning Path Tools** are model text-specific questions associated with Guiding Questions. These questions are included to illustrate the process and possibilities; teachers are encouraged to develop their own text-specific questions based on their own analyses.

QUESTIONING PATH TOOL
Text 1—Classroom Photos

APPROACHING:
I determine my reading purposes and take note of key information about the text. I identify the LIPS domain(s) that will guide my initial reading.

I will initially focus on *ideas* and supporting details.

QUESTIONING: *I use Guiding Questions to help me investigate the text (from the **Guiding Questions Handout**).*

1. What details stand out to me as I examine this image? [I]

2. What do I think this image is mainly about? [I]

ANALYZING: *I question further to connect and analyze the details I find (from the **Guiding Questions Handout**).*

3. How do specific details help me understand what is being depicted in the image? [I]

DEEPENING: *I consider the questions of others.*

4. What do I notice about the arrangement of each classroom? How are the chairs and desks set up?

5. What do the details of the photos suggest about what the students are doing?

6. What connections or comparisons do I notice between the photos?

   What might these connections and comparisons suggest about the nature of education in the classrooms and historical eras they depict?

EXTENDING: *I pose my own questions.*

Examples:

7. Why is there such a big difference between the classrooms?

8. What do I think might influence the way they are set up?

Developing Core Literacy Proficiencies

APPROACHING: FOCUS ON IDEAS AND DETAILS

- Explain to students that they will be focusing on details in the set of images and using those details to understand what the images represent (their information or *ideas*).

QUESTIONING: EXAMINE IMAGES IN SMALL GROUPS

- Students examine the image(s) in small groups and first consider broad Guiding Questions related to ideas from the Questioning section of the *Guiding Questions Handout*, such as "What details stand out to me as I examine this image?" and "What do I think this image is mainly about?"

- In their groups, students find several details that stand out to them, with one group member serving as a recorder of their details.

- Groups may consult the *Guiding Questions Handout* for further questions to help them focus on details.

- Groups discuss what the details suggest to them and identify any new questions they have after examining and discussing the details.

ANALYZING: CONNECT THE DETAILS

- Help students move from simple observations about details they notice to thinking about the connections among details and an understanding of what the images represent.

- Use a Guiding Question related to ideas from the Analyzing section of the *Guiding Questions Handout*, such as "How do specific details help me understand what is being depicted in the image?" As students consider this sort of question, discuss how they have moved from observation to analysis—from what details they notice to what they think about the details.

DEEPENING: INTRODUCE THE CONCEPT OF TEXT-SPECIFIC QUESTIONS

- Lead a discussion on what the groups noticed about the images and the questions they had.

- Introduce them to text-specific questions for each image set (using either the model questions or ones developed in class).

- Discuss how these questions are *text specific* and do the following:
    ⇒ Emerge from looking closely at the image
    ⇒ Prompt a reader to look for more details
    ⇒ Lead to a greater understanding of the image

- Assign one of the three questions to each student group and have the groups develop an observation related to the question and supported by details from the image(s) they have studied closely.

SUMMARIZING: WRITE A CAPTION

- After discussing the image-specific questions, students list three details they think are key for them in understanding something that is going on in one of the photos, returning to the broad Guiding Question, "What do I think this image is mainly about?"

⇒ For example, in the photo from the 1950s, the students are seated in rows and the teacher stands in front of them. Students may have noticed that all the students in the photo are looking at the teacher, who appears to be addressing them as an entire class. How students interpret these details will greatly influence what they think the classroom photo represents—and may present them with a clue about historical differences in approaches to education in the United States.

• Students write a new caption that summarizes what they think their image is about and share and compare their captions, noting the details that have led to what they have written.

EXTENDING: POSE NEW QUESTIONS

If they are ready to practice developing their own text-specific questions, students might write and share a question they have about one or more of the images—possibly a speculative question as seen in the model *Questioning Path Tool*. If time allows, this might be an opportunity to let students explore their extending questions through Internet research— finding out more about different approaches to education in the United States and how they have changed over time.

FORMATIVE ASSESSMENT AND FEEDBACK

Literacy Skills

Have students self-assess, peer assess, and receive informal teacher feedback on their emerging Literacy Skills in the three areas focused on in the previous activities: **Questioning, Attending to Details**, and **Summarizing**. At this stage, definitive answers do not need to be established for questions students use or pose as they examine the images. The purpose of the exercises is for students to get a sense of how close, question-based examination of texts leads to new questions, which in turn lead to further examination of textual detail. This developing understanding, the use of the process, as well as students' developing abilities to summarize what they have discovered and to communicate meaning to others can all be informally assessed.

Academic Habits

Students will also have begun to work informally in small groups on the Academic Habits associated with text-centered discussion. Students might self-assess their behaviors of **Collaborating**, specifically how well they have "paid attention to and worked productively with other participants" in discussing what they have observed.

NOTE

To support self-, peer, and teacher assessment of skills and habits developed during the unit, a formal *RC Literacy Skills and Discussion Habits Rubric* and less formal *Student RC Literacy Skills and Discussion Habits Checklist* are provided in the **RC Literacy Toolbox**.

ACTIVITY 3: READING CLOSELY FOR DETAILS

Students use Guiding Questions to look closely for details in a text.

TEXT NOTES

Text 2 is an excerpt from Helen Keller's autobiography, *The Story of My Life.* In this text, Keller, who was blind and deaf, describes in detail the impact her teacher, Anne Sullivan, had on her development as a child. This is a good first text for close reading because it is vivid and challenging, but it is also relatively short and accessible for most students. Keller's use of descriptive language and characterization enable close attention to details, words, and phrases—and an introduction of close reading that focuses on language and how an author uses it to convey her perspective. If students have had previous experience studying figurative language and characterization, this text can be more formally studied as a powerful example of literary nonfiction and how an autobiographer uses similar literary techniques to those used by writers of fiction.

QUESTIONING PATH TOOL

Text 2—*The Story of My Life,* Helen Keller (Model 1)

APPROACHING: *I determine my reading purposes and take note of key information about the text. I identify the LIPS domain(s) that will guide my initial reading.*

I will initially note that this is an autobiography written in 1905. I will focus on the author's use of *language* to describe the teacher and student.

QUESTIONING: *I use Guiding Questions to help me investigate the text (from the **Guiding Questions Handout**).*

1. What words or phrases stand out to me as powerful and important? [L]
2. How are key ideas or characters described? [L]

ANALYZING: *I question further to connect and analyze the details I find (from the **Guiding Questions Handout**).*

3. What details or words suggest the author's perspective? [L/P]

DEEPENING: *I consider the questions of others.*

4. What words does Keller use to describe her teacher?

   What do these words suggest about how she feels about Anne Sullivan?

5. What does the figurative language phrase "a little mass of possibilities" in the first paragraph suggest about how Keller at first saw herself as a student?

   How does her use of the word *only* with this phrase further develop her view of herself?

   Based on details in this first paragraph, what does she think the role of a teacher is?

6. In paragraph 3, Keller claims that a student "will not work joyously unless he feels that liberty is his."

   What does this statement suggest about Keller's view of students, teachers, and education?

   What must the student experience in order to "dance bravely through a dull routine of textbooks"?

7. In paragraph 4, Keller writes, "How much of my delight in all beautiful things is innate, and how much is due to her influence, I can never tell."

   How does the word *innate* help me understand what Keller means?

   What does this statement suggest Keller thinks the relationship between a teacher and a student should be?

EXTENDING: *I pose my own questions.*

Example:

8. According to Keller, who has more responsibility when it comes to a student's education—the teacher or the student?

APPROACHING: PREREADING FOR TEXT 2

- Help students note the few things they know about this text from the details of its title block: that it was written in 1905, that it is an excerpt from an autobiography by Helen Keller, and that this excerpt is about her teacher, Anne Sullivan. Have students think about what they already understand or might speculate about the text, its author, and the topic based only on this introductory information.

- Direct students to the questions related to language found in the Questioning section of the model **Questioning Path Tool** for Text 2 (or others from the **Guiding Questions Handout**). Explain that they will now be reading this text with a focus on how the author uses descriptive language to detail what she thinks of her teacher.

QUESTIONING: INITIAL READING, FOCUSED ON A GUIDING QUESTION

- Based on students' independent reading skills and previous experiences, determine if they should first follow along as they listen to the text read aloud or if they can do a first, silent reading on their own.

- As they read or listen to the passage, students think about a Guiding Question, such as "What words or phrases stand out to me as powerful and important?" or "How are key ideas or characters described?"

- Ask students to record and share their responses to the question for *one* of the sentences in the text, reminding students to refer to details from the text to support their responses—as they have previously done with the visual details they noted in the images of Text 1.

ANALYZING: ANNOTATING DETAILS AND CONNECTING THEM TO IDEAS

- In groups, students consider a Guiding Question related to language or perspective from the Analyzing section of the **Guiding Questions Handout**, such as "What details or words suggest the author's perspective?"

- Introduce students to the skill of annotating text, in which students note, mark, and interpret key details. (Alternately, review text annotation, if students have previously learned or used these skills.)

  ⇒ Make sure students have print versions of Text 2 on which they can annotate.

  ⇒ Model and have students practice *active reading* and text annotation for one key paragraph of the text by using a pencil, pen, or highlighter to mark short but important sections of text while reading. For this exercise, students might again read and now annotate the first sentence of the second paragraph, which presents a set of descriptive phrases and details for them to note.

  ⇒ Introduce a simple symbol system that can be used for key details students mark. For example, students might use a star (*) to indicate something that seems important to them, a question mark (?) to indicate something that raises a question or is unclear for them, an exclamation point (!) to indicate something that surprises them, and graphic arrows to note possible connections among words, details, or ideas.

  ⇒ Model and have students practice *note-making*, or jotting short comments or questions in the margins of the text that relate to details they have marked or symbols they have inserted in the text.

⇒ Talk through how the modeled text annotations can lead to an observation about "what details or words suggest the author's perspective"—what each of the descriptive phrases conveys and what the words and details suggest about the author's perspective.

- In pairs, students annotate a second descriptive sentence from the text, study their annotations, and decide on an observation, description, or characterization they think is presented in that sentence. [Note: The most challenging sentence in the text, the lengthy, figurative third sentence of paragraph 2, will be examined more deeply in Part 2, Activity 1.]

- Students compare and discuss details across the sections of text they have examined and annotated and the observations, descriptions, or characterizations they have found to be conveyed in those sentences. In small groups or as a class, students think about the author's view or perspective that the text may be presenting, referencing key supporting details they have noted.

ANNOTATING

Teaching students to annotate texts is important because it keeps them focused on the text rather than their own interpretation—at least at first. There are many ways to annotate, including note-making, where students mark a text with comments or symbols to point out a main idea, key word, or important detail. Annotations can be done on a printed copy or electronically.

By staying in the text, students continue to focus on details that emerge from the words and sentences. Later, they will be able to synthesize their annotations.

DEEPENING: INDEPENDENT READING

- Before students reread the passage independently, direct students to text-specific questions such as the examples found in the model *Questioning Path Tool*.

- Students think about one of the questions and focus on specific sections of the overall text. Because the Deepening questions for this text become increasingly complex, students may be assigned questions and the paragraphs they address based on the reading skills they bring to this unit. [Note: Paragraph 2 will be examined more closely in Part 2, Activity 1.]

- While reading independently, students mark and annotate details they notice.

EXTENDING: CLASS REVIEW

As a class, students do the following:

- Compare the details they have noticed and marked and the annotations (comments) they have made.

- Discuss what the details suggest to them.

- Discuss what their question- and paragraph-based observations add up to. What do they as a class notice about how the author has used language to communicate her perspective about her teacher and about education itself?

- Potentially (if they are ready), identify a new text-specific question they have after examining and discussing the details.

PARAPHRASING

As students begin to take notes and describe what is going on in the text, this is a good place to introduce paraphrasing.

Introduce the concept of a *paraphrase* and model paraphrasing a sentence from the passage that presents one or more key details.

- Individually, students draft a paraphrase of one sentence with key details that stood out to them.

FORMATIVE ASSESSMENT AND FEEDBACK

Literacy Skills

Have students self-assess, peer assess, and receive informal teacher feedback on their emerging Literacy Skills in the three areas focused on in the previous activities: **Questioning, Attending to Details**, and **Summarizing**. As students work through the Questioning Path, check to see which students have issues with understanding the text and may need more help determining the meaning of specific words and phrases. Have them reflect on what they have learned about annotating a text as a means of attending to details, compare their annotations, and think about how they might improve their processes and skills. As they examine their paraphrased sentences, have them reflect on the key details they have noted and how clearly they have summarized them.

Academic Habits

Students will have continued to use and develop the Academic Habits associated with text-centered discussion—this time with a print text. Because they have worked as a class, in small groups, and in pairs, they might reflect on how well they have demonstrated the skills of preparing for discussions by reading and annotating the text and considering the questions that have framed discussion.

NOTE

To support self-, peer, and teacher assessment of skills and habits developed during the unit, a formal *RC Literacy Skills and Discussion Habits Rubric* and less formal *Student RC Literacy Skills and Discussion Habits Checklist* are provided in the **RC Literacy Toolbox**.

ACTIVITY 4: ATTENDING TO DETAILS IN MULTIMEDIA

Students use Guiding Questions to look closely for details in a multimedia text and write a few sentences explaining something they have learned.

TEXT NOTES

The multimedia text (Text 3), "Changing Education Paradigms" by Sir Ken Robinson, is a TED Talk from RSA Animate describing the changing educational landscape across the United States and world. Robinson sets out by identifying two reasons why countries are currently reforming education and follows up by pointing out the barriers that traditional education programs pose. The animation that accompanies Robinson's speech supports students' understanding of his specific words, phrases, and ideas with the use of graphs, tables, and drawings. This provides a rich text for students to examine as they listen to and observe Robinson's ideas on models of education.

NOTE

Details to find an online transcript of the TED Talk are available in Media Supports.

QUESTIONING PATH TOOL
Text 3—"Changing Education Paradigms," Ken Robinson, 2010

APPROACHING:
I determine my reading purposes and take note of key information about the text. I identify the LIPS domain(s) that will guide my initial reading.

I will initially focus on *ideas* and supporting details. I will think about the animation helps me to understand the author's words and ideas.

QUESTIONING: *I use Guiding Questions to help me investigate the text (from the Guiding Questions Handout).*

1. What new ideas or information do I find in the text (video)? [I]

2. What do I notice about how the text (video) is organized or sequenced? [S]

ANALYZING: *I question further to connect and analyze the details I find (from the Guiding Questions Handout).*

3. How might I summarize the main ideas of the text and the key supporting details? [I]

DEEPENING: *I consider the questions of others.*

4. Ken Robinson's TED talk is brought to life through illustration and animation. What is one set of visual images from the video that stands out to me? What do these images suggest about Robinson's view of education?

5. What reasons does Robinson present for why "every country on earth is reforming public education"?

   What does he say is the "problem" with current approaches to improving education?

6. What does Robinson say is the old view of the value of education that "our kids don't believe"?

   Why don't students see the value in education that people once did?

   How has the world changed since the development of public education in the age of enlightenment and the industrial revolution?

7. Robinson says that the current model of education is "essentially about conformity." What details does he give to support this claim?

   How does he explain the modern "epidemic" of ADHD?

   Why might students see schoolwork as being about "boring stuff"?

8. Robinson contrasts the two words "aesthetic" and "anaesthetic." How does he define these two words?

   How does he use these words to talk about the differences between education that "puts students to sleep" and education that "wakes them up to what is inside of themselves"?

9. What does Robinson suggest about how and why schools are like factories? Why does he think this is not a good "model of learning"?

10. How does Robinson define the idea of "divergent thinking"?

    Robinson describes a longitudinal study on divergent thinking in young children. How does he use this information to support his claims about what is wrong or missing in current education?

11. The speech is titled, "Changing Education Paradigms." According to Robinson, why do education paradigms (or models) need to change? What evidence does he give to support his claim that a change must occur?

EXTENDING: *I pose my own questions.*

Students might explore a question they generate through Internet research.

APPROACHING: FOCUS ON DETAILS AND IDEAS IN A VIDEO FORMAT

- Inform students that they will now be viewing closely a short video, with the same purpose of attending to details and thinking about ideas that they have used previously with the visual images and first print text.

- Discuss students' perceptions of the similarities and differences between reading and viewing.

QUESTIONING: VIEW THE VIDEO

- Students view the video with no additional context provided other than what they bring from studying the previous texts.

- As students watch the video, they think about a Guiding Question related to ideas from the Questioning section of the *Guiding Question Handout*, such as "What new ideas or information do I find in the text (video)?"

ANALYZING: CLASS DISCUSSION AND RE-VIEW OF VIDEO

- Before re-viewing the video, briefly discuss students' initial observations about what the video is mainly about.

- Use some students' observations to generate a list of ideas presented in the video to guide the re-view. Then, introduce students to a question related to ideas from the Analyzing section of the *Guiding Questions Handout*, such as "How might I summarize a main idea of the text (video) and its key supporting details?"

- As students re-view the video, have them use a system for annotating their viewing through a separate set of notes.

  ⇒ For example, students might record details, symbols, and comments or questions in a two-column notes format.

  ⇒ To do so, they might note details they observe sequentially in the first column of their notes, then go back and highlight details they see as important, and make notes (in the second column) about those selected details and why they see them as important.

DEEPENING: EXAMINE SPECIFIC DETAILS

- Present students with one or more text-specific questions about the video, such as the examples found in the model *Questioning Path Tool*.

If this set of eight Deepening questions is used, all students can individually consider question 4 (about the video's visual images) and think about something that stands out to them. Questions 5 through 10 are arranged sequentially and keyed to phrases Robinson uses and the animators illustrate. Assign student groups one of the six questions and have them locate and watch closely the segment of the video related to their question. The final question (11) provides an opportunity for a concluding all-class discussion of the video's perspective on education, and how it compares to the views in other texts and their own personal perspectives.

- In groups, have students view a segment of the video for a third time and use their two-column notes to think about one or more of the questions.

- Students share and compare their question-based notes and observations in an informal class discussion. Groups can present what they have observed and learned as they have responded to their question.

INSTRUCTIONAL NOTES

EXTENDING: SMALL GROUPS WRITE ABOUT THE VIDEO

- In small groups, students discuss the key details they have found to be important and their thinking about how those details help them understand the video.

- Students share their notes and collaboratively write a few sentences explaining something they have learned from the video, referring to key details that have led to their understanding.

- Volunteers from each group read their sentences to the class.

- As a class, compare what the groups saw, including how clearly and accurately they are able to communicate their understanding.

EXTENDING: FURTHER READING AND DISCUSSION

Following their viewing and discussion of the video, students might engage in informal Internet research about historical or current models of education. They might also explore concepts such as divergent thinking, creativity, or conformity.

FORMATIVE ASSESSMENT AND FEEDBACK

Literacy Skills

Reflect on the close-reading experience of watching a video, using the **Reading Closely Graphic** to guide the reflective discussion. This reflective discussion is an opportunity for students to self-assess their developing skills in the three targeted Literacy Skills areas—**Questioning, Attending to Details**, and **Summarizing**—and to identify areas where they can improve as a reader over the course of this unit.

Academic Habits

Students can also continue to self-assess their use of Academic Habits associated with text-centered discussion—specifically how well they have collaborated with peers as they have viewed and discussed the video.

NOTE

To support self-, peer, and teacher assessment of skills and habits developed during the unit, a formal *RC Literacy Skills and Discussion Habits Rubric* and less formal *Student RC Literacy Skills and Discussion Habits Checklist* are provided in the **RC Literacy Toolbox**.

ACTIVITY 5: INDEPENDENT READING AND RESEARCH

Students use Guiding Questions to independently explore a multimedia website.

INSTRUCTIONAL NOTES

This activity is an optional extension of Part 1, in which students can enrich their skills of looking for details with web-based text. It is recommended for students who have access to a computer either as an individual or in groups. Accessing an informational site can not only help students apply close-reading skills in the context of Internet research but also enrich their understanding of the topic and other texts they will encounter in the unit. Students might be expected to develop deeper understanding of a part of the website through close reading and viewing and to bring details and information they have found back to a small-group discussion.

TEXT NOTES

The recommended website (Text 4) is PBS's Only a Teacher. This site provides students with several avenues for learning about the history and role of the teacher in the US education system. The site includes varied formats of information including pictures, a time line, accompanying videos, and biographies of several education pioneers such as John Dewey and Horace Mann. Students might explore one specific part of the web page or a related link and then report back to their peers.

≡ QUESTIONING PATH TOOL
Only a Teacher, PBS

APPROACHING:
I determine my reading purposes and take note of key information about the text. I identify the LIPS domain(s) that will guide my initial reading.

I will focus on new *ideas* and information I can bring back to the class. I will note key information about the website I visit and its author or source.

QUESTIONING: *I use Guiding Questions to help me investigate the text (from the Guiding Questions Handout).*

1. What do I notice about how the website is organized? [S]

2. What new ideas or information do I find on the website? [I]

ANALYZING: *I question further to connect and analyze the details I find (from the Guiding Questions Handout).*

3. How might I summarize the main ideas of the website and the key supporting details? [I]

DEEPENING: *I consider the questions of others.*

4. What interesting details, examples, or ideas can I find that relate to the other texts we are studying?

5. From the Teaching Timeline, what details do I learn about Normal Schools? What was their primary purpose? How were they related to Common Schools?

6. For one of the Schoolhouse Pioneers or Teachers Today, what do I learn about his or her view of education?

EXTENDING: *I pose my own questions.*

Students might be asked to pose a question and bring back information related to their question.

PART 1: FORMATIVE ASSESSMENT OPPORTUNITIES

LITERACY SKILLS

Focus self-, peer, and teacher assessment at the end of Part 1 on the targeted skills of **Questioning** and **Attending to Details**. Examine students' annotations for Text 2 and their notes for Text 3 (video) to see how well they are using questions to drive their reading and noting of details that relate to the questions they are considering.

Students' captions and paraphrases for Texts 1 and 2 can be reviewed to see if they are able to note key details and generalize from them, and they might provide a preassessment of skills before students read and analyze more challenging passages in Parts 2 through 5. These short, informal writing samples should also be reviewed for initial evidence that students are able to clearly explain their thinking about the texts they are reading.

ACADEMIC HABITS

Student conversations in small groups, particularly in relation to Text 3 (the video), can also provide rich initial evidence of their emerging thinking and of the Academic Habits related to text-centered discussions that they bring into the unit. Students will further develop those habits within the unit's activities and initially demonstrate them in Part 5. At this point, have them think about their discussions in terms of the two Academic Habits developed in Part 1.

NOTE
Students will be introduced to a rubric organized by the habits used in text-centered discussion at the start of Part 5 in this unit.

Academic Habits: Student Reflection Questions

- How have I <u>prepared</u> for the discussion through reading and watching?
- How have I <u>collaborated</u> with other participants?
- What can I <u>improve</u> on as the unit progresses?

NOTE
To support self-, peer, and teacher assessment of skills and habits developed during the unit, a formal *RC Literacy Skills and Discussion Habits Rubric* and less formal *Student RC Literacy Skills and Discussion Habits Checklist* are provided in the **RC Literacy Toolbox**

PART 2

QUESTIONING TEXTS

"The education process begins before the child is born."

OBJECTIVE:	Students use Questioning Paths to guide their approach to reading and deeper analysis of texts. Students read and analyze informational texts.

ESTIMATED TIME: 2–3 days

MATERIALS:

Texts 2 and 5
- *Approaching Texts Tool*
- *Analyzing Details Tool*
- *Questioning Path Tools*
- *Reading Closely Graphic*
- *Guiding Questions Handout*
- *Attending to Details Handout*

☰ LITERACY SKILLS

TARGETED SKILLS	DESCRIPTORS
QUESTIONING	Formulates and responds to questions and lines of inquiry that lead to relevant and important ideas and themes within and across texts
ATTENDING TO DETAILS	Identifies relevant and important textual details, words, and ideas
IDENTIFYING RELATIONSHIPS	Identifies important connections among key details and ideas within and across texts
SUMMARIZING	Recounts the explicit meaning of texts, referring to key details, events, characters, language, and ideas

☰ ACADEMIC HABITS

HABITS DEVELOPED	DESCRIPTORS
COLLABORATING	Pays attention to, respects, and works productively in various roles with all other participants
COMMUNICATING CLEARLY	Uses appropriate language and relevant textual details to clearly present ideas and claims

◰ ALIGNMENT TO CCSS

TARGETED STANDARDS:

CCSS.ELA-LITERACY.RI.9-10.1: Cite strong and thorough textual evidence to support analysis of what the text says explicitly as well as inferences drawn from the text.

CCSS.ELA-LITERACY.RI.9-10.2: Determine a central idea of a text and analyze its development over the course of the text, including how it emerges and is shaped and refined by specific details; provide an objective summary of the text.

SUPPORTING STANDARD:

CCSS.ELA-LITERACY.RI.9-10.4: Determine the meaning of words and phrases as they are used in a text, including figurative, connotative, and technical meanings; analyze the cumulative impact of specific word choices on meaning and tone (e.g., how the language of a court opinion differs from that of a newspaper).

◰ ACTIVITIES

1. HOW SKILLFUL READERS APPROACH TEXTS
The teacher models how to use the *Approaching Texts Tool* to guide initial reading and then pairs practice with a text they have read.

2. APPROACHING A NEW TEXT
Students read a new text and use the *Approaching Texts Tool* to guide their reading.

3. ANALYZING TEXT WITH TEXT-SPECIFIC QUESTIONS
The teacher guides the class through an analysis of the text using the *Analyzing Details Tool*.

4. POSING TEXT-SPECIFIC QUESTIONS
Students develop their own text-specific questions with which to analyze the text.

5. INDEPENDENT WRITING ACTIVITY
Students write a short paragraph explaining their analysis of the text and list supporting textual details.

≡ ACTIVITY 1: HOW SKILLFUL READERS ≡ APPROACH TEXTS

The teacher models how to use the *Approaching Texts Tool* to guide initial reading and then pairs practice on a text they have read.

APPROACHING TEXTS TOOL

The *Approaching Texts Tool* (in the **RC Literacy Toolbox**) is a graphic organizer framed by the first two stages of the questioning process students have encountered using the *Reading Closely Graphic* and *Guiding Questions Handout* in Part 1. It supports students in initiating the question-based process for close reading by guiding them through the Approaching stage—determining their reading purpose and approach, and doing a prereading analysis of key information known about the text. The tool also frames the initial Questioning stage by providing a place for recording Guiding Questions to help students read closely for details. Students learn to use the tool while studying and annotating a text.

INSTRUCTIONAL NOTES

APPROACHING: INTRODUCE THE TOOL

- Walk students through the organization of the *Approaching Texts Tool*, discussing how it relates to the first two stages of the *Reading Closely Graphic* and *Guiding Questions Handout* and how it sets up the question-based reading process they have used in Part 1 Activities. Tell the students that they will use the tool to examine what they know about the text and its author before reading and to focus their initial reading by using one or more questions.

APPROACHING A TEXT

There are many ways to find more information about a text, its author, and publisher. One way is by doing a quick search on the Internet. If students want to know more about an author, they might try to find the author's website or look on *Wikipedia* for quick information—especially for authors who are also historical figures (such as those in this unit). It will then be important for them to reflect on how this background knowledge affects their own understanding of the text(s). For contemporary authors, even Twitter and Facebook accounts and pages can help students find out more about a text and its author.

QUESTIONING: MODEL THE TOOL

Begin by modeling the *Approaching Texts Tool* using Text 2 referring to what students have already done in Part 1. Have students practice recording this information using the tool:

- Think aloud and talk through what to record in the Reading Purposes box of the "Approaching the Text" section. Discuss the initial approach to the text and its focus on ideas and related details.
- Talk through why thinking about the author, text type, and source/publisher can often influence one's reading and analysis of a text. In the case of Text 2, knowing that the text is an autobiography will help students focus on Keller's own perspective. Given that this is a work about her entire life, students may find it important that she chooses to dedicate this part of her life's story to a teacher.

- Model for students how this examination of key information about the text before reading helps them consider and record an insight about the text in response to the question, "What do I already think or understand about the text based on this information?" Have students each record an understanding they had as they approached reading Text 2 for the first time.

- Select one or two questions to consider from the model *Questioning Path Tool* for Text 2 or new questions from the *Guiding Questions Handout* and write them into the Questioning the Text section of the tool. For example, use the Guiding Question from the Questioning section, "How are key details or characters described?"

- Talk through how this question was or could be used to guide a reading of the text and what it suggests a reader might pay attention to. Connect this discussion to students' practice with text annotation in Part 1, and talk through where the question might lead a reader to look in the text, and what details to search for, highlight, and annotate. For example, with the Guiding Question "What details or words suggest the author's perspective?" a reader might pay attention to words and phrases that suggests the author's feelings or attitude about the role of the teacher.

- Reread through a key section of the text (other than paragraph 2, which will be examined more closely by students alter in this activity), searching for details related to the Guiding Question. Model marking and annotating the text—or revisit the annotations recorded in Part 1, Activity 3.

- Review and demonstrate the text annotation skills that were introduced and practiced in Part 1.

ATTENDING TO DETAILS HANDOUT

The *Attending to Details Handout* (in the **RC Literacy Toolbox**) lists examples of details one might typically pay attention to depending on which of the LIPS question domains is the focus for reading and questioning. You may want to introduce this handout now in conjunction with the *Approaching Texts Tool* or wait until students are working independently with the tool.

INSTRUCTIONAL NOTES

ANALYZING: STUDENTS PRACTICE USING THE TOOL IN PAIRS

- Student pairs continue examining Text 2 with the *Approaching Texts Tool*.

- Have student pairs use a *new* text-specific question as a lens for examining the text. For example, students might now approach the text by fully focusing on the language and perspective domains of questions, and consider question 3 from the second Questioning Path for Text 2, which follows.

NOTE

See the following text notes and second model *Questioning Path Tool* for Text 2.

- Student pairs then work together to annotate the text (or make new notes in relationship to previous annotations) in relationship to their question and their question-based thinking about what details to search for.

NOTE

Students may need a second, clean copy of the text if they have already recorded many annotations on Text 2.

Text 2 has previously been used to introduce students to a type of text they will be reading in the unit—personal narratives about experiences with education. Students have also examined Text 2 closely as a powerful example of an author's use of language and characterization to convey her feelings toward a specific teacher in her life. As they practice using the *Approaching Texts Tool* to guide a reading or rereading of the text, they can hone in more specifically on Keller's use of descriptive language and imagery. Revisiting this short text enables students to focus on very specific words and images Keller employs to study how they present her perceptions of the student and teacher in an educational setting.

For this exercise, students might work with the Deepening question from a second model Questioning Path for Text 2 (question 3, following) to guide their final, deep rereading of a single, challenging sentence from the text, then discuss their responses and the conclusions they have drawn, referring to specific details and words they have annotated. Focusing on a single, complex and figurative sentence provides an opportunity for students to attend closely to every word and detail, and to unravel a challenging but critical metaphor Keller uses to express the impact of her teacher on her life.

QUESTIONING PATH TOOL

Text 2—*The Story of My Life,* Helen Keller (Model 2)

APPROACHING:
I determine my reading purposes and take note of key information about the text. I identify the LIPS domain(s) that will guide my initial reading.

I will focus on the author's use of *language* to describe her affection of her teacher and convey her *perspective*.

QUESTIONING: *I use Guiding Questions to help me investigate the text (from the Guiding Questions Handout).*

1. How do specific words or phrases influence the meaning or tone of the text? [L]

ANALYZING: *I question further to connect and analyze the details I find (from the Guiding Questions Handout).*

2. How does the author's choice of words reveal her purposes and perspective? [P]

DEEPENING: *I consider the questions of others.*

3. In the third sentence of paragraph 2, Keller sets up a comparison between a "shallow brook" and a "deep river."

   What language does she use to describe the brook and the river and how do the words help me think about the differences between the two?

   How does this comparison further develop Keller's perspective on what a teacher's role is?

EXTENDING: *I pose my own questions.*

Examples:

4. What does Keller think the role of a student is?

5. What about a teacher—what does she think the teacher's responsibility is?

PAIRS-CHECK: COMPARING APPROACHING TEXTS TOOLS AND ANNOTATIONS

- Transition two student pairs into a group of four for a pairs-check activity. In this informal discussion, each pair introduces their *Approaching Texts Tools* and explains their reading notes, based on the Guiding Question and text-specific question they have considered. Then, each pair explains the annotations they have made in relationship to their questions, comparing them with the annotations completed by the other student pair.

- Pairs-check teams can then share their observations about how their annotations (and readings) were similar and different, based on how they considered the questions recorded on the *Approaching Texts Tool*.

FORMATIVE ASSESSMENT AND FEEDBACK

Literacy Skills

Review (and have students review) the *Approaching Texts Tool* and textual annotations they have completed for Text 2, looking at how they are using the process represented in the *Reading Closely Graphic* for evidence of their developing Literacy Skills in the targeted areas of **Questioning** and **Attending to Details**. Specifically, see how well they are moving from whatever questions they are considering, to a strategic plan for examining the text, to which details they are highlighting in their annotations. They will work more closely on **Identifying Relationships** in the next few activities, so their textual annotations can also be examined as a preassessment of whether they are yet making connections among details.

Academic Habits

The pairs-check activity they have just completed presents an opportunity to reflect on their use of Academic Habits, specifically how clearly they are **Communicating Ideas** and supporting them with references to the text.

NOTE

To support self-, peer, and teacher assessment of skills and habits developed during the unit, a formal *RC Literacy Skills and Discussion Habits Rubric* and less formal *Student RC Literacy Skills and Discussion Habits Checklist* are provided in the **RC Literacy Toolbox**

ACTIVITY 2: APPROACHING A NEW TEXT

Students read a new text and use the *Approaching Texts Tool* to guide their reading.

INTRODUCE AND READ TEXT 5

Text 5 is a related text. Provide minimal context about the passage before students encounter it. Depending on their skills and previous experiences, they can either read the text silently and independently or listen to a reading of the text, concentrating on the author's ideas, use of details, and perspective.

TEXT NOTES

Text 5 is from a speech given by Colin Powell, former Secretary of State and four-star general. In the text, he states his case for children needing structure in their lives. He goes on to discuss the lack of structure leading to many of the problems we see in schools and society. Although this text measures only 900L, the strong description and narration from Powell—his ideas and supporting details—provide an opportunity for students to explore his perspective, which developed during his days in the military.

NOTE

The Media Supports for this unit include information on how to view the TED Talk video recording of Powell's speech. Students might also view the video listed in Media Supports titled "Your first 5 minutes at Marine Corps Recruit Depot—San Diego" to see what kind of structure Powell refers to in his speech.

QUESTIONING PATH TOOL
Text 5—"Kids Need Structure," Colin Powell

APPROACHING:
I determine my reading purposes and take note of key information about the text. I identify the LIPS domain(s) that will guide my initial reading.

I will initially focus on the text's *ideas* and supporting details but will also pay attention to its *perspective* and *language*. I will think about how knowing the text comes from a US General of the Army might influence my reading.

QUESTIONING: *I use Guiding Questions to help me investigate the text (from the **Guiding Questions Handout**).*

1. What new ideas or information do I find in the text? [I]

2. What claims do I find in the text? [I]

ANALYZING: *I question further to connect and analyze the details I find (from the **Guiding Questions Handout**).*

3. What do I learn about the author and the purpose for writing the text? [P]

4. What details or words suggest the author's perspective? [P, L]

DEEPENING: *I consider the questions of others.*

5. Starting in paragraph 4, what does Powell describe?

   How does this description tell me something about his perspective on education?

   What experiences from Powell's life influence what he says in his speech?

6. What does Powell mean when he talks about structure? What examples does he give?

7. What does Powell mean when he makes a claim in paragraph 10 that "the real answer begins with bringing a child to the school with structure in that child's heart and soul to begin with"?

   How does the explanation he gives in the following paragraph help me understand what he means by structure in a child's soul?

8. What details in the final paragraph again point to Powell's perspective?

   How does he use the details he presents to support his view about why American education is not working?

EXTENDING: *I pose my own questions.*

Students will pose a new question in Activity 4.

QUESTIONING: STUDENTS USE THE APPROACHING TEXTS TOOL

- Students independently complete an *Approaching Texts Tool*, considering what they already think or understand about the text based on what they record in the Approaching the Text section of the tool and recording a question they will use for their first reading in the first Questioning the Text section of the tool.

- Students will be gaining new information about an approach to education, so have them begin questioning with a Guiding Question from the Ideas section of the handout such as "What new ideas or information do I find in the text?"

- Before reading, students think about the details they will look for and annotate based on the question(s) they are considering.

ANALYZING, DEEPENING, AND EXTENDING: READ AND DISCUSS TEXT 5 IN PAIRS

- Students use what they have written on the *Approaching Texts Tool* to guide their initial reading of all or part of the text, searching for details related to their Guiding Question.

- Students then consider a more focused question from the Perspective section to use in guiding deeper analysis, such as "What details or words suggest the author's perspective?" Students record the question in the second Questioning section of the tool and think about where they will look for details related to language and perspective and what they will look for.

- Students work in pairs to discuss new information or ideas they have found in the text, based on the Guiding Questions they have thought about and used to guide their reading and the paragraphs they have analyzed.

- Students then consider a new text-specific question related to one of the key sections of the text, such as those found in the Deepening section of the model *Questioning Path Tool*. These questions cause students to (1) search for a specific section of text or quotation, (2) find and think about specific details and words and what they mean, (3) think about how the details and words the author uses suggest his perspective.

NOTE

The model text-specific questions in the model *Questioning Path Tool* for Text 5 focus on different areas of the text and move from more basic, literal analysis questions to more sophisticated, inferential questions. In a differentiated classroom, pairs might be assigned questions based on their levels of skill development.

- Students explain their thinking about their assigned text-specific questions to the class, discussing where they will focus their rereading and what details they will search for and annotate. Discuss how the nature of the question readers are considering influences how they will read (or reread) a section of the text.

- Students (in pairs or individually) do another reading and annotation of a specific section of the text in relationship to their assigned text-specific question.

FORMATIVE ASSESSMENT AND FEEDBACK

Literacy Skills

Review (and have students review) the Approaching Texts Tool and textual annotations they have completed independently for Text 5, looking at how they are using the process represented in the *Reading Closely Graphic* for evidence of their developing Literacy Skills in the targeted areas of **Questioning**, **Attending to Details**, and **Identifying Relationships** (a second preassessment in this last skill area).

Academic Habits

Students' discussions, in pairs and as a class, provide opportunities to reflect on their continuing development of the Academic Habits used in text-centered discussions, specifically **Communicating Clearly** and **Collaborating**.

> **NOTE**
>
> To support self-, peer, and teacher assessment of skills and habits developed during the unit, a formal *RC Literacy Skills and Discussion Habits Rubric* and less formal *Student RC Literacy Skills and Discussion Habits Checklist* are provided in the **RC Literacy Toolbox**.

☰ ACTIVITY 3: ANALYZING TEXT ☰ WITH TEXT-SPECIFIC QUESTIONS

The teacher guides the class through an analysis of the text using the *Analyzing Details Tool*.

ANALYZING DETAILS TOOL

The *Analyzing Details Tool* (in the **RC Literacy Toolbox**) also supports students in the *Reading Closely Graphic*'s process for close reading and in developing skills in the areas of **Questioning**, **Attending to Details**, and **Identifying Relationships**. The tool begins with a place to record a teacher-provided (or self-generated) text-specific question that relates to a Guiding Question. The tool prompts students to reread the text, attending to, marking, and annotating details related to their question. Students then review their details and select those most relevant to their question. Having done so, students analyze and make connections among those details to identify relationships, respond to their question, and deepen their understanding.

INSTRUCTIONAL NOTES

ANALYZING: MODEL THE TOOL

- Guide the class through the *Analyzing Details Tool*, identifying the specific reading purpose, and using an Analyzing question from the model *Questioning Path Tool*, such as "What do I learn about the author and the purpose for writing the text?"
- Read and annotate the opening paragraphs of text 5, marking, highlighting, or flagging details that are related to the reading purpose and question (or revisit previous annotations in relationship to the question).

- Review the details marked and annotated, looking for key details, words, and phrases that relate to the reading purpose and question and that convey or support a central idea.
- Select three of the key details or phrases from the text that are most important or interesting and that have a noteworthy relationship, recording them in the Selecting Details section of the tool. Select at least one detail that is a direct quotation and model how a reader can indicate the source or location of each detail in the Reference section.
- Analyze each detail and record thinking in the "What I Think about . . ." sections of the tool.
- Connect the details by writing a sentence based on the analysis of the three related details.
- Have all students complete their own tool with the information developed as a class. This enables students to get a feel for using the tool and provides them with a model of how to use it to analyze a question they will consider on their own.

DEEPENING: PROVIDE GUIDED PRACTICE IN USING THE TOOL

- Students work in pairs and use the **Approaching Texts** and **Analyzing Details Tools** to examine Guiding Questions and text-specific questions and details related to perspective or language.
- If students need additional guided practice, they can first complete an **Analyzing Details Tool** for a Guiding Question, such as "What details or words suggest the author's perspective?," to guide their reading, annotation, selection of key details, and analysis.
- If ready, students can move directly to the more focused, text-specific question they considered at the end of Activity 2 and complete an **Analyzing Details Tool** based on their annotation and analysis of a section of the text in relationship to that question.
- Student pairs work together to accomplish the following:
  ⇒ Select key details.
  ⇒ Record them on the **Analyzing Details Tool**.
  ⇒ Make accurate references for all details.
  ⇒ Note their meaning and connections.
- Write a **Connecting the Details** statement for each of their questions.

FORMATIVE ASSESSMENT AND FEEDBACK

Literacy Skills

Review (and have students review) the **Analyzing Details Tool(s)** and textual annotations they have completed for Text 5, looking for how they are using the process represented in the **Reading Closely Graphic** and evidence of their developing Literacy Skills in the targeted areas of **Questioning**, **Attending to Details**, **Identifying Relationships**, and **Summarizing**. Specifically, note the following:

- Which details they are attending to and identifying as key
- How they are referencing, analyzing, and understanding those details
- How the type of connections they are making evidences their developing skills in identifying relationships

Their explanatory statements at the bottom of the tool can also be examined for initial abilities in **Interpreting Language** and **Summarizing** what they have observed.

Academic Habits

Students have worked primarily in pairs, and thus can informally peer and self-assess how well they are developing the Academic Habits of **Collaborating** and **Communicating Clearly**.

NOTE

To support self-, peer, and teacher assessment of skills and habits developed during the unit, a formal *RC Literacy Skills and Discussion Habits Rubric* and less formal *Student RC Literacy Skills and Discussion Habits Checklist* are provided in the **RC Literacy Toolbox**.

≡ ACTIVITY 4: POSING TEXT-SPECIFIC QUESTIONS

Students develop their own text-specific questions with which to analyze the text.

INSTRUCTIONAL NOTES

This activity can be done in small groups or individually, depending on how well students have done with previous Questioning, Analyzing, and Deepening Activities.

EXTENDING: STUDENTS USE THE ANALYZING TEXTS TOOL TO EXAMINE THEIR OWN QUESTIONS

- Return to the ***Reading Closely Graphic***, and specifically to the fifth phase of the process, "Extending: Where Does This Lead Me?" Note that readers can extend their reading of a text in many ways:
  ⇒ Posing new text-specific questions
  ⇒ Making a text-based observation or claim
  ⇒ Engaging in further reading or research about something that has captured their interest in the text

- For this activity, students will focus on framing an original text-specific question.

- Students pose a text-specific question that has emerged from their Deepening analysis of Text 5. Because this is the first time that students have posed their own questions, it is an opportunity to consider and discuss what makes a good question. Scaffold or coach students to frame a question that causes them to reexamine textual details and discover something new about the text or to extend their reading to other texts. Consider these possible coaching responses to various kinds of questions students may initially generate:

  ⇒ If students frame a literal question leading to a simple yes-no response (e.g., "Does the military use structure to train soldiers?"), help them reframe the question to focus on key

---

details, relationships, and quotes from the text (e.g., "How does Powell use the military as an example of the importance of structure?").

⇒ If students frame an opinion question that is minimally text-based (e.g., "Does the drill sergeant need to yell at the soldiers to teach them?"), help them reframe the question in direct relationship to something presented in the text (e.g., "What do the fourth and following paragraphs suggest about the process of learning structure?").

⇒ If students frame a question that moves away from the text (e.g., "Does going to a Jesuit school help you to get into college?"), help students first reframe the question to focus on textual details (e.g., "What details from Powell's talk suggest why the Jesuit school's students all go to college?") then develop an extending question that can lead to further research (e.g., "How does a school whose students come from difficult backgrounds succeed in getting all of its graduates to college?").

NOTE

There should be information available through an Internet search that can help students investigate this extension question.

⇒ Think about other ways that students may initially frame questions that are not text-based and plan coaching strategies accordingly. It is important to stress that the various types of questions students might initially come up with are not wrong or bad. The focus of instruction here is to help students become aware of and reflective about different types of questions and their various uses. Students are learning that they can develop questions that help them deeply engage in texts to access information and meaning. They can distinguish these questions from valid questions that cannot be answered within the text but can be used to frame further research.

• Students transfer their question to an ***Analyzing Details Tool***.

• Students annotate their texts by highlighting or marking all the details they feel are relevant to their question.

• Students select three details to analyze, copying them and referencing them in their tool.

• Students analyze the details, recording their thinking.

• Students connect the details, writing a sentence or two explaining their thinking.

• Students share their findings in a group discussion, using their tool to guide their conversations, and reflect as a group on their process of Reading Closely, using the ***Reading Closely Graphic*** as a framework for reflection.

NOTE

Alternately (if they are not yet ready to pose their own text-specific questions), students can consider a final Deepening model question(s) developed by the teacher that causes them to think about the overall ideas and perspective presented in the text.

ACTIVITY 5: INDEPENDENT WRITING

Students write a short paragraph explaining their analysis of the text and reference (or list) supporting textual details.

INSTRUCTIONAL NOTES

In Part 4 of the unit, students will be developing and practicing the skills of writing a detail-based explanation of a text they have read. In this activity, introduce the idea of what a text-based explanation entails, possibly modeling one for Text 2.

- Students work from any of their *Analyzing Details Tools* completed in Activities 3 and 4 (whichever one seems strongest to them in terms of the details and connections they have noted).

- Students write a short paragraph of several clear, coherent, and complete sentences that states and then explains something from their analysis of Text 5, specifically the *connection* they have noted on their *Analyzing Details Tool*. Students should be reminded to use and reference key details they have identified. If students are inexperienced in writing text-based explanations, they can simply list details that support their short explanations. If they are more experienced, they should try to integrate those details into their explanatory sentences.

- In small groups or as a class, have students share and compare their text-based explanations. Note how different the readings and explanations are based on what question students considered as they read, what details they noted, and what connections they made as they analyzed the text. Use this opportunity to discuss the idea that there are many potential readings and interpretations of any text, *all valid as long as they are supported by evidence (details) drawn directly from the text.*

PART 2: FORMATIVE ASSESSMENT OPPORTUNITIES

LITERACY SKILLS

At the end of Part 2, students will have accomplished the following:

- Completed an *Approaching Texts Tool* for Text 2
- Completed an *Approaching Texts Tool* for Text 5
- Annotated their texts to highlight details related to their text questioning
- Completed multiple *Analyzing Details Tools* for Text 5, as a class and independently
- Written an explanation of their analysis of the text, including supporting details
- Engaged in group and class discussions

The primary focus of evaluation at this stage should be on students' use of questioning to focus their reading, annotations, and selection of details. Their work on the tools can manifest and provide concrete evidence of how they are using the Reading Closely process (as represented on the **Reading Closely Graphic**) and what is happening in their heads as they read.

Examine students' ***Approaching Texts Tools*** and annotations in relationship to the Literacy Skills criteria for **Questioning** and **Attending to Details**. Examine their annotated texts and ***Analyzing Details Tools*** to evaluate the relevance of their selected details, their recorded thinking and connections, and their developing skills in **Identifying Relationships**.

Finally, examine the short written explanations for evidence of **Summarizing** skills and as first, baseline examples of their developing writing skills, paying attention to the clarity of the explanation, use of evidence, and to word choice, punctuation, and grammar.

ACADEMIC HABITS

At the end of Part 2, students can more formally self-assess their development of the Academic Habits associated with text-centered discussion. Specifically, they can consider and reflect on these kinds of questions:

- In what ways am I <u>preparing for discussion</u> through close reading and careful consideration of Guiding Questions? How might I improve?
- In what ways am I <u>collaborating with others</u> by paying attention to and respecting their ideas? How might I improve?
- In what ways am I <u>communicating my ideas</u> clearly and with good support from the texts we have read? How might I improve?

NOTE

To support self-, peer, and teacher assessment of skills and habits developed during the unit, a formal ***RC Literacy Skills and Discussion Habits Rubric*** and less formal ***Student RC Literacy Skills and Discussion Habits Checklist*** are provided in the **RC Literacy Toolbox**.

ANALYZING DETAILS

"Never be the obstacle between the child and his experience."

OBJECTIVE:	Students learn to analyze textual details as a key to discovering an author's perspective. Students read, analyze, and compare texts.

ESTIMATED TIME: 3–4 days

MATERIALS:
Texts 5 through 7
- *Approaching Texts Tool*
- *Analyzing Details Tool*

- *Questioning Path Tools*
- *Guiding Questions Handout*
- *Reading Closely Graphic*

≡ LITERACY SKILLS

TARGETED SKILLS	DESCRIPTORS
ATTENDING TO DETAILS	Identifies relevant and important textual details, words, and ideas
IDENTIFYING RELATIONSHIPS	Identifies important connections among key details and ideas within and across texts
INTERPRETING LANGUAGE	Identifies how words and phrases convey meaning and represent an author's or narrator's perspective
RECOGNIZING PERSPECTIVE	Uses textual details to recognize an author's or narrator's relationship to and perspective on a text's topic

≡ ACADEMIC HABITS

HABITS DEVELOPED	DESCRIPTORS
COLLABORATING	Pays attention to, respects, and works productively in various roles with all other participants
COMMUNICATING CLEARLY	Uses appropriate language and relevant textual details to clearly present ideas and claims

☰ ALIGNMENT TO CCSS

TARGETED STANDARDS:

CCSS.ELA-LITERACY.RI.9-10.1: Cite strong and thorough textual evidence to support analysis of what the text says explicitly as well as inferences drawn from the text.

CCSS.ELA-LITERACY.RI.9-10.2: Determine a central idea of a text and analyze its development over the course of the text, including how it emerges and is shaped and refined by specific details; provide an objective summary of the text.

CCSS.ELA-LITERACY.RI.9-10.6: Determine an author's point of view or purpose in a text and analyze how an author uses rhetoric to advance that point of view or purpose.

CCSS.ELA-LITERACY.RI.9-10.9: Analyze seminal US documents of historical and literary significance (e.g., Washington's Farewell Address, the Gettysburg Address, Roosevelt's Four Freedoms speech, King's "Letter from Birmingham Jail"), including how they address related themes and concepts.

SUPPORTING STANDARD:

CCSS.ELA-LITERACY.RI.9-10.4: Determine the meaning of words and phrases as they are used in a text, including figurative, connotative, and technical meanings; analyze the cumulative impact of specific word choices on meaning and tone (e.g., how the language of a court opinion differs from that of a newspaper).

☰ ACTIVITIES

1. ANALYZING TEXTUAL DETAIL
Students closely read and analyze a new text.

2. ANALYZING AND DISCUSSING DETAILS ACROSS TEXTS
The teacher guides and supports students in a comparative discussion of two texts.

3. EXPLAINING AND COMPARING TEXTS
Student groups consider a comparative question and individually write an explanatory paragraph using their question.

4. INDEPENDENT READING ACTIVITY
Students independently read texts using Guiding Questions to frame their first reading.

Developing Core Literacy Proficiencies

ACTIVITY 1: ANALYZING TEXTUAL DETAIL

Students closely read and analyze a new text.

INSTRUCTIONAL NOTES

INTRODUCE AND READ TEXT 6 ALOUD

Students now engage a new text that presents a different perspective on the topic. As before, students can first read the text silently and independently or listen to the text read aloud. Students should be provided with minimal context about the text.

> ### TEXT NOTES
>
> Text 6 is from Maria Montessori, an educational philosopher whose beliefs about educating children have been the foundation for day-care centers, preschools, and elementary schools worldwide. The passage focuses on her beliefs about child development. This text measures at 1270L and contains complex ideas, vividly presented that should be challenging but accessible for most students with the scaffolding and support of the close reading process. In this activity, students will read and analyze descriptive details in the text, examining how Montessori believes children should be developed. Using the questioning process, students will analyze short segments of the text.
>
> In the instructional sequence that follows, the text has been divided or "chunked" into three sections:
>
>
>
> 1. Paragraphs 1 and 2, which students will read first as they practice questioning, focusing on Montessori's use of language to develop her ideas about teaching
> 2. Paragraphs 3 and 4, which students will read and analyze next as they move to Analyzing and Deepening activities and questions
> 3. Paragraphs 5–8 (and the text overall), which students will reread and analyze for their communication of Montessori's perspective on education (and eventually compare to Text 5 in Activity 2)
>
> > #### NOTE
> >
> > Students might also view the video "Montessori—Watch This First," listed in the Media Supports, which presents an overview of Montessori's education pedagogy and school programs.

QUESTIONING PATH TOOL

Text 6—*Dr. Montessori's Own Handbook*, Maria Montessori, 1914

APPROACHING: *I determine my reading purposes and take note of key information about the text. I identify the LIPS domain(s) that will guide my initial reading.*	I will focus on the author's *ideas* and how it reveals her *perspective*. I will think about how the title of this section of text—"Freedom"—is reflected in what I read.
QUESTIONING: *I use Guiding Questions to help me investigate the text (from the **Guiding Questions Handout**).*	1. What words or phrases stand out to me as powerful and important? [L] 2. What ideas stand out to me as significant or interesting? [I]
ANALYZING: *I question further to connect and analyze the details I find (from the **Guiding Questions Handout**).*	3. What seems to be the author's attitude or point of view? [P]
DEEPENING: *I consider the questions of others.*	4. In the first paragraph, what does the word *delicate* suggest about how Montessori thinks a teacher should guide a student? What other words in the first two paragraphs convey similar ideas about how adults should provide "real guidance" to children? How is the subtitle of this section of Montessori's *Handbook*—"Freedom"—reflected in the ideas, details, and words of paragraphs 1 and 2? 5. In paragraphs 3–4, what words are used to describe the child and his or her actions? What words are used to explain what Montessori means with her "motto for the educator": "Wait while observing"? How might I sum up Montessori's perspective about how a teacher should teach? 6. At the end of paragraph 4, Montessori presents a "great educational principle" and an "example of good education." What is that principle? In the following paragraph, what phrases does Montessori use to explain this principle and communicate her view of children? Likewise in paragraph 6, what do the details and words communicate about Montessori's view of how adults treat children? 7. How does Montessori explain what "kindness" is (and is not) in paragraph 6? What does she say about what "kindness consists in" and why it is important to treat children with kindness? 8. Montessori italicizes two key words in paragraphs 7 and 8: *indirect* and *free*. How do these two words communicate Montessori's perspective on child development and teaching children? 9. How does her final paraphrasing of the Biblical quotation about "little children" represent her view of education?
EXTENDING: *I pose my own questions.*	*Example:* 10. How does Montessori's description of how a teacher should teach a child make me think differently about education?

QUESTIONING

- Students complete the first two parts of the ***Approaching Texts Tool***, noting key information in the Approaching the Text section. They may consider who Montessori was. They record Guiding Questions, such as "What words or phrases stand out to me as powerful and important?" or "What ideas stand out to me as significant or interesting?" in the Questioning the Text section.

NOTE

Some groups might work from one Guiding Question and others work from a different Guiding Question, then compare the details they find or annotate based on their question.

- Students think about what details they will look for as they complete a first reading of the text.
- Students read and annotate the first two paragraphs of the text using their Guiding Question(s) to focus them on relevant details they can study and analyze further.
- Discuss as a class what the author's words (such as her repeated use of the word *guide*) have caused students to think about as they read her introductory paragraph.

DEEPENING

- In reading paragraphs 1 and 2, students may naturally focus on the words and phrases that describe *how* a teacher should guide students. If not, help them hone in by considering a deepening text-specific question set such as question 4:
  - ⇒ In the first paragraph, what does the word *delicate* suggest about how Montessori thinks a teacher should guide a student?
  - ⇒ What other words in the first two paragraphs convey similar ideas about how adults should provide "real guidance" to children?
- Have students record the question(s) in the bottom section of the ***Approaching Texts Tool***. Assign student teams to look for details about how Montessori thinks a teacher should guide a student. Have them identify specific words or phrases that bring her perspective to light.
- Share and compare ideas. Then as a class, examine the final phrases in the first two paragraphs to gain a sense of Montessori's driving view on how to educate children.

ANALYZING

- Have students move from thinking about what they notice to what they think about it (analyzing) by recording and considering a Guiding Question, such as "What seems to be the author's attitude or point of view?"
- Ask students to focus their rereading of the text on paragraphs 3 and 4, where Montessori now describes a child. Have them look for words, sentences, and descriptive details that tell them something about how the author views the child with respect to his or her own development and education.
- Discuss the details students find and how they interpret them. Encourage many ways of reading the text, as long as they are supported by details.

- Have students individually complete an ***Analyzing Details Tool*** using the Analyzing Guiding Question (#3) or Deepening question 5.

- In small groups, or as a class, read and compare the connecting details statements students have generated on their ***Analyzing Details Tools***. Emphasize again that there are many ways to read and view the text, all being valid if supported by details and evidence from its paragraphs.

DEEPENING

- To take them further into the text, present students with a text-specific question such as Deepening questions 6 through 8 in the model ***Questioning Path Tool*** (each of the questions might be assigned to a part of the class).

- Students individually complete an ***Analyzing Details Tool*** for their text-specific question.

- Ask students to explain or summarize (either orally to a partner or in a short, informal piece of writing) the main ideas of the text based on the question they have considered, the paragraphs they have reread closely, and the details and connections they have identified.

- In a text-centered discussion, students share explanations by returning to the question "What seems to be the author's attitude or point of view?" and considering what the description and language tell us about how the author views education and what a teacher's role should be in teaching children.

EXTENDING

Montessori's writing under the subsection "Freedom" provides students with a rich description of the student-teacher relationship. It also provides a stark contrast to Colin Powell's own vision of how a teacher should approach a student. Students can extend their understanding of Montessori's perspective by looking into who she was, what she did during her lifetime, and think about how this influenced her views on education.

FORMATIVE ASSESSMENT AND FEEDBACK

Literacy Skills

Students will have just read a very different type of text—a *Handbook*—and applied the Reading Closely process to text intended to instruct others. In self-, peer, and teacher assessments, focus on how they have transferred the process to a different type of text and new questions about language and perspective. Examine their ***Approaching Texts*** and ***Analyzing Details Tools*** (as well as their textual annotations) for evidence of continuing development in the Literacy Skills areas of **Questioning, Attending to Details**, and **Identifying Relationships**. Look to see if the connections and relationships students are noting are moving from literal interpretation of explicit meaning into the newly targeted skill areas of **Interpreting Language** and **Identifying Perspective**.

Academic Habits

Students can reflect on their continuing development of the Academic Habit of **Communicating Clearly** and explaining their ideas with textual support, as evidenced in the comparative discussions of their ***Analyzing Details Tools***.

ACTIVITY 2: ANALYZING AND DISCUSSING DETAILS ACROSS TEXTS

The teacher guides and supports students in a comparative discussion of two texts.

INSTRUCTIONAL NOTES

ANALYZING: CLASS DISCUSSION

- Students use their notes and tools from Texts 5 and 6 to discuss how each author's use of language reflects his or her perspective on the subject.

- Ask students to present evidence from the texts to support their assertions and to connect their comments to the ideas that others have shared.

- In a text-centered discussion, have students take notes and annotate their text, capturing what peers say, how their ideas are changing, or what connections and differences they note between texts.

TEXT NOTES

The Powell and Montessori excerpts provide an interesting contrast in their perspective and point of view. Although the Montessori piece was published in 1914, her views on education expressed in the "Freedom" excerpt, beliefs about respecting a child's own personality during the formative years, are wildly popular and have been applied in thousands of child development centers and elementary schools worldwide. Contrasting this with Powell's thoughts on the importance of "structure" for children from a very early age sets up an interesting comparative analysis. This analysis can be developed further by comparing the differences in perspective between a general and an educational philosopher, a man and a woman, and an op-ed speech and a handbook.

As a lead-in to the comparative discussion of these two contrasting texts, they might return to the ideas presented by Sir Ted Robinson and illustrated in the Text 3 video.

QUESTIONING PATH TOOL
Comparison of Text 5 and Text 6

APPROACHING: *I determine my reading purposes and take note of key information about the text. I identify the LIPS domain(s) that will guide my initial reading.*	I will compare the two text's use of *language* and details to describe what student's need in education and also how they reflect the author's *perspective(s)*. I will think about the differences between the two authors concerning their backgrounds and views about how children should be educated.

QUESTIONING: *I use Guiding Questions to help me investigate the text (from the Guiding Questions Handout).*

1. What details or words suggest the author's perspective? [P-L]

ANALYZING: *I question further to connect and analyze the details I find (from the Guiding Questions Handout).*

2. How does the author's perspective influence the text's presentation of ideas, themes, or claims? [P]

3. How does the author's perspective and presentation of the text compare to others? [P]

DEEPENING: *I consider the questions of others.*

4. In his fourth and following paragraphs, Powell describes the relationships between the drill sergeant and young soldiers. What words are used to describe this relationship?

   In paragraph 6, Montessori describes how we ought to and ought not to treat children. What language does she use to describe the relationship between adult and child?

   Considering each author's choice of language, how do their perspectives about the relationship between teacher and student compare?

5. In his final paragraph, what warning does Powell give the audience about what happens when children have no structure in their lives?

   What is the measurable consequence according to him?

   Montessori also gives a warning, though it is not as obvious. In paragraph 6, what does she mean when she says, "we expect them to be submissive and well-behaved" and "they will imitate us in any case"?

   What is she warning the reader about?

   Each author gives a warning about what happens to children when something specific does not occur. According to each author, what needs to happen so that children are properly taught?

6. Colin Powell is a retired four-star general of the US Army. How might his position influence the ideas and language he uses in his talk?

   Given his perspective, how might he react to the educational philosophy of Montessori?

EXTENDING: *I pose my own questions.*

As an alternative to questions 4–6, students may develop their own comparative questions.

Developing Core Literacy Proficiencies

☰ ACTIVITY 3: EXPLAINING AND COMPARING TEXTS

Student groups consider a comparative question and individually write an explanatory paragraph using their question.

INSTRUCTIONAL NOTES

ANALYZING: SIMILARITIES AND DIFFERENCES BETWEEN TEXTS

- Students work in groups using their analyses of Texts 5 and 6 to come and considering a comparative question from the Deepening section of the Questioning Path. Alternately, if students are ready to do so, they can pose and consider their own text-specific questions.

- Support student groups as they consider or develop their questions.

- Students record their comparative question on an **Analyzing Details Tool**, then annotate and select three to six key related details from the two texts, using the details to discover connections, specifically similarities and differences.

DEEPENING AND EXTENDING: WRITING COMPARATIVE ANALYSES

- Students draw from their notes, tools, annotated texts, and sentences from earlier activities to construct a paragraph that addresses their comparative question. Paragraphs should include these elements:

  ⇒ The comparative question

  ⇒ One to three sentences explaining their analysis of Text 5 and key supporting details

  ⇒ One to three sentences explaining their analysis of Text 6 and key supporting details

  ⇒ One to three sentences explaining a connection they have made between the two texts that addresses their comparative question

- Students construct the paragraph by doing the following:

  ⇒ Introducing the topic, in this case the comparison made between the texts

  ⇒ Organizing their information to clearly and logically express their ideas

  ⇒ Developing the topic with appropriate supporting details

  ⇒ Linking sentences with appropriate transitional words and phrases to clarify relationships and establish coherence

  ⇒ Using precise language and an academic (more formal) style of writing

- In small groups, students read and peer review their comparative paragraphs.

  ⇒ Prior to submission, an optional revision may be asked of students based on peer feedback. Students can use any of the following questions to guide their reviews and revisions:

    1. How clear and text-specific is the comparative <u>question</u> posed by the writer? How well does it lead to close reading and interesting observations about the two texts? How might the question be improved?

    2. In what ways does the writer <u>attend to key details</u>, <u>identify relationships</u>, and <u>compare perspectives</u> in the two texts? How might the thinking about and use of details be improved?

---

3. In what ways does the writer use <u>specific evidence</u> from the text (details, quotes) to support the explanation? How might the use of evidence be improved?

4. In what ways does the writer use <u>clear organization</u> and <u>precise language</u> to explain text-based responses to the comparative question? How might the clarity of the explanation be improved?

- Students submit paragraphs and their supporting materials.

FORMATIVE ASSESSMENT AND FEEDBACK

Literacy Skills

In this part of the unit, students will have completed their first more formal writing assignment, which can now be used to assess the reading skills they are continuing to develop and the writing skills they will work on in Part 4. Review (in peer groups and as a basis for teacher feedback) students' *Analyzing Details Tools* and comparative paragraphs for ongoing evidence of their Literacy Skills in the targeted areas of **Questioning**, **Attending to Details**, **Identifying Relationships**, and **Summarizing**. The paragraphs should also provide initial evidence of how well students are **Interpreting Language** and **Recognizing** (and comparing) **Perspective**. Use the writing samples also to diagnose, provide initial feedback, and plan instruction about the additional Literacy Skill they will be working on in Parts 4 and 5: **Using Evidence**.

Academic Habits

Student peer-review sessions for the writing assignment provide an opportunity to observe and reflect on their ongoing development of Academic Habits related to **Collaborating**, specifically in the area of providing constructive peer feedback.

NOTE

To support self-, peer, and teacher assessment of skills and habits developed during the unit, a formal *RC Literacy Skills and Discussion Habits Rubric* and less formal *Student RC Literacy Skills and Discussion Habits Checklist* are provided in the **RC Literacy Toolbox**.

ACTIVITY 4: INDEPENDENT READING

Students independently read texts using Guiding Questions to frame their first reading.

INSTRUCTIONAL NOTES

This reading, which sets up Parts 4 and 5 of the unit, can be done as homework or in class, with more or less scaffolding depending on how students have been doing in previous reading experiences. On their own, students read Texts 7, 8, and 9—topic-related texts that are connected to previous texts they have read—using one or more of the Guiding Questions in the model

Questioning Path Tool (following) to set up an ***Approaching Texts Tool***. Note that the Guiding Questions now span all four domains of questioning, enabling various approaches to initial close reading. Students might be assigned one of these questions, then compare what they look for and find based on which question they considered.

At this point, students do not need to closely analyze any of the three texts but simply become familiar with them and some of their details so they can prepare themselves for analyzing one of the texts through close reading in Part 4 and for leading a comparative discussion in Part 5.

APPROACHING:
I determine my reading purposes and take note of key information about the text. I identify the LIPS domain(s) that will guide my initial reading.

I will do a first reading of the text, thinking about the sequence of the text and events it presents, the author's use of *language* to describe key events, and the author's *perspective* on those events.

QUESTIONING: *I use Guiding Questions to help me investigate the text (from the* **Guiding Questions Handout***).*

1. What words or phrases stand out to me as powerful and important? [L]

2. What do I think the text is mainly about—what is discussed in detail? [I]

3. What seems to be the author's attitude or point of view? [P]

4. In what ways are ideas and claims linked together in the text? [S]

ANALYZING: *I question further to connect and analyze the details I find (from the* **Guiding Questions Handout***).*

DEEPENING: *I consider the questions of others.*

EXTENDING: *I pose my own questions.*

☰ PART 3: FORMATIVE ASSESSMENT ☰ OPPORTUNITIES

LITERACY SKILLS

In Part 3, students will have accomplished the following:

- Completed an *Approaching Texts Tool* for Text 6 individually and in groups
- Completed three *Analyzing Details Tools*, two for Text 6 and one comparing Texts 5 and 6
- Taken part in a group discussion about connections between Texts 5 and 6
- Written a paragraph explaining their analyses of Texts 5 and 6 and making connections between them

Use these work samples to assess how the class is doing overall in the targeted skills of **Questioning**, **Attending to Details**, **Identifying Relationships**, **Summarizing**, **Interpreting Language**, and **Recognizing** (and comparing) **Perspective**. Diagnostically, use the evidence of individual students' skills to help determine which of the three texts they might be assigned to read and analyze for Parts 4 and 5 of the unit.

Evaluate their paragraphs as evidence of their developing reading and analysis skills and as more formal written exercises (paying increased attention to organization of ideas and how they are using evidence). Thus, their paragraphs potentially serve as formative and diagnostic assessments for Part 4.

ACADEMIC HABITS

As before, student discussions provide opportunities to listen in and informally assess their Academic Habits associated with text-centered discussion in anticipation of Part 5. As students reflect on the discussions they have had in Part 3 of the unit, introduce the idea that the discussion behaviors they have been working on should eventually become habits for them, considering questions such as these:

- In what ways am I demonstrating the habit of <u>collaborating with others</u> by paying attention to and respecting their ideas? How might I improve?
- In what ways am I demonstrating the habit of <u>communicating my ideas</u> clearly and with good support from the texts we have read? How might I improve?

NOTE

To support self-, peer, and teacher assessment of skills and habits developed during the unit, a formal *RC Literacy Skills and Discussion Habits Rubric* and less formal *Student RC Literacy Skills and Discussion Habits Checklist* are provided in the **RC Literacy Toolbox**.

PART 4

EXPLAINING UNDERSTANDING

"The true purpose of education is to produce citizens."

OBJECTIVE:	Students learn how to summarize and explain what they have learned from their reading, questioning, and analysis of texts. Students read and analyze three related texts.

ESTIMATED TIME: 3–4 days

MATERIALS:
Texts 1 through 9
- *Approaching Texts Tool*
- *Analyzing Details Tool*
- *Questioning Path Tools*
- *Guiding Questions Handout*

☰ LITERACY SKILLS

TARGETED SKILLS	DESCRIPTORS
QUESTIONING	Formulates and responds to questions and lines of inquiry that lead to relevant and important ideas and themes within and across texts
ATTENDING TO DETAILS	Identifies relevant and important textual details, words, and ideas
IDENTIFYING RELATIONSHIPS	Identifies important connections among key details and ideas within and across texts
INTERPRETING LANGUAGE	Identifies how words and phrases convey meaning and represent an author's or narrator's perspective
RECOGNIZING PERSPECTIVE	Uses textual details to recognize an author's or narrator's relationship to and perspective on a text's topic

ACADEMIC HABITS

HABITS DEVELOPED	DESCRIPTORS
PREPARING	Reads the texts, researches the topics, and thinks about the questions being studied to prepare for tasks
COLLABORATING	Pays attention to, respects, and works productively in various roles with all other participants
COMMUNICATING CLEARLY	Uses appropriate language and relevant textual details to clearly present ideas and claims

ALIGNMENT TO CCSS

TARGETED STANDARDS:

CCSS.ELA-LITERACY.RI.9-10.1: Cite strong and thorough textual evidence to support analysis of what the text says explicitly as well as inferences drawn from the text.

CCSS.ELA-LITERACY.RI.9-10.2: Determine a central idea of a text and analyze its development over the course of the text, including how it emerges and is shaped and refined by specific details; provide an objective summary of the text.

CCSS.ELA-LITERACY.RI.9-10.6: Determine an author's point of view or purpose in a text and analyze how an author uses rhetoric to advance that point of view or purpose.

SUPPORTING STANDARDS:

CCSS.ELA-LITERACY.RI.9-10.4: Determine the meaning of words and phrases as they are used in a text, including figurative, connotative, and technical meanings; analyze the cumulative impact of specific word choices on meaning and tone (e.g., how the language of a court opinion differs from that of a newspaper).

CCSS.ELA-LITERACY.RI.9-10.10: By the end of grade 9, read and comprehend literacy nonfiction in the grades 9–10 text complexity band proficiently, with scaffolding as needed at the high end of the range.

CCSS.ELA-LITERACY.W.9-10.2: Write informative/explanatory texts to examine and convey complex ideas, concepts, and information clearly and accurately through the effective selection, organization, and analysis of content.

CCSS.ELA-LITERACY.W.9-10.9: Draw evidence from literary or informational texts to support analysis, reflection, and research.

ACTIVITIES

1. INTRODUCTION TO CULMINATING ACTIVITY
The teacher introduces the culminating text-centered writing assignment and comparative discussion.

2. READING AND DISCUSSING RELATED TEXTS
Students read three related texts and discuss them as a class.

3. QUESTIONING AND ANALYZING TEXTS INDEPENDENTLY
Students select (or are assigned) one of the texts to discuss with a small group and then analyze independently.

4. WRITING A TEXT-BASED EXPLANATION
Students use their analysis to independently write a text-based explanation of one of the texts.

≡ ACTIVITY 1: INTRODUCTION TO CULMINATING ACTIVITIES

The teacher introduces the culminating text-centered writing assignment and comparative discussion.

INSTRUCTIONAL NOTES

The final two parts (4 and 5) of the unit are a two-stage culminating activity in which students accomplish the following:

⇒ Analyze one of three related texts and draft a multiparagraph explanation about their text.

⇒ Lead and participate in a comparative discussion about the three texts.

In the first stage (Part 4), students are introduced to the texts and choose one to read closely with a small, "expert" group. Building on their collaborative close reading, students independently analyze and write about their selected text.

In the second stage of the culminating activity (Part 5), students return to their small groups to discuss their writing and draft a question that compares their text to the other texts in the unit. Students then *jigsaw* to a new group and use their analysis, writing, and comparative question to facilitate and participate in a structured text-centered discussion with students who have analyzed the other two texts.

⇒ Discuss the agenda for Parts 4 and 5 with the students, emphasizing that they will now be expected to use the questioning, reading, and analyzing skills they have been developing more independently. Explain that they will need to become an expert for a selected text, which they will choose in Activity 2.

⇒ Introduce (or review) the ***Student Literacy Skills and Discussion Habits Checklist*** (available in the **RC Literacy Toolbox** and Student Edition) as a way of discussing the skills and habits students should try to demonstrate as they write their text-based explanations and prepare for the final text-centered discussion.

≡ ACTIVITY 2: READING AND DISCUSSING RELATED TEXTS

Students read three related texts and discuss them as a class.

INSTRUCTIONAL NOTES

- Students review their initial reading of Texts 7, 8, and 9. Alternatively, have students follow along while strong readers read them aloud.
- Lead a discussion of the students' first impressions of the texts, using the Guiding Questions they considered in Part 3, Activity 4 to help facilitate discussion.

TEXT NOTES

The final three texts all focus on the purposes and value of education in society. The first text, Text 7, is by Eleanor Roosevelt, wife of President Franklin D. Roosevelt, and is more readily accessible for middle school readers than is Text 8. This piece presents her belief that the purpose of a strong education is to prepare educated citizens who can participate in the country's democratic practices. In the first two paragraphs she uses Theodore Roosevelt as an example of a citizen who believed in "service" to one's country, not only militarily but also in politics. She then moves on and discusses the education system in the United States and espouses a very progressive viewpoint about how some teachers and schools are preparing students to be educated, participating citizens and how citizenship is cultivated in their students. This abridged version ends with some candor on teacher pay in the United States and how we value other professions more highly, a discussion which still has relevance for teachers and students seventy-five years later.

Text 8 is a report by Thomas Jefferson in which he describes his carefully crafted plan for creating a compulsory system of schools in Virginia that provides a basic "reading, writing and arithmetic" level of education to all citizens but then pulls the "geniuses" from this level and continues to educate them in higher grades and eventually at the university (William and Mary). He continues by stating the purpose behind educating all citizens is that "every government degenerates when trusted to the rulers of the people alone." His belief is that an educated electorate is needed to hold the elected officials accountable. He uses examples from Great Britain, where corrupt government officials have minimal checks on their authority because "one man in ten has a right to vote for members of parliament."

In Text 9, former Secretary of Education Arne Duncan highlights the importance of raising educational standards in the United States and abroad in order to remain economically competitive. Duncan argues that one purpose for education should be to ensure that students are prepared for the jobs of the current information age and, in turn, are contributing to the economy of our country. Duncan begins this speech by discussing the positive global effects of raising education standards here and abroad and then transitions in the middle by explaining the challenges faced when trying to raise achievement.

The three texts provide interesting perspectives on the role of public education in the United States. The texts are all rich with details and descriptive language, providing a fitting culmination to the unit's focus and topic. However, they present varying degrees of reading challenges for students because of the more archaic language and craft in the Jefferson text (1410L). The Roosevelt text has been abridged to provide a piece that still has complex ideas while being accessible to lower level readers (1250L). The Duncan text (1200L) is much easier to understand because of its modern writing style and vocabulary.

TEXT NOTES

Each text provides opportunities to read closely (and independently) for textual details, to pay close attention to structure, and to study how language illustrates each author's perspective.

NOTE

A number of media sources can be found in the Media Supports section to support understanding and interest.

≡ ACTIVITY 3: QUESTIONING AND ANALYZING TEXTS INDEPENDENTLY

Students select (or are assigned) one of the texts to discuss with a small group and then analyze independently.

INSTRUCTIONAL NOTES

Students may be assigned a text based on their reading comprehension levels, interests, or developing skills (as demonstrated previously in the unit), or they may be allowed to choose a text following their initial reading and small-group discussion of the three. Either way, each student will be responsible for doing a close reading, questioning, analysis, and summary of one of the three related texts.

QUESTIONING PATH TOOL

Text 7—"Good Citizenship: The Purpose of Education," Eleanor Roosevelt, 1930

APPROACHING: *I determine my reading purposes and take note of key information about the text. I identify the LIPS domain(s) that will guide my initial reading.*	I will do a close reading of my text, looking for key details related to its *structure, language, ideas,* or *perspective* in preparation for writing a text-based explanation and leading a comparative discussion. I will think about how the text discusses the role and purpose of education.

QUESTIONING: *I use Guiding Questions to help me investigate the text (from the* **Guiding Questions Handout**).

1. What words or phrases stand out to me as powerful and important? [L]

2. What do I think the text is mainly about—what is discussed in detail? [I]

ANALYZING: *I question further to connect and analyze the details I find (from the* **Guiding Questions Handout**).

3. What seems to be the author's attitude or point of view? [P]

4. In what ways are ideas and claims linked together in the text? [S]

DEEPENING: *I consider the questions of others.*

5. According to paragraph 1, what are the prevailing purposes for education?

   How does Roosevelt structure this paragraph so the reader knows what she believes the purpose of education really should be?

6. Based on paragraphs 3 and 4, how does Roosevelt believe education needs to change in order to meet "these objectives"?

7. What details in paragraphs 5 and 6 point to Roosevelt's perspective on the primary purpose of education?

   What will a child who is educated through the experiences Roosevelt describes be able to "envisage"? What does she suggest will be the result for the child and for society?

8. What shift in focus occurs between paragraphs 7 and 8, and why might Roosevelt have made this shift?

   What claims, and what evidence, does she present about how teachers are treated in the United States?

9. In the final paragraph, Roosevelt presents a comment made to her recently by a "hard-worked businessman."

   What is the implied societal attitude suggested by that comment?

   How does Roosevelt respond, and what does this indicate about her perspective on what needs to happen in United States education?

EXTENDING: *I pose my own questions.*

Students will develop an original question for their text in Part 4 and a comparative question in Part 5.

Developing Core Literacy Proficiencies

QUESTIONING PATH TOOL

Text 8—*Notes on the State of Virginia,* Thomas Jefferson, 1784

APPROACHING:
I determine my reading purposes and take note of key information about the text. I identify the LIPS domain(s) that will guide my initial reading.

I will do a close reading of my text, looking for key details related to its *structure, language, ideas,* or *perspective* in preparation for writing a text-based explanation and leading a comparative discussion. I will think about how the text discusses the role and purpose of education.

QUESTIONING: *I use Guiding Questions to help me investigate the text (from the **Guiding Questions Handout**).*

1. What words or phrases stand out to me as powerful and important? [L]

2. What do I think the text is mainly about—what is discussed in detail? [I]

ANALYZING: *I question further to connect and analyze the details I find (from the **Guiding Questions Handout**).*

3. What seems to be the author's attitude or point of view? [P]

4. In what ways are ideas and claims linked together in the text? [S]

DEEPENING: *I consider the questions of others.*

5. What is the first thing Jefferson discusses in his "note"?

   What details does he present about the process by which "the best geniuses will be raked from the rubbish"?

   Why is this process important in his view of the purpose of education?

6. Jefferson's "note" is presented as a single paragraph, but is actually divided into several sections with different areas of focus.

   How does the focus of his discussion shift with the transitional phrase "But of all the views of this law none is more important…"?

   What do details and words in this section of the text communicate about Jefferson's perspective on the purpose of education?

7. According to Jefferson, why should education focus on the study of history?

8. What does Jefferson mean when he talks about the "degeneracy" of government and says "the people themselves . . . are the only safe depositories"?

   How is this claim related to his call for "an amendment of our constitution" to "come in aid of the public education" and to the Virginia bill and plan he outlines at the start of the text?

   Ultimately, according to Jefferson, what is the purpose of education?

EXTENDING: *I pose my own questions.*

Students will develop an original question for their text in Part 4 and a comparative question in Part 5.

QUESTIONING PATH TOOL

Text 9—"The Vision of Education Reform in the United States," Secretary Arne Duncan, 2010

APPROACHING:
I determine my reading purposes and take note of key information about the text. I identify the LIPS domain(s) that will guide my initial reading.

I will do a close reading of my text, looking for key details related to its *structure, language, ideas,* or *perspective,* in preparation for writing a text-based explanation and leading a comparative discussion. I will think about how the text discusses the role and purpose of education.

QUESTIONING: *I use Guiding Questions to help me investigate the text (from the **Guiding Questions Handout**).*

1. What words or phrases stand out to me as powerful and important? [L]

2. What do I think the text is mainly about—what is discussed in detail? [I]

ANALYZING: *I question further to connect and analyze the details I find (from the **Guiding Questions Handout**).*

3. What seems to be the author's attitude or point of view? [P]

4. In what ways are ideas and claims linked together in the text? [S]

DEEPENING: *I consider the questions of others.*

5. According to what Duncan details in the opening paragraphs of his speech, what purposes does education serve?

6. What details from paragraph 6 explain what the "achievement gap" and "opportunity gap" are?

   In this and the following paragraphs, what details does Duncan provide to support his assertion that "closing the achievement gap and closing the opportunity gap is the civil rights issue of our generation"?

7. Duncan describes "a paradox at the heart of America's efforts to bolster international competitiveness."

   What words and information does he use to explain this paradox?

   What are the implications for education in the United States, and what do "new partnerships" in the world "require" of American students?

8. At the end of the passage, Duncan quotes Nelson Mandela. What does this quotation say about the value of education?

   How are Mandela's words related to the perspective and claims about education that Duncan has presented throughout his speech?

EXTENDING: *I pose my own questions.*

Students will develop an original question for their text in Part 4 and a comparative question in Part 5.

Developing Core Literacy Proficiencies

QUESTIONING: SMALL-GROUP READING USING THE APPROACHING TEXTS TOOL

- Small expert groups read one of the texts collaboratively using the *Approaching Texts Tool*.
- Students record one or more of the Guiding Questions from the model *Questioning Path Tool* for their text in the Questioning the Text section of the tool. *Note:* Depending on skill levels, all students might consider the same Questioning Path (using the same selected questions) or different paths (using questions matched to their interests or skill levels).
- Each group member completes his or her own *Approaching Texts Tool* for the selected text and questions, planning what details he or she will search for, then rereads and annotates a copy of the text based on the question(s) recorded on the tool.
- Each student selects one text-specific question from the Deepening section of the model *Questioning Path Tool* to consider more deeply using the *Analyzing Details Tool*.

ANALYZING: INDEPENDENT ANALYSIS USING THE ANALYZING DETAILS TOOL

- Students independently complete an *Analyzing Details Tool* using a text-specific question from the model *Questioning Path Tool*.
- Students then return to their expert groups to discuss and compare their various analyses of their common text.

EXTENDING: POSING A NEW TEXT-SPECIFIC QUESTION

- Based on their planning on the *Approaching Texts Tool*, their reading and annotations, and the connections they have made using the *Analyzing Details Tool*, students now brainstorm new text-specific questions to consider in their expert groups.
- Students identify one new text-specific question to consider (either their own or one from their group) and complete an additional *Analyzing Details Tool* for that question.

☰ ACTIVITY 4: WRITING A TEXT-BASED EXPLANATION

Students use their analysis to independently write a text-based explanation of one of the texts.

This final activity of Part 4 serves as a more formal assessment of the skills focused on in the unit and as a foundation for students' planning in Part 5, where they will lead a text-centered discussion comparing their text to others read in the unit. Students will submit this writing exercise as part of their summative assessment in Part 5.

- Students return to one of their *Analyzing Details Tools* for their chosen text and think further about the connections they have made, how to explain those connections, and how to support their explanation.

- Review with students the elements of a good text-based explanation, which they have practiced writing in Part 2, Activity 5, and Part 3, Activity 3. Reemphasize the importance of using textual evidence (details they have identified and analyzed) to develop and support their explanations.

- Communicate to students that their task will be to explain a central idea they have discovered in the text through one or more of their Questioning Paths. They will also need to think about the author's purpose and how that has influenced the text's perspective, ideas, language, and structure.

- Have students read through the *Reading Closely Final Writing and Discussion Task handout* found in the Developing Core Literacy Proficiencies Student Edition, which presents them with a short explanation of the assignment and its criteria, as well as a listing of the key Literacy Skills they should try to demonstrate.

- Explain to students that their final written explanations will be evaluated for their demonstration of Literacy Skills and for three key expectations and criteria for the assignment:

  ⇒ Identify a central idea of the text and explain how it is developed through the ideas and details the text presents.

  ⇒ Explain how the central idea is related to the text's purpose and the author's perspective on the topic.

  ⇒ Present and explain a new understanding about the unit's topic that reading the text has led to.

NOTE

The criteria for key skills and discussion habits to be evaluated in Parts 4 and 5 of the unit, are included in the *RC Literacy Skills and Discussion Habits Rubric* in the **RC Literacy Toolbox**.

Teacher Modeling

This final writing assignment will be the first time that students are introduced (informally) to the OE Collaborative Writing Workshop (see the Teacher User Guide for more explanation). In this approach, students will do the following:

1. Consider the Literacy Skills they should demonstrate in their text-based explanations.
2. Receive informal feedback from peers about their first drafts.
3. Do a single revision cycle to improve their explanations in one or more of the skills areas.

Before they draft their explanations and go through the Writer's Workshop cycle, use a short teacher or student paragraph to model the criterion-based writing and review process.

- First model the process of using an *Analyzing Details Tool* to think about and develop an initial written expression of a central idea. Point out how the Connecting Details area on the tool might serve as a central idea that represents an understanding of the text. The Selected and Analyzing Details areas can then be used as supporting evidence in the written explanation. Encourage students also to use details and ideas gathered from their text annotations and notes from previous text-centered discussions.

- Present students with a short written explanation, either one derived in the previous modeling exercise or one written previously in the unit. Tell them that they will be doing a close reading of this text-based explanation looking for evidence of the Literacy Skills used in writing it.

- Next, model how to analyze the written explanation using one or two of the Literacy Skills descriptors (criteria) from the informal **Student RC Literacy Skills and Discussion Habits Checklist** (in the **RC Literacy Toolbox** and Student Edition).

- Read or have students read the criteria that will be used to review the written explanation, pointing out that they are the same criteria that will be used to review students' final written explanations.

- For each of the skills criteria, talk through where evidence of the skill is (or is not) found in the example explanation. Then discuss whether the evidence in the writing "needs work," is "okay" for a first draft, or is "very strong." Ask students to contribute to the review as they become familiar with the process.

Guided Writing

- Using the **Analyzing Details Tool** they developed in Activity 3, students draft a multiparagraph explanation using textual evidence that explains the following:

  ⇒ A central idea of the text and how it is developed through the ideas and details the text presents

  ⇒ How the central idea is related to the text's purpose and the author's perspective on the topic

  ⇒ What they have come to understand about the topic from the text

Students freewrite during class time to generate initial ideas and drafts.

Text-Centered Discussion: Reviewing Text-Based Explanations

- In small groups (which may or may not be the same as the text-specific expert groups), students use the process and criteria previously modeled to review, critique, and revise the drafts of their text-based explanations.

- Students focus on one or more of the criteria, look for evidence in the draft of where the literacy skill is (or is not) demonstrated, and then use the review checklist that follows to indicate if this skill "needs work," is "okay" as demonstrated, or is "very strong." Using the criteria and the evidence they have noted, reviewers provide informal feedback to writers about strengths of the draft or improvements that could be made.

- Either in class or as homework, students use suggestions from peer reviews to revise their drafts into a final product.

Students can use the following informal, *Skills-Based Checklist* to self- and peer assess their explanations or the more complete *Student RC Literacy Skills and Discussion Habits Checklist* (available in the **RC Literacy Toolbox** and Student Edition). Their reviews might focus on any of the criteria or all of them if they are ready to think about multiple issues:

LITERACY SKILLS	DESCRIPTORS: *Find evidence of using the literacy skill in the draft.* *Does the writer's explanation . . .*	NEEDS WORK	OKAY	VERY STRONG
Attending to Details	Identify words, details, or quotations that are important to understanding the text?			
Summarizing	Correctly explain what the text says about the topic?			
Identifying Relationships	Notice important connections among details, ideas, or texts?			
Recognizing Perspective	Identify and explain the author's view of the text's topic?			
Using Evidence	Support the explanation with evidence from the text; use accurate quotations, paraphrases, and references?			

≡ PART 4: SUMMATIVE ASSESSMENT ≡ OPPORTUNITIES

The multiparagraph explanations students draft in Part 4, and their supporting work on *Approaching* and *Analyzing Tools*, should be reviewed closely as evidence of how well they are using the process represented in the *Reading Closely Graphic* and their developing literacy skills of **Questioning, Attending to Details, Identifying Relationships, Summarizing, Interpreting Language**, and **Recognizing Perspective**. At this point, students should be able to do the following:

- Describe accurately the central ideas of a text.
- Explain observations about the author's purpose and perspective.
- Identify something they have learned from their reading that is clearly text-related.
- Reference details related to each of these writing purposes.

Students who can do so are ready to lead discussions in Part 5. Students who have not yet been able to read their text and explain their understanding of it successfully may need additional support before moving on to Part 5.

These multiparagraph explanations should reflect each student's best explanatory writing abilities—especially those related to the *clarity* of their explanations. Students' text-based explanations can be used as a formative assessment of their writing skills in the areas of **Using Evidence**, **Using Language**, and **Using Conventions**. These skills will be more formally assessed in later Developing Core Literacy Proficiencies units.

A Student *RC Literacy Skills and Discussion Habits Checklist* is provided in the **RC Literacy Toolbox** to support students in self- and peer assessment of these targeted skills, as demonstrated in their written explanations and their text-centered discussions. A more formal *RC Literacy Skills and Discussion Habits Rubric* is also provided for evaluation of students' work on the final writing and discussion tasks.

Additionally, students' writing can be reviewed in relationship to the specific grade-level expectations for Writing Standard 2 (Explanatory Writing), especially if students have been working on writing explanations in previous units and are ready for more formal feedback:

CCSS.ELA-LITERACY.W.9-10.2: Write informative/explanatory texts to examine and convey complex ideas, concepts, and information clearly and accurately through the effective selection, organization, and analysis of content.

   a. Introduce a topic; organize complex ideas, concepts, and information to make important connections and distinctions; include formatting (e.g., headings), graphics (e.g., figures, tables), and multimedia when useful to aiding comprehension.

   b. Develop the topic with well-chosen, relevant, and sufficient facts, extended definitions, concrete details, quotations, or other information and examples appropriate to the audience's knowledge of the topic.

   c. Use appropriate and varied transitions to link the major sections of the text, create cohesion, and clarify the relationships among complex ideas and concepts.

   d. Use precise language and domain-specific vocabulary to manage the complexity of the topic.

   e. Establish and maintain a formal style and objective tone while attending to the norms and conventions of the discipline in which they are writing.

   f. Provide a concluding statement or section that follows from and supports the information or explanation presented (e.g., articulating implications or the significance of the topic).

PART 5

DISCUSSING IDEAS

"A great equalizer of the conditions of men"

OBJECTIVE:	Students learn the characteristics of an effective text-based discussion and demonstrate skills in leading and participating in one.

ESTIMATED TIME: 2–3 days

MATERIALS:
Texts 1 through 9
- *Approaching Texts Tool*
- *Analyzing Details Tool*

- *Student Reading Closely Literacy Skills and Discussion Habits Checklist*

☰ LITERACY SKILLS

TARGETED SKILLS	DESCRIPTORS
QUESTIONING	Formulates and responds to questions and lines of inquiry that lead to relevant and important ideas and themes within and across texts
IDENTIFYING RELATIONSHIPS	Identifies important connections among key details and ideas within and across texts
SUMMARIZING	Recounts the explicit meaning of texts, referring to key details, events, characters, language, and ideas
INTERPRETING LANGUAGE	Identifies how words and phrases convey meaning and represent an author's or narrator's perspective
RECOGNIZING PERSPECTIVE	Uses textual details to recognize an author's or narrator's relationship to and perspective on a text's topic

Developing Core Literacy Proficiencies

ACADEMIC HABITS

HABITS DEVELOPED	DESCRIPTORS
PREPARING	Reads the texts, researches the topics, and thinks about the questions being studied to prepare for tasks
COLLABORATING	Pays attention to, respects, and works productively in various roles with all other participants.
COMMUNICATING CLEARLY	Uses appropriate language and relevant textual details to clearly present ideas and claims

ALIGNMENT TO CCSS

TARGETED STANDARD:

CCSS.ELA-LITERACY.SL.9-10.1: Initiate and participate effectively in a range of collaborative discussions (one-on-one, in groups, and teacher-led) with diverse partners on *grades 9–10 topics, texts, and issues,* building on others' ideas and expressing their own clearly and persuasively.

SUPPORTING STANDARDS:

CCSS.ELA-LITERACY.RI.9-10.10: By the end of grade 9, read and comprehend literary nonfiction in the grades 9–10 text complexity band proficiently, with scaffolding as needed at the high end of the range.

CCSS.ELA-LITERACY.W. 9-10.2: Write informative/explanatory texts to examine and convey complex ideas, concepts, and information clearly and accurately through the effective selection, organization, and analysis of content.

CCSS.ELA-LITERACY.W. 9-10.4: Produce clear and coherent writing in which the development, organization, and style are appropriate to task, purpose, and audience.

CCSS.ELA-LITERACY.W. 9-10.9: Draw evidence from literary or informational texts to support analysis, reflection, and research.

 ACTIVITIES

1. UNDERSTANDING TEXT-CENTERED DISCUSSIONS
The teacher leads students in a reflective conversation about productive, text-centered discussions.

2. PREPARING FOR A TEXT-CENTERED DISCUSSION
Students discuss their text explanations in groups and independently prepare for leading a text-centered discussion by crafting a comparative text-specific question.

3. LEADING A TEXT-CENTERED DISCUSSION
Students lead and participate in text-centered discussions with other students who have analyzed different texts.

ACTIVITY 1: UNDERSTANDING TEXT-CENTERED DISCUSSIONS

The teacher leads students in a reflective conversation about productive text-centered discussions.

INSTRUCTIONAL NOTES

Students now move from writing about their texts to leading a comparative text-centered discussion.

- Review and discuss the characteristics of a productive text-centered discussion, that it:
  ⇒ Remains focused on one or more texts and specific evidence from those texts
  ⇒ Uses provocative questions to frame discussion but is not merely focused on answering those questions
  ⇒ Considers various readings, analyses, and views of the text—all potentially valid if well supported
  ⇒ Expects participants (students) to prepare for the discussion, engage actively with the process and each other, collaborate respectfully, and present and explain their ideas clearly and with relevant textual support

Throughout the unit, students have informally practiced and reflected on some of the Academic Habits used in text-centered discussions without formal instruction related to Speaking and Listening **CCSS.ELA-LITERACY.SL.1.** Now, discuss three of the Academic Habits related to participating in text-centered discussions—**Preparing, Collaborating,** and **Communicating Clearly**—what each habit represents, why it is important, and how a participant in a discussion uses and demonstrates the habit.

- Ask students to reflect on how they have—or have not—used and demonstrated the habits in the many small-group discussions throughout the unit.
- Have students refer to specific moments (or evidence) from previous small-group discussions as examples of when they demonstrated—or did not demonstrate—the criteria.
- Students identify skills and behaviors they want to improve on in this last part of the unit as they prepare for and participate in their culminating text-centered discussions.

DISCUSSION HABITS	DESCRIPTORS: *When—and how well—have I demonstrated these habits?*	EXAMPLES FROM TEXT-CENTERED DISCUSSIONS
PREPARING	Reads the text(s) closely and thinks about the questions to prepare for a text-centered discussion	
COLLABORATING	Pays attention to other participants while participating in and leading a text-centered discussion	
COMMUNICATING CLEARLY	Presents ideas and supporting evidence so others can understand them	

NOTE

These same habits and descriptors are also found in the *Student RC Literacy Skills and Discussion Habits Checklist* found in the **RC Literacy Toolbox** and Student Edition.

≡ ACTIVITY 2: PREPARING FOR A ≡ TEXT-CENTERED DISCUSSION

Students discuss their text explanations in groups and independently prepare for leading a text-centered discussion by crafting a comparative text-specific question.

INSTRUCTIONAL NOTES

Students prepare for their culminating activity in the unit—in which they will explain a central idea of their text, identify something they have learned from reading their text (in the context of the other texts of the unit), and pose a comparative text-specific question to facilitate a text-based discussion. The key to this activity is that each student is encouraged to come up with an individual insight or observation that has sprung from reading and studying related texts throughout the unit. For some students, this could be a more literal discovery or comparison, for others an inference supported by the texts, and for others still, an evidence-based claim. Student discoveries need to be text-based, but they do not need to be too carefully structured in relationship to a particular theme, idea, or detail.

ANALYZING: REVIEW EXPLANATIONS IN EXPERT GROUPS

- Students review each other's final written, text-based explanations in expert groups for accuracy and use of details. They compare the observations and discoveries they have made about their common text.

- Students discuss their text in relationship to Texts 5 and 6 and to the other texts of the unit. As a lead-in to this discussion, they might return to the ideas presented by Sir Ted Robinson and illustrated in the Text 3 video.

- Use the discussion habits, as described in the **Discussion Checklist** (previously and at the end of the unit), to help guide their discussion.

- Have students do a self-assessment of their use of these discussion habits following their discussion.

EXTENDING: DEVELOP A COMPARATIVE QUESTION INDEPENDENTLY

- Students review their **Analyzing Details Tools** and the text-based explanations they have developed and think about how to extend their discoveries in relationship to the other texts in the unit.

- Using a new **Analyzing Details Tool**, students independently develop a text-specific question that is based on their selected text (Text 7, 8, or 9) but connects to other texts from the unit.

- This question will be used to set up discussion when they join a new group in Activity 3.

- Depending on student ability, teachers might choose to (1) let students pose a question on their own, (2) model a comparative question, (3) suggest that students work from one of the text-specific questions found in the Deepening sections of the model Questioning Paths for each of the three texts, or (4) work individually with some students to help them develop or improve their own questions.

≡ ACTIVITY 3: LEADING A TEXT-CENTERED DISCUSSION

Students lead and participate in a text-centered discussion with other students who have analyzed different texts.

INSTRUCTIONAL NOTES

In this activity, students *jigsaw* to groups of three (or alternately six, depending on class size) so that each of the final three texts is represented in the group by at least one text expert. In the discussion, students (or student pairs) do the following:

- Have a copy of all three texts to refer to and annotate.
- Take a turn at leading the text-centered discussion for the text they have analyzed and written about.
- Review and summarize what the text is generally about and what they know about its author, source, and purpose.
- Share their explanations of a key central idea of the text (either by summarizing or reading their text-based explanation):
  ⇒ Pointing out key details to the other students in their group
  ⇒ Explaining their analysis of the author's perspective
  ⇒ Pointing out key words that indicate the author's perspective
- Once all students have shared their analyses, they each take turns posing their comparative questions and facilitating the discussion. As they facilitate, they should do the following:
  ⇒ Ask the other participants to reference the texts in their comments
  ⇒ Share the understanding that has emerged for them, connecting it to and deepening it with comments from the others
  ⇒ Direct the group to reread key portions of the texts to support discussion
- Finally, each *jigsaw* group summarizes its discussion for the class, sharing questions, observations, and key textual details that they have identified and discussed.
- Depending on time and their experience participating in text-centered discussions, students might conduct one or more discussions in other *jigsaw* groups. This will enable students to gain more experience in leading discussions, refine their communication of their ideas, and respond to other insights and comments from different groups.
- The class then reflects on what has been learned in the unit—about its topic, various text types and perspectives, close reading, questioning, and text-centered discussion.
- Students individually use the **Student RC Literacy Skills and Discussion Habits Checklist** (available in the **RC Literacy Toolbox** and Student Edition) to reflect on and self-assess their learning in the unit—and potentially to identify areas to work on in future units.

☰ PART 5: SUMMATIVE ASSESSMENT
☰ OPPORTUNITIES

PREASSESSMENT FOR SUBSEQUENT LEARNING

In Parts 4 and 5, students will have written a multiparagraph explanation that presents and supports their individual text-based explanation of one of the culminating texts, then will have led a text-centered discussion about that text. The explanation and the discussion present opportunities to assess students' developing Literacy Skills and their Academic Habits—using the checklist included for student self- and peer assessment and the **Teacher Evaluation Rubric**. Either or both can be used as a basis for evaluation of learning and grading within the unit.

The culminating activity of the unit involves participating in and leading a text-centered discussion, through which students can demonstrate their developing Literacy Skills of **Close Reading**, **Analysis**, and **Questioning** as well as their emerging Academic Habits for text-centered discussion. As such, the activity provides summative assessment of skills targeted within the unit and formative assessment of emerging discussion habits that can inform instruction in future units. To capture evidence, listen in on group conversations and have students self- and peer assess using the **Student RC Literacy Skills and Discussion Habits Checklist** found in the **RC Literacy Toolbox**. If more formal evidence is needed, students can compile an optional collection of evidence that includes a reflective narrative (see the following explanation), or a video of student conversations can be recorded and reviewed later.

A more formal **RC Literacy Skills and Discussion Habits Rubric** (found in the **RC Literacy Toolbox**) should be used by the teacher for evaluating performance and growth as demonstrated in the multiparagraph explanation and final text-based discussion. This rubric includes a four-point developmental scale for indicating where students are on a continuum from "emerging" to "excelling" and also enables the teacher to indicate specific skill areas in which the student has demonstrated noticeable growth. The rubric includes a place for an overall summary evaluation—potentially a grade—or can be used in a point-based grading system by tallying the ratings for each of the thirteen criteria in the rubric.

Notes to the teacher about using this rubric: Find evidence in the student's text-based explanation, planning notes, and participation in a final text-centered discussion to support ratings for each of the component Literacy Skills and overall essay content criteria listed in the rubric. Based on that evidence, use the developmental scale to rate the grade-level performance demonstrated by the student as:

1—**Emerging:** needs improvement
2—**Developing:** shows progress
3—**Becoming Proficient:** demonstrates skills
4—**Excelling:** exceeds expectations

If there is insufficient evidence to make a confident rating, mark **NE** (not enough evidence).

Indicate if the student has demonstrated growth in each skill area during the unit by adding a "+" to the rating. Determine a summary evaluation based on the overall pattern of ratings and strength of evidence. This summary evaluation can be computed based on points or determined by examining the prevalent pattern in the criteria-based ratings.

OPTIONAL—COLLECTION OF EVIDENCE

To extend assessment within this final activity, students could compile a collection of evidence that reflects what they have learned in the unit. The collection could include any or all of these student work samples:

- The written explanation of their final focus text with the tools that have informed and supported that analysis (with a self- or peer assessment using the rubric from Part 4)
- The comparative text-specific question for their discussion group and some reflection about what happened when the group discussed their question
- A self-assessment of skills they have demonstrated as close readers and as group members, using the **Student RC Literacy Skills and Discussion Habits Checklist** to identify and explain their strengths as well as areas they intend to focus on in further work
- A personal narrative in which they tell the story of what they have experienced, discovered, and learned within the unit, including a reflective summary of their reading experience for one or more of the texts
- A reflective self-assessment of their personal literacy development, written using literacy terminology and concepts from the unit

The student collection of evidence can be used for evaluation of learning in the unit, but it will probably be most valuable as a formative assessment to help the teacher, and student, know what to work on in future units.

READING CLOSELY FOR TEXTUAL DETAILS UNIT TEXTS

The unit uses texts that are accessible for free on the Internet without any login information, membership requirements, or purchase. Because of the ever-changing nature of website addresses, specific links are not provided. Teachers and students can locate these texts through web searches using the information provided.

AUTHOR	DATE	PUBLISHER	LEXILE	NOTES
Text 1: Classroom Pictures (Photos)				
NA	1950s & 2012	KJJS—Craig Michaels Inc.	NA	Photos from a 1950s classroom and classrooms in 2012
Text 2: *The Story of My Life* (Personal narrative)				
Helen Keller	1905	Doubleday, Page & Co.	1250L	An excerpt of Keller talking about her teacher, Anne Sullivan
Text 3: "Changing Education Paradigms" (Video)				
Ken Robinson	2010	TED Talk	NA	TED Talk from RSA Animate describing the changing educational landscape across the United States and world
Text 4: Only a Teacher (Website)				
NA	NA	PBS	NA	Website for students to read and search about the history of the role of the teacher in US education
Text 5: "Kids Need Structure" (Speech)				
Colin Powell	2012	TED Talk	900L	Excerpted text of Powell's TED Talk in which he states the importance of structure in kids' lives
Text 6: *Dr. Montessori's Own Handbook* (Informational Text)				
Maria Montessori	1914	Frederick A. Stokes Co.	1270L	Descriptive text describing how children should be allowed to develop through independence and little influence from adults
Text 7: "Good Citizenship: The Purpose of Education" (Personal narrative)				
Eleanor Roosevelt	1930	Pictorial review	1250L	Abridged essay describing Roosevelt's beliefs on the purpose of education

Text 8: *Notes on the State of Virginia* (Government document)				
Thomas Jefferson	1784	University of Chicago Press	1410L	Jefferson's note on the importance of compulsory education
Text 9: "The Vision of Education Reform in the United States" (Speech)				
Arne Duncan	2010	United States Department of Education	1200L	Duncan's argument for raising educational standards in order to remain economically competitive
Extended Reading: "Lectures and Biographical Sketches" (Personal narrative)				
Ralph Waldo Emerson	1863–1864	Houghton Mifflin and Co.	NA	Essay describing Emerson's beliefs on the purpose of education
Extended Reading: "Education and National Welfare" (Speech)				
Horace Mann	1848	Tennessee Criminal Law Resources	NA	Report detailing how education leads to social mobility in society

TEXT 1

Classroom Pictures
1950s and 2012

1950s CLASSROOM

(2012 CLASSROOM)

TEXT 2

The Story of My Life
Helen Keller
Doubleday, Page & Co., 1905

Thus I learned from life itself. At the beginning I was only a little mass of possibilities. It was my   **P1**
teacher who unfolded and developed them. When she came, everything about me breathed of love
and joy and was full of meaning. She has never since let pass an opportunity to point out the beauty
that is in everything, nor has she ceased trying in thought and action and example to make my life
5 sweet and useful.

It was my teacher's genius, her quick sympathy, her loving tact which made the first years of my   **P2**
education so beautiful. It was because she seized the right moment to impart knowledge that made it
so pleasant and acceptable to me. She realized that a child's mind is like a shallow brook which ripples
and dances merrily over the stony course of its education and reflects here a flower, there a bush,
10 **yonder** a **fleecy** cloud; and she attempted to guide my mind on its way, knowing that like a brook
it should be fed by mountain streams and hidden springs, until it broadened out into a deep river,
capable of reflecting in its **placid** surface, **billowy** hills, the **luminous** shadows of trees and the blue
heavens, as well as the sweet face of a little flower.

Any teacher can take a child to the classroom, but not every teacher can make him learn. He will not   **P3**
15 work joyously unless he feels that liberty is his, whether he is busy or at rest; he must feel the flush of

yonder	fleecy	placid
a distant place that is usually within sight	covered or made of fleece, the wool usually from a sheep	peaceful; calm
billowy	**luminous**	
to swell out; puff up	radiating or reflecting light; shining; bright	

victory and the heart-sinking of disappointment before he takes with a will the tasks distasteful to him and resolves to dance his way bravely through a dull routine of textbooks.

My teacher is so near to me that I scarcely think of myself apart from her. How much of my delight in all beautiful things is **innate**, and how much is due to her influence, I can never tell. I feel that her being is inseparable from my own, and that the footsteps of my life are in hers. All the best of me belongs to her—there is not a talent, or an aspiration or a joy in me that has not been awakened by her loving touch.

P4

20

innate		
the essential character of something or someone		

TEXT 3

Changing Paradigms
Ken Robinson
TED Talk, 2010

TEXT 4

Only a Teacher
PBS

TEXT 5

"Kids Need Structure"
Colin Powell
TED Talk, 2012

I want to talk about young people and structure. This was last Wednesday afternoon at a school in   **P1**
Brooklyn, New York, at Cristo Rey High School, run by the **Jesuits**. And I was talking to this group of
students, and take a look at them (shows a picture) . . . And there are about 300 kids in this school, and
the school's been going now for four years, and they're about to graduate their first class. Twenty-two
5 people are graduating, and all 22 are going to college. They all come from homes where there is, for
the most part, just one person in the home, usually the mother or the grandmother, and that's it, and
they come here for their education and for their structure . . .

Now I had this picture taken, and it was put up on my Facebook page last week, and somebody wrote **P2**
in, "Huh, why does he have him standing at attention like that?" And then they said, "But he looks
10 good." (Laughter)

He does look good, because kids need structure, and the trick I play in all of my school appearances **P3**
is that when I get through with my little **homily** to the kids, I then invite them to ask questions,
and when they raise their hands, I say, "Come up," and I make them come up and stand in front of
me. I make them stand at attention like a soldier. Put your arms straight down at your side, look up,
15 open your eyes, stare straight ahead, and speak out your question loudly so everybody can hear. No
slouching, no pants hanging down, none of that stuff. (Laughter) And this young man, his name is—
his last name Cruz—he loved it. That's all over his Facebook page and it's gone viral. (Laughter) So
people think I'm being unkind to this kid. No, we're having a little fun . . .

Jesuits	homily	
a member of a Roman Catholic religious order founded by Ignatius of Loyola in 1534	a sermon, usually religious and of a nondoctrine nature	

But anyway, it's a game I play, and it comes obviously from my military experience. Because for the **P4** majority of my adult life, I worked with young kids, teenagers with guns, I call them. And we would

20 bring them into the army, and the first thing we would do is to put them in an environment of structure, put them in ranks, make them all wear the same clothes, cut all their hair off so they look alike, make sure that they are standing in ranks. We teach them how to go right face, left face, so they can obey instructions and know the consequences of not obeying instructions. It gives them structure.

25 And then we introduce them to somebody who they come to hate immediately, the drill sergeant. And they hate him. And the drill sergeant starts screaming at them, and telling them to do all kinds of awful things. But then the most amazing thing happens over time. Once that structure is developed, once they understand the reason for something, once they understand, "Mama ain't here, son. I'm your worst nightmare. I'm your daddy and your mommy. And that's just the way it is. You got that, son?

30 Yeah, and then when I ask you a question, there are only three possible answers: yes, sir; no, sir; and no excuse, sir. Don't start telling me why you didn't do something. It's yes, sir; no, sir; no excuse, sir."

"You didn't shave." "But sir—"   **P5**

"No, don't tell me how often you scraped your face this morning. I'm telling you you didn't shave."   **P6**

"No excuse, sir." "Attaboy, you're learning fast."   **P7**

35 But you'd be amazed at what you can do with them once you put them in that structure. In 18 weeks, **P8** they have a skill. They are mature. And you know what, they come to admire the drill sergeant and they never forget the drill sergeant. They come to respect him. And so we need more of this kind of structure and respect in the lives of our children.

I spend a lot of time with youth groups, and I say to people, "When does the education process   **P9**
40 begin?" We're always talking about, "Let's fix the schools. Let's do more for our teachers. Let's put more computers in our schools. Let's get it all online."

That isn't the whole answer. It's part of the answer. But the real answer begins with bringing a   **P10** child to the school with structure in that child's heart and soul to begin with.

When does the learning process begin? Does it begin in first grade? No, no, it begins the first time a P11
45 child in a mother's arms looks up at the mother and says, "Oh, this must be my mother. She's the one who feeds me. Oh yeah, when I don't feel so good down there, she takes care of me. It's her language I will learn." And at that moment they shut out all the other languages that they could be learning at that age, but by three months, that's her. And if the person doing it, whether it's the mother or grandmother, whoever's doing it, that is when the education process begins. That's when language
50 begins. That's when love begins. That's when structure begins. That's when you start to imprint on the child that "you are special, you are different from every other child in the world. And we're going to read to you." A child who has not been read to is in danger when that child gets to school. A child who doesn't know his or her colors or doesn't know how to tell time, doesn't know how to tie shoes, doesn't know how to do those things, and doesn't know how to do something that goes by a word
55 that was drilled into me as a kid: mind. Mind your manners! Mind your adults! Mind what you're saying! This is the way children are raised properly. And I watched my own young grandchildren now come along and they're, much to the distress of my children, they are acting just like we did. You know? You imprint them.

And that's what you have to do to prepare children for education and for school. And I'm working P12
60 at all the energy I have to sort of communicate this message that we need preschool, we need Head Start, we need prenatal care. The education process begins even before the child is born, and if you don't do that, you're going to have difficulty. And we are having difficulties in so many of our communities and so many of our schools where kids are coming to first grade and their eyes are blazing, they've got their little **knapsack** on and they're ready to go, and then they realize they're
65 not like the other first graders who know books, have been read to, can do their alphabet. And by the third grade, the kids who didn't have that structure and minding in the beginning start to realize they're behind, and what do they do? They act it out. They act it out, and they're on their way to jail or they're on their way to being dropouts. It's predictable. If you're not at the right reading level at third grade, you are a candidate for jail at age 18, and we have the highest **incarceration** rate because we're not getting our kids the proper start in life.

knapsack	incarceration	
a bag made of nylon or leather and carried on the back of hikers or soldiers, etc.	imprisonment or confining to an enclosure	

TEXT 6

Dr. Montessori's Own Handbook
Maria Montessori
Frederick A. Stokes Co., 1914

Freedom

The success of these results is closely connected with the delicate intervention of the one who guides **P1** the children in their development. It is necessary for the teacher to *guide* the child without letting him feel her presence too much, so that she may be always ready to supply the desired help, but may never be the obstacle between the child and his experience.

5 A lesson in the ordinary use of the word cools the child's enthusiasm for the knowledge of things, just **P2** as it would cool the enthusiasm of adults. To keep alive that enthusiasm is the secret of real guidance, and it will not prove a difficult task, provided that the attitude towards the child's acts be that of respect, calm and waiting, and provided that he be left free in his movements and in his experiences.

Then we shall notice that the child has a personality which he is seeking to expand; he has initiative, **P3**
10 he chooses his own work, persists in it, changes it according to his inner needs; he does not shirk effort, he rather goes in search of it, and with great joy overcomes obstacles within his capacity. He is sociable to the extent of wanting to share with every one his successes, his discoveries, and his little triumphs. There is therefore no need of intervention. "Wait while observing." That is the motto for the educator.

15 Let us wait, and be always ready to share in both the joys and the difficulties which the child **P4** experiences. He himself invites our sympathy, and we should respond fully and gladly. Let us have endless patience with his slow progress, and show enthusiasm and gladness at his successes. If we could say: "We are respectful and courteous in our dealings with children, we treat them as we should like to be treated ourselves," we should certainly have mastered a great educational principle and
20 undoubtedly be setting an *example of good education*.

What we all desire for ourselves, namely, not to be disturbed in our work, not to find hindrances to **P5** our efforts, to have good friends ready to help us in times of need, to see them rejoice with us, to be on terms of equality with them, to be able to confide and trust in them—this is what we need for happy companionship. In the same way children are human beings to whom respect is due, superior

25 to us by reason of their "innocence" and of the greater possibilities of their future. What we desire they desire also.

As a rule, however, we do not respect our children. We try to force them to follow us without regard to **P6** their special needs. We are overbearing with them, and above all, rude; and then we expect them to be **submissive** and well-behaved, knowing all the time how strong is their instinct of imitation and how

30 touching their faith in and admiration of us. They will imitate us in any case. Let us treat them, therefore, with all the kindness which we would wish to help to develop in them. And by kindness is not meant **caresses**. Should we not call anyone who embraced us at the first time of meeting rude, vulgar and ill-bred? Kindness consists in interpreting the wishes of others, in conforming one's self to them, and sacrificing, if need be, one's own desire. This is the kindness which we must show towards children.

35 To find the interpretation of children's desires we must study them scientifically, for their desires are **P7** often unconscious. They are the inner cry of life, which wishes to unfold according to mysterious laws. We know very little of the way in which it unfolds. Certainly the child is growing into a man by force of a divine action similar to that by which from nothing he became a child. Our intervention in this marvelous process is *indirect*; we are here to offer to this life, which came into the world by itself, the

40 *means* necessary for its development, and having done that we must await this development with respect.

Let us leave the life *free* to develop within the limits of the good, and let us observe this inner life **P8** developing. This is the whole of our mission. Perhaps as we watch we shall be reminded of the words of Him who was absolutely good, "Suffer the little children to come unto Me." That is to say, "Do not

45 hinder them from coming, since, if they are left free and unhampered, they will come."

submissive	caresses
passive, obedient	a light touch or embrace

TEXT 7

Good Citizenship: The Purpose of Education
Eleanor Roosevelt
Pictorial Review, 1930

What is the purpose of education? This question agitates scholars, teachers, statesmen, every group **P1** of thoughtful men and women. The conventional answer is the acquisition of knowledge, the reading of books, and the learning of facts. Perhaps because there are so many books and the branches of knowledge in which we can learn facts are so multitudinous today, we begin to hear more frequently

5 that the function of education is to give children a desire to learn. Also to teach them how to use their minds and where to go to acquire facts when their curiosity is aroused. Even more all-embracing than this is the statement made not long ago, before a group of English headmasters, by the Archbishop of York, that "the true purpose of education is to produce citizens." . . .

Theodore Roosevelt was teaching by precept and example. He believed that men owed something **P2**

10 at all times, whether in peace or in war, for the privilege of citizenship. He was saying that, no matter what conditions existed, the blame lay no more heavily on the politician than on the shoulders of the average citizen. For it was he who concerned himself so little with his government that he allowed men to stay in power in spite of his dissatisfaction because he was too indifferent to exert himself to get better men in office …

15 Gradually a change has come about. More young men and more young women (since the latter **P3** have had the vote) are doing political work. And even if they do not hold political office they have felt the need to understand their own government. In our schools are now given courses in civics, government, economics, and current events. Very few children are as ignorant as I was. But there still remains a vast amount to be done before we accomplish our first objective—informed and intelligent

20 citizens. Secondly, to bring about the realization that we are all responsible for the trend of thought and the action of our times.

How shall we arrive at these objectives? We think of course of history as a first means of information.   **P4**
Not the history which is a mere **recital** of facts, dates, wars, and kings, but a study of the life and
growth of other nations. These nations are ones in which we follow the general moral, intellectual,
25 and economic development through the ages. We note what brought about the rise and fall of
nations and what were the lasting contributions of peoples now passed away to the development of
the human family and the world as a whole.

Gradually from this study certain facts emerge. A nation must have leaders, men who have the power   **P5**
to see a little farther, to imagine a little better life than the present. But if this vision is to be fulfilled, it
30 must also have a vast army of men and women capable of understanding and following these leaders
intelligently. These citizens must understand their government from the smallest election district to
the highest administrative office. It must be no closed book to them, and each one must carry his own
particular responsibility or the whole army will lag.

I would have our children visit national shrines, know why we love and respect certain men of the   **P6**
35 past. I would have them see how government departments are run and what are their duties. I
would have them see how courts function, what juries are, what a legislative body is and what it
does. I would have them learn how we conduct our relationships with the rest of the world and what
are our contacts with other nations. The child seeing and understanding these things will begin to
envisage the varied pattern of the life of a great nation such as ours. He will see how his own life and
40 environment fit into the pattern and where his own usefulness may lie . . .

Learning to be a good citizen is learning to live to the maximum of one's abilities and opportunities,   **P7**
and every subject should be taught every child with this in view. The teacher's personality and
character are of the greatest importance. I have known many erudite and scholarly men and women
who were dismal failures as teachers. I have known some less learned teachers who had the gift of
45 inspiring youth and sending them on to heights where perhaps they themselves were unable to
follow . . .

recital		
a formal or public delivery of a memorized nature		

You will be thinking that few teachers of this type exist and you will be right. The blame lies with the **P8** attitude toward teachers and the teaching of our present generation. We have set up a money value, a material gauge by which we measure success. We have frequently given more time and more material
50 compensation to our cooks and chauffeurs and day-laborers, bricklayers, carpenters, and painters than we have to our nurses, governesses, and tutors and teachers in schools and colleges.

We entrust the building of our children's characters and the development of their minds to people **P9** whom we, as a rule, compensate less **liberally** than we do the men and women who build our houses and make our day-by-day existence more comfortable and luxurious. These men and women
55 teachers, paid from $1,200 to $5,000, and in extraordinary cases $10,000 a year, mold the future citizens of our country. We do not treat them with the respect or consideration which their high calling deserves. Nor do we reward them with the only reward which spells success according to our present standards.

One of our hard-worked businessmen said to me not long ago, "Why, these teacher fellows have a **P10**
60 snap. Look at their long summer holidays, and you can't tell me it's as hard to tell a lot of youngsters about logarithms or Scott's novels as it is to handle my board of directors at one end and my shop committee at the other." My thought was that if he and his fellow members on the board of directors and the men on the shop committee had had the right kind of teaching his job would be easier because at both ends he would have men better able to understand the whole problem of **industry**
65 and realize the necessity of cooperation . . .

I believe that each one of us, if we delve in our memories, can find some similar experience which **P11** will uphold my contention that a great teacher is more important than the most gorgeous building. Where no such contacts have been experienced, the most ideal surroundings will not make our school-days anything but a succession of dull and meaningless tasks.

liberally	industry	
allowing freedom of action, particularly with regards to personal belief	the management or ownership of businesses, etc.	

70 There are many inadequate teachers today. Perhaps our standards should be higher, but they cannot   P12
be until we learn to value and understand the function of the teacher in our midst. While we have
put much money in buildings and laboratories and gymnasiums, we have forgotten that they are
but the shell, and will never live and create a vital spark in the minds and hearts of our youth unless
some teacher furnishes the inspiration. A child responds naturally to high ideals, and we are all of us
creatures of habit.

75 Begin young to teach the standards that should prevail in public servants, in governmental   P13
administration, in national and international business and politics, and show by relating to daily life
and known experience the advantages derived from a well-run government. It will then be a logical
conclusion that the ends cannot be achieved without the cooperation of every citizen. This will be
readily grasped by the child because his daily experience in school illustrates the point.

TEXT 8

Notes on the State of Virginia
Thomas Jefferson
University of Chicago Press, 1784

Another object of the revisal is, to **diffuse** knowledge more generally through the mass of the people. **P1**
This bill proposes to lay off every county into small districts of five or six miles square, called hundreds,
and in each of them to establish a school for teaching reading, writing, and arithmetic. The tutor
to be supported by the hundred, and every person in it entitled to send their children three years

5 **gratis**, and as much longer as they please, paying for it. These schools to be under a **visitor**, who is
annually to chuse the boy, of best genius in the school, of those whose parents are too poor to give
them further education, and to send him forward to one of the grammar schools, of which twenty are
proposed to be erected in different parts of the country, for teaching Greek, Latin, geography, and
the higher branches of numerical arithmetic. Of the boys thus sent in any one year, trial is to be made

10 at the grammar schools one or two years, and the best genius of the whole selected, and continued
six years, and the residue dismissed. By this means twenty of the best geniusses will be raked from
the **rubbish** annually, and be instructed, at the public expense, so far as the grammar schools go. At
the end of six years instruction, one half are to be discontinued (from among whom the grammar
schools will probably be supplied with future masters); and the other half, who are to be chosen for

15 the superiority of their parts and disposition, are to be sent and continued three years in the study
of such sciences as they shall chuse, at William and Mary college, the plan of which is proposed to be
enlarged, as will be hereafter explained, and extended to all the useful sciences. The ultimate result
of the whole scheme of education would be the teaching all children of the state reading, writing,
and common arithmetic: turning out ten annually of superior genius, well taught in Greek, Latin,

diffuse	gratis	visitor
to spread or scatter widely or thinly	without charge or payment; free	acting as a superintendent of schools
rubbish		
worthless, unwanted material that is rejected or thrown out; trash		

20 geography, and the higher branches of arithmetic: turning out ten others annually, of still superior

parts, who, to those branches of learning, shall have added such of the sciences as their genius shall

have led them to: the furnishing to the wealthier part of the people convenient schools, at which

their children may be educated, at their own expense. —. But of all the views of this law none is more

important, none more legitimate, than that of rendering the people the safe, as they are the ultimate,

25 guardians of their own liberty. For this purpose the reading in the first stage, where *they* will receive

their whole education, is proposed, as has been said, to be chiefly historical.

History by **apprising** them of the past will enable them to judge of the future; it will avail them of the **P2**

experience of other times and other nations; it will qualify them as judges of the actions and designs

of men; it will enable them to know ambition under every disguise it may assume; and knowing it,

30 to defeat its views. In every government on earth is some trace of human weakness, some germ of

corruption and **degeneracy**, which cunning will discover, and wickedness insensibly open, cultivate,

and improve. Every government **degenerates** when trusted to the rulers of the people alone. The

people themselves therefore are its only safe **depositories**. And to render even them safe their minds

must be improved to a certain degree. This indeed is not all that is necessary, though it be essentially

35 necessary. An amendment of our constitution must here come in aid of the public education. The

influence over government must be shared among all the people. If every individual which composes

their mass participates of the ultimate authority, the government will be safe; because the corrupting

the whole mass will exceed any private resources of wealth: and public ones cannot be provided but

by levies on the people. In this case every man would have to pay his own price. The government

40 of Great-Britain has been corrupted, because but one man in ten has a right to vote for members of

parliament. The sellers of the government therefore get nine-tenths of their price clear. It has been

thought that corruption is restrained by confining the right of suffrage to a few of the wealthier of the

people: but it would be more effectually restrained by an extension of that right to such numbers as

would bid defiance to the means of corruption.

apprising	degeneracy	degenerates
to give notice to; inform; advise	to fall below a normal or desirable level in physical, mental, or moral qualities	to decline in standard
depositories		
a place where something valuable is kept		

TEXT 9

"The Vision of Education Reform in the United States"
Secretary Arne Duncan
United States Department of Education

Remarks to UNESCO in Paris, France, November 4, 2010

The promise of universal education was then a lonely beacon—a light to guide the way to peace and   **P1**
the rebuilding of nations across the globe. Today, the world is no longer recovering from a tragic
global war. Yet the international community faces a crisis of a different sort, the global economic
crisis. And education is still the beacon lighting the path forward—perhaps more so today than ever
5 before.

Education is still the key to eliminating gender inequities, to reducing poverty, to creating a   **P2**
sustainable planet, and to fostering peace. And in a knowledge economy, education is the new
currency by which nations maintain economic competitiveness and global prosperity. . . .

I want to make the case to you today that enhancing educational attainment and economic viability,   **P3**
10 both at home and abroad, is really more of a win-win game; it is an opportunity to grow the economic
pie, instead of carve it up. As President Obama said in his speech to the Muslim world in Cairo last
year, "Any world order that elevates one nation or group of people over another will inevitably fail."

There is so much that the United States has to learn from nations with high- performing education   **P4**
systems. And there is so much that America can share from its experience to the mutual benefit of
15 nations confronting similar educational challenges.

I am convinced that the U.S. education system now has an unprecedented opportunity to get   P5
dramatically better. Nothing—nothing—is more important in the long-run to American prosperity
than boosting the skills and attainment of the nation's students.

In the United States, we feel an economic and moral imperative to challenge the status quo. Closing   P6
20 the achievement gap and closing the opportunity gap is the civil rights issue of our generation.
One quarter of U.S. high school students drop out or fail to graduate on time. Almost one million
students leave our schools for the streets each year. That is economically unsustainable and morally
unacceptable.

One of the more unusual and sobering press conferences I participated in last year was the release   P7
25 of a report by a group of top retired generals and admirals. Here was the stunning conclusion of
their report: 75 percent of young Americans, between the ages of 17 to 24, are unable to enlist in the
military today because they have failed to graduate from high school, have a criminal record, or are
physically unfit.

Now, everyone here today knows that education is taking on more and more importance around the   P8
30 globe. In the last decade, international competition in higher education and the job market has grown
dramatically. As the *New York Times* columnist Thomas Friedman famously pointed out, the world
economy has indeed "flattened." Companies now digitize, automate, and outsource work to the most
competitive individuals, companies, and countries.

In the knowledge economy, opportunities to land a good job are vanishing fast for young workers   P9
35 who drop out of school or fail to get college experience. That is why President Obama often says that
the nation that "out-educates us today is going to out-compete us tomorrow."

Yet there is also a paradox at the heart of America's efforts to bolster international competitiveness.   P10

To succeed in the global economy, the United States, just like other nations, will have to become both P11
more economically competitive and more collaborative.

40 In the information age, more international competition has spawned more international **P12** collaboration. Today, education is a global public good **unconstrained** by national boundaries.

In the United States, for example, concerns are sometimes raised about the large number of foreign- **P13** born students earning masters and doctorates in science and engineering fields. Immigrants now constitute nearly half of America's PhD scientists and engineers, even though they constitute only 12 **45** percent of the workforce overall.

These foreign-born students more often return to the country of origin than in the past. But their **P14** scientific skills and entrepreneurship strengthen not only their native economy but also stimulate innovation and new markets that can help boost the U.S. economy.

The same borderless nature of innovation and ideas is evident when foreign-born students remain **P15** **50** in America. Immigrants to the U.S. started a quarter of all engineering and technology companies from 1995 and 2005, including half of the start-ups in Silicon Valley, our high-tech capital. Sergey Brin, Google's co-founder, was born in Moscow but educated in the United States. Google is now used throughout the globe to gather information and advance knowledge. The brain drain, in short, has become the brain gain.

55 It is no surprise that economic interdependence brings new global challenges and educational **P16** demands.

The United States cannot, acting by itself, dramatically reduce poverty and disease or develop **P17** sustainable sources of energy. America alone cannot combat terrorism or curb climate change. To succeed, we must collaborate with other countries.

60 Those new partnerships require American students to develop better critical thinking abilities, cross- **P18** cultural understanding, and facility in multiple languages. They also will require U.S. students to

unconstrained	
able to act freely	

Unit 1   **99**

strengthen their skills in science, technology, engineering, and math—the STEM fields that anchor much of our innovation in the global economy.

These new partnerships must also inspire students to take a bigger and deeper view of their civic   P19
65 obligations—not only to their countries of origin but to the betterment of the global community. A just and socially responsible society must also be anchored in civic engagement for the public good.

In our view, the United States will be better off, in comparative terms, if we lead the world in   P20
educational attainment, rather than lagging behind. A generation ago, America did in fact lead the world in college attainment. But today among young adults, the U.S. is tied for ninth. That is why
70 President Obama has set a goal that America will once again have the highest proportion of college graduates in the world by 2020, a decade from now.

Yet even as the United States works to strengthen its educational system, it is important to remember P21
that advancing educational attainment and achievement everywhere brings benefits not just to the U.S. but around the globe. In the knowledge economy, education is the new game-changer driving
75 economic growth. Education, as Nelson Mandela says, "is the most powerful weapon which you can use to change the world."

EXTENDED READING

Lectures and Biographical Sketches
Ralph Waldo Emerson
Houghton Mifflin and Co, 1863–1864

I believe that our own experience instructs us that the secret of Education lies in respecting the pupil. **P1**
It is not for you to choose what he shall know, what he shall do. It is chosen and **foreordained**, and
he only holds the key to his own secret. By your **tampering** and **thwarting** and too much governing
he may be **hindered** from his end and kept out of his own. Respect the child. Wait and see the new
5 product of Nature. Nature loves analogies, but not repetitions. Respect the child. Be not too much his
parent. Trespass not on his **solitude**.

But I hear the outcry which replies to this suggestion:—Would you verily throw up the reins of   **P2**
public and private discipline; would you leave the young child to the mad career of his own
passions and **whimsies**, and call this anarchy a respect for the child's nature? I answer,—Respect
10 the child, respect him to the end, but also respect yourself. Be the companion of his thought, the
friend of his friendship, the lover of his virtue,—but no kinsman of his sin. Let him find you so true
to yourself that you are the **irreconcilable** hater of his **vice** and **imperturbable** slighter of
his trifling.

foreordained	tampering	thwarting
to predestine; predetermine	to make changes to something, especially in order to falsify or damage	to prevent from accomplishing a goal or purpose
hindered	**solitude**	**whimsies**
to have caused delay or interruption	the state of being or living alone	excessively playful; fanciful
irreconcilable	**vice**	**imperturbable**
a person who will not agree or compromise	a habit or practice that is immoral; a weakness	incapable of being upset or agitated; not easily excited

I confess myself utterly at a loss in suggesting particular reforms in our ways of teaching. No

15   **discretion** that can be lodged with a school-committee, with the overseers or visitors of an academy,

of a college, can at all avail to reach these difficulties and perplexities, but they solve themselves

when we leave institutions and address individuals. The will, the male power, organizes, imposes its

own thought and wish on others, and makes that military eye which controls boys as it controls men;

admirable in its results, a fortune to him who has it, and only dangerous when it leads the workman

20   to overvalue and overuse it and precludes him from finer means. Sympathy, the female force—

which they must use who have not the first—deficient in instant control and the breaking down of

resistance, is more subtle and lasting and creative. I advise teachers to cherish mother-wit. I assume

that you will keep the grammar, reading, writing and arithmetic in order; 't is easy and of course you

will. But smuggle in a little contraband wit, fancy, imagination, thought. If you have a taste which you

25   have suppressed because it is not shared by those about you, tell them that. Set this law up, whatever

becomes of the rules of the school: they must not whisper, much less talk; but if one of the young

people says a wise thing, greet it, and let all the children clap their hands. They shall have no book

but school-books in the room; but if one has brought in a Plutarch or Shakespeare or Don Quixote or

Goldsmith or any other good book, and understands what he reads, put him at once at the head of

30   the class. Nobody shall he disorderly, or leave his desk without permission, but if a boy runs from his

bench, or a girl, because the fire falls, or to check some injury that a little **dastard** is inflicting behind

his desk on some helpless sufferer, take away the medal from the head of the class and give it on the

instant to the brave rescuer. If a child happens to show that he knows any fact about astronomy, or

plants, or birds, or rocks, or history, that interests him and you, hush all the classes and encourage

35   him to tell it so that all may hear. Then you have made your school-room like the world. Of course you

will insist on modesty in the children, and respect to their teachers, but if the boy stops you in your

speech, cries out that you are wrong and sets you right, hug him!

discretion	dastard	
the power or right to decide or act according to one's own judgment; freedom of judgment or choice	a wrong-doing coward	

Developing Core Literacy Proficiencies

EXTENDED READING

Education and National Welfare
Horace Mann
Tennessee Criminal Law Resources, 1848

**EXCERPT OF THE TWELFTH ANNUAL REPORT OF HORACE MANN AS SECRETARY
OF MASSACHUSETTS STATE BOARD OF EDUCATION**

Now two or three things will doubtless be admitted to be true, beyond all controversy, in regard   P1

to Massachusetts. By its industrial condition, and its business operations, it is exposed, far beyond

any other State in the Union, to the fatal extremes of overgrown wealth and desperate poverty. Its

population is far more dense than that of any other State. It is four or five times more dense than the

5   average of all the other States taken together; and density of population has always been one of the

proximate causes of social inequality. According to population and territorial extent there is far more

capital in Massachusetts—capital which is movable, and instantaneously available—than in any other

State in the Union; and probably both these qualifications respecting population and territory could

be omitted without endangering the truth of the **assertion**. . . .

10 Now surely nothing but universal education can counterwork this tendency to the domination of   P2

capital and the **servility** of labor. If one class possesses all the wealth and the education, while the

residue of society is ignorant and poor, it matters not by what name the relation between them may

be called: the latter, in fact and in truth, will be the servile dependents and subjects of the former.

But, if education be equally diffused, it will draw property after it by the strongest of all attractions;

15 for such a thing never did happen, and never can happen, as that an intelligent and practical body of

proximate	assertion	servility
approximate; fairly accurate	a positive statement or declaration, often without support or reason	oppressed as being in slavery
residue		
a remnant that remains after a part is discarded or removed		

men should be permanently poor. Property and labor in different classes are essentially **antagonistic**; but property and labor in the same class are essentially **fraternal**. The people of Massachusetts have, in some degree, appreciated the truth that the unexampled prosperity of the State—its comfort, its competence, its general intelligence and **virtue**—is attributable to the education, more or less

20 perfect, which all its people have received; but are they sensible of a fact equally important—namely, that it is to this same education that two-thirds of the people are indebted for not being to-day the **vassals** of as severe a **tyranny**, in the form of capital, as the lower classes of Europe are bound to in any form of brute force?

Education then, beyond all other devices of human origin, is a great equalizer of the conditions of   P3
25 men,—the balance wheel of the social machinery. I do not here mean that it so elevates the moral nature as to make men disdain and abhor the oppression of their fellow men. This idea pertains to another of its attributes. But I mean that it gives each man the independence and the means by which he can resist the selfishness of other men. It does better than to disarm the poor of their hostility toward the rich: it prevents being poor. **Agrarianism** is the revenge of poverty against wealth. The
30 wanton destruction of the property of others—the burning of hay-ricks, and corn-ricks, the demolition of machinery because it supersedes hand-labor, the sprinkling of vitriol on rich dresses—is only agrarianism run mad. Education prevents both the revenge and the madness. On the other hand, a fellow-feeling for one's class or caste is the common instinct of hearts not wholly sunk in selfish regard for a person or for a family. The spread of education, by enlarging the cultivated class or caste, will
35 open a wider area over which the social feelings will expand; and, if this education should be universal and complete, it would do more than all things else to obliterate factitious distinctions in society. . . .

For the creation of wealth, then,—for the existence of a wealthy people and a wealthy nation,—   P4
intelligence is the grand condition. The number of improvers will increase as the intellectual

antagonistic	fraternal	virtue
hostile; opposing	a society of men associated with brotherly union	moral excellence; goodness; righteousness
vassals	**tyranny**	**Agrarianism**
servants or slaves	oppressive or severe government	a social movement of the equal division of rural land

constituency, if I may so call it, increases. In former times, and in most parts of the world even at

40 the present day, not one man in a million has ever had such a development of mind as made it

possible for him to become a contributor to art or science. . . . Let this development proceed, and

contributions . . . of inestimable value, will be sure to follow. That political economy, therefore,

which busies itself about capital and labor, supply and demand, interests and rents, favorable and

unfavorable balances of trade, but leaves out of account the elements of a wide-spread mental

45 development, is naught but **stupendous folly**. The greatest of all the arts in political economy is to

change a consumer into a producer; and the next greatest is to increase the producing power,—and

this to be directly obtained by increasing his intelligence. For mere delving, an ignorant man is but

little better than a swine, whom he so much resembles in his appetites, and surpasses in his power of

mischief. . . .

stupendous	folly	
very large or great	an action or idea that is foolish	

READING CLOSELY
FOR TEXTUAL DETAILS

DEVELOPING CORE LITERACY
PROFICIENCIES

GRADE 9

Literacy Toolbox

ODELL
EDUCATION

READING CLOSELY GRAPHIC

1.
APPROACHING
Where do I START?

- I determine my reading purposes and take note of important information about the text.

- Why am I reading this text, and how might that influence how I approach and read it?
- What do I know (or might find out) about the text's title, author, type, publisher, publication date, and history?
- **What sequence of questions might I use to focus my reading and increase my understanding of the text?**

2.
QUESTIONING
What details do I NOTICE?

- I use questions to help me investigate important aspects of the text.

3.
ANALYZING
What do I THINK about the details?

- I question further to analyze the details I notice and determine their meaning or importance.

4.
DEEPENING
How do I deepen my UNDERSTANDING?

- I consider others' questions and develop initial observations or claims.
- I explain why and cite my evidence.

5.
EXTENDING
Where does this LEAD me?

- I pose new questions to extend my investigation of the text and topic.
- I communicate my thinking to others.

ODELL
EDUCATION

READING CLOSELY: GUIDING QUESTIONS HANDOUT

1.
APPROACHING
Where do I START?

- I determine my reading purposes and take note of important information about the text.

- Why am I reading this text, and how might that influence how I approach and read it?
- What do I know (or might find out) about the text's title, author, type, publisher, publication date, and history?
- **What sequence of questions might I use to focus my reading and increase my understanding of the text?**

LANGUAGE (CCSS R.4, L.3, L.4, L.5)	IDEAS (CCSS R.2, W.3, R.8, R.9)	PERSPECTIVE (CCSS R.6)	STRUCTURE (CCSS R.5)
• What words or phrases stand out to me as powerful and important? • What do the author's words and phrases cause me to see, feel, or think? • How are key ideas, events, places, or characters described? • What unfamiliar words do I need to study or define to better understand the text?	• What do I think the text is mainly about—what is discussed in detail? • What new ideas or information do I find in the text? • Who are the main people, voices, or characters presented in the text? • What claims do I find in the text? • What ideas stand out to me as significant or interesting?	• What do I learn about the author and the purpose for writing the text? • What details or words suggest the author's perspective? • What seems to be the author's (narrator's) attitude or point of view?	• What do I notice about how the text is organized or sequenced? • What do I notice about the structure of specific elements (paragraphs, sentences, stanzas, lines, or scenes)? • In what ways does the text begin, end, and develop?

2.
QUESTIONING
What details do I NOTICE?

- I use questions to help me investigate important aspects of the text.

LANGUAGE	IDEAS	PERSPECTIVE	STRUCTURE
• How do specific words or phrases influence the meaning or tone of the text? • How does the author's choice of words reveal his/her purposes and perspective? • How does context define or change the meaning of key words in the text? • How does the text's language influence my understanding of important ideas or themes?	• How might I summarize the main ideas of the text and the key supporting details? • How do the text's main ideas relate to what I already know, think, or have read? • How do the main ideas, events, or people change as the text progresses? • What evidence supports the claims in the text, and what is left uncertain or unsupported?	• How does the author's perspective influence his or her presentation of ideas, themes, or arguments? • How does the author's perspective and presentation of the text compare to others? • How does the author's perspective influence my reading of text?	• In what ways are ideas, events, and claims linked together in the text? • How do specific sections or elements of the text develop its central ideas or themes? • How does the organization of the text influence my understanding of its information, themes, or arguments?

3.
ANALYZING
What do I THINK about the details?

- I question further to analyze the details I notice and determine their meaning or importance.

- **What relationships do I discover among the ideas and details presented, the author's perspective, and the language or structure of the text?**

4.
DEEPENING
How do I deepen my UNDERSTANDING?

- I consider others' questions and develop initial observations or claims.
- I explain why and cite my evidence.

5.
EXTENDING
Where does this LEAD me?

- I pose new questions to extend my investigation of the text and topic.
- I communicate my thinking to others.

ODELL EDUCATION

ATTENDING TO DETAILS HANDOUT

SEARCHING FOR DETAILS	I read the text closely and mark words and phrases that help me answer my question.

SELECTING DETAILS	As I read, I notice authors use a lot of details and strategies to develop their ideas, arguments, and narratives. Following are examples of types of details authors often use in important ways.
I select words or phrases from my search that I think are **important for answering my questions.**	**Author's Facts and Ideas** • Statistics • Examples • Vivid description • Characters and actors • Events **Author's Language and Structure** • Repeated words • Strong language • Figurative language • Tone • Organizational structure and phrases **Opinions and Perspective** • Interpretations • Explanation of ideas or events • Narration • Personal reflection • Beliefs

ANALYZING DETAILS	By reading closely and thinking about the details, I can make connections among them. Following are some ways details can be connected.
I reread parts of the text and think about the **meaning of the details** and what they tell me **about my questions.**	**Facts and Ideas** • Authors use hard facts to illustrate or define an idea. • Authors use examples to express a belief or point of view. • Authors use vivid description to compare or oppose different ideas. • Authors describe different actors or characters to illustrate a comparison or contrast. • Authors use a sequence of events to arrive at a conclusion. **Language and Structure** • Authors repeat specific words or structures to emphasize meaning or tone. • Authors use language or tone to establish a mood. • Authors use figurative language to infer emotion or embellish meaning. • Authors use a specific organization to enhance a point or add meaning. **Opinions and Perspective** • Authors compare or contrast evidence to help define their point of view. • Authors offer their explanation of ideas or events to support their beliefs. • Authors tell their own story to develop their point of view. • Authors use language to reveal an opinion or feeling about a topic.

READING CLOSELY FINAL WRITING AND DISCUSSION TASK HANDOUT

In this unit, you have been developing your skills as an investigator of texts. You have learned to do the following things:

- Ask and think about good questions to help you examine what you read closely
- Uncover key clues in the details, words, and information found in the texts
- Make connections among details and texts
- Discuss what you have discovered with your classmates and teacher
- Cite specific evidence from the texts to explain and support your thinking
- Record and communicate your thinking on graphic tools and in sentences and paragraphs

Your final assignments will provide you with opportunities to use all of these related skills and to demonstrate your proficiency and growth in Reading Closely.

FINAL ASSIGNMENTS

1. **Becoming a Text Expert:** You will first become an expert about one of the three final texts in the unit. To accomplish this, you will do the following:

   a. Read and annotate the text on your own and use Guiding Questions and an *Analyzing Details Tool* to make some initial connections about the text.

   b. Compare the notes and connections you make with those made by other students who are also becoming experts about the same text.

   c. In your expert group, come up with a new text-specific question to think about when rereading the text more closely. Complete a second *Analyzing Details Tool* for this question.

   d. Study your text notes and *Analyzing Details Tools* to come up with your own central idea about the text and topic—something new you have come to understand.

   e. Think about how your text and the central idea you have discovered relates and compares to other texts in the unit.

2. **Writing a Text-Based Explanation:** On your own, you will plan and draft a multiparagraph explanation of something you have come to understand by reading and examining your text. To accomplish this, you will do the following:

   a. Present and explain the central idea you have found in the text—what you think the text is about.

   b. Use quotations and paraphrased references from the text to explain and support the central idea you are discussing.

   c. Explain how the central idea is related to what you have found out about the author's purpose in writing the text and the author's perspective on (view of) the topic.

   d. Present and explain a new understanding about the unit's topic that your text has led you to.

   e. Work with other students to review and improve your draft—and to be sure it is the best possible representation of your ideas and your skills as a reader and writer.

   f. Reflect on how well you have used Literacy Skills in developing this final explanation.

ODELL
EDUCATION

READING CLOSELY FINAL TASK HANDOUT (Continued)

FINAL ASSIGNMENTS (Continued)

3. **Leading and Participating in a Text-Centered Discussion:** After you have become an expert about your text and written an explanation of what you understand, you will prepare for and participate in a final discussion. In this discussion, you and other students will compare your close readings of the final three texts in the unit. To accomplish this, you will do the following:

   a. Prepare a summary of what you have come to understand and written in your explanation to share with the other students in your discussion group.

   b. Reread the other two final texts so that you are prepared to discuss and compare them.

   c. Meet with your expert group to talk about your text and how to lead a discussion of it.

   d. Come up with a new question about your text that will get others to think about the connections between it and the other texts in the unit.

   e. Join a new discussion group, and share your summary about your text and the evidence you have found:

      ⇒ Point out key details to the other students in your group.

      ⇒ Explain your observations about your author's purpose and perspective.

      ⇒ Point out key words, phrases, or sentences that indicate your author's perspective.

      ⇒ Explain what you have come to understand about the topic from your text.

   f. Listen to other students' summaries and think about the connections to your text.

   g. Pose your question to the group, and lead a discussion about the three texts, asking students to present evidence from the texts that supports their thinking.

   h. Reflect on how well you have used Discussion Habits in this final discussion.

SKILLS AND HABITS TO BE DEMONSTRATED

As you become a text expert, write your text-based explanation, and participate in a text-centered discussion, think about demonstrating the Literacy Skills and Discussion Habits you have been working on to the best of your ability. Your teacher will evaluate your work and determine your grade based on how well you do the following things:

- **Attend to Details:** Identify words, details or quotations that you think are important to understanding the text.

- **Interpret Language:** Understand how words are used to express ideas and perspectives.

- **Summarize:** Correctly explain what the text says about the topic.

- **Identify Relationships:** Notice important connections among details, ideas, or texts.

- **Recognize Perspective:** Identify and explain the author's view of the text's topic.

- **Use Evidence:** Use well-chosen details from the text to support your explanation. Accurately paraphrase or quote what the author says in the text.

- **Prepare:** Read the text(s) closely and think about the questions to prepare for a text-centered discussion.

READING CLOSELY FINAL TASK HANDOUT (Continued)

SKILLS AND HABITS TO BE DEMONSTRATED (Continued)

- **Question:** Ask and respond to questions that help the discussion group understand and compare the texts.
- **Collaborate:** Pay attention to other participants while you participate in and lead a text-centered discussion.
- **Communicate Clearly:** Present your ideas and supporting evidence so others can understand them.

NOTE

These skills and habits are also listed on the **Student Literacy Skills and Discussion Habits Checklist**, which you can use to assess your work and the work of other students.

ODELL
EDUCATION

QUESTIONING PATH TOOL

Name: _____ **Text:** _____

APPROACHING: *I determine my reading purposes and take note of key information about the text. I identify the LIPS domain(s) that will guide my initial reading.*	Purpose: Key information: LIPS domain(s):
QUESTIONING: *I use Guiding Questions to help me investigate the text (from the* ***Guiding Questions Handout****).*	1. 2.
ANALYZING: *I question further to connect and analyze the details I find (from the* ***Guiding Questions Handout****).*	1. 2.
DEEPENING: *I consider the questions of others.*	1. 2. 3.
EXTENDING: *I pose my own questions.*	1. 2.

APPROACHING TEXTS TOOL

Name _ _ _ _ _ _ _ _ _ _ _   Text _

APPROACHING THE TEXT	
Before reading, I consider what my specific purposes for reading are.	**What are my reading purposes?**
I also take note of key information about the text.	**Title:** / **Author:** / **Source/Publisher:**
	Text type: / **Publication date:**
	What do I already think or understand about the text based on this information?

QUESTIONING THE TEXT	
As I read the text for the first time, I use Guiding Questions that relate to my reading purpose and focus. (*Can be taken from the Guiding Questions Handout.*)	**Guiding Questions for *my first reading* of the text:**
	As I read I mark details on the text that relate to my Guiding Questions.
As I reread, I use questions I have about specific details that have emerged in my reading to focus my analysis and deepen my understanding.	**Text-specific questions to help focus *my rereading* of the text:**

ANALYZING DETAILS TOOL

Name _____   Text _____

Reading purpose:

A question I have about the text:

SEARCHING FOR DETAILS

I read the text closely and mark words and phrases that help me think about my question.

SELECTING DETAILS

I select words or phrases from my search that I think are the **most important** in thinking about my question.

| Detail 1 (Ref.: |) | Detail 2 (Ref.: |) | Detail 3 (Ref.: |) |

ANALYZING DETAILS

I reread parts of the text and think about the meaning of the details and what they tell me about my question.

| What I think about detail 1: | What I think about detail 2: | What I think about detail 3: |

CONNECTING DETAILS

I compare the details and explain the connections I see among them.

How I connect the details:

PART 4: TEXT-BASED EXPLANATION LITERACY SKILLS CHECKLIST

LITERACY SKILLS	DESCRIPTORS: *Find evidence of using the Literacy Skill in the draft.* *Does the writer's explanation . . .*	NEEDS WORK	OKAY	VERY STRONG
ATTENDING TO DETAILS	Identify words, details, or quotations that are important to understanding the text?			
SUMMARIZING	Correctly explain what the text says about the topic?			
IDENTIFYING RELATIONSHIPS	Notice important connections among details, ideas, or texts?			
RECOGNIZING PERSPECTIVE	Identify and explain the author's view of the text's topic?			
USING EVIDENCE	Support the explanation with evidence from the text; use accurate quotations, paraphrases, and references?			

ODELL
EDUCATION

PART 5: TEXT-CENTERED DISCUSSION ACADEMIC HABITS CHECKLIST

DISCUSSION HABITS	DESCRIPTORS: *When—and how well—have I demonstrated these habits?*	EXAMPLES *FROM TEXT-CENTERED DISCUSSIONS*
PREPARING	Reads the text(s) closely and thinks about the questions to prepare for a text-centered discussion	
COLLABORATING	Pays attention to other participants while participating in and leading a text-centered discussion	
COMMUNICATING CLEARLY	Presents ideas and supporting evidence so others can understand them	

READING CLOSELY TARGETED LITERACY SKILLS

TARGETED SKILLS	DESCRIPTORS
QUESTIONING	Formulates and responds to questions and lines of inquiry that lead to relevant and important ideas and themes within and across texts
ATTENDING TO DETAILS	Identifies relevant and important textual details, words, and ideas
IDENTIFYING RELATIONSHIPS	Identifies important connections among key details and ideas within and across texts
SUMMARIZING	Recounts the explicit meaning of texts, referring to key details, events, characters, language, and ideas
INTERPRETING LANGUAGE	Identifies how words and phrases convey meaning and represent an author's or narrator's perspective
RECOGNIZING PERSPECTIVE	Uses textual details to recognize an author's or narrator's relationship to and perspective on a text's topic

ODELL
EDUCATION

READING CLOSELY ACADEMIC HABITS DEVELOPED

HABITS DEVELOPED	DESCRIPTORS
PREPARING	Reads the texts, researches the topics, and thinks about the questions being studied to prepare for tasks
COLLABORATING	Pays attention to, respects, and works productively in various roles with all other participants
COMMUNICATING CLEARLY	Uses appropriate language and relevant textual details to clearly present ideas and claims

READING CLOSELY LITERACY SKILLS AND DISCUSSION HABITS RUBRIC

Name _ _ _ _ _ _ _ _ _ _ _ _ _ _ **Text** _ _ _ _ _ _ _ _ _ _ _ _ _ _ _

NE: Not enough evidence to make a rating

1—**Emerging:** needs improvement

2—**Developing:** shows progress

3—**Becoming Proficient:** demonstrates skills

4—**Excelling:** exceeds expectations

+—**Growth:** evidence of growth within the unit or task

I. READING SKILLS CRITERIA	NE	1	2	3	4	+
1. **Attends to Details:** Identifies relevant and important textual details, words, and ideas						
2. **Summarizes:** Recounts the explicit meaning of texts, referring to key details, events, characters, language, and ideas						
3. **Interprets Language:** Identifies how words and phrases convey meaning and represent the author's perspective						
4. **Identifies Relationships:** Identifies important connections among key details and ideas within and across texts						
5. **Recognizes Perspective:** Uses textual details to recognize the author's relationship to and perspective on a text's topic						
II. THINKING SKILLS CRITERIA	NE	1	2	3	4	+
1. **Uses Evidence:** Supports all aspects of the explanation with sufficient textual evidence, using accurate quotations, paraphrases, and references						
III. TEXT-CENTERED DISCUSSION CRITERIA	NE	1	2	3	4	+
1. **Prepares:** Reads the texts and thinks about text-specific questions to prepare for a final text-centered discussion task						
2. **Questions:** Formulates and responds to questions that lead to relevant and important ideas and comparisons among texts						
3. **Collaborates:** Pays attention to, respects, and works productively in various roles with all other participants in a text-centered discussion						
4. **Communicates Clearly:** Uses appropriate language and relevant textual details to clearly present ideas and explanations						

ODELL
EDUCATION

READING CLOSELY RUBRIC (Continued)

IV. FINAL ASSIGNMENT CRITERIA	NE	1	2	3	4	+
1. Identifies a central idea in the text and explains how it is developed through supporting ideas and details						
2. Explains how the central idea is related to the text's purpose and the author's perspective on the topic						
3. Communicates a supported understanding of the text clearly through writing and speaking						
SUMMARY EVALUATION		1	2	3	4	

Comments:

1. **Explanation** of ratings—**evidence** found (or not found) in the work:

2. **Strengths** and **areas of growth** observed in the work:

3. **Areas for improvement** in future work:

STUDENT READING CLOSELY LITERACY SKILLS AND DISCUSSION HABITS CHECKLIST

	READING CLOSELY LITERACY SKILLS AND DISCUSSION HABITS	✔	EVIDENCE Demonstrating the SKILLS AND HABITS
READING AND THINKING	1. **Attending to Details:** Identifies words, details, or quotations that are important to understanding the text		
	2. **Interpreting Language:** Understands how words are used to express ideas and perspectives		
	3. **Summarizing:** Correctly explains what the text says about the topic		
	4. **Identifying Relationships:** Notices important connections among details, ideas, or texts		
	5. **Recognizing Perspective:** Identifies and explains the author's view of the text's topic		
	6. **Using Evidence:** Uses well-chosen details from the text to support explanations; accurately paraphrases or quotes		
DISCUSSION	7. **Preparing:** Reads the text(s) closely and thinks about the questions to prepare for a text-centered discussion		
	8. **Questioning:** Asks and responds to questions that help the discussion group understand and compare the texts		
	9. **Collaborating:** Pays attention to other participants while participating in and leading a text-centered discussion		
	10. **Communicating Clearly:** Presents ideas and supporting evidence so others can understand them		
	General comments:		

READING CLOSELY MEDIA SUPPORTS

Because of the ever-changing nature of website addresses, specific links are not provided. Teachers and students can locate these sources through web searches using the information provided.

TITLE	DESCRIPTION	PUBLISHER	FORMAT
"Kids Need Structure"	Video of Colin Powell's TED Talk (excerpted in texts)	TED Talk	TED Talk video
Changing Education Paradigms	Transcript of Sir Ken Robinson's "Changing Paradigms" TED Talk	Royal Society for the encouragement of Arts, Manufactures and Commerce (RSA)	Text
"Your first 5 minutes at Marine Corps Recruit Depot—San Diego"	Video showing the marine recruits during their first experience as US Marines	Live Leak	YouTube video
"MONTESSORI— Watch This First— emontessori.info"	An introduction to Maria Montessori's pedagogy and resulting school programs	Adrian Harrison	YouTube video
"Quiet in school, 1950"	An original instructional video addressing how to behave in class in a 1950s school	mmlearningllc	YouTube video
"Khan Academy: The future of education?"	A video on Kahn Academy, an online learning environment that schools are beginning to use in classrooms	CBS News, *60 Minutes*	Video
"Transparency: Education in America"	A video that uses statistics and facts to compare the US education system to other countries around the world	GOOD.IS	YouTube video
Tenth Amendment	Text of the Tenth Amendment in the United States Constitution	Legal Information Institute	Text
Brown v. Board of Education in PBS's *The Supreme Court*	Short documentary focusing on segregation in 1950s schools, leading to the 1954 Supreme Court case ruling ending racial segregation in K–12	WorldPlot	YouTube video
Only a Teacher— Teaching Timeline	Multimedia time line of the history of US education	PBS	Multimedia time line
"Education in Early America: Birth of Public Schools and Universities"	Animated video chronicling the historical events throughout US education	Study.com	Animated video

UNIT 2

MAKING
EVIDENCE-BASED CLAIMS

DEVELOPING CORE LITERACY
PROFICIENCIES

GRADE 9

"The unexamined life is not worth living"

Apology, Plato

UNIT OVERVIEW

Making evidence-based claims about texts is a Core Literacy and Critical Thinking Proficiency that lies at the heart of the CCSS. The proficiency consists of two component abilities. The first is the ability to extract detailed information from texts and grasp how it is conveyed. Education and personal growth require real exposure to new information from a variety of media. Instruction should push students beyond general understanding of texts into deep engagement with textual content and authorial craft.

The second component of the proficiency is the ability to make valid claims about the new information thus gleaned. This involves developing the capacity to analyze texts, connecting information in literal, inferential, and sometimes novel ways. Instruction should lead students to do more than simply restate the information they take in through close reading. Students should come to see themselves as creators of meaning as they engage with texts.

It is essential that students understand the importance and purpose of making evidence-based claims, which are at the center of many fields of study and productive civic life. Education should help students become invested in developing their ability to explore the meaning of texts. Part of instruction should focus on teaching students how to understand and talk about their skills.

It is also important that students view claims as their own. They should see their interaction with texts as a personal investment in their learning. They are not simply reading texts to report information expected by their teachers; instead, they should approach texts with their own authority and the confidence to support their analysis.

TOPIC AND TEXTS

This unit develops students' abilities to make evidence-based claims through activities based on a close reading of Plato's *Apology* of Socrates, in which the Greek philosopher stands trial for corrupting the youth and being impious toward the gods. The text is available in the unit text section.

LEARNING PROGRESSION

The unit activities are organized into five parts, each associated with a sequential, chunked passage of text. The parts build on each other and can each span a range of instructional time depending on scheduling and student ability.

The sequence of learning activities supports the progressive development of the critical reading and thinking skills involved in making evidence-based claims. Parts 1 and 2 focus on forming and supporting evidence-based claims as readers. Part 3 focuses on preparing to express written evidence-based claims by organizing evidence and thinking. Parts 4 and 5 focus on communicating evidence-based claims in paragraphs and essays. This organization is designed to strengthen the precision of instruction and assessment as well as to give teachers flexibility in their use of the unit.

Independent reading activities are given at the end of Parts 1 through 3. If scheduling and student ability make independent reading outside of class a difficulty, these reading assignments are also included in the subsequent parts as in-class activities.

☰ SEQUENCING LEARNING OVER TIME ☰ AND ACROSS GRADE LEVELS

The learning sequence for this unit and the instructional notes within it have been developed on the assumption that students may be learning the process of *Making Evidence-Based Claims* (EBC) for the first time. Thus, terms are introduced and explained, graphic tools are overviewed and modeled, and lessons move relatively carefully from teacher modeling to guided practice to independent application. The Literacy Skills that are targeted and the Academic Habits that are developed are assumed to be in early stages of development for many students, and thus extensive scaffolding is provided.

However, students may come to this second unit in the Developing Core Literacy Proficiencies Program having developed their Literacy Skills, Academic Habits, and Core Literacy Proficiencies in other contexts. They may have progressed through earlier units in the Developing Core Literacy Proficiencies sequence (*Reading Closely for Textual Details*) and become very familiar with tools, handouts, terminology, skills, and habits addressed in this unit. They may also have experienced the *Making Evidence-Based Claims* instructional sequence in a previous grade or school.

For this reason, teachers should use their professional judgment to plan their instruction for this unit considering not only *what* they are teaching (making claims and the curriculum designed to develop students' skills) but also *whom* they are teaching (their students' backgrounds, previous experiences, and readiness levels). Before beginning the unit, teachers are encouraged to determine what students have previously experienced, learned, or produced.

If students have more advanced skills or extensive previous experience in making claims, instruction can move more rapidly through many sections of this unit, concentrate more on extended reading to deepen students' understanding, and emphasize more complex topics, texts, or academic sources.

OUTLINE

PART 1: UNDERSTANDING EVIDENCE-BASED CLAIMS

- Students learn the importance and elements of making evidence-based claims through a close reading of a section of the text.

PART 2: MAKING EVIDENCE-BASED CLAIMS

- Students develop the ability to make evidence-based claims through a close reading of a second section of text.

PART 3: ORGANIZING EVIDENCE-BASED CLAIMS

- Students learn to develop and explain evidence-based claims through the selection and organization of supporting evidence.

PART 4: WRITING EVIDENCE-BASED CLAIMS

- Students develop the ability to communicate text-based claims and their supporting evidence through writing.

PART 5: DEVELOPING EVIDENCE-BASED WRITING

- Students develop the ability to express global evidence-based claims in writing through a rereading of the text and a review of their previous work.

INTRODUCTION TO THE MAKING EVIDENCE-BASED CLAIMS LITERACY TOOLBOX

In the *Making Evidence-Based Claims* (EBC) unit, students develop a foundational proficiency for reading and analyzing complex texts. To build this proficiency, students learn to select, interpret, and connect significant textual details; articulate their meaning; and form conclusions derived from reading a text closely.

To support the development of this proficiency, the unit uses a series of handouts and tools from the Literacy Toolbox (found in the **Making Evidence-Based Claims Literacy Toolbox**). Students use the *Forming Evidence-Based Claims Tool* to guide their selection of key details, make connections among them, and form a claim that arises from the text. The *Supporting Evidence-Based Claims Tool* is used to strengthen students' ability to find and analyze evidence that supports claims. The

Organizing Evidence-Based Claims Tool aids students in organizing their thinking and supporting evidence in preparation for explaining, defending, and communicating their claims. As they continue to develop and apply the proficiency of reading closely, students also use the handouts and tools introduced in the *Reading Closely* unit. Among these are model *Questioning Path Tools*, which again organize Guiding Questions and text-specific questions for each subsection of text students read in this unit. As a culminating activity, students also use the *Questioning Path Tool* to build their own questioning pathway.

The **Making EBC Literacy Toolbox** also houses detailed tables of targeted Literacy Skills and Academic Habits developed in the unit as well as the *Making EBC Literacy Skills Rubric* and *Student Making EBC Literacy Skills and Academic Habits Checklists*.

If students have previously completed the *Making Evidence-Based Claims* unit, they should already be familiar with these tools and handouts. As they gain independence in practicing the proficiency of reading texts to make evidence-based claims and internalize the concepts and processes detailed in the unit, students might rely less and less on the tools and handouts. Depending on students' abilities and familiarity with the **Making EBC Literacy Toolbox**, teachers might encourage students to use these materials when they encounter difficulties in understanding sections of texts, require assistance in communicating or piecing together analysis, or need to organize their thoughts in preparation for a writing assignment. Otherwise, students can proceed through the readings, annotating, taking notes, and making claims using their own, developing processes. If students are ready to move through the unit without these scaffolds, it is still important that teachers continually verify that they are capturing, analyzing, and communicating salient ideas from the readings.

> **NOTE**
>
> All tools and handouts, including model *Questioning Path Tools*, and *Student Checklists* can also be found in the Student Edition.

LITERACY SKILLS AND ACADEMIC HABITS

TARGETED LITERACY SKILLS

To frame instruction and assessment in the *Making Evidence-Based Claims* unit (and all Developing Core Literacy Proficiencies units), Odell Education has developed a criterion-based framework of component Literacy Skills. The *Making EBC Literacy Skills Rubric* (in the **Making EBC Literacy Toolbox**) lists each Literacy Skill with a descriptor of what students should be able to do when they attain proficiency in that skill.

In this unit, students will be learning about, practicing, developing, and demonstrating skills necessary for **Forming Claims** and **Using Evidence** to support them while continuing to work on foundational skills associated with close reading (**Questioning**, **Attending to Details**, **Interpreting Language**, and **Identifying Relationships**). The following Literacy Skills are targeted throughout the unit:

TARGETED LITERACY SKILLS	DESCRIPTORS
ATTENDING TO DETAILS	Identifies relevant and important textual details, words, and ideas
IDENTIFYING RELATIONSHIPS	Identifies important connections among key details and ideas within and across texts
MAKING INFERENCES	Demonstrates comprehension by using connections among details to make logical deductions about a text
RECOGNIZING PERSPECTIVE	Uses textual details to recognize an author's or narrator's relationship to and perspective on a text's topic
FORMING CLAIMS	Develops meaningful and defensible claims that clearly state valid, evidence-based analysis
USING EVIDENCE	Supports all aspects of claims with sufficient textual evidence, using accurate quotations, paraphrases, and references
PRESENTING DETAILS	Describes and explains important details that effectively develop a narrative, explanation, or argument
ORGANIZING IDEAS	Sequences sentences and paragraphs to establish coherent, logical, and unified narratives, explanations, and arguments
USING LANGUAGE	Selects and combines words that precisely communicate ideas, generate appropriate tone, and evoke intended responses from an audience
PUBLISHING	Uses effective formatting and citations to present ideas for specific audiences and purposes

---

NOTE

Student language versions of these descriptors can be found in the *Student Making EBC Literacy Skills Checklist* in the **Making EBC Literacy Toolbox** and Student Edition.

APPLIED LITERACY SKILLS

In addition to these targeted skills, the unit provides opportunities for students to apply and develop the following Literacy Skills:

- **Deciphering Words**
- **Comprehending Syntax**
- **Interpreting Language**
- **Summarizing**
- **Questioning**
- **Using Conventions**

ACADEMIC HABITS

In conjunction with developing Literacy Skills to meet CCSS expectations, students can also develop Academic Habits associated with being a literate person—working from a framework of key habits developed by Odell Education (the table is available in the **Making EBC Literacy Toolbox**). In this unit, students will have opportunities to further develop habits associated with productive text-centered discussion and will also begin working on habits applied when generating and revising their writing. Although the teacher may choose to teach and assess a range of habits during any activity, some instructional sequences cater to specific habits that have been identified. The descriptors for these habits do not need to be introduced to students immediately; however, if students are ready to think about them, student versions of the descriptors can be found in the *Student EBC Academic Habits Checklist* in the **Making EBC Literacy Toolbox**.

HABITS DEVELOPED	DESCRIPTORS
ENGAGING ACTIVELY	Actively focuses attention on independent and collaborative tasks
COLLABORATING	Pays attention to, respects, and works productively in various roles with all other participants
COMMUNICATING CLEARLY	Uses appropriate language and relevant textual details to clearly present ideas and claims
LISTENING	Pays attention to, acknowledges, and considers thoughtfully new information and ideas from others
REVISING	Rethinks and refines work based on teacher-, peer-, and self-review processes
UNDERSTANDING PURPOSE AND PROCESS	Understands the purpose and uses the process and criteria that guide tasks
REMAINING OPEN	Modifies and further justifies ideas in response to thinking from others

> **NOTE**
>
> Student language versions of these descriptors can be found in the *Student Making EBC Academic Habits Checklist* in the **Making EBC Literacy Toolbox** and Student Edition.

COMMON CORE STATE STANDARDS ALIGNMENT

The primary CCSS alignment of the unit instruction is with **CCSS.ELA-LITERACY.RI.1** and **CCSS.ELA-LITERACY.W.9b** (*cite evidence to support analysis of explicit and inferential textual meaning*).

The evidence-based analysis of the text, including the text-dependent questions and the focus of the claims, address **CCSS.ELA-LITERACY.RI.2** and **CCSS.ELA-LITERACY.RI.3** (*determine a central idea and analyze how it is conveyed and elaborated with details over the course of a text*). Analysis of how authors' choice of words and claims convey and contribute to their perspectives involves **CCSS.ELA-LITERACY.RI.6** (*determine perspective and analyze how it is conveyed with details over the course of a text*).

The numerous paired activities and structured class discussions develop **CCSS.ELA-LITERACY.SL.1** (*engage effectively in a range of collaborative discussions building on others' ideas and expressing their own clearly*).

The evidence-based writing pieces address **CCSS.ELA-LITERACY.W.4** (*produce clear and coherent writing in which the development, organization, and style are appropriate to task, purpose, and audience*).

PART 1

UNDERSTANDING EVIDENCE-BASED CLAIMS

"Just a human sort of wisdom"

OBJECTIVE:	Students learn the importance and elements of making evidence-based claims through a close reading of a section of the text.

ESTIMATED TIME: 2–3 days

TEXT: Plato, *Apology* - paragraphs 1–3

MATERIALS:
- *Guiding Questions Handout*
- *Reading Closely Graphic*
- *Questioning Path Tools*
- *Attending to Details Handout*
- *Forming EBC Tool*
- *Supporting EBC Tool*

OPTIONAL:
- *Approaching Texts Tool*
- *Analyzing Details Tool*

☰ LITERACY SKILLS

TARGETED SKILLS	DESCRIPTORS
ATTENDING TO DETAILS	Identifies relevant and important textual details, words, and ideas
INTERPRETING LANGUAGE	Identifies how words and phrases convey meaning and represent an author's or narrator's perspective
IDENTIFYING RELATIONSHIPS	Identifies important connections among key details and ideas within and across texts

☰ ACADEMIC HABIT

HABIT DEVELOPED	DESCRIPTOR
ENGAGING ACTIVELY	Actively focuses attention on independent and collaborative tasks

ALIGNMENT TO CCSS

TARGETED STANDARD:

CCSS.ELA-LITERACY.RI.9-10.1: Cite strong and thorough textual evidence to support analysis of what the text says explicitly as well as inferences drawn from the text.

SUPPORTING STANDARDS:

CCSS.ELA-LITERACY.RI.9-10.2: Determine a central idea of a text and analyze its development over the course of the text, including how it emerges and is shaped and refined by specific details; provide an objective summary of the text.

CCSS.ELA-LITERACY.RI.9-10.3: Analyze how the author unfolds an analysis or series of ideas or events, including the order in which the points are made, how they are introduced and developed, and the connections that are drawn between them.

CCSS.ELA-LITERACY.RI.9-10.6: Determine an author's point of view or purpose in a text and analyze how an author uses rhetoric to advance that point of view or purpose.

CCSS.ELA-LITERACY.SL.9-10.1: Initiate and participate effectively in a range of collaborative discussions (one-on-one, in groups, and teacher-led) with diverse partners on *grades 9–10 topics, texts, and issues*, building on others' ideas and expressing their own clearly and persuasively.

ACTIVITIES

1. INTRODUCTION TO UNIT
The teacher presents the purpose of the unit and explains the proficiency of making evidence-based claims, making reference to the key characteristics of an evidence-based claim.

2. INDEPENDENT READING
Students independently read part of the text with a Guiding Question to help focus their reading.

3. READ ALOUD AND CLASS DISCUSSION
Students follow along as they listen to the text being read aloud, and the teacher leads a discussion guided by a series of text-specific questions.

4. MODEL THE FORMING OF EBCs
The teacher models a critical reading and thinking process for forming evidence-based claims about texts.

ACTIVITY 1: INTRODUCTION TO THE UNIT

The teacher presents the purpose of the unit and explains the proficiency of making evidence-based claims, making reference to the key characteristics of an evidence-based claim.

INSTRUCTIONAL NOTES

- Introduce the central purpose of the unit and the idea of a claim someone might make.

NOTE

If students have previously completed a *Making Evidence-Based Claims* unit and have an understanding of claims, teachers might follow an abbreviated introduction to the unit by reviewing that students will do the following:

- Work to further develop their proficiency of making evidence-based claims about complex texts.
- Use a series of tools and handouts to guide and organize their analysis (more information in the **Toolbox** section).
- Collaborate with peers to produce written evidence-based claims (EBCs).
- Create original Questioning Paths to guide close reading.
- Read and make original claims independently.

For students new to the *Making Evidence-Based Claims* unit, the following is a possible approach:

- Explain to students that they will be working on honing and deepening their understanding and ability to make evidence-based claims. Introduce the defining characteristic of an evidence-based claim: "A claim states a conclusion you have come to and that you want others to think about."
- Pick a subject that is familiar to students, such as school lunches, and ask them to brainstorm some claim statements they might make about the subject.
- Explain that a claim is only as strong as the evidence that supports it, introducing a second defining characteristic: "All parts of a claim are supported by specific evidence you can point to." Distinguish claims that can be supported by evidence from those that are unsupported opinions using the students' brainstorm list as a reference. Move from experience-based claims to claims in a field such as science. Start with more familiar, fact-based claims. (For example, the claim "It is cold outside" is supported by evidence such as "The outside thermometer reads 13 degrees F.") Then discuss a claim, such as "Smoking is hazardous to your health," and talk about how this claim was once considered to be an opinion until a weight of scientific evidence over time led us to accept this claim as fact.
- Building from this example, discuss the idea that a claim becomes stronger as we expand our knowledge about a subject and find more and better evidence to support the claim. Move from scientific claims to claims that are based in text that has been read closely.

- Use an example of a text read recently in class or one students are likely to be familiar with. Explain that textual claims can start as statements about what a text tells us directly (literal comprehension) such as "Tom Sawyer gets the other boys to paint the fence." Then move to simple conclusions we draw from thinking about the text such as "Tom Sawyer is a clever boy" because (evidence) "he tricks the other boys into doing his work and painting the fence." Then explain how text-based claims can also be more complex and require more evidence (e.g., "Mark Twain presents Tom Sawyer as a contradiction: a 'bad boy' who also is capable of doing good."). Explain that sometimes—as in this example—a text-based claim is supported by evidence from more than one text (i.e., *Tom Sawyer* and *Huckleberry Finn*) or sections of text.

- Tell students that they will be developing and practicing the Literacy Skills of making evidence-based claims that are based in the words, sentences, and ideas of texts by closely reading and analyzing Plato's *Apology*—his account of the defense Socrates presented for himself at his trial before Greek authorities.

In the activities that follow, students will learn to make a text-based claim by moving from literal understanding of the text's details, to simple conclusions or inferences, to claims that arise from and are supported by close examination of textual evidence. This inductive process mirrors what effective readers do and is intended to help students develop a method for moving from comprehension to claim. In addition, the Guiding Questions, model claims, and movement through the text over the course of the unit are sequenced to transition students from an initial, literal understanding of textual details to understand the following:

- Claims about concrete ideas presented in short sections of the text
- Claims about more abstract ideas implied across sections of the text
- More global claims about the entire text and its meaning

> **TEXT NOTES**
>
> The *Apology* is Greek philosopher Plato's account of the defense Socrates gave at his trial in Athens in 399 BCE. Socrates had been accused of various offenses related to the ideas he taught throughout the city, or as Socrates might say, of having a "certain kind of wisdom." Plato's text portrays Socrates in his full glory—principled, ironic, and provocative to the end. Plato recounts Socrates's summary and explanation of his accusation, his defense, the verdict, and his eventual demise.
>
> The text included in this curriculum was excerpted and translated for Odell Education by Peter Heinegg of Union College, Schenectady, New York. Heinegg's fresh and engaging style provides a wonderful introduction to ancient Greek writing for ninth-graders.

ACTIVITY 2: INDEPENDENT READING

Students independently read the first text with a Guiding Question to help focus their reading.

INSTRUCTIONAL NOTES

Students will be using a question-based approach to read and analyze the text, building from and applying learning they may have experienced in a *Reading Closely* unit. Specifically, they will progressively dig deeper into the text using a Questioning Path that begins with Guiding Questions and moves into text-specific questions designed to deepen their understanding. Before students do an initial reading of the text, (re)introduce them to the OE ***Reading Closely Graphic, Questioning Path Tool***, and ***Guiding Questions Handout*** (available in the **Reading Closely Literacy Toolbox**) and the multistage reading process they outline:

- Approaching a text
- Questioning initially to note and annotate details
- Analyzing those details to discern relationships
- Deepening understanding by considering more text-specific questions
- Extending into students' own emerging questions or claims

The following model ***Questioning Path Tool*** (for the first section of the text) is organized by this process and provides example Guiding Questions and text-specific questions students might use as they read and analyze the text. Teachers (and students) are also encouraged to see the example questions as models only—and to select and frame their own questions.

Students might begin the process using an ***Approaching Texts Tool*** (in the **Reading Closely Literacy Toolbox**), which prompts them to consider their reading purpose and what they know about the text *before* reading, then provides a space to record one to two Guiding Questions or text-specific questions that students use to direct their close reading and annotation of the text. This may also be a good time to review (or introduce) the skills, systems, and symbols that students can use as they annotate a section of text:

- Briefly introduce students to the text. The introduction should be kept to naming the author, the speech, and the year and location of its delivery. These details can be recorded in the ***Approaching Texts Tool***.
- Have students reflect on and discuss what they already know about the text based on this basic information.
- Allow students to approach the text freshly and to make their own discoveries, connections, and inferences based on textual content.

The introduction should be kept to naming the author, the text, and the year of publication. To better understand the context of Socrates's "defense," students might read the introductory lines at the beginning of the text. It might also help if students understand that the Greek word *apologia* means "defense."

INSTRUCTIONAL NOTES

- Students independently read the first paragraph of the *Apology* text and consider the first of two Guiding Questions:

  ⇒ What do the author's words and phrases cause me to see, feel, or think?

- After all students have finished reading the paragraphs, lead a brief discussion in which students volunteer something they learned about the speaker (Socrates).

- List their responses on the board, checking those that are repeated.

- Go back to the list and ask this question: "What words or sentences in the paragraph tell you this information?" for each of the listed responses, having students identify the evidence that led them to their answer. Do not worry here about labeling their answers right or wrong but ask them to see if what they think they know is confirmed as they listen to the speech.

- To set up their reading of paragraphs 1 through 3 (and the entire speech), students then move to the second Guiding Question: "What details or words suggest the author's perspective?" Socrates uses the word *slander* a few times in these first three paragraphs. Ask students to find this and other words that point to Socrates's perspective of the trial.

QUESTIONING PATH TOOL

Plato's *Apology*, paragraphs 1–3

APPROACHING:
I determine my reading purposes and take note of key information about the text. I identify the LIPS domain(s) that will guide my initial reading.

I will initially focus on the author's *ideas* and *perspective*, then consider *language*, *structure*, and supporting details.

QUESTIONING: *I use Guiding Questions to help me investigate the text (from the **Guiding Questions Handout**).*

1. What do the author's words and phrases cause me to see, feel, or think? [L]

2. What details or words suggest the author's perspective? [I]

ANALYZING: *I question further to connect and analyze the details I find (from the **Guiding Questions Handout**).*

3. How might I summarize the main ideas of the text and the key supporting details? [I]

4. How are key ideas, events, places, or characters described? [L]

DEEPENING: *I consider the questions of others.*

5. What is Socrates being accused of?

6. What does Socrates's use of the word *slandered* reveal about his position? How does Socrates make it clear that he is innocent?

7. In paragraph 3, Socrates says he is on trial because of "a certain kind of wisdom." According to Socrates, what kind of wisdom does he not have? What does this suggest about the wisdom he does have?

8. In paragraph 2, why does Socrates ask a question to himself as if the audience asked him? How does this paragraph relate to the first and third paragraphs? Why would Socrates pretend the audience is asking him questions?

9. Why is this text titled the *Apology*? What does the word apology mean when translated from the Greek *apologia*? How does this definition help you understand what Socrates is doing?

EXTENDING: *I pose my own questions.*

ACTIVITY 3: READ ALOUD AND CLASS DISCUSSION

Students follow along as they listen to the text being read aloud, and the teacher leads a discussion guided by a series of text-specific questions.

INSTRUCTIONAL NOTES

- Students follow along as they listen to the teacher read the first three paragraphs.

- Students' listening experience is guided by the Guiding Question in the Analyzing section of the model *Questioning Path Tool*: "What do the author's words and phrases cause me to see, feel, or think?" Thinking about this question, students mark and annotate key details.

- Lead a brief, open discussion about students' first impressions of the text and what the speech is about. Some students' observations will likely be very literal, but some may be moving into inferences and even claims. Let students know that all observations are good ones—*if* they are supported by something in the text. Ask students to point out something they have noted in the text that has led to their observation.

- Following this general discussion, introduce students to the text-specific questions from the Deepening section of the model *Questioning Path Tool*—letting them know that the purpose of the questions is to help them deepen their understanding of the text. The questions are designed to progress from more literal comprehension of key details to inferences about the meaning of the text. All students may be asked to read and annotate the text in relationship to all four Deepening questions from the model *Questioning Path Tool* or questions may be differentially assigned to student groups based on their reading readiness levels.

The close reading of the text builds from what students may have done in a *Reading Closely for Textual Details* unit and serves three primary purposes: to ensure comprehension of the literal details of the text (which tell us more about the speaker's life); to apply the skills of close reading (examining specific details, words, phrases, lines, and paragraphs); and to guide students in searching for textual evidence. As each question is discussed, follow it up by asking this:

⇒ What in the text makes you reach your observation or conclusion? Point to specific words or sentences.

- If students have previous experience using an *Analyzing Details Tool* in a *Reading Closely* unit (in the **Reading Closely Literacy Toolbox**), they *might* use it to record one of the text-specific questions assigned to them, key details they annotate as they think about the question, and a connection they might make among the details. Using this tool will set up their initial work with the **Forming EBC Tool** in Activity 4—which parallels and extends the **Analyzing Details** process.

- Use the discussion about the questions (and potentially students' work with the *Analyzing Details Tool*) to review the essential skills of selecting interesting and significant textual details and connecting them inferentially. To help students think about what readers consider when they look for textual details, refer to the *Attending to Details Handout* (introduced in the *Reading Closely* unit and found in the **Reading Closely Literacy Toolbox**), which lists examples of details related to a text's language, ideas, perspective, and structure. This process links directly to the forming of evidence-based claims they will begin in Activity 4.

TEXT NOTES—IDEAS FOR DISCUSSION

The following questions are drawn from the model *Questioning Path Tool* and are numbered as they appear in the Deepening section. All of the questions can be discussed by the class as a whole to deepen understanding of the speech, or questions can be assigned to smaller discussion groups, who might then report their observations back to the class.

1. What is Socrates being accused of?

Discuss with students how beginning with a statement of his accusation sets a foundation for the purpose and meaning of the text. Socrates begins by giving a summary of the charges against him. He cites an affidavit that accuses him: "Socrates is a criminal and meddles in matters where he has no business. He's always poking under the earth and up in the sky. He makes the worse case look better; and he teaches this sort of stuff to others." At this point in the text, it is unclear what it means to be accused of making "the worse case look better" or why Socrates is being put to trial for his curiosity. There are, however, a few concrete accusations that can be extracted from the affidavit, namely, that Socrates is being charged with unlawfully teaching doctrines that are not acceptable.

2. What does Socrates's use of the word *slandered* reveal about his position? How does Socrates make it clear that he is innocent?

One of the pleasures and challenges of this text is figuring out Socrates's various purposes with his speech. This can be a recurrent theme for discussion. Throughout the speech, guide students through Socrates's subtle and ironic language by referring to the text. His use of the word *slandered* makes it clear that he believes he has been falsely accused. It is clear that these accusations against him are longstanding and that he intends to refute them. Socrates immediately gives the example of a play by Aristophanes that portrays him claiming he can "walk on air." Socrates states he knows nothing about Aristophanes's accusations and asks the crowd if they have ever heard him claiming he can do such things. The crowd agrees they never have.

3. In paragraph 3, Socrates says he is on trial because of "a certain kind of wisdom." What kind of wisdom might Socrates be suggesting he has?

In paragraph 3, Socrates introduces his strange account of how he is wiser than everyone else because he admits he knows nothing. As the students will soon read, the Delphi oracle confirms that he is the wisest. Before reading about the oracle, however, draw students to the seemingly contradictory lines 25–28. At first, Socrates says he has a "human wisdom" for which he may really be wise. But then he goes on to say that he might not understand the "superhuman wisdom" of his accusers, bringing the reader to question Socrates's reasoning. Ask the students to reflect on this paragraph and see how Socrates might actually be joking. This form of talking forms one of the defining aspects of the *Apology*: Socrates's use of irony to defiantly defend himself and mock his accusers. In order for students to appreciate Socrates's argument, review the meaning of irony and how it is created in a text. As the unit progresses and students read through paragraph 8 and beyond, return to this question, collecting evidence to help determine how Socrates describes and understands his own kind of wisdom.

TEXT NOTES—IDEAS FOR DISCUSSION

4. In paragraph 2, why does Socrates ask a question to himself as if the audience asked him? How does this paragraph relate to the first and third paragraphs? Why would Socrates pretend the audience is asking him questions?

This paragraph first introduces students to a particular style Socrates used during his conversations and Plato used to recount these "dialogues" with Athenians. Socrates uses an interplay between his questions and responses as if he is performing a kind of dance. He asks questions to set up a response and guide the conversation; Socrates asks questions in order to extrapolate specific information. (As a side note, this is essential to the *Making Evidence-Based Claims* unit.) Here, Socrates asks a question that one can very much expect to be on the audience's mind. Indeed, if Socrates is not guilty as charged, then why do some find his activities suspicious in the first place? Here, Socrates bridges paragraphs 1 and 3 by acknowledging his innocence while also acknowledging that something does set him apart from the crowd, which he will expand on in his defense.

5. Why is this text titled the *Apology*? What does the word *apology* mean when translated from the Greek *apologia*? How does this definition help you understand what Socrates is doing?

Though the text is titled *Apology*, the Greek word *apologia* is better translated into English as "defense." The text is meant to be Socrates's defense of himself, not his apology for something he admits he has done wrong. Discuss with students how this understanding of the meaning of the title helps them understand the purpose of Socrates's speech.

ACTIVITY 4: MODEL THE FORMING OF EBCs

The teacher models a critical reading and thinking process for forming evidence-based claims about texts.

INSTRUCTIONAL NOTES

Based on the class discussion of the text, model a critical reading and thinking process for forming an evidence-based claim: from comprehension of textual details that stand out, to a connection or inference that arises from examining the details, to a basic EBC that is supported by specific references back to the text. Once the class has reached an understanding of the text, the **Attending to Details Handout** (introduced in the *Reading Closely* unit) can be used to help students think about the types of details they might be looking for and to introduce a three-step process for making a text-based claim.

- Introduce the **Forming EBC Tool** (and potentially connect it to the **Analyzing Details Tool** students may have previously used).
- Model the process for using the tool and forming a claim by using details that have emerged from discussion.

FORMING EVIDENCE-BASED CLAIMS TOOL

The *Forming EBC Tool* (in the **Making EBC Literacy Toolbox**) is organized so that students first note details that stand out and that they also see as related to each other. The second section asks them to think about the details and explain a connection they have made among them. Such text-to-text connections should be distinguished from text-to-self connections readers sometimes make between what they have read and their own experiences. These text-to-text connections can then lead them to a claim they can make and record in the final section of the tool—a conclusion they have drawn about the text that can be referenced back to textual details and text-to-text connections.

INSTRUCTIONAL NOTES

- Model the thinking of moving from details, to connections, to a claim as students follow along.
- Provide structured practice for the first two steps by giving students a textual detail on a blank tool—perhaps one related to another text-specific question from the model *Questioning Path Tool*. In pairs, have students use the tool to find other details or quotations that could be related to the one you have provided and then make or explain connections among those details.
- Return to the characteristics of an evidence-based claim that have been discussed in Activity 1:
  ⇒ A claim states a conclusion you have come to after reading a text and that you want others to think about.
  ⇒ All parts of a claim are supported by specific evidence you can point to in the text.
- In pairs or as a class, have students discuss how the model claim developed in class demonstrates these characteristics and where it might be stronger.
- Conduct a final discussion of the insights students have developed by considering the four text-specific question sets from the model *Questioning Path Tool*. As they share their insights, ask them to think about whether they are starting to form claims that are supported by specific evidence from the text—or how their beginning insights might become text-based claims.

NOTE

Here and throughout the entire unit, teachers are encouraged to develop questions and claims based on their own analysis and class discussion. The provided models are possibilities meant more to illustrate the process than to shape textual analysis. Instruction will be most effective if the claims used in modeling arise naturally from the textual ideas and details that students find significant and interesting. Also, although the tools have three places for recording supporting evidence, students should know that not all claims require three pieces of evidence. Sections of the tools can be left blank.

INDEPENDENT READING ACTIVITY

Supporting Evidence-Based Claims Tool

Students read paragraphs 4–10 of the text and use the *Supporting EBC Tool* (in the **Making EBC Literacy Toolbox**) to find evidence to support a teacher-provided claim. Teachers can place their own model claim at the top of the tool. Students look for evidence as they read to support the claim. This activity overlaps with the first activity of Part 2 and can be given as homework or done at the beginning of the next class.

PART 1 FORMATIVE ASSESSMENT OPPORTUNITIES

By the end of Part 1, students will have completed the following:

- *Approaching Texts Tool*
- *Forming EBC Tool* (textual details provided by the teacher)

ASSESSING LITERACY SKILLS

The *Forming EBC Tool* should be evaluated to get an initial assessment of students' grasp of the relationship between claims and textual evidence. Even though the work was done together with the class, filling in the tool helps students get a sense of the critical reading and thinking process and the relationships among the ideas. Also make sure that students are developing the habit of using quotation marks and recording the textual reference for details they identify.

Students will also have annotated the text (paragraphs 1 through 3) and may have recorded key details in an *Analyzing Details Tool*. Their annotations (and notes on the tool) can be reviewed to determine if they are carrying forward and applying the foundational Literacy Skills of **Attending to Details** and **Identifying Relationships** that they may have practiced throughout the *Reading Closely* unit. Students may be given feedback about their developing skills and the evidence they are showing using the **Student Making Literacy Skills Checklist** found in the **Making EBC Literacy Toolbox**.

ASSESSING ACADEMIC HABITS

Student discussions, as a class and in pairs, provide continuing opportunities for students to reflect on and self-assess their developing Academic Habits, specifically those related to **Engaging Actively**. Students might consider these reflection questions:

- What have I done to prepare for discussions by reading the text closely and considering the questions?
- How much have I actively focused my attention on the materials (during reading and annotation) and on the ideas of other participants in the discussion?

> **NOTE**
>
> To support self-, peer, and teacher assessment of skills and habits developed during the unit, a formal *Making EBC Literacy Skills Rubric* and less formal *Student Making EBC Literacy Skills* and *Academic Habits Checklists* are provided in the **Making EBC Literacy Toolbox**.

PART 2

MAKING EVIDENCE-BASED CLAIMS

"I neither know nor think I know."

OBJECTIVE:	Students develop the ability to make evidence-based claims through a close reading of a second section of text.

ESTIMATED TIME: 1–3 days

TEXT: Plato, *Apology* - paragraphs 4–10

MATERIALS:
- *Supporting EBC Tool*
- *Attending to Details Handout*
- *Forming EBC Tool*

≡ LITERACY SKILLS

TARGETED SKILLS	DESCRIPTORS
INTERPRETING LANGUAGE	Identifies how words and phrases convey meaning and represent an author's or narrator's perspective
IDENTIFYING RELATIONSHIPS	Identifies important connections among key details and ideas within and across texts
MAKING INFERENCES	Demonstrates comprehension by using connections among details to make logical deductions about a text
FORMING CLAIMS	Develops meaningful and defensible claims that clearly state valid, evidence-based analysis
USING EVIDENCE	Supports all aspects of claims with sufficient textual evidence using accurate quotations, paraphrases, and references

≡ ACADEMIC HABITS

HABITS DEVELOPED	DESCRIPTORS
COLLABORATING	Pays attention to, respects, and works productively in various roles with all other participants
COMMUNICATING CLEARLY	Uses appropriate language and relevant textual details to clearly present ideas and claims

≡ ALIGNMENT TO CCSS

TARGETED STANDARD:

CCSS.ELA-LITERACY.RI.9-10.1: Cite strong and thorough textual evidence to support analysis of what the text says explicitly as well as inferences drawn from the text.

SUPPORTING STANDARDS:

CCSS.ELA-LITERACY.RI.9-10.2: Determine a central idea of a text and analyze its development over the course of the text, including how it emerges and is shaped and refined by specific details; provide an objective summary of the text.

CCSS.ELA-LITERACY.RI.9-10.3: Analyze how the author unfolds an analysis or series of ideas or events, including the order in which the points are made, how they are introduced and developed, and the connections that are drawn between them.

CCSS.ELA-LITERACY.RI.9-10.6: Determine an author's point of view or purpose in a text and analyze how an author uses rhetoric to advance that point of view or purpose.

CCSS.ELA-LITERACY.SL.9-10.1: Initiate and participate effectively in a range of collaborative discussions (one-on-one, in groups, and teacher-led) with diverse partners on *grades 9–10 topics, texts, and issues*, building on others' ideas and expressing their own clearly and persuasively.

≡ ACTIVITIES

1. INDEPENDENT READING TO FIND SUPPORTING EVIDENCE
Students independently read part of the text and use the **Supporting EBC Tool** to look for evidence to support a claim made by the teacher.

2. READ ALOUD AND CLASS DISCUSSION
Students follow along as they listen to the same section of the text being read aloud and discuss a series of Guiding Questions and text-specific questions.

3. FINDING SUPPORTING EVIDENCE IN PAIRS
In pairs, students use the **Supporting EBC Tool** to look for evidence to support additional claims about the text made by the teacher.

4. CLASS DISCUSSION OF EBCs
The class discusses evidence students have found in support of teacher or class claims.

5. FORMING EBCs IN PAIRS
In pairs, students use the **Forming EBC Tool** to make an evidence-based claim of their own and present it to the class.

≣ ACTIVITY 1: INDEPENDENT READING
≣ TO FIND SUPPORTING EVIDENCE

Students independently read paragraphs 4 through 9 and use the **Supporting EBC Tool** to look for evidence to support a claim made by the teacher.

SUPPORTING EVIDENCE-BASED CLAIMS TOOL

The **Supporting Evidence-Based Claims Tool** (in the **Making EBC Literacy Toolbox**) is organized in a sequence opposite to the **Forming Evidence-Based Claims Tool**. In the first section, students write down a claim established by the teacher, themselves or the class. The second section prompts students to search for textual evidence and details that support the claim and write down where they found the evidence. Teachers can provide their own claims which students can use to practice making connections between valid (or invalid) claims and textual details. Such claims can serve as valuable models for students who are struggling to grasp the concept of a text-based conclusion or text-to-text connection. Students can also use the tool to write down claims as they read through text, then search and write down supporting evidence to determine whether their claims have text-to-text connections or not.

INSTRUCTIONAL NOTES

- Pass out and overview the organization of the **Supporting EBC Tool**—helping students see that it is organized in a sequence opposite to the **Forming EBC Tool** they have been using: moving from an existing claim to its supporting details, rather than from the details to a claim.

- Model the use of the tool with a teacher-developed claim derived from text students have previously read (paragraphs 1–3 of the *Apology*). Have students find and suggest supporting details for the teacher claim and record them on a **Supporting EBC Tool**.

- Present students with a new teacher-developed claim, derived from the next section of text students will read. Students independently read paragraphs 4–10 of the speech, looking for details to support the new teacher-developed claim and recording them on a **Supporting EBC Tool**.

Depending on scheduling and student ability, students can be assigned to read the text and complete the **Supporting EBC Tool** for homework. Teachers should decide what works best for their students. It is essential that students have opportunities to read the text independently at various points in the unit. All students must develop the habit of Perseverance in reading. Assigning the reading as homework potentially gives them more time with the text. Either way, it might be a good idea to provide some time at the beginning of class for students to read the text quietly by themselves, ensuring that all students have had at least some independent reading time.

≡ ACTIVITY 2: READ ALOUD AND CLASS DISCUSSION

Students follow along as they listen to paragraphs 4 through 10 being read aloud and discuss a series of Guiding Questions and text-specific questions.

INSTRUCTIONAL NOTES

- Students follow along as they listen to paragraphs 4–10 of the text being read aloud then share and compare the details they have recorded on a **Supporting EBC Tool** in response to a Guiding Question and a teacher-developed claim.

  ### TEXT NOTES

  Paragraphs 4–10 of Plato's *Apology* develop Socrates's defense as he addresses the question of his particular wisdom. Socrates describes how the oracle of Delphi said there was no one wiser than Socrates, which he considers a riddle because he has never thought of himself being very wise, nor unwise. Discerning what Socrates wants the audience to understand about his quest to find out what the oracle was talking about will require students to examine his perspective and ideas.

   Students will have first read the passage thinking about a broad Guiding Question related to Socrates's perspective ("What seems to be the author's point of view?") and a related claim presented by the teacher (e.g., "Socrates is surprised to hear that the oracle thinks no one is more wise than him."). Considering the question and the claim, students should search first for literal details about what the oracle says and how Socrates responds (his investigation). The questions in the Analyzing and Deepening stages of the model **Questioning Path Tool** should then help them read and annotate the text looking for additional details, words, and images that further reveal Socrates's understanding of the oracle's claim.

QUESTIONING PATH TOOL

Plato's *Apology*, paragraphs 4–10

APPROACHING: *I determine my reading purposes and take note of key information about the text. I identify the LIPS domain(s) that will guide my initial reading.*	I will initially focus on the narrator's *perspective*, then consider his *ideas* and supporting details.

QUESTIONING: *I use Guiding Questions to help me investigate the text (from the **Guiding Questions Handout**).*

1. What seems to be the author's point of view? [P]

2. What claims do I find in the text? [I]

ANALYZING: *I question further to connect and analyze the details I find (from the **Guiding Questions Handout**).*

3. How does the narrator's perspective influence his presentation of ideas or arguments? [P]

4. How do the main ideas, events, or people change as the text progresses? [I]

DEEPENING: *I consider the questions of others.*

5. How does Socrates view the oracle's message? In what way does Socrates use the oracle for his defense?

6. What realization does Socrates come to while trying to prove the oracle wrong? How does Socrates interpret the oracle's words?

7. What does Socrates mean when he says that the god is using him "as an example"? How does his pursuit to understand the oracle come to affect his life?

EXTENDING: *I pose my own questions.*

TEXT NOTES—IDEAS FOR DISCUSSION

Students might begin their rereading and second discussion of the text by considering the question in the Analyzing stage of the model *Questioning Path Tool*: "How does the narrator's perspective influence his presentation of ideas or arguments?" Studying the text for details to understand how Plato portrays Socrates provides practice in close reading for key sentences.

The three Deepening text-specific questions can help students again move from literal comprehension of key details to analysis of Plato's portrayal of Socrates and some of the key ideas in the text. They are numbered here to match the numbering in the model *Questioning Path Tool*. All three questions may be assigned to all students, or they may be differentially assigned based on students' reading readiness levels.

5. How does Socrates view the oracle's message? In what way does Socrates use the oracle for his defense?

Socrates explains that a close friend of his, Chaerephon, went to the oracle and asked if there was anyone wiser than Socrates. The priestess answered that there is no one wiser than Socrates. When Chaerephon relayed this to Socrates, Socrates was confused and wondered, "what ever does the god mean?" Convinced of his own ignorance, but equally convinced of the infallibility of the oracle, Socrates concluded that the statement must be a riddle and set off to solve it. Emphasize that in ancient Greece, the oracle was thought to be a portal through which the gods spoke directly to people. The statements of the oracle were understood to be the word of god, and therefore never doubted. "He can't be telling a lie. That just wouldn't be right," Socrates reasons. If a statement was confusing or seemed incorrect, it was assumed to be a riddle. Therefore, when Socrates heard the oracle's statement that he was the wisest man in Greece, he took it as his life's calling to figure out the truth behind that statement.

Focus students' attention on how Socrates again asks rhetorical questions to analyze his situation and drive forward his defense. It is very interesting how Socrates places the emphasis on the god of Delphi. Socrates uses the oracle to set up a situation where it seems that he wishes he were not so different from the Athenians (wise) and has made it his life's work to prove that the oracle is wrong; Socrates does not wish to be wise, but since it has been uttered by a god it is a matter out of his own hands.

6. What realization does Socrates come to while trying to prove the oracle wrong? How does Socrates interpret the oracle's words?

In order to "prove the oracle wrong," Socrates sought out Athenian citizens who were typically thought of as wise men. When he began to question their wisdom, Socrates found that not only were they not wise but also they were incapable of admitting their ignorance. Socrates comes to the conclusion that the wisdom he has lies in his ability to recognize what he does not know, which no one else seems willing to do: "I neither know nor think I know." This idea is a central theme of the text, and it is worth emphasizing. Socrates points out that people simply assume he knows what he is talking about, when in fact he only reveals the others' own ignorance. Still on course to solving the oracle's riddle, Socrates states that the god must have meant that he is wise because he knows nothing (end of paragraph 8). Discuss Socrates's irony with these

TEXT NOTES—IDEAS FOR DISCUSSION

statements, reminding students of what Socrates is accused of and how it compares to his revelation.

7. **What does Socrates mean when he says that the god is using him "as an example"? How does his pursuit to understand the oracle come to affect his life?**

In his "task of helping god," Socrates exposes the wise as unwise, which he does with apparent lack of satisfaction—he was, after all, simply trying to figure out the god's riddle. As he was doing this, Socrates was aware of the fact that his peers grew angry with him, but he felt it his responsibility to understand the oracle's message. Ask students to focus on the specific words and phrases Socrates chooses to build his irony and innocence. Socrates says he is "sad and fearful" because he has to do this unpleasant work for the god—it is not his fault that he must reveal these peoples' lack of wisdom but the fault of the oracle. In fact, he has gone so far to accept a "poverty-stricken" life because of his sense of obligation to help the god. Socrates paints himself as a victim of the oracle rather than benefiting from it. Have students focus on other areas in the *Apology* where Socrates does the same: turns apparently negative aspects of the trial into positive ones for him, or "makes the worse case look better" as his accusers put it.

- Following discussion, return to the ***Supporting EBC Tool*** and discuss textual details that have emerged as interesting during the discussion of each of the text-dependent questions.

≡ ACTIVITY 3: FINDING SUPPORTING ≡ EVIDENCE IN PAIRS

In pairs, students use the ***Supporting EBC Tool*** to look for evidence to support additional claims about the text made by the teacher.

INSTRUCTIONAL NOTES

- Once the class has reached a solid understanding of this section of the text, connect it to the skill of making claims and supporting them with evidence by presenting a few additional teacher-developed claims—perhaps ones that move from summary of explicit details to interpretation and inference.

- Students work in pairs to consider a new set of teacher-developed claims, find evidence in the text to support the claims, and record the details they find on a ***Supporting EBC Tool***. (*Note:* students may be asked to work with all of the teacher-developed claims, or claims may be assigned to student pairs based on their reading readiness levels.)

Collect each student's ***Supporting EBC Tool(s)*** with the evidence they have found for a teacher-developed claim(s). These should be evaluated to get an assessment of where each student is in the development of the targeted Literacy Skill of **Using Evidence**. Students should use their tools for their work in pairs—identifying and refining their evidence based on the read-aloud and class discussion. Even though students are not finding the evidence independently, they should each fill in separate tools to reinforce their acquisition of the logical structure among the ideas. Students should get into the habit of using quotation marks when recording direct quotes and including the paragraph or line numbers of the evidence they find.

> **NOTE**
>
> This may be a good time to introduce or review the concept and skills of using and citing evidence. Help students understand that it is important for them to record quotations and citations accurately so they can find the evidence again in the text, quote it correctly, and insert a proper citation when they write. Depending on the academic style students are expected to use (MLA, APA, a school or teacher system), have students record identifying citation information so they can use it correctly when they write.

The instructional focus here is on developing familiarity with claims about texts and the use of textual evidence to support them. Students should still not be expected to develop complete sentences to express supporting evidence. The pieces of evidence should be as focused as possible. The idea is for students to identify the precise points in the text that support the claim. This focus is lost if the pieces of evidence become too large. The tools are constructed to elicit a type of pointing at the evidence.

Alternative Instructional Approach: One additional approach for ensuring a close examination of claims and evidence is to provide erroneous claims that contradict textual evidence and ask students to find the places that disprove the claim. Students could then be asked to modify a claim to account for the evidence.

ACTIVITY 4: CLASS DISCUSSION OF EBCs

The class discusses evidence students have found in support of teacher or class claims.

INSTRUCTIONAL NOTES

- After students have finished their work in pairs, regroup for a class discussion.
- Have pairs volunteer to present their evidence to the rest of the class. Discuss the evidence, evaluating how each piece supports the claims. Begin by modeling the evaluation and then call on students to evaluate the evidence shared by the other pairs. They can offer their own evidence to expand the discussion.
- Carefully guide the exchanges, explicitly asking students to support their evaluations with reference to the text.

These constructive discussions are essential for the development of Literacy Skills and related Academic Habits. Listening to and evaluating the evidence of others and providing text-based criticism expand students' capacity to reason through the relationship between claims and evidence—and to reflect on their development of the skill of **Using Evidence** to support a claim. Paying close attention to and providing instructional guidance on the student comments is as important to the process as evaluating the *Supporting EBC Tools* and help develop a class culture of supporting all claims (including oral critiques) with evidence.

Students can also reflect on their participation in class and pair discussions by considering how well they have used and developed the Academic Habits of **Engaging Actively**, **Collaborating**, and **Communicating Clearly**. A reflective discussion or self-assessment could be guided by these questions:

- In what ways have I <u>paid attention to and worked collaboratively</u> with other participants in the discussions? How might I further develop this habit of <u>collaborating</u> in future discussions?

- How clearly have I <u>communicated my ideas</u> and supported them with specific <u>evidence</u>? How might I further develop this habit of communicating and supporting my thinking in future discussions?

ACTIVITY 5: FORMING EBCs IN PAIRS

In pairs, students use the *Forming EBC Tool* to make an evidence-based claim of their own and present it to the class.

INSTRUCTIONAL NOTES

- Once the claims and evidence have been discussed, students return to their collaborative pairs and use the *Forming EBC Tool* to make an evidence-based claim of their own, working again from identifying related details, to making connections among the details, to forming a supported claim. Pairs should develop a single claim, but each student should complete his or her own tool.

- Regroup and discuss the claims and evidence as a class. Pairs can use their tool to present their claims and evidence orally.

- Talk through the process modeled in the tool, including the nature of the details that stood out to students, the reasoning they used to group and relate them, and the claim they developed from the textual evidence.

- Draw on the *Attending to Details Handout* and help develop relevant Literacy Skills and Academic Habits to help guide discussion.

INDEPENDENT READING ACTIVITY

Students read paragraphs 11–18 of the text, guided by a Guiding Question(s) from the model *Questioning Path Tool* and using the *Forming EBC Tool* to make a claim and support it with evidence. This activity overlaps with the first activity of Part 3 and can be given as homework or done at the beginning of the next class.

☰ PART 2 FORMATIVE ASSESSMENT OPPORTUNITIES

At the end of Part 2, students will have completed the following:

- **Supporting EBC Tools** independently (for claims provided by the teacher)
- Class discussions
- **Forming EBC Tool** in pairs

ASSESSING LITERACY SKILLS

The **Supporting EBC Tools** should be evaluated to assess students' understanding of the relationship between claims and textual evidence. They should show progress in terms of the relevance and focus of the evidence they identify. The **Forming EBC Tools** are students' first attempts at crafting their own claims with the help of a peer. Basic claims are fine at this point. Use the Literacy Skills descriptors (or portions of the **Student Making EBC Literacy Skills Checklist** found in the **Making EBC Literacy Toolbox**) to structure the evaluation and feedback to students. Evaluation should focus on the clarity and validity of the claim and the relevance of the evidence. The thinking and connections students record on the tool are also important indicators of students' improving reasoning skills as well as potential evidence of their use of academic vocabulary related to the reading and claim-making process.

Evidence should be presented in quotation marks or paraphrased accurately and the references recorded correctly. Using quotation marks helps students make the distinction between writing quotations and paraphrasing. It also helps them eventually to incorporate quotes properly into their writing. Recording references is critical not only for proper incorporation in writing but also because doing so helps students return to the text to find and reevaluate evidence and make appropriate selections.

ASSESSING ACADEMIC HABITS

In Part 2, students work in small groups and engage in text-centered discussions. They can reflect on how well they have used the fundamental habits of **Collaborating** and **Communicating Clearly** within text-centered discussions.

The Academic Habits descriptors and reflective questions from Activity 4 can be used to evaluate student participation in discussions for formative and diagnostic information. Teachers and students can get a sense of areas where further development of text-centered discussion habits and skills are needed.

NOTE

To support self-, peer, and teacher assessment of skills and habits developed during the unit, a formal **Making EBC Literacy Skills Rubric** and less formal **Student Making EBC Literacy Skills** and **Academic Habits Checklists** are provided in the **Making EBC Literacy Toolbox**.

ORGANIZING EVIDENCE-BASED CLAIMS

"You're not likely to get another gadfly like me."

OBJECTIVE:	Students learn to develop and explain evidence-based claims through the selection and organization of supporting evidence.

ESTIMATED TIME: 2 to 3 days

TEXT: Plato, *Apology* - paragraphs 11–18

MATERIALS:
- *Organizing EBC Tool*
- *Forming EBC Tool*
- **Questioning Path Tool**

☰ LITERACY SKILLS

TARGETED SKILLS	DESCRIPTORS
INTERPRETING LANGUAGE	Identifies how words and phrases convey meaning and represent an author's or narrator's perspective
IDENTIFYING RELATIONSHIPS	Identifies important connections among key details and ideas within and across texts
MAKING INFERENCES	Demonstrates comprehension by using connections among details to make logical deductions about a text
FORMING CLAIMS	Develops meaningful and defensible claims that clearly state valid, evidence-based analysis
USING EVIDENCE	Supports all aspects of claims with sufficient textual evidence using accurate quotations, paraphrases, and references

ACADEMIC HABITS

HABITS DEVELOPED	DESCRIPTORS
COLLABORATING	Pays attention to, respects, and works collaboratively with all other participants in the task, discussion, activity, or process
COMMUNICATING CLEARLY	Uses appropriate language and relevant textual details to clearly present ideas and claims
LISTENING	Pays attention to, acknowledges, and considers thoughtfully new information and ideas from others

ALIGNMENT TO CCSS

TARGETED STANDARD:

CCSS.ELA-LITERACY.RI.9-10.1: Cite strong and thorough textual evidence to support analysis of what the text says explicitly as well as inferences drawn from the text.

SUPPORTING STANDARDS:

CCSS.ELA-LITERACY.RI.9-10.2: Determine a central idea of a text and analyze its development over the course of the text, including how it emerges and is shaped and refined by specific details; provide an objective summary of the text.

CCSS.ELA-LITERACY.RI.9-10.3: Analyze how the author unfolds an analysis or series of ideas or events, including the order in which the points are made, how they are introduced and developed, and the connections that are drawn between them.

CCSS.ELA-LITERACY.RI.9-10.6: Determine an author's point of view or purpose in a text and analyze how an author uses rhetoric to advance that point of view or purpose.

CCSS.ELA-LITERACY.SL.9-10.1: Initiate and participate effectively in a range of collaborative discussions (one-on-one, in groups, and teacher-led) with diverse partners on *grades 9–10 topics, texts, and issues*, building on others' ideas and expressing their own clearly and persuasively.

ACTIVITIES

1. INDEPENDENT READING AND FORMING EBCs
Students independently read a section of the text and use the **Forming EBC Tool** to make an evidence-based claim.

2. COMPARING EBCs
Students compare draft claims, then independently read or follow along as they listen to part of the text being read aloud, looking for additional evidence related to the claims they have made.

3. MODEL THE ORGANIZING OF EBCs
The teacher models organizing evidence to develop and explain claims using student evidence-based claims and the **Organizing EBC Tool**.

4. DEEPENING UNDERSTANDING
As a class, students use text-specific questions to deepen their understanding of the text and produce a second evidence-based claim.

5. ORGANIZING EBCs IN PAIRS
In pairs, students develop and organize a new claim with multiple points using the **Organizing EBC Tool**.

6. CLASS DISCUSSION OF STUDENT EBCs
The class discusses the evidence-based claims developed by student pairs.

ACTIVITY 1: INDEPENDENT READING AND FORMING EBCs

Students independently read paragraphs 11–18 of Plato's *Apology*, guided by a Guiding Question(s) from the model **Questioning Path Tool** and use the **Forming EBC Tool** to make a make an evidence-based claim.

TEXT NOTES

In paragraphs 11–18, Socrates offers his last defense, not for his sake, but for that of Athens. He claims that they will not get anther "gadfly" like him or someone who goads them to think about virtue. Socrates furthers his claims that he is only doing the god's bidding and is acting as a kind of service to the Athenians. When the jury finds him guilty and Meletus requests the death penalty, Socrates maintains his stance of innocence and argues that his accusers have been found guilty by "truth." This section offers complex language as Socrates uses both logic and sarcasm to make his points (e.g. "Then you'd spend the rest of your lives sleeping, unless the god in his kindness were to send you someone else like me."). These sentences will require time and diligence to fully unpack.

The questions in the model **Questioning Path Tool** for this section of the text thus have been selected and developed to help students focus on the ideas Socrates presents in his speech and on his perspective and how it is conveyed through his use of language. Students will first consider one of the general Guiding Questions from the Questioning or Analyzing sections as they do a first reading and develop an initial evidence-based claim.

The text-specific questions in the Deepening section of the Questioning Path are again designed to move students from concrete details and literal understanding of the specific points Socrates makes to defend himself and then to an analysis of how he thinks of his role in Athenian society.

As each question is discussed, follow it up by asking: "What in the text makes you reach your answer or conclusion? Point to specific words or sentences."

Developing Core Literacy Proficiencies

QUESTIONING PATH TOOL
Plato's *Apology*, paragraphs 11–18

APPROACHING:
I determine my reading purposes and take note of key information about the text. I identify the LIPS domain(s) that will guide my initial reading.

I will initially focus on the *ideas* the narrator presents through details and how his perspective influences his ideas.

QUESTIONING: *I use Guiding Questions to help me investigate the text (from the Guiding Questions Handout).*

1. What do I think the text is mainly about—what is discussed in detail? [I]

2. What claims do I find in the text? [I]

ANALYZING: *I question further to connect and analyze the details I find (from the Guiding Questions Handout).*

3. In what ways are ideas, events, and claims linked together in the text? [I]

4. How does the author's perspective influence his presentation of ideas, themes, or claims? [P]

DEEPENING: *I consider the questions of others.*

5. In paragraph 11, Socrates states that he will give his defense, "not for my own sake . . . but for your sake." What details does Socrates give to support this stance? How does Socrates arrive at such a conclusion?

6. The topic of money comes up throughout paragraphs 11–17. Why is it important for Socrates to bring up the issue of poverty? How does he use his economic status in his defense?

7. In paragraph 11, Socrates compares himself to a gadfly. According to him, why is it important for Athenians to have a gadfly? What is the consequence if Athens has no gadfly?

8. In paragraph 13, Socrates says he is "convinced that I never deliberately harmed anyone." Throughout paragraphs 13–17, he claims that it is difficult to persuade the Athenians. Finally, in paragraph 17, Socrates claims that his accusers have been found guilty by truth. What does this language reveal about Socrates's perspective of himself and his audience?

EXTENDING: *I pose my own questions.*

- Students independently work on paragraphs 10–18 from Plato's *Apology*, considering a Guiding Question from the model **Questioning Path Tool**. Depending on scheduling and student ability, students can be assigned to read and complete the **Forming EBC Tool** for homework or to read the text and form a claim at the beginning of class.

- Students record their question at the top of a **Forming EBC Tool**. As they read, they search for and annotate details related to the question.

- After reading, students record key details, connections, and an initial evidence-based claim on the tool.

ACTIVITY 2: COMPARING EBCs

Students compare draft claims, then read independently or follow along as they listen to paragraphs 11-18 being read aloud, looking for additional evidence related to the claims they have made.

INSTRUCTIONAL NOTES

- Either as a class or in small groups, ask students to volunteer claims they have drafted after reading the section of text and considering a specific Guiding Question. Facilitate a short comparative discussion of the student-developed claims, noting how different the claims may be depending on which Guiding Question students have used to frame their reading of the text and the details on which the claim is based.

- Read paragraphs 11–18 aloud to the class while students follow along or have them read independently. Alternatively, use the video recording of the speech or ask students to read aloud to the class. As students listen and read, they should search for and annotate additional details from the text that relate to and support their claims.

NOTE

This unit's Media Supports includes information on how to access an audio reading and a modern-day reenactment of the *Apology*. Although they may not use this unit's translation of the speech, they might give students another perspective of the text.

ACTIVITY 3: MODEL THE ORGANIZING OF EBCs

The teacher models organizing evidence to develop and explain claims using student evidence-based claims and the **Organizing EBC Tool**.

The central focus of Part 3 is learning the thinking processes associated with developing an evidence-based claim:

- Reflecting on how one has arrived at the claim
- Breaking the claim into parts
- Organizing supporting evidence in a logical sequence
- Anticipating what an audience will need to know in order to understand the claim
- Planning a line of reasoning that will substantiate the claim

This is a complex set of cognitive skills, challenging for most students, but these skills are essential so that students can move from the close-reading process of arriving at a claim (Parts 1 and 2 of the unit) to the purposeful writing process of explaining and substantiating that claim (Parts 4 and 5).

How a reader develops and organizes a claim is dependent on the nature of the claim itself and the nature of the text (or texts) from which it arises. In some cases, such as when a claim involves a literal interpretation of the text, it is sufficient to indicate where the claim comes from in the text and explain how the reader arrived at it. This suggests a more straightforward, explanatory organization. More-complex claims, however, often involve multiple parts, points, or premises, each of which needs to be explained and developed, then linked in a logical order into a coherent proof of the claim.

Students learn how to develop and organize a claim only through practice, ideally moving from simpler claims and more familiar organizational patterns to more-complex claims and organizations. Students can be helped in learning how to develop a claim by considering a set of developmental Guiding Questions such as the following.

NOTE
The first few questions might be used with less experienced readers, the latter questions with students who are developing more sophisticated claims.

- What do I mean when I state this claim? What am I trying to communicate?
- How did I arrive at this claim? Can I recount and explain how I moved as a reader from the literal details of the text to a supported claim about the text?
- Can I point to the specific words and sentences in the text from which the claim arises?
- What do I need to explain so that an audience can understand what I mean and where my claim comes from?
- What evidence (quotations) might I use to illustrate my claim? In what order?
- If my claim contains several parts (or premises), how can I break it down, organize the parts, and organize the evidence that goes with them?
- If my claim involves a comparison or a relationship, how might I present, clarify, and organize my discussion of the relationship between parts of text or different texts?

ORGANIZING EVIDENCE-BASED CLAIMS TOOL

Students who are learning how to develop a claim, at any level, can benefit from graphic organizers or instructional scaffolding that helps them organize and record their thinking. Although such models or templates should not be presented formulaically as a how-to for developing a claim, they can be used to support the learning process. The *Organizing EBC Tool* (in the **Making EBC Literacy Toolbox**) can be used to provide some structure for student planning. Alternately, a teacher might use another model or graphic organizer that fits well with the text, the types of claims being developed, and the needs of students.

INSTRUCTIONAL NOTES

ACTIVITY SEQUENCE

- Begin by orienting students to the new tool and the idea of breaking down a claim into parts and organizing the evidence accordingly. Relate the organization of the tool to that of the *Forming* and *Supporting EBC Tools*.

- Ask for a volunteer to present his or her initial claim and identify supporting evidence. Use the example as a basis for a discussion. Discuss what the component parts of the student's claim might be based on the nature of the claim and the evidence that the student has identified.

- Based on the flow of discussion, bring in other volunteers to present their claims and evidence to build and help clarify the points.

- Work with students to hone and develop a student claim, finding additional evidence and thinking about the component parts of the claim.

- As a class, record the organized claim, its parts, and evidence in an *Organizing EBC Tool.*

NOTE

The provided model *Organizing EBC Tool* in the **Making EBC Literacy Toolbox** is one possible way a claim could be expressed and organized.

≡ ACTIVITY 4: DEEPENING ≡ UNDERSTANDING

As a class, students use text-specific questions to deepen their understanding of the text and produce a second evidence-based claim.

TEXT NOTES—IDEAS FOR DISCUSSION

Use the following text-specific questions from the model *Questioning Path Tool* to frame a class (or small group) discussion of the text and to provide a context for a second—and, ideally, deeper—student claim. Students can use a *Forming EBC Tool* to develop their claim as they discuss the text. Depending on whether they work in groups or as a class, all students may work with all five questions, or they may be assigned differentially based on students' reading readiness levels. The questions are numbered here to match the numbering in the model **Questioning Path Tool**.

5. **In paragraph 11, Socrates states that he will give his defense "not for my own sake . . . but for *your* sake." What details does Socrates give to support this stance? How does Socrates arrive at such a conclusion?**

    Socrates boldly states that he gives his defense not for himself but for the sake of the Athenians so that they do not sin against the god that gave them a gadfly like him (paragraph 11). As he narrates previously in paragraphs 4–7, Socrates has made it his mission to figure out the riddle that the oracle of Delphi gave—that there is no other more wise (or unknowing) than Socrates. But Socrates then turns to the metaphor of a gadfly to help explain yet another reason why he makes his defense for Athens's sake. As a gadfly, he is responsible for waking the Athenians up. If they kill him, they are "not likely to get another gadfly like me."

    Part of the joy of reading the *Apology* is to see how craftily Socrates defends himself. Trace or have students trace the logical steps Socrates has taken to begin with a description of the charges against him, to the oracle's message, to his discussions with the supposed wise men of Athens, to this claim that to condemn Socrates is sin against a god. What claims does Socrates to arrive at this bold conclusion and what evidence does he provide along the way?

6. **The topic of money comes up throughout paragraphs 11–17. Why is it important for Socrates to bring up the issue of poverty? How does he use his economic status in his defense?**

     Again, Socrates is the victim of this god-given task as he is doomed to spend his life figuring out the godly riddle. Contrary to the accusations against him that he is a paid educator of the youth (paragraph 1), Socrates claims he is not educating, but merely trying to solve the oracle's riddle. If Socrates is poor (mentioned several times throughout the speech), then he cannot possibly have charged money for any sort of schooling of the youth of Athens. Have students look closely at how Socrates intertwines and connects the details of money, his perceived task as result of the oracle, the charges against him, and his claim that he has been sent by the gods. All are important for understanding how adeptly Socrates defends himself.

7. **In paragraph 11, Socrates compares himself to a gadfly. According to him, why is it important for Athenians to have a gadfly? What is the consequence if Athens has no gadfly?**

    This famous comparison demonstrates what is important to Socrates. As a gadfly he keeps the Athenians from sleeping. But what does this mean—sleeping? What does Socrates wake them up from? Later, in paragraph 15, Socrates says, "the best thing for everyone is to spend some time every day talking about virtue" and that "the unexamined life is not worth living." To Socrates, it is important to discuss virtue (and discuss one's own ignorance of his own wisdom) and ask questions about one's life. In effect, Socrates, as a gadfly, is waking the Athenians up from *un*examined lives and lives where they do not discuss virtues. Students can themselves examine how Socrates connects the gadfly metaphor to the values he espouses. For example, students can closely read paragraphs 17 and 18 to tease out these values.

8. **In paragraph 13, Socrates says he is "convinced that I never deliberately harmed anyone." Throughout paragraphs 13–17, he claims that it is difficult to persuade the Athenians. Finally, in paragraph 17, Socrates claims that his accusers have been found guilty by truth. What does this language reveal about Socrates's perspective of himself and his audience?**

Socrates is completely convinced in not only his innocence before his accusers but also that his action of engaging people in discussions about wisdom and virtue is a good path. Although he is convinced that the "unexamined life is not worth living," he finds it difficult to persuade other Athenians the same (paragraph 15). Instead of telling them what they want to hear (paragraph 16), he stands by his defense that he has done nothing wrong. He would rather die for his conviction than admit any wrongdoing or appease their wishes. Finally, in paragraph 17, Socrates implies that he is on the right side of truth, whereas his accusers have been judged by truth as guilty. Socrates not only believes that he has done no wrongdoing but also that he is living an examined life, a virtuous life, whereas his accusers have been deemed guilty by truth itself. While his accusers think that this trial will put an end to this whole matter with Socrates, the philosopher believes that the trial is connected to something much higher and that will haunt them even after his death. Have students pinpoint why the people of Athens will be "punished immediately after my death" and connect this to Socrates's overall argument (paragraph 18).

ACTIVITY 5: ORGANIZING EBCs IN PAIRS

In pairs, students develop and organize a new claim using the *Organizing EBC Tool*.

INSTRUCTIONAL NOTES

- Based on insights they have gained through reading and discussion of the deepening text-specific questions, students work in pairs, using the *Forming EBC Tool*, to make a new claim about some aspect of paragraphs 11–18. If students' first claims have been of a more concrete or summary nature, this is an opportunity for them to move toward more abstract claims about Socrates's ideas or perspective.

- Students use the *Organizing EBC Tool* to develop subpoints, identify key details and quotations, and organize supporting evidence for their new claim.

- In small pairs-check groups, student pairs use their tools to talk through the development and organization of their claims and compare them to claims developed by another student pair.

ACTIVITY 6: CLASS DISCUSSION OF STUDENT EBCs

The class discusses the evidence-based claims developed by student pairs.

INSTRUCTIONAL NOTES

- After students have finished their work in pairs and small groups, regroup for a class discussion about their evidence-based claims.
- Have pairs volunteer to present their claims, subpoints and evidence to the rest of the class.
- Discuss the evidence and organization, evaluating how each piece supports and develops the claims.
- Use student examples to illustrate how evidence is organized to develop aspects of claims.

> **NOTE**
>
> The model *Organizing EBC Tool* also presents one possible way a claim could be expressed and organized and thus can be used as an alternate example.

- Compare the types of claims students have developed and discuss how the particular Questioning Paths they have followed may have helped lead them to their claims—and may have resulted in varied readings of Socrates's speech.

INDEPENDENT READING ACTIVITY

Students reread paragraphs 1–18 of the *Apology* and use the *Forming EBC Tool* to make a new claim and support it with evidence. This activity overlaps with Activity 3 of Part 4 and can be given as homework or done at the beginning of the class.

PART 3: FORMATIVE ASSESSMENT OPPORTUNITIES

By the end of Part 3, students will have completed the following:

- *Forming EBC Tool* for a claim developed independently
- *Organizing EBC Tool* as a class
- A second *Forming EBC Tool* and *Organizing EBC Tool* for a claim developed in pairs

ASSESSING LITERACY SKILLS

Students' textual annotations and work on tools can be reviewed to see how they are developing the foundational skills of **Interpreting Language** and **Identifying Relationships**, and they should provide direct evidence of their developing skills in making inferences, **Forming Claims**, and **Using Evidence**. Students should now be beginning to develop more complex claims about challenging portions of the text. Their *Forming EBC Tool* should demonstrate a solid grasp of the claim-evidence relationship, but do not expect precision in the wording of their claims. Using the *Organizing EBC Tool* will help them clarify their claims as they break them into parts and organize their evidence. How they have transferred their information from the *Forming to the Organizing Tool* will demonstrate their grasp of the concepts and skills of breaking claims into parts and organizing evidence. Their second *Organizing EBC Tool* should show progress in all dimensions including the clarity of the claim, the reasoning behind subpoints, and the selection and organization of evidence. The *Student Making EBC Literacy Skills Checklist* found in the **Making EBC Literacy Toolbox** can be used to structure formative evaluation and feedback to students.

ASSESSING ACADEMIC HABITS

In Parts 1 and 2, students may have reflected informally on how they are applying the habits of **Engaging Actively**, **Collaborating**, and **Communicating Clearly**. Their pairs, small-group, and class discussions in Activities 4 through 6 of Part 3 can provide an opportunity for a slightly more formal self-assessment (and potentially a peer or teacher assessment) of these habits—along with the habit of **Listening**. Students might be introduced (or reintroduced) to the descriptors for the habits of **Collaborating**, **Communicating Clearly**, and **Listening**, then receive self-, peer, or teacher feedback regarding how well they are applying these habits and how they might improve, using the following *Assessment Checklist* (or the *Student Making EBC Academic Habits Checklist* found in the **Making EBC Literacy Toolbox**):

HABITS DEVELOPED	DESCRIPTORS	EVIDENCE OF USING THE HABIT	THINGS TO IMPROVE ON
COLLABORATING	• Pays attention to and respects other participants • Works productively with others to complete the task and enrich the discussion		
COMMUNICATING CLEARLY	• Uses clear language to communicate ideas and claims • Uses relevant details to explain and support thinking		
LISTENING	• Pays attention to new information and ideas from others • Considers others' ideas thoughtfully		

NOTE

To support self-, peer, and teacher assessment of skills and habits developed during the unit, a formal *Making EBC Literacy Skills Rubric* and less formal *Student Making EBC Literacy Skills* and *Academic Habits Checklists* are provided in the **Making EBC Literacy Toolbox**.

PART 4

WRITING
EVIDENCE-BASED CLAIMS

"The unexamined life is not worth living"

OBJECTIVE:	Students develop the ability to communicate text-based claims and their supporting evidence through writing.

ESTIMATED TIME: 2 to 4 days

TEXT: Plato, *Apology* - paragraphs 1–23

MATERIALS:
- *Writing EBC Handout*
- *Questioning Path Tool*
- *Forming EBC Tool*
- *Organizing EBC Tool*

☰ LITERACY SKILLS

TARGETED SKILLS	DESCRIPTORS
MAKING INFERENCES	Demonstrates comprehension by using connections among details to make logical deductions about a text
FORMING CLAIMS	Develops meaningful and defensible claims that clearly state valid, evidence-based analysis
USING EVIDENCE	Supports all aspects of claims with sufficient textual evidence using accurate quotations, paraphrases, and references
ORGANIZING IDEAS	Sequences sentences and paragraphs to establish coherent, logical, and unified narratives, explanations, and arguments
PRESENTING DETAILS	Describes and explains important details that effectively develop a narrative, explanation, or argument

ACADEMIC HABITS

HABITS DEVELOPED	DESCRIPTORS
UNDERSTANDING PURPOSE AND PROCESS	Understands the purpose and uses the process and criteria that guide tasks
LISTENING	Pays attention to, acknowledges, and considers thoughtfully new information and ideas from others
REVISING	Rethinks and refines work based on teacher-, peer-, and self-review processes

ALIGNMENT TO CCSS

TARGETED STANDARDS:

CCSS.ELA-LITERACY.RI.9-10.1: Cite strong and thorough textual evidence to support analysis of what the text says explicitly as well as inferences drawn from the text.

CCSS.ELA-LITERACY.W.9-10.9b: Draw evidence from literary or informational texts to support analysis, reflection, and research.

SUPPORTING STANDARDS:

CCSS.ELA-LITERACY.RI.9-10.2: Determine a central idea of a text and analyze its development over the course of the text, including how it emerges and is shaped and refined by specific details; provide an objective summary of the text.

CCSS.ELA-LITERACY.RI.9-10.3: Analyze how the author unfolds an analysis or series of ideas or events, including the order in which the points are made, how they are introduced and developed, and the connections that are drawn between them.

CCSS.ELA-LITERACY.RI.9-10.6: Determine an author's point of view or purpose in a text and analyze how an author uses rhetoric to advance that point of view or purpose.

CCSS.ELA-LITERACY.SL.9-10.1: Initiate and participate effectively in a range of collaborative discussions (one-on-one, in groups, and teacher-led) with diverse partners on *grades 9–10 topics, texts, and issues*, building on others' ideas and expressing their own clearly and persuasively.

Developing Core Literacy Proficiencies

ACTIVITIES

1. MODEL THE COMMUNICATION OF AN EBC THROUGH WRITING

The teacher introduces and models the process of writing one or more paragraphs that communicate an evidence-based claim using a claim developed in Parts 2 or 3.

2. MODEL AND PRACTICE THE USE OF QUESTIONS AND CRITERIA TO IMPROVE A WRITTEN EBC

The teacher introduces a collaborative, peer-review process for developing and improving writing using Guiding Questions and criteria from the targeted Literacy Skills.

3. WRITING EBCs IN PAIRS

Students reread the first part of the text and use a *Forming EBC Tool* to make a new claim and support it with evidence. In pairs, students develop a paragraph that communicates an evidence-based claim using one of their claims from Parts 2 or 3.

4. REVIEWING AND IMPROVING WRITTEN EBCs

In small groups, student pairs present their written EBCs and use questions and criteria to identify strengths and possible areas for improvement.

5. INDEPENDENT READING, DEVELOPING QUESTIONING PATHS, AND MAKING EBCs

Students independently read the rest of the text, develop a *Questioning Path Tool* to guide their reading, and use the *Forming EBC Tool* to develop an evidence-based claim.

6. READ ALOUD AND CLASS DISCUSSION

The class discusses their new evidence-based claims from Activity 5 and students listen actively to portions of the text being read or presented.

7. INDEPENDENT WRITING OF EBCs

Students independently complete an *Organizing EBC Tool* for the claim they have formed in Activity 5 and draft a one- to two-paragraph evidence-based claim.

8. USING PEER FEEDBACK TO REVISE A WRITTEN EBC

Students apply the collaborative review process and revise one aspect of their draft evidence-based claims paragraphs.

ACTIVITY 1: MODEL THE COMMUNICATION OF AN EBC THROUGH WRITING

The teacher introduces and models the process of writing one or more paragraphs that communicate an evidence-based claim using a claim developed in Parts 2 or 3.

INSTRUCTIONAL NOTES

Parts 1 through 3 have built a solid foundation of critical thinking and reading skills for developing and organizing evidence-based claims. Parts 4 and 5 focus on expressing evidence-based claims in a written paragraph format. Class discussions and pairs work have given students significant practice in expressing and defending their claims orally. The tools have given them practice in selecting and organizing evidence. Expressing evidence-based claims in writing should now be a natural transition from this foundation.

Writing Evidence-Based Claims Handout

- Begin by explaining that writing an evidence-based claim follows the same basic structure that students have been using with the tools—one states a claim and develops it with evidence.

- Suggest to students that written claims can take various forms. Sometimes the purpose of the writing is merely to explain the claim, what it means, and how it has come from a close reading of textual evidence. At other times, the purpose may be more argumentative in nature—to *prove* the claim through presenting sufficient and relevant textual evidence.

- Have students examine their copy of the **Writing EBC Handout** for this unit (in the **Making EBC Literacy Toolbox**). The handout addresses five key expectations students will need to consider as they write and revise their claims:

  1. Establish the context by connecting the claim to the text.
  2. State the claim clearly to fully communicate their ideas about the text.
  3. Organize supporting evidence found in the text.
  4. Paraphrase and quote from the text.
  5. Reference the evidence drawn from the text.

- Discuss each of these five key aspects of writing a claim in relationship to previous work in the unit. Students will return to this handout and the specific examples it presents when they are writing and reviewing their claims.

- Using the model **Organizing EBC Tool** for this unit (which may have been introduced in Part 3, Activity 3) or another claim developed by the teacher or class, model how a writer moves from an organizational plan to a written explanation of a claim:

  ⇒ Breaking down a claim into its component subpoints and evidence (the Organizing EBC process)

  ⇒ Communicating the claim in complete sentences and paragraphs that explain the subpoints and present the evidence

  ⇒ Integrating evidence as either quotations or paraphrases

- Building a unified explanation or argument from the component paragraphs, ideas, and evidence. A think-aloud approach can be extremely effective here. When modeling the writing process, explain the choices you make. For example, "I'm paraphrasing this piece of evidence because it takes the author four sentences to express what I can do in one." Or, "I'm quoting this piece directly because the author's phrase is so powerful, I want to use the original words."

- Explain that making choices when writing evidence-based claims is easiest when the writer has "lived with the claims." Thinking about a claim—personalizing the analysis—gives a writer an intuitive sense of how to express it.

- Model how reviewing the ideas recorded on the tools and selecting and organizing evidence can help a writer know how to develop a written EBC. Once students are more familiar with their ideas, making links among ideas, subpoints, and evidence will be easier and more intuitive.

ACTIVITY 2: MODEL AND PRACTICE THE USE OF QUESTIONS AND CRITERIA TO IMPROVE A WRITTEN EBC

The teacher introduces a collaborative, peer-review process for developing and improving writing using Guiding Questions and criteria from the targeted Literacy Skills.

INSTRUCTIONAL NOTES

At this point in the unit, before they begin to develop their own written EBCss, students can be introduced to the OE Collaborative Writing Workshop, an approach to developing and strengthening writing through a collaborative, question-based, and text-centered process. This process can help student writers focus on the Literacy Skills they have been working on in the unit, specifically **Forming Claims**, **Using Evidence**, and **Organizing Ideas**. The teaching of the process, here and elsewhere in the Developing Core Literacy Proficiencies units, involves teacher modeling, guided and supported writing, and text-centered discussion.

> **NOTE**
>
> See the User Guide that introduces and supports the Developing Core Literacy Proficiencies units for a detailed discussion of the OE Collaborative Writing Workshop process, principles, and suggestions for instruction.

- **Teacher Modeling:** Present students with a draft paragraph(s) that communicate(s) an evidence-based claim (either a teacher-developed model or a model paragraph from the *Writing EBC Handout* found in the **Making EBC Literacy Toolbox**). Let them know that they will be working with this written claim to learn and practice a process for reading a written draft of an evidence-based claim, using questions and criteria to think about the draft claim, and providing observations and feedback about how to improve the written explanation of the claim.

- **Text-Centered Review and Discussion:** Model and talk through the review process, using the following steps—which students will again apply in Activities 4 and 8 and throughout Part 5 of the unit (when they review each other's final written EBCss).

  1. Introduce a general Guiding Review Question related to the overall content of the writing, such as "What is the writer's claim, and how does it relate to the text we have read?"

2. In review teams, have students reread the draft paragraph in light of the general Guiding Review Question. Student teams then share text-based responses to the question with the class, as if the teacher is the paragraph's author.

3. Focus students' attention on two targeted Literacy Skills criteria: **Forming Claims** and **Using Evidence**. Explain, model, and discuss what each of these criteria causes one to think about, based on previous discussions about claims and textual evidence.

4. Read closely and study the specific language of the skills criteria:

FORMING CLAIMS	Develops a meaningful and defensible claim that clearly states an understanding of the text
USING EVIDENCE	Supports the claim with enough well-chosen evidence from the text; uses accurate quotations, paraphrases, and references

NOTE

Student-language versions of these skills descriptors are also found in the **Student Making EBC Literacy Skills Checklist** included in the **Making EBC Literacy Toolbox**.

5. Model and discuss what specific language in the criterion statements might mean when writing a claim, for example, "What does it mean to develop a claim that is 'meaningful and defensible?' To state a claim that shows an 'understanding of the text'? To support the claim with 'enough well-chosen evidence'?"

6. With the two literacy skills review criteria as a focus, frame one or more text-based question(s) that you might pose to a reviewer who is going to give you specific feedback about the draft paragraph.

- **Text-Based Review Question(s):** Is my claim "clearly stated"? Is my evidence "well chosen," and is there "enough" to explain or "defend" my claim? What might I add (or revise) to help you better get my "understanding of the text"?

7. Students (individually or in review teams) now read the paragraph closely, considering the text-based review question(s) and generating a reviewer's response.

8. Discuss how a text-based response to a draft piece of writing is itself a kind of *claim* that the reviewer makes based on the criteria, question(s), and specific evidence from the writer's draft.

9. Model how you might frame a claim-based response if you were a reviewer of the draft paragraph, emphasizing these points:

  ⇒ A *specific* response that emphasizes a <u>strength</u> of the paragraph and a <u>potential improvement</u>

  ⇒ A *constructive* and respectful articulation of the response

  ⇒ References to *text-based evidence* in the paragraph that has led to and supports your response

10. Guided by this model, students articulate and share their text-based responses and constructive reviewer claims, as if their partners were now the writer of the draft paragraph. Have several students volunteer to present their responses to the whole class and discuss how the responses are (or are not) *specific, constructive, and text-based.*

11. Model the habits a writer should develop when receiving a reviewer's response:

Listening

⇒ Listen fully to what readers have observed.

⇒ Consider their ideas thoughtfully.

⇒ Wait momentarily before responding verbally.

Remaining Open

⇒ Avoid explanations or justifications for what you as a writer have tried to do (no "yes, but . . ." responses).

⇒ Frame additional informal, text-based questions to further probe your readers' observations.

Revising

⇒ Consider the implications of your readers' observations for improving your writing.

⇒ Discuss what you might do as a writer to improve the example written claim after considering the responses you have received to your text-based review questions.

Emphasize throughout this modeling that developing an effective communication of an evidence-based claim through writing is a process—it *cannot* be done in one draft. Revision is fundamental to honing written EBCs.

ACTIVITY 3: WRITING EBCs IN PAIRS

Students reread paragraphs 1–18 of the *Apology* and use a *Forming EBC Tool* to make a new claim and support it with evidence. In pairs, students develop a paragraph that communicates an evidence-based claim, using one of their claims from Parts 2 or 3.

INSTRUCTIONAL NOTES

- Students reread the section of text and make a new claim in class or as homework.

- Students return to the same pairings from Part 3 and review the *Organizing EBC Tools* they developed in Part 3, Activity 5, or one of the *Forming EBC Tool* they just completed independently; they now use these tools to guide their writing of evidence-based claims paragraphs. If they use a *Forming EBC Tool* they just completed or a claim from Part 2, they can organize their evidence using an *Organizing EBC Tool* before moving on.

- Support pairs by answering questions and helping them get comfortable with the techniques for incorporating evidence. Use questions from pairs as opportunities to instruct the entire class.

- In this first phase of the process for writing an evidence-based claim, students should focus on less formal, more fluent writing, trying first to get their ideas out on paper so that they and others can examine them. Students should be given adequate time and opportunity to write in class and be expected to produce something that can be reviewed by others.

- Refocus students' attention on the two Literacy Skills criteria they have just used to review the model written claim: **Forming Claims** and **Using Evidence**. They should think about these skills as they write because they will use them to review the draft claims they develop.

- Explain that the simplest structure for writing evidence-based claims is beginning with a sentence or paragraph stating the claim and its context and then using subsequent sentences or paragraphs logically linked together to explain the claim and develop its necessary points with appropriate evidence. (More-advanced writers can organize the expression differently, for example, establishing a context, building points with evidence, and stating the claim at the end for a more dramatic effect. Let students know that the simplest structure is not the only effective way.)

Incorporating textual evidence into writing is difficult and takes practice. Expect all students to need guidance in deciding what precise evidence to use, how to order it, and when to paraphrase or to quote. They will also need guidance structuring sentence syntax and grammar to smoothly and effectively incorporate textual details while maintaining their own voice and style.

☰ ACTIVITY 4: REVIEWING AND IMPROVING ☰ WRITTEN EBCs

In small groups, student pairs present their written evidence-based claims and use questions and criteria to identify strengths and possible areas for improvement.

- Group student pairs into review groups of four students (two pairs) each.
- Have each student pair read their draft-written EBC paragraph aloud to their partner pair.
- Guide students in using the collaborative, question- and criteria-based review process modeled in Activity 2, as outlined in the following:

  1. Introduce a general Guiding Review Question related to the overall content of the writing, such as "What is the writer's claim, and how does it relate to the text we have read?"

  2. In review teams, have students reread each other's draft paragraphs in light of the general Guiding Review Question. Student teams then share text-based responses to the question with each other.

  3. Focus students' attention again on the two targeted Literacy Skills criteria: **Forming Claims** and **Using Evidence**.

  4. Have student pairs, who have drafted an evidence-based claims paragraph together, each frame a text-specific review question related to one or both of these criteria (if students struggle with this step, they can consider a review question from Activity 2, Step 6).

  5. Student review teams now read the paragraph closely, considering the text-based review questions and generating reviewer's responses. Responses should include these elements:

     ⇒ A *specific* response that emphasizes a <u>strength</u> of the paragraph and a <u>potential improvement</u>

     ⇒ A *constructive* and respectful articulation of the response

     ⇒ References to *text-based evidence* in the paragraph that has led to and supports the response

6. As they listen to their review team's responses, drafting pairs should work on the following behaviors, all related to the Academic Habits of **Listening**, **Remaining Open**, and **Revising**.

   Listening

   ⇒ Listen fully to what readers have observed.

   ⇒ Consider their ideas thoughtfully.

   ⇒ Wait momentarily before responding verbally.

   Remaining Open

   ⇒ Avoid explanations or justifications for what they as writers have tried to do (no "yes, but . . ." responses).

   ⇒ Frame additional informal, text-based questions to further probe their readers' observations.

   Revising

   ⇒ Consider the implications of their readers' observations for improving their writing.

7. Discuss what they might do as writers to improve their written claims after considering the responses they have received.

NOTE

Writers will *not* revise this first claim they have written in pairs, but they will use the same process to revise and improve claims in Activity 8 and Part 5.

- Have a few volunteer pairs present their written claims to the class, explaining the following:
  - ⇒ How they have derived and developed them
  - ⇒ The feedback they received from their reviewers
  - ⇒ What they might do to improve their written claims

- Depending on resources available, students might write or display their claim on the board or share it with the class and teacher electronically. The class together should evaluate the way the writing sets the context, expresses the claim, effectively organizes the evidence, and incorporates the evidence properly.

- Use the targeted Literacy Skills criteria for **Forming Claims** and **Using Evidence** to guide the discussion.

- Let other students lead the discussion of their peers' written claims, reserving guidance when needed and appropriate. It is likely and ideal that other students will refer to their own claims when evaluating the volunteer pair's paragraph.

- Make sure that class discussion maintains a constructive, collegial tone, and all critiques are supported by evidence. This discussion and the previous small-group discussions provide effective opportunities to practice and reflect on the Academic Habits of **Collaborating** and **Communicating Clearly**.

ACTIVITY 5: INDEPENDENT READING, DEVELOPING QUESTIONING PATHS, AND MAKING EBCs

Students independently read the rest of Socrates's defense (paragraphs 19–23), develop a **Questioning Path Tool** to guide their reading, and use the **Forming EBC Tool** to develop an evidence-based claim.

INSTRUCTIONAL NOTES

Depending on scheduling and student ability, students can be assigned to reread the text for homework or do so in class.

INDEPENDENT USE OF A QUESTIONING PATH AND DEVELOPMENT OF A CLAIM

- Students first consider a Questioning Path they might use to frame and guide their close rereading of the text. Using the **Guiding Questions Handout** and previous model **Questioning Path Tools** as examples, students determine an approach they will take in reading the text and identify Guiding Questions they will use as they question and then analyze the text.

- Students initially plan their approach to reading using a blank **Questioning Path Tool** (in the **Making EBC Literacy Toolbox**) and record their Guiding Questions on the tool.

- After their initial reading(s), students independently develop a text-specific question and record it in the Deepening section of the tool.

- Students use this new, independently developed question to guide their deeper reading of the text and the development of an evidence-based claim.

- Students record their question at the top of a **Forming EBC Tool** and search for details related to their question as they develop a new claim.

ACTIVITY 6: READ ALOUD AND CLASS DISCUSSION

The class discusses their new evidence-based claims from Activity 5 and students listen actively to portions of the text being read or presented.

INSTRUCTIONAL NOTES

- The class discusses the text and their new evidence-based claims from Activity 5. Students review the self-developed Questioning Paths they have followed in reading the text and introduce their claims by reading their text-specific questions that led to those claims.

- In pairs, students work together to hone their claims and organize evidence they have found in the speech. Have students transfer their claims from the **Forming EBC Tool** to the **Organizing EBC Tool**, which they will use in Activity 7 to help them organize and refine their evidence in preparation for writing.

- Students should present their evidence-based claims, and the discussion of their claims should determine areas of the text to be read aloud. Students read aloud relevant portions to help the class analyze claims and selected evidence.

ACTIVITY 7: INDEPENDENT WRITING OF EBCs

Students independently complete an *Organizing EBC Tool* for the claim they have formed in Activity 5 and draft a one- to two-paragraph evidence-based claim.

INSTRUCTIONAL NOTES

- Students should have reviewed and reconsidered the claims they wrote in Activity 5 in light of class discussion.

- Students independently develop an *Organizing EBC Tool* and then draft a one- to two-paragraph written EBC based on their tools.

- Direct students to the *Making EBCs Final Writing Task Handout* included in the Student Edition to help review the assignment.

- Because this is the first time students have independently developed a written claim, they may need some support in thinking about how to present and explain the claim, develop it through subpoints, and integrate supporting evidence from the text.

- As students write, remind them to consult the *Writing EBC Handout* that they first reviewed in Part 4, Activity 1. Remind them of the five things they will need to do as they write and revise their claims (from the *Writing EBC Handout*):

  1. Establish the context by connecting the claim to the text.

  2. State the claim clearly to fully communicate their ideas about the text.

  3. Organize supporting evidence found in the text.

  4. Paraphrase and quote from the text.

  5. Reference the evidence drawn from the text.

- Suggest that students read and think about the examples discussed in the handout as they draft, review, and revise their written claims. For some students, thinking about these examples (as models) before they write may be most helpful. For others, writing on their own first and then comparing what they have written to the models may work best. Either way, they should work to successfully do the five things explained and exemplified in the handout.

- Finally, remind students as they draft that the Literacy Skills criteria for **Forming Claims** and **Using Evidence** should continue to be in their minds and that they will review and revise their paragraphs in relationship to these criteria.

ACTIVITY 8: USING PEER FEEDBACK TO REVISE A WRITTEN EBC

Students apply the collaborative review process and revise one aspect of their draft evidence-based claims paragraphs.

- Organize students in editing partners or teams.
- Have students use the same collaborative, question- and criteria-based review process outlined and practiced in Activities 2 and 4:

  1. Read their draft out loud with a general Guiding Review Question.

  2. Listen to reviewers' initial observations based on the Guiding Question.

  3. Consider the Literacy Skills criteria and frame a text-based review question(s) in relationship to those criteria.

  4. Engage in a text-centered discussion of the drafts, referencing the criteria, questions, and specific evidence from the drafts.

  5. Determine strengths and areas for possible improvement based on the discussion of the drafts.

- Following the reviews of their drafts, each student individually determines <u>one aspect</u> of the draft they would like to improve, for example:

  ⇒ The <u>clarity</u> of the claim and its explanation

  ⇒ How <u>defensible</u> their claim is, based on the evidence they have presented

  ⇒ The <u>use of evidence</u> and integration of textual references into their writing

  ⇒ The <u>organization</u> of their subpoints and evidence into a unified written claim

- Students complete one revision of their written claim, focusing on the aspect they have targeted for improvement, then read their revised claims to their editing partners or teams for final feedback.

- As a class, discuss what students have learned about writing a claim, the targeted Literacy Skills of **Forming Claims** and **Using Evidence**, the collaborative process to review and improve writing, and the Academic Habits of **Collaborating** and **Revising**.

INDEPENDENT READING ACTIVITY

Students review the text read in the unit and use a **Forming EBC Tool** to make a new claim of their choice and develop it with evidence. This activity overlaps with the first activity of Part 5 and can be given as homework or done at the beginning of the next class.

≣ PART 4: FORMATIVE ASSESSMENT ≣ OPPORTUNITIES

By the end of Part 4, students will have accomplished the following:

- Written an evidence-based claim paragraph in pairs
- Participated in three rounds of collaborative reviews of written EBCs
- Developed their own Questioning Path on a **Questioning Path Tool**
- Completed a **Forming EBC Tool** and **Organizing EBC Tool** independently
- Written and revised an evidence-based claims paragraph independently

ASSESSING LITERACY SKILLS

At this stage, teachers can assess students' reading and writing skills. Students should be comfortable making claims and supporting them with organized evidence. Their tools should demonstrate evidence of progress or proficiency in targeted reading skills, such as **Attending to Details**, **Identifying Relationships**, **Making Inferences**, and **Forming Claims**. Student writing should begin to demonstrate how well they can organize ideas, use evidence, and present details. Make sure they have properly established the context, that the claim is clearly expressed, and that each paragraph develops a coherent point. Evaluate the writing for an understanding of the difference between paraphrase and quotation when **Using Evidence**. All evidence should be properly referenced. Use the review criteria from Part 4 or the detailed *Student Making EBC Literacy Skills Checklist* in the **Making EBC Literacy Toolbox** to structure evaluation and feedback to students.

ASSESSING ACADEMIC HABITS

Students will have continued to use and develop the habits of **Collaborating** and **Communicating Clearly** in text-centered discussions, and for the first time they will have applied those habits in the context of reviewing and revising a written product. They will have begun to demonstrate how well they can understand and apply a collaborative, criteria-based process for improving their work; in doing so, they will have applied Academic Habits of **Listening** and **Remaining Open** to feedback from peers. Students can reflect informally or receive peer and teacher feedback about any of these habits and might use an expanded habits checklist such as the one below (or the *Student Making EBC Academic Habits Checklist* in the **Making EBC Literacy Toolbox**):

HABITS DEVELOPED	DESCRIPTORS	EVIDENCE OF USING THE HABIT	THINGS TO IMPROVE ON
UNDERSTANDING PURPOSE AND PROCESS	• Understands and uses the collaborative writing workshop process • Uses Literacy Skills criteria to frame questions, responses, and feedback		
LISTENING	• Pays attention to new information and ideas from others • Considers others' ideas thoughtfully		
REMAINING OPEN	• Avoids explanations or justifications for what they as writers have tried to do • Frames text-based questions to probe their readers' observations		
REVISING	• Uses criteria to rethink, refine, or revise work • Uses observations from peers to inform improvement		

NOTE

To support self-, peer, and teacher assessment of skills and habits developed during the unit, a formal *Making EBC Literacy Skills Rubric* and less formal *Student Making EBC Literacy Skills* and *Academic Habits Checklists* are provided in the *Making EBC Literacy Toolbox*.

PART 5

DEVELOPING EVIDENCE-BASED WRITING

"If you think that by killing people you can avoid being taken to task for not living as you should, then you're wrong."

OBJECTIVE:	Students develop the ability to express global evidence-based claims in writing through a rereading of the text in the unit and a review of their previous work.

ESTIMATED TIME: 3 to 4 days

TEXT: Plato, *Apology* - paragraphs 1–23
MATERIALS:

- *Forming EBC Tool*
- *Organizing EBC Tool*
- *Writing EBC Handout*

- *Making EBC Literacy Skills Rubric*
- *Student Making EBC Literacy Skills Checklist*
- *Student Making EBC Academic Habits Checklist*

☰ LITERACY SKILLS

In Part 5, students demonstrate the Literacy Skills they have been working on throughout the unit through a final essay in which they develop, explain, and support a global evidence-based claim. Their essays can be read as evidence of their reading skills (**Attending to Details, Interpreting Language, Identifying Relationships, Making Inferences, Forming Claims**) and their writing skills (**Using Evidence, Presenting Details, Organizing Ideas, Using Language, Using Conventions**). Because their final essay may be their first, more formal piece of writing, it also presents opportunities for them to work on and formatively demonstrate skills associated with Publishing: using effective formatting and citations.

The *Student Making EBC Literacy Skills Checklist* provided in the **Making EBC Literacy Toolbox** can be used for self- and peer assessment, and the *Making EBC Literacy Skills Rubric* can be used for evaluating students' work on the essay.

TARGETED SKILLS	DESCRIPTORS
ATTENDING TO DETAILS	Identifies relevant and important textual details, words, and ideas
INTERPRETING LANGUAGE	Identifies how words and phrases convey meaning and represent an author's or narrator's perspective

TARGETED SKILLS	DESCRIPTORS
IDENTIFYING RELATIONSHIPS	Identifies important connections among key details and ideas within and across texts
MAKING INFERENCES	Demonstrates comprehension by using connections among details to make logical deductions about a text
FORMING CLAIMS	Develops meaningful and defensible claims that clearly state valid, evidence-based analysis
USING EVIDENCE	Supports all aspects of claims with sufficient textual evidence, using accurate quotations, paraphrases, and references
ORGANIZING IDEAS	Sequences sentences and paragraphs to establish coherent, logical, and unified narratives, explanations, and arguments
PRESENTING DETAILS	Describes and explains important details that effectively develop a narrative, explanation, or argument
USING LANGUAGE	Selects and combines words that precisely communicate ideas, generate appropriate tone, and evoke intended responses from an audience
USING CONVENTIONS	Uses effective sentence structure, grammar, punctuation, and spelling to express ideas and achieve writing and speaking purposes
PUBLISHING	Uses effective formatting and citations to present ideas for specific audiences and purposes

ACADEMIC HABITS

Part 5 also presents further opportunities for students to engage in text-centered discussions about the text they have read in the unit and their own written claims. Students can do a final, more formal self-assessment and receive teacher feedback about how well they have developed and are demonstrating the Academic Habits used in discussion and collaborative revision processes. The **Student Making EBC Academic Habits Checklist** provided in the **Making EBC Literacy Toolbox** can be used for self-, peer, and teacher assessment of these habits.

HABITS DEVELOPED	DESCRIPTORS
ENGAGING ACTIVELY	Actively focuses attention on independent and collaborative tasks
COLLABORATING	Pays attention to, respects, and works productively in various roles with all other participants
COMMUNICATING CLEARLY	Uses appropriate language and relevant textual details to clearly present ideas and claims
UNDERSTANDING PURPOSE AND PROCESS	Understands the purpose and uses the process and criteria that guide tasks
LISTENING	Pays attention to, acknowledges, and considers thoughtfully new information and ideas from others
REVISING	Rethinks and refines work based on teacher-, peer-, and self-review processes

ALIGNMENT TO CCSS

TARGETED STANDARDS:

CCSS.ELA-LITERACY.RI.9-10.1: Cite strong and thorough textual evidence to support analysis of what the text says explicitly as well as inferences drawn from the text.

CCSS.ELA-LITERACY.W.9-10.9b: Draw evidence from literary or informational texts to support analysis, reflection, and research.

SUPPORTING STANDARDS:

CCSS.ELA-LITERACY.RI.9-10.2: Determine a central idea of a text and analyze its development over the course of the text, including how it emerges and is shaped and refined by specific details; provide an objective summary of the text.

CCSS.ELA-LITERACY.RI.9-10.3: Analyze how the author unfolds an analysis or series of ideas or events, including the order in which the points are made, how they are introduced and developed, and the connections that are drawn between them.

CCSS.ELA-LITERACY.RI.9-10.6: Determine an author's point of view or purpose in a text and analyze how an author uses rhetoric to advance that point of view or purpose.

CCSS.ELA-LITERACY.W.9-10.4: Produce clear and coherent writing in which the development, organization, and style are appropriate to task, purpose, and audience.

ACTIVITIES

1. INDEPENDENT READING AND CLASS DISCUSSION OF GLOBAL EBCs
Students independently review the text read in the unit and the class discusses the development of more global evidence-based claims.

2. FORMING GLOBAL EBCs
Students review previous claims and use a *Forming EBC Tool* to frame a new global evidence-based claim.

3. REVIEWING AND ORGANIZING EBCs
Students discuss their new claims in pairs and then with the class, considering their supporting evidence and how they will organize it with an *Organizing EBC Tool*.

4. INDEPENDENT DRAFTING OF A FINAL EBC ESSAY
Students independently draft a final evidence-based claim essay using their new claims.

5. USING THE COLLABORATIVE, CRITERIA-BASED PROCESS TO IMPROVE ESSAYS
Students use a *Criteria-Based Checklist* and feedback from peers in a collaborative review process to revise and improve their evidence-based claims essays.

6. CLASS DISCUSSION OF FINAL EBC ESSAYS
The class discusses final evidence-based claims essays of student volunteers and reflects on the Literacy Skills and Academic Habits involved in making and communicating evidence-based claims.

≣ ACTIVITY 1: INDEPENDENT READING AND CLASS DISCUSSION OF EBCs

Students independently review the text read in the unit and the class discusses the development of more global evidence-based claims.

INSTRUCTIONAL NOTES

In Part 5, students move to thinking about the big picture presented to them by considering the text they have read as a whole and also comparing the separate sections of text they have read. Direct students to the **Making EBCs—Final Writing Tasks Handout** included in the Student Edition to help review the assignment.

- Individually, students do the following:
  1. Reread the text.
  2. Review the **Forming EBC** and **Organizing EBC Tools** they have developed.
  3. Reread the two claims they have written in Part 4.

Focused Rereading

- Return to the end of Socrates's speech that students have read and analyzed independently at the end of Part 4. As a stimulus for the discussion of the entire text that will follow, have students read and consider these lines from paragraph 22 of the text: "When my sons grow up, punish them by getting in their face as I've gotten in yours. If you think they care more about money or anything else than they do about virtue; and if they take themselves to be very important when they aren't, rebuke them for, the way I've rebuked you, for not paying attention to what they should and for thinking they're important when they're worthless."

- Have students do a close reading of these lines and then discuss how it relates to Socrates's previous remarks on virtue and statement, "the unexamined life is not worth living."

Group and Class Discussion

- With this analysis as a backdrop, students engage in a discussion—first in small groups, then as a class—about what it all adds up to—what they think about the reading they have completed in the unit.

- These discussions at first should be open-ended so that many different observations or thoughts are shared, but eventually they should be more structured by probing students' observations with the question, "What evidence can you point to in the text(s) that is the basis for and supports your observation?"

- Students will likely move on their own to more global or summative observations and claims about the text. And they may also make comparisons among sections of the text.

Modeling Global Claims

- Move the student discussion into an explanation and modeling of claims that are more "global" in nature: claims that analyze texts based on their ideas, perspective, or language and/or claims that result from analysis and the noting of relationships among sections of a text.

- Present students with a Guiding Question such as this one:
  ⇒ How do the main ideas change as the text progresses?
- Model and discuss a global claim that highlights a significant theme, idea, structure, or perspective that is developed over the course of the *Apology*. Have students suggest evidence from the text that supports this claim.

Generating Informal Global Claims

- Present students with a more global Guiding Question, such as the following:
  ⇒ What relationships do I discover among the ideas and details presented, the narrator's perspective, and the language or structure of the text?
- Model and discuss a global claim that sums up a larger discovery made by considering the entire text, their ideas, perspectives, language, or structure. For Socrates's speech, this might be a claim about what he is trying to convey overall to the Athenians. Have students suggest evidence from the text that supports this claim.
- Have students informally generate, share, and compare their own global claims using details and thinking from the tools they have completed in the unit.

This activity should be seen as an expansion of the skills developed in Part 4. Discuss volunteer student-written claims to review the critical aspects of generating and developing a more global claim. These claims will vary in the amount of text they span and the global nature of the ideas. Use various examples to demonstrate the differences, moving to a discussion of how claims build on each other to produce more global analyses of entire texts.

Throughout the unit, the text has been chunked into sections, and now students have been asked to consider the entire text they have read for their final claim. When modeling the making of a global claim, discuss its relationship to smaller, local claims. Demonstrate how local claims that address less text can become subpoints for broader claims that address more text.

ACTIVITY 2: FORMING GLOBAL EBCs

Students review previous claims and use a *Forming EBC Tool* to frame a new global evidence-based claim.

Having brainstormed and shared various global claims about the text, students are now ready to form a final claim about what they have read to be developed into a multiparagraph essay.

- Using the *Forming EBC* or *Supporting EBC Tool*, students can either work from details across the text to develop a new claim or find supporting evidence for a claim they have come up with in Activity 1.

- In pairs or small groups, students review the claims they have formed and the evidence they have identified, thinking about the Literacy Skills criteria for **Forming Claims** (i.e., Is a claim "clear," meaningful," "defensible," and clearly related to an "understanding of the text"?) and **Using Evidence** (Is there "enough, well-chosen" evidence to support the claim?).

☰ ACTIVITY 3: REVIEWING AND ☰ ORGANIZING EBCs

Students discuss their new claims in pairs and then with the class, considering their supporting evidence and how they will organize it with an *Organizing EBC Tool*.

INSTRUCTIONAL NOTES

- Based on feedback from their peers in Activity 2, students revise claims, find new supporting evidence, and complete an *Organizing EBC Tool* to support their writing of their claim.

- Once the class has a general understanding of the nature of more global claims, break them into pairs to work on the claims they have begun to develop in Activities 1 and 2. Have the pairs discuss whether their claims contain subclaims and how best they might be organized. It may be helpful to provide students with the two-point and three-point organizational tools to best fit their claims.

- Students share their claims and organizational plans, first in pairs and then as a class.
  - ⇒ Volunteer pairs can be asked to discuss the work they did on their claims. At this point they should be able to talk about the nature of their claims and why they have chosen to organize evidence in particular ways.

☰ ACTIVITY 4: INDEPENDENT DRAFTING ☰ OF A FINAL EBC ESSAY

Students independently draft a final evidence-based claims essay using their new claims.

INSTRUCTIONAL NOTES

- Explain to students that they will now be drafting a final, multiparagraph essay that explains, develops, and supports their global evidence-based claim. Let them know that this evidence-based writing piece will be used as a summative assessment to evaluate their development of the Literacy Skills targeted in the unit.

- Communicate to students that their task will be to explain and support a global evidence-based claim they have formed based on their reading and analysis of the text.

- Have students read through the *Making EBC - Final Writing Tasks Handout* found in the Developing Core Literacy Proficiencies Student Edition, which presents them with a short explanation of the assignment and its criteria, as well as a listing of the key Literacy Skills they should try to demonstrate.

- Explain to students that their final written essays will be evaluated for their demonstration of three key expectations and criteria for the assignment:

  1. Demonstrate an accurate reading and insightful analysis of the text.
  2. Develop a supported claim that is clearly connected to the content of the text.
  3. Successfully accomplish the five key elements of a written EBC.

- Students can keep these five key elements in mind by consulting the **Writing EBC Handout** that they first reviewed and used in Part 4, Activities 1 and 7.

  1. Establish the context by connecting the claim to the text.
  2. State the claim clearly to fully communicate their ideas about the text.
  3. Organize supporting evidence found in the text.
  4. Paraphrase and quote from the text.
  5. Reference the evidence drawn from the text.

- Suggest that students again read and think about the examples discussed in the handout as they draft their final written claims. For some students, thinking about these examples (as models) before they write may be most helpful. For others, writing on their own first and then comparing what they have written to the models may work best. Either way, they should work to successfully follow the five components explained and exemplified in the handout.

- Provide students with a copy of the **Student Making EBC Literacy Skills Checklist** for this essay. Explain that they will be using parts of the checklist in Activity 5 to review and revise their draft essays. Review the key criteria they and you will be examining and what the descriptors suggest about the writing of an evidence-based claim essay.

- Provide time and support in class for students to draft their essays, working from the planning they have done on an **Organizing EBC Tool**.

ACTIVITY 5: USING THE COLLABORATIVE, CRITERIA-BASED PROCESS TO IMPROVE ESSAYS

Students use a criteria-based checklist and feedback from peers in a collaborative review process to revise and improve their evidence-based claim essays.

Once students have completed a first draft of their evidence-based claim essays, they will work in writing groups (of two to four students) to complete two review and revision cycles. The first cycle will focus on the essay's content: the <u>clarity</u> of their claim and its explanation and the <u>sufficiency and quality of the evidence</u> they have presented to support their claim. The second cycle will focus on the essay's organization and expression: how they have arranged their ideas in a <u>logical sequence</u>, smoothly integrated <u>textual details</u>, and used <u>language and conventions</u> to communicate their ideas.

INSTRUCTIONAL NOTES

Before beginning the reviews, remind students that as reviewers their observations should include these elements:

- A *specific* response that emphasizes a <u>strength</u> of the essay and a <u>potential improvement</u>
- A *constructive* and respectful articulation of the response
- References to *text-based evidence* in the essay that has led to and supports the response

And that as writers (and receivers of feedback) they should do the following:

- Listen carefully to what their readers have observed.
- Wait momentarily before responding verbally.
- Avoid explanations and justifications for what they as writers have tried to do (no "yes, but . . ." responses).
- Frame additional informal, text-based questions to further probe their readers' observations.

Review 1—Focus on Content

Teacher Modeling

- Return to the Literacy Skills criteria students have been using in Part 4: **Forming Claims** and **Using Evidence**. Talk through how you might apply these criteria in reviewing a draft evidence-based claims essay—beginning with general Guiding Review Questions, such as "What is the claim and how clearly is it expressed and explained? Is there enough, well-chosen evidence to support the claim?" Then model how a writer might develop a more specific text-based review question to guide a second review of the draft.

Text-Centered Review and Discussion

- In writing groups, students read their draft essays aloud, then listen as their reviewers provide initial constructive feedback about the claim and its support.
- Reviewers reread the draft essay with the Guiding Review Questions in mind, noting strengths and places where the clarity of the claim or its support might be improved.
- Based on this initial feedback, each writer determines an area to work on and develops a specific text-based review question.
- Writers revise their essays, focusing on a specific aspect of their claim and its supporting evidence.
- Writers present reviewers with their text-based review question and receive a second text-based review about the draft essay's content.

Review 2—Focus on Organization and Expression

Teacher Modeling

- Determine one or two aspects of organization or expression that students should work on such as

- the logical sequence of the essay's explanation,

- the connections, and transitions among sentences and paragraphs;

- the smooth integration of quotations and paraphrases;

- the clarity or vigor of expression;

- one of more conventions of usage or punctuation;

- the correct citation of textual evidence).

- Avoid asking students to focus on too many issues within this essay's revision cycle. Based on the area(s) chosen to focus on, introduce one or two criteria from the Literacy Skills listed in the **Student Making EBC Literacy Skills Checklist**. Model how these criteria can lead to a general Guiding Review Question and potentially a more specific text-based review question.

Text-Centered Review and Discussion

- In writing groups, reviewers first consider the general Guiding Review Question and complete another reading of the draft while providing constructive feedback.

- Based on this initial feedback, each writer determines an area to work on and develops a specific text-based review question.

- Writers revise their essays, focusing on a specific aspect of their essay's organization, expression, or publication.

- Writers present reviewers with their text-based review question and receive a second text-based review about the draft essay's organization or expression.

FINAL DRAFTING AND PUBLICATION

Using the **Student Making EBC Literacy Skills Checklist** for the evidence-based claims essay and any guidelines provided by the teacher for the formatting and publication of the final product, students complete a final revision and produce an essay to be shared with the class and submitted to the teacher for evaluation.

☰ ACTIVITY 6: CLASS DISCUSSION
☰ OF FINAL EBC ESSAYS

The class discusses final evidence-based claim essays of student volunteers and reflects on the Literacy Skills and Academic Habits involved in making and communicating evidence-based claims.

INSTRUCTIONAL NOTES

- Students present their final evidence-based claim essays to the class. This activity can be done informally, calling on student volunteers, or more formally in a symposium format, in which each student presents his or her work to a group of peers, outside reviewers, or the class as a whole. In reading and presenting their essays, students should explain the following:

  ⇒ The process through which they arrived at their claim—how it emerged from their reading of the text and how they honed it

  ⇒ What they focused on as they rethought, revised, and polished their claim into a final essay

⇒ What they learned about the text and its ideas, about developing claims, and about the Literacy Skills and Academic Habits they worked on during the unit

- The class engages in a final reflective discussion of the text read, the skills and habits worked on, and what they have learned about making evidence-based claims.

Students can complete a self-assessment using the **Student Making EBC Literacy Skills** and **Academic Habits Checklists** and may also compile a review portfolio of the annotated texts, tools, and written EBCs they have produced during the unit.

PART 5: SUMMATIVE ASSESSMENT

By the end of Part 5, students will have completed the following:

- A **Forming EBC Tool** (or **Supporting EBC Tool**) for a global claim
- An **Organizing EBC Tool**
- A rough draft of an evidence-based claim essay on their global claim
- A two-stage collaborative review and revision process
- A final written evidence-based claim essay

ASSESSING LITERACY SKILLS

Students' final evidence-based claim essays, having gone through peer review and revision, should provide evidence of each student's development of the Literacy Skills targeted in the unit—especially the reading and thinking skills that have been the focus of instruction and that are involved in making an evidence-based claim. The **Student Making EBC Literacy Skills Checklist** provided with this unit can be used to guide students during the review and revision process for peer and self-assessment and for informal teacher feedback. A more formal **Making EBC Writing Task Rubric** (found in the **Making EBC Literacy Toolbox**) should be used by the teacher for evaluating performance and growth as demonstrated in the final essay and the reading and thinking exercises that have preceded it. This rubric includes a four-point developmental scale for indicating where students are on a continuum from "emerging" to "excelling" and also enables the teacher to indicate specific skill areas in which the student has demonstrated noticeable growth. The rubric includes a place for an overall summary evaluation—potentially a grade—or can be used in a point-based grading system by tallying the ratings for each of the fifteen criteria in the rubric.

Notes to the teacher about using the *EBC Writing Task Rubric*: Find evidence in the student's essay and planning notes to support ratings for each of the component Literacy Skills and overall essay content criteria listed in the rubric. Based on that evidence, use the developmental scale to rate the grade-level performance demonstrated by the student as:

1—**Emerging:** needs improvement
2—**Developing:** shows progress

3—**Becoming Proficient:** demonstrates skills

4—**Excelling:** exceeds expectations

If there is insufficient evidence to make a confident rating, mark **NE** (no evidence).

Indicate if the student has demonstrated growth in each skill area during the unit by adding a "+" to the rating. Determine a summary evaluation based on the overall pattern of ratings and strength of evidence. This summary evaluation can be computed based on points, or determined by examining the prevalent pattern in the criteria-based ratings.

Evidence of Reading and Thinking

Though the final essay is a written product, it should first and foremost be used as evidence of Literacy Skills associated with close reading and the development of text-based claims: **Attending to Details**, **Interpreting Language**, **Identifying Relationships**, **Recognizing Perspective**, **Making Inferences**, **Forming Claims**, and **Using Evidence**. Students have been working on these skills throughout this and previous Developing Core Literacy Proficiencies units and should be able to demonstrate evidence of them within their essays and the tools they have completed. Specifically, students at this point should show that they can identify key details from the text, note connections and develop inferences from those details, and form an original claim that is well supported by evidence from the text. Students should not be expected to mimic a claim presented by the teacher or suggested by one of the unit's text-specific questions. Rather, they should demonstrate that they can do original thinking based on their own close reading and analysis of the text.

Evidence of Writing

This evidence-based claim essay may be the first piece of more formal writing that students have done in the Developing Core Literacy Proficiencies sequence. If so, it should be viewed as a pre- or formative assessment of students' writing skills—particularly those associated with **Organizing Ideas**, **Using Language**, **Using Conventions**, and correctly citing evidence when **Publishing**. Depending on which of these areas has been a focus for the second round of collaborative review and revision, a teacher might provide more specific evaluation of several targeted criteria but otherwise should use the essay to help each student know which writing skills they might work on in future units.

ASSESSING ACADEMIC HABITS

By the end of the *Evidence-Based Claims* unit, students will have been reflecting on and self-assessing their development of the Academic Habits associated with text-centered discussion and the OE Collaborative Writing Workshop during informal activities at the end of each part of the unit. At the end of the unit, using the **Student Making EBC Academic Habits Checklist**, students can do a more careful self-assessment of their development and demonstration of these habits during the unit—paying particular attention to where and how they have shown (or not shown) evidence of using the habits productively. The teacher can also use this checklist to provide feedback to students. If it is appropriate or desirable to make this feedback evaluative in nature, the **Student Making EBC Academic Habits Checklist** can be used with a three-point system (minus, check, plus) to communicate not only which habits each student has evidenced but also how well.

MAKING EVIDENCE-BASED CLAIMS
UNIT TEXT

Apology
Plato
cir. 360 BCE
Excerpted and translated by Peter Heinegg, 2013

Lexile Measure 980L

In 399 BC, Socrates (an ancient Greek philosopher) was put on trial by his fellow Athenian citizens. The Apology is Plato's account of the speech that Socrates gave in defense of his actions at the trial.

Let me begin by asking what's the charge that has gotten me **slandered** and that gave **Meletus** the   P1
confidence to **indict** me as he has. What did the people who slandered me say? I'll have to read their
sworn statement, as if they were prosecuting me. It runs something like this: "Socrates is a criminal
and meddles in matters where he has no business. He's always poking under the earth and up in the
5   sky. He makes the worse case look better; and he teaches this sort of stuff to others." You yourselves
have seen **Aristophanes** make this claim in his comedy (*The Clouds*), which had a character called
Socrates strolling around sand saying, "I walk on air," and spouting all sorts of other nonsense about
which I know absolutely nothing. And I'm not saying that because I look down on that sort of science,
if someone actually knows it. I just hope Meletus never brings charges against me for that! But,
10 Athenians, I've never gotten mixed up with that sort of thing; and I can call most of you here today as

slandered	Meletus	indict
falsely accused	Ancient Greek Athenian who was the prosecutor in the trial of Socrates	charge with an offense; bring someone to trial
Aristophanes		
Ancient Greek dramatist and comedy playwright		

my witnesses to this. I ask as many of you who've ever heard me speaking in public—and lots of you have—whether anyone ever heard me discussing such things, either briefly or at length.—(*Voices of agreement in the audience.*) You see, and so you'll know what to think of the other accusations most people make against me. None of it's true. And if you've heard anyone say that I set up to be an

15 educator and charge money for it, that's false too.

Perhaps somebody here might reply: "But, Socrates, what's wrong with you? Where do these charges **P2** come from? Surely, none of this talk and publicity about you would have arisen if you behaved like everyone else. So, tell us what your problem is, because we don't want to treat you unfairly." That sounds fair enough to me, and I'll try to show you what has led people to talk about and accuse me.

20 Listen, please. Some of you may think I'm joking, but you can be sure I'll tell you the whole truth.

Athenians, I got this reputation thanks to a certain kind of wisdom I have. What kind of wisdom, you **P3** ask. Just a human sort of wisdom, I'd say; and I may really be wise in this respect. Perhaps the people I just mentioned have some type of superhuman wisdom, or something I can't put into words. That's because I just don't understand it; and anyone who says I do is lying and slandering me.

25 And now please quiet down, Athenians, even if I say something that strikes you as over the top; **P4** because the statement I'm about to make isn't mine. The person I'm referring to deserves to be trusted. The witness I call on with respect to my wisdom—if it be wisdom—is the god of Delphi (Apollo). You know what sort of man **Chaerephon** was, my companion from early on and a friend to your democracy. He took part in the recent **exile** and returned from exile with you. You certainly know

30 what Chaerephon was like, how **impetuous** he was in everything he set his mind to. Well, he went to Delphi and asked the oracle—please don't interrupt—asked the **oracle** if there was anyone wiser than

Chaerephon	exile	impetuous
Ancient Greek Athenian who was the follower and friend of Socrates	banished from your country or place of residence	acting hastily with little thought
oracle		
priest or priestess who could deliver the prophesies of God		

myself. And the priestess of Apollo replied that there was nobody wiser. Chaerephon has since died; but his brother can testify to all of it.

Why do I bring this up? Because I'm going to show you where the accusations against me came from. **P5** When I heard from Chaerephon, I thought, "What ever does the god mean? What is this riddle all about? I'm not aware of being wise, not a lot and not a little. So what does he mean by calling me the wisest? He can't be telling a lie. That just wouldn't be right." So, with great **toil** and trouble I began to look into what he said.

I paid a visit to one of those people with a reputation for being wise. I thought that there, if anywhere, **P6** I could prove the oracle wrong: "Look, this man is wiser than I am; but you said I was the wisest. I checked this man out—there's no need to give his name; he happened to be one of the politicians. And, after conversing with him, I felt that, although many people and especially this gentleman himself took him to be wise, he wasn't. And then I tried to show him that while he thought he was wise, he was no such thing. But that just turned the man and many of those with him against me. As I walked away, I thought to myself, "At least I'm wiser than *this* fellow. Neither of us actually knows what Beauty and Goodness are, but he *thinks* he knows, even though he doesn't; whereas I neither know nor think I know." Then I went to see someone else reputed to be wiser than the first man; but I came away with the same impression, which made me an object of hatred both to him and many others.

Afterwards I went to talk to one person after another, sensing how **odious** I had become to them. I **P7** was sad and fearful; but I felt it was necessary to make the god's work my highest priority. So I had to go consult all those with a reputation for knowing anything, and find out what the oracle's answer meant. And **by the dog**, Athenians, I have to tell you the truth. When I went on my godly quest, I discovered that the people with the finest reputation struck me as just about the most lacking in wisdom, whereas others who were rated lower were actually more sensible.

toil	odious	by the dog
effort; difficulty	disliked; offensive	reference to Anubis, the Egyptian jackal-like god who represented reasoned judgment

55 Now this investigation has made me a lot of bitter enemies, which led in turn to a lot of slander being **P8** spread about me. I've come to be called "the wise man," because the people who listen to me always assume that I know all about the subjects that I show others are ignorant of. But the truth is more likely that the god is the only wise one; and the oracle's response means that human wisdom is worth little or nothing. And it seems that the god isn't talking about Socrates in person; he's just using my

60 name and taking me as an example, as if to say, "O humans, the wisest one among you is somebody like Socrates—he realizes that in fact he's worthless when it comes to wisdom."

That's why I still go around seeking and searching at the god's command for anyone, whether citizen **P9** or foreigner, who I think is wise. And in my task of helping the god, if I find anybody who fails this test, I point out that he's not wise. As a result of this assignment I have no leisure time to devote to any of

65 the city's business worth mentioning or to my own private affairs; and I'm completely poverty-stricken because of my service to the god.

In addition, the young men with the most time on their hands—the ones from the upper classes—like **P10** to come along with me and listen to people being questioned. These fellows often imitate me and try questioning others. I suspect they find a large supply of folks who think they know something when

70 they actually know little or nothing. And then the people who have been grilled by those youngsters get angry, not at themselves, but at me. "This Socrates," they say, "is the most **abominable** man; and he corrupts the youth." When someone asks how I do that, with what sort of actions or teaching, they don't have any answer. They don't know; but rather than appear to be stumped, they repeat the handy old **clichés** about philosophers: "things up in the air" and "things beneath the earth,"

75 "not believing in the gods" and "making the worse case look better." I imagine, they'd rather not tell the truth, that they've been caught pretending to know something when they know nothing. And because there are a lot of them; and they're extremely concerned about their **prestige**, and they line up and speak **plausibly** about me, they've long since filled your ears with violent slander. Meletus

abominable	clichés	prestige
unpleasant; awful	common expression or thought	reputation
plausibly		
speaking with reason		

and **Anytus** and **Lycon** have angrily attacked me: Meletus on behalf of the poets, Anytus on behalf of

80 the craftsmen and the politicians, and Lycon on behalf of the orators. What I've told you, Athenians, is

the truth. I've concealed nothing; I've **evaded** nothing, big or little. And yet I'm pretty sure that what

I've done has made them hate me. That hatred shows that I'm speaking the truth. It's the reason why

they've slandered me, as you'll find out whenever you investigate this, now or later….

Now then, Athenians, I'm going to present my defense, not for my own sake, as one might suppose, P11

85 but for your sake. I mean, so that you don't condemn me and thereby sin against the gift the god gave

you. For if you kill me, you'll find it hard to find someone like me, someone who—if I find someone

like me, someone who—if I can use a **crude** and ridiculous expression— goes after the city the way a

gadfly goes after a big thoroughbred horse that's sluggish because of his great size and that needs to

be **roused** by stinging. It seems to me that the god has inflicted me on the city in some such fashion:

90 I never stop rousing and persuading and **chiding** every one of you, landing on you everywhere all

day long. You're not likely to get another gadfly like me; so take my advice and spare me. You might

get vexed, the way sleepy people do when they're waked up, and you might swat me, if you listen

to Anytus, and easily kill me. Then you'd spend the rest of your lives sleeping, unless the god in his

kindness were to send you someone else like me. I happen to be a gift of the god to the city; and this

95 is how you can tell: Unlike most people, I have neglected all my own interests, and I've put up with

this private neglect for so many years now, while always attending to your business. I've taken each

one of you aside, like a father or elder brother, and encouraged you to have a care for virtue. Now if

I had gotten any profit out of this or been paid for my advice, that would have made sense. But now

you yourselves can see that my accusers, who shamelessly throw every other charge at me, haven't

100 taken their shamelessness so far as to get somebody to testify that I ever charged anyone a fee or

asked for pay. And I think I myself have a witness to the fact that I'm speaking the truth here: my

poverty.

(The jury returns a guilty verdict. Meletus asks for the death penalty.)

Anytus and Lycon	evaded	crude
Athenian prosecutors of Socrates	avoided	unrefined
gadfly	**roused**	**chiding**
a small insect that bites horses	excited, became active	talking with disapproval

There are many reasons, Athenians, why I'm not disturbed by your vote condemning me. It's what
105 I expected. But I was much more surprised by the number of votes for and against. I didn't think I'd
lose by a narrow margin, but by a much wider one. Look, if only thirty votes had gone the other way, I
would have been **acquitted.**

You may think that by arguing this way, as in my remarks about wailing and pleading, I'm just putting
up a bold front. That's not true. No, I'm convinced that I never deliberately harmed anyone; but I
110 can't convince you about this, because we've only had a short time for our discussion. I think that you
would be convinced if you had a law, as other places have, requiring death-penalty cases to be judged
not in a single day but over several days. But, as things stand, it's hard to **quash** these slanders in a
short time. Anyhow, convinced as I am that I never harmed anyone, I'm not about to harm myself by
saying that I deserve anything bad or propose a penalty like that for myself. What do I have to fear?
115 Am I worried about the penalty Meletus proposes, when I've said that I don't know whether death is a
good thing or a bad thing? Should I choose instead something that I'm sure is bad? Should I propose
to be sent to prison? But why should I offer to live in a prison, slaving away for whichever magistrates
have been elected? Should I propose a fine—and be kept in chains until I pay it? But then my old
problem comes up: I don't have any money to pay a fine. Should I propose being sent off into exile?

120 That punishment might suit you. But I would have to be madly in love with life if I failed to realize that
if you, my fellow citizens, can't endure my arguments and discussions—so bothersome and irritating
do you find them that you want to get rid of them for good—then other people wouldn't endure
them either. Not a chance. And what a wonderful life I'd lead if I went off, a man of my age, moving
from one city to another, only to be driven out. Because I'm well aware that wherever I go, the young
125 people will listen to what I say, as they do here. And if I antagonize them, they'll drive me out by
persuading their elders to do so. Or if I don't antagonize them, their fathers and family members will
drive me out on their own.

acquitted	quash	
found not guilty	suppress	

Some might say, "Socrates, why can't you just go away from here, keep quiet and not say anything?"   **P15**
This is the hardest thing to get some of you to understand. Because if I tell you that doing that would
130   mean disobeying the god, and so I can't keep quiet, you'll think I'm putting you on, and you won't
believe me. And if I say that the best thing for everyone is to spend some time every day talking about
virtue and the other things you hear me discussing and examining myself and others about; if I say
that the unexamined life is not worth living, you'll believe me even less. That's how it is, and that's
why it's hard to persuade you.

135   Athenians, you won't save a lot of time by condemning me now. And the people who want to pour   **P16**
abuse on the city will give you a bad name for killing Socrates, "the wise man." That's because the
ones who want to blame you will say that I'm wise, even though I'm not. If you had waited a little
while, you would have gotten your wish without lifting a finger. You see how old I am, how far gone in
life and how close to death. I'm not saying this to all of you, but to those who voted for my death. And
140   I have another thing to tell them. Perhaps you think I've been convicted for lack of arguments that
would have persuaded you—if only I had thought it right to say and do everything possible to win an
acquittal. Far from it. I was convicted not by a lack of arguments, but by my lack of ruthlessness and
shamelessness and willingness to tell you what you most wanted to hear. You would have found it
sweet to hear me groaning and grieving and doing all sorts of things that are beneath me—you know,
145   the kind of things you're used to hearing from others.

But I didn't think then that because I was in danger I ought to do anything unworthy of a free person; **P17**
nor do I now regret defending myself the way I did. I would much rather die for that sort of defense
than to live after giving the other sort. For neither in the courtroom nor on the battlefield should I or
anyone else **scheme** to escape death any which way. It's often clear in battle that you can avoid death
150   by throwing down your weapons and pleading for mercy from those pursuing you. And there are
many other schemes for dodging death amid all sorts of dangers—if you have it in you to do or say
anything at all. It's not hard to escape death; but it's much harder to escape wickedness, because it
runs faster than death. Old and slow as I am, I have been caught by the slower runner, death; while my

scheme		
an underhand plan		

accusers, who are clever and swift, have been caught by the faster runner, wickedness. Now I'm going

155 away, found guilty by you and condemned to death, while they go away—but it's the truth that has found them guilty of evil and injustice. I'll stand by my sentence; and they'll stand by theirs. Perhaps this is how it has to be. I think it's all right.

And now, for those of you who voted to condemn me, I'd like to make a **prophecy**. I am, in fact, at   P18

the place where most people do prophesy: the point when they're about to die. You have killed me;

160 but I have to tell you that you'll be punished immediately after my death. And the punishment will be a lot harsher than the one you gave by putting me to death. You did that, thinking you'd get off the hook, that you wouldn't have to **render** an account of the lives you've led. But I'd say that things will work out very differently for you. There will be *more* people demanding an account of you. You didn't notice it, but I held them back. And they'll be all the harder on you insofar as they'll be younger—

165 which will only make you angrier. Because if you think that by killing people you can avoid being taken to task for not living as you should, then you're wrong. That kind of escape is neither available nor honorable. The easiest and finest escape is not by doing people in, but by making yourself the best person possible. That's my prophecy to those of you who have condemned me. And now I bid you farewell.

170 But for those of you who voted to acquit me, I'd like to say a few words about this event—while the   P19

magistrates are still busy and before I head for where I must die. Stay a bit longer with me. Nothing prevents us from conversing while we can. You're my friends, and I want to show you the meaning of what's just happened to me . . .

Let's think this over in another way. Consider how there's every reason to hope that death is a good   P20

175 thing. To have died means one of two things: either to be in a state of nothingness and to have no awareness of anything; or else, as they say, it's a kind of change and migration of the soul from where it is to somewhere else. If there's no consciousness, as in a sleep where you sleep the whole night through without dreaming, then death would be a marvelous gain. I think that if someone had to

prophesy	render	
a prediction	perform	

pick a night when he or she slept soundest without even dreaming, and then compared it with all the
180 other days and nights of his life, that person would have to say: "How many days and nights of my
life have I lived through more sweetly and pleasantly than this one?" I think that not only an ordinary
individual, but the King of Persia himself could find precious few days or nights like that one. If that's
the nature of death, I'd call it a gain, for then all time turns out to be nothing more than a single night.

But if, on the other hand, death is a departure to another place, and what they say about it is true,   P21
185 and all the dead are there, then what greater good could there be than this? For if a person arrives in
the underworld, having gotten away from these so-called judges, and he or she finds there the real
judges who are said to preside there—**Minos** and **Rhadamanthus** and **Aeacus** and **Triptolemos**
and the demigods who lived righteous lives—that would be a splendid journey. And what would you
give to get together with **Orpheus** and **Musaeus** and **Hesiod** and **Homer**? I'd be willing to die many
190 times over if this is true. And I'd find it marvelous to live there and meet Palamedes or Ajax the son of
Telamon and any other of the ancients who died because of an unjust judgment—I could compare
my troubles with theirs. I think that would be quite pleasurable. Best of all would be to spend my time
examining and questioning the people there as I do here to discover who's wise and who thinks he is
but isn't. What price would you pay, judges, to question Agamemnon, who led the great army against
195 Troy, or Odysseus or Sisiphus and countless others, men and women? Talking to them, and being
with them, examining them—what indescribable happiness. I don't suppose they kill people there for
doing that, since everyone is immortal forever afterwards, as well as being happier in other ways than
people here, if what they say is true.

But now you, my judges, must take a hopeful view of death and reflect on this one truth: nothing evil   P22
200 can befall a good person either in life or in death; and the god will not neglect his or her fate. Thus,

Minos and Rhadamanthus	Aeacus and Triptolemos	Orpheus and Musaeus
in Greek mythology, the judges of the dead in the underworld	in Greek mythology, judges of the dead in the underworld	the earliest and most revered of the Ancient Greek poets and philosophers
Hesiod and Homer		
the earliest and most revered of the Ancient Greek poets and philosophers		

my case didn't play out by chance. It's clear to me that it's better for me to die now and be free from all my troubles. That's why the special sign that I get from heaven never warned me off in this matter. Now I don't hold it against my accusers and the ones who voted to condemn me. Yet in accusing and condemning me, they *did* mean to injure me; and they're to blame for that. But I beg this of them:

205 when my sons grow up, punish them by getting in their face as I've gotten in yours. If you think they care more about money or anything else than they do about virtue; and if they take themselves to be very important when they aren't, rebuke them for, the way I've **rebuked** you, for not paying attention to what they should and for thinking they're important when they're worthless. If you do that, the treatment you give me and my sons will have been fair.

210 But now it's time to leave, time for me to die and for you to live. But which of us is headed to a better   **P23** destiny, nobody knows but God.

rebuked		
expressed disapproval		

         Developing Core Literacy Proficiencies

MAKING
EVIDENCE-BASED CLAIMS

DEVELOPING CORE LITERACY
PROFICIENCIES

GRADE 9

Literacy Toolbox

ODELL
EDUCATION

All materials from the Literacy Toolbox are available as editable and printable PDFs at www.wiley.com/go/coreliteracy. Use the following password: odell2016.

WRITING EVIDENCE-BASED CLAIMS

Writing evidence-based claims is a little different from writing stories or just writing about something. You need to **follow a few steps** as you write.

---

1. ESTABLISH THE CONTEXT

Your readers must know **where your claim is coming from** and **why it's relevant**.

Depending on the scope of your piece and the claim, the context differs. If your whole piece is one claim or if you're introducing the first major claim of your piece, the entire context must be established:

> In Plato's *Apology*, Socrates believes . . .

Purposes of evidence-based writing vary. In some cases, naming the book and author might be enough to establish the relevance of your claim. In other cases, you might want to supply additional information:

> In Plato's *Apology*, Socrates is put on trial for meddling in "matters where he has no business." To begin his defense, Socrates argues that . . .

If your claim is part of a larger piece with multiple claims, then the context might be simpler:

According to Socrates, . . .   *or*   In paragraph 3, Socrates argues . . .

---

2. STATE YOUR CLAIM CLEARLY

How you state your claim is important; it must **precisely and comprehensively express your analysis**. Figuring out how to state claims is a **process**; writers revise them continually as they write their supporting evidence. Here's a claim about Socrates's role in Athenian society from Plato's *Apology*:

> In Plato's *Apology*, Socrates believes that the annoyance he causes helps Athens and they will suffer if they put him to death.

When writing claims it is often useful to describe parts of the claim before providing the supporting evidence. In this case, the writer might want to connect the "annoyance" to Socrates's social role.

> In Plato's *Apology*, Socrates believes that the annoyance he causes helps Athens and they will suffer if they put him to death. Socrates thinks he plays a unique role in Athenian society.

The idea in the second sentence is relevant to the claim and begins connecting the claim to ideas that will be used as evidence.

Remember, you should continually return and rephrase your claim as you write the supporting evidence to make sure you are capturing exactly what you want to say. Writing out the evidence always helps you figure out what you really think.

ODELL
EDUCATION

WRITING EVIDENCE-BASED CLAIMS (Continued)

3. ORGANIZE YOUR SUPPORTING EVIDENCE

Many claims contain multiple parts that require different evidence and should be expressed in separate paragraphs. This claim can be **broken down into two parts:**

The **HELPFUL ANNOYANCE**

and

the **EFFECTS OF SOCRATES'S DEATH ON ATHENS**

Here are two paragraphs that support the claim with evidence organized into these two parts.

A description of the HELPFUL ANNOYANCE:

> Socrates explains that he will argue not for his own sake, but instead for the benefit of the Athenians. He explains that he "goes after the city the way a gadfly goes after a big thoroughbred horse" and that "god has inflicted me on the city" to "never stop rousing and persuading and chiding every one of you, landing on you everywhere all day long" (paragraph 11). Socrates likens himself to a fly that was sent by god to wake up the people from their state of sleep. This suggests that it is the god's will to wrest the Athenian citizens from their ignorance, and Socrates is merely doing what he has been called to do (paragraph 11). In fact, by remaining loyal to this godly calling, Socrates had to put aside his own personal interests and remained impoverished in order to help out the Athenians (paragraph 11). Socrates thus defends himself by proving to the Athenians how much of a help to society he is.

A description of the EFFECTS OF SOCRATES'S DEATH ON ATHENS:

> To strengthen his argument, Socrates tells the Athenians that even though they "might get vexed" and "swat" at him, it is for their own benefit, for without him they will "spend the rest of your lives sleeping" (paragraph 11). Further, he explains that putting him to death will give the Athenians a "bad name" (paragraph 16) and that once he is killed, his accusers' punishment will be much worse than what they gave to Socrates (paragraph 18). Socrates argues that though his condemners have successfully quieted him, they will still be held accountable for their dishonest lives (paragraph 18).

Notice the phrase "to strengthen his argument even further" starting the second paragraph. **Transitional phrases** like this aid the organization by showing how the ideas relate to each other.

4. PARAPHRASE AND QUOTE

Written evidence from texts can be paraphrased or quoted. It's up to the writer to decide which works better for each piece of evidence. Paraphrasing is **putting the author's words into your own.** This works well when the author originally expresses the idea you want to include across many sentences. You might write it more briefly. The fourth line from paragraph 11 paraphrases the evidence from Plato's text. The ideas are his, but the exact way of writing them is not.

> Socrates says that he is not going to make a defense for the benefit of himself, but for the benefit of the Athenians (paragraph 11).

Some evidence is better quoted than paraphrased. If an author has found the quickest way to phrase the idea or the words are especially strong, you might want to use the author's words. The second line from paragraph 11 quotes the text exactly, incorporating important phrases.

> He explains that he "goes after the city the way a gadfly goes after a big thoroughbred horse" and that "god has inflicted me on the city" to "never stop rousing and persuading and chiding every one of you, landing on you everywhere all day long" (paragraph 11).

WRITING EVIDENCE-BASED CLAIMS (Continued)

5. REFERENCE YOUR EVIDENCE

Whether you paraphrase or quote the author's words, you must include **the exact location where the ideas come from**. Direct quotes are written in quotation marks. How writers include the reference can vary depending on the piece and the original text. Here the writer puts the paragraph numbers from the original text in parentheses at the end of the sentence.

ODELL
EDUCATION

MAKING EVIDENCE-BASED CLAIMS FINAL WRITING TASK

In this unit, you have been developing your skills as a reader who can make text-based claims and prove them with evidence from the text.

- Uncovering key clues in the details, words, and central ideas found in the text
- Making connections among details and central ideas in the text
- Using the details, connections, and evidence you find in the text to form a claim—a stated conclusion—about something you have discovered
- Organizing evidence from the text to support your claim and make your case
- Expressing and explaining your claim in writing
- Improving your writing so that others will clearly understand and appreciate your evidence-based claim—and think about the case you have made for it

Your final two writing assignments will provide you with opportunities to use all of these related skills and to demonstrate your proficiency and growth in making evidence-based claims.

FINAL ASSIGNMENTS

1. **Developing and Writing an Evidence-Based Claim:** On your own, you will read the final text in the unit closely and develop an evidence-based claim. To accomplish this, you will do the following:

   a. Read and annotate a section of text on your own and use Guiding Questions and a **Forming Evidence-Based Claims Tool** to develop an initial claim about the text.

   b. Compare the notes and initial claim you make with those made by other students—reframe or revise your claim.

   c. Complete an **Organizing Evidence-Based Claims Tool** to plan subpoints and evidence you will use to explain and support your claim.

   d. Study the **Writing Evidence-Based Claims Handout** to know what a written EBC needs to do and what examples might look like.

   e. Draft a one- to two-paragraph written presentation and explanation of your claim, making sure that you do the things listed on the **Writing Evidence-Based Claims Handout**:

      ⇒ <u>Establish the context</u> by connecting the claim to the text.

      ⇒ <u>State the claim clearly</u> to fully communicate your ideas about the text.

      ⇒ <u>Organize supporting evidence</u> found in the text.

      ⇒ <u>Paraphrase and quote</u> from the text.

      ⇒ <u>Reference the evidence</u> drawn from the text.

   f. Work with other students to review and improve your draft—and to be sure it is the best possible representation of your claim and your skills as a reader and writer. Work on improving at least one of these aspects of your claim:

      ⇒ How <u>clear</u> your presentation and explanation of your claim is

FINAL WRITING TASKS (Continued)

⇒ How <u>defensible</u> (based on the evidence you present) your claim is

⇒ How well you have <u>presented and referenced evidence</u> to support your claim

⇒ How well you have <u>organized</u> your subpoints and evidence into a unified claim

   g. Reflect on how well you have used Literacy Skills in developing this written claim.

2. Writing and Revising a Global Evidence-Based Claims Essay: On your own, you will plan and draft a multiparagraph essay that presents a global claim—one based on connections you have found between details in the text you have read in the unit. To accomplish this, you will do the following:

   a. Review the text you have read, the tools you have completed, and the claims you have formed throughout the unit, looking for connections or comparisons.

   b. Use a **Forming Evidence-Based Claims Tool** to make a new claim that develops a global conclusion about the meaning of the text.

   c. Use an **Organizing Evidence-Based Claims Tool** to plan the subpoints and evidence you will use to explain and support your claim.

   d. Draft a multiparagraph essay that explains, develops, and supports your global claim—keeping in mind these three criteria for this final writing assignment. Your essay should do the following:

      ⇒ Demonstrate an accurate reading and insightful analysis of the text you have read in the unit.

      ⇒ Develop a supported claim that is clearly connected to the content of the text.

      ⇒ Successfully accomplish the five key elements of a written EBC (**Writing Evidence-Based Claims Handout**).

   e. Use a collaborative process with other students to review and improve your draft in two key areas: (1) its content (quality of the claim and its evidence) and (2) its organization and expression (unity of the discussion and clarity of the writing).

   f. Reflect on how well you have used Literacy Skills in developing this final explanation.

SKILLS TO BE DEMONSTRATED

As you become a text expert and write your evidence-based claims, think about demonstrating the Literacy Skills listed in the following to the best of your ability. Your teacher will evaluate your work and determine your grade based on how well you do.

Read

- **Attend to Details:** Identify words, details, or quotations that you think are important to understanding the text
- **Interpret Language:** Understand how words are used to express ideas and perspectives
- **Identify Relationships:** Notice important connections among details, ideas, or texts
- **Recognize Perspective:** Identify and explain the author's view of the unit's topic

ODELL
EDUCATION

FINAL WRITING TASKS (Continued)

Think

- **Make Inferences:** Draw sound conclusions from reading and examining the text closely
- **Form a Claim:** State a meaningful conclusion that is well-supported by evidence from the text
- **Use Evidence:** Use well-chosen details from the texts to support your explanation; accurately paraphrase or quote what the authors say in the text

Write

- **Present Details:** Insert details and quotations effectively into your essay
- **Organize Ideas:** Organize your claim, supporting ideas, and evidence in a logical order
- **Use Language:** Write clearly so others can understand your claim and supporting ideas
- **Use Conventions:** Correctly use sentence elements, punctuation, and spelling to produce clear writing
- **Publish:** Correctly use, format, and cite textual evidence to support your claim

HABITS TO BE DEVELOPED

Your teacher may also want you to reflect on how well you have used and developed the following habits of text-centered discussion when you worked with others to understand the text and improve your writing:

- **Engage Actively:** Focus your attention on the assigned tasks when working individually and with others
- **Collaborate:** Work respectfully and productively to help your discussion or review group be successful
- **Communicate Clearly:** Present your ideas and supporting evidence so others can understand them
- **Listen:** Pay attention to ideas from others and take time to think about them
- **Understand Purpose and Process:** Understand why and how a text-centered discussion or peer writing review should be accomplished
- **Revise:** Rethink your ideas and refine your writing based on feedback from others
- **Remain Open:** Modify and further justify ideas in response to thinking from others.

NOTE

These skills and habits are also listed on the **Student Making EBC Literacy Skills** and **Academic Habits Checklists**, which you can use to assess your work and the work of other students.

FORMING EVIDENCE-BASED CLAIMS TOOL

Name _ _ _ _ _ _ _ _ _ _ _ _ _ **Text** _ _ _ _ _ _ _ _ _ _ _ _ _

A question I have about the text:

FINDING DETAILS	**Detail 1 (Ref.:)**	**Detail 2 (Ref.:)**	**Detail 3 (Ref.:**
I find interesting details that are related and that stand out to me from reading the text closely.			

CONNECTING THE DETAILS	**What I think about detail 1:**	**What I think about detail 2:**	**What I think about detail 3:**
I reread and think about the details, and <u>explain</u> the connections I find among them.			
	How I connect the details:		

MAKING A CLAIM	**My claim about the text:**
I state a conclusion that I have come to and can support with <u>evidence</u> from the text after reading and thinking about it closely.	

ODELL
EDUCATION

SUPPORTING EVIDENCE-BASED CLAIMS TOOL

Name _ _ _ _ _ _ _ _ _ _ _ _ _ _ **Text** _ _ _ _ _ _ _ _ _ _ _ _ _ _ _ _ _ _

CLAIM:

Supporting Evidence	Supporting Evidence

(Reference:) (Reference:)

(Reference:)

CLAIM:

Supporting Evidence	Supporting Evidence

(Reference:) (Reference:)

(Reference:)

ODELL EDUCATION

ORGANIZING EVIDENCE-BASED CLAIMS TOOL (2 POINTS)

Name _ _ _ _ _ _ _ _ _ _ _ _ _ _   Text _ _ _ _ _ _ _ _ _ _ _ _ _ _ _ _

CLAIM:

Point 1

A   Supporting Evidence

(Reference:)

B   Supporting Evidence

(Reference:)

C   Supporting Evidence

(Reference:)

D   Supporting Evidence

(Reference:)

Point 2

A   Supporting Evidence

(Reference:)

B   Supporting Evidence

(Reference:)

C   Supporting Evidence

(Reference:)

D   Supporting Evidence

(Reference:)

ODELL
EDUCATION

ORGANIZING EVIDENCE-BASED CLAIMS TOOL (3 POINTS)

Name _ _ _ _ _ _ _ _ _ _ _ _ _ _ _ _ Text _ _ _ _ _ _ _ _ _ _ _ _ _ _ _ _ _ _

CLAIM:

Point 1

Point 2

Point 3

	Supporting Evidence	Supporting Evidence	Supporting Evidence
A			
	(Reference:)	(Reference:)	(Reference:)
B			
	(Reference:)	(Reference:)	(Reference:)
C			
	(Reference:)	(Reference:)	(Reference:)

MODEL ORGANIZING EVIDENCE-BASED CLAIMS TOOL

Name Model   **Text** Plato's "Apology"

CLAIM:	Socrates believes that the annoyance he causes helps the Athenians and they will suffer if they put him to death.		

Point 1 The annoyance Socrates causes helps Athens.

A **Supporting Evidence**	B **Supporting Evidence**
"For if you kill me, you'll find it hard to find someone like me"	"goes after the city the way a gadfly goes after a big thoroughbred horse that's sluggish because of his great size and that needs to be roused by stinging."
(**Reference:** paragraph 11)	(**Reference:** paragraph 11)

C **Supporting Evidence**	D **Supporting Evidence**
"You're not likely to get another gadfly like me; so take my advice and spare me."	"I happen to be a gift of the god to the city"
(**Reference:** paragraph 11)	(**Reference:** paragraph 11)

Point 2 Athens will suffer if they put Socrates to death.

A **Supporting Evidence**	B **Supporting Evidence**
"Then you'd spend the rest of your lives sleeping"	"And the people who want to pour abuse on the city will give you a bad name for killing Socrates, 'the wise man.'"
(**Reference:** paragraph 11)	(**Reference:** paragraph 16)

C **Supporting Evidence**	D **Supporting Evidence**
"You have killed me; but I have to tell you that you'll be punished immediately after my death. And the punishment will be a lot harsher than the one you gave by putting me to death."	"Because if you think that by killing people you can avoid being taken to task for not living as you should, then you're wrong. That kind of escape is neither available nor honorable. The easiest and finest escape is not by doing people in, but by making yourself the best person possible."
(**Reference:** paragraph 18)	(**Reference:** paragraph 18)

ODELL EDUCATION

QUESTIONING PATH TOOL

Name: _____ **Text:** _____

APPROACHING: *I determine my reading purposes and take note of key information about the text. I identify the LIPS domain(s) that will guide my initial reading.*	Purpose: Key information: LIPS domain(s):

QUESTIONING: *I use Guiding Questions to help me investigate the text (from the **Guiding Questions Handout**).*

1.

2.

ANALYZING: *I question further to connect and analyze the details I find (from the **Guiding Questions Handout**).*

1.

2.

DEEPENING: *I consider the questions of others.*

1.

2.

3.

EXTENDING: *I pose my own questions.*

1.

2.

PART 3: STUDENT ACADEMIC HABITS CHECKLIST

HABITS DEVELOPED	DESCRIPTORS	EVIDENCE OF USING THE HABIT	THINGS TO IMPROVE ON
COLLABORATING	• Pays attention to and respects other participants • Works productively with others to complete the task and enrich the discussion		
COMMUNICATING CLEARLY	• Uses clear language to communicate ideas and claims • Uses relevant details to explain and support thinking		
LISTENING	• Pays attention to new information and ideas from others • Considers others' ideas thoughtfully		

ODELL
EDUCATION

PART 4: STUDENT ACADEMIC HABITS CHECKLIST

HABITS DEVELOPED	DESCRIPTORS	EVIDENCE OF USING THE HABIT	THINGS TO IMPROVE ON
UNDERSTANDING PURPOSE AND PROCESS	• Understands and uses the collaborative writing workshop process • Uses Literacy Skills criteria to frame questions, responses, and feedback		
LISTENING	• Pays attention to new information and ideas from others • Considers others' ideas thoughtfully		
REMAINING OPEN	• Avoids explanations or justifications for what they as writers have tried to do • Frames text-based questions to probe their readers' observations		
REVISING	• Uses criteria to rethink, refine, or revise work • Uses observations from peers to inform improvement		

MAKING EVIDENCE-BASED CLAIMS
TARGETED LITERACY SKILLS

TARGETED SKILLS	DESCRIPTORS
ATTENDING TO DETAILS	Identifies relevant and important textual details, words, and ideas
IDENTIFYING RELATIONSHIPS	Identifies important connections among key details and ideas within and across texts
MAKING INFERENCES	Demonstrates comprehension by using connections among details to make logical deductions about a text
RECOGNIZING PERSPECTIVE	Uses textual details to recognize an author's or narrator's relationship to and perspective on a text's topic
FORMING CLAIMS	Develops meaningful and defensible claims that clearly state valid, evidence-based analysis
USING EVIDENCE	Supports all aspects of claims with sufficient textual evidence, using accurate quotations, paraphrases, and references
PRESENTING DETAILS	Describes and explains important details that effectively develop a narrative, explanation, or argument
ORGANIZING IDEAS	Sequences sentences and paragraphs to establish coherent, logical, and unified narratives, explanations, and arguments
PUBLISHING	Uses effective formatting and citations to present ideas for specific audiences and purposes
USING LANGUAGE	Selects and combines words that precisely communicate ideas, generate appropriate tone, and evoke intended responses from an audience

ODELL
EDUCATION

MAKING EVIDENCE-BASED CLAIMS
ACADEMIC HABITS DEVELOPED

HABITS DEVELOPED	DESCRIPTORS
ENGAGING ACTIVELY	Actively focuses attention on independent and collaborative tasks
COLLABORATING	Pays attention to, respects, and works productively in various roles with all other participants
COMMUNICATING CLEARLY	Uses appropriate language and relevant textual details to clearly present ideas and claims
LISTENING	Pays attention to, acknowledges, and considers thoughtfully new information and ideas from others
REVISING	Rethinks and refines work based on teacher-, peer-, and self-review processes
UNDERSTANDING PURPOSE AND PROCESS	Understands the purpose and uses the process and criteria that guide tasks
REMAINING OPEN	Modifies and further justifies ideas in response to thinking from others

MAKING EVIDENCE-BASED CLAIMS LITERACY SKILLS RUBRIC

Name _ _ _ _ _ _ _ _ _ _ _ _ _ **Text** _ _ _ _ _ _ _ _ _ _ _ _ _ _ _ _

NE: Not enough evidence to make a rating

1—**Emerging:** needs improvement

2—**Developing:** shows progress

3—**Becoming Proficient:** demonstrates skills

4—**Excelling:** exceeds expectations

+—**Growth:** evidence of growth within the unit or task

I. READING SKILLS CRITERIA	NE	1	2	3	4	+
1. **Attends to Details:** Identifies relevant and important textual details, words, and ideas						
2. **Interprets Language:** Identifies how words and phrases convey meaning and represent the author's perspective						
3. **Identifies Relationships:** Identifies important connections among key details and ideas within and across texts						
4. **Recognizes Perspective:** Uses textual details to recognize the author's relationship to and perspective on a text's topic						
II. THINKING SKILLS CRITERIA	NE	1	2	3	4	+
1. **Makes Inferences:** Demonstrates comprehension by using connections among details to make logical deductions about the text(s)						
2. **Forms Claims:** Develops meaningful and defensible claims that clearly state valid, evidence-based analysis						
3. **Uses Evidence:** Supports all aspects of the claim with sufficient textual evidence, using accurate quotations, paraphrases, and references						
III. WRITING SKILLS CRITERIA	NE	1	2	3	4	+
1. **Presents Details:** Describes and explains important details that effectively develop an explanation or argument for the claim						
2. **Organizes Ideas:** Sequences sentences and paragraphs to establish a coherent, logical, and unified explanation or argument						
3. **Uses Language:** Selects and combines words that precisely communicate the claim and its supporting ideas						
4. **Uses Conventions:** Uses effective sentence structure, grammar, punctuation, and spelling to communicate ideas						
5. **Publishes:** Uses effective formatting and citations when integrating textual evidence to support the claim						

ODELL
EDUCATION

MAKING EBC SKILLS AND HABITS RUBRIC (Continued)

IV. ESSAY CONTENT CRITERIA	NE	1	2	3	4	
1. Demonstrates an accurate reading and insightful analysis of the text(s)						
2. Develops a supported claim that is clearly connected to the content of the text(s)						
3. Accomplishes the five key elements of an evidence-based claims essay (See *Writing EBC Handout*.)						
SUMMARY EVALUATION		1	2	3	4	

Comments:

1. Explanation of ratings—**evidence** found (or not found) in the work:

2. Strengths and **areas of growth** observed in the work:

3. Areas for improvement in future work:

STUDENT MAKING EVIDENCE-BASED CLAIMS LITERACY SKILLS CHECKLIST

	LITERACY SKILLS USED IN THIS UNIT	✓	EVIDENCE Demonstrating the SKILLS
READING	1. **Attending to Details:** Identifies words, details, or quotations that are important to understanding the text		
READING	2. **Interpreting Language:** Understands how words are used to express ideas and perspectives		
READING	3. **Identifying Relationships:** Notices important connections among details, ideas, or texts		
READING	4. **Recognizing Perspective:** Identifies and explains the author's view of the text's topic		
THINKING	5. **Making Inferences:** Draws sound conclusions from reading and examining the text closely		
THINKING	6. **Forming Claims:** States a meaningful conclusion that is well supported by evidence from the text		
THINKING	7. **Using Evidence:** Uses well-chosen details from the text to explain and support claims; accurately paraphrases or quotes		
WRITING	8. **Presenting Details:** Inserts details and quotations effectively into written or spoken explanations		
WRITING	9. **Organizing Ideas:** Organizes claims, supporting ideas, and evidence in a logical order		
WRITING	10. **Using Language:** Writes and speaks clearly so others can understand claims and ideas		
WRITING	11. **Using Conventions:** Correctly uses sentence elements, punctuation, and spelling to produce clear writing		
WRITING	12. **Publishing:** Correctly uses, formats, and cites textual evidence to support claims		
	General comments:		

ODELL EDUCATION

STUDENT MAKING EVIDENCE-BASED CLAIMS ACADEMIC HABITS CHECKLIST

Academic Habits Used in This Unit	✓	EVIDENCE Demonstrating the HABITS
1. **Engaging Actively:** Focuses attention on the task when working individually and with others		
2. **Collaborating:** Works respectfully and productively to help a group be successful		
3. **Communicating Clearly:** Presents ideas and supporting evidence so others can understand them		
4. **Listening:** Pays attention to ideas from others and takes time to think about them		
5. **Understanding Purpose and Process:** Understands why and how a task should be accomplished		
6. **Revising:** Rethinks ideas and refines work based on feedback from others		
7. **Remaining Open:** Modifies and further justifies ideas in response to thinking from others		
General comments:		

MAKING EVIDENCE-BASED CLAIMS
MEDIA SUPPORTS

Because of the ever-changing nature of website addresses, specific links are not provided. Teachers and students can locate these sources through web searches using the information provided.

TITLE	DESCRIPTION	PUBLISHER	FORMAT
Apology by Plato	Audiobook version of Plato's *Apology* read by Bob Neufeld. Please note that, because the OE version is an original translation by Peter Heinegg, the wording will not be an exact copy of this audio version. The OE version starts at 5:48 of the video.	The 16th Cavern	Audiobook via YouTube
Apology	Complete text version of Plato's *Apology* translated by Benjamin Jowett. Please note that, because the OE version is an original translation by Peter Heinegg, the wording will not be an exact copy of this translation.	Project Guttenberg	Ebook
"Plato's *Apology*"	A modern-day reenactment of Socrates's trial and speech. Although this reenactment does not use the OE translation, it is interesting to see it read on a modern set and conveys one interpretation of Socrates's tone during his speech. The OE version starts at 1:32 of the video.	Doug Blackburn	YouTube video
Apologia de Socrates	Spanish translation of *Apology* by Plato	Biblioteca Virtual Universal	Online PDF
"2. Socratic Citizenship: Plato's *Apology*"	A lecture from Yale University on the political and philosophical contexts of Socrates' trial. Although this is an advanced analysis of Plato's *Apology*, students can benefit from watching how an expert discusses an important text in Western civilization. Also, this video can serve as a jumping-off point if the class pursues a topic from or related to the *Apology*.	YaleCourses	YouTube video

ODELL
EDUCATION

UNIT 3

MAKING
EVIDENCE-BASED
CLAIMS ABOUT LITERARY
TECHNIQUE

DEVELOPING CORE LITERACY
PROFICIENCIES

GRADE 9

**"Macomber laughed, a very
natural hearty laugh."**

ODELL
EDUCATION

UNIT OVERVIEW

Making evidence-based claims about texts is a Core Literacy and Critical Thinking Proficiency that lies at the heart of the CCSS. The proficiency consists of two component abilities. The first is the ability to extract detailed information from texts and grasp how it is conveyed. Education and personal growth require real exposure to new information from a variety of media. Instruction should push students beyond general understanding of texts into deep engagement with textual content and authorial craft.

The second component of the proficiency is the ability to make valid claims about the new information thus gleaned. This involves developing the capacity to analyze texts, connecting information in literal, inferential, and sometimes novel ways. Instruction should lead students to do more than simply restate the information they take in through close reading. Students should come to see themselves as creators of meaning as they engage with texts.

It is essential that students understand the importance and purpose of making evidence-based claims, which are at the center of many fields of study and productive civic life. Education should help students become invested in developing their ability to explore the meaning of texts. Part of instruction should focus on teaching students how to understand and talk about their skills.

It is also important that students view claims as their own. They should see their interaction with texts as a personal investment in their learning. They are not simply reading texts to report information expected by their teachers; instead, they should approach texts with their own authority and the confidence to support their analysis.

This unit extends students' abilities to make evidence-based claims into the realm of literary analysis. The unit explicitly focuses on teaching students to attend to the ways authors use literary techniques to shape textual meaning and reader experience.

TOPIC AND TEXTS

This unit develops students' abilities to make evidence-based claims about literary technique through activities based on a close reading of Ernest Hemingway's short story, "The Short Happy Life of Francis Macomber." The full text of the short story is not provided in the materials. The instructional activities and materials can be used with any unabridged publication of the short story that teachers choose to use.

LEARNING PROGRESSION

The unit activities are organized into five parts, each associated with sequential, chunked portions of text. The parts build on each other and can each span a range of instructional time depending on scheduling and student ability.

The sequence of learning activities supports the progressive development of the critical reading and thinking skills involved in making evidence-based claims. Parts 1 and 2 focus on forming and supporting evidence-based claims as readers. Part 3 focuses on preparing to express written evidence-based claims by organizing evidence and thinking. Parts 4 and 5 focus on communicating evidence-based claims in paragraphs and essays. This organization is designed to strengthen the precision of instruction and assessment as well as to give teachers flexibility in their use of the unit.

Independent reading activities are given at the end of Parts 1 through 3. If scheduling and student ability make independent reading outside of class a difficulty, these reading assignments are also included in the subsequent parts as in-class activities.

SEQUENCING LEARNING OVER TIME AND ACROSS GRADE LEVELS

The learning sequence for this unit and the instructional notes within it have been developed on the assumption that students may be learning the process of *Making Evidence-Based Claims* for the first time. Thus, terms are introduced and explained, graphic tools are overviewed and modeled, and lessons move relatively carefully from teacher modeling to guided practice to independent application. The Literacy Skills that are targeted and the Academic Habits that are developed are assumed to be in early stages of development for many students, and thus extensive scaffolding is provided.

However, students may come to this unit in the Developing Core Literacy Proficiencies Program having developed their Literacy Skills, Academic Habits, and Core Literacy Proficiencies in other contexts. They may have progressed through earlier units in the Developing Core Literacy Proficiencies sequence and become very familiar with tools, handouts, terminology, skills, and habits addressed in this unit. They may also have experienced the *Making Evidence-Based Claims* instructional sequence in a previous unit, grade, or school.

For this reason, teachers should use their professional judgment to plan their instruction for this unit considering not only *what* they are teaching (making claims and the curriculum designed to develop students' skills) but also *whom* they are teaching (their students' backgrounds, previous experiences, and readiness levels). Before beginning the unit, teachers are encouraged to determine what students have previously experienced, learned, or produced.

If students have more advanced skills or extensive previous experience in making claims, instruction can move more rapidly through many sections of this unit, concentrating more on textual analysis to deepen students' understanding.

OUTLINE

PART 1: UNDERSTANDING EVIDENCE-BASED CLAIMS

- Students learn the importance and elements of making evidence-based claims through a close reading of a section of the text.

PART 2: MAKING EVIDENCE-BASED CLAIMS

- Students develop the ability to make evidence-based claims through a close reading of a second section of text.

PART 3: ORGANIZING EVIDENCE-BASED CLAIMS

- Students learn to develop and explain evidence-based claims through the selection and organization of supporting evidence.

PART 4: WRITING EVIDENCE-BASED CLAIMS

- Students develop the ability to communicate text-based claims and their supporting evidence through writing.

PART 5: DEVELOPING EVIDENCE-BASED WRITING

- Students develop the ability to express global evidence-based claims in writing through a rereading of the texts in the unit and a review of their previous work.

INTRODUCTION TO THE MAKING EVIDENCE-BASED CLAIMS LITERACY TOOLBOX

In the *Making Evidence-Based Claims* (EBC) unit, students develop a foundational proficiency for reading and analyzing complex texts. To build this proficiency, students learn to select, interpret, and connect significant textual details; articulate their meaning; and form conclusions derived from reading a text closely.

To support the development of this proficiency, the unit uses a series of handouts and tools from the Literacy Toolbox (found in the **Making Evidence-Based Claims Literacy Toolbox**). Students use the **Forming Evidence-Based Claims Tool** to guide their selection of key details, make connections among them, and form a claim that arises from the text. The **Supporting Evidence-Based Claims Tool** is used to strengthen students' ability to find and analyze evidence that supports claims. The **Organizing Evidence-Based Claims Tool** aids students in organizing their thinking and supporting evidence in preparation for explaining, defending, and communicating their claims. As they continue to develop and apply the proficiency of reading closely, students also use the handouts and tools introduced in the *Reading Closely* unit.

The **Making EBC Literacy Toolbox** also houses detailed tables of targeted Literacy Skills and Academic Habits developed in the unit as well as the *Making EBC Literacy Skills Rubric* and *Student Making EBC Literacy Skills and Academic Habits Checklists*.

If students have previously completed the *Making Evidence-Based Claims* unit, they should already be familiar with these tools and handouts. As they gain independence in practicing the proficiency of reading texts to make evidence-based claims and internalize the concepts and processes detailed in the unit, students might rely less and less on the tools and handouts. Depending on students' abilities and familiarity with the **Making EBC Literacy Toolbox**, teachers might encourage students to use these materials when they encounter difficulties in understanding sections of texts, require assistance in communicating or piecing together analysis, or need to organize their thoughts in preparation for a writing assignment. Otherwise, students can proceed through the readings, annotating, taking notes, and making claims in using their own, developing processes. If students are ready to move through the unit without these scaffolds, it is still important that teachers continually verify that they are capturing, analyzing, and communicating salient ideas from the readings.

NOTE

All tools and handouts, including model *Questioning Path Tools*, and *Student Checklists* can also be found in the Student Edition.

LITERACY SKILLS AND ACADEMIC HABITS

TARGETED LITERACY SKILLS

To frame instruction and assessment in the *Making Evidence-Based Claims* unit (and all Developing Core Literacy Proficiencies units), Odell Education has developed a criterion-based framework of component Literacy Skills. The *Making Evidence-Based Claims Literacy Skills Rubric* (in the **Making EBC Literacy Toolbox**) lists each Literacy Skill with a descriptor of what students should be able to do when they attain proficiency in that skill.

In this unit, students will be learning about, practicing, developing, and demonstrating skills necessary for **Forming Claims** and **Using Evidence** to support them while continuing to work on foundational skills associated with close reading (**Questioning, Attending to Details, Interpreting Language**, and **Identifying Relationships**). The following Literacy Skills are targeted throughout the unit:

TARGETED LITERACY SKILLS	DESCRIPTORS
ATTENDING TO DETAILS	Identifies relevant and important textual details, words, and ideas
IDENTIFYING RELATIONSHIPS	Identifies important connections among key details and ideas within and across texts
MAKING INFERENCES	Demonstrates comprehension by using connections among details to make logical deductions about a text
RECOGNIZING PERSPECTIVE	Uses textual details to recognize an author's or narrator's relationship to and perspective on a text's topic

TARGETED LITERACY SKILLS	DESCRIPTORS
FORMING CLAIMS	Develops meaningful and defensible claims that clearly state valid, evidence-based analysis
USING EVIDENCE	Supports all aspects of claims with sufficient textual evidence, using accurate quotations, paraphrases, and references
PRESENTING DETAILS	Describes and explains important details that effectively develop a narrative, explanation, or argument
ORGANIZING IDEAS	Sequences sentences and paragraphs to establish coherent, logical, and unified narratives, explanations, and arguments
USING LANGUAGE	Selects and combines words that precisely communicate ideas, generate appropriate tone, and evoke intended responses from an audience
PUBLISHING	Uses effective formatting and citations to present ideas for specific audiences and purposes

NOTE

Student language versions of these descriptors can be found in the *Student Making EBC Literacy Skills Checklist* in the **Making EBC Literacy Toolbox** and Student Edition.

APPLIED LITERACY SKILLS

In addition to these targeted skills, the unit provides several opportunities for students to apply and develop the following Literacy Skills:

- Deciphering Words
- Comprehending Syntax
- Interpreting Language
- Summarizing
- Questioning
- Using Conventions

ACADEMIC HABITS

In conjunction with developing Literacy Skills to meet CCSS expectations, students can also develop Academic Habits associated with being a literate person—working from a framework of key habits developed by Odell Education (the table is available in the **Making EBC Literacy Toolbox**). In this unit, students will have opportunities to further develop habits associated with productive text-centered discussion and will also begin working on habits applied when generating and revising their writing. Although the teacher may choose to teach and assess a range of habits during any activity, some instructional sequences cater to specific habits that have been identified. The descriptors for these habits do not need to be introduced to students immediately; however, if students are ready to think about them, student versions of the descriptors can be found in the *Student Making EBC Academic Habits Checklist* in the **Making EBC Literacy Toolbox.**

HABITS DEVELOPED	DESCRIPTORS
ENGAGING ACTIVELY	Actively focuses attention on independent and collaborative tasks
COLLABORATING	Pays attention to, respects, and works productively in various roles with all other participants
COMMUNICATING CLEARLY	Uses appropriate language and relevant textual details to clearly present ideas and claims
LISTENING	Pays attention to, acknowledges, and considers thoughtfully new information and ideas from others
REVISING	Rethinks and refines work based on teacher-, peer-, and self-review processes
UNDERSTANDING PURPOSE AND PROCESS	Understands the purpose and uses the process and criteria that guide tasks
REMAINING OPEN	Modifies and further justifies ideas in response to thinking from others

> **NOTE**
>
> Student language versions of these descriptors can be found in the *Student EBC Academic Habits Checklist* in the **Making EBC Literacy Toolbox** and Student Edition.

☰ COMMON CORE STATE STANDARDS ☰ ALIGNMENT

The primary CCSS alignment of the unit instruction is with **CCSS.ELA-LITERACY.RL.1** and **CCSS.ELA-LITERACY.W.9b** (*cite evidence to support analysis of explicit and inferential textual meaning*).

The evidence-based analysis of the text, including the text-dependent questions and the focus of the claims, address **CCSS.ELA-LITERACY.RL.3** (*analyze how characters are developed over the course of a text*), **CCSS.ELA-LITERACY.RL.5** (*analyze the effects an author's use of structure have on a text*), and **CCSS.ELA-LITERACY.RL.6** (*analyze an author's choices concerning the development of characters, structure, and point of view over the course of a text*).

The numerous paired activities and structured class discussions develop **CCSS.ELA-LITERACY.SL.1** (*engage effectively in a range of collaborative discussions building on others' ideas and expressing their own clearly*).

The evidence-based writing pieces address **CCSS.ELA-LITERACY.W.4** (*produce clear and coherent writing in which the development, organization, and style are appropriate to task, purpose, and audience*).

PART 1

UNDERSTANDING EVIDENCE-BASED CLAIMS

"I'll have a gimlet too. I need something."

OBJECTIVE:	Students learn the importance and elements of making evidence-based claims through a close reading of part of the text.

ESTIMATED TIME: 2–3 days

MATERIALS:
- *Guiding Questions Handout*
- *Reading Closely Graphic*
- *Questioning Path Tools*

- *Attending to Details Handout*
- *Forming EBC Tool*
- *Supporting EBC Tool*

OPTIONAL:
- *Approaching Texts Tool*

- *Analyzing Details Tool*

LITERACY SKILLS

TARGETED SKILLS	DESCRIPTORS
ATTENDING TO DETAILS	Identifies relevant and important textual details, words, and ideas
INTERPRETING LANGUAGE	Identifies how words and phrases convey meaning and represent an author's or narrator's perspective
IDENTIFYING RELATIONSHIPS	Identifies important connections among key details and ideas within and across texts

ACADEMIC HABITS

HABIT DEVELOPED	DESCRIPTOR
ENGAGING ACTIVELY	Actively focuses attention on independent and collaborative tasks

ALIGNMENT TO CCSS

TARGETED STANDARD:

CCSS.ELA-LITERACY.RL.9-10.1: Cite strong and thorough textual evidence to support analysis of what the text says explicitly as well as inferences drawn from the text.

SUPPORTING STANDARDS:

CCSS.ELA-LITERACY.RL.9-10.3: Analyze how complex characters (e.g., those with multiple or conflicting motivations) develop over the course of a text, interact with other characters, and advance the plot or develop the theme.

CCSS.ELA-LITERACY.RL.9-10.5: Analyze how an author's choices concerning how to structure a text, order events within it (e.g., parallel plots), and manipulate time (e.g., pacing, flashbacks) create such affects as mystery, tension, or surprise.

CCSS.ELA-LITERACY.SL.9-10.1: Initiate and participate effectively in a range of collaborative discussions (one-on-one, in groups, and teacher-led) with diverse partners on *grades 9–10 topics, texts, and issues,* building on others' ideas and expressing their own clearly and persuasively.

ACTIVITIES

1. INTRODUCTION TO UNIT
The teacher presents the purpose of the unit and explains the proficiency of making evidence-based claims about literary technique.

2. INDEPENDENT READING
Students independently read the first sentence of the text with a Guiding Question to help focus their reading.

3. READ ALOUD AND CLASS DISCUSSION
Students follow along as they listen to a section of text being read aloud, and the teacher leads a discussion guided by a series of text-specific questions.

4. MODEL THE FORMING OF EBCs
The teacher models a critical reading and thinking process for forming evidence-based claims about texts.

ACTIVITY 1: INTRODUCTION TO UNIT

The teacher presents the purpose of the unit and explains the proficiency of making evidence-based claims about literary technique.

INSTRUCTIONAL NOTES

This unit extends students' abilities to make evidence-based claims into the realm of literary analysis. The unit explicitly focuses on teaching students to attend to the ways authors use literary techniques to shape textual meaning and reader experience. Unit instruction follows that of the previous *Making Evidence-Based Claims* unit: students are introduced to the instructional concepts, read text closely, practice forming claims, work on organizing claims, and eventually develop their claims in writing. It is recommended that teachers sequence this unit after students work on the general concept of making evidence-based claims in the previous unit. If teachers choose, instead, to substitute this unit for the general *Making Evidence-Based Claims* unit, they should incorporate the discussion of evidence-based claims from Part 1, Activity 1 of that unit into this introductory class discussion.

Introduce students to the central focus of the unit: making evidence-based claims about literary works and the close reading skills of literary analysis. This is the domain of scholars and critics but also that of active and skillful readers who intuitively sense and appreciate the multidimensional aspects of writing craft when they read a poem, short story, novel, play, or essay. Let students know that in this unit they will be focusing and applying their skills of reading closely for textual details and making evidence-based claims in the realm of literary analysis.

Use an example text read recently by most students to suggest what it means to read a literary work for meaning while also attending to its craft. Discuss with students that when reading and analyzing a literary work (as with any text), a reader attends to details that are related to comprehending the text, finding meaning, and understanding the author's perspective. But a skillful reader of a literary work also pays attention to what authors do—the language, elements, devices, and techniques they use, and the choices they make that influence a reader's experience with and understanding of the literary work—the craft of writing. Explain that literary scholars classify, name, and discuss the elements, devices, and techniques characteristic of a literary genre to help us analyze and think about texts. Students should already be familiar with some of these techniques (i.e., plot, characterization, imagery, rhyme). Throughout this unit, they will discuss specific techniques, develop their ability to identify and analyze the use of those techniques, and make evidence-based claims about the effects of those techniques on textual meaning.

It is important for students to come to understand that in a great literary work, the many aspects of its craft are interdependent, creating what Cleanth Brooks and Robert Penn Warren have described as the "organic unity" of a work, in which all aspects "are significant and have some bearing on the total significance" of the work (*The Scope of Fiction*, 1960). However, students will also need to practice and develop the skills of examining specific aspects of a work and the relationship of those aspects to other aspects—and to the overall meaning of the work. Thus, this unit will focus on specific elements, devices, or techniques that are particularly relevant, and students will initially make claims related to those targeted aspects of craft.

The text notes and text-dependent questions are designed to emphasize these targeted techniques, but teachers and students are also encouraged to extend beyond or outside of the unit's models into the study of other literary techniques, themes, and meanings that transcend what is suggested here. No matter what approach is emphasized during reading, discussion, and analysis, the close-reading process should be guided by these broad questions:

1. What specific aspect(s) of the author's craft am I attending to? (Through what lens(es) will I focus my reading?)

2. What choices do I notice the author making, and what techniques do I see the author using? What textual details do I find as evidence of those choices and techniques?

3. How do the author's choices and techniques influence my reading of the work and the meaning that emerges for me? How can I ground my claims about meaning in specific textual evidence?

In this unit, reading, discussion, and literary analysis will focus on the short story genre, using Ernest Hemingway's "The Short Happy Life of Francis Macomber." Students will read this text closely, search for evidence of techniques used by Hemingway, and develop claims about specific passages, eventually forming and writing more global claims about how the techniques and choices they have identified contribute to the story's overall meaning and unity. Broad Guiding Questions, specific textual notes, and text-dependent questions will guide teachers and students as they examine how Hemingway has evidenced the following targeted elements and devices of the short story:

Character development (exposition, description, internal conflict, evolution):

Whose story is it? How do we come to know its characters (exposition)? What internal conflicts do they seem to face? What details suggest how or why they change (or don't)? How does characterization influence our reading and understanding of the story?

Focus of narration (narrative point of view, narrator's voice):

Who tells the story? What do details and language reveal about the point of view of its narrator and characters? How might we characterize the narrator's voice? How does the focus of the narration influence our reading and understanding of the narrative? How does narrative point of view shift in third person omniscient and what are the effects of those shifts?

Narrative structure (use of time, flashback, foreshadowing):

How is the narrative structured? How does it unfold in time—chronologically or not? What details stand out in the sequence of the plot? What effects do those details—and the order and ways in which they are presented—have on our reading and understanding of the narrative?

TEXT NOTES

Ernest Hemingway's "The Short Happy Life of Francis Macomber" was originally published by *Cosmopolitan* magazine in 1936. In the story, which draws from his own experience hunting in Africa, Hemingway explores some of his favorite themes: travel and adventure, nature, codes of masculinity, and relationships between men and women. The story also illustrates some of Hemingway's classic techniques: rich, subtle characterization; vivid description; economy; irony; and ambiguity.

The engaging topic, plot, and themes make the story a good, accessible introduction to Hemingway for ninth-graders. The powerful use of important literary techniques provides fertile ground for developing student's ability to analyze literary works. The text offers rich opportunity for numerous analytic claims and interpretations, enabling the students to develop their own views of the story and its characters, all of which can be supported by textual evidence. Apart from the several read-alouds, it is also recommended to find and play a recording of the story for students.

ACTIVITY 2: INDEPENDENT READING

Students independently read the first sentence of the text with a Guiding Question to help focus their reading.

INSTRUCTIONAL NOTES

Students might begin the process using an **Approaching Texts Tool** (in the **Reading Closely Literacy Toolbox**), which prompts them to consider their reading purpose and what they know about the text *before* reading, then provides a space to record one to two Guiding Questions or text-specific questions that students use to direct their close reading and annotation of the text. This may also be a good time to review (or introduce) the skills, systems, and symbols that students can use as they annotate a section of text:

- Briefly introduce students to the text. The introduction should be kept to naming the author, the speech, and the year and location of its delivery. These details can be recorded in the **Approaching Texts Tool**.

- Have students reflect on and discuss what they already know about the text based on this basic information.

- Allow students to approach the text freshly and to make their own discoveries, connections, and inferences based on textual content.

Students independently read the first sentence of the story guided by this question:

- How does the text begin?

Allow students to spend some time independently focusing on the information Hemingway presents in the first sentence. Encourage students to consider each word and phrase, annotating and making notes informally to express what they think.

≡ ACTIVITY 3: READ ALOUD AND CLASS ≡ DISCUSSION

Students follow along as they listen to the first seventeen paragraphs of the text being read aloud, and the teacher leads a discussion guided by a series of text-specific questions.

Students follow along as they listen to the student read aloud the first sentence of "The Short Happy Life of Francis Macomber." The teacher leads a discussion guided by this question:

- How does the text begin?
- Have students discuss all the information they have found in the first sentence. In your discussion, draw out what can already be learned from the various phrases:
  ⇒ "It was now lunch time" establishes the time and the organizing activity—lunch, while also indicating through "It was now" that the shared experience of those having lunch preceded this moment into the morning.
  ⇒ "they were all" establishes a group. The story seems to have a "they," and "they" are all present for lunch.
  ⇒ "sitting under the double green fly of the dining tent" establishes a physical setting. A "dining tent" suggests at least an outdoor and possibly a camping or expedition context for the story. Students will probably need some help with the word *fly*. Direct instruction on its meaning should be given if necessary, but first see if any students are familiar with this usage.
  ⇒ "pretending that nothing had happened" confirms that something has happened prior to lunchtime in which "they" were all involved. It also further brings the "they" together, because they are all involved in the same cognitive-physical activity of "pretending." This shared intention of "pretending" also suggests that they all wish that whatever happened before lunch hadn't happened.
- Remind students of the focus on literary techniques, explain that one technique is called *in medias res*—when authors choose to start telling a story in the middle of the action instead of at the beginning. Point out that Hemingway uses this technique in this story.

Students follow along as a student reads from the beginning of the story to the end of paragraph 17 (". . . very publicly, to be a coward.").

- Tell students that another literary technique is called *characterization*. Explain that characterization can be defined as the various ways authors develop characters. Throughout the unit, they will be learning strategies for analyzing those ways, but for now, a simple definition will suffice.

- Ask students to annotate their texts in response to this question:

  ⇒ Who does "they" refer to in the first sentence, and what details from the text give clues about each of their personalities?

- Students should be able to identify Francis Macomber, Mrs. Macomber, and Robert Wilson as "they." Students will likely begin by pointing out traits directly provided by the narrator. Have them be specific and directly reference the details they pick. As the discussion progresses, push students to make a few basic inferences about the characters based on the traits provided by the author as well as the things they say and what they do. For example, explore what the differences in the quite-similar attire worn by Wilson and Macomber reveal about each of the men. Explore, too, what Wilson and Macomber's stating-questioning and teaching-learning modes of communicating suggest about each of them and their relationships to each other.

ACTIVITY 4: MODEL THE FORMING OF EBCs

The teacher models a critical reading and thinking process for forming evidence-based claims about texts.

INSTRUCTIONAL NOTES

Based on the class discussion of the text, model a critical reading and thinking process for forming an evidence-based claim: from comprehension of textual details that stand out, to a connection or inference that arises from examining the details, to a basic evidence-based claim that is supported by specific references back to the text.

Once the class has reached an understanding of the text, the **Attending to Details Handout** (introduced in the *Reading Closely* unit) can be used to help students think about the types of details they might be looking for and to introduce a three-step process for making a text-based claim.

- Introduce the **Forming EBC Tool**.
- Model the process for using the tool and forming a claim by using details that have emerged from discussion of one of the questions. Form a model claim related to the literary technique characterization (e.g., the way Macomber continually asks Wilson questions suggests that Wilson is a type of teacher or authority).

Developing Core Literacy Proficiencies

The *Forming EBC Tool* (in the **EBC Literacy Toolbox**) is organized so that students first note details that stand out and that they also see as related to each other. The second section asks them to think about the details and explain a connection they have made among them. Such text-to-text connections should be distinguished from text-to-self connections readers sometimes make between what they have read and their own experiences. These text-to-text connections can then lead them to a claim they can make and record in the final section of the tool—a conclusion they have drawn about the text that can be referenced back to textual details and text-to-text connections.

INSTRUCTIONAL NOTES

- Model the thinking of moving from details, to connections, to a claim, as students follow along If necessary, provide structured practice for the first two steps by giving students a textual detail on a blank tool. In pairs, have students use the tool to find other details or quotations that could be related to the one provided and then make and explain connections among those details.

- Return to the characteristics of an evidence-based claim that have been discussed in Activity 1:
  - ⇒ A claim states a conclusion you have come to after reading a text and that you want others to think about.
  - ⇒ All parts of a claim are supported by specific evidence you can point to in the text.

- In pairs or as a class, have students discuss how the model claim developed in class demonstrates these characteristics and where it might be stronger.

- Conduct a final discussion of the insights students have developed through discussion of the first part of the story. As they share their insights, ask them to think about whether they are starting to form claims that are supported by specific evidence from the text—or how their beginning insights might become text-based claims.

NOTE

Here and throughout the entire unit, teachers are encouraged to develop questions and claims based on their own analysis and class discussion. The provided models are possibilities meant more to illustrate the process than to shape textual analysis. Instruction will be most effective if the claims used in modeling arise naturally from the textual ideas and details that students find significant and interesting. Also, although the tools have three places for recording supporting evidence, students should know that not all claims require three pieces of evidence. Sections of the tools can be left blank.

INDEPENDENT READING ACTIVITY

Supporting Evidence-Based Claims Tool

Students read paragraphs 18 through 106, until the line "Anyone could be upset by his first lion. That's all over," and use the *Supporting EBC Tool* (in the **Making EBC Literacy Toolbox**) to find evidence to support a teacher-provided claim. Teachers can place their own model claim at the top of the tool. Students look for evidence as they read to support the claim. This activity overlaps with the first activity of Part 2 and can be given as homework or done at the beginning of the next class.

☰ PART 1: FORMATIVE ASSESSMENT ☰ OPPORTUNITIES

By the end of Part 1, students will have completed the following:

- *Approaching Texts Tool*
- *Forming EBC Tool* (textual details provided by the teacher)

ASSESSING LITERACY SKILLS

The *Forming EBC Tool* should be evaluated to get an initial assessment of students' grasp of the relationship between claims and textual evidence. Even though the work was done together with the class, filling in the tool helps students get a sense of the critical reading and thinking process and the relationships among the ideas. Also make sure that students are developing the habit of using quotation marks and recording the textual reference for details they identify.

Students will also have annotated the text (paragraphs 1 through 17) and may have recorded key details in an *Analyzing Details Tool*. Their annotations (and notes on the tool) can be reviewed to determine if they are carrying forward and applying the foundational Literacy Skills of **Attending to Details** and **Identifying Relationships** that they may have practiced throughout the *Reading Closely* unit. Students may be given feedback about their developing skills and the evidence they are showing using the *Student Making EBC Literacy Skills Checklist* found in the **Making EBC Literacy Toolbox**.

ASSESSING ACADEMIC HABITS

Student discussions, as a class and in pairs, provide continuing opportunities for students to reflect on and self-assess their developing Academic Habits, specifically those related to **Engaging Actively**. Students might consider these reflection questions:

- What have I done to prepare for discussions by reading the text closely and considering the questions?
- How much have I actively focused my attention on the materials (during reading and annotation) and on the ideas of other participants in the discussion?

NOTE

To support self-, peer, and teacher assessment of skills and habits developed during the unit, a formal *Making EBC Literacy Skills Rubric* and less formal *Student Making EBC Literacy Skills* and *Academic Habits Checklists* are provided in the **Making EBC Literacy Toolbox**.

MAKING EVIDENCE-BASED CLAIMS ABOUT LITERARY TECHNIQUE

"Still drinking their whisky"

OBJECTIVE:	Students develop the ability to make evidence-based claims through a close reading of the text.

ESTIMATED TIME: 1 to 3 days

MATERIALS:
- *Supporting EBC Tool*
- *Attending to Details Handout*
- *Forming EBC Tool*
- *Questioning Path Tool*

≣ LITERACY SKILLS

TARGETED SKILLS	DESCRIPTORS
INTERPRETING LANGUAGE	Identifies how words and phrases convey meaning and represent an author's or narrator's perspective
IDENTIFYING RELATIONSHIPS	Identifies important connections among key details and ideas within and across texts
MAKING INFERENCES	Demonstrates comprehension by using connections among details to make logical deductions about a text
FORMING CLAIMS	Develops meaningful and defensible claims that clearly state valid, evidence-based analysis
USING EVIDENCE	Supports all aspects of claims with sufficient textual evidence using accurate quotations, paraphrases, and references

ACADEMIC HABITS

HABITS DEVELOPED	DESCRIPTORS
COLLABORATING	Pays attention to, respects, and works productively in various roles with all other participants
COMMUNICATING CLEARLY	Uses appropriate language and relevant textual details to clearly present ideas and claims

ALIGNMENT TO CCSS

TARGETED STANDARD:

CCSS.ELA-LITERACY.RL.9-10.1: Cite strong and thorough textual evidence to support analysis of what the text says explicitly as well as inferences drawn from the text.

SUPPORTING STANDARDS:

CCSS.ELA-LITERACY.RL.9-10.3: Analyze how complex characters (e.g., those with multiple or conflicting motivations) develop over the course of a text, interact with other characters, and advance the plot or develop the theme.

CCSS.ELA-LITERACY.RL.9-10.5: Analyze how an author's choices concerning how to structure a text, order events within it (e.g., parallel plots), and manipulate time (e.g., pacing, flashbacks) create such effects as mystery, tension, or surprise.

CCSS.ELA-LITERACY.SL. 9-10.1: Initiate and participate effectively in a range of collaborative discussions (one-on-one, in groups, and teacher-led) with diverse partners on *grades 9–10 topics, texts, and issues,* building on others' ideas and expressing their own clearly and persuasively.

 **ACTIVITIES**

1. INDEPENDENT READING TO FIND SUPPORTING EVIDENCE
Students independently read a section of the text and use the ***Supporting EBC Tool*** to look for evidence to support a claim made by the teacher.

2. READ ALOUD AND CLASS DISCUSSION
Students follow along as they listen to the same part of the text being read aloud and discuss a series of Guiding Questions and text-specific questions.

3. FINDING SUPPORTING EVIDENCE IN PAIRS
In pairs, students use the ***Supporting EBC Tool*** to look for evidence to support additional claims about the text made by the teacher.

4. CLASS DISCUSSION OF EBCs
The class discusses evidence students have found in support of teacher or class claims.

5. FORMING EBCs IN PAIRS
In pairs, students use the ***Forming EBC Tool*** to make an evidence-based claim of their own and present it to the class.

≡ ACTIVITY 1: INDEPENDENT READING
≡ TO FIND SUPPORTING EVIDENCE

Students independently read paragraphs 18 through 106 and use the **Supporting EBC Tool** to look for evidence to support a claim made by the teacher.

SUPPORTING EVIDENCE-BASED CLAIMS TOOL

The **Supporting Evidence-Based Claims Tool** (in the **Making EBC Literacy Toolbox**) is organized in a sequence opposite to the **Forming Evidence-Based Claims Tool**. In the first section, students write down a claim established by the teacher, themselves or the class. The second section prompts students to search for textual evidence and details that support the claim and write down where they found the evidence. Teachers can provide their own claims which students can use to practice making connections between valid (or invalid) claims and textual details. Such claims can serve as valuable models for students who are struggling to grasp the concept of a text-based conclusion or text-to-text connection. Students can also use the tool to write down claims as they read through text, then search and write down supporting evidence to determine whether their claims have text-to-text connections or not.

INSTRUCTIONAL NOTES

- Pass out and overview the organization of the **Supporting EBC Tool**—helping students see that it is organized in a sequence opposite to the **Forming EBC Tool** they have been using: moving from an existing claim to its supporting details rather than from the details to a claim.

- Model the use of the tool with a teacher-developed claim derived from text students have previously read. Have students find and suggest supporting details for the teacher claim and record them on a **Supporting EBC Tool**.

- Present students with a new teacher-developed claim, derived from the next section of text students will read.

Students independently read paragraphs 18 through 106, up until "Anyone could be upset by his first lion. That's all over," looking for details to support the new teacher-developed claim and recording them on a **Supporting EBC Tool**.

Depending on scheduling and student ability, students can be assigned to read the text and complete the **Supporting EBC Tool** for homework. Teachers should decide what works best for their students. It is essential that students have opportunities to read the text independently at various points in the unit. All students must develop the habit of **Perseverance** in reading. Assigning the reading as homework potentially gives them more time with the text. Either way, it might be a good idea to provide some time at the beginning of class for students to read the section quietly by themselves, ensuring that all students have had at least some independent reading time.

☰ ACTIVITY 2: READ ALOUD
☰ AND CLASS DISCUSSION

Students follow along as they listen to the same section of the text being read aloud and discuss a series of Guiding Questions and text-specific questions.

INSTRUCTIONAL NOTES

Students follow along as they listen to the next section of the story up until "Anyone could be upset by his first lion. That's all over." being read aloud, then share and compare the details they have recorded on a **_Supporting EBC Tool_** in response to a Guiding Question and a teacher-developed claim.

TEXT NOTES

In this second section of the story Hemingway builds his characterization of the key characters through dialogue. The section provides rich opportunity to continue to extend the analysis of characterization that was begun with the discussion on their physical descriptions. It is also a good section to introduce two additional literary techniques students will be analyzing: narrative chronology and point of view.

APPROACHING:
I determine my reading purposes and take note of key information about the text. I identify the LIPS domain(s) that will guide my initial reading.

I will initially focus on the author's *language*, *ideas*, and *supporting details*.

QUESTIONING: *I use Guiding Questions to help me investigate the text (from the **Guiding Questions Handout**).*

1. How are key characters described? [L]

2. What seems to be the narrator's attitude or point of view?

ANALYZING: *I question further to connect and analyze the details I find (from the **Guiding Questions Handout**).*

3. How does the text's language influence my understanding of important characters or themes?

4. How does the narrator's perspective influence the presentation of themes or characterizations?

DEEPENING: *I consider the questions of others.*

5. Why does Margaret begin to cry in paragraph 36? What specific details provide clues? How do these details develop the characterization of Francis and Margaret Macomber?

6. In paragraph 55, why does Wilson think it is "bad form" for Macomber to ask if anyone will hear about "the lion business"? What specific details provide clues? How do these details develop the characterization of Macomber and Wilson? How does the use of point of view in this section affect the characterization of Wilson and Macomber?

7. Who does Wilson like more, Francis or Margaret? What details provide clues? How do these details develop the characterization of Wilson, Francis, and Margaret?

EXTENDING: *I pose my own questions.*

Students might begin their rereading and second discussion of the text by considering a question in the Analyzing stage of the model *Questioning Path Tool*: "How does the text's language influence my understanding of important characters or themes?"

The three deepening text-specific questions can then help students again move from literal comprehension of key details to analysis of Hemingway's characterization of the three main characters: Macomber, Wilson, and Margaret. They are numbered here to match the numbering in the model *Questioning Path Tool*. All three questions may be assigned to all students, or they may be differentially assigned based on students' reading readiness levels.

5. Why does Margaret begin to cry in paragraph 36? What specific details provide clues? How do these details develop the characterization of Francis and Margaret Macomber?

The initial exchanges about the lion provide a good context to explore how Hemingway develops the characterization of the three through their conversation and action. It is also a good place to discuss the impact that beginning the story *in medias res* has on emphasis and tension. Beginning with lunch emphasizes the meaning of the "lion business" for the characters and their relationships with each other over the incident itself. Because that meaning is developed through their conversation—including Margaret's crying—we begin to get a sense of each character and the interpersonal dynamics that preceded the incident and which it serves to compound.

6. In paragraph 55, why does Wilson think it is "bad form" for Macomber to ask if anyone will hear about "the lion business"? What specific details provide clues? How do these details develop the characterization of Macomber and Wilson? How does the use of point of view in this section affect the characterization of Wilson and Macomber?

This story is excellent for teaching the effects of point of view in general and especially with respect to characterization. Discuss Hemingway's use of the third-person omniscient. Discuss that third-person omniscient enables the narrator to see and enter any of the characters' perspectives and minds. Authors can shift among perspectives to relate specific events from specific (and even multiple) characters. This shifting shapes the way the reader experiences the story and contributes to the characterization. Help students become attuned to when Hemingway shifts the perspective from character to character (and later, the lion) and to an impersonal view. Having students annotate the text when reported thoughts, feelings, and judgments shift is a good strategy for developing their sense of point of view and engaging them deeply in the story. Starting with "So they sat there" (paragraph 42) and continuing to "Anyone could be upset by his first lion. That's all over." (paragraph 106), the perspective is that of Wilson. This frames this early characterization of Macomber and Margaret through Wilson's perspective, giving the reader an assessment of the couple from someone who is extremely knowledgeable about their current context—a "professional"—as well as giving the reader a good sense of Wilson himself. In this exchange, we learn about Macomber's insecurity, pride, and naiveté. We also learn about Wilson's knowledge, experience, "codes" of behavior, pride, and his fluctuating opinion of Macomber. And we learn about the dynamic between the two men.

7. Who does Wilson like more, Francis or Margaret? What details provide clues? How do these details develop the characterization of Wilson, Francis, and Margaret?

There may be no answer to this question—at least at this point in the story. Discussing Wilson's view of the pair (and having students look for evidence of those views while they read) is a good way to engage students in an analysis of characterization, point of view, as well as the issues of gender present in the story. Have students defend their answers with direct textual evidence. Use the verb "like" as a mechanism for moving to precise analysis of textual detail. Encourage students to probe whether the evidence suggests "liking" or more subtle judgments. Explore, too, according to the evidence, why Wilson would have those judgments.

- Following discussion, return to the **Supporting EBC Tool** and discuss textual details that have emerged as interesting during the discussion of each of the text-dependent questions.

☰ ACTIVITY 3: FINDING SUPPORTING EVIDENCE IN PAIRS

In pairs, students use the **Supporting EBC Tool** to look for evidence to support additional claims about the text made by the teacher.

INSTRUCTIONAL NOTES

- Once the class has reached a solid understanding of this section of the text, connect it to the skill of making claims and supporting them with evidence by presenting a few additional teacher-developed claims—perhaps ones that move from summary of explicit details to interpretation and inference.

- Students work in pairs to consider a new set of teacher-developed claims, find evidence in the text to support the claims, and record the details they find on a **Supporting EBC Tool**.

> **NOTE**
>
> Students may be asked to work with all of the teacher-developed claims, or claims may be assigned to student pairs based on their reading readiness levels.

Collect each student's **Supporting EBC Tool(s)** with the evidence they have found for a teacher-developed claim(s). These should be evaluated to get an assessment of where each student is in the development of the targeted Literacy Skill of **Using Evidence**. Students should use their tools for their work in pairs—identifying and refining their evidence based on the read-aloud and class discussion. Even though students are not finding the evidence independently, they should each fill in separate tools to reinforce their acquisition of the logical structure among the ideas. Students should get into the habit of using quotation marks when recording direct quotes and including the paragraph or line numbers of the evidence they find.

> **NOTE**
>
> This may be a good time to introduce or review the concept and skills of using and citing evidence. Help students understand that it is important for them to record quotations and citations accurately so they can find the evidence again in the text, quote it correctly, and insert a proper citation when they write. Depending on the academic style students are expected to use (MLA, APA, a school or teacher system), have students record identifying citation information so they can use it correctly when they write.

The instructional focus here is on developing familiarity with claims about texts and the use of textual evidence to support them. Students should still not be expected to develop complete sentences to express supporting evidence. The pieces of evidence should be as focused as possible. The idea is for students to identify the precise points in the text that support the claim. This focus is lost if the pieces of evidence become too large. The tools are constructed to elicit a type of pointing at the evidence.

Alternative Instructional Approach: One additional approach for ensuring a close examination of claims and evidence is to provide erroneous claims that contradict textual evidence and ask students to find the places that disprove the claim. Students could then be asked to modify a claim to account for the evidence.

☰ ACTIVITY 4: CLASS DISCUSSION OF EBCs

The class discusses evidence students have found in support of teacher or class claims.

INSTRUCTIONAL NOTES

- After students have finished their work in pairs, regroup for a class discussion.
- Have pairs volunteer to present their evidence to the rest of the class. Discuss the evidence, evaluating how each piece supports the claims. Begin by modeling the evaluation and then call on students to evaluate the evidence shared by the other pairs. They can offer their own evidence to expand the discussion.
- Carefully guide the exchanges, explicitly asking students to support their evaluations with reference to the text.

These constructive discussions are essential for the development of Literacy Skills and related Academic Habits. Listening to and evaluating the evidence of others and providing text-based criticism expand students' capacity to reason through the relationship between claims and evidence—and to reflect on their development of the skill of **Using Evidence** to support a claim. Paying close attention to and providing instructional guidance on the student comments are as important to the process as evaluating the *Supporting EBC Tools* and help develop a class culture of supporting all claims (including oral critiques) with evidence.

Students can also reflect on their participation in class and pair discussions by considering how well they have used and developed the Academic Habits of **Engaging Actively**, **Collaborating**, and **Communicating Clearly**. A reflective discussion or self-assessment could be guided by these questions:

- In what ways have I paid attention to and worked collaboratively with other participants in the discussions? How might I further develop this habit of collaborating in future discussions?
- How clearly have I communicated my ideas and supported them with specific evidence? How might I further develop this habit of communicating and supporting my thinking in future discussions?

ACTIVITY 5: FORMING EBCs IN PAIRS

In pairs, students use the **Forming EBC Tool** to make an evidence-based claim of their own and present it to the class.

INSTRUCTIONAL NOTES

- Once the claims and evidence have been discussed, students return to their collaborative pairs and use the **Forming EBC Tool** to make an evidence-based claim of their own, working again from identifying related details, to making connections among the details, to forming a supported claim. Pairs should develop a single claim, but each student should complete his or her own tool.

- Regroup and discuss the claims and evidence as a class. Pairs can use their tool to present their claims and evidence orally.

- Talk through the process modeled in the tool, including the nature of the details that stood out to students, the reasoning they used to group and relate them, and the claim they developed from the textual evidence.

- Draw on the **Attending to Details Handout** and the descriptors of relevant Literacy Skills and Academic Habits to help guide discussion.

INDEPENDENT READING ACTIVITY

Students read paragraphs 107 through 237 ("No one had said anything more until they were back at camp.") guided by a Guiding Question(s) from the model **Questioning Path Tool** and using the **Forming EBC Tool** to make a claim and support it with evidence. This activity overlaps with the first activity of Part 3 and can be given as homework or done at the beginning of the next class.

PART 2: FORMATIVE ASSESSMENT OPPORTUNITIES

At the end of Part 2, students will have completed the following:

- **Supporting EBC Tools** independently (for claims provided by the teacher)
- Class discussions
- **Forming EBC Tool** in pairs

ASSESSING LITERACY SKILLS

The **Supporting EBC Tools** should be evaluated to assess students' understanding of the relationship between claims and textual evidence. They should show progress in terms of the relevance and focus of the evidence they identify. The **Forming EBC Tools** are students' first attempts at crafting their own claims with the help of a peer. Basic claims are fine at this point. Use the Literacy Skills descriptors (or portions of the *Student Making EBC Literacy Skills Checklist* found in the **Making EBC Literacy Toolbox**) to structure the evaluation and feedback to students. Evaluation should focus on the clarity and validity of the claim and the relevance of the evidence. The thinking and connections students record on the tool are also important indicators of students' improving reasoning skills as well as potential evidence of their use of academic vocabulary related to the reading and claim-making process.

Evidence should be presented in quotation marks or paraphrased accurately, and the references recorded correctly. Using quotation marks helps students make the distinction between writing quotations and paraphrasing. It also helps them eventually to incorporate quotes properly into their writing. Recording references is critical not only for proper incorporation in writing but also because doing so helps students return to the text to find and reevaluate evidence and make appropriate selections.

ASSESSING ACADEMIC HABITS

In Part 2, students work in small groups and engage in text-centered discussions. They can reflect on how well they have used the fundamental habits of Collaborating for and Communicating Clearly within text-centered discussions.

The Academic Habits descriptors and reflective questions from Activity 4 can be used to evaluate student participation in discussions for formative and diagnostic information. Teachers and students can get a sense of areas in which further development of text-centered discussion habits and skills are needed.

NOTE
To support self-, peer, and teacher assessment of skills and habits developed during the unit, a formal *Making EBC Literacy Skills Rubric* and less formal *Student Making EBC Literacy Skills* and *Academic Habits Checklists* are provided in the **Making EBC Literacy Toolbox**.

PART 3
ORGANIZING EVIDENCE-BASED CLAIMS
"Hell of a fine lion"

OBJECTIVE:	Students learn to develop and explain evidence-based claims through the selection and organization of supporting evidence.

ESTIMATED TIME: 2–3 days

MATERIALS:
- *Forming EBC Tool*
- *Organizing EBC Tool*
- *Questioning Path Tool*

☰ LITERACY SKILLS

TARGETED SKILLS	DESCRIPTORS
INTERPRETING LANGUAGE	Identifies how words and phrases convey meaning and represent an author's or narrator's perspective
IDENTIFYING RELATIONSHIPS	Identifies important connections among key details and ideas within and across texts
MAKING INFERENCES	Demonstrates comprehension by using connections among details to make logical deductions about a text
FORMING CLAIMS	Develops meaningful and defensible claims that clearly state valid, evidence-based analysis
USING EVIDENCE	Supports all aspects of claims with sufficient textual evidence using accurate quotations, paraphrases, and references

ACADEMIC HABITS

HABITS DEVELOPED	DESCRIPTORS
COLLABORATING	Pays attention to, respects, and works collaboratively with all other participants in the task, discussion, activity, or process
COMMUNICATING CLEARLY	Uses appropriate language and relevant textual details to clearly present ideas and claims
LISTENING	Pays attention to, acknowledges, and considers thoughtfully new information and ideas from others

ALIGNMENT TO CCSS

TARGETED STANDARD:

CCSS.ELA-LITERACY.RL.9-10.1: Cite strong and thorough textual evidence to support analysis of what the text says explicitly as well as inferences drawn from the text.

SUPPORTING STANDARDS:

CCSS.ELA-LITERACY.RL.9-10.3: Analyze how complex characters (e.g., those with multiple or conflicting motivations) develop over the course of a text, interact with other characters, and advance the plot or develop the theme.

CCSS.ELA-LITERACY.RL.9-10.5: Analyze how an author's choices concerning how to structure a text, order events within it (e.g., parallel plots), and manipulate time (e.g., pacing, flashbacks) create such effects as mystery, tension, or surprise.

CCSS.ELA-LITERACY.SL. 9-10.1: Initiate and participate effectively in a range of collaborative discussions (one-on-one, in groups, and teacher-led) with diverse partners on *grades 9–10 topics, texts, and issues,* building on others' ideas and expressing their own clearly and persuasively.

ACTIVITIES

1. INDEPENDENT READING AND FORMING EBCs
Students independently read a section of the text and use the ***Forming EBC Tool*** to make an evidence-based claim.

2. COMPARING EBCs
Students compare draft claims, returning to the text as necessary to look for additional evidence related to the claims they have made.

3. MODEL THE ORGANIZING OF EBCs

The teacher models organizing evidence to develop and explain claims using student evidence-based claims and the *Organizing EBC Tool*.

4. DEEPENING UNDERSTANDING

Students follow along as they listen to the text being read aloud, use text-specific questions to discuss a section of the text, and produce a second evidence-based claim.

5. ORGANIZING EBCs IN PAIRS

In pairs, students develop and organize a new claim with multiple points using the *Organizing EBC Tool*.

6. CLASS DISCUSSION OF STUDENT EBCs

The class discusses the evidence-based claims developed by student pairs.

ACTIVITY 1: INDEPENDENT READING AND FORMING EBCs

Students independently read paragraphs 107 through 237 ("No one had said anything more until they were back at camp.") guided by a Guiding Question(s) from the model *Questioning Path Tool* and use the *Forming EBC Tool* to make an evidence-based claim.

TEXT NOTES

This section of the story covers the flashback description of the "story of the lion." Instruction should continue the analysis of characterization (including the new lion character), but it should shift to emphasize narrative point of view and chronology. This is a lengthy section and should be thought of as a whole, but given its length, should take a few days to get through.

The questions in the model **Questioning Path Tool** for this section of the speech's text thus have been selected and developed to help students focus on perspective and structure. Students will first consider one of the general Guiding Questions from the Questioning or Analyzing sections as they do a first reading and develop an initial evidence-based claim.

The text-specific questions in the Deepening section of the **Questioning Path Tool** are again designed to move students from concrete details and literal understanding of the events of the story to a deeper appreciation and analysis of Hemingway's use of literary technique.

- As each question is discussed, follow it up by asking "What in the text makes you reach your answer or conclusion? Point to specific words or sentences."

APPROACHING: *I determine my reading purposes and take note of key information about the text. I identify the LIPS domain(s) that will guide my initial reading.*

I will initially focus on how the author uses narrative *perspective* and *structure* to convey *ideas*.

QUESTIONING: *I use Guiding Questions to help me investigate the text (from the Guiding Questions Handout).*

1. What do I notice about how the text is organized or sequenced? [S]

2. What are the narrators' points of view? [P]

ANALYZING: *I question further to connect and analyze the details I find (from the Guiding Questions Handout).*

3. What details or words suggest the narrators' perspectives? [P, L]

4. How do the narrators' perspectives influence their presentation of ideas and themes? [P]

5. How does the organization of the text influence my understanding of its information and themes? [S]

DEEPENING: *I consider the questions of others.*

6. How does the shift in perspective of narration in this section relate to the sequence of action?

7. How does the shift to the lion's perspective during points in the hunt affect the characterization of Macomber?

8. How does Hemingway show Wilson's perspective in this section? Are there any moments when his thoughts are reported? How does Hemingway develop Wilson's character in this section?

EXTENDING: *I pose my own questions.*

- Students independently work on paragraphs 107 through 237 ("No one had said anything more until they were back at camp.") considering a Guiding Question from the model *Questioning Path Tool*. Depending on scheduling and student ability, students can be assigned to read and complete the *Forming EBC Tool* for homework or to read the text and form a claim at the beginning of class.
- Students record their question at the top of a *Forming EBC Tool*. As they read, they search for and annotate details related to the question.
- After reading, students record key details, connections, and an initial evidence-based claim on the tool.

ACTIVITY 2: COMPARING EBCs

Students compare draft claims, returning to the text as necessary to look for additional evidence related to the claims they have made.

INSTRUCTIONAL NOTES

- Either as a class or in small groups, ask students to volunteer claims they have drafted after reading the section of text and considering a specific Guiding Question. Facilitate a short comparative discussion of the student-developed claims, noting how different the claims may be depending on which Guiding Question students have used to frame their reading of the text and the details on which the claim is based.

ACTIVITY 3: MODEL THE ORGANIZING OF EBCs

The teacher models organizing evidence to develop and explain claims using student evidence-based claims and the *Organizing EBC Tool*.

INSTRUCTIONAL NOTES

The central focus of Part 3 is learning the thinking processes associated with developing an evidence-based claim:

- Reflecting on how one has arrived at the claim
- Breaking the claim into parts
- Organizing supporting evidence in a logical sequence

- Anticipating what an audience will need to know in order to understand the claim
- Planning a line of reasoning that will substantiate the claim

This is a complex set of cognitive skills, challenging for most students, but these skills are essential so that students can move from the close-reading process of arriving at a claim (Parts 1 and 2 of the unit) to the purposeful writing process of explaining and substantiating that claim (Parts 4 and 5).

How a reader develops and organizes a claim is dependent on the nature of the claim itself and the nature of the text (or texts) from which it arises. In some cases, such as when a claim involves a literal interpretation of the text, it is sufficient to indicate where the claim comes from in the text and explain how the reader arrived at it. This suggests a more straightforward, explanatory organization. More-complex claims, however, often involve multiple parts, points, or premises, each of which needs to be explained and developed, then linked in a logical order into a coherent proof of the claim.

Students learn how to develop and organize a claim only through practice, ideally moving from simpler claims and more familiar organizational patterns to more-complex claims and organizations. Students can be helped in learning how to develop a claim by considering a set of developmental Guiding Questions such as the following.

NOTE

The first few questions might be used with less experienced readers, the latter questions with students who are developing more sophisticated claims.

- What do I mean when I state this claim? What am I trying to communicate?
- How did I arrive at this claim? Can I recount and explain how I moved as a reader from the literal details of the text to a supported claim about the text?
- Can I point to the specific words and sentences in the text from which the claim arises?
- What do I need to explain so that an audience can understand what I mean and where my claim comes from?
- What evidence (quotations) might I use to illustrate my claim? In what order?
- If my claim contains several parts (or premises), how can I break it down, organize the parts, and organize the evidence that goes with them?
- If my claim involves a comparison or a relationship, how might I present, clarify, and organize my discussion of the relationship between parts of text or different texts?

ORGANIZING EVIDENCE-BASED CLAIMS TOOL

Students who are learning how to develop a claim, at any level, can benefit from graphic organizers or instructional scaffolding that helps them organize and record their thinking. Although such models or templates should not be presented formulaically as a how-to for developing a claim, they can be used to support the learning process. The *Organizing EBC Tool* (in the **Making EBC Literacy Toolbox**) can be used to provide some structure for student planning. Alternately, a teacher might use another model or graphic organizer that fits well with the text, the types of claims being developed, and the needs of students.

ACTIVITY SEQUENCE

- Begin by orienting students to the new tool and the idea of breaking down a claim into parts and organizing the evidence accordingly. Relate the organization of the tool to that of the *Forming* and *Supporting EBC Tools*.

- Ask for a volunteer to present his or her initial claim and identify supporting evidence. Use the example as a basis for a discussion. Discuss what the component parts of the student's claim might be based on the nature of the claim and the evidence that the student has identified.

- Based on the flow of discussion, bring in other volunteers to present their claims and evidence to build and help clarify the points.

- Work with students to hone and develop a student claim, finding additional evidence and thinking about the component parts of the claim.

- As a class, record the organized claim, its parts, and evidence in an *Organizing EBC Tool.*

NOTE

The provided model *Organizing EBC Tool* in the **Making EBC Literacy Toolbox** is one possible way a claim could be expressed and organized.

ACTIVITY 4: DEEPENING UNDERSTANDING

Students follow along as they listen to paragraphs 107 through 237 being read aloud, use text-specific questions to discuss a section of the text, and produce a second evidence-based claim.

TEXT NOTES—IDEAS FOR DISCUSSION

Use the following text-specific questions from the model *Questioning Path Tool* to frame a class (or small-group) discussion of the text and to provide a context for a second—and ideally deeper—student claim. Students can use a *Forming EBC Tool* to develop their claim as they discuss the text. Depending on whether they work in groups or as a class, all students may work with all five questions, or they may be assigned differentially based on students' reading readiness levels.

Either prior to or as they discuss the questions, students listen to the story of the lion being read aloud, focusing on how 1) how Hemingway chooses to sequence the telling of the events and 2) how Hemingway alternates the narrative point of view to relate the events. To do this, students might read the section annotating the chronological breaks in the narrative and the precise points where the narrative perspective shifts. Once these breaks and shifts have been identified, students can reflect on how Hemingway's use of these techniques affects the reader's experience of the story.

Additionally, students might re-read and annotate these narrative breaks and shifts as homework in preparation for the class discussion.

- If re-reading as a class, work through paragraphs 107 to 237 ("No one had said anything more until they were back at camp.") reading aloud and stopping for discussion based on questions and claims. It's important to move slowly to ensure all students have gained basic comprehension and have practiced making and organizing claims. A good possible stopping point within the section is at paragraph 187 ("Yes, Bwana.") after the initial shooting and before the lion charge. Discussion of this section should focus on how Hemingway masterfully uses narrative structure and point of view to reveal important aspects of the characters.

- Use the following text-specific questions from the model **Questioning Path Tool** to guide students thinking during discussion.

6. How does the shift in narrative perspective in this section relate to the sequence of action?

Some students will be able to identify this section as a "flashback." Before discussing perspective, probe the impact of Hemingway's use of flashback, connecting this discussion to the earlier one on *in medias res*. Explore how the knowledge we already have of the characters and the meaning the "lion business" had for them affects our experience of the narration of the hunt.

Some students will have identified (and annotated) the shift to Macomber as the dominant organizing perspective of narration for this flashback. Students can explore the relationship between perspective and action by analyzing the impact of experiencing the hunt through Macomber has on the story in general. Discuss how this emphasizes what the hunt and his failure mean for Macomber over the other characters. How would we experience the lion differently if we hadn't been introduced to the characters at lunch?

Highlight, too, how close to reality the situation of the flashback in the story is—how anyone who this had happened to would be lying in bed late that night recounting the events, dealing with newfound fear and cowardice. Later on in the unit, students can reflect on the fact that while Macomber is thinking about the incident, Margaret and Wilson are acting out part of its consequences.

7. How does the shift to the lion's perspective during points in the hunt affect the characterization of Macomber?

Before asking this question, see if students have identified when the perspective shifts to the lion. First discuss the impact that seeing and feeling the lion's perspective had on the students' experience with the story. Then discuss how Hemingway's choice affects the characterization of Macomber. What comparisons are established between the two through the retelling of their experiences of the same event? Have students cite specific evidence in discussion. For example: "The lion still stood looking majestically and coolly toward this object" versus "He only knew that his hands were shaking and as he walked away from the car it was almost impossible for him to make his legs move. They were stiff in the thighs, but he could feel the muscles fluttering."

8. How does Hemingway show Wilson's perspective in this section? Are there any moments when his thoughts are reported? How does Hemingway develop Wilson's character in this section?

This is a good section to explore various ways of characterization. The perspective and primary methods of characterization are reversed now from the previous section. Whereas at first we learned about Wilson from his reported thoughts and Macomber from his words and actions, now it is the opposite. Discuss the impact of that shift, drawing out how Wilson as an experienced hunter demonstrates his character through his actions here. What is he doing and saying throughout the hunt? Focus on specific actions and words of Wilson that develop his character. A good sequence to focus on might be Macomber's initial questioning about the distance from which he should shoot at the lion. We do not have access to Wilson's thoughts, but we do read, "Wilson looked at him quickly" (paragraph 123). What does that quick look suggest of Wilson's assessment of Macomber? This quick look can eventually be connected to the one line in this section when Wilson's thoughts and feelings are reported in paragraph 201: "Robert Wilson, whose entire occupation had been with the lion and the problem he presented, and who had not been thinking about Macomber except to note that he was rather windy, suddenly felt as though he had opened the wrong door in a hotel and seen something shameful." These lines are fruitful to explore in several ways. What does the image mean? What do the lines tell us about Macomber, Wilson, and Wilson's image of Macomber? What impact does reporting these thoughts and feelings of Wilson, and only these during this section, have? Incidentally, if students have identified this shift in perspective in their annotations, they should be celebrated and "carried [around the room] in triumph on the arms and shoulders" of the teacher and their fellow students (paragraph 11). How would the story be different if we experienced this retelling largely through Wilson's perspective?

ACTIVITY 5: ORGANIZING EBCs IN PAIRS

In pairs, students develop and organize a new claim with multiple points using the *Organizing EBC Tool*.

INSTRUCTIONAL NOTES

- Based on insights they have gained through reading and discussion of the deepening text-specific questions, students work in pairs, using the *Forming EBC Tool*, to make a new claim about some aspect of the text. If students' first claims have focused more on localized aspects of the story, this is an opportunity for them to move toward more general claims about Hemingway's use of narration and structure.

- Students use the ***Organizing EBC Tool*** to develop subpoints, identify key details and quotations, and organize supporting evidence for their new claims.

- In small pairs-check groups, student pairs use their tools to talk through the development and organization of their claims and compare them to claims developed by another student pair.

ACTIVITY 6: CLASS DISCUSSION OF STUDENT EBCs

The class discusses the evidence-based claims developed by student pairs.

- After students have finished their work in pairs and small groups, regroup for a class discussion about their evidence-based claims.

- Have pairs volunteer to present their claims, subpoints, and evidence to the rest of the class.

- Discuss the evidence and organization, evaluating how each piece supports and develops the claims.

- Use student examples to illustrate how evidence is organized to develop aspects of claims.

NOTE

The model ***Organizing EBC Tool*** also presents one possible way a claim could be expressed and organized and thus can be used as an alternate example.

INDEPENDENT READING ACTIVITY

Students read from paragraph 238 ("That was the story of the lion.") to the end of the story and use the ***Forming EBC Tool*** to make a new claim and support it with evidence. This activity overlaps with Activity 5 of Part 4 and can be given as homework or done at the beginning of the next class.

PART 3: FORMATIVE ASSESSMENT OPPORTUNITIES

By the end of Part 3, students will have completed the following:

- ***Forming EBC Tool*** for a claim developed independently
- ***Organizing EBC Tool*** as a class
- A second ***Forming EBC Tool*** while discussing text-specific questions
- ***Forming EBC Tool*** and ***Organizing EBC Tool*** for a claim developed in pairs

ASSESSING LITERACY SKILLS

Students' textual annotations and work on tools can be reviewed to see how they are developing the foundational skills of **Interpreting Language** and **Identifying Relationships**. They should also provide direct evidence of their developing skills in **Making Inferences, Forming Claims,** and **Using Evidence.** Students should now be beginning to develop more complex claims about challenging portions of the text. Their *Forming EBC Tools* should demonstrate a solid grasp of the claim-evidence relationship, but do not expect precision in the wording of their claims. Using the *Organizing EBC Tool* will help them clarify their claims as they break them into parts and organize their evidence. How they have transferred their information from the *Forming* to the *Organizing EBC Tool* will demonstrate their grasp of the concepts and skills of breaking claims into parts and organizing evidence. Their second *Organizing EBC Tool* should show progress in all dimensions including the clarity of the claim, the reasoning behind subpoints, and the selection and organization of evidence. The *Student Making EBC Literacy Skills Checklist* found in the **Making EBC Literacy Toolbox** can be used to structure formative evaluation and feedback to students.

ASSESSING ACADEMIC HABITS

In Parts 1 and 2, students may have reflected informally on how they are applying the habits of **Engaging Actively, Collaborating,** and **Communicating Clearly.** Their pairs, small-group, and class discussions in Activities 4 through 6 of Part 3 can provide an opportunity for a slightly more formal self-assessment (and potentially a peer or teacher assessment) of these habits—along with the habit of **Listening.** Students might be introduced (or reintroduced) to the descriptors for the habits of **Collaborating, Communicating Clearly,** and **Listening,** then receive self-, peer, or teacher feedback regarding how well they are applying these habits and how they might improve, using the following Assessment Checklist (or the *Student Making EBC Academic Habits Checklist* found in the **Making EBC Literacy Toolbox**):

HABITS DEVELOPED	DESCRIPTORS	EVIDENCE OF USING THE HABIT	THINGS TO IMPROVE ON
COLLABORATING	• Pays attention to and respects other participants • Works productively with others to complete the task and enrich the discussion		
COMMUNICATING CLEARLY	• Uses clear language to communicate ideas and claims • Uses relevant details to explain and support thinking		
LISTENING	• Pays attention to new information and ideas from others • Considers others' ideas thoughtfully		

> **NOTE**
>
> To support self-, peer, and teacher assessment of skills and habits developed during the unit, a formal *Making EBC Literacy Skills Rubric* and less formal *Student Making EBC Literacy Skills* and *Academic Habits Checklists* are provided in the **Making EBC Literacy Toolbox.**

PART 4

WRITING EVIDENCE-BASED CLAIMS ABOUT LITERARY TECHNIQUE

"Like a dam bursting"

OBJECTIVE:	Students develop the ability to communicate text-based claims and their supporting evidence through writing.

ESTIMATED TIME: 2 to 4 days

MATERIALS:
- *Writing EBC Handout*
- *Questioning Path Tool*
- *Forming EBC Tool*
- *Organizing EBC Tool*

≡ LITERACY SKILLS

TARGETED SKILLS	DESCRIPTORS
MAKING INFERENCES	Demonstrates comprehension by using connections among details to make logical deductions about a text
FORMING CLAIMS	Develops meaningful and defensible claims that clearly state valid, evidence-based analysis
USING EVIDENCE	Supports all aspects of claims with sufficient textual evidence using accurate quotations, paraphrases, and references
ORGANIZING IDEAS	Sequences sentences and paragraphs to establish coherent, logical, and unified narratives, explanations, and arguments
PRESENTING DETAILS	Describes and explains important details that effectively develop a narrative, explanation, or argument

ACADEMIC HABITS

HABITS DEVELOPED	DESCRIPTORS
UNDERSTANDING PURPOSE AND PROCESS	Understands the purpose and uses the process and criteria that guide tasks
LISTENING	Pays attention to, acknowledges, and considers thoughtfully new information and ideas from others
REVISING	Rethinks and refines work based on teacher-, peer-, and self-review processes

ALIGNMENT TO CCSS

TARGETED STANDARDS:

CCSS.ELA-LITERACY.RL.9-10.1: Cite strong and thorough textual evidence to support analysis of what the text says explicitly as well as inferences drawn from the text.

CCSS.ELA-LITERACY.W.9-10.9b: Draw evidence from literary or informational texts to support analysis, reflection, and research.

SUPPORTING STANDARDS:

CCSS.ELA-LITERACY.RL.9-10.3: Analyze how complex characters (e.g., those with multiple or conflicting motivations) develop over the course of a text, interact with other characters, and advance the plot or develop the theme.

CCSS.ELA-LITERACY.RL.9-10.5: Analyze how an author's choices concerning how to structure a text, order events within it (e.g., parallel plots), and manipulate time (e.g., pacing, flashbacks) create such effects as mystery, tension, or surprise.

CCSS.ELA-LITERACY.SL. 9-10.1: Initiate and participate effectively in a range of collaborative discussions (one-on-one, in groups, and teacher-led) with diverse partners on *grades 9–10 topics, texts, and issues,* building on others' ideas and expressing their own clearly and persuasively.

# ACTIVITIES

1. MODEL THE COMMUNICATION OF AN EBC THROUGH WRITING

The teacher introduces and models the process of writing one or more paragraphs that communicate an evidence-based claim using a claim developed in Parts 2 or 3.

2. MODEL AND PRACTICE THE USE OF QUESTIONS AND CRITERIA TO IMPROVE A WRITTEN EBC

The teacher introduces a collaborative, peer-review process for developing and improving writing using Guiding Questions and criteria from the targeted Literacy Skills.

3. WRITING EBCs IN PAIRS

In pairs, students develop a paragraph that communicates an evidence-based claim using one of their claims from Parts 2 or 3.

4. REVIEWING AND IMPROVING WRITTEN EBCs

In small groups, student pairs present their written evidence-based claims and use questions and criteria to identify strengths and possible areas for improvement.

5. INDEPENDENT READING, DEVELOPING QUESTIONING PATHS, AND MAKING EBCs

Students independently read the rest of the text, develop a *Questioning Path Tool* to guide their reading, and use the *Forming EBC Tool* to develop an evidence-based claim.

6. READ ALOUD AND CLASS DISCUSSION

The class discusses their new evidence-based claims from Activity 5 and students listen actively to portions of the text being read or presented.

7. INDEPENDENT WRITING OF EBCs

Students independently complete an *Organizing EBC Tool* for the claim they have formed in Activity 5 and draft a one- to two-paragraph evidence-based claim.

8. USING PEER FEEDBACK TO REVISE A WRITTEN EBC

Students apply the collaborative review process and revise one aspect of their draft evidence-based claims paragraphs.

NOTE TO TEACHER

In the first two activities of part 4, teachers model writing and revising evidence-based claims. These activities duplicate instruction in the earlier *Making Evidence-Based Claims* unit on Plato's *Apology*. Depending on the needs of their students, teachers might choose to skip the first two activities and move directly to Activity 3 where students begin work on writing claims in pairs.

Developing Core Literacy Proficiencies

ACTIVITY 1: MODEL THE COMMUNICATION OF AN EBC THROUGH WRITING

The teacher introduces and models the process of writing one or more paragraphs that communicate an evidence-based claim using a claim developed in Parts 2 or 3.

INSTRUCTIONAL NOTES

Parts 1 through 3 have built a solid foundation of critical thinking and reading skills for developing and organizing evidence-based claims. Parts 4 and 5 focus on expressing evidence-based claims in a written paragraph format. By discussing as a class and working in pairs, students have gained significant practice in expressing and defending their claims orally. The tools have given them practice in selecting and organizing evidence. Expressing evidence-based claims in writing should now be a natural transition from this foundation.

Writing Evidence-Based Claims Handout

- Begin by explaining that writing an evidence-based claim follows the same basic structure that students have been using with the tools—one states a claim and develops it with evidence.

- Suggest to students that written claims can take various forms. Sometimes the purpose of the writing is merely to explain the claim, what it means, and how it has come from a close reading of textual evidence. At other times, the purpose may be more argumentative in nature—to *prove* the claim through presenting sufficient and relevant textual evidence.

- Have students examine their copy of the **Writing EBC Handout** for this unit (in the **Making EBC Literacy Toolbox**). The handout addresses five key expectations students will need to consider as they write and revise their claims:

  1. Establish the context by connecting the claim to the text.

  2. State the claim clearly to fully communicate their ideas about the text.

  3. Organize supporting evidence found in the text.

  4. Paraphrase and quote from the text.

  5. Reference the evidence drawn from the text.

- Discuss each of these five key aspects of writing a claim in relationship to previous work in the unit. Students will return to this handout and the specific examples it presents when they are writing and reviewing their claims.

- Using the model **Organizing EBC Tool** for this unit (which may have been introduced in Part 3, Activity 3) or another claim developed by the teacher or class, model how a writer moves from an organizational plan to a written explanation of a claim:

  ⇒ Breaking down a claim into its component subpoints and evidence (the Organizing Evidence-Based Claims process)

  ⇒ Communicating the claim in complete sentences and paragraphs that explain the subpoints and present the evidence

  ⇒ Integrating evidence as either quotations or paraphrases

- Building a unified explanation or argument from the component paragraphs, ideas, and evidence A think-aloud approach can be extremely effective here. When modeling the writing process, explain the choices you make. For example, "I'm paraphrasing this piece of evidence because it takes the author four sentences to express what I can do in one." Or, "I'm quoting

> this piece directly because the author's phrase is so powerful that I want to use the original words."
>
> - Explain that making choices when writing evidence-based claims is easiest when the writer has "lived with the claims." Thinking about a claim—personalizing the analysis—gives a writer an intuitive sense of how to express it.
>
> - Model how reviewing the ideas recorded on the tools and selecting and organizing evidence can help a writer know how to develop a written EBC. Once students are more familiar with their ideas, making links among ideas, subpoints, and evidence will be easier and more intuitive.

ACTIVITY 2: MODEL AND PRACTICE THE USE OF QUESTIONS AND CRITERIA TO IMPROVE A WRITTEN EBC

The teacher introduces a collaborative, peer-review process for developing and improving writing using Guiding Questions and criteria from the targeted Literacy Skills.

INSTRUCTIONAL NOTES

At this point in the unit, before they begin to develop their own written EBCs, students can be introduced to the OE Collaborative Writing Workshop, an approach to developing and strengthening writing through a collaborative, question-based, and text-centered process. This process can help student writers focus on the Literacy Skills they have been working on in the unit, specifically **Forming Claims**, **Using Evidence**, and **Organizing Ideas**. The teaching of the process, here and elsewhere in the Developing Core Literacy Proficiencies units, involves teacher modeling, guided and supported writing, and text-centered discussion.

> **NOTE**
>
> See the Users Guide that introduces and supports the Developing Core Literacy Proficiencies units for a detailed discussion of the OE Collaborative Writing Workshop process, principles, and suggestions for instruction.

- **Teacher Modeling:** Present students with a draft paragraph(s) that communicate(s) an evidence-based claim (either a teacher-developed model or a model paragraph from the *Writing EBC Handout* found in the **Making EBC Literacy Toolbox**). Let them know that they will be working with this written claim to learn and practice a process for reading a written draft of an evidence-based claim, using questions and criteria to think about the draft claim, and providing observations and feedback about how to improve the written explanation of the claim.

- **Text-Centered Review and Discussion:** Model and talk through the review process, using the following steps—which students will again apply in Activities 4 and 8 and throughout Part 5 of the unit (when they review each other's final written evidence-based claims).

1. Introduce a general Guiding Review Question related to the overall content of the writing, such as "What is the writer's claim, and how does it relate to the text we have read?"

2. In review teams, have students reread the draft paragraph in light of the general Guiding Review Question. Student teams then share text-based responses to the question with the class, as if the teacher is the paragraph's author.

3. Focus students' attention on two targeted Literacy Skills criteria: **Forming Claims** and **Using Evidence**. Explain, model, and discuss what each of these criteria causes one to think about, based on previous discussions about claims and textual evidence.

4. Read closely and study the specific language of the skills criteria:

FORMING CLAIMS	Develops a meaningful and defensible claim that clearly states an understanding of the text
USING EVIDENCE	Supports the claim with enough well-chosen evidence from the text; uses accurate quotations, paraphrases, and references

NOTE

Student-language versions of these skills descriptors are also found in the ***Student Making EBC Literacy Skills Checklist*** included in the **Making EBC Literacy Toolbox**.

5. Model and discuss what specific language in the criterion statements might mean when writing a claim, for example, "What does it mean to develop a claim that is 'meaningful and defensible'? To state a claim that shows an 'understanding of the text'? To support the claim with 'enough well-chosen evidence'?"

6. With the two literacy skills review criteria as a focus, frame one or more text-based question(s) that you might pose to a reviewer who was going to give you specific feedback about the draft paragraph.

- **Text-Based Review Question(s):** Is my claim "clearly stated"? Is my evidence "well chosen," and is there "enough" to explain or "defend" my claim? What might I add (or revise) to help you better get my "understanding of the text"?

7. Students (individually or in review teams) now read the paragraph closely, considering the text-based review question(s) and generating a reviewer's response.

8. Discuss how a text-based response to a draft piece of writing is itself a kind of *claim* that the reviewer makes based on the criteria, question(s), and specific evidence from the writer's draft.

9. Model how you might frame a claim-based response if you were a reviewer of the draft paragraph, emphasizing these points:

  ⇒ A *specific* response that emphasizes a <u>strength</u> of the paragraph and a <u>potential improvement</u>

  ⇒ A *constructive* and respectful articulation of the response

  ⇒ References to *text-based evidence* in the paragraph that has led to and supports your response

10. Guided by this model, students articulate and share their text-based responses and constructive reviewer claims, as if their partners were now the writer of the draft paragraph. Have several students volunteer present their responses to the whole class and discuss how the responses are (or are not) *specific, constructive, and text-based.*

11. Model the habits a writer should develop when receiving a reviewer's response:

Listening

⇒ Listen fully to what readers have observed.

⇒ Consider their ideas thoughtfully.

⇒ Wait momentarily before responding verbally.

Remaining Open

⇒ Avoid explanations or justifications for what you as a writer have tried to do (no "yes, but . . ." responses).

⇒ Frame additional informal, text-based questions to further probe your readers' observations.

Revising

⇒ Consider the implications of your readers' observations for improving your writing.

⇒ Discuss what you might do as a writer to improve the example written claim after considering the responses you have received to your text-based review questions.

Emphasize throughout this modeling that developing an effective communication of an evidence-based claim through writing is a process—it *cannot* be done in one draft. Revision is fundamental to honing written evidence-based claims.

ACTIVITY 3: WRITING EBCs IN PAIRS

In pairs, students develop a paragraph that communicates an evidence-based claim, using one of their claims from Parts 2 or 3.

- Students return to the same pairings from Part 3 and review the **Organizing EBC Tool** they developed; they now use these tools to guide their writing of EBC paragraphs. Support pairs by answering questions and helping them get comfortable with the techniques for incorporating evidence. Use questions from pairs as opportunities to instruct the entire class.

- In this first phase of the process for writing an evidence-based claim, students should focus on less formal, more fluent writing, trying first to get their ideas out on paper so that they and others can examine them. Students should be given adequate time and opportunity to write in class and be expected to produce something that can be reviewed by others.

- Refocus students' attention on the two Literacy Skills criteria they have just used to review the model written claim in Part 3: **Forming Claims** and **Using Evidence**. They should think about these skills as they write because they will use them to review the draft claims they develop.

- Explain that the simplest structure for writing evidence-based claims is beginning with a sentence or paragraph stating the claim and its context and then using subsequent sentences or paragraphs logically linked together to explain the claim and develop its necessary points with appropriate evidence. (More advanced writers can organize the expression differently, for example, establishing a context, building points with evidence, and stating the claim at the end for a more dramatic effect. Let students know that the simplest structure is not the only effective way.)

Incorporating textual evidence into writing is difficult and takes practice. Expect all students to need guidance in deciding what precise evidence to use, how to order it, and when to paraphrase or to quote. They will also need guidance in structuring sentence syntax and grammar to smoothly and effectively incorporate textual details while maintaining their own voice and style.

☰ ACTIVITY 4: REVIEWING AND IMPROVING WRITTEN EBCs

In small groups, student pairs present their written evidence-based claims and use questions and criteria to identify strengths and possible areas for improvement.

INSTRUCTIONAL NOTES

- Group student pairs into review groups of four students (two pairs) each.

- Have each student pair read their draft written EBCs paragraph aloud to their partner pair.

- Guide students in using the collaborative, question- and criteria-based review process modeled in Activity 3, as outlined in the following:

  1. Introduce a general Guiding Review Question related to the overall content of the writing, such as "What is the writer's claim, and how does it relate to the text we have read?"

  2. In review teams, have students reread each other's draft paragraphs in light of the general Guiding Review Question. Student teams then share text-based responses to the question with each other.

  3. Focus students' attention again on the two targeted Literacy Skills criteria: **Forming Claims** and **Using Evidence**.

  4. Have student pairs, who drafted an EBC paragraph together, each frame a text-specific review question related to one or both of these criteria (if students struggle with this step, they can consider a review question from Activity 3, Step 6).

  5. Student review teams now read the paragraph closely, considering the text-based review questions and generating reviewer's responses. Responses should include these elements:

     ⇒ A *specific* response that emphasizes a <u>strength</u> of the paragraph and a <u>potential improvement</u>

     ⇒ A *constructive* and respectful articulation of the response

     ⇒ References to *text-based evidence* in the paragraph that has led to and supports the response

  6. As they listen to their review team's responses, drafting pairs should work on the following behaviors, all related to the Academic Habits of **Listening**, **Remaining Open**, and **Revising**.

Listening

⇒ Listen fully to what readers have observed.

⇒ Consider their ideas thoughtfully.

⇒ Wait momentarily before responding verbally.

Remaining Open

⇒ Avoid explanations or justifications for what they as writers have tried to do (no "yes, but..." responses).

⇒ Frame additional informal, text-based questions to further probe their readers' observations.

Revising

⇒ Consider the implications of their readers' observations for improving their writing.

7. Discuss what they might do as writers to improve their written claims after considering the responses they received.

NOTE

Writers will *not* revise this first claim they have written in pairs, but they will use the same process to revise and improve claims in Activity 8 and Part 5.

- Have a few volunteer pairs present their written claims to the class, explaining the following:

  ⇒ How they have derived and developed them

  ⇒ The feedback they received from their reviewers

  ⇒ What they might do to improve their written claims

- Depending on resources available, students might write or display their claim on the board or share it with the class and teacher electronically. The class together should evaluate the way the writing sets the context, expresses the claim, effectively organizes the evidence, and incorporates the evidence properly.

- Use the targeted Literacy Skills criteria for **Forming Claims** and **Using Evidence** to guide the discussion.

- Let other students lead the discussion of their peers' written claims, reserving guidance when needed and appropriate. It is likely and ideal that other students will refer to their own claims when evaluating the volunteer pair's paragraph.

- Make sure that class discussion maintains a constructive, collegial tone, and all critiques are supported by evidence. This discussion and the previous small-group discussions provide effective opportunities to practice and reflect on the Academic Habits of **Collaborating** and **Communicating Clearly**.

ACTIVITY 5: INDEPENDENT READING, DEVELOPING QUESTIONING PATHS, AND MAKING EBCs

Students independently read from paragraph 238 ("That was the story of the lion.") to the end and use the **Forming EBC Tool** to develop an evidence-based claim.

INSTRUCTIONAL NOTES

Depending on scheduling and student ability, students can be assigned to read and complete the tool for homework or do so in class.

INDEPENDENT USE OF A QUESTIONING PATH AND DEVELOPMENT OF A CLAIM

- Students first consider a Questioning Path they might use to frame and guide their close reading of the text. Using the **Guiding Questions Handout** and previous model **Questioning Path Tools** as examples, students determine an approach they will take in reading the text and identify Guiding Questions they will use as they initially question and then analyze the text.

- Students initially plan their approach to reading using a blank **Questioning Path Tool** (in the **Making EBC Literacy Toolbox**) and record their Guiding Questions on the tool.

- After their initial reading(s), students independently develop a text-specific question and record it in the Deepening section of the tool.

- Students use this new, independently developed question to guide their deeper reading of the text and the development of an evidence-based claim.

- Students record their question at the top of a **Forming EBC Tool** and search for details related to their question as they develop a new claim.

ACTIVITY 6: READ ALOUD AND CLASS DISCUSSION

The class discusses their new evidence-based claims from Activity 5 and students listen actively to portions of the text being read or presented.

INSTRUCTIONAL NOTES

- The class discusses the text and their new evidence-based claims from Activity 5. Students review the self-developed Questioning Paths they have followed in reading the text and introduce their claims by reading their text-specific questions that led to those claims.

- In pairs, students work together to hone their claims and organize evidence they have found in the text. Have students transfer their claims from the **Forming EBC Tool** to the **Organizing EBC Tool**, which they will use in Activity 7 to help them organize and refine their evidence in preparation for writing.

- Students follow along as they listen to the final four paragraphs read. Students should present their evidence-based claims, and the discussion of their claims should determine areas of the text to be read aloud. Students read aloud relevant portions to help the class analyze claims and selected evidence.

ACTIVITY 7: INDEPENDENT WRITING OF EBCs

Students independently complete an *Organizing EBC Tool* for the claim they have formed in Activity 5 and draft a one- to two-paragraph evidence-based claim.

INSTRUCTIONAL NOTES

Students should have reviewed and reconsidered the claims they wrote in Activity 5 in light of class discussion.

- Students independently develop an *Organizing EBC Tool* and then draft a one- to two-paragraph written EBC based on their tools.

- Direct students to the *Making EBCs about Literary Technique—Final Writing Task Handout* included in the Student Edition to help review the assignment.

Because this is the first time students have independently developed a written claim, they may need some support in thinking about how to present and explain the claim, develop it through subpoints, and integrate supporting evidence from the text.

- As students write, remind them to consult the *Writing EBC Handout* that they first reviewed in Part 4, Activity 1. Remind them of the five things they will need to do as they write and revise their claims (from the *Writing EBC Handout*):
  1. Establish the context by connecting the claim to the text.
  2. State the claim clearly to fully communicate their ideas about the text.
  3. Organize supporting evidence found in the text.
  4. Paraphrase and quote from the text.
  5. Reference the evidence drawn from the text.

- Suggest that students read and think about the examples discussed in the handout as they draft, review, and revise their written claims. For some students, thinking about these examples (as models) before they write may be most helpful. For others, writing on their own first and then comparing what they have written to the models may work best. Either way, they should work to successfully do the five things explained and exemplified in the handout.

- Finally, remind students as they draft that the Literacy Skills criteria for **Forming Claims** and **Using Evidence** should continue to be in their minds and that they will review and revise their paragraphs in relationship to these criteria.

ACTIVITY 8: USING PEER FEEDBACK TO REVISE A WRITTEN EBC

Students apply the collaborative review process and revise one aspect of their draft evidence-based claims paragraphs.

Developing Core Literacy Proficiencies

- Organize students in editing partners or teams.
- Have students use the same collaborative, question- and criteria-based review process outlined and practiced in Activities 3 and 4:
  1. Read their draft out loud with a general Guiding Review Question.
  2. Listen to reviewers' initial observations based on the Guiding Question.
  3. Consider the Literacy Skills criteria and frame a text-based review question(s) in relationship to those criteria.
  4. Engage in a text-centered discussion of the drafts, referencing the criteria, questions, and specific evidence from the drafts.
  5. Determine strengths and areas for possible improvement based on the discussion of the drafts.
- Following the reviews of their drafts, each student individually determines <u>one aspect</u> of the draft they would like to improve, for example:
  ⇒ The <u>clarity</u> of the claim and its explanation
  ⇒ How <u>defensible</u> their claim is, based on the evidence they have presented
  ⇒ The <u>use of evidence</u> and integration of textual references into their writing
  ⇒ The <u>organization</u> of their subpoints and evidence into a unified written claim
- Students complete one revision of their written claim, focusing on the aspect they have targeted for improvement, then read their revised claims to their editing partners or teams for final feedback.
- As a class, discuss what students have learned about writing a claim, the targeted Literacy Skills of **Forming Claims** and **Using Evidence**, the collaborative process to review and improve writing, and the Academic Habits of **Collaborating** and **Revising**.

INDEPENDENT READING ACTIVITY

Students review the entire story and use a **_Forming EBC Tool_** to make a new claim of their choice and develop it with evidence. This activity overlaps with Activity 1 of Part 5 and can be given as homework or done at the beginning of the next class.

☰ PART 4: FORMATIVE ASSESSMENT ☰ OPPORTUNITIES

By the end of Part 4, students will have accomplished the following:

- Written an evidence-based claim paragraph in pairs
- Participated in three rounds of collaborative reviews of written EBCs
- Develop their own Questioning Path on a **_Questioning Path Tool_**
- Completed a **_Forming EBC Tool_** and **_Organizing EBC Tool_** independently
- Written and revised an EBC paragraph independently

ASSESSING LITERACY SKILLS

At this stage, teachers can assess students' reading and writing skills. Students should be comfortable making claims and supporting them with organized evidence. Their tools should demonstrate evidence of progress or proficiency in targeted reading skills, such as **Attending to Details**, **Identifying Relationships**, **Making Inferences**, and **Forming Claims**. Student writing should begin to demonstrate how well they can organize ideas, use evidence, and present details. Make sure they have properly established the context, that the claim is clearly expressed, and that each paragraph develops a coherent point. Evaluate the writing for an understanding of the difference between paraphrase and quotation when using evidence. All evidence should be properly referenced. Use the review criteria from Part 4 or the detailed *Student Making EBC Literacy Skills Checklist* in the **Making EBC Literacy Toolbox** to structure evaluation and feedback to students.

ASSESSING ACADEMIC HABITS

Students will have continued to use and develop the habits of **Collaborating** and **Communicating Clearly** in text-centered discussions, and for the first time they will have applied those habits in the context of reviewing and revising a written product. They will have begun to demonstrate how well they can understand and apply a collaborative, criteria-based process for improving their work; in doing so, they will have applied the Academic Habits of **Listening** and **Remaining Open** to feedback from peers. Students can reflect informally or receive peer and teacher feedback about any of these habits and might use an expanded *Habits Checklist* such as the one below (or the *Student Making EBC Academic Habits Checklist* in the **Making EBC Literacy Toolbox**):

HABITS DEVELOPED	DESCRIPTORS	EVIDENCE OF USING THE HABIT	THINGS TO IMPROVE ON
UNDERSTANDING PURPOSE AND PROCESS	Understands and uses the collaborative writing workshop process Uses Literacy Skills criteria to frame questions, responses, and feedback		
LISTENING	Pays attention to new information and ideas from others Considers others' ideas thoughtfully		
REMAINING OPEN	Avoids explanations or justifications for what they as writers have tried to do Frames text-based questions to probe their readers' observations		
REVISING	Uses criteria to rethink, refine, or revise work Uses observations from peers to inform improvement		

> **NOTE**
>
> To support self-, peer, and teacher assessment of skills and habits developed during the unit, a formal *Making EBC Literacy Skills Rubric* and less formal *Student Making EBC Literacy Skills* and *Academic Habits Checklists* are provided in the **Making EBC Literacy Toolbox**.

Developing Core Literacy Proficiencies

PART 5

DEVELOPING EVIDENCE-BASED WRITING

"Mrs. Macomber, in the car, had shot at the buffalo"

OBJECTIVE:	Students develop the ability to express global evidence-based claims in writing through a rereading of the texts in the unit and a review of their previous work.

ESTIMATED TIME: 3 to 4 days

MATERIALS:
- *Forming EBC Tool*
- *Organizing EBC Tool*
- *Writing EBC Handout*
- *Making EBC Literacy Skills Rubric*
- *Student Making EBC Literacy Skills Checklist*
- *Student Making EBC Academic Habits Checklist*

≡ LITERACY SKILLS

In Part 5, students demonstrate the Literacy Skills they have been working on throughout the unit through a final essay in which they develop, explain, and support a global evidence-based claim. Their essays can be read as evidence of their reading skills (**Attending to Details, Interpreting Language, Identifying Relationships, Making Inferences, Forming Claims**) and their writing skills (**Using Evidence, Presenting Details, Organizing Ideas, Using Language, Using Conventions**). Because their final essay may be their first, more formal piece of writing, it also presents opportunities for them to work on and formatively demonstrate skills associated with **Publishing**: using effective formatting and citations.

The *Student Making EBC Literacy Skills Checklist* provided in the **Making EBC Literacy Toolbox** can be used for self- and peer assessment, and the *Making EBC Literacy Skills Rubric* can be used for evaluating students' work on the essay.

TARGETED SKILLS	DESCRIPTORS
ATTENDING TO DETAILS	Identifies relevant and important textual details, words, and ideas
INTERPRETING LANGUAGE	Identifies how words and phrases convey meaning and represent an author's or narrator's perspective
IDENTIFYING RELATIONSHIPS	Identifies important connections among key details and ideas within and across texts
MAKING INFERENCES	Demonstrates comprehension by using connections among details to make logical deductions about a text
FORMING CLAIMS	Develops meaningful and defensible claims that clearly state valid, evidence-based analysis

TARGETED SKILLS	DESCRIPTORS
USING EVIDENCE	Supports all aspects of claims with sufficient textual evidence, using accurate quotations, paraphrases, and references
ORGANIZING IDEAS	Sequences sentences and paragraphs to establish coherent, logical, and unified narratives, explanations, and arguments
PRESENTING DETAILS	Describes and explains important details that effectively develop a narrative, explanation, or argument
USING LANGUAGE	Selects and combines words that precisely communicate ideas, generate appropriate tone, and evoke intended responses from an audience
USING CONVENTIONS	Uses effective sentence structure, grammar, punctuation, and spelling to express ideas and achieve writing and speaking purposes
PUBLISHING	Uses effective formatting and citations to present ideas for specific audiences and purposes

ACADEMIC HABITS

Part 5 also presents further opportunities for students to engage in text-centered discussions about the text(s) they have read in the unit and their own written claims. Students can do a final, more formal self-assessment and receive teacher feedback about how well they have developed and are demonstrating the Academic Habits used in discussion and collaborative revision processes. The *Student Making EBC Academic Habits Checklist* provided in the **Making EBC Literacy Toolbox** can be used for self-, peer, and teacher assessment of these habits.

HABITS DEVELOPED	DESCRIPTORS
ENGAGING ACTIVELY	Actively focuses attention on independent and collaborative tasks
COLLABORATING	Pays attention to, respects, and works productively in various roles with all other participants
COMMUNICATING CLEARLY	Uses appropriate language and relevant textual details to clearly present ideas and claims
UNDERSTANDING PURPOSE AND PROCESS	Understands the purpose and uses the process and criteria that guide tasks
LISTENING	Pays attention to, acknowledges, and considers thoughtfully new information and ideas from others
REVISING	Rethinks and refines work based on teacher-, peer-, and self-review processes

ALIGNMENT TO CCSS

TARGETED STANDARDS:

CCSS.ELA-LITERACY.RL.9-10.1: Cite strong and thorough textual evidence to support analysis of what the text says explicitly as well as inferences drawn from the text.

CCSS.ELA-LITERACY.W.9-10.9b: Draw evidence from literary or informational texts to support analysis, reflection, and research.

SUPPORTING STANDARDS:

CCSS.ELA-LITERACY.RL.9-10.3: Analyze how complex characters (e.g., those with multiple or conflicting motivations) develop over the course of a text, interact with other characters, and advance the plot or develop the theme.

CCSS.ELA-LITERACY.RL.9-10.5: Analyze how an author's choices concerning how to structure a text, order events within it (e.g., parallel plots), and manipulate time (e.g., pacing, flashbacks) create such affects as mystery, tension, or surprise.

CCSS.ELA-LITERACY.W.9-10.4: Produce clear and coherent writing in which the development, organization, and style are appropriate to task, purpose, and audience.

ACTIVITIES

1. **INDEPENDENT READING AND CLASS DISCUSSION OF GLOBAL EBCs ABOUT LITERARY TECHNIQUE**
   Students independently reread the entire text and the class discusses the development of global evidence-based claims about literary technique.

2. **FORMING GLOBAL EBCs ABOUT LITERARY TECHNIQUE**
   Students review previous claims and use a *Forming EBC Tool* to frame a new global evidence-based claim about literary technique.

3. **REVIEWING AND ORGANIZING EBCs**
   Students discuss their new claims in pairs and then with the class, considering their supporting evidence and how they will organize it with an *Organizing EBC Tool*.

4. **INDEPENDENT DRAFTING A FINAL EBC ESSAY**
   Students independently draft a final evidence-based essay using their new claims.

5. **USING THE COLLABORATIVE, CRITERIA-BASED PROCESS TO IMPROVE ESSAYS**
   Students use a criteria-based rubric and feedback from peers in a collaborative review process to revise and improve their evidence-based claims essays.

6. **CLASS DISCUSSION OF FINAL EBC ESSAYS**
   The class discusses final evidence-based essays of student volunteers and reflects on the Literacy Skills and Academic Habits involved in making and communicating evidence-based claims.

ACTIVITY 1: INDEPENDENT READING AND CLASS DISCUSSION OF GLOBAL EBCs ABOUT LITERARY TECHNIQUE

Students independently reread the entire text, and the class discusses the development of global evidence-based claims about literary technique.

INSTRUCTIONAL NOTES

In Part 5, students move to thinking about the big picture presented to them by considering "The Short Happy Life of Francis Macomber" in its entirety both with respect to its content as well Hemingway's use of literary techniques. Students have been focusing on specific sections of the story and Hemingway's use of characterization, narrative point of view, and chronology in those specific contexts. Now they should expand their view and consider the cumulative effect of those techniques.

Making global claims about literary technique will be challenging for students, and they can be supported in a number of ways. Encourage students to begin with one of their smaller claims about a specific portion of the story. Have them apply that same insight to a wider range of text, looking for evidence throughout the story that supports and clarifies the claim.

For example, students may have developed a claim about how Hemingway's physical description of Wilson's clothes gives the reader a sense of his experience and authority. If so, students could be encouraged to search for every place where Hemingway gives a physical description of Wilson. Once the evidence has been collected, they could be encouraged to think what the global effect the physical description gives. They might also highlight a few instances in which the description possesses significant importance for the story as a whole.

Another way students might be supported in developing global claims about literary technique is to have them start their thinking from the standpoint of the content or themes of the story. Encourage students to identify a specific event or line from the story that they feel is significant. Once the event or line is identified, they can draw on their analysis of Hemingway's techniques to interpret its significance.

For example, a classic way to interpret this story as a whole is to consider the meaning of its title. What might Hemingway have meant by Macomber's "happy life"? How was it "short"? As students consider the meaning of the parts of the title, encourage them to draw on their analysis of Hemingway's techniques to develop and support their thinking. They might explain the various methods of characterization Hemingway uses to express how Macomber changes through the events of the story.

In addition to the title, many other single lines could be used to provide students a jumping-off point for their global claim essays. For instance, "like a dam bursting" or "he felt a sudden white-hot, blinding flash explode inside his head and that was all he ever felt."

If students have focused discussion on narrative point of view, the line, "he felt a sudden white-hot, blinding flash explode inside his head and that was all he ever felt" could be used as an anchor for a global claim. How does Hemingway's shift to Macomber's perspective in the telling of this episode affect the reader's experience? How does this description and use of point of view relate to the description of the lion's experience of the initial hunt? How do these parallel uses of narrative point of view affect the meaning of the story as a whole?

- Using these or other teacher-developed examples model and explain a global claim about literary technique.

- Direct students to the *Making EBCs about Literary Technique—Final Writing Task Handout* included in the Student Edition to help review the assignment.

- In pairs or groups, have students do the following:
  1. Reread the text.
  2. Review the *Forming EBC* and *Organizing EBC Tools* they have developed.
  3. Reread the claims they have written in Part 4

- Students engage in a discussion—first in small groups, then as a class—about what it all adds up to—what they think about some of the stories' larger meanings.

- Have students informally generate, share, and compare their own global claims using details and analysis from their work throughout the unit.

☰ ACTIVITY 2: FORMING GLOBAL EBCs
☰ ABOUT LITERARY TECHNIQUE

Students review previous claims and use a *Forming EBC Tool* to frame a new global evidence-based claim about literary technique.

INSTRUCTIONAL NOTES

Having brainstormed and shared various global claims about the text, students are now ready to form a final claim about what they have read to be developed into a multiparagraph essay.

- Using the *Forming EBC* or *Supporting EBC Tool*, students can either work from connected details to develop a new claim or find supporting evidence for a claim they have come up with in Activity 1.

- In pairs or small groups, students review the claims they have formed and the evidence they have identified, thinking about the Literacy Skills criteria for forming claims (i.e., Is a claim "clear," "meaningful," "defensible," and clearly related to an "understanding of the text"?) and using evidence (Is there "enough, well-chosen" evidence to support the claim?).

☰ ACTIVITY 3: REVIEWING AND ☰ ORGANIZING EBCs

Students discuss their new claims in pairs and then with the class, considering their supporting evidence and how they will organize it with an *Organizing EBC Tool*.

INSTRUCTIONAL NOTES

- Based on feedback from their peers in Activity 2, students revise claims, find new supporting evidence and complete an *Organizing EBC Tool* to support their writing of their claim.
- Students share their claims and organizational plans, first in pairs and then as a class.
  - ⇒ Volunteer pairs can be asked to discuss the work they did on their claims. At this point they should be able to talk about the nature of their claims and why they have chosen to organize evidence in particular ways.

☰ ACTIVITY 4: INDEPENDENT DRAFTING ☰ OF A FINAL EBC ESSAY

Students independently draft a final evidence-based claims essay using their new claims.

INSTRUCTIONAL NOTES

- Explain to students that they will now be drafting a final, multiparagraph essay that explains, develops, and supports their global EBC. Let them know that this evidence-based writing piece will be used as a summative assessment to evaluate their development of the Literacy Skills targeted in the unit.
- Communicate to students that their task will be to explain and support a global EBC they have formed based on their reading and analysis of the text.
- Have students read through the *Final Evidence-Based Claim Writing Assignment* found in the Developing Core Literacy Proficiencies Student Edition, which presents them with a short explanation of the assignment and its criteria, as well as a listing of the key Literacy Skills they should try to demonstrate.
- Explain to students that their final written essays will be evaluated for their demonstration of three key expectations and criteria for the assignment:
  1. Demonstrate an accurate reading and insightful analysis of the text.
  2. Develop a supported claim that is clearly connected to the content of the text.
  3. Successfully accomplish the five key elements of a written EBC.
- Students can keep these five key elements in mind by consulting the *Writing EBC Handout* that they first reviewed and used in Part 4, Activities 1 and 7.
  1. Establish the context by connecting the claim to the text.
  2. State the claim clearly to fully communicate their ideas about the text.
  3. Organize supporting evidence found in the text.

4. Paraphrase and quote from the text.

5. Reference the evidence drawn from the text.

- Suggest that students again read and think about the examples discussed in the handout as they draft their final written claims. For some students, thinking about these examples (as models) before they write may be most helpful. For others, writing on their own first and then comparing what they have written to the models may work best. Either way, they should work to successfully follow the five components explained and exemplified in the handout.

- Direct students to consult the **Student Making EBC Literacy Skills Checklist** for this essay. Explain that they will be using parts of the checklist in Activity 5 to review and revise their draft essays. Review the key criteria they and you will be examining and what the descriptors suggest about the writing of an evidence-based claims essay.

- Provide time and support in class for students to draft their essays, working from the planning they have done on an **Organizing EBC Tool**.

ACTIVITY 5: USING THE COLLABORATIVE, CRITERIA-BASED PROCESS TO IMPROVE ESSAYS

Students use a criteria-based rubric and feedback from peers in a collaborative review process to revise and improve their evidence-based claims essays.

INSTRUCTIONAL NOTES

Once students have completed a first draft of their evidence-based claims essays, they will work in writing groups (of two to four students) to complete two review and revision cycles. The first cycle will focus on the essay's content: the <u>clarity</u> of their claim and its explanation and the <u>sufficiency and quality of the evidence</u> they have presented to support their claim. The second cycle will focus on the essay's organization and expression: how they have arranged their ideas in a <u>logical sequence</u>, smoothly integrated <u>textual details</u>, and used <u>language and conventions</u> to communicate their ideas.

Before beginning the reviews, remind students that as reviewers their observations should include these elements:

- A *specific* response that emphasizes a <u>strength</u> of the essay and a <u>potential improvement</u>
- A *constructive* and respectful articulation of the response
- References to *text-based evidence* in the essay that has led to and supports the response

And that as writers (and receivers of feedback) they should do the following:

- Listen carefully to what their readers have observed.
- Wait momentarily before responding verbally.
- Avoid explanations and justifications for what they as writers have tried to do (no "yes, but . . ." responses).
- Frame additional informal, text-based questions to further probe their readers' observations.

Review 1—Focus on Content

Teacher Modeling

- Return to the Literacy Skills criteria students have been using in Part 4: Forming Claims and Using Evidence. Talk through how you might apply these criteria in reviewing a draft evidence-based claims essay—beginning with general Guiding Review Questions, such as "What is the claim and how clearly is it expressed and explained? Is there enough, well-chosen evidence to support the claim?" Then model how a writer might develop a more specific text-based review question to guide a second review of the draft.

Text-Centered Review and Discussion

- In writing groups, students read their draft essays aloud, then listen as their reviewers provide initial constructive feedback about the claim and its support.

- Reviewers reread the draft essay with the Guiding Review Questions in mind, noting strengths and places where the clarity of the claim or its support might be improved.

- Based on this initial feedback, each writer determines an area to work on and develops a specific text-based review question.

- Writers revise their essays, focusing on a specific aspect of their claim and its supporting evidence.

- Writers present reviewers with their text-based review question and receive a second text-based review about the draft essay's content.

Review 2—Focus on Organization and Expression

Teacher Modeling

- Determine one or two aspects of organization or expression that students should work on such as:
  ⇒ the logical sequence of the essay's explanation;
  ⇒ the connections, and transitions among sentences and paragraphs;
  ⇒ the smooth integration of quotations and paraphrases;
  ⇒ the clarity or vigor of expression;
  ⇒ one of more conventions of usage or punctuation;
  ⇒ the correct citation of textual evidence.

- Avoid asking students to focus on too many issues within this essay's revision cycle. Based on the area(s) chosen to focus on, introduce one or two criteria from the Literacy Skills listed in the **Student EBC Literacy Skills Checklist**. Model how these criteria can lead to a general Guiding Review Question and potentially a more specific text-based review question.

Text-Centered Review and Discussion

- In writing groups, reviewers first consider the general Guiding Review Question and complete another reading of the draft while providing constructive feedback.

- Based on this initial feedback, each writer determines an area to work on and develops a specific text-based review question.

- Writers revise their essays, focusing on a specific aspect of their essay's organization, expression, or publication.
- Writers present reviewers with their text-based review question and receive a second text-based review about the draft essay's organization or expression.

FINAL DRAFTING AND PUBLICATION

Using the *Student Making EBC Literacy Skills Checklist* for the evidence-based claims essay and any guidelines provided by the teacher for the formatting and publication of the final product, students complete a final revision and produce an essay to be shared with the class and submitted to the teacher for evaluation.

ACTIVITY 6: CLASS DISCUSSION OF FINAL EBC ESSAYS

The class discusses final evidence-based claims essays of student volunteers and reflects on the Literacy Skills and Academic Habits involved in making and communicating evidence-based claims.

- Students present their final evidence-based claims essays to the class. This activity can be done informally, calling on student volunteers, or more formally in a symposium format, in which each student presents his or her work to a group of peers, outside reviewers, or the class as a whole. In reading and presenting their essays, students should explain the following:
  - ⇒ The process through which they arrived at their claim—how it emerged from their reading of the text and how they honed it
  - ⇒ What they focused on as they rethought, revised, and polished their claim into a final essay
  - ⇒ What they learned about the text and its ideas, developing claims, and the Literacy Skills and Academic Habits they worked on during the unit
- The class engages in a final reflective discussion of the text read, the skills and habits worked on, and what they have learned about making evidence-based claims.

Students can complete a self-assessment using the *Student EBC Literacy Skills* and *Academic Habits Checklists* and may also compile a review portfolio of the annotated texts, tools, and written EBCs they have produced during the unit.

PART 5: SUMMATIVE ASSESSMENT

By the end of Part 5, students will have completed the following:

- A *Forming EBC Tool* (or *Supporting EBC Tool*) for a global claim
- An *Organizing EBC Tool*

- A rough draft of an evidence-based claims essay about their global claim
- A two-stage collaborative review and revision process
- A final written EBCs essay

ASSESSING LITERACY SKILLS

Students' final evidence-based claims essays, having gone through peer review and revision, should provide evidence of each student's development of the Literacy Skills targeted in the unit—especially the reading and thinking skills that have been the focus of instruction and that are involved in making an evidence-based claim. The *Student Making EBC Literacy Skills Checklist* provided with this unit can be used to guide students during the review and revision process for peer and self-assessment and for informal teacher feedback. A more formal **EBC Writing Task Rubric** (found in the **Making EBC Literacy Toolbox**) should be used by the teacher for evaluating performance and growth as demonstrated in the final essay and the reading and thinking exercises that have preceded it. This rubric includes a four-point developmental scale for indicating where students are on a continuum from "emerging" to "excelling" and also enables the teacher to indicate specific skill areas in which the student has demonstrated noticeable growth. The rubric includes a place for an overall summary evaluation— potentially a grade—or can be used in a point-based grading system by tallying the ratings for each of the fifteen criteria in the rubric.

Notes to the teacher about using the *EBC Writing Task Rubric*: Find evidence in the student's essay and planning notes to support ratings for each of the component Literacy Skills and overall essay content criteria listed in the rubric. Based on that evidence, use the developmental scale to rate the grade-level performance demonstrated by the student as:

1—**Emerging:** needs improvement

2—**Developing:** shows progress

3—**Becoming Proficient:** demonstrates skills

4—**Excelling:** exceeds expectations

If there is insufficient evidence to make a confident rating, mark **NE** (no evidence).

Indicate if the student has demonstrated growth in each skill area during the unit by adding a "+" to the rating. Determine a summary evaluation based on the overall pattern of ratings and strength of evidence. This summary evaluation can be computed based on points, or determined by examining the prevalent pattern in the criteria-based ratings.

Evidence of Reading and Thinking

Though the final essay is a written product, it should first and foremost be used as evidence of Literacy Skills associated with close reading and the development of text-based claims: **Attending to Details**, **Interpreting Language**, **Identifying Relationships**, **Recognizing Perspective**, **Making Inferences**, **Forming Claims**, and **Using Evidence**. Students have been working on these skills throughout this and previous Developing Core Literacy Proficiencies units and should be able to demonstrate evidence of them within their essays and the tools they have completed. Specifically, students at this point should show that they can identify key details from the text, note connections and develop inferences from those details, and form an original claim that is well supported by evidence from the text. Students should not be expected to mimic a claim presented by the teacher or suggested by one of the unit's text-specific questions. Rather, they should demonstrate that they can do original thinking based on their own close reading and analysis of the text.

Evidence of Writing

This evidence-based claims essay may be the first piece of more formal writing that students have done in the Developing Core Literacy Proficiencies sequence. If so, it should be viewed as a pre- or formative assessment of students' writing skills—particularly those associated with **Organizing Ideas**, **Using Language**, **Using Conventions**, and correctly citing evidence when **Publishing**. Depending on which of these areas has been a focus for the second round of collaborative review and revision, a teacher might provide more specific evaluation of several targeted criteria but otherwise should use the essay to help each student know which writing skills they might work on in future units.

ASSESSING ACADEMIC HABITS

By the end of the *Evidence-Based Claims* unit, students will have been reflecting on and self-assessing their development of the Academic Habits associated with text-centered discussion and the OE Collaborative Writing Workshop during informal activities at the end of each part of the unit. At the end of the unit, using the ***Student Making EBC Academic Habits Checklist***, students can do a more careful self-assessment of their development and demonstration of these habits during the unit—paying particular attention to where and how they have shown (or not shown) evidence of using the habits productively. The teacher can also use this checklist to provide feedback to students. If it is appropriate or desirable to make this feedback evaluative in nature, the ***Student Making EBC Academic Habits Checklist*** can be used with a three-point system (minus, check, plus) to communicate not only which habits each student has evidenced but also how well.

MAKING
EVIDENCE-BASED CLAIMS
ABOUT LITERARY
TECHNIQUE

DEVELOPING CORE LITERACY PROFICIENCIES

GRADE 9

Literacy Toolbox

ODELL
EDUCATION

WRITING EVIDENCE-BASED CLAIMS

Writing evidence-based claims is a little different from writing stories or just writing about something. You need to **follow a few steps** as you write.

1. ESTABLISH THE CONTEXT

Your readers must know **where your claim is coming from** and why it's relevant.

Depending on the scope of your piece and claim, the context differs.

If your whole piece is one claim or if you're introducing the first major claim of your piece, the entire context must be established:

> In "The Short Happy Life of Francis Macomber," Ernest Hemingway develops …

Purposes of evidence-based writing vary. In some cases, naming the book and author might be enough to establish the relevance of your claim. In other cases, you might want to supply additional information:

> In literature, authors often use the technique *in media res* where they begin a story in the middle of the action rather than at the beginning. In his short story "The Short Happy Life of Francis Macomber," Ernest Hemingway develops …

If your claim is part of a larger piece with multiple claims, then the context might be simpler:

> To create this effect, Hemingway …   *or*   In paragraph 5, Hemingway …

2. STATE YOUR CLAIM CLEARLY

How you state your claim is important; it must **precisely and comprehensively express your analysis.** Figuring out how to state claims is a **process**; writers revise them continually as they write their supporting evidence. Here's a claim about how Hemingway uses various points of view to characterize the character of Francis Macomber:

> In "The Short Happy Life of Francis Macomber," Ernest Hemingway develops the characters of the short story by jumping from one character's point of view to another.

When writing claims, it is often useful to describe parts of the claim before providing the supporting evidence. In this case, the writer might want to briefly identify and describe the encounter between Macomber and the lion:

> In "The Short Happy Life of Francis Macomber," Ernest Hemingway develops the characters of the short story by jumping from one character's point of view to another. Although the hunting scene is largely told from Macomber's perspective, Hemingway alternates the perspective of both the lion and Macomber to highlight his fear and cowardice character.

The explanation in the second sentence about how Hemingway uses a shifting point of view is relevant to the claim. It also begins connecting the claim to ideas that will be used as evidence.

Remember, you should continually return to and re-phrase your claim as you write the supporting evidence to make sure you are capturing exactly what you want to say. Writing out the evidence always helps you figure out what you really think.

WRITING EVIDENCE-BASED CLAIMS (Continued)

3. ORGANIZE YOUR SUPPORTING EVIDENCE

Many claims contain multiple aspects that require different evidence that can be expressed in separate paragraphs. This claim can be organized sequentially, contrasting each perspective throughout the stages of the hunt: An account of **THE START OF THE ENOUNTER**, an account of **AFTER THE INITAL SHOTS**, and an account of **THE FINAL ENCOUNTER**.

Here are two paragraphs that support the claim with evidence for the first two stages.

An account of **THE START OF THE ENCOUNTER**:

> The comparison starts with the different ways the lion and Macomber begin their encounter. As Macomber got out of the car "the lion still stood looking majestically and coolly toward this object that his eyes only showed in silhouette, bulking like some super-rhino" (p168). This majestic coolness is contrasted with what the heavily armed Macomber was feeling at the time: "He only knew his hands were shaking and as he walked away from the car it was almost impossible for him to make his legs move. They were stiff in the thighs, but he could feel the muscles fluttering" (p169). Standing fearfully atop his "fluttering" thighs, Macomber manages to wound the lion with a few "gut-shot(s)" (p172).

An account of **AFTER THE INITAL SHOTS**:

> The next sequence of shifting perspective sets up another contrast of character. The lion, now facing an enemy who has just shot and wounded him unprovoked, prepares bravely and calmly for their next encounter: "He galloped toward the high grass where he could crouch and not be seen and make them bring the crashing thing close enough so he could make a rush and get the man that held it" (p168). In contrast, Macomber does everything he can to avoid going into the grass after the lion. "Can't we set the grass on fire? … Can't we send beaters? … What about the gun-bearers? … Why not just leave him?" (p195). He will put other men's lives in danger to avoid confronting the lion. At one point, he even blurts out uncontrollably, "I don't want to go in there" (p 197).

Notice the phrase, "The next sequence," starting the second paragraph. Transitional phrases like this one aid the organization by showing how the ideas relate to each other or are further developed.

4. PARAPHRASE AND QUOTE

Written evidence from texts can be paraphrased or quoted. It's up to the writer to decide which works better for each piece of evidence. Paraphrasing is **putting the author's words into your own**. This works well when the author originally expresses the idea you want to include across many sentences. You might write it more briefly.

The second sentence from paragraph 2 begins by paraphrasing Hemingway's description of the lion. The ideas are his, but the exact way of writing is not.

> The lion, now facing an enemy who has just shot and wounded him unprovoked, prepares bravely and calmly for their next encounter.

Some evidence is better quoted than paraphrased. If an author has found the quickest way to phrase the idea or the words are especially strong, you might want to **use the author's words**.

The second sentence in paragraph 1 quotes Hemingway exactly:

> As Macomber got out of the car "the lion still stood looking majestically and coolly toward this object that his eyes only showed in silhouette, bulking like some super-rhino" (p168).

ODELL
EDUCATION

WRITING EVIDENCE-BASED CLAIMS (Continued)

5. REFERENCE YOUR EVIDENCE

Whether you paraphrase or quote the author's words, you must include **the exact location where the ideas come from**. Direct quotes are written in quotation marks. How writers include the reference can vary depending on the piece and the The Short Stories of Ernest Hemingway, Charles Scribner's Sons. Here the writer puts the line numbers from the original text in parentheses at the end of the sentence.

MAKING EVIDENCE-BASED CLAIMS ABOUT LITERARY TECHNIQUE FINAL WRITING TASKS

In this unit, you have been developing your skills as a reader who can make text-based claims about literary techniques and prove them with evidence from the text.

- Attending to various techniques authors use, such as characterization, narration, and chronology
- Uncovering key clues in the details, words, and central ideas found in the texts
- Making connections among details, central ideas, and texts
- Using the details, connections, and evidence you find in texts to form a claim—a stated conclusion—about something you have discovered
- Organizing evidence from the text to support your claim and make your case
- Expressing and explaining your claim in writing
- Improving your writing so that others will clearly understand and appreciate your evidence-based claim—and think about the case you have made for it.

Your final two writing assignments will provide you with opportunities to use all of these related skills and to demonstrate your proficiency and growth in making evidence-based claims about literary technique.

FINAL ASSIGNMENTS

1. **Developing and Writing an Evidence-Based Claim:** On your own, you will read the final part of the text in the unit closely and develop an evidence-based claim. To do this, you will do the following:

   a. Read and annotate the text (or section of text) on your own and use Guiding Questions and a **Forming EBC Tool** to develop an initial claim about the effects of a technique Hemingway uses.

   b. Compare the notes and initial claim you make with those made by other students—reframe or revise your claim.

   c. Complete an **Organizing EBC Tool** to plan subpoints and evidence you will use to explain and support your claim.

   d. Study the **Writing EBC Handout** to know what a written EBC needs to do and what examples might look like.

   e. Draft a one- to two-paragraph written presentation and explanation of your claim, making sure that you do the things listed on the **Writing EBC Handout**:

      ⇒ <u>Establish the context</u> by connecting the claim to the text.

      ⇒ <u>State the claim clearly</u> to fully communicate your ideas about the text.

      ⇒ <u>Organize supporting evidence</u> found in the text.

      ⇒ <u>Paraphrase and quote</u> from the text.

      ⇒ <u>Reference the evidence</u> drawn from the text.

FINAL WRITING TASKS (Continued)

   f. Work with other students to review and improve your draft—and to be sure it is the best possible representation of your claim and your skills as a reader and writer. Work on improving at least one of these aspects of your claim:

      ⇒ How <u>clear</u> your presentation and explanation of your claim is

      ⇒ How <u>defensible</u> (based on the evidence you present) your claim is

      ⇒ How well you have <u>presented and referenced evidence</u> to support your claim

      ⇒ How well you have <u>organized</u> your subpoints and evidence into a unified claim

   g. Reflect on how well you have used Literacy Skills in developing this written claim.

2. **Writing and Revising a Global Evidence-Based Claim Essay:** On your own, you will plan and draft a multiparagraph essay that presents a global claim about the cumulative effects of a technique Hemingway uses. To accomplish this, you will do the following:

   a. Review the short story, the tools you have completed, and the claims you have formed throughout the unit, looking for connections or comparisons.

   b. Use a **Forming EBC Tool** to make a new claim that develops a global conclusion about the meaning of the text and Hemingway's use of a literary technique.

   c. Use an **Organizing EBC Tool** to plan the subpoints and evidence you will use to explain and support your claim.

   d. Draft a multiparagraph essay that explains, develops, and supports your global claim—keeping in mind these three criteria for this final writing assignment. Your essay should do the following:

      ⇒ Demonstrate an accurate reading and insightful analysis of the text.

      ⇒ Develop a supported claim that is clearly connected to the text.

      ⇒ Successfully accomplish the five key elements of a written EBC (**Writing EBC Handout**).

   e. Use a collaborative process with other students to review and improve your draft in two key areas: (1) its content (quality of the claim and its evidence) and (2) its organization and expression (unity of the discussion and clarity of the writing).

   f. Reflect on how well you have used Literacy Skills in developing this final explanation.

SKILLS TO BE DEMONSTRATED

As you become a text expert and write your evidence-based claims, think about demonstrating the Literacy Skills listed in the following to the best of your ability. Your teacher will evaluate your work and determine your grade based on how well you do.

Read

- **Attend to Details:** Identify words, details, or quotations that you think are important to understanding the text

- **Interpret Language:** Understand how words are used to express ideas and perspectives

- **Identify Relationships:** Notice important connections among details, themes, or sections of the text

- **Recognize Perspective:** Identify and explain the author's or narrator's perspective and how it affects the story

FINAL WRITING TASKS (Continued)

SKILLS TO BE DEMONSTRATED (Continued)

Think

- **Make Inferences:** Draw sound conclusions from reading and examining the text closely
- **Form a Claim:** State a meaningful conclusion that is well supported by evidence from the texts
- **Use Evidence:** Use well-chosen details from the text to support your explanation; accurately paraphrase or quote the text

Write

- **Present Details:** Insert details and quotations effectively into your essay
- **Organize Ideas:** Organize your claim, supporting ideas, and evidence in a logical order
- **Use Language:** Write clearly so others can understand your claim and supporting ideas
- **Use Conventions:** Correctly use sentence elements, punctuation, and spelling to produce clear writing
- **Publish:** Correctly use, format, and cite textual evidence to support your claim

HABITS TO BE DEVELOPED

Your teacher may also want you to reflect on how well you have used and developed the following habits of text-centered discussion when you worked with others to understand the text and improve your writing:

- **Engage Actively:** Focus your attention on the assigned tasks when working individually and with others
- **Collaborate:** Work respectfully and productively to help your discussion or review group be successful
- **Communicate Clearly:** Present your ideas and supporting evidence so others can understand them
- **Listen:** Pay attention to ideas from others and take time to think about them
- **Understand Purpose and Process:** Understand why and how a text-centered discussion or peer writing review should be accomplished
- **Revise:** Rethink your ideas and refine your writing based on feedback from others
- **Remain Open:** Modify and further justify ideas in response to thinking from others.

NOTE

These skills and habits are also listed on the **Student Making EBC Literacy Skills** and **Academic Habits Checklists**, which you can use to assess your work and the work of other students.

FORMING EVIDENCE-BASED CLAIMS TOOL

Name _ _ _ _ _ _ _ _ _ _ _ _ _ _ _ _ _ _   Text _ _ _ _ _ _ _ _ _ _ _ _ _ _ _ _ _ _

A question I have about the text:

FINDING DETAILS	**Detail 1 (Ref.:)**	**Detail 2 (Ref.:)**	**Detail 3 (Ref.:)**
I find interesting details that are related and that stand out to me from reading the text closely.			

CONNECTING THE DETAILS	**What I think about detail 1:**	**What I think about detail 2:**	**What I think about detail 3:**
I reread and think about the details, and explain the connections I find among them.			
	How I connect the details:		

MAKING A CLAIM	**My claim about the text:**
I state a conclusion that I have come to and can support with evidence from the text after reading and thinking about it closely.	

ODELL EDUCATION

SUPPORTING EVIDENCE-BASED CLAIMS TOOL

Name _ _ _ _ _ _ _ _ _ _ _ _ **Text** _ _ _ _ _ _ _ _ _ _ _ _ _

CLAIM:

Supporting Evidence	Supporting Evidence	Supporting Evidence

(Reference:) **(Reference:**) **(Reference:**)

CLAIM:

Supporting Evidence	Supporting Evidence	Supporting Evidence

(Reference:) **(Reference:**) **(Reference:**)

ODELL EDUCATION

ORGANIZING EVIDENCE-BASED CLAIMS TOOL (2 POINTS)

Name _____   Text _____

CLAIM:

Point 1

A	Supporting Evidence	B	Supporting Evidence

(Reference:)   (Reference:)

C	Supporting Evidence	D	Supporting Evidence

(Reference:)   (Reference:)

Point 2

A	Supporting Evidence	B	Supporting Evidence

(Reference:)   (Reference:)

C	Supporting Evidence	D	Supporting Evidence

(Reference:)   (Reference:)

ODELL
EDUCATION

ORGANIZING EVIDENCE-BASED CLAIMS TOOL (3 POINTS)

Name _ _ _ _ _ _ _ _ _ _ _ _ Text _ _ _ _ _ _ _ _ _ _ _ _ _ _ _ _

CLAIM:

Point 1		Point 2		Point 3	
A	Supporting Evidence	**A**	Supporting Evidence	**A**	Supporting Evidence
(Reference:	)	(Reference:	)	(Reference:	)
B	Supporting Evidence	**B**	Supporting Evidence	**B**	Supporting Evidence
(Reference:	)	(Reference:	)	(Reference:	)
C	Supporting Evidence	**C**	Supporting Evidence	**C**	Supporting Evidence
(Reference:	)	(Reference:	)	(Reference:	)

MODEL ORGANIZING EVIDENCE-BASED CLAIMS TOOL

Name Model ----------- **Text** "The Short Happy Life of Francis Macomber," Hemingway

CLAIM:	Hemingway develops strong comparisons between Macomber and the lion by alternating between their perspectives during the hunt.

Point 1	LION		Point 2	MACOMBER	

A Supporting Evidence	**B** Supporting Evidence	**A** Supporting Evidence	**B** Supporting Evidence
"The lion still stood looking majestically and coolly toward this object"	"Then it crashed again and he felt the blow as it hit his lower ribs and ripped on through, blood sudden hot and frothy in his mouth, and he galloped toward the high grass where he could crouch and not be seen and make them bring the crashing thing close enough so he could make a rush and get the man that held it."	"He only knew his hands were shaking and as he walked away from the car it was almost impossible for him to make his legs move. They were stiff in the thighs, but he could feel the muscles fluttering."	"Can't we set the grass on fire?" "Can't we send beaters?" "What about the gun-bearers?" "I don't want to go in there," said Macomber. It was out before he knew he'd said it. "You mean you'd go in by yourself? Why not leave him there?"
(Reference: P168)	**(Reference:** P168)	**(Reference:** P169)	**(Reference:** PP191–200)

C Supporting Evidence	**D** Supporting Evidence	**C** Supporting Evidence	**D** Supporting Evidence
"His ears were back and his only movement was a slight twitching up and down of his long, black-tufted tail . . . All of him, pain, sickness, hatred and all of his remaining strength, was tightening into an absolute concentration for a rush."	"As he heard their voices his tail stiffened to twitch up and down, and, as they came into the edge of the grass, he made a coughing grunt and charged."	"He sat there, sweating under his arms, his mouth dry, his stomach hollow feeling, wanting to find courage to tell Wilson to go on and finish off the lion without him."	"The next thing he knew he was running; running wildly, in panic in the open, running toward the stream"
(Reference: P227)	**(Reference:** P227)	**(Reference:** P221)	**(Reference:** P228)

ODELL
EDUCATION

QUESTIONING PATH TOOL

Name: _____ **Text:** _____

APPROACHING: *I determine my reading purposes and take note of key information about the text. I identify the LIPS domain(s) that will guide my initial reading.*	Purpose: Key information: LIPS domain(s):
QUESTIONING: *I use Guiding Questions to help me investigate the text (from the **Guiding Questions Handout**).*	1. 2.
ANALYZING: *I question further to connect and analyze the details I find (from the **Guiding Questions Handout**).*	1. 2.
DEEPENING: *I consider the questions of others.*	1. 2. 3.
EXTENDING: *I pose my own questions.*	1. 2.

ODELL EDUCATION

PART 3: STUDENT ACADEMIC HABITS CHECKLIST

HABITS DEVELOPED	DESCRIPTORS	EVIDENCE OF USING THE HABIT	THINGS TO IMPROVE ON
COLLABORATING	Pays attention to and respects other participants Works productively with others to complete the task and enrich the discussion		
COMMUNICATING CLEARLY	Uses clear language to communicate ideas and claims Uses relevant details to explain and support thinking		
LISTENING	Pays attention to new information and ideas from others Considers others' ideas thoughtfully		

PART 4: STUDENT ACADEMIC HABITS CHECKLIST

HABITS DEVELOPED	DESCRIPTORS	EVIDENCE OF USING THE HABIT	THINGS TO IMPROVE ON
UNDERSTANDING PURPOSE AND PROCESS	Understands and uses the collaborative writing workshop process Uses Literacy Skills criteria to frame questions, responses, and feedback		
LISTENING	Pays attention to new information and ideas from others Considers others' ideas thoughtfully		
REMAINING OPEN	Avoids explanations or justifications for what they as writers have tried to do Frames text-based questions to probe their readers' observations		
REVISING	Uses criteria to rethink, refine, or revise work Uses observations from peers to inform improvement		

ODELL
EDUCATION

MAKING EVIDENCE-BASED CLAIMS
TARGETED LITERACY SKILLS

TARGETED SKILLS	DESCRIPTORS
ATTENDING TO DETAILS	Identifies relevant and important textual details, words, and ideas
IDENTIFYING RELATIONSHIPS	Identifies important connections among key details and ideas within and across texts
MAKING INFERENCES	Demonstrates comprehension by using connections among details to make logical deductions about a text
RECOGNIZING PERSPECTIVE	Uses textual details to recognize an author's or narrator's relationship to and perspective on a text's topic
FORMING CLAIMS	Develops meaningful and defensible claims that clearly state valid, evidence-based analysis
USING EVIDENCE	Supports all aspects of claims with sufficient textual evidence, using accurate quotations, paraphrases, and references
PRESENTING DETAILS	Describes and explains important details that effectively develop a narrative, explanation, or argument
ORGANIZING IDEAS	Sequences sentences and paragraphs to establish coherent, logical, and unified narratives, explanations, and arguments
PUBLISHING	Uses effective formatting and citations to present ideas for specific audiences and purposes
USING LANGUAGE	Selects and combines words that precisely communicate ideas, generate appropriate tone, and evoke intended responses from an audience

MAKING EVIDENCE-BASED CLAIMS
ACADEMIC HABITS DEVELOPED

HABITS DEVELOPED	DESCRIPTORS
ENGAGING ACTIVELY	Actively focuses attention on independent and collaborative tasks
COLLABORATING	Pays attention to, respects, and works productively in various roles with all other participants
COMMUNICATING CLEARLY	Uses appropriate language and relevant textual details to clearly present ideas and claims
LISTENING	Pays attention to, acknowledges, and considers thoughtfully new information and ideas from others
REVISING	Rethinks and refines work based on teacher-, peer-, and self-review processes
UNDERSTANDING PURPOSE AND PROCESS	Understands the purpose and uses the process and criteria that guide tasks
REMAINING OPEN	Modifies and further justifies ideas in response to thinking from others

ODELL
EDUCATION

MAKING EVIDENCE-BASED CLAIMS LITERACY SKILLS RUBRIC

Name _ _ _ _ _ _ _ _ _ _ _ _ _ _ _ _ _ **Text** _ _ _ _ _ _ _ _ _ _ _ _ _ _ _ _ _ _ _

NE: Not enough evidence to make a rating

1—**Emerging:** needs improvement

2—**Developing:** shows progress

3—**Becoming Proficient:** demonstrates skills

4—**Excelling:** exceeds expectations

+—**Growth:** evidence of growth within the unit or task

I. READING SKILLS CRITERIA	NE	1	2	3	4	+
1. **Attends to Details:** Identifies relevant and important textual details, words, and ideas						
2. **Interprets Language:** Identifies how words and phrases convey meaning and represent the author's perspective						
3. **Identifies Relationships:** Identifies important connections among key details and ideas within the text						
4. **Recognizes Perspective:** Uses textual details to recognize how the author's or narrator's perspective or point of view impacts the text						
II. THINKING SKILLS CRITERIA	NE	1	2	3	4	+
1. **Makes Inferences:** Demonstrates comprehension by using connections among details to make logical deductions about the text						
2. **Forms Claims:** Develops meaningful and defensible claims that clearly state valid, evidence-based analysis						
3. **Uses Evidence:** Supports all aspects of the claim with sufficient textual evidence, using accurate quotations, paraphrases, and references						
III. WRITING SKILLS CRITERIA	NE	1	2	3	4	+
1. **Presents Details:** Describes and explains important details that effectively develop an explanation or argument for the claim						
2. **Organizes Ideas:** Sequences sentences and paragraphs to establish a coherent, logical, and unified explanation or argument						
3. **Uses Language:** Selects and combines words that precisely communicate the claim and its supporting ideas						
4. **Uses Conventions:** Uses effective sentence structure, grammar, punctuation, and spelling to communicate ideas						

MAKING EBC SKILLS AND HABITS RUBRIC (Continued)

	NE	1	2	3	4	
5. **Publishes:** Uses effective formatting and citations when integrating textual evidence to support the claim						
IV. ESSAY CONTENT CRITERIA	NE	1	2	3	4	
1. Demonstrates an accurate reading and insightful analysis of the text						
2. Develops a supported claim that is clearly connected to the content of the text						
3. Accomplishes the five key elements of an evidence-based claims essay (See **Writing EBC Handout**.)						
SUMMARY EVALUATION		1	2	3	4	

Comments:

1. **Explanation** of ratings—**evidence** found (or not found) in the work:

2. **Strengths** and **areas of growth** observed in the work:

3. **Areas for improvement** in future work:

ODELL
EDUCATION

STUDENT MAKING EVIDENCE-BASED CLAIMS LITERACY SKILLS CHECKLIST

	LITERACY SKILLS USED IN THIS UNIT	✔	EVIDENCE Demonstrating the SKILLS
READING	1. **Attending to Details:** Identifies words, details, or quotations that are important to understanding the text		
	2. **Interpreting Language:** Understands how words are used to express ideas and perspectives		
	3. **Identifying Relationships:** Notices important connections among details, ideas, or texts		
	4. **Recognizing Perspective:** Identifies and explains the author's or narrator's perspective		
THINKING	5. **Making Inferences:** Draws sound conclusions from reading and examining the text closely		
	6. **Forming Claims:** States a meaningful conclusion that is well supported by evidence from the text		
	7. **Using Evidence**: Uses well-chosen details from the text to explain and support claims; accurately paraphrases or quotes		
WRITING	8. **Presenting Details:** Inserts details and quotations effectively into written or spoken explanations		
	9. **Organizing Ideas:** Organizes claims, supporting ideas, and evidence in a logical order		
	10. **Using Language:** Writes and speaks clearly so others can understand claims and ideas		
	11. **Using Conventions:** Correctly uses sentence elements, punctuation, and spelling to produce clear writing		
	12. **Publishing:** Correctly uses, formats, and cites textual evidence to support claims		

General comments:

STUDENT MAKING EVIDENCE-BASED CLAIMS ACADEMIC HABITS CHECKLIST

ACADEMIC HABITS USED IN THIS UNIT	✔	EVIDENCE demonstrating the HABITS
1. Engaging Actively: Focuses attention on the task when working individually and with others		
2. Collaborating: Works respectfully and productively to help a group be successful		
3. Communicating Clearly: Presents ideas and supporting evidence so others can understand them		
4. Listening: Pays attention to ideas from others and takes time to think about them		
5. Understanding Purpose and Process: Understands why and how a task should be accomplished		
6. Revising: Rethinks ideas and refines work based on feedback from others		
7. Remaining Open: Modifies and further justifies ideas in response to thinking from others		
General comments:		

ODELL
EDUCATION

UNIT 4

RESEARCHING TO DEEPEN
UNDERSTANDING

DEVELOPING CORE LITERACY
PROFICIENCIES

GRADE 9

Music: What Role Does It Play
in Our Lives?

UNIT OVERVIEW

The ability to inquire and research—to explore critically—is a proficiency. Students can develop skills, methods, and Academic Habits to lead them ever deeper into the experiences accessed through critical research. These skills involve being open to new knowledge, asking questions, and finding new and better answers. They involve listening to others, building on what they know and have experienced, and incorporating that knowledge into students' own exploration. Critical research also involves making connections and organizing what is found, then returning to and refining the questions that have led to inquiry. As they explore, students also develop the ability to explain what they have come to think and show why they think it. Eventually this exploration, the process of research, leads to an evolving perspective rooted in deep knowledge and understanding.

This unit develops that explorative proficiency: researching to deepen understanding. It lays out a process through which students learn to explore topics with their learning community, posing and refining questions, listening to experiences, and discovering areas they wish to investigate. It develops their ability to determine what they do not know or understand and where and how to find that information. The unit also develops and supports students' abilities to archive and organize information in order to see and analyze connections in ways that aid comprehension, deepen their understanding, and prepare them to express their evolving perspective.

Learning Progression

Instruction in this unit is built on four components:

1. Choosing a *topical area* of interest to research
2. Conducting a *research process*
3. Compiling a *Research Portfolio*
4. Communicating a *researched perspective*

The unit activities integrate these components in a learning progression that develops and supports proficiency in the entire research process. While doing so, the activities further develop students' reading and analysis skills through independent application and target specific skill areas that are components of good research, for example, the skills of assessing and evaluating sources.

Part 1 introduces students to the idea of researching to deepen understanding and immerses students in a collaborative process for exploring a topic, reading to gain background knowledge, choosing an Area of Investigation, and developing an initial Inquiry Question. They begin to compile a Research Portfolio.

Part 2 addresses essential skills for assessing, annotating, and making notes on sources to answer Inquiry Questions. Introduced here, these skills will be developed throughout the remainder of the unit.

In Part 3, students apply their skills of reading closely and making evidence-based claims as they analyze key sources and develop a deeper understanding of their Area of Investigation.

In Part 4, students review and evaluate their materials and analysis, refining their Inquiry Questions and extending their research where necessary, and returning to the skills introduced in Parts 2 and 3.

In Part 5 students organize their research and synthesize their analysis in order to develop an evidence-based perspective about their area of investigation. Students communicate this understanding in the form of a reflective research narrative or an optional multimedia presentation.

☰ SEQUENCING LEARNING OVER TIME
☰ AND ACROSS GRADE LEVELS

The learning sequence for this unit and the instructional notes within it have been developed on the assumption that students may be learning the process of Researching to Deepen Understanding for the first time. Thus, terms are introduced and explained, graphic tools are overviewed and modeled, and lessons move relatively carefully from teacher modeling to guided practice to independent application. The Literacy Skills that are targeted and the Academic Habits that are developed are assumed to be in early stages of development for many students, and thus extensive scaffolding is provided.

However, students may come to this fourth unit in the Developing Core Literacy Proficiencies Program having developed their Literacy Skills, Academic Habits, and Core Literacy Proficiencies in other contexts. They may have progressed through earlier units in the Developing Core Literacy Proficiencies sequence (*Reading Closely for Textual Details* and *Making Evidence-Based Claims*) and become very familiar with tools, handouts, terminology, skills, and habits addressed in this unit. They may also have experienced the *Researching to Deepen Understanding* instructional sequence in a previous grade or school.

For this reason, teachers should use their professional judgment to plan their instruction for this unit considering not only *what* they are teaching (the research process and the curriculum designed to develop students' skills) but also *whom* they are teaching (their students' backgrounds, previous experiences, and readiness levels). Before beginning the unit, teachers are encouraged to determine what students have previously experienced, learned, or produced.

If students have more advanced skills or extensive previous experience in researching, instruction can move more rapidly through many sections of this unit, concentrate more on extended reading to deepen students' understanding, and emphasize more complex topics, texts, or academic sources.

COMPONENT SKILL LESSONS

In addition to and included in these five parts are Component Skill lessons. These lessons cover a range of skills that are specific to developing the research proficiency, but they can be taught individually or out of this unit's context. Some lessons, such as A through C, touch on skills that should be familiar to students if they have completed the *Reading Closely for Textual Details* and *Making Evidence-Based Claims* units. Other lessons, such as Assessing and Evaluating Sources (Component Skill Lesson E), will be new to students.

 OUTLINE

The following outline summarizes the overall instructional purpose and focus of each part of the unit and also lists Component Skill lessons that can be taught individually to support less formal student research in other learning contexts.

PART 1: INITIATING INQUIRY

- Students learn the purposes and processes of using inquiry and research to deepen understanding. Students initially explore a topic and build background knowledge through reading and text-centered discussion, then initiate inquiry by generating questions collaboratively that can frame and direct their research. By the end of Part 1, students will have chosen an Area of Investigation and developed one or more Inquiry Questions.

Component Skill Lessons:

    A. Reading a Foundational Source Closely

    B. Using Questions to Explore a Topic

    C. Writing an Inquiry Question

PART 2: GATHERING INFORMATION

- Students learn how to conduct searches, assess, and annotate sources, and keep an organized record of their findings. By the end of Part 2, students will have framed their inquiry and gathered their main body of research material.

Component Skill Lessons:

    D. Searching for Information

    E. Assessing and Evaluating Sources

    F. Making and Recording Notes

PART 3: DEEPENING UNDERSTANDING

- Students read and analyze key sources closely to deepen their understanding and draw personal conclusions about their Area of Investigation. By the end of Part 3, students will have a series of evidence-based claims addressing each Inquiry Path of their Research Frame.

Component Skill Lessons:

    G. Analyzing a Source's Perspective and Bias

PART 4: FINALIZING INQUIRY

- Students analyze and evaluate their material with respect to their Inquiry Questions and refine their research. By the end of Part 4, students will have an analyzed body of research addressing their Inquiry Questions from which to develop and communicate an evidence-based perspective on their Area of Investigation.

- Students draw from their research and personal analysis to develop and communicate an evidence-based perspective. By the end of Part 5, students will have an organized body of research and have written a reflective research narrative that communicates their evidence-based perspective on their area of investigation, which can also be expressed in an optional multimedia presentation.

≣ INTRODUCTION TO THE RESEARCHING TO DEEPEN UNDERSTANDING LITERACY TOOLBOX

In the *Researching to Deepen Understanding* (RDU) unit, students develop a foundational proficiency for conducting a research process. The proficiency involves questioning, reading closely, analyzing and recording information, organizing thinking, and generating relevant, research-based claims.

To support the development of this proficiency, the unit uses a series of handouts and tools found in the **Researching to Deepen Understanding Literacy Toolbox**.

Reading and Questioning Tools: The toolbox includes resources carried forward from previous Developing Core Literacy Proficiencies units that emphasize reading skills applied in the research process. As they explore and read texts associated with the topic, students continue to use the *Guiding Questions Handout* and *Questioning Path Tool* to focus their reading—now applying those resources more independently. They may also use an *Approaching Texts Tool* or *Analyzing Details Tool* to frame and support their initial background reading.

Initiating Inquiry Tools: The second set of tools is introduced early in this unit to support students as they initiate and frame inquiry. The *Exploring a Topic Tool* helps students explore potential Areas of Investigation within a topic *before* choosing the one they will focus on. Students use the *Potential Sources Tool* to record general information about potential sources they may use for the research project. The *Area Evaluation Checklist* guides the class in the process of evaluating potential Areas of Investigation. The *Posing Inquiry Questions Handout* serves as a guide to help students develop compelling questions that reflect their curiosity to learn and also direct their research experience. The Research Frame Tool provides students the space to organize their questions into more structured Inquiry Paths that address one Area of Investigation.

Analyzing Sources Tools: As students identify, read, and analyze sources, they use tools that help them be more critical readers and note-takers. The *Assessing Sources Handout* is a key component to the research process. It helps students understand and practice the important skill of vetting a source for its accessibility and interest, credibility, and relevance and richness; they use this handout to inform the assessment of sources they have listed on the *Potential Sources Tool*. With a column to take notes and another to make comments, the *Taking Notes Tool* helps students make and organize notes as they read their sources closely.

Research Process Tools: Several key resources support students in managing and evaluating their research processes. The *Student Research Plan* outlines the process they will follow within the unit and also can remind them of steps they should take in any extended research project. (A fuller

Teacher Research Unit Guide is also available in the toolbox.) Students use the **Research Portfolio** to organize information and analysis *throughout the research process*. The **Research Evaluation Tool** guides students in a process for evaluating their research and consists of three parts to structure collaborative reviews with teachers and peers to determine whether findings are credible, relevant, and sufficient.

Developing Researched Claims Tools: As students build their understanding of their Area of Investigation through research, they develop evidence-based claims that summarize what they have learned and lead to the development of their Research-Based Perspective. In doing so, they can use tools brought forward from previous units. The **Forming Evidence-Based Claims Research Tool, Attending to Details Handout, Writing Evidence-Based Claims Handout,** and **Connecting Ideas Handout** can all be used to help students write claims related to their Inquiry Question(s) and research findings. The **Organizing Evidence-Based Claims Research Tool** helps students organize multiple claims and supporting evidence stemming from their Inquiry Question(s) as they develop and then communicate the perspective they have come to within their Area of Investigation. Students use the **RDU Final Writing Task Handout** to plan for and execute their papers.

Assessment Tools: The **RDU Literacy Toolbox** also houses detailed tables of targeted Literacy Skills and Academic Habits developed in the unit as well as the **RDU Literacy Skills and Academic Habits Rubric** and **Student RDU Literacy Skills and Academic Habits Checklist**.

If students have previously completed a *Researching to Deepen Understanding* unit, they should already be familiar with these tools and handouts. As they gain independence in practicing the proficiency of researching to deepen understanding, students might rely less and less on these support resources. Depending on students' ability and familiarity with the **RDU Literacy Toolbox**, teachers might encourage students to use these materials when they encounter difficulties getting started researching a topic, assessing and choosing sources, or developing a Research Plan. Otherwise, students can proceed through reading, annotating, taking notes, and developing Research Plans using their own, developing processes. If students are ready to move through the unit without these scaffolds, it is still important that teachers continually verify that they are choosing relevant, quality sources and developing effective Research Plans as a foundation for taking notes and making claims.

> **NOTE**
>
> The tools and handouts and the **Student RDU Literacy Skills and Academic Habits Checklist** can also be found in the Student Edition.

≣ LITERACY SKILLS AND ACADEMIC HABITS

TARGETED LITERACY SKILLS

In this unit, students learn about and develop the skills necessary to conduct research on a topic they wish to explore. They develop a researched-based perspective on the topic and learn how to organize and express their findings in a variety of ways. The following Literacy Skills are targeted with explicit instruction and assessment throughout the unit (in the **RDU Literacy Toolbox**).

LITERACY SKILLS	DESCRIPTORS
IDENTIFYING RELATIONSHIPS	Identifies important connections among key details and ideas within and across texts
MAKING INFERENCES	Demonstrates comprehension by using connections among details to make logical deductions about a text
SUMMARIZING	Recounts the explicit meaning of texts, referring to key details, events, characters, language, and ideas
QUESTIONING	Formulates and responds to questions and lines of inquiry that lead to the identification of important ideas and themes
RECOGNIZING PERSPECTIVE	Uses textual details to recognize an author's or narrator's relationship to and perspective on a text's topic
EVALUATING INFORMATION	Assesses the relevance and credibility of information, ideas, evidence, and logic presented in texts
FORMING CLAIMS	Develops meaningful and defensible claims that clearly state valid, evidence-based analysis
USING EVIDENCE	Supports all aspects of claims with sufficient textual evidence, using accurate quotations, paraphrases, and references
PRESENTING DETAILS	Describes and explains important details that effectively develop a narrative, explanation, or argument.
ORGANIZING IDEAS	Sequences sentences and paragraphs to establish coherent, logical, and unified narratives, explanations, and arguments
PUBLISHING	Uses effective formatting and citations to present ideas for specific audiences and purposes
REFLECTING CRITICALLY	Uses literacy terminology and concepts to reflect on, discuss, and evaluate personal and peer literacy development

APPLIED LITERACY SKILLS

In addition to these targeted skills, the unit provides opportunities for students to apply and develop the following Literacy Skills:

- Attending to Details
- Interpreting Language
- Using Logic
- Using Language

- Publishing
- Using Conventions

ACADEMIC HABITS

In this unit, students will be introduced to specific Academic Habits associated with managing a research process: organizing a portfolio, developing Inquiry Paths on a specific topic, analyzing resources, compiling and synthesizing information, and completing work within a time frame. The habits students use and develop are listed in the following table.

NOTE
Student versions of the Academic Habits descriptors can be found in the **Student RDU Literacy Skills and Academic Habits Checklist** in the **RDU Literacy Toolbox** and Student Edition.

HABITS DEVELOPED	DESCRIPTORS
GENERATING IDEAS	Generates and develops ideas, positions, products, and solutions to problems
ORGANIZING WORK	Maintains work and materials so that they can be used effectively and efficiently in current and future tasks
COMPLETING TASKS	Finishes short and extended tasks by established deadlines
UNDERSTANDING PURPOSE AND PROCESS	Understands the purpose and uses the process and criteria that guide tasks

≡ HOW THIS UNIT ALIGNS WITH CCSS
≡ FOR ELA AND LITERACY

The instructional focus of this unit is on building student proficiency in a process for conducting research: developing and refining Inquiry Questions; finding, assessing, analyzing, and synthesizing multiple sources to answer those questions; and organizing and using evidence from those sources to explain understanding in ways that avoid plagiarism. As such, the unit primarily aligns with these standards:

CCSS.ELA-LITERACY.W.9-10.7: (Conduct short as well as more sustained research projects to answer a question (including a self-generated question) or solve a problem; narrow or broaden the inquiry when appropriate; synthesize multiple sources on the subject, demonstrating understanding of the subject under investigation.)

CCSS.ELA-LITERACY.W.9-10.8: (Gather relevant information from multiple authoritative print and digital sources, using advanced searches effectively; assess the usefulness of each source in answering the research question; integrate information into the text selectively to maintain the flow of ideas, avoiding plagiarism and following a standard format for citation.)

CCSS.ELA-LITERACY.W.9-10.9: (Draw evidence from literary or informational texts to support analysis, reflection, and research.)

This process involves key moments of collaboration and also of independence. As the unit leads students through structured collaborative processes for initiating and refining inquiry, it develops their ability in **CCSS.ELA-LITERACY.SL.1** (*Prepare for and participate effectively in a range of conversations and collaborations with diverse partners, building on others' ideas and expressing their own clearly and persuasively*). At other moments, students are alone in their search for and analysis of sources, building their proficiency for **CCSS.ELA-LITERACY.RI.10** (*Read and comprehend complex texts independently and proficiently*).

The task of writing from researched sources is an important part of larger writing processes. Thus, the unit develops student ability in key aspects of the production of writing expressed in the expectations of **CCSS.ELA-LITERACY.W.4** (*Produce clear and coherent writing in which the development, organization, and style are appropriate to task, purpose, and audience*) and **CCSS.ELA-LITERACY.W.5** (*Develop and strengthen writing as needed by planning, revising, editing, rewriting, or trying a new approach*). And as they strategically write organized analyses, students develop their ability to do explanatory writing and meet the expectations of **CCSS.ELA-LITERACY.W.2** (*Write informative/ explanatory texts to examine and convey complex ideas and information clearly and accurately through the effective selection, organization, and analysis of content*). With their final writing assignment, a reflective research narrative, students also experience narrative writing and thus address **CCSS. ELA-LITERACY.W.3** (*Write narratives to develop real or imagined experiences or events using effective technique, well-chosen details, and well-structured event sequences*).

Students develop these skills throughout the unit through direct instruction and guided practice, and they are assessed continuously through activities, graphic organizers, and written products.

As students develop these primary targeted CCSS skill sets, they also practice and use related reading skills from supporting CCSS. Throughout the research process, they read key sources closely and analyze textual details to answer their Inquiry Questions, particularly building their growing proficiency in the following standards areas:

CCSS.ELA-LITERACY.RI.1: (*Read closely to determine what the text says explicitly and to make logical inferences from it; cite specific textual evidence when writing or speaking to support conclusions drawn from the text.*)

CCSS.ELA-LITERACY.RI.2: (*Determine central ideas or themes of a text and analyze their development; summarize the key supporting details and ideas.*)

CCSS.ELA-LITERACY.RI.4: (*Interpret words and phrases as they are used in a text, including determining technical, connotative, and figurative meanings, and analyze how specific word choices shape meaning or tone.*)

CCSS.ELA-LITERACY.RI.6: (*Assess how point of view or purpose shapes the content and style of a text.*)

CCSS.ELA-LITERACY.RI.9: (*Analyze how two or more texts address similar themes or topics in order to build knowledge or to compare the approaches the authors take.*)

☰ TERMS AND DEFINITIONS USED
☰ IN THIS UNIT

Topic: the general topic chosen for class exploration

Area of Investigation: a particular theme, question, problem, or more focused subtopic within the general topic that warrants investigation

Inquiry Questions: questions posed by researchers about their Areas of Investigation to be answered through inquiry

Inquiry Path: a realm of inquiry stemming from one or more related Inquiry Questions; a path can be framed by a general question that summarizes more specific questions or subtopics

Research Frame: an organized set of Inquiry Questions or Paths that guide the research process

Research Plan: a handout presenting the process students follow to guide them through the various stages of inquiry

Research Portfolio: the binder or electronic folder where students physically or electronically store and organize all the material related to their personal research

RESEARCH TOPICS

This unit has been intentionally designed to support student research in a variety of curricular contexts. The activities and materials can be used regardless of the subject matter students choose or need to investigate or their purposes for that investigation.

A topical focus and a set of possible sources are provided to support the unit. Depending on their needs and goals, teachers can use the topic and one or more of the sources included to teach the research process, or they can connect the instruction of this unit to different texts and topics of their choice. They can choose topics related to those in their ELA classroom as well as those that students are learning in other academic and technical disciplines.

The unit is also designed to support the simultaneous research of students into different Areas of Investigation, Inquiry Questions, and even offshoot topics. It is recommended, however, for coherence, mutual support, and enrichment, that students initially all explore a general topic, choosing different but related Areas of Investigation within it.

In this unit, titled "Music: What Role Does It Play in Our Lives?," the topic and Common Sources address different aspects of music and its impact in our lives.

COMMON SOURCE SET

This unit comes with a Common Source Set (found at the end of the unit's materials and in the Student Edition) that models and briefly explains a text sequence focused on a particular Area of Investigation. These—or similar—Common Sources can be used to build background information, for teacher modeling, and as the focus for skill development lessons. Teachers and students determine which Common Texts to use and how to use them, depending on the degree to which they want to focus their own inquiry on the Areas of Investigation suggested by the set. For each possible text, the Common Source Set provides information to help locate the source, a brief overview, and several questions that might be used to guide initial reading and discussion. The Common Source Set is referenced within relevant activities in the unit plan to help teachers think about which of the provided texts they might use or what they might search for in compiling their own set of Common Texts. The Common Source Set thus can be used as any of the following:

- The core sources students use in their research
- Commonly read sources used to model and develop reading and research skills
- A starting point for students to jump off from as they follow their own Research Paths and find new sources
- A model to guide teachers as they compile Common Sources on a different topic

SOURCE SEARCH LOCATIONS

In conducting research, students should be encouraged to search for sources in a variety of ways, such as investigating the school library, visiting and observing sites and places related to the topic, using search engines such as Google and Bing, and researching within online databases such as EBSCO Host and Gale. In expanding the circle of potential resources for research and in realigning their strategic searches, students should use the expertise of library or media specialists in their school or community and learn from them how to access additional search vehicles that may be available to them.

Many state and school district library systems provide free public access to research portals that enable teachers and students to access various informational databases. Many of these have been organized so that articles can be searched for by text difficulty level (Lexile measure) as well as topic, enabling teachers and students to find information at a variety of text complexity levels. Some national content and news aggregators that identify sources by Lexile level are EBSCO, Gale, Grolier Online, Net Trekker, News Bank, Pro Quest, Questia, and Newsela. Contact a library or media specialist for information on how to connect students to and navigate their state's or district's database portals.

PART 1

INITIATING INQUIRY

OBJECTIVE:	Students learn the purposes and processes of using inquiry and research to deepen understanding. Students initially explore a topic and build background knowledge through reading and text-centered discussion, then initiate inquiry by generating questions collaboratively that can frame and direct their research. By the end of Part 1, students will have chosen an Area of Investigation and developed one or more Inquiry Questions.

MATERIALS:

Common Sources 1 through 4

- *Student Research Plan*
- *Questioning Path Tool*
- *Exploring a Topic Tool*
- *Approaching Texts Tool*
- *Analyzing Details Tool*

- *Guiding Questions Handout (RC Literacy Toolbox)*
- *Potential Sources Tool*
- *Area Evaluation Checklist*
- *Posing Inquiry Questions Handout*

≡ LITERACY SKILLS

TARGETED SKILLS	DESCRIPTORS
IDENTIFYING RELATIONSHIPS	Identifies important connections among key details and ideas within and across texts
SUMMARIZING	Recounts the explicit meaning of texts, referring to key details, events, characters, language, and ideas
QUESTIONING	Formulates and responds to questions and lines of inquiry that lead to the identification of important ideas and themes

Developing Core Literacy Proficiencies

ACADEMIC HABITS

HABITS DEVELOPED	DESCRIPTORS
GENERATING IDEAS	Generates and develops ideas, positions, products, and solutions to problems
COMPLETING TASKS	Finishes short and extended tasks by established deadlines
UNDERSTANDING PURPOSE AND PROCESS	Understands the purpose and uses the process and criteria that guide tasks

ALIGNMENT TO CCSS

TARGETED STANDARDS:

CCSS.ELA-LITERACY.W.9-10.7: Conduct short as well as more sustained research projects to answer a question (including a self-generated question) or solve a problem; narrow or broaden the inquiry when appropriate; synthesize multiple sources on the subject, demonstrating understanding of the subject under investigation.

CCSS.ELA-LITERACY.W.9-10.8: Gather relevant information from multiple authoritative print and digital sources, using advanced searches effectively; assess the usefulness of each source in answering the research question; integrate information into the text selectively to maintain the flow of ideas, avoiding plagiarism and following a standard format for citation.

CCSS.ELA-LITERACY.W.9-10.9: Draw evidence from literary or informational texts to support analysis, reflection, and research.

SUPPORTING STANDARDS:

CCSS.ELA-LITERACY.W.9-10.4: Produce clear and coherent writing in which the development, organization, and style are appropriate to task, purpose, and audience.

CCSS.ELA-LITERACY.RI.9-10.1: Cite strong and thorough textual evidence to support analysis of what the text says explicitly as well as inferences drawn from the text.

CCSS.ELA-LITERACY.RI.9-10.2: Determine a central idea of a text and analyze its development over the course of the text, including how it emerges and is shaped and refined by specific details; provide an objective summary of the text.

CCSS.ELA-LITERACY.SL.9-10.1: Initiate and participate effectively in a range of collaborative discussions (one-on-one, in groups, and teacher-led) with diverse partners on *grades 9–10 topics, texts, and issues*, building on others' ideas and expressing their own clearly and persuasively.

 ACTIVITIES

1. INTRODUCTION TO THE UNIT

The teacher explains how critical readers use research to deepen their understanding and develop an evidence-based perspective on a topic. Students are introduced to the purposes, process, and products of the unit.

2. EXPLORING A TOPIC

The teacher leads a class exploration of a topic. Students independently explore the research topic.

3. CONDUCTING PRE-SEARCHES

Students conduct pre-searches for sources pertaining to one or two Areas of Investigation to assess availability of information.

4. VETTING AREAS OF INVESTIGATION

Students vet their potential Areas of Investigation and develop a research question or problem.

5. GENERATING INQUIRY QUESTIONS

Students generate one or more Inquiry Questions to guide their searches for information within their Areas of Investigation.

Developing Core Literacy Proficiencies

≡ ACTIVITY 1: INTRODUCING THE UNIT

The teacher explains how critical readers use inquiry and research to deepen their understanding and develop an evidence-based perspective on a topic. Students are introduced to the purposes, process, and products of the unit.

INSTRUCTIONAL NOTES

INTRODUCTORY DISCUSSION OF RESEARCH

The teacher begins the unit with a discussion of the nature, process, and tools of research. This unit approaches research as a critical process people do to deepen their understanding of topics and develop a perspective that evolves as they find, analyze, and incorporate new evidence.

Discuss with students these issues:

- How this kind of research differs from having an initial opinion and trying to find support for it
- How successful researchers follow an iterative process and use tools and strategies to find, analyze, and organize information
- How this process leads researchers to adopt different points of view and to explore different paths as a consequence of their findings
- How a researched understanding and perspective serves many purposes, among them the following:
  ⇒ Writing an article, essay, or academic paper on a topic or text
  ⇒ Developing a position on a controversial issue
  ⇒ Developing business plans
  ⇒ Designing and building objects
  ⇒ Informing personal and community decision making
  ⇒ Developing processes and plans
  ⇒ Writing fictional or historical narratives
  ⇒ Delivering presentations

INTRODUCE THE PURPOSES, PROCESS, AND PRODUCTS OF THE UNIT

Purposes

- Introduce the purposes of the unit:
  ⇒ To develop the skills and habits used in conducting research to deepen understanding
  ⇒ To use those skills and habits in developing and communicating an evidence-based perspective on a topical area they wish to explore

Process

Use the **Student Research Plan** to overview the research process students will embark on, briefly explaining the elements and importance of each stage. It is important that students have an initial understanding of the process so they can explore the topic and sources before feeling like they need to develop a final position or thesis.

Products

Tell students they will create three primary products:

- Research Portfolio
- Reflective research narrative
- Optional final multimedia presentation

Research Portfolio

Using the Student Research Portfolio Handout (found in the **RDU Literacy Toolbox** and Student Edition), discuss how the portfolio is a structured collection of the research and analysis students compile in their investigation. Its purpose is to organize information and analysis *throughout the research process,* as opposed to compiling and organizing information *at the end of the process.* The components of the portfolio guide and archive students' work in a way that teaches them key critical thinking, Academic Habits, and organizational skills.

The research portfolio is the primary product that students will generate throughout the unit, and should be assessed and evaluated as evidence of their developing research skills. In addition, students will produce a final written or multimedia product that communicates the perspective they have developed as they have conducted inquiry and compiled their research portfolio. Teachers should identify their preferred final product at the start of the unit, and guide student research in light of that product.

Reflective Research Narrative

The recommended written product for grade 9 is a reflective research narrative, in which students will communicate their perspective on the topic and reflect on their experiences during research by telling the story of their inquiry process.

If this is the final product students will work toward, explain that at the end of the research process, students will use their portfolios and analyses to write a reflective research narrative that tells a story about their search, how they came to their perspective on the topic, and their experience of inquiry and conducting research.

Explain that while researching, students should concentrate on recording not only what they find but also what they did to find it, tracking their inquiry questions as they relate to various sources. Their claims should be seen as results of their search, and their perspective should be seen as the end point of the research "journey" they have been on.

Discuss how they might maintain reflective journals in conjunction with their research portfolios, and also how to be reflective about their thinking and discoveries as they "make" notes. Peers can be used to help them reflect along the way and as an audience for their developing narratives. If students wish to produce a video or audio recording as their product, they might consider recording peer and teacher reviews with a recording device for the duration of the project.

Optional or Alternate Products

Teachers and students can consider other options for a final product of their research; they should decide on what this product will be before embarking on their research project so that they can customize their portfolios and begin planning. Students might also use their reflective research narrative as a jumping-off point for a final product. Options for communicating their evidence-based perspectives might include but are not limited to the following:

1. An informational presentation incorporating text, graphics, and multimedia
2. A research-based explanation of a phenomenon, issue, event, process, or device
3. A thesis-driven academic argument, research-based essay, or op-ed piece

Full descriptions and suggested approaches to these possible products are located at the end of Part 5. Teachers are encouraged to discuss the characteristics and expectations of students' final products as they begin the unit and to guide instruction and student research accordingly.

> **NOTE**
>
> The ***RDU Final Writing Task Handout*** is an overview for students of this unit's three tasks and is included in the Student Edition.

ACTIVITY 2: EXPLORING A TOPIC

The teacher leads a class exploration of a topic. Students independently explore the research topic.

Note on Exploring Unit Topics

Teachers can use the Common Source Set provided with this unit in multiple ways, depending on their students and curricular context. If the teacher chooses to focus on the grade-level topic, the source set can be used to provide background knowledge, inform students' initial research, and practice independent reading and research skills with Common Sources. Alternately, the source set can be used as a model for a different topic and source set selected by the teacher (or students).

In either case, it will still be important to decide if the class will all focus on a single, more-narrow topic area, or if students will be allowed to explore offshoots of the topic based on their individual interests. If the entire class initially focuses on one topic area, each student might still pursue a separate Area of Investigation within this topic. Limiting topics enables students to learn about other aspects of a topic from each other and enables deeper class discussions, helping students evaluate their plan, their strategic approach to the inquiry, and their findings. It also enables the teacher to model skills using Common Sources related to students' research and a wider curricular context. Regardless of the chosen approach, teachers can use the topics and model sources provided with the unit or choose their own topics and sources of similar richness and suitability.

It is important for students to explore the topic for a few days to build an initial knowledge base and to discover various aspects of the topic that are of real interest to them. This exploration should take place in and outside of class—supported by interaction with a few Common Sources as well as general discussion of the topic with their peers, teachers, and wider learning community.

By the end of these several days, each student should be able to summarize the growing conversation and to articulate a few areas that she or he would like to investigate. The *Exploring a Topic Tool* (in the **RDU Literacy Toolbox**) supports that work and captures it for evaluation by the teacher.

Continuing Proficiency: Reading Closely and Questioning Paths

At this stage of literacy development in the Developing Core Proficiencies program, students have several tools and approaches at their disposal to help read and analyze text. If students have completed the *Reading Closely for Textual Details* and *Making Evidence-Based Claims* units in the Developing Core Proficiencies program, they should be familiar with the **Questioning Path Tool** and **Guiding Questions Handout**. Depending on student proficiency and preference, they might continue to use the **Guiding Questions Handout** and form their own Questioning Paths as they work through the texts in this unit. Because it is not the primary focus of instruction, model Questioning Paths are not provided; however, source notes in the Common Source Set (found at the end of this unit) include selected Guiding Questions and text-specific questions. If needed and helpful, teachers might use these questions or their own to provide students with model Questioning Paths, as in previous units.

Introducing a Topic—Opening Avenues for Inquiry

- Begin the research process with the idea of exploring a general topic and considering possible directions for inquiry and research.

- Introduce the general topic.

- Make connections to curricular contexts if relevant, including texts the class has previously read.

- Suggest to students that a key step in any research investigation is to read or view something that stimulates thinking about what makes the topic interesting and opens up possible areas to investigate. Tell them they will be watching a video and then reading a Common Text to get them started.

- Review with students the value of having a few Guiding Questions in mind to focus their viewing or reading. Use the **Reading Closely Graphic** (located in the **RC Literacy Toolbox**) to remind students about the question-based process—moving from first approaching a text, to questioning and analyzing, then on to deepening and extending their understanding. Let them know that they will be learning to apply this process independently as they do their research in this unit.

- Using the **Guiding Questions Handout** (located in the **RC Literacy Toolbox**), have the class select several questions that they think might help them view and think about the video more actively. Alternately, narrow the list for students and have them select from among these applicable questions:

  ⇒ What new ideas or information do I find in the text?

  ⇒ What ideas stand out to me as significant or interesting?

  ⇒ How do the text's main ideas relate to what I already know, think, or have read?

TEXT NOTES: SOURCE 1

The first informational source students encounter in the unit (preferably a video or multimedia text) should be selected and used to help introduce the topic and to stimulate students' thinking and interest. It should be a general text that opens up, rather than closes down, possible directions for inquiry and research and one that naturally builds curiosity and leads to discussion.

The video listed as Source 1 in the Common Source Set for the Music topic asks the audience to "Imagine Life Without Music." This five-minute video introduces the topic by demonstrating the many ways that music plays a role in our lives. Through a montage of pictures and video, enhanced by a classical music soundtrack, the videographer provides many ideas about how music plays an essential role in our lives, including its impact on leisure, self-expression, and culture. The video is intended to spark students' interest in the topic of music and can provide opportunities for exploration of how music relates to almost all aspects of our lives, even our joy. The video is a good starting point for brainstorming different aspects of the topic that might be interesting for students to research.

- Students view the video and take notes related to the Guiding Questions they have selected to focus on.
- In groups of three and then as a class, students summarize what they have noted and thought about as they have watched the video. Have students compare the notes they have taken—in terms of their content and their approach to note-taking.
- Open a broad brainstorming discussion by asking students to share what they currently know or think about the topical area of music and its many connections to performance, self-expression, culture, movies, and our emotions. Start the discussion with the unit's overarching title and question:

  ⇒ Music: What role does it play in our lives?

- Have students first respond to the question in terms of what the video has suggested about how music influences our lives. Then open the discussion to consider students' own thoughts about the ways music affects our lives.
- Next ask students to think about what they might want to know more about—topic areas that might be interesting to research. Conduct an open-ended brainstorm in which as many topics as possible are listed, stemming from the connections identified in the first brainstorm.
- As a class, go back and star those possible topics that meet these key criteria:

  ⇒ The topic *matters*—it is worth spending time learning and thinking about.

  ⇒ The topic is *interesting*—it interests many members of the class.

  ⇒ The topic is somewhat *complex*—there are various aspects and sides to it.

  ⇒ The topic is likely to be *researchable*—there is probably information out there about it.

- Finish the discussion by talking about why these criteria are important to consider when starting out in a direction for research—and how they may help a researcher avoid a dead end early in the research process.

- Identify up to five good possibilities for Areas of Investigation the class might begin to examine—but keep the entire list to return to later.

READING TO EXPAND UNDERSTANDING OF THE TOPIC

Having initially explored directions for possible research, students will now read a Common Source independently to expand their background and thinking about the general topic and about the possible directions for research they have brainstormed and identified. This activity uses a Common Text and expects students to apply skills they have developed and tools they have used in previous Developing Core Literacy Proficiencies units.

NOTE

This lesson addresses a Component Skill of Research and may be extracted from the instructional sequence of this unit and taught on its own to support students in a different learning context.

COMPONENT SKILL LESSON A

READING A FOUNDATIONAL SOURCE CLOSELY

- Have students go to the **RDU Literacy Toolbox** and take out tools they have used previously to support their reading processes: the *Guiding Questions Handout* (in the **RC Literacy Toolbox**), the *Questioning Path Tool*, the *Approaching Texts Tool*, and the *Analyzing Details Tool*.
- Remind students how they have used these tools previously to read texts more closely. Let them know that now they will be trying to use the tools and their skills and processes *independently* as they engage in research—because they will be reading texts that have not been preselected for them (as in the past), oftentimes on their own.
- They will practice the independent use of the tools and close reading with a Common Text so that they can compare the reading paths they use to read the source closely.

TEXT NOTES: SOURCE 2

The source students use should be a foundational print text that presents general background information about the topic area and builds from their earlier viewing or reading experiences. Reading this text should expand students' thinking about the topic and its possibilities and build their background knowledge. Because they will read it independently, it should be an accessible text for most students in the class, but it should also be one that presents them with some complexity.

TEXT NOTES: SOURCE 2

The text listed as Source 2 in the Common Source Set for the Music topic, "A Brief History of the Music Industry" by Theo Smith, again addresses the broad topic of music and what role it plays in our lives, but it focuses a bit more specifically on the history of the music industry. Because it touches on so many facets of music, it can provoke students to think more broadly about the topic and begin to explore people or things they did not know previously about music. The author, Theo Smith, provides an overview of the life and history of the music industry with insights into current and future states. Through nonfiction narrative and graphics, it describes the roles played by technological advancements, such as the printing press and the Internet, and the differences among live music, published music, and recorded music. The article also addresses how digital rights issues, such as copyright and piracy, shape the music industry as we know it today. The article measures 1500L, but is written in student-friendly way with short paragraphs and should be an accessible foundational text for most students.

- Tell students that the text they will be reading is Internet-based and that they will be navigating on the web to find and read the text. (Alternately, provide students with a hard copy if they are not able to access the text via a computer or tablet.)

- Present them with enough information to search for and find the text, then individually (or in small learning teams), have them find the site. Observe students as they search to note aspects of using the Internet and search engines to work on later.

- Once they have found the text, have students scan its web page and record any key details they find at the top of an *Approaching Texts Tool* (in the **RDU Literacy Toolbox**). Briefly compare their annotations and discuss what they already know about the text before they read it.

- Based on this information and their purpose for reading (to gain more information about the topic and think further about where they might want their research to go), students *independently and individually* identify several Guiding Questions they will use initially to question and analyze the text. The questions might come from the *Guiding Questions Handout* or from students' own developing question banks. Each student can record his or her questions on either the *Approaching Texts Tool* or a *Questioning Path Tool* (in the **RDU Literacy Toolbox**).

- Students *independently* do an initial reading of the text, recording informal notes (or annotating their hard copies) in relationship to the questions they are considering.

- In small groups or as a class, students compare the questions they have used, the notes they have taken, and initial text-based observations they can make after this first reading. Students then brainstorm text-specific questions they might ask to deepen their reading of the text.

- Each student records a text-specific question on an *Analyzing Details Tool* and then uses the question to frame a deeper rereading of the text—looking for details and connections related to the individual question each is considering.

- Return to the broad topic area that the class is investigating and ask students to discuss how the source they have just read relates to the topic, the video they have previously viewed, their list of possible directions for further investigation, and their interests. Several Guiding Questions can be used to frame this discussion:

  ⇒ What ideas stand out to me as significant or interesting?

  ⇒ How do the text's main ideas relate to what I already know, think, or have read?

- Conclude the discussion by considering several reflective questions:

  ⇒ What more have we learned about the topic that might move us forward in our research?

  ⇒ What have we learned about using questions to frame our independent reading of possible sources?

  ⇒ How does the type of question we consider influence how we read and what we find in a source?

- Let students know that from this point forward they will be using the skills, processes, and (potentially) tools that they have just applied, but they will be doing so primarily on their own. It will be up to them to decide which questions to consider, which tools to use, and what to pay attention to, based on their own skill sets and the nature of the texts they will find and use as they do their research.

In this series of activities, students will generate questions about an area they are interested in investigating, then use those questions to begin exploring the topic.

NOTE

This lesson addresses a Component Skill of research and may be extracted from the instructional sequence of this unit and taught on its own to support students in a different learning context.

COMPONENT SKILL LESSON B

USING QUESTIONS TO EXPLORE A TOPIC

Students are familiar (or reacquainted) with the strategy of using questions to drive close reading and analysis of a text. They will now think about how good questions can also be used to frame a direction for research—for doing question-based inquiry. This is an opportunity to teach the academic vocabulary associated with the word *inquiry*—what it means and why it is so important in many academic fields, most notably science and social science.

- Introduce the concept of *inquiry*, discussing the word, its roots, and related words (e.g., *exploration, investigation, review,* etc.). Discuss circumstances in school in which students may have heard the word used (e.g., in a science classroom) and the reasons why *inquiry* is fundamental in many academic fields.

- Return to and reconsider the list of possible directions for research brainstormed and identified previously (or a list from a different learning context). Most likely, this list has been expressed as a series of short phrases or topic area titles.

- For each of the areas on the list, ask students to think about these or similar questions:
  - ⇒ What questions do we have about this topic area?
  - ⇒ What do we want to learn more about?
  - ⇒ What are some things we might investigate to understand the topic better?
- As students think about and respond to these questions, ask them to phrase their responses in a *question form*.
- Model an example. If using the model topic and Common Source Set, an example might be this:

  - ⇒ Subtopic of interest: Music on the web
  - ⇒ Possible questions: What are the benefits and drawbacks to having music available on the web? How does the Internet affect how music is bought and sold? What is music piracy? Why is music piracy beneficial or harmful to the music industry?
- Have the class work on a second example. If using the model topic and text set, a subtopic of interest might be "Relationship between Music and the Brain" or "Role of Music in History."
- Students individually (or alternately in small groups) each consider an additional (third) subtopic area of interest and list a set of questions they have about the topic: what they want to learn more about and what they might investigate.

INSTRUCTIONAL NOTES

- Each student should now have done some thinking about three possible areas of interest for further investigation:
  1. One modeled by the teacher
  2. One identified by the class
  3. One identified by the student

For each of these areas, students will also have generated one or more informal questions that can be used to explore the subtopic and initiate inquiry. They will now begin the exploration through a process of teacher modeling, guided practice, and independent investigation. As they do so, students will want to think about these issues:

- **What they have already learned** from previous class reading and discussions—as a starting point for their exploration
- **What they have become interested** in as a possible area for investigation
- **Why they are potentially interested** in learning more about this area
- **How they might frame questions** to explore the potential area of interest

Students will now use their initial questions to begin exploring several possible topics, using a new tool from the **RDU Literacy Toolbox** that is organized to support students and record their thinking as they consider these four aspects of initiating research: the ***Exploring a Topic Tool***.

EXPLORING A TOPIC TOOL

The ***Exploring a Topic Tool*** (in the **RDU Literacy Toolbox**) helps students explore potential Areas of Investigation within a topic *before* choosing the one they will focus on. The tool prompts them to describe potential Areas of Investigation and examine why those areas are of interest to them. They are then prompted to express their interest in the form of a question (or problem statement). This tool will also be used to guide student discussions in parts of the collaborative exploration process.

INSTRUCTIONAL NOTES

- Based on their previous discussions for the first two sources, the class's brainstorm for possible areas of interest, and their own work generating initial research questions, students can complete the following sections on page one of the ***Exploring a Topic Tool***:
  ⇒ Name
  ⇒ Topic
  ⇒ Brief account of the class conversation about the topic
- Return to the example modeled previously for the class as the first possible Area of Investigation. Model moving from a brief summary of the topic area, to an explanation of why it might be interesting to investigate, to a further expression of the question(s) initially modeled for the class. If using the model topic and text set, this example might be related to the subtopic area of "Music on the Web." Have students paraphrase the thinking from the class discussion and record it in the first Area of Investigation section of the ***Exploring a Topic Tool***.
- Then, in small groups, students practice the thinking process by using the topic area and questions previously developed by the class and filling in the tool's second Area of Investigation section:
  ⇒ Students write a sentence describing the area that they would like to know more about.
  ⇒ Then, they write several sentences explaining why they are interested in this area of the topic and how they came to this question or problem statement.
  ⇒ Finally, they write a question that they might try to answer through research.
- Individually, each student now applies the thinking process for the third possible Area of Investigation previously identified independently. Students should now have three possible Areas of Investigation to explore: two that are common with the rest of the class and one that is specific to each student and her or his interests.

Possible Areas of Investigation

Several possible areas related to the model topic and source set have already been identified and potentially considered in class. If these do not match up well with student interests or the curricular context, or if students need additional help identifying an area of interest, the following list of topics related to the role music plays in our lives might be helpful.

Topics Already Considered

1. Music on the Web
2. Relationship between Music and the Brain
3. Role of Music in History

Other Possible Topics

1. The Relationship between Faith and Music
2. How Music Influences Culture, Policy, and Society
3. Music and Therapy
4. The Physics and Psychoacoustics of Music
5. The Emergence and Influence of Music Genres

Exploring a Topic Independently

Students will now use their ***Exploring a Topic Tool*** to direct their exploratory research into several possible Areas of Investigation. They will begin to develop or apply strategies and skills for conducting searches for information, initially open-ended explorations and later more focused follow-up searches for potential resources. If students have previous academic experience in conducting searches, they may begin this process somewhat independently—with observation and monitoring by the teacher. If not, the following instructional sequence can support their development of effective initial searching strategies.

- Explain to students that their goals will be to (1) explore the three Areas of Investigation from their ***Exploring a Topic Tool*** to see what others think about the topics and extend their own thinking and (2) identify one additional possible Area of Investigation that may be an offshoot of another topic or a new interest.

- Students spend time outside of class exploring and doing further reading and thinking about the topic. A strategic approach for having students do this involves moving outward from sources of information most familiar to them to sources that may be farther from their previous experience. For example, students might do the following:

  1. Initially talk informally with family members, friends, advisors, other teachers, or other members of their immediate learning community. Ask them what they know about the topics and what interests them and share their own thinking from the ***Exploring a Topic Tool***.

  2. Survey possible sources of information they may have in their own homes or communities. These might include books or other print resources or videos, but they could also be people who are experts in the field (e.g., a music teacher, musician, or music store owner).

  3. Confer with a librarian or media specialist in the school, first to think about the topic, then to identify locally available resources, then to learn more about ways to search for more information (e.g., online database portals available through the local library).

  4. Informally search the Internet to begin exploring various dimensions of the topic. These initial Internet searches might use the following strategies discussed and practiced later in Part 2, Activity 3: Conducting Pre-searches.

    ⇒ Key word searches

    ⇒ Searches for websites managed by organizations closely related to the topic (e.g., American Music Therapy Association)

    ⇒ Searches that follow a trail from a previous source. They might work from a reference on a website, a citation in the text, or a name that is identified as an expert. For example, if using the Common Source Set for this unit, they might search using terminology used in Source 2 such as "Napster" or "iTunes" to learn more about how these download services shed light on the topic of "Music on the Web."

- Make it clear to students that they are not yet searching for definitive sources or knowledge on the topic but rather exploring various aspects of it through accessing the knowledge, questions, and perspectives of their learning community.

Completing the Exploring a Topic Tool

Students should return to class with some additional information and thinking about the three possible Areas of Investigation they previously identified on their *Exploring a Topic Tool*. They may have learned things that have increased their interest in the topic, expanded their understanding, caused them to refine their initial questions, or led them potentially to abandon the topic as a likely Area of Investigation. They should also have identified and completed the tool for at least one new potential Area of Investigation, using the fourth section of the *Exploring a Topic Tool* to record their thinking. They follow the same process they did for the first through third Areas of Investigation (explored in class and identified independently), and write sentences to explain these points:

1. The potential Area of Investigation
2. Why they are interested in this new area—and how they became interested
3. How they have initially framed the area as a question (or problem statement)

For the last two areas (the ones students have identified individually), students write and refine their explanations and questions so that the writing exhibits the following qualities:

Clear: A reader should immediately understand the meaning of the explanatory sentence(s). An easy way for students to check for clarity is to read each sentence to parents or peers, without giving them any clarification, and ask their reviewers to explain what they understood.

Concise: They must provide a direct response to each of the prompts, contain no unnecessary words and provide immediate direction for further investigation.

Correct: They should be well-written sentences with no grammatical or spelling errors.

Collect the tools to confirm completion and to evaluate for initial coherence.

ORGANIZING THE RESEARCH PORTFOLIO

Instruct students to store their material in Section 1 of their Research Portfolios: Defining an Area of Investigation. If students are going to produce a reflective research narrative as a final product in the unit, they might also record discoveries they have made thus far about the topic or research process in a reflective research journal.

☰ ACTIVITY 3: CONDUCTING
☰ PRE-SEARCHES

Students conduct pre-searches for sources pertaining to one or two Areas of Investigation to assess availability of information.

INSTRUCTIONAL NOTES

- Introduce the process of performing searches using Inquiry Questions and emphasize the importance of recording the potential sources found.

- Explain to students that as they have framed, reconsidered, and refined their exploratory questions in Activity 2, they have begun to develop one or more Inquiry Questions that can be used to direct further research and reading, expand their background knowledge, and potentially lead to a strategic research process that will culminate in the development of a personal but evidence-based perspective on the topic.

USING INQUIRY QUESTIONS TO DIRECT FURTHER RESEARCH AND READING

Using Inquiry Questions is absolutely essential to the research process articulated in this unit. Developing student proficiency in posing general and specific questions to direct inquiry and deepen understanding is a central instructional focus. This questioning process, itself, is iterative and serves specific functions at different stages throughout the process. To this point, the goal of questioning has been explorative. Students have identified general areas of interest and explored those areas to confirm their interest and the viability of the area to support research. They will now use their evolving questions to do further research and reading, still working in the pre-search stage of the inquiry process.

At this stage, students' Inquiry Questions are still general. By the time their pre-searches (and eventual vetting) for additional sources are done, students should be able to articulate each potential Area of Investigation in a clear and coherent question (or problem statement) to guide their research. Once a research direction has been established, the role and nature of the Inquiry Question will change. The question then becomes more specific and serves to guide investigation and the eventual development of a coherent and comprehensive, evidence-based perspective within their Area of Investigation. These more specific Inquiry Questions will also eventually organize a frame for ensuring sufficient research. At this stage, however, students should continue the questioning processes they have learned previously, moving from more general questions that explore their potential Areas of Investigation to more specific questions that will help them analyze sources, deepen their understanding of the topic, and extend their research.

- Explain the basic principles of using Inquiry Questions to guide initial pre-searches for additional sources. Inquiry questions can be simply defined as *questions that identify things you need to know about a topic and that will help guide your research and analysis.*

- Have students review (individually, in small groups, or as a class) the questions they have already written, thinking about them now as initial Inquiry Questions that will help them conduct pre-searches within one or more of their potential Areas of Investigation.

- Remind students that at this stage of research they will be looking for general information that will help them gain background knowledge and understanding of their potential Areas of Investigation—and also determine if there are good sources of information in that area.

IDENTIFYING AND EXAMINING POTENTIAL SOURCES

Students will now use their questions and explanations from their *Exploring a Topic Tool* to conduct a pre-search for sources in at least two of their potential Areas of Investigation. To begin this process, they will read and analyze an additional Common Source, enabling the teacher to provide modeling and guided practice in the pre-search process. They will then conduct further independent searches for sources related to their topics of interest. For each source, they will record key identifying information and some initial impressions of the source—observations about its general content, identification of key ideas, and notes and comments about the source. To support their recording of information about the potential sources, they will use another new tool from the **RDU Literacy Toolbox**, the *Potential Sources Tool*. Later, they will also use this tool to assess the credibility, relevance, and accessibility or interest of the potential sources they find.

Students use the *Potential Sources Tool* (in the **RDU Literacy Toolbox**) to record general information about potential sources that they may use for the research project. They can also write a brief description of the content and personal comments.

USING THE POTENTIAL SOURCES TOOL TO RECORD SOURCES

- Introduce the structure and purposes of the *Potential Sources Tool*.
- Model its use by recording identifying information for one of the Common Sources previously examined by the class (Source 1 or 2, if using the Common Source Set, or other books, or Internet-based sources, of similar complexity and richness) at the top of one section of the tool.
- Discuss how the source is connected to one (or more) of the general Inquiry Questions from class discussion, and show students where on the tool they might record this information (on the right side of each section of the tool).
- When modeling, spend some time explaining different ways that notes for the section on "General Content/Key Ideas/Personal Comments" can be made: brief description of the content, personal impressions and evaluation of the quality of the content, quotes, facts, and numbers, and so on. Explain how this information will be used in the next activity to assess the direction of the research and the availability of sources of information.
- Have students practice using the *Potential Sources Tool* with Source 3 (or a similar text provided by the teacher, if not using the Common Source Set).

TEXT NOTES: SOURCE 3

The next common resource that students examine should again provide general background information, but it should be more focused on a subtopic area that might become an Area of Investigation for the class or individual students. This Common Source should be accessible to students, but it also should provide some additional reading challenges, often by referencing technical information or terminology. The Common Source ideally will also provide references or a bibliography that can lead students to additional sources.

The Common Source Set for this unit provides several options for Source 3 that teachers or students can select from. All of the sources address issues within the larger topic area of "Music and Its Role in Our Lives" but have been chosen because they are relevant to one of the possible areas of investigation that students may be exploring, as follows:

Source 3A: Music on the Web: "What Is Online Piracy?" by the Recording Industry Association of America (RIAA), Date (NA). This source can be found on the RIAA website.—1210L

Source 3B: Relationship between Music and the Brain: "Why Your Brain Craves Music" by Michael D. Lemonick, April 15, 2013. This source can be found on the *Time Magazine* website.—1350L

Source 3C: Role of Music in History: "The 25 Most Important Civil Rights Moments in Music History" by Matthew Trammel, David Drake, Ernest Baker, Insanul Ahmed, and Rob Kenner, February 7, 2013. This source can be found on the complex.com website.

Source 3A: The Recording Industry Association of America (RIAA) is the trade organization that supports and promotes the creative and financial aspects of the major music companies. Its members are the music labels that comprise the most vibrant record industry in the world. This website, through its links, provides explanation about the topic of music piracy and why it is harmful to the music industry at large.

Source 3B: The article "Why Your Brain Craves Music" explores the physiological and neurological reasons for why we like music, but it also considers intellectual factors such as how paying for music stimulates our brains more than free music. The article considers how music affects our brains, thus our emotions, and how music might have even affected our evolutionary progress.

Source 3C: "25 Most Important Civil Rights Moments in Music History" shows the important role music and musicians can play during historical events and movements and presents several avenues for further research—either by artist or event. The article features images and commentary on key moments in history when civil rights and music collided, from the 1956 integration of southern dancehalls to Elton John and Eminem's Duet at the 2001 Grammys.

Teachers can use these Common Sources as a model in several ways, depending on the classroom context and emerging student interests:

- Select a single source for modeling that matches with the direction for investigation that the class is likely to pursue. All students read and work with this single Common Source.
- Use one source for modeling and a second for guided practice. All students read both sources, working with one as a class and the other in small groups.
- Use all three sources (and additional ones if helpful), grouping students by possible topic interests and modeling and practicing within groups.
- Find other, similar Common Source(s) related to the topic and subtopics the class is examining.

Once one or more Common Sources have been selected, students will now examine and read the source to practice the skills of close, independent reading and research and the use of the Potential Sources Tool. Students may be provided with a hard copy of the Common Source or asked to navigate to the website where the text can be accessed, depending on classroom circumstances.

- Model the recording of information about the source at the top of one section of the tool. Discuss with students how this work connects to what they have previously done when they approach a text, referencing the **Approaching Texts Tool** or the **Questioning Path Tool**.
- In small groups, students discuss a purpose for reading the Common Source and some questions (a Questioning Path) they might use to read it. If helpful, students might record their question(s) on an **Analyzing Details Tool** (or if they have internalized the process, they may note details and connections as they annotate the text).

NOTE

If students have trouble identifying or generating questions, good general questions might be, "What information in this source relates to the Area of Investigation I am interested in? What new information do I find that might lead me to other sources of information?"

- Students individually and independently read the Common Source, making annotations related to their Area of Investigation and their text questions (or making notes if using an online version of the text).
- Students record initial impressions of the text in the "General Content/Key Ideas/Personal Comments" section of the **Potential Sources Tool**.
- In small groups, students compare their annotations or notes for the source and their initial impressions recorded on the tool.
- As a class, students discuss what they have learned from the Common Source(s) and how this influences their thinking about the Area(s) of Investigation they are considering.

CONDUCTING PRE-SEARCHES INDEPENDENTLY

- Students select two of their potential Areas of Investigation based on their previous assessment of relevance and interest. For each area, they should try to find at least two new sources. When finished searching, they should then have at least five total sources listed on **Potential Sources Tools** (including the Common Source 3).

- Students conduct pre-searches and gather initial basic information, guided by some of their general Inquiry Questions. More than likely, students will do these pre-searches using the Internet. If so, remind them of the suggestions for searching introduced in Activity 2:

  ⇒ Key word searches—phrases that combine key words from their Area of Investigation (e.g., "music on the web issues")

  ⇒ Searches for websites managed by organizations closely related to the topic (e.g., the American Music Therapy Organization). These sites often present overviews and links to other pages or sites that present more specific information.

  ⇒ Searches that follow a trail from a previous source. They might work from a reference on a website, a citation in the text, or a name that is identified as an expert. For example, if using the Common Source Set for this unit, they might search using a citation quoted in Source 2 to learn more about that particular source's relationship to music and its impact on human lives.

- The goals of the pre-searches are as follows:

  1. Assess the availability of information.

  2. Confirm further the student's level of interest in the potential Areas of Investigation.

  3. Refine the question or problem statement and the scope of the area if necessary.

- For the purpose of this activity, students only use part of the tool:

  ⇒ Name

  ⇒ Topic

  ⇒ Source (—Title—Author—Location—Publication Date)

  ⇒ General Content/Key Ideas/Personal Comments

  ⇒ Later on, they will record more information—related to their evaluation of the source's credibility, richness, and interest—when they use the **Assessing Sources Handout** (in the **RDU Literacy Toolbox**).

- Remind students that at this point, their notes must serve two main purposes: recording general identifying information about a source and noting relevant information about its content.

TEXT NOTES: SOURCE 4

If using the model topic and Common Sources Set for this unit, students might be supported in beginning their searches by starting with one of the following Source 4 texts or websites that can lead to further narrowing of their topic and search or to other sources of related information.

Source 4A: Music on the Web: "The True Cost of Sound Recording Piracy to the U.S. Economy" by Stephen E. Siwek, August 21, 2007. This article is available on The Institute for Policy Innovation website and provides a study by the conservative think tank discussing the adverse economic influence of music piracy. This article may help students narrow their interest and investigation to specific areas within music piracy.

Source 4B: Relationship between Music and the Brain: "Study Shows Some Are Unmoved by Music" by the *Los Angeles Times*, adapted by Newsela staff, March, 11, 2014. This article is available on the Newsela website. If the school or classroom does not already have an account, tell students they will have to create a username and password to log in to the Newsela website. This article explores how some people find it difficult to relate to music because of certain biological conditions. Students can use this article to springboard into research of certain brain conditions such as anhedonia that are related to the connection between the brain and music.

Source 4C: Role of Music in History: "The Evolution of Music: How Genres Rise and Fall Over Time" by Kyle Kim, May 6, 2015. This article is available on the *Los Angeles Times* website. The article provides research on how scientists used Billboard music charts from the past to track how music genres evolved since 1960. The researchers were able to chart the popularity of thirteen different musical categories including hip-hop and country music. Students can use this article to springboard into further articles or research about the evolution of certain musical genres and how culture during that time period may have influenced certain types of music popularity.

ACTIVITY 4: VETTING AREAS OF INVESTIGATION

Students vet their potential Areas of Investigation and develop a research question or problem statement.

USING THE AREA EVALUATION CHECKLIST TO EVALUATE AN AREA OF INVESTIGATION

As they move forward in their research, students will need to make decisions about which of their potential Areas of Investigation is the most promising, considering what they have now learned about the area, their evolving interests, and the potential sources they have identified. To determine if a topic has the potential to work for them as an area for extended investigation, they will need to consider several key issues:

1. **Coherence:** The topic area is one that the student is beginning to understand in a way that enables her or him to talk about it clearly and coherently with others.

2. **Scope:** The topic area is broad enough to sustain research but also focused enough to be investigated using the questions the student has identified. There are likely to be enough accessible and credible sources about the topic area but not so many as to be confusing.

3. **Relevance:** The topic area matters in relationship to the general topic and also to the world or the student.

4. **Interest:** The topic area continues to be clearly interesting to the student, and she or he can explain why. The student recognizes why investigating the topic area will be valuable.

AREA EVALUATION CHECKLIST

To think about and discuss these characteristics of a promising Area of Investigation, students will use a new resource and tool from the **RDU Literacy Toolbox** that is organized by these four issues to consider. This new tool, the *Area Evaluation Checklist*, provides spaces for recording comments about the four issues based on what the student has learned or can communicate at any point in the research process and for articulating the emerging Inquiry Question(s). The teacher uses the checklist with the class to determine if an area warrants investigation.

INSTRUCTIONAL NOTES

REVIEWING STUDENT PROGRESS

At this formative point in the developing research process, the teacher reviews each student's progress and assesses what needs to be done to ensure that all students have chosen good topics, set up promising Areas of Investigation, and are ready to write good Inquiry Questions. The teacher may first model this process for the entire class, evaluating the Area of Investigation that has been used as a classroom example or, if students are ready, move directly into individual student conferencing, as outlined in the following steps:

- Students hand in their *Exploring a Topic* and *Potential Sources Tools* and any initial notes they have from their pre-searches.
- Review the material in preparation for student-teacher conferences.
- Schedule an in-class conference with each student individually.
- The other students can be given time to work on their pre-searches or read additional sources while individual student conferences occur.
- Begin each conference by introducing the *Area Evaluation Checklist*. Show students how this tool will guide the conversation. Explain the different criteria.
- Work through the checklist with the student, probing and discussing the area based on the criteria.

NOTE

Students may have narrowed their interests to one area or may be still considering the two areas for which they identified potential sources and have written initial Inquiry Questions.

- The goals of the conference are for the student to decide on a promising area for further investigation, affirm that area through evaluation (or think how it might need to be reframed), and arrive at a more focused written research question or problem statement.

- This is also a good opportunity to discuss and assess the student's Academic Habit of **Understanding Purpose and Process**. Understanding this beginning process of probing potential topics and sources is crucial to a student's success throughout the research unit. Ask the student to describe what is being asked of him or her and why it is important to explore a topic.

- At the end of the conference, students file their *Exploring a Topic Tools*, notes, and *Area Evaluation Checklists* in Section 1 of their Research Portfolios: Defining an Area of Investigation.

- If students are going to produce a reflective research narrative as a final product in the unit, they might also record discoveries they have made thus far about the topic or research process in a reflective research journal.

ACTIVITY 5: GENERATING INQUIRY QUESTIONS

Students generate one or more Inquiry Questions to guide their searches for information regarding their Areas of Investigation.

INSTRUCTIONAL NOTES

NOTE

This lesson addresses a Component Skill of research and may be extracted from the instructional sequence of this unit and taught on its own to support students in a different learning context.

Students should now have decided on a potential Area of Investigation based on their exploration, pre-searches, and vetting discussion. They will have expressed their area in the form of a problem or overarching question. They now brainstorm and articulate one or more specific Inquiry Question(s) about their Area of Investigation that will guide their research.

COMPONENT SKILL LESSON C

WRITING AN INQUIRY QUESTION

Having generated a list of informal questions, students will now work on articulating several well-written Inquiry Questions—more focused questions that can frame and drive their continuing research. Depending on the class circumstances, these questions might be generated as follows:

- *A single subtopic area of interest to the entire class:* The class as a whole frames a central Inquiry Question, and then students individually write a second question of their own.

- *Several related interest areas within the overall topic:* Students group based on interests and frame an Inquiry Question for their area, then students individually write a second question of their own.
- *Student-directed inquiry:* Each student chooses a subtopic of interest (or identifies a new, related subtopic) and writes one to two Inquiry Questions related to their area of interest.

Introduce the expectation that students will generate and write one to two Inquiry Questions that they can explore as they begin their research. Explain to students the purpose of an Inquiry Question and some characteristics of useful questions. Useful questions are as follows:

1. **Interesting:** The question focuses on an area that the researcher is genuinely interested in and thinks others may be, too.

2. **Answerable:** The question puts the researcher on a Research Path that can be followed and promises to lead to new discoveries, understandings, or, in some cases, answers.

3. **Clear:** The question is expressed in a way that the researcher and others understand exactly what it is asking and where it will lead.

4. **Rich:** The question can support deep investigation and is likely to lead to new information, multiple answers, and further questions (i.e., it is not a simple yes-no question).

5. **Open-ended:** The question addresses a topic or issue that the researcher is interested in but for which the researcher has not already formed an opinion or arrived at an answer.

6. **Focused:** Although being rich and open-ended, the question also narrows down the topic area into a specific pathway for conducting research, rather than being a broad, general question.

These key characteristics are explained and discussed for students in a resource handout found in the **RDU Literacy Toolbox**, the *Posing Inquiry Questions Handout*. Introduce this handout to students.

POSING INQUIRY QUESTIONS HANDOUT

The *Posing Inquiry Questions Handout* serves as a guide to help students develop *questions about things they need to know to help guide their research and analysis.* The teacher introduces the principles of using Inquiry Questions and models how to generate good questions.

- Model writing useful questions related to the earlier teacher subtopic example. If using the model topic and the text set, example questions might be as follows:
  ⇒ Subtopic of interest: Music on the web
  ⇒ Inquiry Questions: What is the difference between downloading and streaming music? How does downloading or streaming music affect musicians? Why is music piracy such a controversial issue? How does music piracy affect musicians and consumers? How has music piracy emerged from the invention of the Internet?

- Have students discuss the example questions in relationship to the characteristics of a useful Inquiry Question found on the ***Posing Inquiry Questions Handout***.

- Model posing other types of questions about additional Areas of Investigation, building from students' reading of Common Texts**.**

- As a class or in small groups, brainstorm additional possible Inquiry Questions (students can share and build from the questions they have previously generated and recorded on various tools).

- Students should help each other pose questions exploring as many possible aspects of their Areas of Investigation as possible. Similar to any brainstorming activity, volume should be the initial goal, enabling students to build from each other's ideas.

- Using the criteria in the ***Posing Inquiry Questions Handout***, discuss whether specific selected questions are either inadequate or sufficient to sustain a research avenue. Students will use this handout as a guide while generating their own questions.

- Model and discuss how questions can be reframed and refined to become fruitful questions that require and will sustain research.

- In pairs, students draft Inquiry Questions, building from their earlier informal question sets or questions generated by the class. Student pairs then discuss their draft questions with another pair (in a pairs-check format).

- Individually, each student drafts (or redrafts) an individual Inquiry Question.

- Using the OE Collaborative Writing model, students then review and revise their questions, considering the characteristics of a useful inquiry question found on the ***Posing Inquiry Questions Handout***.

- Set a goal: at the end of the process, each student should have one or two well-written Inquiry Questions to guide further research in Parts 2 through 5.

PART 1: FORMATIVE ASSESSMENT OPPORTUNITIES

By the end of Part 1, students will have produced the following:

- *Questioning Path Tool*
- *Approaching Texts Tool*
- *Analyzing Details Tool*
- *Exploring a Topic Tools*

- *Potential Sources Tool*
- *Area Evaluation Checklist*
- *Inquiry Questions*

LITERACY SKILLS

In this part of the unit students will have begun exploring a topic by reading texts, writing sentences that identify and explain their Areas of Investigation, posing and discussing Inquiry Questions, and reflecting on their research process.

Focus formative evaluation of these products on the targeted Literacy Skills. Look for evidence of students' abilities in the skill areas of **Summarizing** and **Identifying Relationships** demonstrated while conducting pre-searches and completing *Potential Sources Tools*. In their *Exploring a Topic Tools*, look for how well they summarize the class conversation, identify relationships among the various ideas, and use language to exhibit clear descriptions and thinking about potential Areas of Investigation. Most important, formatively assess where students are in developing **Questioning** skills as demonstrated by how they formulate their potential Areas of Investigations and how they generate Inquiry Questions.

ACADEMIC HABITS

The Academic Habit of **Generating Ideas** is key to successful inquiry-based research. Teaching a research process can be understood as teaching *productive curiosity*. Students are naturally curious and interested in things. In this unit students learn approaches and methods to make their curiosity productive—to nurture and focus their curiosity in ways that deepen their understanding and lead to the development of materials to support the expression of their perspective. The habit of **Generating Ideas** is a concrete expression of curiosity. The activities of topic exploration, developing Inquiry Questions, and determining Areas of Investigation are all opportunities to assess how students generate ideas in discussion and in their independent work.

Research involves sustained independent work. **Completing Tasks**, large and small, is essential for compiling a comprehensive set of materials to support an evidence-based perspective. The tasks associated with initiating inquiry, including determining an Area of Investigation, provide the opportunity for teachers to assess how well students can complete small but important tasks in the process. This initial evaluation can enable teachers to give specific and early feedback to students before they are assigned longer and more complex tasks to complete collaboratively and independently.

In Part 1, teachers discuss the research process taught in the unit, including its various purposes. Because students are explicitly learning an important process, it is essential that they develop an understanding of it and use that understanding as they participate in the activities. Formatively assess how well students initially demonstrated the habit of **Understanding Purpose and Process** as they worked collaboratively to initiate inquiry. An interesting and appropriate Area of Investigation is a good indicator of how well a student understands purpose and process.

Academic Habits—Student Reflection Questions

- How have I generated ideas in the class discussions?
- How have I completed the tasks assigned to me?

- How have I applied my understanding of the process to the activities?
- What can I improve on as the unit progresses?
- If students are going to produce a reflective research narrative as a final product in the unit, they might also record discoveries they have made thus far about the topic or research process in a reflective research journal.

NOTE

To support self-, peer, and teacher assessment of skills and habits developed during the unit, a formal *RDU Literacy Skills and Academic Habits Rubric* and less formal *Student RDU Literacy Skills and Academic Habits Checklist* can be found in the **RDU Literacy Toolbox.**

PART 2

GATHERING INFORMATION

OBJECTIVE:	Students learn how to conduct searches, assess and annotate sources, and keep an organized record of their findings. By the end of Part 2, students will have framed their inquiry and gathered their main body of research material.

MATERIALS:
Common Sources 1 through 4
- **Student-identified sources**
- **Potential Sources Tool**
- **Assessing Sources Handout**

- **Taking Notes Tool**
- **Posing Inquiry Questions Handout**
- **Research Frame Tool**

LITERACY SKILLS

TARGETED SKILLS	DESCRIPTORS
IDENTIFYING RELATIONSHIPS	Identifies important connections among key details and ideas within and across texts
SUMMARIZING	Recounts the explicit meaning of texts, referring to key details, events, characters, language, and ideas
QUESTIONING	Formulates and responds to questions and lines of inquiry that lead to the identification of important ideas and themes
EVALUATING INFORMATION	Assesses the relevance and credibility of information, ideas, evidence, and logic presented in texts
ORGANIZING IDEAS	Sequences sentences and paragraphs to establish coherent, logical, and unified narratives, explanations, and arguments

ACADEMIC HABITS

HABITS DEVELOPED	DESCRIPTORS
GENERATING IDEAS	Generates and develops ideas, positions, products, and solutions to problems
COMPLETING TASKS	Finishes short and extended tasks by established deadlines
ORGANIZING WORK	Maintains work and materials so that they can be used effectively and efficiently in current and future tasks
UNDERSTANDING PURPOSE AND PROCESS	Understands the purpose and uses the process and criteria that guide tasks

ALIGNMENT TO CCSS

TARGETED STANDARDS:

CCSS.ELA-LITERACY.W.9-10.7: Conduct short as well as more sustained research projects to answer a question (including a self-generated question) or solve a problem; narrow or broaden the inquiry when appropriate; synthesize multiple sources on the subject, demonstrating understanding of the subject under investigation.

CCSS.ELA-LITERACY.W.9-10.8: Gather relevant information from multiple authoritative print and digital sources, using advanced searches effectively; assess the usefulness of each source in answering the research question; integrate information into the text selectively to maintain the flow of ideas, avoiding plagiarism and following a standard format for citation.

CCSS.ELA-LITERACY.W.9-10.9: Draw evidence from literary or informational texts to support analysis, reflection, and research.

SUPPORTING STANDARDS:

CCSS.ELA-LITERACY.W.9-10.4: Produce clear and coherent writing in which the development, organization, and style are appropriate to task, purpose, and audience.

CCSS.ELA-LITERACY.RI.9-10.1: Cite strong and thorough textual evidence to support analysis of what the text says explicitly as well as inferences drawn from the text.

CCSS.ELA-LITERACY.RI.9-10.2: Determine a central idea of a text and analyze its development over the course of the text, including how it emerges and is shaped and refined by specific details; provide an objective summary of the text.

CCSS.ELA-LITERACY.RI.9-10.4: Determine the meaning of words and phrases as they are used in a text, including figurative, connotative, and technical meanings; analyze the cumulative impact of specific word choices on meaning and tone (e.g., how the language of a court opinion differs from that of a newspaper).

CCSS.ELA-LITERACY.RI.9-10.6: Determine an author's point of view or purpose in a text and analyze how an author uses rhetoric to advance that point of view or purpose.

CCSS.ELA-LITERACY.RI.9-10.10: By the end of grade 9, read and comprehend literary nonfiction in the grades 9–10 text complexity band proficiently, with scaffolding as needed at the high end of the range.

 **ACTIVITIES**

1. PLANNING SEARCHES FOR INFORMATION

The teacher works with students to determine organizing strategies and types and locations of sources in order to plan for searches.

2. BUILDING AN INITIAL RESEARCH FRAME

Students reflect on their emerging understanding of their Inquiry Question and the pathways it can lead to and build an initial Research Frame that will guide their continuing investigation.

3. CONDUCTING SEARCHES FOR BACKGROUND SOURCES USING INQUIRY QUESTIONS AND PATHS

Keeping in mind their Inquiry Questions, emerging Inquiry Paths, and strategies for finding sources, students conduct initial searches.

4. ASSESSING SOURCES

The teacher explains and models how to assess sources to determine their credibility and relevance to Inquiry Questions.

5. MAKING AND RECORDING NOTES

The teacher explains how to annotate sources and record key information, personal impressions, and ideas for further exploration of the Area of Investigation.

6. CONDUCTING SEARCHES INDEPENDENTLY

Students use their Inquiry Questions and Inquiry Paths to conduct strategic searches for potential sources; they annotate promising sources, then make and record notes.

7. REVIEWING AND REVISING THE RESEARCH FRAME

Students reflect on their research strategy based on their findings and review or revise their Research Frames to guide their further investigation.

NOTE

Activities 1, 4, and 5 introduce and explain key research proficiencies that students will use with various degrees of independence when searching for sources. Although the skills of finding, assessing, and annotating sources are introduced here, support and instruction on their development should continue as students progress through their research. The activities use Common Texts and student-found material to model searching for and assessing sources as well as a method for annotating texts and making notes. Instruction on these critical skill areas should be integrated and sustained. A cyclical approach of introductory discussion, modeling, independent practice, and group reflection on experience, taking place over several days, is suggested. Discussion is key for students to process new information and ideas and learn successful practices from their peers. Teachers will need to determine which activities need more time and support based on the proficiency of students.

≡ ACTIVITY 1: PLANNING SEARCHES ≡ FOR INFORMATION

The teacher works with students to determine organizing strategies and types and locations of sources in order to plan for searches.

INSTRUCTIONAL NOTES

> **NOTE**
>
> This lesson addresses a Component Skill of research and may be extracted from the instructional sequence of this unit and taught on its own to support students in a different learning context.

COMPONENT SKILL LESSON D

SEARCHING FOR INFORMATION

Search processes in any type of research involve strategic planning and skills. Students should understand that although the research process relates to informal searching they may have done, one of the purposes of this unit is to develop and hone students' academic research skills. Students will have likely performed online searches based on personal curiosities. The goal here is to encourage that same curiosity and make it more productive by teaching them ways to approach searching in a research context. Discuss four aspects of planning for searches:

1. Following Inquiry Questions <u>to new pathways for research</u>
2. Determining where to look for sources
3. Choosing key words or phrases for online searches
4. Following a research trail from one source to other, related sources

Following Inquiry Questions to New Pathways for Research

It is impossible to look for answers to all the questions a researcher may have at once. Effective and efficient searches for information begin with a focus—which is not to say that they don't lead to new and unforeseen directions. An initial focus, however, guides searching in productive directions. In addition to the simple use of questions to guide inquiry, it is also helpful to consider how one might sequence those searches, building a base of knowledge that will help inform and direct subsequent inquiry. Students should not feel constrained by a rigid and static system but rather should build a sense that strategic planning can make research more productive, efficient, and successful—especially when dealing with deadlines.

- Introduce students to a few guidelines for planning Inquiry Question–based searches:
  ⇒ Focus searches on specific Inquiry Questions.

⇒ Move from general Inquiry Questions to more specific ones.

⇒ Move from Inquiry Questions more easily answered to more complex questions.

⇒ Think about how a broad Inquiry Question leads outward in multiple directions to related subtopics and to new, more focused questions. A helpful analogy for students might be to think about a path they follow on a hike, which then branches in different directions—each of which might be interesting to explore. In a similar way, their first Inquiry Questions can frame or direct their research and lead to new, more focused searches, which can be referred to as Inquiry Paths.

⇒ Emphasize that the plan is not static but can evolve as knowledge and understanding of the area deepens.

- Model how to organize class Inquiry Questions into an initial set of pathways using student work or model questions and Areas of Investigation. A cluster diagram might help students visualize this model. If using the Common Source Set and topic, an example of a question-based set of pathways might look like the following:

⇒ Area of Interest: Music on the web

⇒ Inquiry Question: Why is music piracy such a controversial issue? How does music piracy affect musicians and consumers? How has music piracy emerged from the invention of the Internet?

Pathways and questions:

1. *Consumers and music piracy*: How do you know if you have committed music piracy? How can you share music in a legal way? In what ways is the sharing of music limited for the consumer?

2. *Current controversy*: Why are people concerned about music piracy? What are the different ways of thinking about the issue? Who are the people or interest groups on various sides of the issue?

3. *Music piracy and current online companies*: How have cases such as Naptser affected current models for online music providers such as Spotifiy, Pandora, and iTunes?

- Explain that questions can lead to all sorts of pathways, depending on the topic.

- Ask the class to work from a starting Inquiry Question, identify pathways (subtopics or questions) that branch off from the Inquiry Question, and give the pathways headings or titles. As a class, come up with two to three pathways stemming from an initial question.

- In groups, students now turn to their own Inquiry Questions and come up with two to three pathways that branch off from each question.

- As students move to the next phase of research, searching for additional sources, they will continue to consider their broad Inquiry Question(s) but will also search within each of the pathways they have identified.

Determining Where to Look for Sources

A crucial aspect of planning for searches is determining where to look for information depending on the questions asked.

- Open with a class discussion about the various kinds of sources students found in their pre-searches (articles, images, video or multimedia, research studies, primary and secondary sources, interviews, expert opinions, essays, fiction, etc.), highlighting those that might be especially relevant to the class topic(s).
- Discuss various places where sources can be found and the associated search methods. Direct the class discussion by asking these questions:
  ⇒ Which locations would seem to be a good choice in looking for reliable information?
    ⇒ If I am looking for answers to questions relating to specific domains such as medicine, biology, history, art, law, or architecture, I should be looking for specialized libraries, library sections, research databases, or websites.
    ⇒ If I don't know where to look for specialized information, I might want to ask a librarian for guidance.
  ⇒ What sorts of sources should I look for, depending on the kinds of information I want?
    ⇒ If I am looking for facts and numbers, I might want to search for reports.
    ⇒ If I am looking for an explanation of a historical or political event, I might look into articles in specialized websites, magazines, or books on the subject.
    ⇒ If I am looking for information on a public figure's opinion on a subject, I might look for speeches delivered or articles written by this person or interviews with this person on the topic.

    ⇒ If I am investigating a subject such as the music business, I might consider visiting a local radio station or music store.
- Using the Inquiry Questions and Pathways of a student volunteer, choose one or two pathways or questions and model planning where to look for sources.
- Then have students work in pairs to discuss where they would look for sources to answer their own Inquiry Questions.
- They can keep their notes in Section 2 of their Research Portfolios: Gathering and Analyzing Information.

Choosing Key Words or Phrases for Online Searches

Successful online searches can be performed most effectively by using appropriate words and phrases. The search engine will provide a list of sites based on a request. The more focused, clear, precise, and domain-specific requests are, the more accurate and relevant the search results will be.

Modeling Internet and database searches presents a great opportunity for vocabulary development:

- Focus on key domain-specific words.
- Examine variations of words and word families.
- Highlight key distinctions among synonyms.

- One activity might involve doing a search with two particular words associated with a student's Area of Investigation:
  - ⇒ After briefly examining the lists of possible sources resulting from a particular key word or phrase, change one of the words to a *synonym*.
  - ⇒ Discuss the differences in the resulting titles that the search engine generates based on differences between the two words.
- Explain the notion of *domain-specific vocabulary* by discussing how any topic uses specific words and phrases to describe things. This is the case of anything from baseball to geography. Just as students need to know something about the game and its rules to talk about baseball, they will need to become familiar with the domain-specific vocabulary of their own topic.
- Encourage students to keep track of domain-specific vocabulary they come across in their notes. These terms will help them complete searches and refine their Inquiry Questions.

    An example for the topic of "Music and the Role It Plays in Our Lives" could look like the following:

  - ⇒ Area of Investigation: Music on the web
  - ⇒ Initial Inquiry Questions: How has the Internet affected copyright laws for recorded music? How can you share music in a legal way? In what ways is the sharing of music limited for the consumer? How do the rights of musicians compare to those of the consumer? Why is music piracy currently such a controversial issue?

  - ⇒ Synonyms:
    - ⇒ Rights: entitlements, privileges
    - ⇒ Piracy: stealing, robbery, theft
    - ⇒ Controversy: disagreement, debate, dispute, argument
  - ⇒ Domain-specific vocabulary: recording industry, musicians, copyright infringement, intellectual property, downloading music, music consumption, distribution, noncommercial file sharing
- Using a short common text students have read previously (either Source 2 or Source 3 if using the Common Source Set), model how key words (synonyms or domain-specific vocabulary) can be found in the source. Highlight (or point out) examples of key words embedded in the source. Explain how the vocabulary in this source can help students find key words to use in their searches and how a key word search could lead back to this source.
- Using their Inquiry Questions and the sources found during their pre-searches, students prepare an initial set of key words or phrases.
- Instruct students to mark and record domain-specific terms that are relevant to their research in order to use them in their work.

Partnering with the public or school librarian or media center specialist (perhaps actually holding class in the library or media center) may help facilitate modeling of appropriate searches. If technology permits, modeling how to conduct search engine and online repository searches should be done live for the class.

Following a Research Trail from One Source to Other, Related Sources

Students can and should also learn to search progressively, by following a trail from previous sources to new, related information. In this process, students might conduct the following kinds of searches:

- Searches for websites managed by organizations closely related to the topic (e.g., the Recording Industry Association of America, RIAA). These sites often present overviews and links to other pages or sites that present more specific information.

- Searches that follow a trail from a previous source. They might work from a reference on a website, a citation in the text, or a name that is identified as an expert. For example, if using the Common Source Set for this unit, they might search for artists or events cited in the article on the "25 Most Important Civil Rights Moments in Music History" (Source 3C).

ACTIVITY 2: BUILDING AN INITIAL RESEARCH FRAME

Students reflect on their emerging understanding of their Inquiry Question and the pathways it can lead to and build an initial Research Frame that will guide their continuing investigation.

INSTRUCTIONAL NOTES

USING QUESTIONS TO ORGANIZE A RESEARCH FRAME

Students have been developing and using Inquiry Questions to guide their initial searches and examination of an Area of Investigation. Now, they will begin to organize their questions and pathways into more structured Inquiry Paths using the **Research Frame Tool** (in the **RDU Literacy Toolbox**).

- Connect the concept of an Inquiry Path to students' previous listing of pathways that branch off from an Inquiry Question. An Inquiry Path is a subtopic or question that defines a crucial aspect of the Area of Investigation. Students will need to explore a set of related Inquiry Paths to conduct their research, organize their information, and develop an evidence-based perspective. An Inquiry Path can be made up of more specific Inquiry Questions, subtopic areas, or key words that guide research.

- Revisit the analogy of pathways students might follow when doing an exploratory hike. Let them know that their Research Frame will now let them map out those pathways so that they will not get lost as they explore their Area of Investigation and head off toward the end point of their journey—the development of their own evidence-based perspective on the topic.

RESEARCH FRAME TOOL

The **Research Frame Tool** is one way for students to frame their inquiry. The teacher may compare it to a detective's investigation plan. The **Research Frame Tool** helps students map out their exploration of the research topic and the chosen Area of Investigation. It guides students throughout the research process and helps them organize their findings. It contains a brief description of the topic, the Area of Investigation, and several Inquiry Paths containing lists of questions, subtopics, and key words to guide the research strategically. Students initially use the tool to set direction for their searches for sources, then return to it and refine their frame as they read and assess those sources, gather information through note-taking, and further develop their guiding Inquiry Questions.

INSTRUCTIONAL NOTES

Teacher Models the Research Frame Tool

- Use the **Research Frame Tool** to model how the informal pathways stemming from an Inquiry Question that the class and students have identified can become Inquiry Paths. Point out how these paths address different aspects of the topic and the Area of Investigation. In the teacher model, explain how these paths might be used to frame and direct the next steps in inquiry and research—how they might guide the reading and assessing of sources.

- Give each path a title expressed in the form of a question or subtopic area. Assign each path a number or key word so that the path can be easily referenced when finding sources and taking notes.

Students Practice Using the Research Frame Tool

- Students review their Inquiry Questions for their Area of Investigation and the possible branching pathways they have identified in Activity 1. Encourage students to refine, combine, elaborate, and add pathways and questions as they review them.

- Students set up an Inquiry Path for each of the informal pathways that they think they want to follow as they explore the topic. They should give each path a title—preferably in the form of a question—that they can use to refer to the path as they move forward. Initially, students might try to identify three Inquiry Paths stemming from their broad Inquiry Question and record them in the three columns of the tool.

- For each Inquiry Path, students group questions, titling phrases for subtopics, and key words they have identified that are relevant to that path. Each group becomes an Inquiry Path.

- Students can also determine new Inquiry Paths based on their findings at this point and then develop a series of Inquiry Questions and key words that will help them address each path.

- Depending on ability, students could develop their paths independently and then review them with a partner, or they could reverse the process, working first with a partner and then completing them independently.

- Students might also work in teams to research a common Area of Investigation. Each team member could be responsible for developing Inquiry Questions, subtopics, and key words for an Inquiry Path she or he would then research within a collaborative process.

- After the work is completed, ask students to reflect on their Area of Investigation and review all the titles of their Inquiry Paths to make sure that they do the following:

  ⇒ Cover a wide range of aspects and questions about the Area of Investigation

  ⇒ Are clearly distinct from one another

  ⇒ Seem to be important

- Students may choose to regroup paths covering similar questions and subtopics or create new paths to cover missing questions about the Area of Investigation.

Framing inquiry through Inquiry Paths enables students to have a plan for comprehensively exploring a topic. At every step of the investigation, students should go back to their **Research Frame Tool** and ask themselves what they've learned, what questions they have answered, and what questions they should investigate next based on the results of their investigation at that point.

It is important to explain that the Research Frame is not meant to be static. It will evolve as the student progresses. Questions within the Inquiry Paths may change, become obsolete, or new questions may be added. Entire Inquiry Paths may need to be abandoned or added as well. Even the framing of the Area of Investigation may evolve, because students may refine their angle of investigation. The **Research Frame Tool** will also be revised in class as part of the process in Part 4.

Having a plan also frames inquiry as ideas to be explored and questions to be answered rather than beliefs to be proven. At this point in the process, it should be clearly stressed to students that they do not need to know what they think about their Area of Investigation or have a definitive opinion or perspective on it before they go through the next steps in the investigation. It is important to be explicit with students that they will come to an understanding from which they can develop an evidence-based perspective as a result of the research process—*after* they investigate, not *before*.

☰ ACTIVITY 3: CONDUCTING SEARCHES FOR BACKGROUND ☰ SOURCES USING INQUIRY QUESTIONS AND PATHS

Keeping in mind their Inquiry Questions, emerging Inquiry Paths, and strategies for finding sources, students conduct initial searches.

INSTRUCTIONAL NOTES

During and outside of class, students are given time to consult a librarian or media specialist and conduct web- or library-based searches. At this time, direct students to focus on finding sources that are more broad in scope and that address several different paths or questions. These texts can potentially be used for background information on the topic.

- Encourage students to find sources that address their initial Inquiry Questions and Inquiry Paths. They should focus on finding one to two sources per path.

- Emphasize the importance of using the key words they have identified for each path as a starting point for more focused searches.

- Remind students (or model an example) that one source is often a gateway to another source; they should be looking for names, references, or citations that might lead them from an initial source to other, related sources.

Students can use a **Potential Sources Tool** to record their findings, expanding the list of sources they have already identified in Part 1.

ACTIVITY 4: ASSESSING SOURCES

The teacher explains and models how to assess sources to determine their credibility and relevance to Inquiry Questions.

INSTRUCTIONAL NOTES

- Explain why the assessment of a source's credibility, richness, and interest is fundamental to the selection of sources for the research:

  ⇒ To reflect on and evaluate the source of the information

  ⇒ To purge one's research during the process (eliminating the least credible and relevant sources)

  ⇒ To identify the most important sources to analyze more deeply through close reading

  NOTE

  This lesson addresses a Component Skill of research and may be extracted from the instructional sequence of this unit and taught on its own to support students in a different learning context.

COMPONENT SKILL LESSON E

ASSESSING AND EVALUATING SOURCES

Previously, students have used Questioning Paths, Guiding Questions, and text-specific questions to frame their reading and rereading of texts. To support their questioning, they have used tools such as the **Guiding Questions Handout** and the **Questioning Path Tool**. Students have also been generating questions that can frame their research. Ideally, they will have begun to internalize their own processes for selecting, developing, and using questions as a way to deepen their understanding.

In this phase of the research process, they will use questions to read sources more critically and assess how suitable they are for use in their continuing research. A source's suitability is based on many factors, some specific to the Area of Investigation and some to the students' own background, interests, and reading skills. Three key factors should be considered:

1. **Accessibility and interest:** How readable and understandable is the source for the researcher, and how interesting or useful does it seem to be?
2. **Credibility:** How trustworthy and believable is the source, based on what the researcher knows about its publisher, date of publication, author (and author's perspective), and purpose?
3. **Relevance and richness:** How closely connected is the source to the topic, Area of Investigation, and Inquiry Path(s)? How extensive and valuable is the information in the source?

These domains for assessing a source's suitability are somewhat equivalent to the organizing domains in the LIPS questioning framework (of the **Guiding Questions Handout**) that students have used previously, but now they address aspects of a source's suitability rather than aspects of the author's craft. Similarly, within each of these source assessment domains, it can be helpful to have and use a bank of Guiding Questions that readers can bring to any text. These kinds of questions are organized in a new resource that students will use to assess their sources (ones they have already found and ones they will find): the **Assessing Sources Handout**. As with the previously used **Guiding Questions Handout**, students will select helpful questions from this new handout and use them to assess the suitability of their sources. Based on their text-based responses to the questions, they will rate the accessibility, credibility, or relevance of each source as high, medium, or low. They will then record their ratings of suitability on the **Potential Sources Tools** they have begun to use previously in the unit.

ASSESSING SOURCES HANDOUT

The **Assessing Sources Handout** (in the **RDU Literacy Toolbox**) is a key component in the research process. It helps students understand and practice the important skill of vetting a source for its accessibility, interest, credibility, relevance, and richness. Students can use the handout's Guiding Questions under each area of review (Accessibility, Interest and Meaning, Credibility, Relevance, and Scope and Richness) as they review potential sources. These Guiding Questions help students think more clearly about each area as they review a text.

INSTRUCTIONAL NOTES

DISCUSSING ACCESSIBILITY, CREDIBILITY, AND RELEVANCE OF SOURCES

Instruction aimed at helping students assess sources begins with some understanding of what is meant by a source's *accessibility, interest, credibility, relevance,* and *richness.* Working with these terms, as represented on the **Potential Sources Tool** and the **Assessing Sources Handout**, provides an opportunity for the development of students' academic vocabulary.

- **Accessibility:** Using examples from day-to-day life, discuss what the word *accessible* means (e.g., what it means for a building to be handicap accessible). With this frame as an analogy, explain to students that sources are more or less accessible to a researcher based on her or his background and reading skills as well as the format, text level, and technicality of the source itself.

  Ideally, sources used by students in their research will be accessible to them as readers. Initially, students should search for sources that are not a stretch for them—that they can read and comprehend with relative ease—and that build from (rather than exceed) their background knowledge. Later, as students learn more about their topic and its terminology, they can then move to more challenging sources. One way initially to assess the accessibility of a source for a particular researcher is to compare the complexity level of the text to the reading level of the student researcher. For this reason, many sources available through libraries and Internet research databases have been "Lexiled" (measured for the complexity of their sentences and the familiarity of their vocabulary). And many research databases enable students and teachers to search for relevant sources by Lexile range. If students know their own Lexile level (based on a reading assessment or their experiences with other Lexiled texts), they can use the match (or mismatch) between their level and the text's level as they assess its accessibility. Alternately, students can read a sample section of the source's text and ask themselves if they comprehend what it is talking about during a first reading.

  Using either a Common Text from the Common Source Set or a Lexiled text found in the library or through a database search, talk to students about the text's complexity level and what that means for its accessibility. Based on their experience in trying to read the text and their sense of their own reading skill levels, have students individually rate the example text's accessibility for each of them as a reader.

- **Credibility:** Discuss the word *credibility* and what it means. How do we know if a source is credible or can be trusted or believed? If students are unfamiliar with the term or how it applies to analyzing sources, ask students first to think about a courtroom analogy, where the jury would be trying to determine the credibility (believability) of witnesses and their testimonies. Then have students compare several sample sources, thinking about their credibility. These sources might be on a topic outside of classroom content with which the students are familiar (e.g., sports, current events, school events, etc.). Or compare a questionable blog from an unknown author with a website from a government agency.

- **Relevance:** Discuss the meaning of the word *relevant* in terms of its roots and related words. Help students understand that a source's relevance is relative—dependent on the context, topic, and inquiry questions being asked. Using sources previously examined by students (Sources 1 through 3 if using the Common Source Set), talk about each source's relevance to various Inquiry Questions. Note that a source such as Source 3 on "music on the web" becomes highly relevant if that is the Area of Investigation but much less so if research branches off into an area such as the "relationship between music and the brain."

NOTE

If the teacher or students are interested in the more technical aspects of Internet search engines, studying this term can also lead to some discussion of how search engines determine relevance based on the frequency of key word occurrence. For more information about this, search for the dictionary.com definition of *relevance* relative to *technology* and *information science*.

MODELING AND GUIDED PRACTICE

- Introduce students to the process of assessing a source's accessibility, credibility, and relevance to determine its suitability to use in their research.

- Using the *Assessing Sources Handout*, model for students how to do a quick analysis of a Common Source read or viewed previously in the unit.

- Have students reread the text themselves using selected Guiding Questions from the handout to help them look for specific details about the texts' accessibility, interest, credibility, relevance, and richness. Ask them to annotate the text and take notes about details that stand out to them and that relate to the Guiding Questions from the *Assessing Sources Handout*. (Alternately, pair this activity with Activity 5, in which students learn and practice skills of systematic note-taking.)

- **Accessibility and interest:** Have students consider and discuss whether, based on their analysis, the source is accessible and potentially interesting to them, making sure they support the answers with evidence from the text.

- **Credibility and relevance:** Walk students through the handout's Guiding Questions for assessing credibility and relevance, asking how credible and relevant they think the text is and what evidence they have found to support their thinking. Note that their assessment of relevance will be influenced by the Area of Investigation and Inquiry Questions(s) they are thinking about.

- Show how the resulting assessment will be recorded on the *Potential Sources Tool* (high, medium, low).

- Model and discuss assessing sources of uncertain credibility or suitability for specific Inquiry Questions. (One or more of the Source 5 options from the Common Source Set might be used—see Part 3, Activity 2.)

- Before students move on to assessing their own background sources, they can practice the use of the Assessing Sources process with any of the previously read Source 3 options from the model Source Set, working in pairs to talk through their preliminary analysis of the text's *accessibility, interest, credibility,* and *relevance*.

INDEPENDENT ASSESSMENT OF SOURCES

- Students go back to the sources they have recorded on their *Potential Sources Tools*.

- Using the *Assessing Sources Handout*, students assess their sources for accessibility and interest, credibility, and relevance and richness.

- Students may take this opportunity to purge their sources based on their assessment and make an additional note in the comments box to record the general outcome of the assessment when relevant.

- The class discusses the outcome of their independent assessment of their sources.

- Students comment about their strategies for assessing and purging sources and the difficulties encountered, if any.

ORGANIZING THE RESEARCH PORTFOLIO

Instruct students to store all their tools, notes, and handouts in Section 2 of their Research Portfolios: Gathering and Analyzing Information. If students are going to produce a reflective research narrative as a final product in the unit, they might also record discoveries they have made thus far about the topic or research process in a reflective research journal.

ACTIVITY 5: MAKING AND RECORDING NOTES

The teacher explains how to annotate sources and record key information, personal impressions, and ideas for further exploration of the Area of Investigation.

INSTRUCTIONAL NOTES

> **NOTE**
>
> This lesson addresses a Component Skill of research and may be extracted from the instructional sequence of this unit and taught on its own to support students in a different learning context.

COMPONENT SKILL LESSON F

MAKING AND RECORDING NOTES

In previous units and previous activities within this Research unit, students have been making text annotations and taking text notes using their own approaches and systems. In reviewing these notes, the teacher should assess where students are as systematic note-takers and how much support they need to develop better skills and systems. In this part of the unit, students will learn and use a widely accepted process for taking notes based on the Cornell two-column system. They may need more or less instruction, modeling, and scaffolding depending on their previous experience with this system and the note-taking processes they have developed and demonstrated previously.

> **NOTE**
>
> This activity may be introduced and done in conjunction with Activity 4, in which students are assessing sources. Or their initial assessments may be done and then their more formal notes taken for sources they have deemed to be accessible, interesting, credible, and relevant.

ANNOTATING SOURCES

The first step in recording important information about a source is annotating a printed version of the source with pencil, highlighter, or markers or an electronic version of the source with electronic highlighting and commenting tools. Students may have learned and used systems for annotating texts in previous units; now they will be using their annotation systems in specific ways to support research.

Students can use either of the Source 3 texts for modeling and independent work on annotation (or similar texts selected by the teacher).

- The annotation process includes these steps:
    ⇒ Marking or highlighting key information, words, and concepts

⇒ Recording initial impressions, questions, or comments (*making* notes)

⇒ Identifying areas for possible further exploration

⇒ Making connections to other sources

⇒ Coding details to Inquiry Questions or Inquiry Paths

- The teacher models the process with part of a Common Text and provides suggestions for annotating a text when reading for specific purposes such as research.

- Students practice annotating the rest of the text individually.

- Student volunteers share their annotations and the class discusses their relevance.

 • Explain that annotated texts are valuable sources of information and should always be stored and organized in Section 2 of the Research Portfolio.

SYSTEMATIC NOTE-TAKING

Having read and annotated an example text closely, students will now practice the interconnected skills of taking, recording, and organizing notes in a systematic way. They should come to understand the connections and differences between the processes of *note-taking* (recording as accurately as possible key pieces of information, details, paraphrased ideas, and quotations) and *note-making* (recording impressions, questions, comments, and other notes that reflect the reader's analysis of the text's content and the informational notes that have been taken). To set up their systematic note-taking and note-making, students will use a new tool from the **RDU Literacy Toolbox**, the *Taking Notes Tool*.

THE TAKING NOTES TOOL

The *Taking Notes Tool* helps students make and organize notes for each of their sources and also with respect to their Inquiry Questions. It is based on the principle of two-column notes (also known as the Cornell system), providing spaces for note-taking (recording information) and note-making (commenting on that information). It sets up detail-based textual and cross-textual analysis and claim making. The sheet is divided into three sections: source reference, details, and comments.

INSTRUCTIONAL NOTES

USING THE TAKING NOTES TOOL

Teacher Modeling

- Introduce the *Taking Notes Tool*.

- Using an Inquiry Question to guide the reading of one of the Common Texts that students have previously read and annotated, model taking notes on details addressing that Inquiry Question. Repeat the process with multiple Inquiry Questions and texts as necessary.

- Then, go back to the notes taken and *make* notes, adding personal comments or insights about the details recorded.

Independent Practice with a New Text

- Students read a new Common Text. In small groups, they annotate it and take and make notes on a *Taking Notes Tool*.

- Students will initially use a *Taking Notes Tool* for each source, because it is an easy way of organizing notes when reading a specific source.

- Students can also use the tool to reread some of their sources from their initial search using their Inquiry Questions and Inquiry Paths.

USING VARIOUS SOURCES TO ANSWER AN INQUIRY QUESTION

Now that students have a few different *Taking Notes Tools* filled out for different sources (texts), the teacher models how to combine information gleaned from separate sources onto a *Taking Notes Tool* that addresses one Inquiry Question or Inquiry Path.

This enables students to develop a series of key details and comments addressing the same Inquiry Question or Inquiry Path. Connections can be made and related information can thus be analyzed throughout the research process instead of at the end. This will help students to accomplish the following:

⇒ See information that is repeated across multiple sources.

⇒ Identify gaps as they assess information per each Inquiry Question or Inquiry Path.

⇒ Make connections among the details collected and draw conclusions.

⇒ Identify new investigation paths based on their analysis of the information collected to this point.

⇒ Determine the need to make adjustments to their Inquiry Questions or Inquiry Paths.

⇒ Analyze more easily the information collected for each Inquiry Question or Inquiry Path when they develop their evidence-based perspectives.

Teacher Modeling

- Explain another way of taking notes is based on organizing information by Inquiry Question rather than by source. Ask the class if anyone has noticed during their annotating and note-taking that multiple sources often address the same question or path and can offer an example.

- Taking several *Taking Notes Tools* as models, assign each Inquiry Question or Inquiry Path a color code and use colored pencils or markers to mark notes addressing the same Inquiry Questions or Inquiry Paths across multiple sources.

- Talk through a rereading of a *Taking Notes Tool*, identifying notes that pertain to the specific Inquiry Question or Inquiry Path, highlighting any notes that are identified with the designated color code.

- Repeat for subsequent Inquiry Questions or Inquiry Paths, using different colors each time to highlight relevant notes.

- Finally, model gathering various highlighted notes from different tools and compiling them onto one tool organized by an Inquiry Question or Inquiry Path.

- Alternatively, this can be done on electronic PDFs by cutting and pasting notes from source-specific tools to Inquiry Path–specific tools.

Taking Notes Independently

- Students go back to the sources they have found through their independent searches and select the ones that rated higher during the assessing sources process.
- They use their notes in the General Content box in the *Potential Sources Tool* to connect sources to specific Inquiry Questions or Inquiry Paths.
- They reread these sources closely using their Inquiry Questions as Guiding Questions and take notes on a *Taking Notes Tool*.
- They can also use their annotations on paper or on file to identify important details that can be noted on the *Taking Notes Tool*.
- Finally, they can compile notes from different sources onto Inquiry Path–specific *Taking Notes Tools* so that their notes are now organized by Inquiry Questions or Inquiry Paths.

This process will encourage students to analyze and connect the details drawn from their sources. After doing so, they will have information that will enable them to review and revise their emergent Research Frames.

ORGANIZING THE RESEARCH PORTFOLIO

Instruct students to store their material in Section 2 of their Research Portfolios: Gathering and Analyzing Information. If students are going to produce a reflective research narrative as a final product in the unit, they might also record discoveries they have made thus far about the topic or research process in a reflective research journal.

☰ ACTIVITY 6: CONDUCTING SEARCHES ☰ INDEPENDENTLY

Students use their Inquiry Questions and Inquiry Paths to conduct strategic searches for potential sources; they annotate promising sources, then make and record notes.

INSTRUCTIONAL NOTES

Students conduct research, reproducing the steps outlined in Activities 1 through 5.

1. Generate and consider Inquiry Questions that define and drive the research direction.
2. Use Inquiry Questions and keywords to conduct searches for sources.
3. Assess each source for accessibility, interest, credibility, relevance, and richness.
4. Make and record notes about each new source
5. Revisit and revise the Research Frame as necessary.

Students can use the Student Research Plan to guide them in the sequence of steps to follow and the supporting materials to use (tools and handouts).

Teachers should expect students to conduct some searches and find sources outside of class. Teachers should also work with students on their research in class. It is important for students to understand that developing their research proficiencies is central to their literacy education. It is not something they do outside of class, as in-class instruction continues on something else (another book, unit, topic, etc.).

Class time during this process can be given to support students' development of their searching, source assessing, and note-taking as well as their managing and monitoring of progress through the research process. The teacher can choose to have students work independently while he or she moves around the room monitoring and supporting, using issues and questions from individual students to instruct the entire class. Students can also work in groups on texts that are relevant to multiple students, enabling collaboration and peer support.

ORGANIZING THE RESEARCH PORTFOLIO

Throughout all these activities, it is important that students build and maintain an organized Research Portfolio. They should be storing all their sources, tools, and notes, coding and organizing them with respect to their Research Frames. If students are going to produce a reflective research narrative as a final product in the unit, they might also record discoveries they have made thus far about the topic or research process in a reflective research journal.

≡ ACTIVITY 7: REVIEWING AND REVISING ≡ THE RESEARCH FRAME

Students reflect on their research strategy based on their findings and review or revise their Research Frames to guide their further investigation.

INSTRUCTIONAL NOTES

- Considering the additional research they have now done, students individually review their **Research Frame Tools** and think about changes they may want to make in their organizing Inquiry Questions and their Inquiry Paths. This may involve adding new paths, questions, subtopics, or key words, rethinking the organizing name and question for a given path, or even eliminating paths that may not seem fruitful or relevant any more.

- In collaborative research teams (organized by Area of Investigation, if multiple students are investigating the same or similar topics), students talk through their Research Frames and share general summaries of what they have learned so far in each Inquiry Path area.

- Other team members offer observations, affirmations, and suggestions based on what they hear.

- Each researcher then records any relevant rethinking or revisions on a **Research Frame Tool** (either a new tool or their previous one, if revisions are minor).

- Students store their **Research Frame Tool** in Section 2 of their Research Portfolios: Gathering and Analyzing Information.

- Individually or in research teams, students can reflect on the habits a researcher should develop when thinking about developing a Research Frame.

Generating Ideas

⇒ Develops and considers many different Inquiry Questions

⇒ Thinks about how these questions make up different Inquiry Paths

Organizing Work

⇒ Keeps track of texts and how they relate to each specific Inquiry Path

⇒ Maintains an orderly portfolio that can be used and modified to accompany the research process

Understanding Purpose and Process

⇒ Recognizes and reflects on each step in the research process and understands why it is important

⇒ Understands where she or he is in the inquiry process—where the research has come from and where it should go next

PART 2: FORMATIVE ASSESSMENT OPPORTUNITIES

By the end of Part 2 students will have produced the following:

- *Research Frame Tool(s)*
- *Potential Sources Tools*
- *Annotated Common Texts*
- Annotated sources
- *Taking Notes Tools*

LITERACY SKILLS

As students begin to use various texts to address one Inquiry Question or Path, they continue to refine their skills of **Summarizing** and **Identifying Relationships**. They also now begin **Evaluating Information** in sources to determine the credibility of each source and its relevance in addressing their Inquiry Questions and Research Frame.

ACADEMIC HABITS

As students push their Research Plans forward by drafting and grouping Inquiry Questions, conducting searches and assessing sources, and defining their Research Paths, there are several opportunities for students and teachers to reflect on how well students are addressing the Academic Habits of **Generating Ideas** and **Understanding Purpose and Process**. The habit of **Organizing Work** becomes more and more critical as they compile additional materials into their Research Portfolios and develop Research Paths.

Students might reflect on the following questions:

- What have I done to generate ideas related to the topic I am researching?
- How have I begun to organize my notes and tools?
- What can I do to improve?

NOTE

To support self-, peer, and teacher assessment of skills and habits developed during the unit, a formal **RDU Literacy Skills and Academic Habits Rubric** and less formal **Student RDU Literacy Skills and Academic Habits Checklist** can be found in the **RDU Literacy Toolbox**.

PART 3

DEEPENING UNDERSTANDING

OBJECTIVE:	Students read and analyze key sources closely to deepen their understanding and draw personal conclusions about their Area of Investigation. By the end of Part 3, students will have a series of evidence-based claims addressing each Inquiry Path of their Research Frame.

MATERIALS:
Common Source 5
Student-identified sources
- *Research Frame Tool*
- *Analyzing Details Tool*
- *Assessing Sources Handout*

- *Forming EBC Research Tool*
- *Attending to Details Handout*
- *Writing EBC Handout*
- *Connecting Ideas Handout*

☰ LITERACY SKILLS

TARGETED SKILLS	DESCRIPTORS
MAKING INFERENCES	Demonstrates comprehension by using connections among details to make logical deductions about a text
RECOGNIZING PERSPECTIVE	Uses textual details to recognize an author's or narrator's relationship to and perspective on a text's topic
EVALUATING INFORMATION	Assesses the relevance and credibility of information, ideas, evidence, and logic presented in texts
FORMING CLAIMS	Develops meaningful and defensible claims that clearly state valid, evidence-based analysis
USING EVIDENCE	Supports all aspects of claims with sufficient textual evidence using accurate quotations, paraphrases, and references
ORGANIZING IDEAS	Sequences sentences and paragraphs to establish coherent, logical, and unified narratives, explanations, and arguments

ACADEMIC HABITS

HABITS DEVELOPED	DESCRIPTORS
GENERATING IDEAS	Generates and develops ideas, positions, products, and solutions to problems
COMPLETING TASKS	Finishes short and extended tasks by established deadlines
UNDERSTANDING PURPOSE AND PROCESS	Understands the purpose and uses the process and criteria that guide tasks
ORGANIZING WORK	Maintains work and materials so that they can be used effectively and efficiently in current and future tasks

ALIGNMENT TO CCSS

TARGETED STANDARDS:

CCSS.ELA-LITERACY.W.9-10.7: Conduct short as well as more sustained research projects to answer a question (including a self-generated question) or solve a problem; narrow or broaden the inquiry when appropriate; synthesize multiple sources on the subject, demonstrating understanding of the subject under investigation.

CCSS.ELA-LITERACY.W.9-10.8: Gather relevant information from multiple authoritative print and digital sources, using advanced searches effectively; assess the usefulness of each source in answering the research question; integrate information into the text selectively to maintain the flow of ideas, avoiding plagiarism and following a standard format for citation.

CCSS.ELA-LITERACY.W.9-10.9: Draw evidence from literary or informational texts to support analysis, reflection, and research.

CCSS.ELA-LITERACY.RI.9-10.7: Analyze various accounts of a subject told in different mediums (e.g., a person's life story in both print and multimedia), determining which details are emphasized in each account.

CCSS.ELA-LITERACY.RI.9-10.9: Analyze seminal U.S. documents of historical and literary significance (e.g., Washington's Farewell Address, the Gettysburg Address, Roosevelt's Four Freedoms speech, King's "Letter from Birmingham Jail"), including how they address related themes and concepts.

CCSS.ELA-LITERACY.RI.9-10.10: By the end of grade 9, read and comprehend literary nonfiction in the grades 9–10 text complexity band proficiently, with scaffolding as needed at the high end of the range.

ACTIVITIES

1. SELECTING KEY SOURCES
The teacher discusses how to identify the most relevant sources and helps students select key sources to analyze through close reading.

2. ANALYZING A SOURCE'S PERSPECTIVE
The teacher models analyzing a source's perspective and relevance using a Common Source, and students practice the process with a second Common Source.

3. READING KEY SOURCES CLOSELY—FORMING CLAIMS
Students use their Inquiry Questions to read key sources closely, analyzing them for content, perspective, and relevance.

4. WRITING EBCs ABOUT SOURCES
Students develop evidence-based summaries and explanations of relevant sources using their notes and annotations.

ACTIVITY 1: SELECTING KEY SOURCES

The teacher discusses how to identify the most relevant sources and helps students select key sources to analyze through close reading.

INSTRUCTIONAL NOTES

CONNECTING SOURCES TO INQUIRY PATHS

By the end of Part 2, students should have gathered and annotated additional sources related to their Inquiry Paths and Area of Investigation. They are now ready to select their key sources and relate them to specific Inquiry Paths.

- Model connecting sources to Inquiry Paths using the Research Frame, the general comments on content in the **Potential Sources Tools**, and the notes on **Taking Notes Tools**.
- The connections can be recorded in the Connection to Inquiry Paths box using the reference number assigned to each Inquiry Path on the **Potential Sources Tools**.
- Students now practice connecting their sources to their Inquiry Paths.

SELECTING KEY SOURCES

- Introduce the idea that to determine the exact relevance of a source to an Inquiry Path, some require additional close reading in order to extract important details and to analyze more deeply their ideas and perspectives.
- The selection should be based on the assessment of accessibility, interest, credibility, relevance, and richness recorded on the **Potential Sources Tool**. Personal notes recorded on the same tool may also help select key sources.
- Model using the information recorded on a **Potential Sources Tool** to select key sources (the **Assessing Sources Handout** can also be used).
- Then have students review their notes on **Potential Sources** and **Taking Notes Tools** and their annotation on the sources to determine which sources need additional close reading.
- Students select at least one key source per Inquiry Path to analyze further through close reading.

ACTIVITY 2: ANALYZING A SOURCE'S PERSPECTIVE

The teacher models analyzing a source's perspective and relevance using a Common Source, and students practice the process with a second Common Source.

INSTRUCTIONAL NOTES

NOTE

This lesson addresses a Component Skill of research and may be extracted from the instructional sequence of this unit and taught on its own to support students in a different learning context.

ANALYZING A SOURCE'S PERSPECTIVE AND BIAS

When they have analyzed previous texts in other units and used the LIPS domains from the **Guiding Questions Handout**, students will have considered the author's *perspective* and how it is conveyed within a text. Students will now apply what they have learned about analyzing perspective:

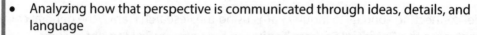

- Determining an author's purpose for writing a text
- Identifying the author's relationship to a topic
- Describing the author's view of or perspective on the topic
- Analyzing how that perspective is communicated through ideas, details, and language

In the research context, they will need to apply these skills independently as they read, analyze, and evaluate their key sources more closely. They will also need to compare the perspectives of multiple sources and authors in relationship to their Area of Investigation and its inherent issues or controversies. In order to develop their own perspective on the Area of Investigation, they will ideally examine and consider multiple perspectives of others. In preparation for applying these critical reading and thinking skills within their own source sets, students will analyze and compare perspectives on two Common Sources, one through teacher modeling and one in research teams for guided practice.

INSTRUCTIONAL NOTES

TEXT NOTES: SOURCE 5

The Common Sources used in this activity should be selected to present clear and different perspectives on some aspect of the general topic of the unit or one of the subtopics students have been investigating. If the Common Source Set is used for this purpose, Source Set 5 includes four texts that present different perspectives on the subtopic of music piracy. The teacher can use any of these texts to model the examination of a source's perspective (and its credibility), then have students use another to practice the skill in small groups.

Source 5A: In his article, "Why I Pirate," Sebastian Anthony justifies his practice of music piracy. Citing profit sharing between labels and musicians, criticizing the value of a music product, and highlighting the access of music for the economically disadvantaged, this argumentative piece lays out a position defending the controversial, if not illegal, practice of pirating and sharing music content regardless of copyright laws. Reading and discussion could focus on his perspective and whether or not Sebastian's claims are credible. This text measures at 1200L, and so it might be a good one for teacher modeling.

TEXT NOTES: SOURCE 5

Source 5B: In his article, "Why I No Longer Give Away My Music: How the digital music biz makes it difficult for musicians to offer free downloads," sound artist Bob Ostertag recounts the unexpected issues concerned with giving away his music for free. Specifically, he talks about the idea that a large audience downloading more music than they will actually be able to listen to over a lifetime cheapens music and how other laws negatively affect Creative Commons licenses. This text measures at 1300L and is written in an informal, narrative style while providing an interesting perspective quite different than that of Source 5A.

Source 5C: In the article, "How the web changed music forever: it's both a boon and a bane to musicians," the author explores how smaller music groups are getting by in the new era of music streaming services such as Spotify and Pandora. She explains that unknown musicians release their music on free, open, and public networks in order to become known, but then they might not make any money. This article considers the freedom of music access, exposing vulnerabilities in traditional music markets while admitting that open-source music platforms provide economic opportunities for lesser-known artists. This text measures at 1310L and is one that more advanced students should be able to read and analyze.

Source 5D: In the article "Are Musicians Going Up a Music Stream Without a Fair Payout?," the author explores several musicians' arguments that music should not be streamed and should, instead, be purchased. The author discusses why musicians such as Taylor Swift feel that the art form of making music should be valued and therefore purchased, not streamed for pennies. This text measures at 1180L and should be accessible for most students (Newsela.com also allows students to switch between different Lexiles).

INSTRUCTIONAL NOTES

TEACHER MODELING: ANALYZING A SOURCE'S PERSPECTIVE

Using one of the Common Texts or a similar text related to a class Area of Investigation, the teacher models a process for reading closely and analyzing a source's perspective—and also its bias and credibility.

- Remind students that they have previously used Guiding Questions from the Guiding Questions Handout as a starting point for examining the perspective of an author and its influence on and reflection in a text. This may entail reviewing the meaning of the term *perspective* as it applies to texts—and talking about the range of ways we can think about perspective. Remind students that an author's perspective is usually a function of various factors but that the author's *purpose* in writing the text and *relationship to the topic* are always important to examine.

- Present students with a set of Guiding Questions that can be helpful in thinking about perspective, or have them identify questions themselves from the **Guiding Questions Handout**

(GQH) and the **Assessing Sources Handout** (ASH) they have used previously. A useful set of questions, drawn from the two sources, might be as follows:

⇒ What do I learn about the author and the purpose for writing the text? (GQH)

⇒ What are the author's qualifications or credentials relative to the topic area? (ASH)

⇒ What is the author's personal relationship to the topic area? (ASH)

⇒ What details or words suggest the author's perspective? (GQH)

⇒ How does the author's perspective influence the text's presentation of ideas or arguments? (GQH)

⇒ How does the author's perspective and presentation of the text compare to others? (GQH)

⇒ How does the author's perspective influence my reading of the text—and my use of the text in research? (GQH)

- Have students read the model Common Text individually, considering one or more Guiding Questions to focus their reading.

- Ask students to make initial text-based observations in relationship to the question(s) they have considered.

- Using a projected text, model the process of highlighting information, statements, ideas, details, or language in the text that indicate or reflect the author's perspective. For example, if using Text 5A, mark information that identifies the text as coming from a specific perspective or viewpoint and suggests its purpose in explaining why music piracy can be considered a valid practice.

- Discuss with students how knowing that the text comes from an author who was an editor and writer for a website title ExtremeTech might affect their reading of it and use in research.

- Return to the issue of *credibility* considered when assessing sources previously. Remind students that a source's credibility is likely influenced by its author's background, relationship to the topic, credentials, purpose, and, in some cases, bias. Talk a bit about the concept of *bias* and ask students to reread the text to see if they can find any evidence that the author has a bias about his subject.

- Compare and discuss students' findings about bias in the article. Ask them to draw conclusions about its perspective and usability to support research in the main topic area of music and its role in our lives and the subtopic area of music on the web.

STUDENT PRACTICE IN RESEARCH TEAMS

- Organize students in reading and research teams. They may be organized by common Areas of Investigation or based on differentiated reading levels.

- Assign one of the additional Common Texts to each team.

- In text-based teams, students read their assigned text individually, considering one or more of the Guiding Questions related to *perspective* (from either the GQH or ASH). Students annotate the text, noting details related to perspective and their Guiding Question(s).

- After reading, team members compare their annotations and observations. As a team, they identify and describe the purpose and perspective of the text. If they think that the text has a bias or that its perspective affects its credibility, they note this.

- Student teams report their findings to the class, briefly summarizing what they have observed about their text's purpose, perspective, bias, and credibility; they support their summaries with evidence from the text.

- As a class, compare and discuss what student teams have observed and reported. Compare the purposes and perspectives of the various texts, including the text used for teacher modeling. Ask students to consider the set of sources as a whole and whether they together would represent a valuable range of perspectives on the topic of music on the web. Ask them to think about what is missing or problematic in the source set.

- Inform students that they will next independently (or in topic-related research teams) apply the same question-based process to read closely and analyze the perspective, bias, and credibility of their identified key sources. Tell them that they will do this analysis as part of the process of examining the sources in relationship to their Inquiry Questions and Inquiry Paths from their Research Frame.

≡ ACTIVITY 3: READING KEY SOURCES ≡ CLOSELY—FORMING CLAIMS

Students use their Inquiry Questions to read key sources closely, analyzing them for content, perspective, and relevance.

INSTRUCTIONAL NOTES

In this activity, students employ skills developed in the *Reading Closely for Textual Details* and *Making Evidence-Based Claims* units to analyze selected sources for content and perspective. The approach to close reading developed in those units and incorporated here involves strategically questioning texts to access deep meaning associated with key textual details. In the *Reading Closely for Textual Details* unit, students develop this proficiency using general Guiding Questions and a Questioning Path Framework. Now, in the context of their research, students use their Inquiry Questions to guide their analysis. If students need further work on developing independence in close reading, teachers are encouraged to use the additional materials such as the **Questioning Path** and **Analyzing Details Tools** introduced in the *Reading Closely* unit.

Students will be analyzing their sources to identify their perspectives (and any resulting issues related to bias or credibility) while they also examine their content and information more closely. They will study each source for supporting information related to one or more Inquiry Questions. Their goal will be to develop an evidence-based claim for each source that stems from the Inquiry Question they are considering. To guide this process, they will use a modified version of a tool from the *Making Evidence-Based Claims* unit, the **Forming EBC Research Tool**.

ADDRESSING INQUIRY QUESTIONS USING THE FORMING EVIDENCE-BASED CLAIMS RESEARCH TOOL

The **Forming Evidence-Based Claims Research Tool** (in the **RDU Literacy Toolbox**) incorporates skills students developed in the *Reading Closely for Textual Details* and *Making Evidence-Based*

Claims units. Students use an Inquiry Question to guide their reading, marking details that help them respond to this question. Then, they select details that seem most relevant to their Inquiry Question, record their thoughts and connections, and make a claim based on their analysis that responds to their Inquiry Question.

Modeling Using the Forming EBC Research Tool

- Model close reading to answer an Inquiry Questions using the Common Text modeled previously in Activity 2. (If using the Common Source Set, this might likely be Text 5A.)

- Orient students to the **Forming EBC Research Tool**.

- Identify a model Inquiry Question from a Research Frame related to the topic of the article and record it at the top of the tool.

- Model working through several paragraphs of the text, guiding the reading with the Inquiry Question, noting relevant details, and selecting key ones. The class might contribute by sharing what they think are important details that address the Inquiry Question.

- Record what the class thinks about the details and the connections among them.

- Finally, develop several claims that respond to the Inquiry Question and are based on the textual evidence identified.

- Model a claim that presents a straightforward *summary* of the text's information and a second claim that presents an *interpretation* of the author's perspective—both in relationship to the Inquiry Question being considered.

Independent Close Reading of Sources

- Using the **Forming EBC Research Tool**, students read the sources they have selected in Activity 1 closely. Students start from an identified Inquiry Question related to each source, annotate the text, note key details related to the question, make connections, and form an evidence-based claim stemming from the source. The claim they develop may be a *summary claim* that is based on information from the text or an *interpretive claim* that analyzes the author's perspective on the topic.

- Support students as they work, helping them select details that relate to their Inquiry Questions and make connections among them.

- Students may work across several days in class, reading closely and analyzing each of their key sources. By the end of the activity, they should have drafted claims for all of the key sources they intend to use.

ORGANIZING THE RESEARCH PORTFOLIO

Instruct students to store their **Forming EBC Research Tools** in Section 2 of their Research Portfolios: Gathering and Analyzing Information. If students are going to produce a reflective research narrative as a final product in the unit, they might also record discoveries they have made thus far about the topic or research process in a reflective research journal.

≡ ACTIVITY 4: WRITING EBCs ABOUT
≡ SOURCES

Students develop evidence-based summaries and explanations of relevant sources using their notes and annotations.

INSTRUCTIONAL NOTES

At this point, students will have analyzed several key sources and developed initial evidence-based claims related to their Inquiry Questions for each source. They now further develop and write evidence-based claims in relationship to their Inquiry Questions, using evidence from one or more of their analyzed sources.

- Students select one of the **Forming EBC Research Tools** that contains their analysis of a source based on an Inquiry Question.

- Students review the **Forming EBC Research Tool** and assess whether they have made an appropriately meaningful and supported claim. They consider the Literacy Skills related to forming claims:

FORMING CLAIMS	States a meaningful conclusion that is well supported by evidence from the text
USING EVIDENCE	Uses well-chosen details from the text to explain and support claims; accurately paraphrases or quotes

- In collaborative review teams, students present and explain their claims, citing evidence from one or more of their sources. Using the Literacy Skills criteria, review team members present initial feedback about how well the writer has *formed the claim* and *used evidence* to support it.

- Students revise their claim statements based on the collaborative, criteria-based review.

- Using their **Forming EBC Research Tool**, students develop the claim into a written paragraph.

  ⇒ The paragraph should state and explain the claim and incorporate supporting evidence from one or more of the student's key sources through direct quotations and paraphrasing.

  ⇒ Proper transitional phrases and citations should be included.

- The **Writing EBC Handout** (introduced and used in the *Making EBC* unit and available in the **Making EBC Literacy Toolbox**) and **Connecting Ideas Handout** can be used to support instruction on writing evidence-based claims.

USING SKILLS CRITERIA TO REVIEW WRITTEN CLAIMS

- Organize students in collaborative writing review teams.

- Discuss the following criteria from the Literacy Skills that can be used to evaluate a written evidence-based claim:

FORMING CLAIMS	States a meaningful conclusion that is well supported by evidence from the text
USING EVIDENCE	Uses well-chosen details from the text to explain and support claims; accurately paraphrases or quotes

- Taking either a teacher or student example, model(1) how to determine whether the example accomplishes what is stated in the criteria and (2) how to discuss the merits or shortcomings of the example using language from the skills descriptors.

- In review teams, students use the OE Collaborative Writing Process to read each other's paragraphs; make constructive, text-based comments in reference to the Literacy Skills criteria; and consider ways to improve the written claims.

- Students revise their paragraphs to improve the clarity or accuracy of the claim and the use of researched evidence to support it.

- Using what they have learned from the collaborative review of their first claim, students consider a second key source and write a second evidence-based claim that appropriately addresses another Inquiry Question.

ORGANIZING THE RESEARCH PORTFOLIO

Students file their two written evidence-based claims in Section 2 of their Research Portfolios. If students are going to produce a reflective research narrative as a final product in the unit, they might also record discoveries they have made thus far about the topic or research process in a reflective research journal.

≡ PART 3: FORMATIVE ASSESSMENT ≡ OPPORTUNITIES

By the end of Part 3 students will have produced the following:

- *Forming EBC Research Tools*
- Annotated Common Texts
- Annotated sources
- Written evidence-based claims

ASSESSING LITERACY SKILLS

By the end of Part 3, students will have compiled most of their researched information and begun to express their analysis in the form of evidence-based claims that address their Inquiry Questions. Their annotated sources can be used to evaluate their developing skills of **Making Inferences**, **Recognizing Perspective**, **Evaluating Information**, and **Organizing Ideas**.

Their *Forming EBC Research Tools* and written claims can be used to evaluate how well students are extending their basic skills of **Forming Claims** and **Using Evidence** into a more independent, inquiry-driven context.

ASSESSING ACADEMIC HABITS

The habits of **Organizing Work** and **Completing Tasks** are particularly important in Part 3. Student Research Portfolios at this stage are a strong demonstration of their development of these habits.

Students might use the following questions to reflect on the development of their Academic Habits:

- Is my Research Portfolio well organized? What practices can I employ to keep my work better organized?
- Is my Research Portfolio complete? Have I completed all the tasks necessary for compiling my portfolio?
- What can I do to improve my organization?

PART 4

FINALIZING INQUIRY

OBJECTIVE:	Students analyze and evaluate their material with respect to their Inquiry Questions and refine their inquiry. By the end of Part 4, students will have an analyzed body of research addressing their Inquiry Questions from which to develop and communicate an evidence-based perspective on the Area of Investigation.

MATERIALS:
- *Research Frame Tool*
- *Forming EBC Research Tool*
- *Organizing EBC Research Tool*
- *Connecting Ideas Handout*
- *Research Evaluation Tool*

☰ LITERACY SKILLS

TARGETED SKILLS	DESCRIPTORS
FORMING CLAIMS	Develops meaningful and defensible claims that clearly state valid, evidence-based analysis
EVALUATING INFORMATION	Assesses the relevance and credibility of information, ideas, evidence, and logic presented in texts
ORGANIZING IDEAS	Sequences sentences and paragraphs to establish coherent, logical, and unified narratives, explanations, and arguments
REFLECTING CRITICALLY	Uses literacy terminology and concepts to reflect on, discuss, and evaluate personal and peer literacy development

☰ ACADEMIC HABITS

HABITS DEVELOPED	DESCRIPTORS
GENERATING IDEAS	Generates and develops ideas, positions, products, and solutions to problems
COMPLETING TASKS	Finishes short and extended tasks by established deadlines
UNDERSTANDING PURPOSE AND PROCESS	Understands the purpose and uses the process and criteria that guide tasks
ORGANIZING WORK	Maintains work and materials so that they can be used effectively and efficiently in current and future tasks

ALIGNMENT TO CCSS

TARGETED STANDARDS:

CCSS.ELA-LITERACY.W.9-10.2: Write informative/explanatory texts to examine and convey complex ideas, concepts, and information clearly and accurately through the effective selection, organization, and analysis of content.

CCSS.ELA-LITERACY.W.9-10.7: Conduct short as well as more sustained research projects to answer a question (including a self-generated question) or solve a problem; narrow or broaden the inquiry when appropriate; synthesize multiple sources on the subject, demonstrating understanding of the subject under investigation.

CCSS.ELA-LITERACY.W.9-10.8: Gather relevant information from multiple authoritative print and digital sources, using advanced searches effectively; assess the usefulness of each source in answering the research question; integrate information into the text selectively to maintain the flow of ideas, avoiding plagiarism and following a standard format for citation.

CCSS.ELA-LITERACY.W.9-10.9: Draw evidence from literary or informational texts to support analysis, reflection, and research.

CCSS.ELA-LITERACY.RI.9-10.7: Analyze various accounts of a subject told in different mediums (e.g., a person's life story in both print and multimedia), determining which details are emphasized in each account.

CCSS.ELA-LITERACY.RI.9-10.9: Analyze seminal U.S. documents of historical and literary significance (e.g., Washington's Farewell Address, the Gettysburg Address, Roosevelt's Four Freedoms speech, King's "Letter from Birmingham Jail"), including how they address related themes and concepts.

CCSS.ELA-LITERACY.RI.9-10.10: By the end of grade 9, read and comprehend literary nonfiction in the grades 9–10 text complexity band proficiently, with scaffolding as needed at the high end of the range.

SUPPORTING STANDARDS:

CCSS.ELA-LITERACY.W.9-10.4: Produce clear and coherent writing in which the development, organization, and style are appropriate to task, purpose, and audience.

CCSS.ELA-LITERACY.W.9-10.5: Develop and strengthen writing as needed by planning, revising, editing, rewriting, or trying a new approach, focusing on addressing what is most significant for a specific purpose and audience.

CCSS.ELA-LITERACY.RI.9-10.1: Cite strong and thorough textual evidence to support analysis of what the text says explicitly as well as inferences drawn from the text.

CCSS.ELA-LITERACY.RI.9-10.2: Determine a central idea of a text and analyze its development over the course of the text, including how it emerges and is shaped and refined by specific details; provide an objective summary of the text.

ACTIVITIES

1. ADDRESSING INQUIRY PATHS
Students review their notes and analyses for the sources that address one of their Inquiry Paths.

2. ORGANIZING EVIDENCE
Students review and organize their research and analysis, establishing connections to address all the Inquiry Paths of their Research Frame.

3. EVALUATING RESEARCH
Students review and discuss their Research Frames and researched materials to determine relevance, coherence, and sufficiency.

4. REFINING AND EXTENDING INQUIRY
Students refine and extend their scope of inquiry based on teacher and peer feedback.

ACTIVITY 1: ADDRESSING INQUIRY PATHS

Students review their notes and analyses for the sources that address one of their Inquiry Paths.

INSTRUCTIONAL NOTES

At this point, students will have analyzed several key sources and used evidence from those sources to develop and write source-specific, evidence-based claims in response to Inquiry Questions. They now should begin to review and compare their notes and analyses for multiple sources that address the Inquiry Paths framing their research. Teachers may choose to model this process for the class.

- Students return to their Research Frames and identify one Inquiry Path to work on first.
- Students should compile all their notes, annotated sources, and *Forming EBC Research Tools* that have been coded to that Inquiry Path.
- Students think about what all of their source annotations, notes, and claims for a particular Inquiry Path add up to—how they can connect and synthesize their analyses for several sources.
- Students form a new, more global evidence-based claim that combines information from multiple sources and represents their research and thinking for the Inquiry Path and its question(s).
- Students think about the parts of this new claim—either represented by other subclaims they have developed or the questions and subtopics within the Inquiry Path they have identified earlier in Parts 2 and 3. Students can then use an *Organizing EBC Research Tool* to help them distinguish and organize relevant information into multiple parts that support a *synthesizing* evidence-based claim for that Inquiry Path.

ORGANIZING EVIDENCE-BASED CLAIMS RESEARCH TOOL

The *Organizing EBC Research Tool* (in the **RDU Literacy Toolbox**) has been introduced in the *Making Evidence-Based Claims* unit. It helps students organize results of their findings, including their personal claims and the key ideas and information they have identified in the sources, into a more general claim that synthesizes their findings. Using one or more *Organizing EBC Research Tools*, students will be able to organize the necessary information to help them in the process of writing synthesizing claims for their Inquiry Paths.

INSTRUCTIONAL NOTES

WRITING SYNTHESIZING CLAIMS THAT ADDRESS INQUIRY PATHS

To tie multisource analyses relative to Inquiry Paths more tightly to the close-reading process, students can use a *Forming EBC Research Tool* to build multisource claims.

- Based on their *Organizing EBC Research* or *Forming EBC Research Tools*, students develop an appropriate claim that addresses one of their Inquiry Paths and write a paragraph that presents and explains the global claim.

The paragraph should state and explain the claim and incorporate supporting evidence from multiple sources through direct quotations and paraphrasing. Proper transitional phrases and citations should be included. Students can use the **Connecting Ideas Handout** for guidance.

- As students write their global, synthesizing claims for their identified Inquiry Paths, they again consider the Literacy Skills for forming claims and using evidence.

FORMING CLAIMS	States a meaningful conclusion that is well supported by evidence from the text
USING EVIDENCE	Uses well-chosen details from the text to explain and support claims; accurately paraphrases or quotes

- In collaborative review teams or pairs, students read each other's paragraphs and make constructive comments in relationship to the Literacy Skills criteria.
- Students revise their paragraphs to improve the clarity or accuracy of the global claim and the quality of the supporting evidence.

ORGANIZING THE RESEARCH PORTFOLIO

At the end of the activity, students file their material in Section 3 of the Research Portfolios: Drawing Conclusions. If students are going to produce a reflective research narrative as a final product in the unit, they might also record discoveries they have made thus far about the topic or research process in a reflective research journal.

ACTIVITY 2: ORGANIZING EVIDENCE

Students review and organize their research and analysis, establishing connections to address all the Inquiry Paths of their Research Frame.

- Once students have had the experience of organizing and writing evidence-based claims to address one Inquiry Path, they should review and organize their research to address the other Inquiry Paths from their Research Frame.
- Students develop **Organizing EBC Research Tools** to address each of their Inquiry Paths.
- Depending on how they organize evidence, students may develop multiple claims to address some of their Inquiry Paths.
- The emphasis here is on forming claims and organizing evidence, not writing additional paragraphs. Remind students to file all their work in Section 3 of their portfolios.

ACTIVITY 3: EVALUATING RESEARCH

Students review and discuss their Research Frames and researched materials to determine relevance, coherence, and sufficiency.

INSTRUCTIONAL NOTES

In this reflective activity, students will use a new, comprehensive tool from the **RDU Literacy Toolbox**, the *Research Evaluation Tool*. They will use this tool to consider the important characteristics of a developing body of research, to receive feedback from the teacher and peers, and to plan revisions to their Research Frame and its components based on that feedback and their own self-assessments.

RESEARCH EVALUATION TOOL

The Research Evaluation Tool guides students in a process for evaluating their research. The tool consists of three parts to structure collaboration with teachers and peers to determine whether findings are *credible*, *relevant*, and *sufficient*. Part 1, the Research Evaluation Checklist, is used by teachers in teacher-student conferences. Part 2, the Peer Evaluation of Research, presents a protocol for peer reviews. Part 3, Revising Research, is used by students to respond to feedback from the teacher and peers. Based on this structured process, students consider alternative approaches to their investigation, which may result in the modification of their Inquiry Paths and the revision of their research frames.

INSTRUCTIONAL NOTES

PEER AND TEACHER REVIEWS USING THE RESEARCH EVALUATION TOOL

Students should have an opportunity to present their findings for evaluation and respond to feedback by redirecting and extending their research. Teachers can structure this process through a simultaneous series of teacher-student conferences and peer discussions. Before getting started, teachers might model the peer-review process by using criteria from the *Research Evaluation Checklist* (Part 1 of the *Research Evaluation Tool*) to comment on a student's or sample work. Remind students to think about the following behaviors as they conduct peer reviews, all related to the Academic Habits of **Listening**, **Remaining Open**, and **Revising**:

Listening

⇒ Listen fully to what readers have observed.

⇒ Consider their ideas thoughtfully.

⇒ Wait momentarily before responding verbally.

Remaining Open

⇒ Avoid explanations or justifications for what they as writers have tried to do (no "yes, but . . ." responses).

⇒ Frame additional informal, text-based questions to further probe their readers' observations.

Revising:

⇒ Consider the implications of their readers' observations for improving their writing.

TEACHER-STUDENT CONFERENCING

- Introduce the **Research Evaluation Tool** and its three parts and their various purposes. Using the left column of the **Research Evaluation Checklist** (Part 1 of the tool), discuss the four components of an effective body of research:
  1. Adequacy and sufficiency of research
  2. Credibility and richness of sources
  3. Range of perspectives
  4. Coherence of the researcher's developing evidence-based perspective

- Schedule in-class teacher-student conferences for each student.

- While individual students engage in a teacher-student conference, have the other students form groups of three to conduct peer reviews. This two-part process enables students to build presentation and peer-review skills and gain multiple perspectives on their research, ensuring a deep evaluation of the research by multiple reviewers.

- Have students prepare for class by organizing their Research Portfolios and reviewing their claims addressing each Inquiry Path.

- Break students into groups of three, each taking turns presenting while the other two review and provide feedback.

- Talk students through the questioning protocol in Part 2 of the **Research Evaluation Tool**: Peer Evaluation of Research to guide their discussion and assessment.

- Following the protocol, model how presenters might present their research and how reviewers might craft observations or suggestions in response to the presentation and the tool's Guiding Questions.

- In a rotating process, each student in the collaborative review team summarizes her or his Research Frame and inquiry-based claims, and the other members of the team use the six Guiding Questions from the **Review Tool** to make constructive comments and suggestions.

- While peer groups are discussing, meet with individual students to evaluate their research using the **Research Evaluation Checklist**.

- Students complete Part 3: Revising Research and develop a plan for responding to peer and teacher feedback.

- The Research Evaluation should be kept in Section 3 of the Research Portfolio: Drawing Conclusions.

☰ ACTIVITY 4: REFINING AND EXTENDING ☰ INQUIRY

Students refine and extend their scope of inquiry based on teacher and peer feedback.

INSTRUCTIONAL NOTES

Based on teacher and peer feedback, students identify how they will refine their scope of inquiry. Responding to feedback may include a combination of the following three activities:

Refining Investigation: Students refine and extend their Research Frames.

Extending Research: Students search for additional sources based on their revised Research Frames.

Reading and Analyzing New Sources: Students read new sources closely to develop relevant evidence-based claims using the **Potential Sources** and **Taking Notes Tools** as necessary.

REFINING INVESTIGATION

- Based on teacher and peer review discussions, students reconsider the scope of their initial Research Frame.
- Students use the **Research Evaluation Tool** to help revise their Research Frame.
- Students may need to pose new questions within existing paths or add a new Inquiry Path. They may need to reorganize questions, subtopics, or claims in their existing Inquiry Paths.
- Students submit a revised Research Frame that addresses peer and teacher feedback for the teacher to review.

EXTENDING RESEARCH

- Feedback may have pointed out gaps in information or perspectives or information lacking credibility or deemed untrustworthy.
- Students return to their sources and search for new ones to address these gaps.

READING AND ANALYZING NEW SOURCES

- Using approaches and materials outlined in Parts 2 and 3, students find and analyze new sources to address their revised Research Frame.
- Students revise their evidence-based claims that were deemed unsupported and develop new ones using **Organizing EBC Research Tools** that address additional Inquiry Paths.

ORGANIZING THE RESEARCH PORTFOLIO

Instruct students to store all their notes and tools in Section 2 of their Research Portfolios: Gathering and Analyzing Information. If students are going to produce a reflective research narrative as a final product in the unit, they might also record discoveries they have made thus far about the topic or research process in a reflective research journal.

☰ PART 4: FORMATIVE ASSESSMENT
☰ OPPORTUNITIES

In this part of the unit students will have produced the following:

- *Forming EBC Research Tools*
- Annotated Common Texts
- Annotated sources
- Written evidence-based claims
- *Organizing EBC Research Tools*
- Revised Research Frame
- *Potential Sources Tools*
- *Taking Notes Tools*

ASSESSING LITERACY SKILLS

Students' evidence-based claims and their Inquiry Paths can be reviewed to see how well they are developing their skills of **Forming Claims** and **Evaluating Information**. As students prepare for and conduct teacher and peer reviews of their Research Frames, students can be evaluated on how well they are **Organizing Ideas**. Students can also be evaluated on **Reflecting Critically** as they consider teacher and peer feedback, and rethink and revise their Research Frames as necessary.

ASSESSING ACADEMIC HABITS

The Academic Habits of **Understanding Purpose and Process**, **Organizing Work**, and **Completing Tasks** are all key to completing Part 4. The research evaluation sessions with peers and the teacher provide a clear demonstration of how well students are demonstrating an understanding of purpose and process.

To prepare their portfolios for the evaluation sessions, students will demonstrate their habits of **Completing Tasks** and **Organizing Work**. Their demonstration of these habits here will provide a good assessment of how prepared they are to organize, plan, and execute their culminating product that communicates their evidence-based perspective. Students who are struggling with these habits can be given extra support and accountability as they plan and complete their final products.

Student participation in the peer- and teacher-review sessions can also be evaluated for the Academic Habits associated with text-centered discussions, including **Remaining Open**, **Listening**, and **Revising**.

Students might use the following questions to reflect on the development of their Academic Habits:

- Is my Research Portfolio well organized? What practices can I employ to keep my work better organized?
- Is my Research Portfolio complete? Have I completed all the tasks necessary for compiling my portfolio?

- How open was I to others' evaluation of my work?
- How well did I listen to the feedback from my peers and revise my work accordingly?
- What can I do to improve?

NOTE
To support self-, peer, and teacher assessment of skills and habits developed during the unit, a formal ***RDU Literacy Skills and Academic Habits Rubric*** and less formal ***Student RDU Literacy Skills and Academic Habits Checklist*** can be found in the **RDU Literacy Toolbox**.

PART 5

DEVELOPING AND COMMUNICATING AN EVIDENCE-BASED PERSPECTIVE

OBJECTIVE:	Students draw from their research and personal analysis to develop and communicate an evidence-based perspective. By the end of Part 5, students will have an organized body of research and will have written a reflective research narrative on the topic and inquiry experience, which can optionally be expressed in a multimedia presentation.

MATERIALS:
- *Research Frame Tool*
- *Potential Sources Tools*
- *Organizing EBC Research Tool*
- *Connecting Ideas Handout*
- *Writing EBC Handout*
- *RDU Final Writing Task Handout*

☰ LITERACY SKILLS

TARGETED SKILLS	DESCRIPTORS
IDENTIFYING RELATIONSHIPS	Identifies important connections among key details and ideas within and across texts
RECOGNIZING PERSPECTIVE	Uses textual details to establish a relationship to and perspective on a topic
EVALUATING INFORMATION	Assesses the relevance and credibility of information, ideas, evidence, and logic presented in texts
FORMING CLAIMS	Develops meaningful and defensible claims that clearly state valid, evidence-based analysis
USING EVIDENCE	Supports all aspects of claims with sufficient textual evidence, using accurate quotations, paraphrases, and references
PRESENTING DETAILS	Describes and explains important details that effectively develop a narrative, explanation, or argument.
ORGANIZING IDEAS	Sequences sentences and paragraphs to establish coherent, logical, and unified narratives, explanations, and arguments
REFLECTING CRITICALLY	Uses literacy terminology and concepts to reflect on, discuss and evaluate personal and peer literacy development.

ACADEMIC HABITS

HABITS DEVELOPED	DESCRIPTORS
GENERATING IDEAS	Generates and develops ideas, positions, products, and solutions to problems
COMPLETING TASKS	Finishes short and extended tasks by established deadlines
UNDERSTANDING PURPOSE AND PROCESS	Understands the purpose and uses the process and criteria that guide tasks
ORGANIZING WORK	Maintains work and materials so that they can be used effectively and efficiently in current and future tasks

ALIGNMENT TO CCSS

TARGETED STANDARDS:

CCSS.ELA-LITERACY.W.9-10.3: Write narratives to develop real or imagined experiences or events using effective technique, well-chosen details, and well-structured event sequences.

CCSS.ELA-LITERACY.W.9-10.4: Produce clear and coherent writing in which the development, organization, and style are appropriate to task, purpose, and audience.

CCSS.ELA-LITERACY.W.9-10.5: Develop and strengthen writing as needed by planning, revising, editing, rewriting, or trying a new approach, focusing on addressing what is most significant for a specific purpose and audience.

CCSS.ELA-LITERACY.W.9-10.7: Conduct short as well as more sustained research projects to answer a question (including a self-generated question) or solve a problem; narrow or broaden the inquiry when appropriate; synthesize multiple sources on the subject, demonstrating understanding of the subject under investigation.

CCSS.ELA-LITERACY.W.9-10.8: Gather relevant information from multiple authoritative print and digital sources, using advanced searches effectively; assess the usefulness of each source in answering the research question; integrate information into the text selectively to maintain the flow of ideas, avoiding plagiarism and following a standard format for citation.

CCSS.ELA-LITERACY.W.9-10.9: Draw evidence from literary or informational texts to support analysis, reflection, and research.

CCSS.ELA-LITERACY.RI.9-10.7: Analyze various accounts of a subject told in different mediums (e.g., a person's life story in both print and multimedia), determining which details are emphasized in each account.

CCSS.ELA-LITERACY.RI.9-10.9: Analyze seminal U.S. documents of historical and literary significance (e.g., Washington's Farewell Address, the Gettysburg Address, Roosevelt's Four Freedoms speech, King's "Letter from Birmingham Jail"), including how they address related themes and concepts.

CCSS.ELA-LITERACY.RI.9-10.10: By the end of grade 9, read and comprehend literary nonfiction in the grades 9–10 text complexity band proficiently, with scaffolding as needed at the high end of the range.

SUPPORTING STANDARDS:

CCSS.ELA-LITERACY.RI.9-10.1: Cite strong and thorough textual evidence to support analysis of what the text says explicitly as well as inferences drawn from the text.

CCSS.ELA-LITERACY.RI.9-10.2: Determine a central idea of a text and analyze its development over the course of the text, including how it emerges and is shaped and refined by specific details; provide an objective summary of the text.

CCSS.ELA-LITERACY. RI.9-10.4: Determine the meaning of words and phrases as they are used in a text, including figurative, connotative, and technical meanings; analyze the cumulative impact of specific word choices on meaning and tone (e.g., how the language of a court opinion differs from that of a newspaper).

CCSS.ELA-LITERACY.RI.9-10.6: Determine an author's point of view or purpose in a text and analyze how an author uses rhetoric to advance that point of view or purpose.

CCSS.ELA-LITERACY.W.9-10.2: Write informative/explanatory texts to examine and convey complex ideas, concepts, and information clearly and accurately through the effective selection, organization, and analysis of content.

ACTIVITIES

1. REVIEWING RESEARCH PORTFOLIOS
Students review and organize their Research Portfolios in preparation for communicating their evidence-based perspectives through a reflective research narrative.

2. COMMUNICATING AN EVIDENCE-BASED PERSPECTIVE
Considering what they have learned and developed for their Inquiry Paths and Questions, students write a reflective research narrative explaining how they came to their understanding of the topic, the steps they took to reach that understanding, and what they have learned about the inquiry process.

3. WRITING A BIBLIOGRAPHY
Students use their *Potential Sources Tools* to write bibliographies listing all their sources.

4. COMMUNICATING A FINAL EVIDENCE-BASED PRODUCT
Students develop a multi-media presentation to share their research experience or formal paper to fully communicate their perspective.

≡ ACTIVITY 1: REVIEWING RESEARCH
≡ PORTFOLIOS

Students review and organize their research portfolios in preparation for communicating their evidence-based perspectives through a reflective research narrative.

INSTRUCTIONAL NOTES

After extending and refining their research, students organize their Research Portfolios in preparation for crafting their final written product(s), which should communicate the evidence-based perspective on the topic that they have developed through their inquiry process. Section 2 should be complete, containing all the sources, annotated copies, notes, and EBCs used or developed by the student during Parts 2 through 4 of the unit. The portfolios should also contain **Organizing EBC Research Tools** for each Inquiry Path that synthesize information related to its Inquiry Question(s). The claim addressing at least one of the Inquiry Paths should be written in a paragraph form. The claims addressing students' Inquiry Paths and Questions become the first part of Section 3 (Drawing Conclusions) of their portfolios and form the basis for developing and explaining their evidence-based perspective through a final written or multimedia product.

≡ ACTIVITY 2: COMMUNICATING AN
≡ EVIDENCE-BASED PERSPECTIVE

Considering what they have learned and developed for their Inquiry Paths and Questions, students write a reflective research narrative explaining how they came to their understanding of the topic, the steps they took to reach that understanding, and what they have learned about the inquiry process.

INSTRUCTIONAL NOTES

The focus of the *Researching to Deepen Understanding* activity sequence has been on what the unit's title implies: deepening each student's understanding of a chosen area of investigation while also developing and applying the skills of effective inquiry and research: questioning, reading closely, analyzing and recording information, organizing thinking, and generating relevant, research-based claims. At this point, students should have developed a well-supported perspective on their focused topic—a particular way of seeing that topic that has emerged through their inquiry. This perspective, and the understanding it represents, is an important outcome of any good research process. However, research is less meaningful (and potentially less rigorous) if there is no tangible result or product that communicates a student's understanding and perspective. Students and teachers, therefore, should emphasize an intended purpose and an anticipated result or product from the start of their investigation. At this final point in the unit, class activities should then focus on fulfilling students' purposes and generating those anticipated results and products.

For grade 9, the recommended final product is a reflective research narrative, through which students communicate what they have come to understand about the topic and tell the story of the inquiry process that led them to that understanding.

Based on the context for the research and its primary purpose(s), however, students might develop other written or multimedia products, as explained at the end of the unit. Teachers who plan on having students move on to the *Building Evidence-Based Arguments* unit, which includes a comprehensive writing component, may consider having students create a presentation to communicate their perspective rather than an essay, or even to use their research in this unit as a starting point for their arguments in the next.

Writing a Reflective Narrative

- **Purpose and Result:** In this unit, the primary purposes for research have been open-ended, to follow an Inquiry Path to wherever it may lead, and to learn about the processes of effective research along the way. Accordingly, students can develop a reflective narrative that documents the story of their search and communicates their reflections about both the process and the results. The results of their inquiry should be both a deepened understanding of their topic and an emerging personal process for conducting research that they can apply in future situations.

- **Product(s):** Students can use the claims they have developed and the evidence they have gathered as components of their reflective narratives, as they recount the steps that led to these outcomes and the story of their experiences in the search. This kind of reflective narrative as a research product was first championed by Ken Macrorie, who referred to the product as an "I-Search paper," the purpose of which is to document the search as much as to present its results (Macrorie, *The I-Search Paper*, Heinemann, 1988).

  Students typically use a chronological, narrative structure to organize and present their thinking, moving from "What I wanted to learn" to "How I searched and what I found" to "What I ultimately learned," discussing search processes, close readings, evidence gathered, claims formed, and emerging understandings along the way. For this sort of communication to be most valuable, students should be expected to be reflective about what worked and what didn't, what they would do again, and how they would improve their research processes in the future. Students can write a narrative paper to communicate their evidence-based perspective and how they arrived at it, but they might alternately create a presentation (e.g. Prezi, PowerPoint, video, radio, etc.) that tells the story of their research experience, process, and resulting perspective. This style and method of presenting research can often be found in radio reporting on programs such as "This American Life," "The Radio Lab," and "Planet Money."

Instructional Sequence: Within the unit, students should concentrate on recording not only what they find but also what they did to find it, tracking their Inquiry Paths as they bend, branch, and are rerouted. Similarly, they should keep track of Inquiry Paths or sources that were perhaps valuable or interesting but did not pertain to their eventual research focus. Their claims should be seen as results of their search, and their perspective should be seen as the current end point of the research journey they have been on. Students can be more open-ended in their search processes, following leads as much as trying to accumulate purposeful information, if a reflective narrative rather than an informational paper or argument is their intended product.

It is a good idea for them to maintain reflective journals in conjunction with their research portfolios (where information is recorded) and also to be reflective about their thinking and discoveries as they make notes. Peers can be used to help them reflect along the way and as an audience for their developing narratives. If students wish to produce a video or audio recording as their product, they might consider recording peer and teacher reviews with a recording device for the duration of the project.

Activity Sequence

- Communicate to students that their task will be to draw from their research portfolios to write a multipage reflective research narrative. Their narrative should express and support the evidence-based perspective they have arrived at through their research and reflect on their experiences with the inquiry process. Their "evidence-based perspective" is their *particular view or understanding of the topic resulting from their investigation of it.*

- In this narrative, students tell the "story" of their search, including the following reflective points:
  - ⇒ Their initial understanding of the topic of Music and its importance in our lives
  - ⇒ Their culminating understanding or view of the topic
  - ⇒ The steps they took to reach their evidence-based perspective
  - ⇒ Their personal experience learning about and using the inquiry process to research the issues connected to the topics they have investigated.

- Explain to students that even though they are writing a narrative, they will also need to be sure to communicate their evidence-based perspective.

- The result should be a deepened understanding of both their topic and the experience of inquiry.

- To begin, ask students to ponder these questions:
  1. Before starting my inquiry, what did I think about the topic? How did I view or understand it?
  2. What specific steps did I take to research the topic? How did I address and answer my Inquiry Questions?
  3. Which sources were the most interesting to me and why? What specifically did I find interesting about the sources?
  4. What did I learn and discover about my Area of Investigation and Inquiry Question(s)?
  5. What did I learn from my peers about the topic?
  6. What do I now think about the topic I have investigated, based on the research and reading I have done? What is my own perspective?
  7. What did I learn about the research process? Where did I struggle and where did I triumph?

Their answers to these questions—supported by the claims they have written—are the basis for their reflective research narrative.

- Following discussion of these questions, have students brainstorm various ways of understanding the topic that have emerged for the class through their reading and research. Each student should then select one or two of these ideas that seem to match his or her own understanding, and return to the question: What do I now think about the topic we have researched? As they articulate an answer to this question, they will be expressing their evidence-based perspective for the first time, which can then be refined and further developed.

- Have students read through the guidelines for the **RDU Final Writing Task Handout** (in the Student Edition), which presents them with a short explanation of the assignment and its criteria, as well as a listing of the key literacy skills they should try to demonstrate.

- Explain to students that their final written narratives will be evaluated for their demonstration of key expectations and criteria for the assignment, specifically, how well they do the following:

  1. Express their original understanding of the research topic and tell the story of how they arrived at their new understanding.

  2. Communicate a new perspective on the topic that is clearly connected to the area of investigation and supported by their analysis.

  3. Explain and support the new perspective by discussing claims they have derived from inquiry questions.

  4. Discuss evidence from relevant texts by accurately quoting and paraphrasing.

  5. Use a clear narrative structure to sequence sentences and paragraphs and to present a coherent explanation of the perspective.

  6. Use an informal narrative voice (first person) and effective words and phrases to communicate and connect ideas.

- Note: The **Writing EBC** and the **Connecting Ideas Handouts** can be used to support students as they complete their written reflective research narratives.

- These written narratives should clearly and logically express students' views on the area of investigation, but they do not need to fully summarize all of their research. The purposes of this writing are to tell the story of how they arrived at their perspective on the topic through their research and to communicate their experience with the inquiry process.

Once students have completed an initial draft, the review process for their reflective research narrative can be organized as an OE Collaborative Writing Workshop, which students may have used in the *Making EBC* unit. In this approach, students develop and strengthen writing through a collaborative, question-based, and text-centered process. This process can help student writers focus on the literacy skills they have been working on in the unit, specifically **Forming Claims**, **Using Evidence**, **Using Language**, and **Organizing Ideas**; they will also think about issues specific to writing a reflective narrative and work on the related literacy skills of **Presenting Details** and **Reflecting Critically**. As previously, the teaching of the process involves teacher modeling, guided and supported writing, and text-centered discussion.

> ### NOTE
>
> See the Users Guide that introduces and supports the Developing Core Literacy Proficiencies units for a detailed discussion of the OE Collaborative Writing Workshop process, its principles, and suggestions for teaching it.

TEACHER MODELING

- Prepare a model reflective research narrative that tells the story of the class's overall research process, and that communicates an evidence-based perspective that may have emerged through class research.

- Select and use ideas, claims, and evidence that have been recorded on tools during class modeling sessions. Include several claims, derived from inquiry questions, in the draft narrative. The model narrative should be written chronologically to illustrate a basic narrative organization. It might begin with an initial understanding of the topic, recount steps taken to address inquiry questions and analyze texts, then explain how a culminating research-based perspective emerged. It should include reflections on the inquiry process, either integrated within the narrative or presented in its conclusion.

- Present the example narrative to students. Let them know that they will be working with this written reflective research narrative as a model for their own writing and to practice a process for reading and improving a draft narrative. In that process, they will use questions and criteria to think about the draft and provide observations and feedback about how to improve the narrative.

- Explain how materials from the Research Portfolios have been used to arrive at and develop the evidence-based perspective that is communicated in the model narrative and to help tell a story about the research process. These materials might include the following:
  ⇒ *Taking Notes Tools*
  ⇒ *Forming EBC Research Tools*
  ⇒ *Organizing EBC Research Tools*
  ⇒ Written EBCs

- Demonstrate how a claim derived from an Inquiry Question, with information and ideas from accompanying *Organizing EBC Research Tools*, has been incorporated into the example narrative.

- Point out details that carry over from the tools to the narrative.

- Referring to language from the *Connecting Ideas Handout*, explain to students how transitional words and phrases have been used to help link the sequence of events in the narrative and its claims and ideas.

- Point out how the narrative is constructed chronologically and is told like a story with a first person narrator (for the class model, this might be "we," but in students' papers it will be "I").

- Note examples of proper paraphrasing and quoting in the model narrative.

TEXT-CENTERED REVIEW AND DISCUSSION

Model and talk through the review process with the example narrative, using the following steps:

1. Introduce general Guiding Review Questions related to the overall content of the writing, such as, "What is the writer's perspective? How does the narrative tell the story of arriving at this perspective?"

2. In review teams (which can be the same teams that worked together in Part 4 to evaluate one another's research), have students read the model narrative in light of the general Guiding Review Questions. Students then share text-based responses to the questions within their team.

3. Focus students' attention on the targeted literacy skills criteria: **Forming Claims, Using Evidence, Using Language,** and **Organizing Ideas.** Explain, model, and discuss what each of these criteria cause one to think about based on previous discussions about claims and textual evidence, and the current task of writing a chronological narrative.

4. Discuss how the narrative uses a chronological sequence of steps to communicate an original understanding, steps taken to address Inquiry Questions and the Area of Investigation, and a culminating perspective on the topic. Students can consider questions such as:

   ⇒ Does the narrative communicate how the writer originally thought of the topic before starting to research it?

   ⇒ Does the narrative recount the specific steps taken to think of Inquiry Questions around the Area of Investigation?

   ⇒ Does the narrative explain the process of reading and analyzing texts to help answer Inquiry Questions?

   ⇒ Does the narrative clearly communicate how the writer arrived at a final research-based perspective?

5. Students (individually or in review teams) now read the model reflective narrative closely, considering the text-based review question(s) and generating a reviewer's response.

6. Discuss how a text-based response to a draft piece of writing is itself a kind of claim that the reviewer makes based on the criteria, question(s), and specific evidence from the writer's draft.

7. Model how you might frame a claim-based response if you were a reviewer of the paper, emphasizing these points:

   ⇒ A *specific* response that emphasizes both a strength of the narrative and a potential improvement

   ⇒ A *constructive* and respectful articulation of the response

   ⇒ *Text-based evidence* in the narrative that has led to and supports your response

8. Guided by this model, students articulate and share their text-based responses and constructive reviewer claims, as if their review partner (or the teacher) has written the model narrative. Have several students volunteer to present their responses to the whole class and discuss how the responses are (or are not) *specific, constructive, and text-based.*

9. For these volunteer responses, model the habits a writer should develop when receiving a reviewer's response:

   Listening

   ⇒ Listen fully to what readers have observed.

   ⇒ Consider their ideas thoughtfully.

   ⇒ Wait momentarily before responding verbally.

   Remaining Open

   ⇒ Avoid explanations or justifications for what you as a writer have tried to do (no "yes, but . . ." responses).

   ⇒ Frame additional informal, text-based questions to further probe your readers' observations.

   Revising

   ⇒ Consider the implications of your readers' observations for improving your writing.

   ⇒ Discuss what you might do as a writer to improve the example written claim after considering the responses you have gotten to your text-based review questions.

Emphasize throughout this modeling that developing an effective communication of an evidence-based perspective through narrative writing is a process—it *cannot* be done in one draft. Revision is fundamental to honing written papers.

Writing Reflective Research Narratives

With the model narrative as an example, students now draft their own reflective research narratives, working from the draft narrative and the statement of their perspective they have developed previously, using evidence from their tools, and incorporating claims they have developed in response to Iquiry Questions. Emphasize that in this draft, students should "talk out" their thinking and explain the story of how it developed as clearly as possible, so that a reader will understand how their perspective has emerged from and is supported by the class's research.

Suggest that most students use a basic chronological organization for their narratives, moving from where they started, to what they did and learned along the way, to how they arrived at their final perspective and their reflections on the process. However, also support students who may be ready to take a more sophisticated approach, for example: starting with a thorough explanation of their research-based perspective, then going back in time to explain how this perspective emerged, with reflections on the process and their learning integrated into their narrative sequences.

- Students can write their narratives as an in-class writing assignment for which they have prepared by organizing and finalizing their Research Portfolios.

- Because this may be the first time in the Developing Core Proficiencies program sequence that students have written a narrative, they may want to consider the specific expectations of CCSS W.3 at ninth grade:

- **CCSS W.9-10.3:** Write narratives to develop real or imagined experiences or events using effective technique, well-chosen details, and well-structured event sequences.

   a. Engage and orient the reader by setting out a problem, situation, or observation, establishing one or multiple point(s) of view, and introducing a narrator and/or characters; create a smooth progression of experiences or events.

   b. Use narrative techniques, such as dialogue, pacing, description, reflection, and multiple plot lines, to develop experiences, events, and/or characters.

   c. Use a variety of techniques to sequence events so that they build on one another to create a coherent whole.

   d. Use precise words and phrases, telling details, and sensory language to convey a vivid picture of the experiences, events, setting, and/or characters.

   e. Provide a conclusion that follows from and reflects on what is experienced, observed, or resolved over the course of the narrative.

- Discuss key phrases from the standard that students should attend to, such as:

   ⇒ *orient the reader by establishing a context*

   ⇒ *organize an event sequence that unfolds naturally and logically*

   ⇒ *provide a conclusion that ... reflects on the narrated experiences.*

- Additionally, students and teachers can use the following relevant criteria from the literacy skills to review students' narratives:

LITERACY SKILLS	DESCRIPTORS
PRESENTING DETAILS	Describes and explains important details that effectively develop a narrative, explanation, or argument.
ORGANIZING IDEAS	Sequences sentences and paragraphs to establish coherent, logical, and unified narratives, explanations, and arguments
REFLECTING CRITICALLY	Uses literacy terminology and concepts to reflect on, discuss and evaluate personal and peer literacy development.

Text-Centered Review and Revision

- After drafting their perspectives, students engage in text-centered review and discussion, using the same process, questions, and protocol modeled previously in this activity, only this time focusing on their own narratives.

  1. Consider general Guiding Review Questions related to the overall content of the writing, such as, "What is the writer's perspective? How does the narrative tell the story of arriving at this perspective?"

  2. Think about one or more of the expectations for narrative writing and/or targeted literacy skills, and how the narrative does or does not yet demonstrate those expectations or skills.

  3. As writers, frame text-based questions for reviewers to consider, such as:

     ⇒ Do I orient my readers to the research context and topic, and to where I started my inquiry?

     ⇒ Are my perspective and claims that I developed through research clearly stated?

     ⇒ Is my evidence well chosen, and have I presented details that effectively develop my narrative?

     ⇒ What might I add (or revise) to help you better understand my perspective and how I arrived at it?

     ⇒ Is my narrative organized and sequenced in a chronological order? Do I clearly, naturally, and logically tell the story of how I arrived at my understanding?

     ⇒ Do I provide a conclusion that clearly explains and reflects on my experiences while researching, including any difficulties or successes I had? Do I use terms and concepts from the unit when talking about my experiences?

  4. As reviewers (after closely reading the writer's draft), articulate feedback to writers that is *specific, constructive,* and *text-based.*

  5. As writers, practice the habits of **Listening**, **Remaining Open**, and **Revising**.

- Based on peer feedback, students revise their papers. Allow sufficient class time for students to do so, and if necessary engage them in additional collaborative reviews of other aspects of their papers.

- If students are not developing an additional product, they might participate in a final class discussion in which each student summarizes and explains something important learned in the unit.

ORGANIZING THE RESEARCH PORTFOLIO

Students should store their written explanations of their perspectives and all of the tools they have used to develop them in Section 3 of their Research Portfolios: Drawing Conclusions.

ACTIVITY 3: WRITING A BIBLIOGRAPHY

Students use their **Potential Sources Tools** to write bibliographies listing all of their sources.

As accreditation of the sources that led to their Reflective Research Narrative and to complete their Research Portfolios, students compile a bibliography that lists entries for all of their sources. Students can work from their **Potential Sources Tools**, transferring the relevant information. Teachers should introduce the bibliography format they prefer and provide direct instruction and models for students on formatting their information accordingly. Students can use the following criterion to think about their work:

PUBLISHING	Uses effective formatting and citations when paraphrasing, quoting, and listing sources

ACTIVITY 4: COMMUNICATING A FINAL EVIDENCE-BASED PRODUCT (OPTIONAL)

Students develop a multi-media presentation to share their research experience or formal paper to fully communicate their perspective.

If the teacher chooses not to have students complete a final reflective research narrative, or if students choose to present their research and experiences in a format other than a written one, any of several possible alternative final assignments might be considered.

1. An Informational Presentation Incorporating Text, Graphics, and Multimedia

2. A Research-Based Explanation of a Phenomenon, Issue, Event, Process, or Device

3. A Thesis-Driven Academic Argument, Research-Based Essay, or Op-Ed Piece

For each possible product option described in the following explanations, the instructional notes briefly explain the purpose and result, product, and instructional sequence that a teacher and students might consider. Whichever option is selected, or if another product is intended, teachers are encouraged to use their own best practices for delivering instruction and supporting their students.

An Informational Presentation Incorporating Text, Graphics, and Multimedia

- **Purpose and Result:** If the primary purpose for research is to build the student's own understanding (to inform a decision or support personal development), with an eye to sharing that understanding, then students might aim their research at producing an informational presentation that recaptures and presents what they have learned. This could be a multimedia presentation of their reflective research narrative, or might focus on a topic of personal or community interest.

- **Product(s):** Students will link the claims they have developed and organize the evidence they have gathered into an informational presentation, most likely one that involves the use of multimedia (e.g., a PowerPoint presentation or website). Students should think about how text, graphics, audio, and video can be combined to communicate what they have learned, potentially using links to and content from websites they have searched.

- **Instructional Sequence:** Within the unit, students should focus their research on gaining as much information about their topic as possible, think about how others might use that information, and identify good websites, videos, or graphics that they might use to convey what they have learned to others. As they conclude their research, they should learn how to use presentation or web-design tools to organize and communicate what they want to present. They should focus on how text can be used sparingly but effectively in conjunction with other ways of communicating information. Peers can be seen as practice and real audiences for student products and presentations.

A Research-Based Explanation of a Phenomenon, Issue, Event, Process, or Device

- **Purpose and Result:** If the primary purpose for research is to deepen students' understanding of how something works, has occurred, is done by experts, or affects our lives, with the intent that they can explain it in detail, then students should aim their research and thinking at developing a technical, scientific, social, or historical explanation that uses research to help others understand a particular phenomenon, issue, event, process, or device.

- **Product(s):** Students will link the claims they have developed and organize the evidence they have gathered into an explanatory sequence that moves from background information to increasingly sophisticated details and analysis. The result might be a technical paper, manual, or something less formal intended for a general audience (a good model for this kind of writing might be Discovery Learning's "How It Works" web-based explanations), or a historical–social science analysis. In most cases, this will result in a piece of explanatory writing that may be accompanied by visual support, but it could also result in a multimedia presentation or speech.

- **Instructional Sequence:** Within the unit, students should focus on informational sources that will build their understanding of the topic they are investigating and will ultimately need to explain in detail. They should read texts that exemplify how things are analyzed and explained in a particular field (science, social science, technical, the arts, consumer-related, etc.). As they complete their research, they should organize their claims and evidence into an explanatory sequence aimed at a particular audience and purpose. Peer reviews might play a major role in helping them develop explanations that are clear, coherent, and effective.

A Thesis-Driven Academic Argument, Research-Based Essay, or Op-Ed Piece

- **Purpose and Result:** If the primary purpose for research is to find, organize, and use evidence to build an argument (whether more formal and academic or less formal and utilitarian) then students' research should result in a set of claims that can be seen as premises from which to construct an argument for the research-based perspective and position they have developed.

- **Product(s):** Students will link the claims they have developed and organize the evidence they have gathered into a logical sequence of premises that make a case for their position on their topic. If the product is to be a written argument, then students may move on to *Developing Core Literacy Proficiencies Unit 5: Building Evidence-Based Arguments*. To prepare for the writing instruction in that unit, students can produce a well-developed plan for their argument, either in outline or diagrammatic form or in product forms that resemble a legal brief or a précis. Students might also engage in a class symposium, in which they outline their argument and the evidence behind it in a peer or jury-type review before other students in the class.

- [Note: Pursuing this option of linking the *Research* and *Argument* units means that teachers will likely use the instructional sequence and activities from *Building Evidence-Based Arguments* but not the model source set that accompanies that unit at this grade level. Alternately, teachers might choose to use the model source set for the argumentation unit in place of the topic and source set for this research unit.]

- **Instructional Sequence:** Within the unit, students should read and analyze multiple examples of argumentation in their chosen topic area to build their understanding of various perspectives and to study how arguments are constructed (or misconstructed). As they complete their research, students will need to study the relationships among their perspective, claims, and evidence to determine a reasoned plan for argumentation. The instructional focus should be on the logical progression of claims, the adequacy of evidence, and the effectiveness of the case they can make for their position. Peer reviews might play a major role in preparing them to write a final argument.

≡ PART 5: SUMMATIVE ASSESSMENT ≡ OPPORTUNITIES

After students have completed Part 5, teachers should assess if students have been able to successfully complete a cycle of independent research.

Students will have finalized their Research Portfolios, written a reflective research narrative or produced or presented an alternative final research-based product. These products can be used as evidence for the development of the full range of targeted Literacy Skills and Academic Habits as reflected in the **RDU Literacy Skills and Academic Habits Rubric**.

Notes to the teacher about using this rubric: When evaluating students' research portfolios, reflective narratives, and other evidence from the unit, the following process for using the Teacher Rubric is recommended:

- Find evidence in the student's portfolio and reflective narrative to support ratings for each of the component Literacy Skills and overall research content criteria listed in the rubric.

- Based on that evidence, use the developmental scale to rate the grade-level performance demonstrated by the student as:

  1—**Emerging:** needs improvement

  2—**Developing:** shows progress

  3—**Becoming Proficient:** demonstrates skills

  4—**Excelling:** exceeds expectations

- If there is insufficient evidence to make a confident rating, mark **NE** (not enough evidence).
- Indicate if the student has demonstrated growth in each skill area during the unit by adding a "+" to the rating.
- Determine a summary evaluation based on the overall pattern of ratings and strength of evidence. This summary evaluation can be computed based on points, or determined by examining the prevalent pattern in the criteria-based ratings.

EVIDENCE OF READING AND THINKING

Students' Research Portfolios, reflective research narrative, and final research-based products can be used as evidence of Literacy Skills associated with close reading, evaluation of information, and recognition of authorial perspective. The following Literacy Skills (listed in section 1 of the in the *Researching to Deepen Understanding Skills and Academic Habits Rubric*) can be used as criteria to review student work: **Making Inferences, Summarizing, Interpreting Language, Identifying Relationships, Evaluating Information**, and **Recognizing Perspective**. Students have been working on these skills throughout this and previous Developing Core Literacy Proficiencies units and should be able to demonstrate evidence of them within their written and final evidence-based products. Specifically, students at this point should show that they can identify and summarize key details from research texts, note connections and develop inferences from those details, evaluate information presented in sources for its credibility and relevance, and use language to analyze an author's perspective on a topic.

EVIDENCE OF WRITING

If they have completed the *Making EBC* unit, students' reflective research narratives will be the second piece of more formal writing that students have done in the Developing Core Literacy Proficiencies instructional sequence, but the first narrative. Their narratives might thus be viewed as a formative assessment of students' writing skills—particularly those associated with **Forming Claims, Using Evidence, Presenting Details, Organizing Ideas, Publishing**, and **Reflecting Critically**. A teacher might provide more specific evaluation of several targeted criteria but otherwise should use the narrative to help students know which writing skills they still need to work on. Other products that provide written evidence include students' *Exploring a Topic Tools*, EBC statements, and paragraphs explaining claims related to Inquiry Paths. Depending on which option the class or students choose, students' alternative final evidence-based products or presentations may be evaluated for their writing as well.

ASSESSING ACADEMIC HABITS

By the end of the Research unit, students will have been informally reflecting on and self-assessing their development of the Academic Habits associated with the research process and the development of an evidence-based perspective. Using the *Student Researching to Deepen Understanding Skills and Academic Habits Checklist* found in the **RDU Literacy Toolbox**, students can do a more careful self-assessment of their development and demonstration of these habits during the unit—paying particular attention to where and how they have shown (or not shown) evidence of using the habits productively. The teacher can use these same criteria, as listed in section II of the Rubric, to provide feedback to students about how well they have exhibited the following research habits: **Questions, Generates Ideas, Understands Process and Purpose, Completes Tasks, Organizes Work, Reflects Critically**.

RESEARCHING TO DEEPEN UNDERSTANDING COMMON SOURCE SET

≡ MUSIC: WHAT ROLE DOES IT PLAY ≡ IN OUR LIVES?

Source 1: The first Common Source introduces a broad topic area in which to conduct research. It should be a high-interest source, preferably a video or multimedia resource. This source is used to stimulate curiosity and thinking about the topic and opens up many possibilities for research questions and learning within the topic area. This source is introduced and used in Part 1, Activity 2.

Common Source: "Imagine Life Without Music"—Leah Stevens. This video can be found on YouTube.com and was published on May 18, 2013.

Overview: This five-minute video introduces the topic of music by demonstrating the many ways that music influences our lives. Through a montage of pictures and video, enhanced by a classical music soundtrack, the videographer provides many ideas about how music plays an essential role in our lives including its impact on leisure, self-expression, and culture.

Discussion Questions: What does the video suggest about the topic area of music? What other questions about the topic of music does the video make you think about?

Source 2: The second Common Source provides background information and is used to extend discussion about the topic area. It also provides an opportunity to work on close-reading skills used during an independent research project. It is a print source that presents new information but is fairly easy to read and understand, and may be an Internet-based text. The source should expand thinking about the topic and open up additional paths for asking questions and learning within the topic area. All students read this source. This source is introduced and used in Part 1, Activity 2.

Common Source 2A: "A Brief History of the Music Industry" by Theo Smith, June 7, 2012. This Internet-based article can be found on the musicthinktank.com website.

Overview: In this article, the author provides an overview of the life and history of the music industry with insights into current and future states. Because it touches on so many facets of music, the article can provoke students to think more broadly about the topic and begin to explore people or things they did not know previously about music. Through nonfiction narrative and graphics, it describes the roles played by technological advancements, such as the printing press and the Internet, and the differences among live music, published music, and recorded music. The article also addresses how digital rights issues, such as copyright and piracy, shape the music industry as we know it today.

Discussion Questions: What does the text suggest about the topic area, "Music: What Role Does It Play in Our Lives?" What other connections to music does it make you think about?

Source 3: The third Common Source is a set of resources that introduce various subtopics within the general topic area. These sources provide additional background information and thinking to help make decisions about a more focused direction for research. The texts in this source set are also used to practice the skills of assessing sources for their relationship to research questions, their accessibility and interest, and their credibility and relevance within the topic area. Students read *one* of these sources, depending on their interests. This source is introduced and used in Part 1, Activity 3.

Common Sources:

Source 3A: Music on the Web: "What is Online Piracy?" by the Recording Industry Association of America (RIAA), Date (NA). This source can be found on the RIAA website.—1210L

Source 3B: Relationship between Music and the Brain: "Why Your Brain Craves Music" by Michael D. Lemonick, April 15, 2013. This source can be found on the *Time Magazine* website.—1350L

Source 3C: Role of Music in History: "The 25 Most Important Civil Rights Moments in Music History" by Matthew Trammel, David Drake, Ernest Baker, Insanul Ahmed, and Rob Kenner, February 7, 2013. This source can be found on the complex.com website.

Overview: These three sources each focus on different aspects of the topic of "Music: What Role Does It Play in Our Lives?" and open up possible subtopic areas for research.

Source 3A: The Recording Industry Association of America (RIAA) is the trade organization that supports and promotes the creative and financial aspects of the major music companies. Its members are the music labels that comprise the most vibrant record industry in the world. This website, through its links, provides explanation about the topic of music piracy and why it is harmful to the music industry at large.

Source 3B: The article "Why Your Brain Craves Music" explores the physiological and neurological reasons for why we like music, but it also considers intellectual factors such as how paying for music stimulates our brains more than free music. The article considers how music affects our brains, thus our emotions, and how music might have even affected our evolutionary progress.

Source 3C: "25 Most Important Civil Rights Moments in Music History" shows the important role music and musicians can play during historical events and movements and presents several avenues for further research—either by artist or event. The article features images and commentary on key moments in history when civil rights and music collided, from the 1956 integration of southern dancehalls to Elton John and Eminem's Duet at the 2001 Grammys.

Discussion Questions: What does the text suggest about the topic area "Music: What Role Does It Play in Our Lives?" What questions or directions for research does it suggest to you?

Text Assessment Questions: How accessible and interesting is the text for you? How credible and relevant is the source as a starting point for further research?

Source 4: The fourth Common Source Set provides information about websites (or other resources) that can be used to start a search for new sources and information in one of several possible subtopic areas. Students investigate *one* of these websites, depending on their interests. This source is introduced and used in Part 1, Activity 3.

Common Sources and Overviews

Source 4A: Music on the Web: "The True Cost of Sound Recording Piracy to the U.S. Economy" by Stephen E. Siwek, August 21, 2007. This article is available on The Institute for Policy Innovation website and provides a study by the conservative think tank discussing the adverse economic influence of music piracy.

Source 4B: Relationship between Music and the Brain: "Study Shows Some Are Unmoved by Music" by the *Los Angeles Times*, adapted by Newsela staff, March, 11, 2014. This article is available on the Newsela website. If the school or classroom does not already have an account, tell students they will have to create a username and password to log in to the Newsela website. This article explores how some people find it difficult to relate to music because of certain biological conditions.

Source 4C: Role of Music in History: "The Evolution of Music: How Genres Rise and Fall Over Time" by Kyle Kim, May 6, 2015. This article is available on the *Los Angeles Times* website. The article provides research on how scientists used Billboard music charts from the past to track how music genres evolved since 1960. The researchers were able to chart the popularity of thirteen different musical categories including hip-hop and country music.

Discussion Questions: What does the website suggest about the topic area "Music: What Role Does It Play in Our Lives?" What questions or directions for research does it suggest to you?

Text Assessment Questions: How accessible and interesting is the website's text for you? How credible and relevant is the source as a starting point for further research?

Source 5: The fifth Common Source is a set of texts that present a range of perspectives on a subtopic within the overall topic area. These texts are ones that have been written for various purposes by a range of organizations or authors who view the topic area in somewhat different ways. This Source Set is used to practice the skills of reading to understand a text's perspective on a topic and to compare perspectives and the ways they are presented by different authors. Students read *one* of these sources as a class and *another* individually. This source is introduced and used in Part 3, Activity 2.

Common Sources

Source 5A: "Why I Pirate" by Sebastian Anthony, January 18, 2012. This source is an article on the Extreme Tech website and is available through Extremetech.com.

Source 5B: "Why I No Longer Give Away My Music: How the digital music biz makes it difficult for musicians to offer free downloads" by Bob Ostertag, June 6, 2013. This source is an article on the *Commons Magazine* website and is available through Onthecommons.org.

Source 5C: "How the web changed music forever: it's both a boon and a bane to musicians" by Veronica Majerol, March 11, 2013. This source can be found using the Gale Virtual Reference Library.

Source 5D: "Are Musicians Going Up a Music Stream Without a Fair Payout?" by the *Philadelphia Inquirer*, adapted by Newsela staff, November 12, 2014. Available through the Newsela website.

Overview: These four sources all present specific and differing perspectives on the subtopic area of music piracy. They can be used to further understanding in the subtopic area and also to practice the skills of determining a source's perspective and therefore also its bias, credibility, and relevance to research in the topic area.

Source 5A: In his article, "Why I Pirate," Anthony Sebastian justifies his practice of music piracy. Citing profit sharing between labels and musicians, criticizing the value of a music product, and highlighting the access of music for the economically disadvantaged, this argumentative piece lays out a position defending the controversial, if not illegal, practice of pirating and sharing music content regardless of copyright laws. Reading and discussion could focus on his perspective and whether or not Sebastian's claims are credible.

Source 5B: In his article "Why I No Longer Give Away My Music: How the digital music biz makes it difficult for musicians to offer free downloads," sound artist Bob Ostertag recounts the unexpected issues concerned with giving away his music for free. Specifically, he talks about the idea that a large audience downloading more music than they will actually be able to listen to over a lifetime actually cheapens or degrades music. The author also describes how other laws negatively affect Creative Commons licenses.

Source 5C: "How the web changed music forever: it's both a boon and a bane to musicians" explores how smaller music groups are getting by in the new era of music streaming services such as Spotify and Pandora. The author explains that unknown musicians release their music on free, open, and public networks in order to become known, but then they might not make any money. This article considers the freedom of music access, exposing vulnerabilities in traditional music markets while admitting that open-source music platforms provide economic opportunities for lesser-known artists.

Source 5D: In the article "Are Musicians Going Up a Music Stream Without a Fair Payout?," the author explores several musicians' arguments that music should not be streamed and should, instead, be purchased. The author discusses why musicians such as Taylor Swift feel that the art form of making music should be valued and therefore purchased, not streamed for small payouts.

Evaluating Perspective Questions:
- What do I learn about the author and the purpose for writing the text? (GQH)
- What are the author's qualifications or credentials relative to the topic area? (ASH)
- What is the author's personal relationship to the topic area? (ASH)
- What details or words suggest the author's perspective? (GQH)
- How does the author's perspective influence the text's presentation of ideas or arguments? (GQH)
- How does the author's perspective and presentation of the text compare to others? (GQH)
- How does the author's perspective influence my reading of the text—and my use of the text in research? (GQH)

NOTE

Questions are referenced to handouts from the toolbox: GQH is the **Guiding Questions Handout** and ASH is the **Assessing Sources Handout**.

ADDITIONAL RESOURCES IN THE TOPIC AREA

Music on the Web

- "Spotify's Daniel Ek: The Most Important Man In Music" by Steven Bertoni, January 4, 2012. Available through the Forbes.com website.

- "SoundScan Mid-Year: Albums Down, Stream Equivalents Nearly Double, Vinyl Continues Gain" by Ed Christman, July 3, 2014. Available through the Billboard.com website.

- "Are YOU Ruining the Music Industry?" by Suzanne Fitzpatrick, July 1, 2010. Available through the Siouxtrick.hubpages.com.

- "Digital Music Consumption on the Internet: Evidence from Clickstream Data" by Luis Aguiar and Bertin Martens, March 2013. Available through the Institute for Prospective Technological Studies as part of the Joint Research Centre.

- "The Music Video, Before Music Television" by History.Com staff, August 1, 2011. Available through the History.com website.

- "Are Musicians Going Up a Music Stream Without a Fair Payout?" by the Philadelphia Inquirer, adapted by Newsela staff, November 12, 2014. Available through the Newsela.com website.

Music and Therapy

- "What is Music Therapy," American Music Therapy Association. Available through the Musictherapy.org website.

- "The transformative power of classical music," Benjamin Zander, TED Talk, February 2008. Available through the Ted.com website.

- "Music is medicine, music is sanity," Robert Gupta, TED Talk, February 2010. Available through the Ted.com website.

RESEARCHING TO DEEPEN UNDERSTANDING

DEVELOPING CORE LITERACY PROFICIENCIES

GRADE 9

Literacy Toolbox

ODELL
EDUCATION

TEACHER RESEARCH UNIT GUIDE

TEACHER RESEARCH UNIT GUIDE - GRADE 8		MATERIALS
I. INITIATING INQUIRY *Students determine what they want to know about a topic and develop Inquiry Questions that they will investigate.*	**1. Introducing the Unit**	Student Research Plan Research Portfolio
	2. Exploring a Topic	Guiding Questions Handout Questioning Path Tool, Approaching Texts Tool Analyzing Details Tool Exploring a Topic
	3. Conducting Pre-searches	Potential Sources
	4. Vetting Areas of Investigation	Area Evaluation Checklist
	5. Generating Inquiry Questions	Posing Inquiry Questions
II. GATHERING INFORMATION *Students find and take notes on sources that will help them answer their Inquiry Questions and define the scope of their investigation.*	**1. Planning Searches for Information**	
	2. Building an Initial Research Frame	*Research Frame Tool*
	3. Conducting Searches for Background Sources Using Inquiry Paths	Potential Sources Assessing Sources Handout
	4. Assessing Sources	*Guiding Questions Handout* *Assessing Sources Handout* *Potential Sources Tools*
	5. Making and Recording Notes	*Taking Notes Tool* Research Frame
	6. Conducting Searches Independently	*Student Research Plan* *Research Portfolio* *Research Frames* *Students repeat steps 1–3*
	7. Review and Rethinking the Research Frame	*Research Frame Tool*
III. DEEPENING UNDERSTANDING *Students analyze key sources to deepen their understanding and answer their Inquiry Questions.*	**1. Selecting Key Sources**	Research Frame Tool Potential Source Tool Taking Notes Tool Assessing Sources Handout

TEACHER RESEARCH UNIT GUIDE (Continued)

TEACHER RESEARCH UNIT GUIDE - GRADE 8		MATERIALS
	2. Analyzing a Source's Perspective	Guiding Question Handout Assessing Sources Handout Research Frame
	3. Reading Sources Closely- Forming Claims	*Forming Evidence-Based Claims Research Tool*
	4. Writing and Peer Reviewing Evidence-Based Claims about Sources	*Forming Evidence-Based Claims Research Tool* Writing Evidence-Based Claims Handout Connecting Ideas Handout Research Portfolio
IV. FINALIZING INQUIRY *Students synthesize their information to determine what they have learned and what more they need to know about their area of investigation. They gather and analyze more information to complete their inquiry.*	**1. Writing Claims that Address Inquiry Paths**	Research Frame Forming Evidence-Based Claims Research Tool *Organizing Evidence-Based Claims Research Tool* Research Portfolio
	2. Organizing Evidence	Research Frame *Research Evolution Tool* *Organizing Evidence-Based Claims Research Tool*
	3. Evaluating Research	Research Frame *Research Evaluation Tool* Research Portfolio
	4. Refining and Extending Inquiry	Research Frame
V. DEVELOPING AND COMMUNICATING AN EVIDENCE-BASED PERSPECTIVE *Students review and synthesize their research to develop and communicate an evidence-based perspective on their area of investigation.*	**1. Reviewing Research Portfolios**	Research Portfolio
	2. Expressing an Evidence-Based Perspective	*Writing Evidence-Based Claims Handout* *Connecting Ideas Handouts* *Organizing Evidence-Based Claims Research Tools* Student Research Literacy Skills and Discussion Habits Checklist
	3. Writing a Bibliography	*Potential Sources Tools*
	4. Communicating a Final Evidence-Based Product	Student Research Literacy Skills and Discussion Habits Checklist

ODELL
EDUCATION

STUDENT RESEARCH PLAN

STUDENT RESEARCH PLAN		TOOLS AND HANDOUTS
I. INITIATING INQUIRY *I determine what I want to know about a topic and develop Inquiry Questions that I will investigate.*	**1. Exploring a Topic**	Exploring a Topic Potential Sources Area Evaluation Checklist Posing Inquiry Questions Handout
	2. Choosing an Area of Investigation	
	3. Generating Inquiry Questions	
II. GATHERING INFORMATION *I find and take notes on sources that will help me answer my Inquiry Questions and define the scope of my investigation.*	**1. Finding and Assessing Sources**	Potential Sources Assessing Sources Handout Taking Notes Research Frame Posing Inquiry Questions Handout
	2. Making and Recording Notes	
	3. Framing Inquiry	
III. DEEPENING UNDERSTANDING *I analyze key sources to deepen my understanding and answer my Inquiry Questions.*	**1. Selecting Key Sources**	Potential Sources Assessing Sources Handout Taking Notes Forming Evidence-Based Claims Student Research Literacy Skills and Discussion Habits Checklist Connecting Ideas Handout
	2. Analyzing Researched Information	
	3. Writing Evidence-Based Claims	
IV. FINALIZING INQUIRY *I synthesize my information to determine what I have learned and what more I need to know about my Area of Investigation. I gather and analyze more information to complete my inquiry.*	**1. Organizing Evidence**	Research Frame Forming Evidence-Based Claims Organizing Evidence-Based Claims Student Research Literacy Skills and Discussion Habits Checklist *Repeat parts II and III*
	2. Evaluating Research	
	3. Refining and Extending Inquiry	
V. DEVELOPING AND COMMUNICATING AN EVIDENCE-BASED PERSPECTIVE *I review and synthesize my research to develop and communicate an evidence-based perspective on my area of investigation.*	**1. Reviewing Research**	Research Frame Organizing Evidence-Based Claims Student Research Literacy Skills and Discussion Habits Checklist Connecting Ideas Handout
	2. Expressing an Evidence-Based Perspective	
	3. Communicating an Evidence-Based Perspective	

STUDENT RESEARCH PORTFOLIO DESCRIPTION

The research portfolio helps you store and organize your findings and analysis throughout every step of the research process. Various tools help you develop a research strategy and record, analyze, and annotate your sources. Every time you complete a tool or annotate a source, file it in the corresponding section of your portfolio. Keeping an organized portfolio helps you make connections, see what you already have, and determine what you still have left to investigate. It will also provide everything you need to write your conclusions when you finish your research. The portfolio may be in either electronic or paper format.

PORTFOLIO SECTIONS	CONTENT
SECTION 1: DEFINING AN AREA OF INVESTIGATION *This section stores all the work you do exploring the topic and choosing an Area of Investigation.*	Exploring a Topic Area Evaluation Checklist Potential Sources (from pre-searches)
SECTION 2: GATHERING AND ANALYZING INFORMATION *This section stores all the information you gather throughout your investigation. It also stores your notes and analysis of sources. All the tools should be grouped by source.*	Potential Sources Annotated Sources Personal Drafts Taking Notes (about sources) Forming Evidence-Based Claims
SECTION 3: DRAWING CONCLUSIONS *This section stores your notes and evidence-based claims about Inquiry Paths, your research evaluations, and the personal perspective that you come to at the end of your inquiry.* *Group the Taking Notes, Forming Evidence-Based Claim, or Organizing Evidence-Based Claim by Inquiry Path.*	Taking Notes (about Inquiry Paths) Forming Evidence-Based Claims Organizing Evidence-Based Claims Research Evaluation
SECTION 4: DISCARDED MATERIAL *This section stores all the sources and analysis that you have discarded throughout your investigation.* *The purpose of this section is to keep a record of discarded materials until the end of the research process in case you change your mind and want to use them.*	

ODELL
EDUCATION

RESEARCHING TO DEEPEN UNDERSTANDING—FINAL WRITING TASK

In this unit, you have been developing your skills as a researcher of a topic. You have learned to do the following things:

- Explore topics with your learning community
- Pose and refine inquiry questions
- Discover areas you wish to investigate
- Develop and refine a Research Frame (Area of Investigation with Inquiry Paths)
- Identify and assess pertinent sources
- Make claims about sources you find and connect them to your Research Frame
- Develop an evidence-based perspective on the topic

RESEARCH PORTFOLIO

- The Research Portfolio helps you store and organize your findings and analysis throughout every step of the research process. Various tools help you develop a research strategy and record, analyze, and annotate your sources. Every time you complete a tool or annotate a source, file it in the corresponding section of your portfolio.

- Keeping an organized portfolio helps you make connections, see what you already have, and determine what you still have left to investigate. It will also provide everything you need to write your reflective narrative when you finish your research. The portfolio may be in either electronic or paper format.

FINAL WRITING TASK: REFLECTIVE RESEARCH NARRATIVE

As you complete your research, you will have an opportunity to share what you've learned in a short reflective research narrative. Your narrative should clearly express your understanding of the topic and "tell the story" of how you have developed your new knowledge. *It does not need to fully summarize and include all of your research.*

In the reflective research narrative you will:

- Tell a story about what you've learned about the topic through your investigation
- Use notes and claims from your portfolio that you have already written
- Clearly connect your ideas to the sources where you have found them
- Reflect on what you have learned about the research process

To write this narrative, you will:

1. Review your Research Portfolio.
    a. Review the materials you have compiled and organized in your Research Portfolio:
       ⇒ *Taking Notes Tools*
       ⇒ *Forming EBC-Research Tools*

FINAL WRITING TASK (Continued)

⇒ *Organizing EBC-Research Tools*

⇒ *Written EBC(s)*

b. Identify key materials that have helped you develop your thinking about the topic.

c. Arrange key materials in a chronological order, to help you organize the narrative you will write.

2. Think of several different ways you and your classmates have come to understand the topic of "Music: What Role Does It Play in Our Lives?" based on the texts you have read.

a. Select one or two of these ideas that match your own understanding, and return to the question:

⇒ *What do I think about this aspect of the topic of Music and its Importance in Our Lives?*

b. Your response to this question is the basis for your evidence-based perspective, which you will work into your narrative.

3. Think further about your perspective and your research by considering and discussing any of the following questions:

⇒ *Before starting my inquiry, what did I think about the topic? How did I view or understand it?*

⇒ *What specific steps did I take to research the topic? How did I address and answer my Inquiry Questions?*

⇒ *Which sources were the most interesting to me and why? What specifically did I find interesting about the sources?*

⇒ *What did I learn and discover about my Area of Investigation and Inquiry Question(s)?*

⇒ *What Inquiry Questions did I research but did not lead me anywhere?*

⇒ *What did I learn from my peers about the topic?*

⇒ *What moments were key in developing my understanding of the topic? When did I "get" something major about the topic?*

⇒ *What do I now think about the topic I have investigated, based on the research and reading I have done? What is my own perspective?*

⇒ *What did I learn about the research process? Where did I struggle and where did I triumph?*

4. Develop a plan or outline for your reflective research narrative.

a. Think about telling the story of how you reached your perspective in a *chronological order*—from what you first thought or knew, through what you did to learn more about the topic, to how you arrived at your new understanding and perspective.

b. Use your **Forming EBC Tools**, Written EBCs and **Organizing EBC Tools** to develop a detailed plan for your narrative.

5. Write a first draft of your reflective research narrative.

a. Tell the story of how you researched the topic and arrived at your new perspective on it.

b. Use your **Taking Notes Tools** to include evidence from relevant texts to support your story and your claims, accurately quoting and paraphrasing.

c. Tell your story in the first person ("I"), present interesting details to help your reader understand it, and make good word choices to express and connect your ideas.

ODELL
EDUCATION

FINAL WRITING TASK (Continued)

FINAL WRITING TASK: REFLECTIVE RESEARCH NARRATIVE (Continued)

    d. Your reflective research narrative should do the following things, which will be evaluated in your final draft:

⇒ Express your original understanding of the research topic and tell the story of how you arrived at your new understanding.

⇒ Communicate a new perspective on the topic that is clearly connected to the area of investigation and supported by your research.

⇒ Explain and support the new perspective by discussing claims you have derived from inquiry questions.

⇒ Discuss evidence from relevant texts by accurately quoting and paraphrasing.

⇒ Use a clear narrative structure to sequence sentences and paragraphs and to present a coherent explanation of the perspective.

⇒ Use an informal narrative voice (first person) and effective words and phrases to communicate and connect ideas.

⇒ Present your reflections on what you have learned about the research process, using specific terminology from the unit.

6. Work with other students to review and improve your reflective research narrative.

    a. Use the following Guiding Review Questions to guide self and peer reviews of your narrative:

⇒ *Do I reflect on how I originally thought of the topic before I started to research it?*

⇒ *Do I recount the specific steps I took to think of Inquiry Questions around the Area of Investigation?*

⇒ *Do I tell how I found, read, and analyzed texts to help answer my Inquiry Questions?*

⇒ *Do I clearly communicate how I arrived at my research-based perspective?*

⇒ *What is the perspective and is it clearly stated?*

⇒ *Are the claims I present in my narrative "well supported," and is there enough evidence to explain or defend my perspective?*

⇒ *Are the sources cited accurately and consistently?*

⇒ *What can be added or revised to better express the perspective?*

7. Complete any additional drafts and peer reviews of your paper as instructed.

SKILLS AND HABITS TO BE DEMONSTRATED:

As you develop and communicate a fine-tuned perspective on the topic, think about demonstrating the Literacy Skills and Academic Habits listed below to the best of your ability. Your teacher will evaluate your work and determine your grade based on how well you:

- **IDENTIFY RELATIONSHIPS:** Notice important connections among details, ideas, and texts
- **MAKE INFERENCES:** Draw sound conclusions from examining a text closely
- **SUMMARIZE:** Correctly explain what a text says about a topic
- **QUESTION:** Develop questions and lines of inquiry that lead to important ideas

FINAL WRITING TASK (Continued)

- **RECOGNIZE PERSPECTIVE:** Identify and explain the author's view of the text's topic
- **EVALUATE INFORMATION:** Assess the relevance and credibility of information in sources
- **FORM CLAIMS:** State a meaningful conclusion that is well supported by evidence from sources
- **USE EVIDENCE:** Use well-chosen details from sources to explain and support claims. Accurately paraphrase or quote.
- **ORGANIZE IDEAS:** Organize the narrative and its claims, supporting ideas, and evidence in a logical order
- **PRESENT DETAILS:** Describe and explain important details to tell the story
- **PUBLISH:** Use effective formatting and citations when paraphrasing, quoting and listing sources
- **REFLECT CRITICALLY:** Use research concepts and terms to discuss and evaluate learning
- **GENERATE IDEAS:** Generate and develop ideas, perspectives, products, and solutions to problems
- **ORGANIZE WORK:** Maintain materials so that they can be used effectively and efficiently
- **COMPLETE TASKS:** Finish short and extended tasks by established deadlines
- **UNDERSTAND PURPOSE AND PROCESS:** Understand why and how a task should be accomplished

NOTE

These skills and habits are also listed on the ***Student RDU Literacy Skills and Academic Habits Checklist*** in your **Literacy Toolbox**, which you can use to assess your work and the work of other students.

ODELL
EDUCATION

POSING INQUIRY QUESTIONS

Successful research results from posing good Inquiry Questions. When you have to solve a difficult problem or want to investigate a complex idea or issue, **developing questions about things you need to know helps guide your research and analysis**. But not all questions are created equal. Some lead to dead ends, and others open up vistas of knowledge and understanding . . . or best of all: *more questions!*

GENERATING QUESTIONS

Generating questions is most fun and effective with friends—the more minds the merrier. And **starting with lots of questions** helps you find the best ones. When brainstorming questions, consider many things about your Area of Investigation, for instance:

- **How is it defined?**
- **Where did it originate?**
- **What is its history?**
- **What are its important places, things, people, and experts?**
- **What are its major aspects?**
- **What are its causes and implications?**
- **What other things is it connected to or associated with?**

SELECTING AND REFINING QUESTIONS

Once you have a huge list of possible questions, select and refine them by asking yourself a few things about them:

Are you genuinely interested in answering your question?

Research requires hard work and endurance. If you don't care about your questions you won't do the work to answer them. The best questions are about things you actually want and need to know.

Can your question truly be answered through your research?

Some questions are unanswerable (How many walnuts are there in the world?) or take years to answer (What is the meaning of life?). Your Inquiry Questions must put you on a reachable path.

Is your question clear?

Can you pose your question in a way that you and others understand what you are asking? If it's confusing, then perhaps you are asking more than one thing. That's great: just break it into two questions. The more good Inquiry Questions you have the better.

What sort of answers does your question require?

Interesting, meaningful research comes from interesting questions. Good Inquiry Questions are rich enough to support lots of investigation that may even lead to multiple answers and more questions. Questions that can be answered with a simple yes or no generally do not make good Inquiry Questions.

Do you already know what the answer is?

Good Inquiry Questions are actually questions. If you already have answered the questions for yourself, then you won't really be inquiring through your research. If you already know what you think, then you won't get the true reward of research: a deeper knowledge and understanding of things you want to know about.

ASSESSING SOURCES

ASSESSING A SOURCE'S ACCESSIBILITY AND INTEREST LEVEL

Consider your initial experience in reading the text, how well you understand it, and whether it seems interesting to you:

ACCESSIBILITY TO YOU AS A READER	INTEREST AND MEANING FOR YOU AS A READER
• Am I able to read and comprehend the text easily? • How do the text's structure and formatting either help or hinder me in reading it? • Do I have adequate background knowledge to understand the terminology, information, and ideas in the text?	• Does the text present ideas or information that I find interesting? • Which of my Inquiry Paths will the text provide information for? • Which Inquiry Questions does the text help me answer? How?

ASSESSING A SOURCE'S CREDIBILITY

Look at the information you can find about the text in the following areas, and consider the following questions to assess a source text's credibility:

PUBLISHER	DATE	AUTHOR	TYPE
• What is the publisher's relationship to the topic area? • What economic stake might the publisher have in the topic area? • What political stake might the publisher have in the topic area?	• When was the text first published? • How current is the information on the topic? • How does the publishing date relate to the history of the topic?	• What are the author's qualifications or credentials relative to the topic area? • What is the author's personal relationship to the topic area? • What economic or political stakes might the author have in the topic area?	• What type of text is it: explanation, informational article, feature, research study, op-ed, essay, argument, other? • What is the purpose of the text with respect to the topic area?

ASSESSING A SOURCE'S RELEVANCE AND RICHNESS

Using your Research Frame as a reference, consider the following questions:

RELEVANCE TO TOPIC AND PURPOSE	RELEVANCE TO AREA OF INVESTIGATION	SCOPE AND RICHNESS
• What information does the text provide on the topic? • How might the text help me accomplish the purpose for my research? • Does the text provide accurate information?	• How is the text related to the specific area I am investigating? • Which of my Paths of Inquiry might the text provide information for? • Which Inquiry Questions might the text help me address? How?	• How long is the text and what is the scope of the topic areas it addresses? • How extensive and supported is the information it provides? • How does the information in the text relate to other texts?

CONNECTING IDEAS

USING TRANSITIONAL WORDS AND PHRASES

Transitional words and phrases create links between your ideas when you are speaking and writing. They help your audience understand the logic of your thoughts. When using transitional words, make sure that they are the right match for what you want to express. And remember, transition words work best when they are connecting two or more strong ideas that are clearly stated. Here is a list of transitional words and phrases that you can use for different purposes.

ADD RELATED INFORMATION	GIVE AN EXAMPLE OR ILLUSTRATE AN IDEA	MAKE SURE YOUR THINKING IS CLEARLY UNDERSTOOD	COMPARE IDEAS OR SHOW HOW IDEAS ARE SIMILAR	CONTRAST IDEAS OR SHOW HOW THEY ARE DIFFERENT
• furthermore • moreover • too • also • again • in addition • next • further • finally • and, or, nor	• to illustrate • to demonstrate • specifically • for instance • as an illustration • for example	• that is to say • in other words • to explain • i.e., (that is) • to clarify • to rephrase it • to put it another way	• in the same way • by the same token • similarly • in like manner • likewise • in similar fashion	• nevertheless • but • however • otherwise • on the contrary • in contrast • on the other hand

EXPLAIN HOW ONE THING CAUSES ANOTHER	EXPLAIN THE EFFECT OR RESULT OF SOMETHING	EXPLAIN YOUR PURPOSE	LIST RELATED INFORMATION	QUALIFY SOMETHING
• because • since • on account of • for that reason	• therefore • consequently • accordingly • thus • hence • as a result	• in order that • so that • to that end, to this end • for this purpose • for this reason	• First, second, third . . . • First, then, also, finally	• almost • nearly • probably • never • always • frequently • perhaps • maybe • although

QUESTIONING PATH TOOL

Name: _____ **Text:** _____

APPROACHING: *I determine my reading purposes and take note of key information about the text. I identify the LIPS domain(s) that will guide my initial reading.*

Purpose:

Key information:

LIPS domain(s):

QUESTIONING: *I use Guiding Questions to help me investigate the text (from the **Guiding Questions Handout**).*

1.

2.

ANALYZING: *I question further to connect and analyze the details I find (from the **Guiding Questions Handout**).*

1.

2.

DEEPENING: *I consider the questions of others.*

1.

2.

3.

EXTENDING: *I pose my own questions.*

1.

2.

ODELL EDUCATION

APPROACHING TEXTS TOOL

Name _____ **Text** _____

APPROACHING THE TEXT		
Before reading, I consider what my specific purposes for reading are.	**What are my reading purposes?**	
I also take note of key information about the text.	**Title:**	**Source/Publisher:**
	Text type:	**Publication date:**
	What do I already think or understand about the text based on this information?	

QUESTIONING THE TEXT	
As I read the text for the first time, I use Guiding Questions that relate to my reading purpose and focus. (*Can be taken from the Guiding Questions Handout.*)	**Guiding Questions for *my first reading* of the text:**
	As I read I mark details on the text that relate to my Guiding Questions.
As I reread, I use questions I have about specific details that have emerged in my reading to focus my analysis and deepen my understanding.	**Text-specific questions to help focus *my rereading* of the text:**

ODELL EDUCATION

ANALYZING DETAILS TOOL

Name _ _ _ _ _ _ _ _ _ _ _ _ _ _ _ _ **Text** _

Reading purpose:

A question I have about the text:

SEARCHING FOR DETAILS

I read the text closely and mark words and phrases that help me think about my question.

SELECTING DETAILS

I select words or phrases from my search that I think are the most important in thinking about my question.

Detail 1 (Ref.:)	Detail 2 (Ref.:)	Detail 3 (Ref.:)

ANALYZING DETAILS

I reread parts of the text and think about the meaning of the details and what they tell me about my question.

What I think about detail 1:	What I think about detail 2:	What I think about detail 3:

CONNECTING DETAILS

I compare the details and explain the connections I see among them.

How I connect the details:

EXPLORING A TOPIC TOOL

Name _ _ _ _ _ _ _ _ _ _ _ _ **Topic** _ _ _ _ _ _ _ _ _

Write a brief account of the class conversation about the topic describing what you know at this point about some of its aspects:

_____

_____

_____

_____

_____

_____

_____

_____

_____

_____

_____

_____

POTENTIAL AREA OF INVESTIGATION 1
In a few words, describe an area within the topic that you would like to know more about:
Explain why you are interested in this area of the topic:
Express your potential Area of Investigation as a question or problem:

ODELL EDUCATION

EXPLORING A TOPIC TOOL (Continued)

Name _   Topic _

POTENTIAL AREA OF INVESTIGATION 2	POTENTIAL AREA OF INVESTIGATION 3	POTENTIAL AREA OF INVESTIGATION 4
In a few words, describe what you would like to know more about within the topic:	In a few words, describe what you would like to know more about within the topic:	In a few words, describe what you would like to know more about within the topic:
Explain why you are interested in this:	Explain why you are interested in this:	Explain why you are interested in this:
Express your potential area of investigation as a question or problem:	Express your potential area of investigation as a question or problem:	Express your potential area of investigation as a question or problem:

POTENTIAL SOURCES TOOL

Name _ _ _ _ _ _ _ _ _ _ _ Topic _

Area of Investigation _ _ _ _ _ _ _ _ _ _ _ _ _ _ _ _ _ _ _

SOURCE

No.	Title:	Location:
	Author:	Text type:	Publication date:

General Content/Key Ideas/Personal Comments:

Connection to Inquiry Paths:

Accessibility/Interest: [ ] High [ ] Medium [ ] Low | Credibility: [ ] High [ ] Medium [ ] Low | Relevance/Richness: [ ] High [ ] Medium [ ] Low

SOURCE

No.	Title:	Location:
	Author:	Text type:	Publication date:

General Content/Key Ideas/Personal Comments:

Connection to Inquiry Paths:

Accessibility/Interest: [ ] High [ ] Medium [ ] Low | Credibility: [ ] High [ ] Medium [ ] Low | Relevance/Richness: [ ] High [ ] Medium [ ] Low

SOURCE

No.	Title:	Location:
	Author:	Text type:	Publication date:

General Content/Key Ideas/Personal Comments:

Connection to Inquiry Paths:

Accessibility/Interest: [ ] High [ ] Medium [ ] Low | Credibility: [ ] High [ ] Medium [ ] Low | Relevance/Richness: [ ] High [ ] Medium [ ] Low

RESEARCH FRAME

Name – – – – – – – – – – **Topic** – – – – – – – – – –

Area of Investigation – – – – – – – –

INQUIRY PATH	INQUIRY PATH	INQUIRY PATH
Reference: IP No.	**Reference: IP No.**	**Reference: IP No.**
Name this Inquiry Path in the form of a brief description or question:	Name this Inquiry Path in the form of a brief description or question:	Name this Inquiry Path in the form of a brief description or question:
List all the questions in this Inquiry Path:	List all the questions in this Inquiry Path:	List all the questions in this Inquiry Path:

TAKING NOTES TOOL

Name _

Source(s) _ _ _ _ _ _ _ _ _ _ _ _ _ _ _ _ _ _ _

Inquiry Question/Path _ _ _ _ _ _ _ _ _ _ _ _

REFERENCE	DETAILS	COMMENTS
Source no. and location in the source:	*I record details, ideas, or information that I find in my sources that help me answer my Inquiry Questions:*	*I explain the reason why I think they are important and write personal comments:*

FORMING EVIDENCE-BASED CLAIMS RESEARCH TOOL

Name _ _ _ _ _ _ _ _ _ _ **Source(s)** _

Inquiry Question:

SEARCHING FOR DETAILS	I read the sources closely and mark words and phrases that help me answer my question.		
SELECTING DETAILS I select words or phrases from my search that I think are the most important for answering my question. I write the reference next to each detail.	**Detail 1** (Ref.:)	**Detail 2** (Ref.:)	**Detail 3** (Ref.:)
ANALYZING AND CONNECTING DETAILS I reread parts of the texts and think about the meaning of the details and what they tell me about my question. Then I compare the details and explain the connections I see among them.	What I think about the details and how I connect them:		
MAKING A CLAIM I state a conclusion I have come to and can support with evidence from the texts after reading them closely.	My claim that answers my Inquiry Question:		

ODELL
EDUCATION

ORGANIZING EVIDENCE-BASED CLAIMS
RESEARCH TOOL (2 POINTS)

Name _ _ _ _ _ _ _ _ _ _ _ _ _ _ _ _ **Inquiry Path** _ _ _ _ _ _ _ _ _ _ _ _ _ _ _ _

CLAIM:

Point 1

A Supporting Evidence	B Supporting Evidence

(Reference:)   (Reference:)

C Supporting Evidence	D Supporting Evidence

(Reference:)   (Reference:)

Point 2

A Supporting Evidence	B Supporting Evidence

(Reference:)   (Reference:)

C Supporting Evidence	D Supporting Evidence

(Reference:)   (Reference:)

ODELL EDUCATION

ORGANIZING EVIDENCE-BASED CLAIMS
RESEARCH TOOL (3 POINTS)

Name _____   - - - - - - - - - - **Inquiry Path** -

CLAIM:

	Point 1	Point 2	Point 3
A	Supporting Evidence	Supporting Evidence	Supporting Evidence
	(Reference:)	(Reference:)	(Reference:)
B	Supporting Evidence	Supporting Evidence	Supporting Evidence
	(Reference:)	(Reference:)	(Reference:)
C	Supporting Evidence	Supporting Evidence	Supporting Evidence
	(Reference:)	(Reference:)	(Reference:)

PART 1 RESEARCH EVALUATION CRITERIA CHECKLIST

Name_____ Area of Investigation_____ Date_____

RESEARCH EVALUATION CRITERIA CHECKLIST		√	COMMENTS
I. ADEQUACY AND SUFFICIENCY OF RESEARCH *The researcher's investigation follows the research frame and the information gathered is sufficient.*	**Adequacy of the research:** The researcher's investigation is based on the Research Frame and the claims and information presented link directly to the Inquiry Questions.	☐	
	Sufficiency of the answers: The answers formulated by the researcher based on his or her investigation are sufficient to cover the scope of each Inquiry Question.	☐	
	Adequacy of the scope and focus of the research: No Inquiry Questions or Paths of the research seem irrelevant with respect to the research frame.	☐	
II. CREDIBILITY AND RICHNESS OF SOURCES *The sources gathered by the researcher are credible and rich.*	**Credibility of sources:** The sources gathered by the researcher are credible.	☐	
	Richness of sources: The researcher found a reasonable amount of rich sources that provide important information that is relevant to the inquiry.	☐	
III. RANGE OF PERSPECTIVES *The researcher has considered a wide range of perspectives.*	**Richness of perspectives:** The researcher has considered and explored multiple perspectives.	☐	
	Sufficiency of perspectives: No important perspective has been ignored.	☐	
	Balance among perspectives: There is no overreliance on any one source or perspective.	☐	
IV. COHERENCE OF THE PERSPECTIVE *The evidence-based claims drawn from the analysis of the sources are coherent, sound, and supported.*	**Coherence of evidence-based claims:** The evidence-based claims drawn from the analysis of the sources are coherent with respect to the research frame.	☐	
	Soundness of evidence-based claims: The evidence-based claim demonstrates knowledge of and sound thinking about the area of investigation.	☐	
	Support for evidence-based claims: The evidence-based claims are supported by quotations and examples from the texts.	☐	

PART 2 PEER EVALUATION OF RESEARCH

Presenter: _ _ _ _ _ _ _ _ _ _ _ _ _ _ **Reviewer:** _ _ _ _ _ _ _ _ _ _ _ _ _ _

Work in small groups to evaluate each other's research. Rotate roles in your group.

AS A PRESENTER:

- **Present your Area of Investigation and Research Frame.** Describe the general scope of your research and explain why you are interested in this area.

- **Summarize from your written claims** for each of your answers to the Inquiry Paths. Make sure you reference evidence from sources to support your claims.

- **Present two key sources.** Explain why you think they are key, summarize their content and explain your analysis of these sources to your peers. Show your peers and comment on your annotations, notes, and EBCs about these sources.

- Make sure you **give your peers the opportunity to ask you questions** during the entire presentation.

- **Take notes** on a Revising Research tool to determine actions you may take to revise your research based on your peers review.

AS A REVIEWER:

- **Listen** carefully to the presentation. **Ask clarifying questions** to the presenter when necessary.

- Using the table below, **make comments and suggestions** about the presentation answering the guiding questions.

GUIDING QUESTIONS	COMMENTS AND SUGGESTIONS
What have you learned about the presenter's area of investigation?	
What was interesting to you in the presentation?	
What new information does the presenter need to find to more fully address existing or new Inquiry Paths?	
What was not clear to you in the presentation?	
What would you like to know more about the presenter's area of investigation?	
Do you have any other comment or suggestions that you think would help the presenter improve his/her work?	

PART 3 REVISING RESEARCH

Presenter: _ _ _ _ _ _ _ _ _ _ _ _ _ _ _ _   **Reviewer:** _ _ _ _ _ _ _ _ _ _ _ _

Review the feedback on your Research and think about ways you should revise your work. For each action you choose, explain what specific steps you are planning to take.

GUIDING QUESTIONS	MY NOTES, COMMENTS, AND FUTURE STEPS
What adjustments and additions do I need to make to my Research Frame?	
Are there sources lacking in credibility that I need to replace?	
What new information do I need to find to more fully address existing or new Inquiry Paths?	
What missing perspectives do I need to research?	
Are there any parts of my research I should discard?	
Other:	

AREA EVALUATION CHECKLIST

Date   **Name**

Area of Investigation

AREA EVALUATION CHECKLIST	√	COMMENTS
I. COHERENCE OF AREA *What is the Area of Investigation?*	The researcher can speak and write about the Area of Investigation in a way that makes sense to others and is clearly understood.	
II. SCOPE OF AREA *What do I need to know to gain an understanding of the Area of Investigation?*	The questions necessary to investigate for gaining an understanding require more than a quick review of easily accessed sources. The questions are reasonable enough so that the researcher is likely to find credible sources that address the issue in the time allotted for research.	
III. RELEVANCE OF AREA *How is this Area of Investigation related to a larger topic?*	The Area of Investigation is relevant to the larger topic.	
IV. INTEREST IN AREA *Why are you interested in this Area of Investigation?*	The researcher is able to communicate genuine interest in the Area of Investigation. Gaining an understanding of the area would be valuable for the student.	

In one or two sentences express the potential Area of Investigation in the form of a problem or overarching question:

....

....

....

ODELL EDUCATION

RESEARCHING TO DEEPEN UNDERSTANDING TARGETED LITERACY SKILLS

TARGETED SKILLS	DESCRIPTORS
IDENTIFYING RELATIONSHIPS	Identifies important connections among key details and ideas within and across texts
MAKING INFERENCES	Demonstrates comprehension by using connections among details to make logical deductions about a text
SUMMARIZING	Recounts the explicit meaning of texts, referring to key details, events, characters, language, and ideas
QUESTIONING	Formulates and responds to questions and lines of inquiry that lead to the identification of important ideas and themes
RECOGNIZING PERSPECTIVE	Uses textual details to recognize an author's or narrator's relationship to and perspective on a text's topic
EVALUATING INFORMATION	Assesses the relevance and credibility of information, ideas, evidence, and logic presented in texts
FORMING CLAIMS	Develops meaningful and defensible claims that clearly state valid, evidence-based analysis
USING EVIDENCE	Supports all aspects of claims with sufficient textual evidence, using accurate quotations, paraphrases, and references
ORGANIZING IDEAS	Sequences sentences and paragraphs to establish coherent, logical, and unified narratives, explanations, and arguments
REFLECTING CRITICALLY	Uses literacy terminology and concepts to reflect on, discuss, and evaluate personal and peer literacy development

RESEARCHING TO DEEPEN UNDERSTANDING ACADEMIC HABITS DEVELOPED

HABITS DEVELOPED	DESCRIPTORS
GENERATING IDEAS	Generates and develops ideas, positions, products, and solutions to problems
ORGANIZING WORK	Maintains work and materials so that they can be used effectively and efficiently in current and future tasks
COMPLETING TASKS	Finishes short and extended tasks by established deadlines
UNDERSTANDING PURPOSE AND PROCESS	Understands the purpose and uses the process and criteria that guide tasks

ODELL
EDUCATION

RESEARCHING TO DEEPEN UNDERSTANDING LITERACY SKILLS AND ACADEMIC HABITS RUBRIC

Name _ _ _ _ _ _ _ _ _ _ _ _ _ _ _ **Text** _ _ _ _ _ _ _ _ _ _ _ _ _ _ _ _

NE— not enough evidence to make a rating

1—**Emerging:** needs improvement

2—**Developing:** shows progress

3—**Becoming Proficient:** demonstrates skills

4—**Excelling:** exceeds expectations+—**Growth:** evidence of growth within the unit or task

I. READING SKILLS CRITERIA	NE	1	2	3	4	+
1. Makes Inferences: Demonstrates comprehension by using connections among details to make logical deductions about a text						
2. Summarizes: Recounts the explicit meaning of texts, referring to key details, events, characters, language, and ideas						
3. Interprets Language: Identifies how words and phrases convey meaning and represent the author's perspective						
4. Identifies Relationships: Identifies important connections among key details and ideas within and across texts						
5. Evaluating Information: Assesses the relevance and credibility of information, ideas, evidence, and logic presented in texts						
6. Recognizes Perspective: Uses textual details to recognize the author's relationship to and perspective on a text's topic						
II. RESEARCH PROCESS SKILLS AND HABITS CRITERIA	NE	1	2	3	4	+
1. Questions: Formulates and responds to questions and lines of inquiry that lead to the identification of important ideas and themes						
2. Generates Ideas: Generates and develops ideas, positions, products, and solutions to problems						
3. Understands Process and Purpose: Understands the purpose and uses the process and criteria that guide tasks						
4. Completes Tasks: Finishes short and extended tasks by established deadlines						
5. Organizes Work: Maintains work and materials so that they can be used effectively and efficiently in current and future tasks						
6. Reflects Critically: Uses literacy terminology and concepts to reflect on discuss and evaluate personal and peer literacy development						

RESEARCH SKILLS AND HABITS RUBRIC (Continued)

III. EVIDENCE-BASED WRITING CRITERIA	NE	1	2	3	4	+
1. Forms Claims: Develops meaningful and defensible claims that clearly state valid, evidence-based analysis						
2. Uses Evidence: Supports all aspects of the explanation with sufficient textual evidence, using accurate quotations, paraphrases, and references						
3. Uses Language: Selects and combines words that precisely communicate ideas, generate appropriate tone, and evoke intended responses from an audience						
4. Presents Details: Describes and explains important details that effectively develop a narrative, explanation, or argument.						
5. Organizes Ideas: Sequences sentences and paragraphs to establish coherent, logical, and unified narratives, explanations, and arguments						
6. Publishes: Uses effective formatting and citations to present ideas for specific audiences and purposes						
IV. FINAL ASSIGNMENT CRITERIA	**NE**	**1**	**2**	**3**	**4**	**+**
1. Compiles a complete and organized Research Portfolio						
2. Develops a reflective research narrative that tells the story of how the researcher moved from an initial understanding of the research topic to a new, evidence-based perspective						
3. Communicates a new perspective on the topic that is clearly connected to the area of investigation, supported by research, and explained through claims derived from inquiry questions						
4. Presents and discusses personal reflections on the research experience and process, using specific terminology from the unit						
SUMMARY EVALUATION		**1**	**2**	**3**	**4**	

ODELL
EDUCATION

RESEARCH SKILLS AND HABITS RUBRIC (Continued)

Comments:

1. Explanation of ratings—**evidence** found (or not found) in the work:

2. Strengths and **areas of growth** observed in the work:

3. Areas for improvement in future work:

STUDENT RESEARCHING TO DEEPEN UNDERSTANDING LITERACY SKILLS AND ACADEMIC HABITS CHECKLIST

	RESEARCH LITERACY SKILLS AND ACADEMIC HABITS	✔	EVIDENCE Demonstrating the SKILLS AND HABITS
READING	1. **Identifying Relationships:** Notices important connections among details, ideas, and texts		
	2. **Making Inferences:** Draws sound conclusions from examining a text closely		
	3. **Summarizing:** Correctly explains what a text says about a topic		
	4. **Questioning:** Develops questions and lines of inquiry that lead to important ideas		
THINKING	5. **Recognizing Perspective:** Identifies and explains the author's view of the text's topic		
	6. **Evaluating Information:** Assesses the relevance and credibility of information in sources		
	7. **Forming Claims:** States a meaningful conclusion that is well supported by evidence from sources		
	8. **Using Evidence:** Uses well-chosen details from sources to explain and support claims; accurately paraphrases or quotes		
	9. **Presenting Details:** Describes and explains details that are important in the story of the research process		
	10. **Organizing Ideas:** Organizes the narrative and its claims, supporting ideas, and evidence in a logical order		
	11. **Publishing:** Uses effective formatting and citations when paraphrasing, quoting, and listing sources		
ACADEMIC HABITS	12. **Reflecting Critically:** Uses research concepts and terms to discuss and evaluate learning		
	13. **Generating Ideas:** Generates and develops ideas, perspectives, products, and solutions to problems.		
	14. **Organizing Work:** Maintains materials so that they can be used effectively and efficiently		
	15. **Completing Tasks:** Finishes short and extended tasks by established deadlines		
	16. **Understanding Purpose and Process:** Understands why and how a task should be accomplished		
	General comments:		

ODELL EDUCATION

UNIT 5

BUILDING
EVIDENCE-BASED
ARGUMENTS

DEVELOPING CORE LITERACY
PROFICIENCIES

GRADE 9

"What is the virtue of a proportional response?"

UNIT OVERVIEW

Literacy—the integrated abilities to read texts, to investigate ideas and deepen understanding through research, to make and evaluate evidence-based claims, and to communicate one's perspective in a reasoned way—is fundamental to participation in civic life. Thus, the importance of a literate citizenry was understood and expressed by Thomas Jefferson early in the life of our democratic nation. Today, students face the prospect of participating in a civic life that stretches beyond the boundaries of a single nation and has become increasingly contentious, characterized by entrenched polarization in response to complex issues.

Learning the skills and habits of mind associated with argumentation—how to conceive and communicate **CCSS.ELA-LITERACY.W.1** (*arguments to support claims, using valid reasoning and sufficient evidence*) as well as **CCSS.ELA-LITERACY.R.8** (*how to delineate and evaluate the argument*[s] and *the validity of the reasoning and relevance and sufficiency of the evidence* presented by others)—is therefore central to students' civic and academic lives. In order to participate in thoughtful, reasoned, and civil discussion about societal issues, students must learn to (1) investigate and understand an issue; (2) develop an evidence-based perspective and position; (3) evaluate and respond to the perspectives and positions of others; (4) make, support, and link claims as premises in a logical chain of reasoning; and (5) communicate a position so that others can understand and thoughtfully evaluate their thinking.

Thus, this unit, as the culminating set of instructional activities in the Developing Core Literacy Proficiencies series, focuses on aspects of argumentation involving evidence, reasoning, and logic rather than on persuasive writing and speaking. It moves away from an *op-ed* approach that asks students to form an opinion, take a stand, and convince others to agree. Instead, students are expected first to understand a complex issue through exploratory inquiry and close reading of information on the topic and then to study multiple perspectives on the issue before they establish their own position. From their reading and research, they are asked to craft an argumentative plan that explains and supports their position, acknowledges the perspectives and positions of others, and uses evidence gleaned through close reading and analysis to support their claims. Having developed a logical and well-supported chain of reasoning, they use an iterative process to develop an argumentative essay in the spirit in which Montaigne first used the word *essay*—as a progression of attempts to communicate their thinking and contribute to reasoned debate about the issue.

The unit's pedagogy and instructional sequence are based on the idea that students (and citizens) must develop a *mental model* of what effective—and reasoned—argumentation entails to guide them in reading, evaluating, and communicating arguments concerning issues to which there are many more than two sides (i.e., most issues in our world today). The unit therefore focuses on learning about and applying academic concepts related to argumentation, such as *issue, perspective, position, premise, evidence,* and *reasoning.* Thus, the unit provides numerous opportunities to build students' academic vocabularies while emphasizing close reading and research skills, critical thinking, evidence-based discussion, collaborative development, and an iterative approach to writing.

Developing Core Literacy Proficiencies

TOPIC AND TEXTS—TERRORISM

The topic area and texts focus on terrorism and, more specifically, what is meant by terrorism, the events leading up to 9/11, an analysis of the responses to the attacks, and terrorism in context of the recent developments in war. Responses to terrorism, and policy related to and resulting from terrorism, is a complex topic with many perspectives and positions—not a simple pro and con arena for debate—which enables the teacher and students to approach and study the issue from many possible angles.

The texts in this unit are offered in the form of text sets, in which texts are grouped together for instructional and content purposes. It is not required that students read all texts in all text sets in order for them to develop the skills associated with the unit or learn about the unit topic. This gives greater flexibility to teachers and students as they make decisions based on student reading levels (texts have different complexities), student groupings, and time limitations.

LEARNING PROGRESSION

The unit activities are organized into five parts, each associated with a sequence of texts and writing activities. The parts build on each other and can each span a range of instructional time depending on scheduling and student ability.

Part 1 introduces students to the concept of evidence-based argumentation in the context of societal issues. Students read and write about a variety of informational texts to build an understanding of terrorism as a definition and concept.

Part 2 develops students' abilities to analyze arguments through learning close-reading skills and terminology used in delineating argumentation. Students read and analyze several arguments associated with terrorism, responses to terrorism, and terrorism policy.

Part 3 deepens students' abilities to read and think about arguments, moving them into evaluation. Students begin to synthesize their analysis and evaluation of other arguments into the development of their own position.

Part 4 focuses students on identifying and crafting the structure of their own arguments, including their sequence of claims and their supporting evidence.

Part 5 engages students in a collaborative, question-based process to develop and strengthen their argumentative essays. Students work with their teachers and peers to draft, revise, and publish their own argumentative essay on the unit's issue.

OUTLINE

PART 1: UNDERSTANDING THE NATURE OF AN ISSUE
• Students apply their close-reading skills to understand a societal issue as a context for various perspectives, positions, and arguments.

PART 2: ANALYZING ARGUMENTS
• Students delineate and analyze the position, premises, reasoning, evidence, and perspective of arguments.

PART 3: EVALUATING ARGUMENTS AND DEVELOPING A POSITION
• Students evaluate arguments, determine which arguments they find most convincing, and synthesize what they have learned so far to establish their own positions.

PART 4: ORGANIZING AN EVIDENCE-BASED ARGUMENT
• Students establish and sequence evidence-based claims as premises for a coherent, logical argument concerning a position related to the unit's issue.

PART 5: DEVELOPING WRITING THROUGH A COLLABORATIVE PROCESS
• Students learn and practice a collaborative, question-based approach to developing and improving their writing, using Literacy Skills criteria and Guiding Questions to draft and revise argumentative essays.

SEQUENCING LEARNING OVER TIME AND ACROSS GRADE LEVELS

The learning sequence for this unit and the instructional notes within it have been developed on the assumption that students may be learning the process of building an evidence-based argument for the first time. Thus, terms are introduced and explained, graphic organizers (tools) are overviewed and modeled, and lessons move relatively carefully from teacher modeling to guided practice to independent application. The Literacy Skills that are targeted and the Academic Habits that are developed are assumed to be in early stages of development for many students, and thus extensive scaffolding is provided.

However, students may come to this fifth unit in the Developing Core Literacy Proficiencies series having developed their Literacy Skills, Academic Habits, and Core Literacy Proficiencies in other contexts. They may have progressed through earlier units in the Developing Core Literacy Proficiencies sequence (*Reading Closely, Making Evidence-Based Claims, Researching to Deepen Understanding*) and become very familiar with tools, handouts, terminology, skills, and habits addressed in this unit. They may also have experienced the Building Evidence-Based Arguments instructional sequence in a previous grade or school.

For this reason, teachers should use their professional judgment to plan their instruction for this unit considering not only *what* they are teaching (argumentation and the curriculum designed to develop students' skills) but also *whom* they are teaching (their students' backgrounds, previous experiences, and readiness levels). Before teaching the unit, teachers are encouraged to determine what students have previously experienced, learned, or produced.

If students have more advanced skills or extensive previous experience in building arguments, instruction can move more rapidly through many sections of this unit, concentrate more on extended reading to deepen students' understanding, and emphasize more complex topics, texts, or academic arguments.

☰ INTRODUCTION TO BUILDING EVIDENCE-BASED ARGUMENTS LITERACY TOOLBOX

In the *Building Evidence-Based Arguments* (EBA) unit, students learn and develop skills associated with building an argument, including researching a topic, recognizing perspective and purpose, analyzing arguments, forming one's own perspective, building a logical progression of evidence-based claims, and using a peer-review process to clearly communicate an argument. Much of this unit serves as an opportunity for students to apply and demonstrate the literacy proficiencies they have developed over the course of the previous three units; students will be reading closely, analyzing, and evaluating texts to understand an issue and form a concrete, evidence-based position on it.

As students largely draw from skills they have worked on up to this point, they will revisit tools and handouts from the **Reading Closely, Making Evidence-Based Claims,** and **Researching to Deepen Understanding Toolboxes**. Students can reach into these toolboxes to help guide their reading as they first familiarize themselves with the topic and then work to fully understand the content, vocabulary, and perspectives associated with it. Students will use a slightly modified **Forming Evidence-Based Claims Tool** for this unit that helps them deeply analyze their own questions about texts while also making claims.

Tools to Support Argumentation: Students also learn to use new tools that are specific to argumentation. The **Evidence-Based Arguments Terms Handout** defines key words students will be using throughout the unit in order to analyze and express arguments. The **Delineating Arguments Tool** graphically outlines the organizing components of an argument, beginning with areas to note the *issue, perspective,* and *position* that define the argument and including columns in which to record the *premises* and *supporting evidence* of the argument. The **Model Arguments** provided with the unit offer synopses of conflicts that should be familiar to students.

These **Model Arguments** provided within the unit serve as practice examples for students to analyze and delineate as they familiarize themselves with argument concepts and vocabulary.

The **Evaluating Arguments Tool** provides students with a checklist to guide their process in evaluating an argument, either one they have read or written. The tool is organized to support evaluation of eight related elements of an argument: the argument's *issue, perspective, credibility and bias, position, claims, evidence, reasoning and logic,* and *conclusions.* The tool also provides a place to make a summary rating of whether the argument is, overall, *convincing* to the evaluator. Reading and evaluation for each of these nine criteria areas is supported by two or three Guiding Questions.

The ***Building Evidence-Based Arguments —Final Writing Task Handout*** gives students a detailed overview of how to apply skills they have learned throughout the unit to a final argumentative writing task.

The **Building Evidence-Based Arguments Literacy Toolbox** also houses complete tables of targeted Literacy Skills and Academic Habits developed in the unit as well as the ***EBA Literacy Skills Rubric*** and ***Student EBA Literacy Skills and Academic Habits Checklist***.

If students have previously completed a *Building Evidence-Based Arguments* unit, they should already be familiar with these tools and handouts. As they gain independence in practicing the proficiency of analyzing and delineating positions and developing their own evidence-based perspectives and arguments, students can internalize the concepts and processes detailed in the unit and might rely less and less on these tools and handouts. Depending on students' abilities and familiarity with the **EBA Literacy Toolbox**, teachers might encourage students to use these materials when they encounter difficulties in understanding sections of texts, require assistance in communicating or piecing together analysis, or need to organize their thoughts in preparation for a writing assignment. Otherwise, students can proceed through the texts, delineating and evaluating arguments using their own developing processes. If students are ready to move through the unit without these scaffolds, it is still important that teachers continually verify that they are capturing, analyzing, and communicating with evidence salient ideas from the readings.

> **NOTE**
>
> Tools, handouts, and the ***Student EBA Literacy Skills and Academic Habits Checklist*** can also be found in the Student Edition.

HOW THIS UNIT TEACHES VOCABULARY

This unit draws on a variety of strategies for teaching academic and disciplinary vocabulary. The primary strategy involves the way critical disciplinary vocabulary and concepts are built into instruction. Students are taught words such as *claims, perspective, position, evidence,* and *criteria* through their explicit use in activities.

Students come to understand and use these words as they think about and evaluate their own analysis and that of their peers. The handouts and tools play a key role in this process. By the end of the unit, students will have developed deep conceptual knowledge of key vocabulary that they can transfer to a variety of academic and public contexts.

The texts and activities also provide opportunities for academic vocabulary instruction. Many of the activities focus directly on analyzing the way authors use language and key words to develop ideas and achieve specific purposes. The sequence of topical texts also builds vocabulary knowledge and connections, supporting textual comprehension and vocabulary acquisition. The argumentative essays students write at the end of the unit give them the opportunity to immediately use new academic and disciplinary vocabulary they have learned in their reading.

LITERACY SKILLS AND ACADEMIC HABITS

TARGETED LITERACY SKILLS

In this unit, students will be learning about, practicing, developing, and demonstrating foundational skills necessary to analyze, develop, and write evidence-based arguments. The following Literacy Skills are targeted with explicit instruction and assessment throughout the unit and are included in the **EBA Literacy Skills Rubric** (found in the **EBA Literacy Toolbox**):

LITERACY SKILLS	DESCRIPTORS
RECOGNIZING PERSPECTIVE	Uses textual details to recognize and establish a perspective on a topic
EVALUATING INFORMATION	Assesses the relevance and credibility of information, ideas, evidence, and logic presented in texts
DELINEATING ARGUMENTATION	Identifies and analyzes the components and accuracy of claims, evidence, and reasoning in explanations and arguments
FORMING CLAIMS	Establishes and presents a clear and defensible position that is supported by a series of valid premises and set in the context of the topic
USING EVIDENCE	Presents a comprehensive view of the issue by providing textual evidence to support claims and using sufficient and accurate quotations, paraphrases, and references
USING LOGIC	Establishes and supports a position through a logical sequence of related premises and supporting evidence
ORGANIZING IDEAS	Sequences sentences, paragraphs, and parts of an essay to establish a coherent, logical, and unified argument
USING CONVENTIONS	Uses effective sentence structure, grammar, punctuation, and spelling to express ideas and achieve writing and speaking purposes
PUBLISHING	Uses effective formatting and citations to present ideas for specific audiences and purposes
REFLECTING CRITICALLY	Uses literacy terminology and concepts to reflect on, discuss, and evaluate personal and peer literacy development

> ### NOTE
> Student language versions of these descriptors can be found in the **Student EBA Literacy Skills and Academic Habits Checklist** in the **EBA Literacy Toolbox** and Student Edition.

APPLIED LITERACY SKILLS

In addition to these targeted skills, the unit provides several opportunities for students to apply and develop the following Literacy Skills:

- **Attending to Details**
- **Identifying Relationships**
- **Making Inferences**
- **Summarizing**
- **Using Language**
- **Presenting Details**

ACADEMIC HABITS

In this unit, students will be introduced to specific Academic Habits associated with exploring societal issues and developing an evidence-based position. Teachers may choose to introduce students to the habits formally at the beginning of the unit and reflect on them informally throughout the unit activities. Discussion of the skills is incorporated into the instructional notes of key activities.

The following Academic Habits are targeted throughout the unit:

HABITS DEVELOPED	DESCRIPTORS
REVISING	Rethinks and refines work based on teacher-, peer-, and self-review processes
REMAINING OPEN	Adopts a stance of inquiry—asking questions to learn more—rather than arguing for entrenched positions
QUALIFYING VIEWS	Modifies and further justifies ideas in response to thinking from others

NOTE

Student language versions of these descriptors can be found in the *Student EBA Literacy Skills and Academic Habits Checklist* in the **EBA Literacy Toolbox** and Student Edition.

☰ COMMON CORE STATE STANDARDS ALIGNMENT

The instructional focus of this unit is on analyzing and writing evidence-based arguments with specific attention to argumentative perspective, position, claims, evidence, and reasoning.

Accordingly, the primary alignment of the unit—the targeted CCSS—are **CCSS.ELA-LITERACY.RI.1**, **CCSS.ELA-LITERACY.RI.8,** and **CCSS.ELA-LITERACY.W.1**, **CCSS.ELA-LITERACY.W.2,** and **CCSS.ELA-LITERACY.W.9**.

The sequences of texts and instruction emphasize helping students analyze the way various authors' perspectives and points of view relate to their argumentation. Thus, **CCSS.ELA-LITERACY.RI.6** and **CCSS.ELA-LITERACY.RI.9** are also targeted standards.

In Parts 1 through 3, students write short pieces analyzing arguments on a societal issue. In Parts 4 and 5, instruction supports students in the organization, development, revision, and production of a significant and original argumentative essay. As such, **CCSS.ELA-LITERACY.W.4** and **CCSS.ELA-LITERACY.W.5** become targeted standards.

As students develop these primary targeted reading and writing skills, they are also practicing their abilities to engage in text-centered discussions. Thus, **CCSS.ELA-LITERACY.SL.1** is also an emerging targeted standard as the unit progresses, and this standard is central to the collaborative process students use in Part 5 for developing and strengthening their writing.

As students develop these primary targeted CCSS skill sets, they also practice and use related reading and writing skills from supporting CCSS. Analysis of texts focuses on interpreting key words and phrases (**CCSS.ELA-LITERACY.RI.4**), determining central ideas (**CCSS.ELA-LITERACY.RI.2**), and the way they interact over the course of a text (**CCSS.ELA-LITERACY.RI.3**), as well as the way authors have structured their particular arguments (**CCSS.ELA-LITERACY.RI.5**). The sequence of texts engages students in the analysis of information presented in a variety of media and formats (**CCSS.ELA-LITERACY.RI.7**).

PART 1

UNDERSTANDING
THE NATURE OF AN ISSUE

"What does it mean when we say something is 'terrorism' and why does it matter?"

OBJECTIVE:	Students apply their close-reading skills to understand a societal issue as a context for various perspectives, positions, and arguments.

MATERIALS:
Text Sets 1 and 2
- *Guiding Questions Handout*
- *Questioning Path Tool*
- *Forming EBC Tool*

- *Organizing EBC Tool*
- *EBA terms*

LITERACY SKILLS

TARGETED SKILLS	DESCRIPTORS
FORMING CLAIMS	Establishes and presents a clear and defensible position that is supported by a series of valid claims (premises) and set in the context of the topic
USING EVIDENCE	Presents a comprehensive view of the issue by providing textual evidence to support claims and using sufficient and accurate quotations, paraphrases, and references

ACADEMIC HABITS

HABITS DEVELOPED	DESCRIPTORS
REMAINING OPEN	Adopts a stance of inquiry—asking questions to learn more—rather than arguing for entrenched positions

ALIGNMENT TO CCSS

TARGETED STANDARDS:

CCSS.ELA-LITERACY.RI.9-10.1: Cite strong and thorough textual evidence to support analysis of what the text says explicitly as well as inferences drawn from the text.

CCSS.ELA-LITERACY.RI.9-10.2: Determine a central idea of a text and analyze its development over the course of the text, including how it emerges and is shaped and refined by specific details; provide an objective summary of the text.

CCSS.ELA-LITERACY.RI.9-10.3: Analyze how the author unfolds an analysis or series of ideas or events, including the order in which the points are made, how they are introduced and developed, and the connections that are drawn between them.

CCSS.ELA-LITERACY.W.9-10.2: Write informative/explanatory texts to examine and convey complex ideas, concepts, and information clearly and accurately through the effective selection, organization, and analysis of content.

SUPPORTING STANDARDS:

CCSS.ELA-LITERACY.SL.9-10.1: Initiate and participate effectively in a range of collaborative discussions (one-on-one, in groups, and teacher-led) with diverse partners on *grades 9–10 topics, texts, and issues*, building on others' ideas and expressing their own clearly and persuasively.

CCSS.ELA-LITERACY.RI.9-10.4: Determine the meaning of words and phrases as they are used in a text, including figurative, connotative, and technical meanings; analyze the cumulative impact of specific word choices on meaning and tone (e.g., how the language of a court opinion differs from that of a newspaper).

ACTIVITIES

1. INTRODUCING THE UNIT
The teacher presents an overview of the unit and its societal issue.

2. EXPLORING THE ISSUE
Students read and analyze a background text to develop an initial understanding of the issue.

3. DEEPENING UNDERSTANDING OF THE ISSUE
Students read and analyze an additional background text from Text Set 2 to expand and deepen their understanding of the issue.

4. QUESTIONING TO REFINE UNDERSTANDING
Students develop text-dependent questions and use them to refine their analysis.

5. WRITING AN EBC ABOUT THE NATURE OF THE ISSUE
Students develop and write multipart evidence-based claims about the nature of the issue.

ACTIVITY 1: INTRODUCING THE UNIT

The teacher presents an overview of the unit and its societal issue.

INSTRUCTIONAL NOTES

Introduce Argumentation

Introduce the central purpose of the unit: to develop, practice, and apply the skills of argumentation in the context of a societal issue by doing the following:

1. Understanding the nature of a challenging issue for which there are various perspectives and positions
2. Understanding and comparing perspectives and arguments on the issue
3. Developing an evidence-based position on the issue
4. Linking claims as premises in an evidence-based argument for one's position
5. Supporting one's premises with logical reasoning and relevant evidence
6. Writing and revising an argumentative essay

Emphasize that in this unit, students will learn and think about a complex societal issue for which there are many explanations, perspectives, and opinions, not simply two sides of an argument to be debated. Let them know that they will read and research to better understand the issue and various perspectives on it *before* they form a position of their own and develop an argument in support of that position. Explain that the unit will culminate in a collaborative process for developing and strengthening an argumentative essay that each student will write on the unit's societal issue.

- Establish a clear definition of the term *issue* in general. An issue can be defined as *an important aspect of human society for which there are many differing opinions on an appropriate course of action*. Brainstorming a list of societal issues might be helpful.
- Using examples from various fields and topical areas, discuss the general question, "How do strategic thinkers discuss and understand challenging issues or problems?" Brainstorm a list of approaches and skills used by experts who regularly have to propose and support responses to issues or problems.

Present the Topic

The topic area and texts focus on terrorism and, more specifically, what is meant by terrorism, the events leading up to 9/11, an analysis of the responses to the attacks, and terrorism in context of the recent developments in war. Responses to terrorism, and policy related to and resulting from terrorism, is a complex topic with many perspectives and positions—not a simple pro and con arena for debate—which enables the teacher and students to approach and study the issue from many possible angles.

Formulate a Problem-Based Question

Formulate a problem-based question from which students can begin their discussions, reading, and development of an argumentative position. Choose or develop a general, though still focused, question that causes students to think about the problem with many directions for argumentation and that connects to students' backgrounds and interests. This might be done as a class, in groups, or individually, accompanied with a discussion on what students already know or want to know about the topic. An example or option for problem-based questions is as follows:

- How does a government decide whether a violent attack can be considered terrorism, and how does this decision influence the government's response? What are appropriate responses to terrorist attacks?

If this question is selected, or a similar one developed, provide a little background to get students thinking. In this case, showing them a video entitled "Proportional Response" from Season 1, Episode 3 on the television series *West Wing* [video is 2:28 long and can be found on YouTube. com]. In this scene, President Bartlet asks his military staff in the situation room after the United States has recently been attacked, "What is the virtue of a proportional response?"

Formulate a Text-Specific Question

As students analyze the *West Wing* video, they can apply the text-questioning skills they have developed in previous Developing Core Literacy Proficiency units. They will be using these skills more independently in the context of analyzing and evaluating arguments. As an opportunity to review the text-questioning process, the video provides a first opportunity for close reading and analysis, using a text-specific question set such as these:

- In the video, President Bartlet asks his military staff, "What is the virtue of a proportional response?" How do he and his staff define the concept?
- How does "proportional response" apply to the subject of terrorism?

Let students know that they will be returning to these questions often as they read texts related to terrorism. Emphasize that their task in this argumentation unit is not simply to answer them but rather to use them as a stimulus for reading and discussion. Thinking about these questions as they read, analyze, and discuss will lead them eventually to a perspective on terrorism and finally to a position about current decisions related to terrorism and war from which they can build an evidence-based argument.

KWL

Teachers might choose to introduce the topic by using an activity such as a KWL, class brainstorm, image brainstorm, or freewrite to help students access their prior knowledge of the subject. These activities can help bring to light erroneous prior conceptions of the topic that can be addressed as students study it further.

ACTIVITY 2: EXPLORING THE ISSUE

Students read and analyze a background text to develop an initial understanding of the issue.

INSTRUCTIONAL NOTES

NOTE ON USING TEXT SETS

Instruction in this unit links to a sequence of text sets. Each text set provides multiple entry points into the issue, giving teachers and students flexibility with respect to the time and depth with which they wish to explore the topic.

> **NOTE**
>
> All students should not be required to read all texts.

All students should not be required to read all texts.

As with all text sets, teachers may choose to use Text Set 1: Background Informational Texts in a variety of ways:

1. Select one of the three texts for all students to read, analyze, and discuss. Provide links to the other two so that students can do additional reading if desired.
2. Have all students read, analyze, and discuss all three texts (or two of the three) in a more extended instructional time sequence.
3. Place students in expert groups and have them read and analyze one of the three texts. Then have students jigsaw into cross-text discussion groups to share and compare what they have learned from the text each has read.

> **NOTE**
>
> Students might be grouped by reading level and assigned texts based on their complexity or difficulty.

4. Use the text set as a model only and substitute other, similar background texts.

TEXT NOTES AND MODEL QUESTIONING PATHS

In previous Developing Core Literacy Proficiencies units, students have been provided with comprehensive sets of text-dependent questions organized in model Questioning Paths to scaffold and guide them through multiple, progressively closer readings of texts. By this unit, students should have begun to develop independence as readers who can approach and initially question any text. They should be bringing useful questions from such handouts as the **Guiding Questions** and **Assessing Sources Handouts** into their reading processes, and they should not require prescriptive scaffolding. However, students will also be reading, analyzing, and evaluating complex arguments in this unit, perhaps for the first time. They may need the support of text-dependent questions that help them attend to the elements and reasoning within arguments.

For this reason, the **EBA Toolbox** contains abbreviated versions of the model *Questioning Path Tools* found in other units. These resources include suggested Guiding Questions for analyzing arguments and a few model text-specific questions for deepening students' understanding of specific aspects of the arguments they will read closely. Students may be expected to use their own processes and questions as they approach and initially question the texts—or the teacher can scaffold their reading by providing a reading purpose, background information about the text, and one or two initial Guiding Questions to initiate the multistage close-reading process.

TEXT NOTES: TEXT SET 1

BACKGROUND INFORMATIONAL TEXTS

Text Set 1 includes three texts that can be used to provide initial background information about terrorism including what constitutes an act of terror (terrorist act), whether foreign or domestic, and whether all acts that cause fear can be considered as terrorism.

Text 1.1: "What Is Terrorism?"

Author: Laura Beth Nielsen, associate professor of sociology and director of legal studies, Northwestern University, and research professor for the American Bar Foundation

Source/Publisher: Aljazeera.com

Date: April 17, 2013

Complexity level: The text measures at 1200L and should be accessible to most ninth-grade students.

Text Notes

This text introduces the question of what is terrorism and what constitutes a terrorist act. It addresses several historical "terrorist" acts students may need to investigate and discusses the various claims made about those acts and whether they were indeed terrorist acts or not. The author also explains why it is important to arrive at a clearer understanding of the term *terrorism* when talking about violent events on the national level.

APPROACHING:
I determine my reading purposes and take note of key information about the text. I identify the LIPS domain(s) that will guide my initial reading.

QUESTIONING: *I use Guiding Questions to help me investigate the text (from the **Guiding Questions Handout**).*

ANALYZING: *I question further to connect and analyze the details I find (from the **Guiding Questions Handout**).*

1. How might I summarize the main ideas of the text and the key supporting details?

2. How do the text's main ideas relate to what I already know, think, or have read?

3. In what way are ideas, events, and claims linked together in the text?

DEEPENING: *I consider the questions of others.*

4. Throughout the article, the author asks several questions. Why does the author do this? How do the questions develop the author's point of view about the complexity of terrorism?

5. Toward the end of the article the author asks, "What work is the word 'terrorism' doing in these conversations?" How does the author use the word *work* in the context of this question?

EXTENDING: *I pose my own questions.*

6. What evidence does this text provide that builds my understanding of the issue of terrorism?

Text 1.2: "Terrorists or Freedom Fighters: What's the Difference?"

Author: John Bolt

Source/Publisher: Acton Institute (Acton.org)

Date: November 14, 2001

Complexity level: This text measures at 1070L. Because of some domain-specific vocabulary and new concepts (e.g., freedom fighter, deadly sins, oppressed/ marginalized people), this text might challenge some ninth-grade readers. Teachers might pre-teach the vocabulary or assign the text in heterogeneous reading teams.

Text Notes

This text attempts to distinguish the difference between a terrorist and a freedom fighter by considering the differing philosophical motives of both, specifically envy versus greed. The difference between the two will be important for students to discuss, especially in light of the 9/11 terrorist attacks, as addressed in the text. This text enables students to think about the motives of terrorists versus freedom fighters and how those motives can play a role in how others respond to the acts committed by both groups.

QUESTIONING PATH TOOL

Text 1.2—"Terrorists or Freedom Fighters: What's the Difference?"

APPROACHING:
I determine my reading purposes and take note of key information about the text. I identify the LIPS domain(s) that will guide my initial reading.

QUESTIONING: *I use Guiding Questions to help me investigate the text (from the **Guiding Questions Handout**).*

ANALYZING: *I question further to connect and analyze the details I find (from the **Guiding Questions Handout**).*

1. How might I summarize the main ideas of the text and the key supporting details?

2. How does the author's choice of words reveal his purposes and perspective?

3. What evidence supports the claims in the text, and what is left uncertain or unsupported?

DEEPENING: *I consider the questions of others.*

4. The author uses the word *perception* to explain the difference between a terrorist and freedom fighter. What does he mean by "perception" and how does this contrast with a "metaphysical difference"?

5. How does the author use two of the seven deadly sins (greed and envy) to characterize terrorists and freedom fighters? How does he use one of the sins to ultimately categorize those who carried out the attacks of 9/11?

EXTENDING: *I pose my own questions.*

6. What evidence does this text provide that builds my understanding of the issue of terrorism?

Developing Core Literacy Proficiencies

Text 1.3: "Militant Extremists in the United States"

Author: Jonathan Masters;

Source/Publisher: Council on Foreign Relations (cfr.org)

Date: February 7, 2011

Complexity level: The text measures at 1470L. Although this text is more complex, the headings and subheadings help organize the information into sections. Students could jigsaw the article, each group focusing on different sections.

Text Notes

This text provides an overview of the distinction between "domestic terrorism" and "violent extremism." It also lists four categories of domestic extremists that will help students understand the different nuances to the concept of terrorism. The article also introduces or reinforces students' knowledge of several cases of violent acts that are often included in conversations about terrorism.

QUESTIONING PATH TOOL

Text 1.3— "Militant Extremists in the United States"

APPROACHING:
I determine my reading purposes and take note of key information about the text. I identify the LIPS domain(s) that will guide my initial reading.

QUESTIONING: *I use Guiding Questions to help me investigate the text (from the **Guiding Questions Handout**).*

ANALYZING: *I question further to connect and analyze the details I find (from the **Guiding Questions Handout**).*

1. How might I summarize the main ideas of the text and the key supporting details?

2. In what ways are ideas, events, and claims linked together in the text?

DEEPENING: *I consider the questions of others.*

3. The author uses the words *terrorist* and *extremist* throughout the article. What distinctions, if any, are drawn between the two concepts?

4. According to the article, what are some of the outcomes of this new era of facing terrorism?

EXTENDING: *I pose my own questions.*

5. What evidence does this text provide that builds my understanding of the issue of terrorism?

Developing Core Literacy Proficiencies

READING

Students initially read one or more of the texts independently, annotating and making notes on how the text relates to the unit's problem-based question.

- Following the initial reading of each text, students discuss its relationship to the unit's problem-based question. These discussions can involve the entire class (if all students have read the text) or can occur in reading teams (if only some students have read it).

- Introduce one or more text-specific questions (from the Deepening sections of the model Questioning Paths) to drive a closer reading of the text(s). Students reread (or follow along as the text is presented to them), considering the new text-specific question(s).

- In reading teams, students discuss the Deepening text-based questions and search for relevant details, annotating and making notes for their text.

- As a class, students return to the unit's problem-based question and discuss what they have learned about the issue from closely reading the background texts.

WRITING CLAIMS

Having read and discussed one or more of the background texts, students will now form a claim that explains something they have learned about the issue. At this point, students' claims should be *explanatory* in nature, not *evaluative* or *argumentative*. Students are only beginning to develop background understanding of the issue from which to read further and eventually develop a position. They should practice the Academic Habit of **Remaining Open** to new information and thinking about the issue.

- Introduce and discuss the Academic Habit of **Remaining Open**. Discuss that exploring an issue starts with gathering as much information as possible before developing one's own position on the issue. Remaining open to multiple perspectives enables one's understanding to grow by not closing off paths of inquiry and exploration, including self-exploration. Discuss how the habit of **Remaining Open** can apply to new information and ideas as well as the various perspectives of source texts they will read and of their peers. Considering the unit topic issue of terrorism, have students suggest examples (and nonexamples) of what the habit of **Remaining Open** might mean.

- For one of the texts from Text Set 1, model the development and writing of an explanatory claim that addresses something the text has presented about the unit's issue. The claim is explanatory, not argumentative at this point.

- Students individually develop explanatory claims about a text they have read and analyzed, explaining something it has presented about the issue and citing specific details and evidence from the text(s) for support (a **Forming EBC Tool** can be used).

- In reading teams, students compare claims and the evidence they have found to derive and support them. Teams may be organized by common texts or in a jigsaw format if students have read different texts.

Examples of explanatory claims for Text 1.1: "What is Terrorism?" might be as follows:

- The article "What Is Terrorism?" explains that it is not always clear what crimes or violent acts can be classified as terrorism because the term is used so broadly in different types of situations.

- In the article "What Is Terrorism?" the author points to the ambiguity of the definition of *terrorism* and *terrorist* by answering several rhetorical questions.

> **NOTE**
>
> Emphasize that at this point in the process, student claims should focus on interpreting what the text says about the nature of the issue, not on the validity of the text's perspective or position and not on articulating the student's own, still-developing position. Those sorts of claims will come later.

STUDENT PORTFOLIOS

As students explore additional texts about the issue, they will begin to collect text annotations, responses to questions, tools, claims, and written exercises. Either suggest or require that students keep an organized portfolio of their work. This will help them immensely as they compile these materials to generate their own position on the issue and write their argumentative essay.

☰ ACTIVITY 3: DEEPENING ☰ UNDERSTANDING OF THE ISSUE

Students read and analyze an additional background text from Text Set 2 to expand and deepen their understanding of the issue.

TEXT NOTES: TEXT SET 2

Text Set 2 includes texts that can be used to provide additional background information about terrorism and more specifically the subtopic area of the events of September 11, 2001.

Text 2.1: "Major Terrorism Cases: Past and Present"

Author: Federal Bureau of Investigation

Source/Publisher: FBI.gov

Date: NA

Complexity level: These texts should be accessible to most ninth-graders.

 Text Notes

This website by the FBI contains several links under the "terrorism" category that provide stories and accounts of many different terrorist attacks in the United States. This site should be used prior to learning about 9/11 because it gives students background information on different types of terrorist attacks as defined by the FBI, including the USS *Cole* bombing, the 1993 World Trade Center bombing, and the Oklahoma City bombing. The site also gives a historical perspective to the issue of terrorism because it includes cases back to the 1920s. This website can be used for students to learn about other terrorists acts including domestic acts of terrorism.

≡ QUESTIONING PATH TOOL

Text 2.1—"Major Terrorism Cases: Past and Present"

APPROACHING:
I determine my reading purposes and take note of key information about the text. I identify the LIPS domain(s) that will guide my initial reading.

QUESTIONING: *I use Guiding Questions to help me investigate the text (from the Guiding Questions Handout).*

ANALYZING: *I question further to connect and analyze the details I find (from the Guiding Questions Handout).*

1. How might I summarize the main ideas of the text and the key supporting details?

2. How does the text's language influence my understanding of important ideas or themes?

DEEPENING: *I consider the questions of others.*

3. How does the FBI develop their point of view or perspective in their descriptions of the various terrorist attacks?

EXTENDING: *I pose my own questions.*

4. What evidence does this text provide that builds my understanding of the issue of terrorism?

Text 2.2: "9/11: Timeline of Events"

Author/Source: History.com

Publisher: History.com

Date: NA

Complexity level: NA

Text Notes

The unit focuses on terrorism as a subject, so it is important that students have an understanding of the events of 9/11—a day that has a tremendous impact on how the United States thinks of war and terrorism. This website has several multimedia sources that students can use to explore the events of 9/11. The videos should be used in conjunction with the background text. These are primary source and informational videos that include some footage from the day and also reenactments of some of the events of the day.

QUESTIONING PATH TOOL

Text 2.2—"9/11: Timeline of Events"

APPROACHING:
I determine my reading purposes and take note of key information about the text. I identify the LIPS domain(s) that will guide my initial reading.

QUESTIONING: *I use Guiding Questions to help me investigate the text (from the **Guiding Questions Handout**).*

ANALYZING: *I question further to connect and analyze the details I find (from the **Guiding Questions Handout**).*

1. How might I summarize the main ideas of the text and the key supporting details?

2. In what ways are ideas, events, and claims linked together in the text?

DEEPENING: *I consider the questions of others.*

3. How do the images and information presented in the time line fit the description of terrorism that you are familiar with or have read about in this unit so far?

EXTENDING: *I pose my own questions.*

4. What evidence does this text provide that builds my understanding of the issue of terrorism?

Text 2.3: "September 11 Attacks Timeline"

Author/Source/Publisher: National September 11 Memorial and Museum, available at 911memorial.org.

Date: NA

Complexity level: This time line and accompanying text and multimedia are very accessible to students.

Text Notes

This time line is part of the National September 11 Memorial and Museum and provides a rich and detailed account of the events of 9/11. At each slide in the time line, students are able to click on sound, photo, and video files that are all accompanied by short descriptions.

≡ QUESTIONING PATH TOOL
Text 2.3—"September 11 Attacks Timeline"

APPROACHING: *I determine my reading purposes and take note of key information about the text. I identify the LIPS domain(s) that will guide my initial reading.*

QUESTIONING: *I use Guiding Questions to help me investigate the text (from the **Guiding Questions Handout**).*

ANALYZING: *I question further to connect and analyze the details I find (from the **Guiding Questions Handout**).*

1. How might I summarize the main ideas of the text and the key supporting details?

2. In what ways are ideas, events, and claims linked together in the text?

DEEPENING: *I consider the questions of others.*

3. How do the images and information presented in the time line fit the description of 9/11 or terrorism that you are familiar with or have read about in this unit so far?

EXTENDING: *I pose my own questions.*

4. What evidence does this text provide that builds my understanding of the issue of terrorism?

READING

Students read one or more additional background texts from Text Set 2 independently, annotating and making notes about how it relates to questions from the model Questioning Path the unit's problem-based question. Similar to Text Set 1, teachers may choose to use Text Set 2: Additional Background Informational Texts in a variety of ways:

1. Select one of the three texts for all students to read, analyze, and discuss. Provide links to the other two so that students can do additional reading if desired.
2. Have all students read, analyze, and discuss all three texts (or two of the three) in a more extended instructional time sequence.
3. Place students in expert groups and have them read and analyze one of the three texts. Then have students jigsaw into cross-text discussion groups to share and compare what they have learned from the text each has read.
4. Use the text set as a model only and substitute other, similar background texts.

NOTE

Students might be grouped by reading level and assigned texts based on their complexity or difficulty.

- Introduce one or more text-based questions to drive a closer reading of the text. Students then follow along as the text is presented to them.
- In reading teams, students discuss the text-based questions and search for relevant details, highlighting and annotating them in their text. (Students might use a **Forming EBC Tool** to record their thinking.)

WRITING CLAIMS

Having read and discussed several more focused background texts, students will now form a second claim that explains something they have learned about the issue. At this point, students' claims continue to be *explanatory* in nature, not *evaluative* or *argumentative*. Students are building background understanding of the issue from which to read further and eventually develop a position. They should continue to practice the Academic Habit of **Remaining Open** to new information and thinking about the issue.

- Model the development and writing of an explanatory claim that addresses something one of the texts has presented about the unit's issue.
- Students individually develop explanatory claims about one of the texts and its presentation of the issue, citing specific details and evidence to support their explanatory claim (a **Forming EBC Tool** can be used).
- In reading teams, students compare claims and the evidence they have found to derive and support them.

An example of an explanatory claim about the nature of the issue or problem might be as follows:

- The 9/11 time lines show that it was not until later, after the attacks, that Americans became aware that the events of the day might be associated with terrorism.

NOTE

Emphasize again that student claims should focus on interpreting what the text says about the nature of the issue, not on the validity of the text's perspective or position and not on articulating the student's own, still-developing position. Those sorts of claims will come later.

≡ ACTIVITY 4: QUESTIONING TO REFINE ≡ UNDERSTANDING

Students develop text-specific questions and use them to refine their analysis.

INSTRUCTIONAL NOTES

QUESTIONING TEXTS

Students now apply skills they have developed in the *Reading Closely for Textual Details* and *Researching to Deepen Understanding* units to frame their own, more focused questions about the issue and texts. They use these questions to drive a deeper reading of the previous texts or of additional texts providing more background and perspectives on the topic. Students can continue to use the **Guiding Questions Handout** and **Questioning Path Tool** to guide and track their questioning of any given text, using the Extending area to note their own text-specific question related to the problem or issue.

- Starting from the unit's problem-based question, students work in reading teams to develop a set of more focused text-specific questions to drive further inquiry into the issue. These questions should address areas of the topic students feel they need to explore to understand the issue.

- Individually, students can use these new questions to reread or review *one of the background texts,* find additional details, and further refine their explanatory claim.

If additional background information is necessary or desired, students can also use their question sets to drive close reading and analysis of one or more additional texts.

NOTE

Suggested texts are listed in the instructional notes or may be identified by the teacher or found by the students. Students might work in teams to become experts and develop explanatory claims about one or more of these additional texts, then jigsaw into new groups and share what they have learned. In this way, all students can become familiar with a wider range of background texts.

- Students write or revise one or more explanatory claim(s) based on additional evidence they have found through further or deeper reading.

ADDITIONAL BACKGROUND TEXTS

To expand their understanding of the topic, students might be assigned any of the texts from Text Sets 1 and 2 that have *not* been read by the class. They might also access other sources found by the teacher (or by students themselves) or the additional sources listed in the unit texts list (indicated by "AT").

These additional source texts provide supplementary and different information about terrorism as a legal term and events that shape our understanding of terrorism. These sources can be used to expand students' understanding and used as independent reading or research assignments. The definition of *international terrorism*, as provided by Cornell Law, is from the US Code and can be used to provide students with further clarity about how terrorism is defined while also reminding them that the term is a legal one that is vital for court cases. "A Brief History of Terrorism in the United States" by Brian Resnick gives a brief summary of several attacks, domestic and international, on the United States. CNN's "USS *Cole* Bombing Fast Facts" provides information on the USS *Cole* attack in Yemen, which many consider to be a factor leading to 9/11. Finally, the About.com time line, "The History of Terrorism" by Amy Zalman, gives an even broader, historical view of terrorism and helps further define the term in its modern development.

ACTIVITY 5: WRITING AN EBC ABOUT THE NATURE OF THE ISSUE

Students develop and write multipart evidence-based claims about the nature of the issue.

INSTRUCTIONAL NOTES

In the culminating activity for Part 1, students now develop a more global claim about the nature of the issue that they will expand and revise when drafting their final argument. Before they can take a position and make their case for a response, they must be able to use evidence to explain their understanding of the issue or problem.

- Model the development of an evidence-based claim that combines information from multiple sources and demonstrates an understanding of the unit's issue.

- The model could use a *Forming EBC Tool* and details from more than one text to form a global claim.

- Alternately, use an *Organizing EBC Tool (2 or 3 Points)* to demonstrate how the overall claim might be built from two or more supporting claims. Begin by writing down supporting claims that may have arisen from students' initial claims about the background texts. Using these, a more global claim might be formed.

- In reading teams, students go back to the background texts, their annotations, and notes to find additional evidence and details that support a global claim. (A *Forming* or *Organizing EBC Tool* can be used to record key details.)

- In reading teams, students do the following:
  ⇒ Review the explanatory claims they wrote about each text.
  ⇒ Brainstorm alternative ways of viewing or understanding the problem, based on evidence from the background texts.

- Remind students that they are practicing the Academic Habit of **Remaining Open**. Their claims should be written in a way that *describes the nature of the issue without defining a particular position*.

- Individually, students use an *Organizing EBC Tool* (or *Forming EBC Tool*) to develop a global claim that presents how they have come (so far) to view and understand the nature of the issue and its components.

- In reading teams, students compare their global claims and the evidence that supports them.

- As a formative assessment and a building block for their final argument (in Part 5), students write a one- to three-paragraph explanation of their multipart claim about the nature of the issue, organized by their thinking on the *Forming* or *Organizing EBC Tool*. This written explanation of their EBC should do the following:
  ⇒ Present what they have learned about the nature of the unit's issue.
  ⇒ Present their current way of understanding the issue and its components.
  ⇒ Present evidence from multiple sources that explains and supports their understanding.
  ⇒ Represent their best thinking and clearest writing.

- As a class, return to the unit's problem-based question (or question set) to consider revising the question(s) based on the emerging understanding of the issue.

≡ PART 1: FORMATIVE ASSESSMENT ≡ OPPORTUNITIES

By the end of Part 1, students will have produced these items:

- *Questioning Path Tool* (if they have used this tool to record their questions)
- Evidence-based claims about two background texts (*Forming EBC Tools*)
- *Organizing EBC Tools*
- Final written EBC about the nature of the issue

LITERACY SKILLS

Focus self-, peer, and teacher assessment at the end of Part 1 on the targeted skills of **Forming Claims** and **Using Evidence**. Examine students' claims for their respective background texts to see how well they are identifying and analyzing details.

As a formative assessment for these targeted skills, review students' global claims about the issue. The multipart claim should do the following:

- Synthesize what they have learned about the nature of the unit's issue.
- Present their current way of understanding the issue and its components.

- Cite evidence from multiple sources that explains and substantiates their understanding.
- Represent their best thinking and clearest writing.

Use their writing to formatively assess their basic understanding of the topic as well as their development of the **Forming Claims** and **Using Evidence Literacy Skills**.

ACADEMIC HABITS

Continue to focus on the Academic Habit of **Remaining Open**. As a class, reflect on how well students have remained open to information about the issue without predetermining their positions. As students complete their explanatory claims about various texts and synthesis claim about the issue, they can reflect on how well they have remained open to understanding the issue based on what they have read or viewed in the unit. They will be developing this habit within the unit's activities and initially demonstrating their development in Part 5 when they express their position on the issue in an argumentative essay.

Academic Habits—Student Reflection Question

- How have I remained open to new ideas and information I have read on the issue or problem?

NOTE

To support self-, peer, and teacher assessment of skills and habits developed during the unit, a formal *EBA Literacy Skills and Academic Habits Rubric* and less formal *Student Checklist* are provided in the **EBA Literacy Toolbox**.

ANALYZING ARGUMENTS

"They [terrorists] are usually clever enough to cloak their motives by hijacking the popular will of an oppressed people, but their wrath is not appeased when they acquire what they say they want."

OBJECTIVE:	Students delineate and analyze the position, premises, reasoning, evidence, and perspective of arguments.

MATERIALS:

Text Sets 3 through 5
- *Guiding Questions Handout*
- *Forming EBC Tool*
- *Delineating Arguments Tool*

- *Model Arguments*
- *EBA Terms*

OPTIONAL:
- *Questioning Path Tool*

- *Organizing EBC Tool*

≣ LITERACY SKILLS

TARGETED SKILLS	DESCRIPTORS
FORMING CLAIMS	Establishes and presents a clear and defensible position that is supported by a series of valid claims (premises) and set in the context of the topic
USING EVIDENCE	Presents a comprehensive view of the issue by providing textual evidence to support claims and using sufficient and accurate quotations, paraphrases, and references
RECOGNIZING PERSPECTIVE	Uses textual details to recognize and establish a relationship to and perspective on a topic
DELINEATING ARGUMENTATION	Identifies and analyzes the components and accuracy of claims, evidence, and reasoning in explanations and arguments

ACADEMIC HABITS

HABITS DEVELOPED	DESCRIPTORS
REMAINING OPEN	Adopts a stance of inquiry—asking questions to learn more—rather than arguing for entrenched positions

ALIGNMENT TO CCSS

TARGETED STANDARDS:

CCSS.ELA-LITERACY.RI.9-10.6: Determine an author's point of view or purpose in a text and analyze how an author uses rhetoric to advance that point of view or purpose.

CCSS.ELA-LITERACY.RI.9-10.8: Delineate and evaluate the argument and specific claims in a text, assessing whether the reasoning is valid and the evidence is relevant and sufficient; identify false statements and fallacious reasoning.

CCSS.ELA-LITERACY.RI.9-10.9: Analyze seminal U.S. documents of historical and literary significance (e.g., Washington's Farewell Address, the Gettysburg Address, Roosevelt's Four Freedoms speech, King's "Letter from Birmingham Jail"), including how they address related themes and concepts.

CCSS.ELA-LITERACY.W.9-10.2: Write informative/explanatory texts to examine and convey complex ideas, concepts, and information clearly and accurately through the effective selection, organization, and analysis of content.

SUPPORTING STANDARDS:

CCSS.ELA-LITERACY.RI.9-10.1: Cite strong and thorough textual evidence to support analysis of what the text says explicitly as well as inferences drawn from the text.

CCSS.ELA-LITERACY.RI.9-10.2: Determine a central idea of a text and analyze its development over the course of the text, including how it emerges and is shaped and refined by specific details; provide an objective summary of the text.

CCSS.ELA-LITERACY.RI.9-10.3: Analyze how the author unfolds an analysis or series of ideas or events, including the order in which the points are made, how they are introduced and developed, and the connections that are drawn between them.

CCSS.ELA-LITERACY.RI.9-10.4: Determine the meaning of words and phrases as they are used in a text, including figurative, connotative, and technical meanings; analyze the cumulative impact of specific word choices on meaning and tone (e.g., how the language of a court opinion differs from that of a newspaper).

☰ ACTIVITIES

1. UNDERSTANDING ARGUMENTATIVE POSITION
The teacher introduces the concept of an argumentative position through a discussion of the unit's issue.

2. IDENTIFYING ELEMENTS OF AN ARGUMENT
The teacher introduces and the class explores the elements of argumentation in a familiar context.

3. DELINEATING ARGUMENTS
Student teams read and delineate arguments and write evidence-based claims about one author's argument.

4. UNDERSTANDING PERSPECTIVE
The teacher leads an exploration of the concept of perspective in a familiar context.

5. DELINEATING AND COMPARING ARGUMENTS
Students analyze and compare perspectives and positions in argumentative texts.

6. DELINEATING ADDITIONAL ARGUMENTS
As needed, students read and analyze additional arguments related to the unit's issue.

7. WRITING TO ANALYZE ARGUMENTS
Students write short essays analyzing an argument.

≡ ACTIVITY 1: UNDERSTANDING
≡ ARGUMENTATIVE POSITION

The teacher introduces the concept of an argumentative position through a discussion of the unit's issue.

INSTRUCTIONAL NOTES

In Part 2, discussion and instruction shifts from the previous focus on understanding the background and nature of the unit's issue to a focus on the various controversies or differences of opinion that have surrounded the issue and have led to various positions and arguments. The class can now begin to define the issue and identify specific positions about the problem.

POINTS OF CONTROVERSY—CLASS BRAINSTORM

- As a class, brainstorm a list of questions that highlight various points of controversy or debate within the issue. If applicable, this can be related to the initial prior knowledge or KWL activity. Questions might look like the following:
  - ⇒ How do we arrive at a definition of what a terrorist attack is? Does it come down to the amount of or how people are killed? Does the definition rely on the attackers' motives? Does it matter whether they are successful or not?

The questions might address the current realm for debate related to terrorism. For example:

- ⇒ Which violent events today are labeled as terrorist attacks and which are not? Why?
- ⇒ They might also examine aspects of the topic that are more peripheral to the central debate, but may still be very relevant. For example:
- ⇒ Why might it be important to understand why terrorists carry out their attacks?

INTRODUCE THE CONCEPT OF POSITION

All questions, however, should be framed in a manner that accomplishes the following:

1. Suggests multiple ways of responding
2. Prepares students to examine various perspectives from which an answer could come
3. Prepares students to examine various positions that might be taken in response to the topic and question

- Discuss with students how each of the example questions can be responded to in various ways.
- Introduce the term *position,* which can be defined as *someone's stance on what to do or think about a clearly defined issue based on their perspective and understanding of it.* When writing an argumentative essay, one's position may be expressed as a *thesis.*
- Discuss how the term relates to points of controversy in the issue.

ANALYZING POSITIONS—POLITICAL CARTOONS

To begin practicing the skills of analyzing position, students will first look at visual examples of arguments. Political cartoons often address controversial issues about which multiple positions are taken. Although a cartoon is not a formal argument, a political cartoon often combines words and imagery to communicate a stance or position on the issue it addresses—often in an extreme or dramatic way. In the unit topic area of terrorism, there exists a wealth of historical and contemporary political cartoons. By examining them, students can also expand their background knowledge on the issue.

- Distribute Text Set 3, a set of political cartoons related to the unit's issue (or have students navigate to the selected bank of cartoons on the Internet). Use one example to model how the cartoon can be seen as expressing a position on the issue.

- As a class discuss the various positions expressed in example cartoons. Discuss how argumentative essays develop arguments to support positions. Ask if students see the beginnings of any basic arguments to support the position in the visual details or captions of the cartoons, and discuss the evidence they identify.

TEXT NOTES: TEXT SET 3

Text 3.1: "Political Cartoons: The Human Aspect of Modern Conflict"

Source/Publisher: College of Education at the University of Texas—Austin

Date: N/A

Text Notes

In Part 2, students move from reading to build their background knowledge about the issue and problem to reading for analysis of topical arguments. Initially, their focus should be on determining the position an argument takes on the issue. To develop and practice their analytical reading skills, students can first work with relatively simple, skeletal arguments—either short passages that clearly communicate a position or political cartoons that visually represent their positions and may therefore be more readily accessible to some students.

Recommended is a site with political cartoons from the University of Texas. The teacher (and students) can browse this source and find cartoons that relate to the unit's focus, the problem-based question, and the set of debatable questions generated in Activity 1. Teachers are encouraged to conduct their own web searches in order to include the most current political cartoons or cartoons appropriate for the specific classroom context.

Once cartoons are selected, students should read them closely by visually scanning for key details and presentation techniques, considering also any text that may be presented with the cartoon. Ideally a cartoon set will provide examples that come from several different perspectives and take several different positions as they communicate political commentary through their imagery and words.

- Model how one can read a cartoon and its details to determine the point or commentary communicated by the cartoon and thus determine its position (which may or may not be stated). Finally, model how a cartoon artist presents visual details as evidence that establishes and supports the cartoon's position. In groups, students can use questions to drive discussions about the positions reflected in the cartoons on the issue.

Guiding Questions

- Following this modeling and some guided practice, students might then work in teams with a cartoon set. The questioning and analysis sequence might begin with a general text question(s) from the **Guiding Questions Handout**, such as these:
  1. What words, phrases, or images stand out to me as powerful and important?
  2. What details or words suggest the author's perspective?
  3. What seems to be the author's (narrator's) attitude or point of view?

☰ ACTIVITY 2: IDENTIFYING ELEMENTS OF ARGUMENTATION

The teacher introduces and the class explores the elements of argumentation in a familiar context.

INSTRUCTIONAL NOTES

INTRODUCE THE ELEMENTS OF ARGUMENTATION

Once students have a good understanding of the concept of a position on an issue and the idea that positions are supported with argumentation, instruction can shift to the specific elements authors use to explain and defend their positions. The objective of this activity is for students to have a solid conceptual understanding of the elements of an argument and to be able to use a set of terms to identify and analyze arguments. The terms for elements of argumentation used in this ninth-grade unit are as follows:

- Issue
- Relationship To Issue
- Perspective
- Position
- Thesis
- Implications
- Premises

- Evidence
- Reasoning
- Chain Of Reasoning
- Claim
- Evidence-Based Claim

These terms are defined in a handout entitled **Evidence-Based Arguments Terms**, available at the end of this Teacher's Edition and in the Student Edition for this unit.

Teachers may have already worked with students using different nomenclature and might elect to use that terminology instead. For instance, some might call a *position* a *thesis,* and the *claims* that make up an argument might be called the argument's *premises.* Whatever nomenclature a teacher chooses, it should be used consistently so students develop an understanding and facility with the terminology.

- Introduce and describe how authors explain and defend their positions with a series of linked *claims* (or *premises),* developed through a *chain of reasoning,* and supported by *evidence.* When introducing these concepts, it may be best to model and practice their use with familiar topics from students' personal experiences and everyday life that do not require background information.
- For this reason, several model arguments (in the **EBA Literacy Toolbox**) are provided with the unit. These model arguments address issues about Facebook, Twitter, School Conflict and Course Scheduling.

PRACTICE USING ARGUMENTATION TERMS WITH EVERYDAY, MODEL ARGUMENTS

Students read a model argument to practice identifying the elements of argumentation and using the academic vocabulary associated with those elements. Teachers or students might also create their own scenarios that highlight more familiar arguments.

DELINEATING ARGUMENTS TOOL

A **Delineating Arguments Tool** (in the **EBA Literacy Toolbox**) can be used to support instruction and students' analysis of the model arguments. This graphic organizer includes places to record sentences or notes that represent what the *issue* is, what a particular *perspective* on that issue is, and what *position* concerning the issue is established in the argument. The tool then provides spaces for recording the claims and evidence that support the position. Students may record their thinking on the tool in various ways. They might first identify evidence and then claims, as they have previously when using the **Analyzing Details** and **Forming Claims Tools**, then deduce the argument's position from the claims and evidence (working from bottom to top of the tool). Or, for more transparent arguments, they might first identify the position when it is stated early in the argument, then record claims and evidence as they are introduced to support the position (working from top to bottom).

Students can use this tool to take structured notes specific to an argument while also practicing the use of argumentation terms such as *perspective, position,* and *claim*. As mentioned previously, students do not always need to fill the tool in from top to bottom but might work on identifying claims first and then deducing what the author's perspective is. The teacher might encourage students to write down the issue as defined by the author so that his or her perspective might be more readily understood.

PRACTICE USING ARGUMENTATION TERMS AND DELINEATING ARGUMENTS

For this activity, focus on the terms *position, claim,* and *evidence*. Have the students read one or more of the model arguments.

- If using the **Guiding Questions Handout** and **Questioning Path Tool**, teachers can guide students to use questions related to argumentation from the ideas and structure columns.

Guiding Questions (from the *Guiding Questions Handout*)

1. What claims do I find in the text?
2. What evidence supports the claims in the text, and what is left uncertain or unsupported?
3. In what ways are ideas and claims linked together in the text?

Modeling the Tool

- After students read the model argument, the teacher models how to use the **Delineating Arguments Tool** to think about the elements of the argument.
- Create a model **Delineating Arguments Tool** for one of the model arguments.
- Begin by showing students a basic example of the **Delineating Arguments Tool** and its use.
- Talk through the tool by associating each section with the model argument's *issue* and the *position* and *claims* presented by one of the characters (for the Facebook model argument, this might be the teacher's position).

Independent Practice with the Tool

- Now, on a blank tool, students can delineate the second position expressed in the model argument (for Facebook, the student's position) by writing down the *position* and *claims (they can come back to perspective later)*.
- Finally, have students identify and discuss *alternative* premises and evidence to defend the same position and the reasoning that would connect them.
- In reading teams, have students work with blank tools to develop a *different position* and *argument* on the issue. (For the Facebook model, this, for example, might be what the student's parents could argue.)
- Have reading teams present their positions and arguments, explaining each element: *position, claims,* and *evidence*. As a class, discuss the way the reading teams used each element as they built an alternative argument.

- Encourage students to use the vocabulary terms they have learned. Write the new vocabulary on the board so they can use the words as references for discussion.
- Once students have some facility with the elements, explain to them that they will be using the terminology to analyze and compare various arguments related to the unit's issue.

ACTIVITY 3: DELINEATING ARGUMENTS

Student teams read and delineate arguments and write evidence-based claims about one author's argument.

Students next read and analyze Text 4.1, an accessible, foundational argument related to the unit's issue. Use text-dependent questions to help students attend to key details related to the argument's position, claims (premises), structure and reasoning, and supporting evidence. Emphasize that at this point students are reading to *delineate* and not yet *evaluate* the argument.

TEXT NOTES: TEXT SET 4

Text 4.1: "Authorization for Use of Military Force"

Author: Public Law 107—40

Source/Publisher: 107th Congress, gpo.gov, fas.org

Date: 9/18/2001

Text Notes

This document is the law expressing the resolution of the 107th Congress to authorize President Bush to use the United States Armed Forces against those responsible for the attacks against the United States. The authorization was signed on September 18, just one week after the attacks. This law is an important historical document for understanding how the United States responded to the attacks of 9/11, as well as to terrorist attacks more generally. The law provides students with a clear argument for an initial experience in delineation.

QUESTIONING PATH TOOL

Text 4.1—"Authorization for Use of Military Force," 107th Congress

APPROACHING:
I determine my reading purposes and take note of key information about the text. I identify the LIPS domain(s) that will guide my initial reading.

QUESTIONING: *I use Guiding Questions to help me investigate the text (from the **Guiding Questions Handout**).*

ANALYZING: *I question further to connect and analyze the details I find (from the **Guiding Questions Handout**).*

1. What evidence supports the claims in the text, and what is left uncertain or unsupported?

2. How does the author's choice of words reveal his purposes and perspective?

3. In what ways are ideas, events, and claims linked together in the text?

DEEPENING: *I consider the questions of others.*

4. Which sentences or paragraphs best communicate the position of 107th Congress?

5. What powers does the law give to President Bush?

6. What reasons does the Congress provide for giving President Bush authorization to use the United States Armed Forces?

EXTENDING: *I pose my own questions.*

7. What argumentative premises and evidence does this text provide that influence your understanding of or perspective on the issue and problem of terrorism?

Developing Core Literacy Proficiencies

READING

- Students first read the argument independently, considering general Guiding Questions, such as "What claims do I find in the text?" (***Guiding Questions Handout***)

- Guiding Questions might focus on ideas or structure because the argument in this text is clearly organized and presented.

- Introduce a set of text-specific questions to drive a closer reading and analysis of the text's argument; then have students follow along as the text is read aloud or presented to them.

- In reading teams, students discuss the text-specific questions and search for relevant details, annotating and making notes about the various elements of argumentation.

Delineating

- Students use a blank ***Delineating Arguments Tool*** to structure and capture their *delineation*.

- Assign each team one or more of the elements of the argument (position, claims, reasoning, evidence) and have the members prepare a short presentation for the class about what they have discovered through their analysis of the argument. Emphasize that teams will need to cite specific evidence from the text that supports their analysis.

- As a class delineate the article's argument by having teams identify and explain its *position*, *claims*, *reasoning*, and *evidence*.

Writing an Evidence-Based Claim

- Model the writing of a claim about how the author has presented and developed one element of the argument (e.g., its *position*).

- Then have students individually write a claim about the author's use of the element their team studied.

☰ ACTIVITY 4: UNDERSTANDING ☰ PERSPECTIVE

The teacher leads an exploration of the concept of perspective in a familiar context.

NOTE

If a teacher chooses to begin the exploration of perspective by having students first refer back to the model argument, its characters, and their positions, students might use a Socratic discussion model to explore the various positions and the reasons why the various actors might hold those positions. After students have come to an initial understanding of perspective through these familiar examples, teachers can then introduce the terms and their definitions, reversing the order of the activities outlined here.

- Introduce the terms *relationship to an issue* and *perspective* to the class.

  ⇒ *Relationship to an issue* can be defined in this context as a person's particular personal involvement with an issue, given his or her experience, education, occupation, socioeconomic-geographical status, interests, or other characteristics.

  ⇒ *Perspective* can be defined as how someone understands and views an issue based on his or her current relationship to it and analysis of the issue.

- Spend some time exploring the various meanings of perspective and how they might relate to how the term is used here. If relevant, review students' experience in analyzing the author's *perspective* in previous units, particularly in *Researching to Deepen Understanding*.

- Compare the author's perspective to an iceberg, in which the author's particular argument or position is clearly seen, but his or her personal relationship and perspective on the issue may or may not be explicitly revealed in the text. Without this perspective, however, the author's position would not be possible; the author's perspective influences how he or she approaches and ultimately defines an issue and eventually a particular position on it.

- Remind students about the academic habit of **Remaining Open**. Discuss the idea that understanding someone else's perspective begins by listening to (or reading) closely that person's ideas and thinking without immediate evaluation. Evaluation comes later and is best informed by a deeper understanding of the perspective from which the argument comes.

- Revisit the model argument that the class explored in Activity 2. Use Guiding Questions concerning perspective to help drive a discussion of the various perspectives of the actors in those situations. Discuss how the actors' personal relationship to the issue influences their perspectives and how their perspective influences their understanding of the issue and their position.

Guiding Questions (from the *Guiding Questions Handout*)

1. What seems to be the person' attitude or point of view?

2. How does the person's perspective influence his or her presentation of ideas or arguments?

3. How does each person's perspective compare to others?

Students can use their responses to these questions to fill in the Perspective sections of their **Delineating Arguments Tools** for the model argument(s) as well as for their own hypothetical argument about the sample issue.

ACTIVITY 5: DELINEATING AND COMPARING ARGUMENTS

Students analyze and compare perspectives and positions in argumentative texts.

INSTRUCTIONAL NOTES

TEXT 4.1 AND PERSPECTIVE

Students revisit Text 4.1 after developing an understanding of how perspective helps shape an author's position and argument.

- Model a claim that analyzes how an author's position on an issue is directly influenced by his or her relationship to it and perspective on it. The model argument from Activity 2 can be referred to, with a claim based on how one of the actor's perspective on the issue influences his or her position. For example:
  - ⇒ "As a teacher, Mr. Higgins feels he must maintain some personal separation from his students, so he is uncomfortable being 'friended' by a student on Facebook." Remind students again about the Academic Habit of **Remaining Open** that understanding someone else's perspective begins by listening to (or reading) closely that person's ideas and thinking without immediate evaluation.

- In reading teams, students think about how the perspective of Text 4.1's author influences his position on the issue, then individually write and compare claims about this relationship.

READING AND COMPARING SEMINAL ARGUMENTS

The remaining texts in Text Set 4 present students with different perspectives, positions, and arguments for them to read and analyze. Students will use these texts to move from guided to independent practice of the close-reading skills associated with analyzing an argument. Students might all read both arguments or be assigned one of them for delineation, then compare what they learn about the arguments and their elements.

> #### TEXT NOTES: TEXT SET 4
>
> Texts 4.2 and 4.3 provide two very different arguments about the issues of terrorism, specifically the United States' response to the terrorist events of 9/11. Each argument takes a very different position and comes from very distinct perspectives (based a great deal on each author's personal relationship to the issue). Either or both can provide an interesting text for students to use in analyzing and comparing perspectives.
>
>
>
> #### *Additional Texts*
>
> Included in the unit's text set are three additional arguments that further expose students to more positions and perspectives surrounding the issue of terrorism and the United States' response to the terrorist attacks of 9/11. In "Joint Resolution to authorize the use of United States Armed Forces against those responsible for the recent attacks launched against the United States," the 107th Congress invokes the

TEXT NOTES: TEXT SET 4

right of self-defense against attacks on the United States and its civilians and gives President Bush war-time powers. In a PBS *News Hour* interview in the days after 9/11, Deputy Secretary of Defense Paul Wolfowitz discusses a shift toward a new kind of war given the recent terrorist attacks. In an article entitled "U.S. Response to Terrorism: A Strategic Analysis of the Afghanistan Campaign," author Valentina Taddeo examines certain facets of the United States' response to global terrorism in general and Afghanistan in particular.

Text 4.2: "George W. Bush's Address to the Nation on September 11, 2001"

Author: President George W. Bush

Source/Publisher: Salempress.com, YouTube.com

Date: September 11, 2001

Complexity level: This text measures at 1380L and should be accessible for most ninth-graders.

Text Notes

In his first appearance in the Oval Office after the 9/11 attacks, President Bush addressed the nation to define what happened and inform the public of the next moves the government will take. He immediately takes a clear position, first by directly labeling the attacks as terrorist attacks and describing why America has been attacked and proclaiming that America's resolve remains strong. Of particular interest, Bush invokes religion in this time of chaos and struggle. As the president, Bush clearly has a particular perspective toward the attacks, which can be explored by analyzing what details he chooses to address in one of the most important speeches in his presidency. The piece is relatively short, but contains rich language and strong central ideas. Students might also explore the other resources offered in this Salem Press publication. These include an overview on the context of President Bush's speech and history of terrorism in the Middle East (including a time line), as well as an analysis of the speech, its audience, and how it affected national policy. Additional readings and study questions are also provided. This speech can also be viewed on YouTube.

QUESTIONING PATH TOOL

Text 4.2—"George W. Bush's Address to the Nation on September 11, 2001"

APPROACHING: *I determine my reading purposes and take note of key information about the text. I identify the LIPS domain(s) that will guide my initial reading.*

QUESTIONING: *I use Guiding Questions to help me investigate the text (from the **Guiding Questions Handout**).*

ANALYZING: *I question further to connect and analyze the details I find (from the **Guiding Questions Handout**).*

1. How does the author's perspective influence his presentation of ideas, themes, or arguments?

2. How does the author's choice of words reveal his purposes and perspective?

DEEPENING: *I consider the questions of others.*

3. How does President Bush use rhetoric (such as religious language and metaphors) in his speech? How does his rhetoric further develop his purpose?

4. President Bush establishes a series of claims in favor of his position. How does one of these claims relate to his overall argument, and what specific evidence does he provide to support the claim?

EXTENDING: *I pose my own questions.*

5. What argumentative premises and evidence does this text provide that influence your understanding of or perspective on the issue and problem of terrorism?

Text 4.3: "A Place of Peace: For a 9/11 Victim's Widow, Revenge Is Not the Answer"

Author: Laura Frohne

Source/Publisher: The *Boston Globe* (the video available through the article "Four families, Four Stories of Loss, Love, and Resilience" by Jenna Russell)

Date: September 4, 2011

Complexity level: N/A (The video is highly accessible to ninth-graders.)

Text Notes

In a video by the *Boston Globe*, Andrea Leblanc, wife of a victim of 9/11, speaks about the decision to go to war after the attacks. Her opinion is radically different from that of President Bush's in that she argues against the use of force as a just means for retaliation. Her position is of particular interest given her strong perspective on the issue: Andrea Leblanc's husband was on one of the planes that crashed on 9/11. The video raises interesting questions about how individuals who were directly affected actually feel about government responses to the attacks and how their loved ones who were victims might have responded.

QUESTIONING PATH TOOL

Text 4.3—"A Place of Peace: For a 9/11 Victim's Widow, Revenge Is Not the Answer"

APPROACHING: *I determine my reading purposes and take note of key information about the text. I identify the LIPS domain(s) that will guide my initial reading.*

QUESTIONING: *I use Guiding Questions to help me investigate the text (from the **Guiding Questions Handout**).*

ANALYZING: *I question further to connect and analyze the details I find (from the **Guiding Questions Handout**).*

1. How does the author's choice of words reveal her purposes and perspective?

2. How does the author's perspective influence her presentation of ideas, themes, or arguments?

DEEPENING: *I consider the questions of others.*

3. What is Leblanc's perspective on the response to the attacks of 9/11? How does her perspective help shape her position? How does her perspective differ from that of President Bush's?

4. How does Leblanc use language to convey her position?

5. Leblanc talks about a "frightening patriotism" that followed 9/11. How does she describe this idea? How does this sentiment fit into her overall argument?

EXTENDING: *I pose my own questions.*

6. What argumentative premises and evidence does this text provide that influence your understanding of or perspective on the issue and problem of terrorism?

INSTRUCTIONAL NOTES

READING

- Students first read one or more of the arguments independently, considering general Guiding Questions (from the **Guiding Questions Handout**), such as these:
  - ⇒ What details or words suggest the author's perspective?
  - ⇒ What seems to be the author's attitude or point of view?
  - ⇒ How does the author's perspective influence his or her presentation of ideas or arguments?
- Consider one or more of the text-specific questions in the Deepening sections of each text's model Questioning Path to drive a closer reading and analysis of the text's argument; then have students follow along as the text is read aloud or presented to them.
- In reading teams, students discuss the text-specific questions and search for relevant details, annotating and making notes about them.

Delineating

- Students use a **Delineating Arguments Tool** to delineate the author's argument for each of the texts they have read.
- Discuss as a class the author's position, argument, and perspective for each of the arguments students have read, as a class or in text-specific teams.

Writing Comparative Evidence-Based Claims

- Discuss the ways in which the arguments compare in terms of their authors' perspectives, positions, lines of reasoning, and use of evidence. Ask students to make observations and then support those observations with evidence from one or more of the texts.
- Model developing an evidence-based claim that compares how the authors have used one of the elements of argumentation differently, as influenced by their perspectives.
- Then have students individually develop their own comparative EBCs using two or more of the texts (these can be developed orally, on paper, or using an **Organizing EBC Tool**).

NOTE

The teacher may also choose to discuss the various ways authors structure the logical reasoning of arguments.

☰ ACTIVITY 6: DELINEATING ADDITIONAL ☰ ARGUMENTS

As needed, students read and delineate additional arguments related to the unit's issue.

INSTRUCTIONAL NOTES

To more fully understand the issue, students may need to explore additional arguments. If students will benefit from reading additional background or historical arguments, possibilities related to the unit's issue are listed in Text Set 4 (Historical Arguments). Students should also become familiar with the most current positions and arguments around the issue. If more contemporary arguments are relevant, Text Set 5 includes several examples, or teachers and students can use key word searches of the Internet related to the general topic of *terrorism, terrorism and national security, terrorist acts,* and other terms or names that have emerged during the reading of the foundational sources.

NOTE

This is the point in the unit at which students might embark on further research, guided by the *Researching to Deepen Understanding* unit's activities and resources. See in particular Part 2, Activity 1 of that unit, "Planning Searches for Information."

For each argument read, students can follow the same process of reading, delineating the argument, and writing an explanatory or comparative evidence-based claim as modeled and practiced in Activity 5. To broaden the class's access to many arguments, students might work in expert teams focused on one or more of the arguments, then jigsaw to share their team's findings with students from other teams

☰ ACTIVITY 7: WRITING TO ANALYZE ☰ ARGUMENTS

Students write short essays analyzing an argument.

INSTRUCTIONAL NOTES

- Students use their notes, annotations, and tools to write paragraphs analyzing one of the arguments they have read thus far in the unit. In their written analyses, students do the following:
  ⇒ State the author's position.
  ⇒ Identify the elements of the argument (perspective, claims, key evidence).
  ⇒ Make an evidence-based claim about how the author's perspective shapes the position and argumentation.
  ⇒ Use evidence from the text to support their analysis.

INSTRUCTIONAL NOTES

- Students select one of the arguments they have read and delineated, either from the Text Set 4 collection or one found by the teacher or students themselves. Students use the **Delineating Arguments Tool** they have developed for their chosen argument to organize their explanatory paragraph.

- After drafting their paragraphs, students work in collaborative review teams, focusing on one or more of the literacy skills criteria listed in the chart below as they review and improve their written analyses of arguments. Students may be grouped according to the argument they have selected for analysis or in cross-text teams. If a more structured review process is needed, students can use the collaborative, question-based writing workshop practiced in other units, and fully outlined in Part 5 of this unit.

LITERACY SKILLS	DESCRIPTORS
RECOGNIZING PERSPECTIVE	Identifies and explains the author's view of the text's topic
DELINEATING ARGUMENTATION	Identifies and analyzes the claims, evidence, and reasoning in arguments
FORMING CLAIMS	States a meaningful position that is well supported by evidence from texts
USING EVIDENCE	Uses well-chosen details from texts to explain and support claims; accurately paraphrases or quotes

- Students submit their revised explanatory essays for review by the teacher.

≡ PART 2: FORMATIVE ASSESSMENT ≡ OPPORTUNITIES

At the end of Part 2, students will have accomplished the following:

- Discussed the positions of political cartoons
- Completed a **Delineating Arguments Tool** for a model argument
- Completed a **Delineating Arguments Tool** and written an EBC for Text 4.1
- Completed **Delineating Arguments Tools** and written comparative EBC for other arguments in Text Set 4
- Written short essays analyzing one of the arguments they have read

LITERACY SKILLS

Part 2 presents many opportunities for formative assessment. Teachers can use the tools, claims, and conversations from Activities 2 and 4 to assess how the class is doing overall in the targeted skills of **Forming Claims, Using Evidence, Recognizing Perspective**, and **Delineating Argumentation**.

Evaluate their claim-based essays as evidence of these same reading and analysis skills and as more formal written exercises (paying increased attention to organization of their ideas and how they are using evidence).

ACADEMIC HABITS

Teachers might also lead a class discussion about how well students have practiced the Academic Habit of **Remaining Open**. Students might be asked to talk about moments when they consciously decided to consider new perspectives and ideas in order to deepen their own understanding of the issue.

NOTE

To support self-, peer, and teacher assessment of skills and habits developed during the unit, a formal *EBA Literacy Skills and Academic Habits Rubric* and less formal *Student Checklist* are provided in the **EBA Literacy Toolbox**.

PART 3

EVALUATING ARGUMENTS AND DEVELOPING A POSITION

"Terrorist attacks can shake the foundations of our biggest buildings, but they cannot touch the foundation of America."

OBJECTIVE:	Students evaluate arguments, determine which arguments they find most convincing, and synthesize what they have learned so far to establish their own positions.

MATERIALS:
Text Sets 3 through 5
- *Forming EBC Tool*
- *Delineating Arguments Tool*
- *Evaluating Arguments Tool*

- *Organizing EBC Tool*
- *Student EBA Literacy Skills and Academic Habits Checklist*
- *EBA terms*

☰ LITERACY SKILLS

TARGETED SKILLS	DESCRIPTORS
FORMING CLAIMS	Establishes and presents a clear and defensible position that is supported by a series of valid claims (premises) and set in the context of the topic
USING EVIDENCE	Presents a comprehensive view of the issue by providing textual evidence to support claims and using sufficient and accurate quotations, paraphrases, and references
RECOGNIZING PERSPECTIVE	Uses textual details to recognize and establish a relationship to and perspective on a topic
EVALUATING INFORMATION	Assesses the relevance and credibility of information, ideas, evidence, and logic presented in texts
DELINEATING ARGUMENTATION	Identifies and analyzes the components and accuracy of claims, evidence, and reasoning in explanations and arguments

Developing Core Literacy Proficiencies

ACADEMIC HABITS

HABITS DEVELOPED	DESCRIPTORS
REMAINING OPEN	Adopts a stance of inquiry—asking questions to learn more—rather than arguing for entrenched positions
QUALIFYING VIEWS	Modifies and further justifies ideas in response to thinking from others

ALIGNMENT TO CCSS

TARGETED STANDARDS:

CCSS.ELA-LITERACY.RI.9-10.6: Determine an author's point of view or purpose in a text and analyze how an author uses rhetoric to advance that point of view or purpose.

CCSS.ELA-LITERACY.RI.9-10.8: Delineate and evaluate the argument and specific claims in a text, assessing whether the reasoning is valid and the evidence is relevant and sufficient; identify false statements and fallacious reasoning.

CCSS.ELA-LITERACY.RI.9-10.9: Analyze seminal U.S. documents of historical and literary significance (e.g., Washington's Farewell Address, the Gettysburg Address, Roosevelt's Four Freedoms speech, King's "Letter from Birmingham Jail"), including how they address related themes and concepts.

CCSS.ELA-LITERACY.W.9-10.1: Write arguments to support claims in an analysis of substantive topics or texts, using valid reasoning and relevant and sufficient evidence.

CCSS.ELA-LITERACY.W.9-10.2: Write informative/explanatory texts to examine and convey complex ideas, concepts, and information clearly and accurately through the effective selection, organization, and analysis of content.

SUPPORTING STANDARDS:

CCSS.ELA-LITERACY.RI.9-10.1: Cite strong and thorough textual evidence to support analysis of what the text says explicitly as well as inferences drawn from the text.

CCSS.ELA-LITERACY.RI.9-10.2: Determine a central idea of a text and analyze its development over the course of the text, including how it emerges and is shaped and refined by specific details; provide an objective summary of the text.

CCSS.ELA-LITERACY.RI.9-10.3: Analyze how the author unfolds an analysis or series of ideas or events, including the order in which the points are made, how they are introduced and developed, and the connections that are drawn between them.

ACTIVITIES

1. EVALUATING ARGUMENTS
Students review and evaluate arguments using objective criteria and their own developing perspectives on the issue.

2. DEVELOPING A PERSPECTIVE AND POSITION
Students synthesize what they have learned about the issue and related arguments to clarify their own developing perspectives and to establish positions for their own arguments.

3. DEEPENING UNDERSTANDING
If needed, students conduct further research to help develop and support their positions.

4. USING OTHERS' ARGUMENTS TO SUPPORT A POSITION
Students identify an argument that supports their positions and write evidence-based claims about why the argument is convincing or makes sense to them.

5. RESPONDING TO OPPOSING ARGUMENTS
Students identify an argument that opposes their position and write an evidence-based claim that either acknowledges the argument's position, points out its limitations, counters its claims, or refutes it as invalid, illogical, or unsupported.

≡ ACTIVITY 1: EVALUATING ARGUMENTS

Students review and evaluate arguments using objective criteria and their own developing perspectives on the issue.

INSTRUCTIONAL NOTES

Having analyzed and compared the perspectives, positions, premises, and evidence for various arguments related to the unit's issue, students are ready to evaluate the logic and quality of various positions and arguments in order to determine which ones make sense to them. To do so, students will reconsider the elements of the arguments they have delineated, as well as some key characteristics of effective arguments, and evaluate how successful and convincing are the arguments they have read. For each of the elements or characteristics, they will think about a short set of Guiding Questions that will help them do an evaluative reading of the argument. They will then rate the argument for its effectiveness in each of the areas and overall as a convincing argument that they may want to use as a foundation for the argument they will develop and write. To guide the evaluation process, record their evaluations, and make notes about evidence from the text that supports those evaluations, they will use a new tool from the **EBA Literacy Toolbox**, the *Evaluating Arguments Tool*.

EVALUATING ARGUMENTS TOOL

The *Evaluating Arguments Tool* (in the **EBA Literacy Toolbox**) is organized to support evaluation of eight related elements or characteristics of an argument: the argument's *issue, perspective, credibility* and *bias, position* or *thesis, claims, evidence, reasoning* and *logic*, and *conclusions*. The tool also provides a place to make a summary rating of whether the argument is, overall, convincing to the evaluator. Reading and evaluation for each of these eight criteria areas are supported by two to three Guiding Questions. Students thus apply skills they have developed in previous units with the *Guiding Questions Handout, Questioning Path Tool*, and *Assessing Sources Handout*— using questions to guide close, evaluative reading of a given argument. The tool includes a simple three-point scale, enabling students to rate each of the eight criteria as *questionable/weak, acceptable*, or *strong*. Because students should base their evaluations on specific evidence from the argument's text, a space is included for notes about text-based observations as well as one for overall comments.

INSTRUCTIONAL NOTES

TEACHER MODELING

- Introduce the *Evaluating Arguments Tool* as a set of criteria for evaluating arguments. Explain that this tool will be used to support students' close reading and evaluation of arguments they have encountered in the unit. Using the tool should also help students think about the characteristics of an effective argument when they write, review, and revise their final argumentative essays.

- Overview and discuss the organization of the tool, noting the following:
  - ⇒ The elements and characteristics of an argument that organize the tool, listed in its first column; connect these criteria to the elements students have analyzed when delineating arguments and to related Literacy Skills criteria that they have been working on (e.g., **Forming Claims** and **Using Evidence**)
  - ⇒ The column of Guiding Questions for Evaluating an Argument, which they will think about as they read, analyze, discuss, and evaluate argumentative texts
  - ⇒ The three-point rating scale, which asks them to consider evidence from the text in evaluating if a part of the argument is *questionable, acceptable,* or a *strength*

- Model how to use the **Evaluating Arguments Tool** to review and evaluate an argument, using a familiar text from Part 2. Focus initially on questions and ratings for the elements of the argument that have already been delineated, its issue, perspective, position, claims, and evidence. Think aloud as you consider a question, such as "How accurate and current is the explanation of the issue?" Use your answer to this question to inform your rating of the argument's presentation of the issue. Model the use of textual evidence in your evaluation. Work with the class to consider other questions related to the elements of the argument, asking students to support their thinking and ratings with specific evidence from the text.

- Move the modeling and discussion to other, less familiar criteria: credibility and bias, reasoning and logic, and conclusions. Explain to students what you need to look for and think about for each of these areas. Potentially support students with an examination of these terms as academic vocabulary, and review what students have learned and thought about when they have assessed, credibility, bias, and perspective in the *Researching to Deepen Understanding* unit.

- Talk through what students' observations and ratings in the eight areas add up to—whether they find the argument to be a convincing one. Let them know that they will be making similar summary evaluations for each argument they analyze and that those evaluations will help them know how to use or respond to the argument when they write their own essays.

EVALUATING ARGUMENTS IN READING TEAMS

- In reading teams, students use the **Evaluating Arguments Tool** and review process to evaluate an argument they have read thus far in the unit. Have each group share and discuss their ratings with the class. Ask students to support their evaluations with textual evidence.

- To close the discussion, remind students that they will be striving to develop and write a convincing argument themselves in Parts 4 and 5 of the unit and that the criteria and the Guiding Questions from this tool may help them do so. Relate those criteria and questions to skills students have been working on throughout the unit (and the Developing Core Literacy Proficiencies curriculum overall): **Evaluating Information**, **Delineating Argumentation**, **Forming Claims**, and **Using Evidence**. Let them know that they will continue working on these skills as they move forward in the unit.

> ### NOTE
>
> Students should be familiar with text-centered discussions if they have completed Units 1 through 4 of the Developing Core Literacy Proficiencies program. If not, the teacher may need to model how to lead and participate in a text-centered discussion in which students use questions, criteria, and textual evidence to discuss, analyze, or evaluate a text. The following *Habits-Based Text-Centered Discussion Checklist* (found in the **RC Literacy Toolbox**) can be used to self-evaluate their discussions.

DISCUSSION HABITS	DESCRIPTORS: *When—and how well—have I demonstrated these habits?*	EXAMPLES FROM TEXT-CENTERED DISCUSSIONS
PREPARING	Reads the text(s) closely and thinks about the questions to prepare for a text-centered discussion	
COLLABORATING	Pays attention to other participants while participating in and leading a text-centered discussion	
COMMUNICATING CLEARLY	Presents ideas and supporting evidence so others can understand them	

DETERMINING IF AN ARGUMENT IS COMPELLING OR CONVINCING

- Explain to students that evaluating an argument involves an objective, criteria-based assessment of its strengths and weaknesses (as practiced using the *Evaluating Arguments Tool*) and the consideration of one's own developing position about the issue. Discuss ways in which readers can determine if an argument is *convincing*.

> ### NOTE
>
> This is an opportunity to develop students' academic vocabulary for the term *convincing* and its connotations in the realm of argumentation.

- In reading teams, have students review and evaluate another argument previously read in the unit. Students use the same eight criteria from the *Evaluating Arguments Tool* to rate objectively (as a team) the elements or characteristics of the argument. Students then, individually, make a final summary rating based on the criteria but also considering their own emerging perspectives and positions relative to the issue. When finished, students compare and discuss their summary evaluations and opinions about whether the argument is convincing and makes sense to them. Some may find the argument to be more convincing than others. They should use evidence from the text, as well as from their own thinking, to support their summary evaluations.

INDIVIDUALLY EVALUATE AND SELECT CONVINCING ARGUMENTS

- Individually, students review the arguments they have read in the unit and initially determine which they find most convincing.

- For the arguments whose positions they rate as acceptable or strong, students do a full rating using the ***Evaluating Arguments Tool*** to be certain that the arguments they favor are ones that meet the criteria.

Arguments students find to be questionable, but that may need to be countered, will be considered further in Part 4.

ACTIVITY 2: DEVELOPING A PERSPECTIVE AND POSITION

Students synthesize what they have learned about the issue and related arguments to clarify their own developing perspectives and to establish positions for their own arguments.

INSTRUCTIONAL NOTES

- Return to the unit's problem-based question and the set of debatable questions that students brainstormed and discussed in Parts 1 (Activity 1) and 2 (Activity 1)—perhaps even to the original KWL activity—to again take a wide-angle view of the topical issue. Review the various positions students have encountered in the arguments they have read. Have students suggest and discuss various ways of thinking about the issue and responding to the debatable questions, given what they now know about the unit's issue. Ask students to discuss how their thinking is leading them to a position.

- As a foundation for taking a position, have students review the multipart, evidence-based claim about the nature of the issue they wrote at the end of Part 1. Have them revise their initial claim based on their current understanding of the issue. They should include new evidence from arguments they encountered in Part 2. They can again use an ***Organizing EBC Tool*** to help develop their evidence-based claims.

- In reading teams, students review and discuss their revised evidence-based claims about the nature of the issue.

Teacher Modeling

- Using a sample ***Delineating Arguments Tool***, model for students how to use the tool now to generate thinking rather than analyze an existing argument, how to communicate one's own perspective, position, and supporting claims. Point out that their evidence-based claims about the nature of the issue can serve as their thinking for the first section of the tool. Then model how to articulate a short explanation of perspective based on your own, developing view of the issue. Note that your explanation of your position might be the result of the recent thinking the class has done or stem from a previous claim recorded on an ***Organizing EBC Tool***.

- Referring to the ***Delineating Arguments Tool***, now demonstrate how to move either of two ways in your thinking as you identify and articulate claims related to your position:

  1. **Downward** (deductively): From the position to a set of supporting claims by thinking about what you will have to prove to support your position. This thinking may be similar to what students have done previously with an ***Organizing EBC Tool.***

  2. **Upward** (inductively): From the details of supporting arguments and evidence they have found in their reading to a set of claims that can be built into an argument for the position. This thinking may be similar to what they have done previously with a ***Forming EBC Tool.***

Independent Practice

- Using their own ***Delineating Arguments Tool***, students independently record a summary of their explanation of the issue and one to two sentences articulating their perspective and position, considering how those elements have now developed through reading and discussion. Students then list claims to support their position, either working from the position to a set of supporting claims or from evidence to claims that lead to the position. They will likely need to consult prior texts, annotations, notes, and tools in this process.

- Using the ***Delineating Arguments Tool*** as an organizer, students write a paragraph explaining the position they want to take on the issue, the perspective from which it comes, and the claims that will be used to support their argument.

- Students consider the criteria from the ***Evaluating Arguments Tool*** as they write and review the explanations of their positions, asking themselves if what they are thinking is likely to lead to a convincing argument.

Peer Review of Positions

In informal peer-review teams or partners, students read and present their explanations of their positions. Reviewers discuss whether they think the argument is likely to be convincing. Because student paragraphs are written demonstrations of Literacy Skills targeted in the unit, peer reviewers can also consider and discuss criteria from the Student ***EBA Literacy Skills and Academic Habits Checklist*** and make constructive suggestions about strengths and areas for future improvement. Students might focus on the following criteria, using this informal rubric:

LITERACY SKILLS	DESCRIPTORS: *Find evidence of using the Literacy Skill in the draft.* *Does the writer's paragraph . . .*	NEEDS WORK	OKAY	VERY STRONG
FORMING CLAIMS	State a meaningful position that is well supported by evidence from the unit texts?			
USING EVIDENCE	Use well-chosen details from texts to explain and support the position?			
USING LOGIC	Support the position through a logical sequence of related premises and supporting evidence?			

≡ ACTIVITY 3: DEEPENING
≡ UNDERSTANDING

If needed, students conduct further research to help develop and support their positions.

INSTRUCTIONAL NOTES

At this point, students may have sufficient background information, knowledge, and evidence to develop an argument related to their position. If not—and especially if they have ventured into an area related to but also somewhat divergent from the focus of texts in the unit—they may need to do additional reading or research. Unread texts from the text sets and additional suggested texts provide options for this further research.

However, it will almost certainly be revealing and helpful for students to find and consider the most current arguments on the issue, which the fixed text set for the unit cannot possibly include. To do so, students (or the teacher) will likely need to use the Internet and do key word searches related to terms and concepts from the unit. Activities, materials, and resources from the *Researching to Deepen Understanding* unit and Literacy Toolbox may be helpful here. See in particular Part 2, Activity 1 of that unit, "Planning Searches for Information." Additionally, an approach articulated in the *Research* unit that is relevant here is the idea of framing inquiry with a set of questions to be investigated. Before conducting additional research, students could identify Inquiry Paths and Inquiry Questions they still need to explore to develop their argument. This will help them effectively frame their research for better efficiency and success.

≡ ACTIVITY 4: USING OTHERS' ARGUMENTS
≡ TO SUPPORT A POSITION

Students identify an argument that supports their position and write an evidence-based claim about why the argument is convincing and makes sense to them.

INSTRUCTIONAL NOTES

In developing and supporting their chosen positions, students will need to reference others' arguments related to the unit's issue and to use those arguments as evidence to support their own. Here, students will write a claim that establishes a supporting argument's position and also explains its relevance to their own position.

- Students individually select one or more arguments to use as building blocks for their own argument. This is likely to be an argument(s) that they have previously evaluated and found to be sound as well as convincing for them.

- Students use a **Delineating Arguments Tool** (or return to one they already produced) to identify the author's position, perspective, and the claims used to support the position.

Developing Core Literacy Proficiencies

- Students then use the ***Delineating Arguments Tool*** to help write a multipart evidence-based claim—or adapt a previously written claim about the nature of the argument—that establishes what the argument's position is. They explain why that argument makes sense and is relevant to their own position, citing specific evidence from the argument that they will use to support their own argument. Students should be encouraged to incorporate the perspective and position they drafted in Activity 2.

- Introduce and discuss the Academic Habit of **Qualifying Views**. Discuss how our own views generally originate from and are influenced by the ideas of others. Discuss how as we remain open to others' ideas and perspectives, we have opportunities to qualify our own perspectives and positions based on what we learn.

≡ ACTIVITY 5: RESPONDING TO OPPOSING ≡ ARGUMENTS

Students identify an argument that opposes their position and write an evidence-based claim that either acknowledges the argument's position, points out its limitations, counters its claims, or refutes it as invalid, illogical, or unsupported.

INSTRUCTIONAL NOTES

In developing their own positions and arguments, students must also (CCSS W.9-10.1b) "Develop claim(s) and counterclaims fairly, supplying evidence for each while pointing out the strengths and limitations of both." This expectation could be addressed by writing a counterclaim or counterargument—expressing why they think the opposed perspective and position are wrong. However, students should also learn that there are many ways to respond to a divergent or opposing argument. Discuss with students how including and addressing opposing arguments within their writing bolsters their credibility as authors as they demonstrate a fuller comprehension of the issue and are able to refute other's positions objectively.

- Explain and model the various ways that one might respond to an argument that emanates from a different perspective and position:

  1. By acknowledging the argument's position and the quality of its reasoning but explaining why one has not found it relevant or convincing

  2. By noting the limitations of the argument, especially as it applies to one's own position and response

  3. By countering one or more of the argument's claims, offering opposing evidence that calls the claims into question

  4. By pointing out the argument's poor reasoning or lack of valid evidence, analyzing and evaluating it as invalid, illogical, or specious

  5. Other approaches based on the nature of the argument itself

- If desired, argumentative fallacies such as a *straw man, ad hominem,* and *red herrings* can be discussed, noting that these techniques should be avoided in academic argumentation.

- Either as a class or in reading teams, identify texts in which authors have addressed opposing points of view in their argument. Ask students to reflect on these issues:

  ⇒ Why the author decided to address the opposing view or position

  ⇒ How the author acknowledges and responds to the opposing view or position

  ⇒ How including the opposing view or position strengthens (or weakens) the argument

- In reading teams, students discuss an opposing argument and determine ways in which they might respond to it. If this is an argument they have previously evaluated, they review their ratings and the evidence they have cited to support those ratings.

- Students individually select an argument that they want or need to acknowledge and respond to. They determine which of the strategies is best suited to that argument and their own positions and arguments. If this is an argument they have previously evaluated, they review their ratings and the evidence they have cited to support those ratings. If it is an argument they have judged not to be convincing but have not fully evaluated, they may choose to use an *Evaluating Arguments Tool* to more carefully analyze the argument.

- Students write a multipart evidence-based claim—or adapt a previously written claim about the argument they are acknowledging—that establishes what the argument's position is and then responds to that argument using one of the modeled strategies. Student claims should cite specific evidence from the argument (potentially from an *Evaluating Arguments Tool*) to support their evaluation of the argument and response to it.

≡ PART 3: FORMATIVE ASSESSMENT ≡ OPPORTUNITIES

By the end of Part 3, students will have accomplished the following:

- Analyzed and discussed compelling arguments based on their quality of argumentation and relevance to students' own positions
- Rewritten multipart, evidence-based claims about the nature of the issue
- Completed *Evaluating Arguments Tools* to evaluate arguments they have read so far
- Completed (or reviewed) a *Delineating Arguments Tool* to express their own position
- Written a paragraph expressing their position on the issue
- Completed a *Delineating Arguments Tool* for a supporting argument
- Written a multipart evidence-based claim about the supporting argument's position and why it is relevant to their own position
- Written a multipart evidence-based claim about an opposing argument's position and how they will respond to or counter it

LITERACY SKILLS

As a formative task and building block for their final argument, students have now revised their evidence-based claim about the nature of the issue based on their developing perspective. In a paragraph, they have also expressed a position they wish to take on the issue, and they have written several multipart claims that accomplish the following:

1. Presents analyses and evaluations of an argument related to the unit's issue
2. Establishes the relevance of the argument's position and evidence to their own argument
3. Responds to a divergent or opposing argument in an appropriate and strategic way
4. Cites evidence from texts to support their analyses and evaluations
5. Represents their best thinking and clearest writing

These pieces should be evaluated for students' growing proficiency in the Literacy Skills of **Forming Claims**, **Using Evidence**, **Recognizing Perspective**, **Delineating Argumentation**, and **Evaluating Information**.

ACADEMIC HABITS

As students begin to form their own perspective and positions on the issue, they have the opportunity to reflect on how well they are practicing the habits of **Remaining Open** and **Qualifying Views**. Students should base their developing position not solely on prior convictions but primarily on the arguments they have read in the unit. As they continue to add to their knowledge of the issue, they should also continually qualify their thoughts and even their position. Students might ask themselves the following questions to reflect on their Academic Habits:

- In what ways am I demonstrating the habit of Remaining Open by reading about the issue and arguments with an open mind? How might I improve?
- In what ways am I demonstrating the habit of **Qualifying My Views** on the topic by thinking about and using new information we have read? How might I improve?

> **NOTE**
>
> To support self-, peer, and teacher assessment of skills and habits developed during the unit, a formal *EBA Literacy Skills and Academic Habits Rubric* and less formal *Student Checklist* are provided in the **EBA Literacy Toolbox**.

PART 4

ORGANIZING AN EVIDENCE-BASED ARGUMENT

"There's no doubt that al Qaeda will continue to pursue attacks against us. We must—and we will—remain vigilant at home and abroad."

OBJECTIVE:	Students establish and sequence evidence-based claims as premises for a coherent, logical argument that establishes a position related to the unit's issue.

MATERIALS:
- *Forming EBC Tool*
- *Organizing EBC Tool*
- *Delineating Arguments Tool*
- *EBA Terms*

≣ LITERACY SKILLS

TARGETED SKILLS	DESCRIPTORS
FORMING CLAIMS	Establishes and presents a clear and defensible position that is supported by a series of valid claims (premises) and set in the context of the topic
USING EVIDENCE	Presents a comprehensive view of the issue by providing textual evidence to support claims and using sufficient and accurate quotations, paraphrases, and references
USING LOGIC	Establishes and supports a position through a logical sequence of related claims, premises, and supporting evidence
ORGANIZING IDEAS	Sequences sentences, paragraphs, and parts of an essay to establish a coherent, logical, and unified argument

ACADEMIC HABITS

HABITS DEVELOPED	DESCRIPTORS
ORGANIZING WORK	Maintains work and materials so that they can be used effectively and efficiently in current and future tasks
REVISING	Rethinks and refines work based on teacher-, peer-, and self-review processes

ALIGNMENT TO CCSS

TARGETED STANDARDS:

CCSS.ELA-LITERACY.W.9-10.1: Write arguments to support claims in an analysis of substantive topics or texts, using valid reasoning and relevant and sufficient evidence.

CCSS.ELA-LITERACY.W.9-10.5: Develop and strengthen writing as needed by planning, revising, editing, rewriting, or trying a new approach, focusing on addressing what is most significant for a specific purpose and audience.

CCSS.ELA-LITERACY.W.9-10.9: Draw evidence from literary or informational texts to support analysis, reflection, and research

SUPPORTING STANDARDS:

CCSS.ELA-LITERACY.RI.9-10.1: Cite strong and thorough textual evidence to support analysis of what the text says explicitly as well as inferences drawn from the text.

CCSS.ELA-LITERACY.SL.9-10.1: Initiate and participate effectively in a range of collaborative discussions (one-on-one, in groups, and teacher-led) with diverse partners on *grades 9–10 topics, texts, and issues*, building on others' ideas and expressing their own clearly and persuasively.

ACTIVITIES

1. IDENTIFYING SUPPORTING EVIDENCE
Students review their notes, tools, and previously written claims to determine what they will use as evidence to develop and support their positions.

2. DEVELOPING AND SEQUENCING CLAIMS AS PREMISES OF THE ARGUMENT
Students review the claims they have previously written (and potentially develop new claims) to determine how they will use them as premises to develop their arguments. Students determine a potential sequence for their premises and plan a chain of reasoning for their arguments.

3. ORGANIZING EVIDENCE TO SUPPORT CLAIMS
Students list and sequence their claims and then organize and cite sources for the evidence they will use to explain and support each of their premises of their arguments.

4. REVIEWING A PLAN FOR WRITING AN ARGUMENT
Students review and revise their plans to ensure that they are clear, relevant, coherent, strategically sequenced, well reasoned, and sufficiently supported by evidence.

Developing Core Literacy Proficiencies

ACTIVITY 1: IDENTIFYING SUPPORTING EVIDENCE

Students review their notes, tools, and previously written claims to determine what they will use as evidence to develop and support their positions.

INSTRUCTIONAL NOTES

PREVIEWING THE FINAL ASSIGNMENT

Through their reading and work in Parts 1 through 3 of the unit, students will have developed an understanding of a controversial issue, analyzed and evaluated various arguments about the issue, developed their own perspective about the issue, and begun to formulate a supported position from which they can build an argument. In Activity 2 of Part 3, they will have written a short explanation of their position and proposed a set of evidence-based claims they will use as the building blocks of their argument. As the instructional emphasis in the unit shifts from reading and analysis to thinking and writing, students should be introduced to their final task, writing an essay that effectively communicates a reasoned, evidence-based argument. Students will organize a plan for that essay in Part 4 and then draft and revise the essay in Part 5.

- Have students read and discuss the ***Building Evidence-Based Arguments—Final Writing Task Handout*** found in their **Student Edition Toolbox**.

- Emphasize that their task will be to produce a convincing argument that represents to the best of their ability all that they have learned in this unit (as well as the entire Developing Core Literacy Proficiencies sequence of units).

- Introduce the three-assignment criteria for the argument, which will be used (along with the Literacy Skills criteria they have been working on during the unit) to evaluate their final products. Their written argument should do the following:

  1. Present a convincing argument that comes from an understanding of the issue and a clear perspective and position.

  2. Organize a set of claims in an order that explains and supports the position.

  3. Use relevant and trustworthy evidence to support all claims and the overall position.

IDENTIFYING EVIDENCE (ASSIGNMENT CRITERION 3)

Having initially established their perspectives and positions related to the issue, students now inventory what they have learned and what they can use to develop and support their positions.

During the course of Activities 1 through 3, students develop a coherent plan for their argument by reviewing their notes and tools, discussing their emerging plan with peers, determining what is lacking, and revising their plan accordingly. Students may repeat these activities a few times before finalizing their plan.

- To start this process, students gather all their previous reading notes, tools, and short writing pieces for review, looking for information, arguments, and evidence that will help them develop and support their position.

> **NOTE**
>
> This will be much easier if students have previously maintained a working file or portfolio.

- Students review their notes and materials to identify potential evidence, sorting out what is relevant to their position and what is not. Students also evaluate how credible, or trustworthy, the sources of their evidence are.

- Students determine if what they have is sufficient or if they need to do any additional reading or research.

ACTIVITY 2: DEVELOPING AND SEQUENCING CLAIMS AS PREMISES OF THE ARGUMENT

Students review the claims they have previously written (and potentially develop new claims) to determine how they will use them as building blocks to develop their position. Students determine a potential order for their premises and plan the organization for their arguments.

INSTRUCTIONAL NOTES

- Review with students that an argument's premises are a series of claims that need to be backed up by evidence and that lead to the position. Claims become the argument's premises (building blocks) that defend, support, or prove the position.

- Students return to and review the claims they have written in the unit, thinking about their relationship to their emerging plan for their argument. They will have produced the following written claims:

  ⇒ An explanatory EBC that presents their understanding of the issue (Part 1, Activity 5)

  ⇒ An explanatory EBC that analyzes an author's use of one of the elements of argumentation (Part 2, Activity 2)

  ⇒ A comparative EBC contrasting two authors' perspectives and use of elements of argumentation (Part 2, Activity 5)

  ⇒ Additional comparative EBCs for new arguments they find and analyze (Part 2, Activity 6)

  ⇒ A short essay that analyzes an argument and its use of the elements (Part 2, Activity 7)

  ⇒ A **Delineating Arguments Tool** that communicates their understanding of the issue, perspective on it, emerging position, and claims that might be used to develop and support the position (Part 3, Activity 2)

  ⇒ A paragraph that explains the student's emerging position on the issue (Part 3, Activity 2)

  ⇒ An analytical and evaluative EBC about an argument that may be used for support (Part 3, Activity 4)

  ⇒ An analytical and evaluative EBC about an opposed argument that may need a response (Part 3, Activity 5)

- Students revisit their previous claims and materials, looking for patterns and ideas that relate to their position.

- Students determine what they can use and how they might adapt or revise each written claim so that it fits coherently into their argument.

- Students gather their relevant supporting claims and present them to a peer-review team, explaining their relationships to each other and to their overall position.

- Through review and discussion in peer review teams, students determine what they still need so that they can develop and prove their argument. Based on peer feedback, they identify additional claims they will need to write and evidence they will need to locate in support of those claims.

- Students think about a logical sequence or order in which to present their claims—an initial chain of reasoning. For students who need some support or scaffolding, this sequence might be as follows:

  ⇒ Paragraph 1: Explanation of the issue

  ⇒ Paragraph 2: Presentation of the position

  ⇒ Paragraphs 3+: Explanation of and evidence for claims that present supporting arguments and acknowledge opposing claims

- Final paragraph: Presentation of final claims, conclusions, and recommendations.

- Thinking about what seems to be the most logical approach and line of reasoning, students organize their claims into a tentative sequence of premises for their argument and record them on an *Organizing EBC Tool* or a *Delineating Arguments Tool.*

- Students might return to and refine the *Delineating Arguments Tool* they initially used to express their developing position in Part 3, Activity 2.

ACTIVITY 3: ORGANIZING EVIDENCE TO SUPPORT CLAIMS

Students list and sequence their claims and then organize and cite sources for the evidence they will use to explain and support each of the premises of their arguments.

Teacher Modeling

- Model the use of an *Organizing EBC Tool* or a *Delineating Arguments Tool* for a teacher-developed argument related to the unit's issue or problem. Record a statement of a position and three example claims that might be used to develop and support the position.

- In reading teams, have students identify evidence that might be used to support the teacher-developed argument and its claims.

Organizing Evidence

- Based on this modeling, students identify evidence from the sources they have read and analyzed that might be used to support their positions, claims, and arguments. Students might do this by returning to their text annotations and notes and color-coding evidence that is relevant to each of their premises. (See the *Researching to Deepen Understanding* unit for more extensive discussion of this method of identifying and organizing information.)

- Students individually list supporting evidence and cite sources on an *Organizing EBC Tool* or a *Delineating Arguments Tool* for each of the claims they will use in their argument. They should briefly identify the evidence they will use so that they will know where to find it when they begin writing.

- Students categorize evidence under the most relevant of their identified claims or develop and write new claims to account for important evidence that does not fit under any of their existing premises.

≡ ACTIVITY 4: REVIEWING A PLAN FOR ≡ WRITING AN ARGUMENT

Students review and revise their plans to ensure that they are clear, relevant, coherent, strategically sequenced, well reasoned, and sufficiently supported by evidence.

INSTRUCTIONAL NOTES

- Introduce and discuss the Academic Habit of **Revising**. Discuss how literate people are always revising their ideas, perspectives, positions, arguments, and writing. Sometimes revision is done independently, and other times it is done in collaboration with peers. Sometimes revising is done informally, and other times it is part of set processes. Inform students that in the final part of the unit, they will be practicing the Academic Habit of **Revising** as part of the Collaborative Writing Workshop. For this activity they should work on the habit by improving at least one part of their plan based on feedback from one of their peers.

- In reading teams, students individually talk through their organizational plans, using specific vocabulary and their *Organizing EBC Tool* or *Delineating Arguments Tool* to explain the following:

  ⇒ Their understanding of the issue

  ⇒ Their chosen perspective and position

  ⇒ Their organizational approach and the order of their claims

  ⇒ Each of their claims (by reading their claim statements)

  ⇒ The evidence they will use to support their claims and substantiate their argument

- Students consider whether the proposed argument is likely to be convincing (considering issues from the *Evaluating Arguments Tool*) and use the *Student EBA Literacy Skills and Academic Habits Checklist* to discuss and peer review each other's organizational plans. Students should focus on the following Literacy Skills criteria:

LITERACY SKILLS	DESCRIPTORS: *Find evidence of using the literacy skill in the draft.* *Does the writer's plan . . .*	NEEDS WORK	OKAY	VERY STRONG
FORMING CLAIMS	Establish a clear position that is supported by valid claims (premises)?			
USING EVIDENCE	Use well-chosen information and arguments from texts to explain and support claims?			
USING LOGIC	Support the position through a logical sequence of related claims, premises, and supporting evidence?			

NOTE

- Students adjust, revise, or further develop their plans based on criterion-based peer feedback and self-reflection.

PART 4: FORMATIVE ASSESSMENT OPPORTUNITIES

By the end of Part 4, students will have accomplished the following:

- Organized their previous annotations, questions, tools, and written assignments into a coherent compilation
- Sequenced supporting premises by completing *Organizing EBC* or *Delineating Arguments Tools*
- Compiled evidence for their premises on *Organizing EBC* or *Delineating Arguments Tools*
- Discussed, evaluated, and revised their argument plans with peers

LITERACY SKILLS

Students submit their *Organizing EBC* or *Delineating Arguments Tools* to the teacher for formative assessment and criterion-based review and feedback before beginning to write their final arguments in Part 5. Their plans for writing an argument can be evaluated for the targeted skills of **Forming Claims**, **Using Evidence**, **Using Logic**, and **Organizing Ideas**. The plans can be used for a final check of each student's understanding of the issue and the coherence of his or her position and initial argument. Based on these materials, the teacher can determine which students need extra help before they begin drafting their essays.

ACADEMIC HABITS

As a class or in groups, discuss the students' informal experience with **Organizing** and **Revising**. At this point, they have organized their collective notes and tools and used them to arrive at a plan to write an argument. Based on this experience and feedback from peers, they might also have needed to revise their thinking, approach, or position. Have some students share something they changed in their plan based on peer feedback.

> **NOTE**
>
> To support self-, peer, and teacher assessment of skills and habits developed during the unit, a formal *EBA Literacy Skills and Academic Habits Rubric* and less formal *Student Checklist* are provided in the **EBA Literacy Toolbox**.

Developing Core Literacy Proficiencies

DEVELOPING WRITING THROUGH A COLLABORATIVE PROCESS

"For students, writing is a key means of asserting and defending claims, showing what they know about a subject, and conveying what they have experienced, imagined, thought, and felt."

CCSS ELA Literacy Standards, p. 41

OBJECTIVE:	Students learn and practice a collaborative, question-based approach to developing and improving their writing, using Literacy Skills criteria and Guiding Questions to draft and revise argumentative essays.

MATERIALS:
- *Student EBA Literacy Skills and Academic Habits Checklist*
- *Connecting Ideas Handout*
- *Organizing EBC Tool*
- *EBA Terms*

☰ LITERACY SKILLS

TARGETED LITERACY SKILLS	DESCRIPTORS
ORGANIZING IDEAS	Sequences sentences, paragraphs, and parts of an essay to establish a coherent, logical, and unified argument
USING CONVENTIONS	Uses effective sentence structure, grammar, punctuation, and spelling to express ideas and achieve writing and speaking purposes
PUBLISHING	Uses effective formatting and citations to present ideas for specific audiences and purposes
REFLECTING CRITICALLY	Uses literacy terminology and concepts to reflect on, discuss, and evaluate personal and peer literacy development

ACADEMIC HABITS

HABITS DEVELOPED	DESCRIPTORS
REVISING	Rethinks and refines work based on teacher-, peer-, and self-review processes
REMAINING OPEN	Adopts a stance of inquiry—asking questions to learn more—rather than arguing for entrenched positions

ALIGNMENT TO CCSS

TARGETED STANDARDS:

CCSS.ELA-LITERACY.W.9-10.1: Write arguments to support claims in an analysis of substantive topics or texts, using valid reasoning and relevant and sufficient evidence.

CCSS.ELA-LITERACY.W.9-10.4: Produce clear and coherent writing in which the development, organization, and style are appropriate to task, purpose, and audience.

CCSS.ELA-LITERACY.W.9-10.5: Develop and strengthen writing as needed by planning, revising, editing, rewriting, or trying a new approach, focusing on addressing what is most significant for a specific purpose and audience.

CCSS.ELA-LITERACY.W.9-10.9: Draw evidence from literary or informational texts to support analysis, reflection, and research.

CCSS.ELA-LITERACY.SL.9-10.1: Initiate and participate effectively in a range of collaborative discussions (one-on-one, in groups, and teacher-led) with diverse partners on *grades 9–10 topics, texts, and issues*, building on others' ideas and expressing their own clearly and persuasively.

SUPPORTING STANDARDS:

CCSS.ELA-LITERACY.RI.9-10.1: Cite strong and thorough textual evidence to support analysis of what the text says explicitly as well as inferences drawn from the text.

CCSS.ELA-LITERACY.RI.9-10.5: Analyze in detail how an author's ideas or claims are developed and refined by particular sentences, paragraphs, or larger portions of a text (e.g., a section or chapter).

CCSS.ELA-LITERACY.RI.9-10.6: Determine an author's point of view or purpose in a text and analyze how an author uses rhetoric to advance that point of view or purpose.

CCSS.ELA-LITERACY.RI.9-10.8: Delineate and evaluate the argument and specific claims in a text, assessing whether the reasoning is valid and the evidence is relevant and sufficient; identify false statements and fallacious reasoning.

ACTIVITIES

1. **STRENGTHENING WRITING COLLABORATIVELY: PRINCIPLES AND PROCESSES**
   Students learn and practice a collaborative, question-based approach to developing and improving writing, using criteria from the unit and Guiding Questions to begin the drafting and revision process.

2. **FOCUS ON CONTENT: INFORMATION AND IDEAS**
   Students write, discuss, and revise with a focus on articulating their overall ideas with necessary information.

3. **FOCUS ON ORGANIZATION: UNITY, COHERENCE, AND LOGICAL SEQUENCE**
   Students write, discuss, and revise with a focus on the unity of their initial drafts, coherence among their ideas and information, and logic of their organizational sequence.

4. **FOCUS ON SUPPORT: INTEGRATING AND CITING EVIDENCE**
   Students write, discuss, and revise with a focus on their selection, use, and integration of evidence.

5. **ADDITIONAL ROUNDS OF FOCUSED REVIEW AND REVISION**
   Students write, discuss, and revise with a focus on additional issues of expression, conventions, or publication, as determined by the teacher.

ACTIVITY 1: STRENGTHENING WRITING COLLABORATIVELY: PRINCIPLES AND PROCESSES

Students learn and practice a collaborative, question-based approach to developing and improving writing, using criteria from the unit and guiding questions to begin the drafting and revision process.

INSTRUCTIONAL NOTES

FOCUSING ON THE CRITERIA FOR AN EFFECTIVE ARGUMENT

As students prepare for and begin writing their final arguments, they should read or reread the **Building Evidence-Based Arguments—Final Writing Task Handout** and reconsider the three central expectations (criteria) for the assignment:

1. *Present a convincing argument that stems from an understanding of the issue, a reasoned perspective, and a clear, defensible position.*
2. *Organize a set of evidence-based claims in a logical sequence that explains and supports the thesis of the argument.*
3. *Use and cite relevant and credible (trustworthy) evidence to support all claims, counterarguments, and the overall position.*

These three criteria will be used, respectively, to organize three rounds of review and revision within a collaborative writing process, which students will learn, practice, and apply to produce a high-quality final written essay. As they move through the multistage writing and review process, they will first take a wide-angle view of the content of their argument, then focus progressively on its organization and its use of evidence. In each stage of the process, students will also consider how well they are demonstrating the Literacy Skills targeted in this unit that are relevant to the overall content of the argument, its organization, and reasoning and its use of evidence.

DEMONSTRATING LITERACY SKILLS

The skills described in the following table, and targeted throughout the unit, will be applied and demonstrated as students develop their final arguments. As students draft, review, and revise their essays, they will think about how their work provides evidence of proficiency in the following areas:

LITERACY SKILLS	DESCRIPTORS
RECOGNIZING PERSPECTIVE	Uses textual details to recognize an author's or narrator's relationship to and perspective on a text's topic
EVALUATING INFORMATION	Assesses the relevance and credibility of information, ideas, evidence, and logic presented in texts
DELINEATING ARGUMENTATION	Identifies the claims, evidence, and reasoning in explanations and arguments
FORMING CLAIMS	Establishes and presents a clear and defensible position that is supported by a series of valid premises and set in the context of the topic

INSTRUCTIONAL NOTES

LITERACY SKILLS	DESCRIPTORS
USING EVIDENCE	Presents a comprehensive view of the issue by providing textual evidence to support claims and using sufficient and accurate quotations, paraphrases, and references
USING LOGIC	Establishes and supports a position through a logical sequence of related premises and supporting evidence
ORGANIZING IDEAS	Sequences sentences, paragraphs, and parts of an essay to establish a coherent, logical, and unified argument

LEARNING A COLLABORATIVE APPROACH TO DEVELOPING WRITING

In this first activity, students learn about the collaborative, question-based approach to developing and improving writing and initially practice that approach in the context of talking out a first draft. Each of the activities in the sequence addresses the four components of the Collaborative Workshop as described in the User Guide (*Modeling, Guided Writing, Text-Centered Discussion, Read Aloud*), following the format and model that is first practiced in Activity 1. As students experience each phase of the activity, explain the purpose and focus of each of these components as students begin work to develop and strengthen their writing.

Recommended Resource

One of the finest and most helpful resources to support writers as they work to develop and strengthen their writing, and teachers as they facilitate the learning process, is John R. Trimble's *Writing with Style: Conversations on the Art of Writing* (Longman, 2010; ISBN: 9780205028801). Trimble begins by discussing the critical importance of "thinking well" and of both "selling and serving" one's reader, and moves from there to concrete tips about writing, revision, and editing. Trimble's central premise is that effective writers "have accepted the grim reality that nine tenths of all writing is rewriting" (p. 9). Trimble's ideas will occasionally be referenced in the unit's activity sequence and can provide a valuable supplement to the brief discussions of effective writing presented here. Here are his "four essentials" (p. 6):

1. Have something to say that's worth a reader's attention.
2. Be sold on its validity and importance yourself so you can pitch it with conviction.
3. Furnish strong arguments that are well supported with concrete proof.
4. Use confident language—vigorous verbs, strong nouns, and assertive phrasing.

Teacher Modeling

Because students may begin their first draft from different places of readiness and resources, model (or at least discuss) several possible approaches to drafting, for example:

Working from Previous Thinking and Planning: In Part 4, Activity 5, students have used the tools to frame and review an initial plan for their argument that included their written EBC about the nature of the problem, their position, their logical approach and line of reasoning, the claims that formed the building blocks of their argument, and the evidence they might use to substantiate those claims. Students will also have completed a series of tools and written claims about various arguments they have read. Model how one might use these materials to talk out a first draft as guided and organized by these resources and this emerging plan or outline.

> ### NOTE
>
> This approach may work best for students who know what they want to argue, have been able to plan a structure for their argument, and are most comfortable writing from a preexisting plan.

Working from a Previously Written Paragraph(s):   Throughout Parts 1 through 4, students will have composed paragraphs that present and support claims about the nature of the issue and various arguments written in response to it. One or more of these paragraphs may be a starting point from which to build their argument. Using either a teacher or student example paragraph, model how one can take an existing draft paragraph, and either write from it or expand it to produce a more fleshed-out, multipoint argument.

> ### NOTE
>
> This approach may work best for students who are very happy with something they have already written or who have trouble getting started and putting words to paper but are more comfortable moving forward once they are started.

Writing to Discover or Clarify Thinking: Some students may have moved through Parts 1 through 4 with many thoughts in their head about the topic and what they have been reading, but they may still be unclear about exactly what position they want to take or how they might argue for it. For these students, model how a less formal freewrite about the topic—and various questions or ideas that have arisen during the unit—might help them get their thinking out on paper and then discuss it with others. Emphasize that with this approach, they are writing their way to an emergent understanding and sense of direction.

> ### NOTE
>
> This approach may work best for students who are still uncertain how they feel about the topic or problem or who have difficulty writing a thesis and developing an outline prior to writing.

No matter what approach to drafting students follow, remind them that they are trying to work out their thinking so that others can examine it—and to follow Trimble's essential advice to "have something to say that's worth a reader's attention."

Guided and Supported Writing

In this first phase of the writing process, students should focus on less formal, more fluid writing, trying first to get their ideas out on paper so that they and others can examine them. Students should be given adequate time and opportunity to write in class and be expected to produce something on demand that can be reviewed by others. They may be taking very different approaches to talking out their first drafts, but they should be able to explain to others what they are doing and why.

Guiding Questions

Present students with one or more general question to think about as they begin to talk out their initial drafts, and model how those questions might relate to any of the three approaches to talking out a draft. Use Guiding Questions that prompt reflection, such as these:

> ⇒ What do I know and think about this topic or issue?
>
> ⇒ How can I help others understand my thinking?

Text-Centered Discussion

As students write, they may also begin to check in informally with others—teacher and peers.

- Initially, they might simply communicate what their approach to generating a first draft is and why.

- As their drafts begin to emerge, conversations can be organized by the Guiding Questions suggested previously.

- When most students have gotten a first draft out on paper, organize them into review pairs for their first, modeled close-reading session. For this reading, students will use a process (that should be familiar from Units 1 through 3) to examine their partner's emerging argument a first time. For this session, explain and model the following guidelines:

    > ⇒ Reading partners initially listen to each draft as it is read aloud by the writer.
    >
    > ⇒ Partners then exchange papers with no additional discussion of what they have written.
    >
    > ⇒ Readers analyze the draft, looking especially for textual evidence that expresses the writer's understanding of the issue, perspective, and position. Readers do not evaluate or make suggestions for improvement at this stage.
    >
    > ⇒ Readers share their analyses with writers, striving to be non-evaluative and specific, constructive, and text-based in their observations. (Model observations that either meet or do not meet these criteria for a good response, which will become even more important in later activities.)
    >
    > ⇒ As they listen to their partner's responses, drafting pairs should work on the following behaviors, all related to the Academic Habits of Listening, Remaining Open, and Revising:

Listening

> ⇒ Listen fully to what readers have observed.
>
> ⇒ Consider their ideas thoughtfully.
>
> ⇒ Wait momentarily before responding verbally.

Remaining Open

> ⇒ Avoid explanations or justifications for what they as writers have tried to do (no "yes, but . . ." responses).
>
> ⇒ Frame additional informal, text-based questions to further probe their readers' observations.

Revising

> ⇒ Consider the implications of their readers' observations for improving their writing.

- Based on their partners' observations and responses to text-based questions, writers determine what they want to continue to work on as they revisit their initial drafts and return to in-class writing.

- Throughout the process, circulate in the room and ask students to share their observations, questions, and reflections with you. Provide feedback and guidance when necessary.

Read-Alouds

In this initial activity, read-alouds occur informally, in pairs, at the start of text-centered discussions.

☰ ACTIVITY 2: FOCUS ON CONTENT: IDEAS ☰ AND INFORMATION

Students write, discuss, and revise with a focus on articulating their overall ideas with necessary information.

INSTRUCTIONAL NOTES

In this phase of the writing, review, and revising process, students will focus on the overall content of their argument, considering the first of the assignment's three criteria. Their essay should do the following:

1. *Present a convincing argument that comes from an understanding of the issue and a clear perspective and position.*

In this classroom writing activity (and all subsequent activity sequences), the same general process and procedures are followed—in this case to support students as they continue to draft or redraft an argument that will eventually serve as their final product and summative assessment in the unit. In Activity 1, students have focused on getting their ideas and information on paper and listening as a reader analyzes what their draft communicates about their understanding, perspective, and position. Students will begin this activity with a new, criteria- and question-based text-centered discussion that more formally helps them examine and think about the content of their emerging drafts.

Remind them that they will be engaged in thoughtful conversations, to French essayist Montaigne "the most fruitful and natural exercise of our minds," and that they will be using those conversations to address Trimble's second essential for an effective written argument, to "be sold on its validity and importance yourself so you can pitch it with conviction" (*Essais,* 1580).

Teacher Modeling

The demonstration lesson focuses on the first of the three assignment criteria and on the related Literacy Skills of **Forming Claims**, **Evaluating Information**, and **Using Evidence**. Begin the demonstration lesson by again clarifying what the overall writing task is, what the final product will be, and a general time line for generating, improving, and finalizing that product. Review the three assignment criteria and the *Student EBA Literacy Skills and Academic Habits Checklist* to clarify that students' final products will be analyzed and evaluated in terms of their content, organization, and evidence and their demonstration of the skills associated with **Forming Claims, Evaluating Information**, and **Using Evidence**.

- Introduce a general guiding review question related to the overall content of the writing, and the criteria, such as "What is the writer's central position, and how does it reflect an understanding of the issue?"

- Provide students with a draft paragraph that represents a skeletal or emerging argument (either teacher-developed or taken from an anonymous student) and read the paragraph aloud.

- In review teams, have students reread the draft paragraph in light of the general guiding question. Student teams then share text-based responses to the question with the class, as if the teacher is the paragraph's author.

- Focus students' attention on the first assignment criterion—regarding the essay's content and analysis—and its key components.

- Present a convincing argument that comes from an understanding of the issue and a clear perspective and position.

- Also read closely and study the specific language of one of the criteria from the *Student EBA Literacy Skills and Academic Habits Checklist:*

LITERACY SKILL	DESCRIPTOR
FORMING CLAIMS	States a meaningful position that is well supported by evidence from texts

- Model and discuss what specific language in the assignment and skills criteria might mean within an argument, for example, what does it mean to state a *position*, that is also *meaningful*, that is "supported by evidence." and that is *well supported by evidence from texts*. Discuss these key phrases with students—and their implications for developing a *convincing argument*. With the review criteria as a focus, frame one or more text-based question(s) that you might pose to a reviewer who was going to give you specific feedback about the draft paragraph.

Text-Based Review Question(s)

⇒ Is my position clear? Meaningful?

⇒ In sentences 3 to 5, what helps you as a reader understand the issue and my perspective on it?

⇒ What might I add (or revise) to help you understand that my perspective is based on thoughtful examination and evaluation of evidence and other arguments?

- Students (individually or in review teams) now read the paragraph closely, considering one or more of the text-based review questions and generating a reviewer's response.

- Discuss how a text-based response to a draft piece of writing is a kind of claim that the reviewer makes based on the criteria, question(s), and specific evidence from the draft.

- Model how you might frame a claim-based response if you were a reviewer of the draft paragraph, emphasizing characteristics:

  ⇒ A specific response that emphasizes a strength of the paragraph and a potential improvement

  ⇒ A constructive and respectful articulation of the response

  ⇒ Text-based evidence in the paragraph that has led to and supports your response

- Guided by this model, students articulate and share their text-based responses and constructive reviewer claims, as if their partners were now the writer of the draft paragraph. Have several student volunteers present their responses to the whole class and discuss how the responses are (or are not) specific, constructive, and text-based.

- Model the writer's behaviors introduced and practiced in Activity 1: (1) listen fully to what readers have observed, (2) wait momentarily before responding verbally, (3) avoid explanations or justifications for what you as a writer have tried to do (no "yes, but . . ." responses), and (4) frame additional informal, text-based questions to further probe your readers' observations.

- Discuss what you might do as a writer after considering the responses you have gotten to your text-based review questions.

Text-Centered Discussion

- Before continuing the drafting process, students will engage in their first criterion- and question-based review of their own writing. This initial review team conference is structured and facilitated by the teacher based on the modeling and practice just completed with the draft paragraph. Discussions follow this protocol:

  1. Each discussion begins with a focus on the assignment and Literacy Skills criteria and a related general Guiding Review Question.

  2. The student whose work is being reviewed poses a specific text-based review question to guide the reading and review. Reviewers can probe this question to clarify what specifically the writer wants to know about his or her draft.

  3. The close reading and review of the draft (or section of draft) focuses on discussing specific responses to the question, making and sharing reviewers' claims, and citing specific textual evidence from the draft. Reviewers present and support claims about the writing's overall strengths in terms of ideas and content and about possible areas for improvement of its thinking and the explanation of that thinking.

- With a reading partner, students engage in and practice this protocol using their emerging draft arguments previously reviewed in Activity 1. Students first frame and share their specific text-based review question. Reading partners read and review the draft, using the question to drive their close reading and search for specific textual evidence. In response to the question, reviewers then share observations and (potentially, if students are ready to do so) suggestions for improvement.

- Writers practice exhibiting the behaviors of a constructive text-centered discussion:

Listening

⇒ Listen fully to what readers have observed.

⇒ Consider their ideas thoughtfully.

⇒ Wait momentarily before responding verbally.

Remaining Open

⇒ Avoid explanations or justifications for what they as writers have tried to do (no "yes, but . . ." responses).

⇒ Frame additional informal, text-based questions to further probe their readers' observations.

Guided and Supported Writing

- Students will be working to further develop and strengthen their initial draft of their final product, focusing on the overall criteria for content, ideas, and information and the feedback they have gotten from reviewers. They will work to improve how well the essay presents a convincing argument that stems from an understanding of the issue, a reasoned perspective, and a clear, defensible position.

- Based on constructive feedback from their readers, students frame a direction and strategy for what they want to work on to improve the ideas and information of their arguments.

- Students work on all or parts of their writing in light of this direction and strategy.

- Informal conferences—either with the teacher or other students—can occur throughout this writing time, with check-ins about what the writer is working on and how it is going.

Read-Alouds

Periodically, students might read emerging sections of their drafts, talking about what they are working on in terms of questions and criteria. As some students complete their initial drafts, they might simply read what they have written so that students who are not yet finished get a chance to hear what a completed and strengthened first draft might sound like.

≡ ACTIVITY 3: FOCUS ON ORGANIZATION: UNITY, ≡ COHERENCE, AND LOGICAL SEQUENCE

Students write, discuss, and revise with a focus on the unity of their initial drafts, coherence among their ideas and information, and logic of their organizational sequence.

INSTRUCTIONAL NOTES

In this phase of the writing, review, and revising process, students will focus on the organization, reasoning, and logic of their argument, considering the second of the assignment's three criteria. Their final essay should do the following:

2. *Organize a set of claims in an order that explains and supports the position.*

The third activity in the sequence emphasizes issues related to the overall line of reasoning and unity of the argument. In conjunction with the assignment criterion for organization, related criteria from the **Student EBA Literacy Skills and Academic Habits Checklist** are considered as students develop and strengthen their writing. The Literacy Skills focused on in Activity 3 are as follow:

LITERACY SKILLS	DESCRIPTORS
FORMING CLAIMS	States a meaningful position that is well supported by evidence from texts
ORGANIZING IDEAS	Sequences sentences and paragraphs to establish coherent, logical, and unified narratives, explanations, and arguments
DELINEATING ARGUMENTATION	Identifies the claims, evidence, and reasoning in explanations and arguments

Teacher Modeling

- The demonstration lesson focuses on the expectations of the second assignment criterion for organization and the skills criteria for **Using Logic** and **Organizing Ideas**.

- Begin the lesson with a close reading and discussion of the assignment and skills criteria. Emphasize the importance of phrases such as *logical sequence, valid claims,* and *coherent and unified argument.*

- To examine the unity, coherence, and logic of an argument's line of reasoning, students can benefit from studying their writing drafts in a skeletal form. Model how they might do this with either a teacher-developed or anonymous student draft (or even a text from the unit's reading). With a highlighter, shade the key sentences of the argument—those that establish its position and each of the premises presented in support of that position—often, but not always, the topic sentences. (Alternately, extract these sentences into a separate document or record them on a **Delineating Arguments** or **Organizing EBC Tool**.)

- Read the skeletal sentences aloud, with students following. Present students with the Guiding Question and focal criteria (presented in the following "Text-Centered Discussion" notes).

- Ask them to reread the skeletal text and offer observations directly connected to the question and criteria and to specific evidence from the draft.

- Based on these observations, model how you might determine a strategy for rethinking or revising the draft's organization, and present a specific text-based review question to guide your work in developing and strengthening the draft—and your readers' review of that draft.

Text-Centered Discussion

Text-centered review discussions will likely happen at the start of the writing and revising phase of the activity, and again, less formally, with the teacher and peers during writing time. Students should begin by extracting their skeletal argument (either through highlighting or cutting and pasting) so that readers can focus on the line of reasoning. Before asking a reader to review a draft, students should formulate their own text-based review questions to direct close reading and evidence-based feedback.

Guiding Question

⇒ What is the order in which claims are presented by the writer in this argument?

Criteria

Focus reading, review, and writing on the key words of the assignment's second criterion—organization:

⇒ Organize a set of claims in an order that explains and supports the position.

As students focus on this expectation for the assignment, they will also consider these criteria from the *Literacy Skills Checklist*.

LITERACY SKILLS	DESCRIPTORS
ORGANIZING IDEAS	Organizes claims, supporting ideas, and evidence in a logical order
USING LOGIC	Establishes and supports a position through a logical sequence of related claims, premises, and supporting evidence

Examples of Text-Based Review Questions

⇒ Is my sequence of related claims logical? Does it make sense as a way of explaining and supporting my position?

⇒ Is my essay unified into a coherent argument?

⇒ How might I rethink, re-sequence, or reorganize my four premises to improve the clarity or logic of my argument?

Guided and Supported Writing

Students will be working to improve the overall line of reasoning and organization of their draft arguments. This may entail resequencing their premises, adding additional premises, deleting sections that take the argument off course, or adopting a different organizational plan. In classroom conferences, remind them to focus less at this point on specific issues of expression or conventions and more on their overall line of thinking from introduction to conclusion. It may be easiest for students to do this work within the skeletal or outlined version of their draft and then revise its paragraphs within the new organizational plan they develop.

Read-Alouds

Periodically, students might read their skeletal arguments aloud and share what they are doing (or have done) to improve the essay's organization and their line of reasoning.

≡ ACTIVITY 4: FOCUS ON SUPPORT: ≡ INTEGRATING AND CITING EVIDENCE

Students write, discuss, and revise with a focus on their selection, use, and integration of evidence.

INSTRUCTIONAL NOTES

In this phase of the writing, review, and revising process, students will focus on their use of evidence to support their argument, considering the third of the assignment's three criteria. Their final essay should do the following:

3. *Use relevant and trustworthy evidence to support all claims and the overall position.*

Point out that this expectation for the assignment is closely related to the Literacy Skill of **Using Evidence** that they have worked on throughout this and other units:

USING EVIDENCE	Uses well-chosen details from texts to explain and support claims; accurately paraphrase or quote

Teacher Modeling

- The demonstration lesson focuses on the assignment criteria for use of supporting evidence (see previous).

- Begin the lesson with a close reading and discussion of key words from the criterion for evidence: "relevant and trustworthy evidence, support all claims . . . and the overall position." Emphasize that the first step in using *well-chosen details from texts* is to select evidence that is closely related to their position (relevant) and comes from sources they can trust (*trustworthy*).

- Review what students have learned about the relevance and trustworthy nature of sources and discuss what this means in terms of the evidence they select to support an argument. Focus on the Literacy Skills they should use and demonstrate in order to ensure that their evidence is relevant and credible:

LITERACY SKILLS	DESCRIPTORS
RECOGNIZING PERSPECTIVE	Identifies and explains the author's view of the text's topic
EVALUATING INFORMATION	Assesses the relevance and credibility of information in texts
DELINEATING ARGUMENTATION	Identifies and analyzes the claims, evidence, and reasoning in arguments

- Discuss the ways in which a writer can use and cite evidence within an argument. Remind students that supporting evidence may be integrated into an argument through references to other texts or information, citing of data, direct quotations, or paraphrasing. Emphasize also Trimble's reminder that "strong arguments" require "concrete proof" and that writers do not merely insert quotations but rather select and use them thoughtfully to develop or support their ideas.

- Select a single draft paragraph (one with a highlighted claim from Activity 3) to use in modeling. With a second color highlighter (or with underlining or a symbol system), annotate the paragraph to indicate the evidence that is presented to support the claim.
- Have students read the paragraph, using the Guiding Question (presented in the following "Text-Centered Discussion" notes) to make observations about the nature and use of evidence. Introduce one or more of the criteria and discuss how you might use those criteria to review and rethink the use of evidence in the paragraph, including discussing where evidence might need to be reconsidered that may not be relevant or credible and where new evidence might be added to better support the claim.

Text-Centered Discussion

As in the demonstration lesson, students might begin reviewing and revising a single paragraph of their drafts to develop their thinking and practice their skills. The writing phase of the activity might begin with a short text-centered discussion using the Guiding Question and one or more criteria to get a sense of issues in the paragraph's use of evidence. Based on this first review, students frame a specific text-based review question and set a direction for revision. As students revise paragraphs, they can discuss with the teacher and peers, using the text-based review question to guide close reading, discussion, and feedback.

Guiding Question

- What sort of evidence has the writer used to support the claim? (Data? References? Quotations? Paraphrasing?)

Criteria

Focus reading, review, and writing on the assignment's criterion for evidence:

- Use relevant and trustworthy evidence to support all claims and the overall position.

For each claim they present as a premise or building block of their argument, students thus need to think about these points:

- The relevance and credibility of the evidence they use
- How to integrate that evidence smoothly within their writing—how they use and cite it and whether they quote or paraphrase
- How to provide enough, convincing evidence to support their position and to prove their argument

Depending on which of these issues students are working on, they should try to think about, use, and demonstrate any or all of these criteria from *Student EBA Literacy Skills and Academic Habits Checklist*:

LITERACY SKILLS	DESCRIPTORS
EVALUATING INFORMATION	Assesses the relevance, credibility, and logic of information in texts

DELINEATING ARGUMENTATION	Identifies and analyzes the claims, evidence, and reasoning in arguments
USING EVIDENCE	Uses well-chosen details from texts to explain and support claims; accurately paraphrases or quotes

Example of Text-Based Review Questions

⇒ Is my evidence clearly presented? Relevant? Credible? Sufficient (is there enough)?

⇒ How might I better integrate the evidence in sentences 4 and 5 with the overall discussion?

⇒ Should I quote or paraphrase? Where will each approach be most effective?

Guided and Supported Writing

Students will be working to strengthen their use of evidence, which may entail rethinking the evidence itself, inserting new evidence, or reconsidering how they have presented and integrated the evidence into their paragraphs. The guided writing process will be iterative, with students potentially working through several cycles with a single paragraph, then moving on to other sections of their drafts.

Read-Alouds

Periodically, students might share single paragraphs they are working on, reading them aloud and then discussing what they have come to think about their use and integration of supporting evidence.

ACTIVITY 5: ADDITIONAL ROUNDS OF FOCUSED REVIEW AND REVISION

Students write, discuss, and revise with a focus on additional issues of expression, conventions, or publication, as determined by the teacher.

INSTRUCTIONAL NOTES

Activities 1 through 4 enable students to become comfortable with the collaborative process for developing and strengthening their writing. The review and revision activities cause them to reflect on and strengthen their writing skills as they learn how to build an evidence-based argument. At this point, review activities and revision should focus on aspects of writing that are involved in translating good thinking into a clear, effective, and polished written product: connections and transitions; clarity and impact of language; grammar, punctuation, and spelling; and final editing and formatting for publication. Reviews for these rounds can be organized to examine and improve any of these relevant Literacy Skills from the ***Student EBA Literacy Skills and Academic Habits Checklist***:

LITERACY SKILLS	DESCRIPTORS
USING LANGUAGE	Writes and speaks clearly so others can understand claims and ideas
USING CONVENTIONS	Correctly uses sentence elements, punctuation, and spelling to produce clear writing
PUBLISHING	Correctly uses, formats, and cites textual evidence to support claims

Based on their specific instructional objectives, students' needs, and time restrictions, teachers should select one or more of these additional aspects for students to focus on in additional rounds of collaborative review and revision. The additional review activities should follow the same principles and processes with which students have now become familiar.

As now established, the process should involve these steps:

- Teacher modeling
- Text-centered discussion
- Guided and supported writing
- Read-alouds

Review discussions should incorporate these elements:

- Guiding Questions
- Criteria
- Text-based review questions

At each round of review, model how to use the language of the **Student EBA Literacy Skills and Academic Habits Checklist** as criteria from which to develop questions and provide feedback. You may choose to work with a model paragraph or one from a student as you talk through ways to think about areas for improvement in the writing's use of language or use of conventions.

PREPARING A FINAL DRAFT FOR PUBLICATION

As students complete their final review and revision processes, they should reread the **Building Evidence-Based Arguments—Final Writing Task Handout** and reflect on how well they have demonstrated the assignment criteria and the Literacy Skills targeted in the unit. They should format the essay and build a bibliography or source list following conventions prescribed by the teacher. The publication of their argument will potentially be more meaningful for them if they have been considering a specific audience and purpose, which the teacher might establish early in the unit or during the final revision stage. As they submit or present their final essays, students might also write a less formal reflection about what they have learned in the unit and how their essay represents their learning. This activity can also be combined with a final class discussion about the unit's issue, the various positions on it students have taken, and what they have learned about argumentation.

ACADEMIC HABITS

Throughout the multistage collaborative review process, students can reflect on how well they demonstrate Academic Habits associated with **Revising** and **Remaining Open**. They might ask themselves the following questions either individually or in their peer working groups:

- In what ways am I demonstrating the habit of revising my essay based on my reflection and the analyses of others? How might I improve?
- In what ways am I demonstrating the habit of remaining open as my peers give me observations and insights about my writing and ideas? How might I improve?

PART 5: SUMMATIVE ASSESSMENT OPPORTUNITIES

By the end of Part 5, students will have completed the following:

- An initial rough draft of their argument
- A draft that focuses on establishing a clear position and a convincing argument
- A draft that focuses on organizing, sequencing, and connecting ideas
- A draft that focuses on using sufficient evidence and citing sources correctly
- Drafts that focus on issues of clarity and impact of the writing, such as transitions, language and expression, usage and conventions, or publication.
- A multistage collaborative review and revision process
- A final written argumentative essay

ASSESSING LITERACY SKILLS

Having gone through peer review and revision, students' final argumentative essays should provide evidence of each student's development of the Literacy Skills targeted in the unit—especially the reading and thinking skills that have been the focus of instruction and that are involved in building an evidence-based argument. The *Student EBA Literacy Skills and Academic Habits Checklist* in the **Evidence-Based Argument Literacy Toolbox** can be used to guide students during the review and revision process, to frame peer and self-assessment, and to provide informal teacher feedback. A more formal *EBA Literacy Skills and Academic Habits Rubric* should be used by the teacher for evaluating performance and growth as demonstrated in the final essay and the reading and thinking exercises that have preceded it. This rubric includes a four-point developmental scale for indicating where students are on a continuum from "emerging" to "excelling" and also enables the teacher to indicate specific skill areas in which students have demonstrated noticeable growth.

The rubric lists the three assignment criteria for the argumentative essay that students have focused on during the writing and review process to enable evaluation of their written product as well as the Literacy Skills and Academic Habits they have demonstrated in developing that product. At the bottom of the rubric is a place for an overall summary evaluation—potentially a grade. A grade can also be computed in a point-based grading system by tallying the ratings for each of the criteria in the rubric (some of which may be weighted by the teacher as more important).

Notes to the teacher about using this rubric: When evaluating students' argumentative essays and other evidence from the unit, the following process for using the Teacher Rubric is recommended:

Find evidence in the student's essays and tools to support ratings for each of the component Literacy Skills and overall essay content criteria listed in the rubric. Based on that evidence, use the developmental scale to rate the grade-level performance demonstrated by the student as:

1—**Emerging:** needs improvement

2—**Developing:** shows progress

3—**Becoming Proficient:** demonstrates skills

4—**Excelling:** exceeds expectations

If there is insufficient evidence to make a confident rating, mark **NE** (not enough evidence).

Indicate if the student has demonstrated growth in each skill area during the unit by adding a "+" to the rating. Determine a summary evaluation based on the overall pattern of ratings and strength of evidence. This summary evaluation can be computed based on points, or determined by examining the prevalent pattern in the criteria-based ratings.

(See the Users Guide for more complete discussion about how to use the rubric as a tool for evaluating and grading students' work.)

Evidence of Reading and Thinking

Though the final essay is a written product, it should first and foremost be used as evidence of Literacy Skills associated with delineating and producing Arguments. In addition to **Delineating Argumentation**, students have been working on and demonstrating many of the following literacy skills throughout the Developing Core Literacy Proficiencies multiunit sequence: **Recognizing Perspective, Evaluating Information, Forming Claims, Using Evidence, Using Logic, Organizing Ideas, Using Conventions, Publishing,** and **Reflecting Critically.** In their summative assignment, students should be able to demonstrate evidence of developing proficiency in these skill areas within their final essays and through the formative tools and written exercises they have completed. Specifically, students should show that they can identify and analyze the following:

- A topic and the specific issues it presents
- Key components of an argumentative text
- An author's position and perspective on a given issue
- Relevant, credible, and sufficient supporting evidence for a position
- The chain of reasoning of an argument

Students should also show that they are able to do the following:

- Develop evidence-based claims about arguments
- Form a clear and evidence-based position on an issue
- Organize a string of claims in a logical sequence that supports a stated position

- Cite texts appropriately and sufficiently
- Write using appropriate grammar and tone for a desired audience

Students should not be expected to mimic a position presented by the teacher or suggested by one of the unit's texts. Rather, they should demonstrate that they can do original thinking based on their own analysis of several texts on a given issue.

Evidence of Writing

This argumentative essay may be the first long piece of formal writing that students have done in which they are required to develop a position that is supported by their analysis, evaluation, and citation of multiple texts from a given topic area. As such, it can serve as a formative assessment of their proficiency in the complex task of building and communicating an evidence-based argument.

However, students' essays can also be viewed and evaluated as a culminating assessment of students' general writing skills—skills they have developed and demonstrated throughout the Developing Core Literacy Proficiencies program. As such, the essay should provide evidence of students' writing skills associated with **Organizing Ideas**, **Using Language**, **Using Conventions**, and **Correctly Citing Evidence** when publishing.

ASSESSING ACADEMIC HABITS

By the end of the *Building Evidence-Based Arguments* unit, students will have been informally reflecting on and self-assessing their development of the Academic Habits associated with the process of discovering and analyzing an important issue that affects society. These include **Remaining Open** as they explore the topic, qualifying views of prior understanding they bring into or develop within the research process, and **Revising** their thinking and writing within a collaborative process.

Using the *Student EBA Literacy Skills and Academic Habits Checklist* provided with the unit, students can do a more careful self-assessment of their development and demonstration of these habits during the unit—paying particular attention to where and how they have shown (or have not shown) evidence of using the habits productively. The teacher can also use this checklist to provide feedback to students. If it is appropriate or desirable to make this feedback evaluative in nature, the checklist can be used with a three-point system (minus, check, plus) to communicate not only which habits each student has evidenced but also how well.

BUILDING EVIDENCE-BASED ARGUMENTS UNIT TEXTS

This table lists the unit texts, organized by the text sets connected to the progression of instructional activities. Additional texts for some of the sets are indicated with an *AT*.

The unit uses texts that are accessible for free on the Internet without any login information, membership requirements, or purchase. Because of the ever-changing nature of website addresses, links are not provided. Teachers and students can locate these texts through web searches using the information provided.

NO.	TITLE	AUTHOR	DATE	SOURCE/ PUBLISHER
Text Set 1: Background Informational Texts				
1.1	"What Is Terrorism?"	Laura Beth Nielsen	4/17/2013	Al Jazeera—English
1.2	"Terrorists or Freedom Fighters: What's the Difference?"	John Bolt	11/14/2001	Acton Institute
1.3	"Militant Extremists in the United States"	Jonathan Masters	2/7/2011	Council on Foreign Relations
Text Set 2: Additional Background Informational Texts				
2.1	Major Terrorism Cases: Past and Present	FBI	NA	FBI.gov
2.2	September 11 Attacks Timeline	National September 11 Memorial and Museum	NA	9/11memorial.org
2.3	Events of 9/11	History.com	NA	History.com
AT	"Title 18: Crimes and Criminal Procedure; Part 1—Crimes; Chapter 113B—Terrorism"	Cornell Law	NA	*Cornell Law*
AT	"A Brief History of Terrorism in the United States"	Brian Resnick	4/16/2013	*National Journal*
AT	USS *Cole* Bombing Fast Facts	CNN Library	9/18/2013	CNN
AT	The History of Terrorism	Amy Zalman	NA	About.com

Text Set 3: Political Cartoons			
3.1	"Political Cartoons: The Human Aspect of Modern Conflict"	Various	NA	College of Education at the University of Texas—Austin
Text Set 4: Seminal Arguments			
4.1	"Authorization for Use of Military Force"	Public Law 107—40	9/18/2001	107th Congress gpo.gov, fas.org
4.2	George W. Bush's Address to the Nation on September 11, 2001 (text)	President Bush	9/11/2001	Salem Press
4.2	"George W. Bush's Address to the Nation on September 11, 2001" (video)	President Bush	9/11/2001	CNN/YouTube.com
4.3	"A Place of Peace: For a 9/11 Victim's Widow, Revenge Is Not the Answer"	Lauren Frohne	9/4/2011	*Boston Globe*
AT	Osama bin Laden's Declaration of Jihad against Americans	Osama bin Laden	1996	Salem Press
AT	9/11 Paul Wolfowitz Interview PBS *News Hour* with Jim Lehrer	Paul Wolfowitz	9/14/2001	PBS.org— NewsHour with Jim Lehrer (transcript)/ YouTube.com (video)
AT	"U.S. Response to Terrorism: A Strategic Analysis of the Afghanistan" "Campaign	Valentina Taddeo	Summer 2010	*Journal of Strategic Security* (http:// scholarcommons. usf.edu)
Text Set 5: Additional Arguments			
5.1	Our War on Terrorism	Howard Zinn	11/2004	Progressive.org
5.2	"Obama's Speech on Drone Policy"	President Obama	5/23/2013	*New York Times*
5.3	Remarks by President Obama on the death of Osama bin Laden	President Obama	5/2/2011	Whitehouse.gov
5.4	"Why Drones Work: The Case for Washington's Weapon of Choice"	Daniel L. Byman	2013	Brookings.edu
AT	"Terrorism Can Only Be Defeated by Education, Tony Blair Tells the UN"	NA	11/22/2013	*UN News* (news article and video)

BUILDING EVIDENCE-BASED ARGUMENTS

DEVELOPING CORE LITERACY PROFICIENCIES

GRADE 9

Literacy Toolbox

ODELL
EDUCATION

EVIDENCE-BASED ARGUMENTS TERMS

ISSUE	An important aspect of human society for which there are many different opinions about what to think or do; many issues can be framed as a problem-based question
RELATIONSHIP TO ISSUE	A person's particular personal involvement with an issue, given his or her experience, education, occupation, socioeconomic-geographical status, interests, or other characteristics
PERSPECTIVE	How someone understands and views an issue based on his or her current relationship to it and analysis of the issue
POSITION	Someone's stance on what to do or think about a clearly defined issue based on his or her perspective and understanding of it; when writing an argumentative essay, one's position may be expressed as a thesis
THESIS	Another word for *position* sometimes used when writing an argument to support it
IMPLICATIONS	The practical and logical consequences of a position that has been supported by evidence-based argumentation
PREMISES	The claims of an argument that are linked together logically using evidence and reasoning to support a position or thesis
EVIDENCE	The topical and textual facts, events, and ideas from which the claims of an argument arise and which are cited to support the argument's position
REASONING	The logical relationships among ideas, including claims, premises, and evidence
CHAIN OF REASONING	The logical relationships linking the premises of an argument that lead to the demonstration and support of a position
CLAIM	A personal conclusion about a text, topic, event, or idea
EVIDENCE-BASED CLAIM	A personal conclusion that arises from and is supported by textual and topical evidence

ODELL
EDUCATION

BUILDING EVIDENCE-BASED ARGUMENTS—FINAL WRITING TASK

In this unit, you have been developing your skills as a presenter of reasoned arguments. You have learned to do the following things:

- Understand the background and key aspects of an important issue
- Look at various viewpoints on the issue
- Read the arguments of others closely and thoughtfully
- Develop your own view of the issue and take a position on it
- Make and prove your case by using sound evidence and reasoning to support it
- Improve your thinking and writing so that others will clearly understand and appreciate your evidence-based argument—and think about the case you have made for it

Your final writing assignment—the development of an evidence-based argumentative essay—will provide you with opportunities to use all of these related skills and to demonstrate your proficiency and growth in building evidence-based arguments. The assignment will also represent your final work in the Developing Core Literacy Proficiencies sequence and should demonstrate all that you have learned as a reader, thinker, and writer this year.

FINAL ASSIGNMENT

Developing, Writing, and Revising an Evidence-Based Argumentative Essay

Having read a collection of informational texts and arguments related to the unit's issue, you will develop a supported position on the issue. You will then plan, draft, and revise a multiparagraph essay that makes a case for your position. To do this, you will do the following:

1. Review the texts you have read, the tools you have completed, and the claims you have formed throughout the unit to determine the position you will take on the issue.
2. Write a paragraph that clearly states and explains your position—and the support you have found for it.
3. Read or reread arguments related to your position, looking for evidence you might use to support your argument.
4. Read or reread arguments that take an opposed or different position and think about how you might respond to these arguments.
5. Use a ***Delineating Arguments Tool*** to plan a multiparagraph essay that presents a series of claims, supported by evidence, to develop an argument in favor of your position.
6. Draft a multiparagraph essay that explains, develops, and supports your argumentative position—keeping in mind these criteria for this final writing assignment. Your essay should accomplish the following:
    ⇒ Present a convincing argument that comes from your understanding of the issue and a clear perspective and position.

FINAL WRITING TASK (Continued)

FINAL ASSIGNMENTS (Continued)

⇒ Organize a set of claims in an order that explains and supports your position.

⇒ Use relevant and trustworthy evidence to support all claims and your overall position.

⇒ Represent the best thinking and writing you can do.

7. Use a collaborative process with other students to review and improve your draft in key areas:

⇒ The information and ideas that make up your argument

⇒ The organization (unity and logical sequence) of your argument

⇒ Your selection, use, and integration of supporting evidence (quotations, facts, statistics, references to other arguments, etc.)

⇒ The clarity of your writing—in areas identified by your teacher

8. Reflect on how well you have used Literacy Skills and Academic Habits throughout the unit and in developing your final written argument.

SKILLS AND HABITS TO BE DEMONSTRATED

As you become an expert on your issue and develop your evidence-based position and argument, think about demonstrating the Literacy Skills and Academic Habits you have been working on to the best of your ability. Your teacher will evaluate your work and determine your grade based on how well you are able to do the following things:

Read

Recognize Perspective: Identify and explain each author's view of the unit's issue.

Evaluate Information: Assess the relevance and credibility of information in texts about the issue.

Delineate Arguments: Identify and analyze the claims, evidence, and reasoning of arguments related to the issue.

DEVELOP ACADEMIC HABITS

Remain Open to New Ideas: Ask questions of others rather than arguing for your own ideas or opinions.

Qualify Your Views: Explain and change your ideas in response to thinking from others.

Revise: Rethink your position and refine your writing based on feedback from others.

Reflect Critically: Discuss and evaluate your learning, using the criteria that describe the Literacy Skills and Academic Habits you have been developing.

Write

Form Claims: State meaningful positions and conclusions that are well supported by evidence from texts you have examined.

Use Evidence: Use well-chosen details from the texts to support your position and claims. Accurately paraphrase or quote what the authors say in the texts.

FINAL WRITING TASK (Continued)

DEVELOP ACADEMIC HABITS (Continued)

Use Logic: Argue for your position through a logical sequence of related claims, premises, and supporting evidence.

Organize Ideas: Organize your argument, supporting claims, and evidence in an order that makes sense to others.

Use Language: Write clearly so others can understand your position, claims, and supporting ideas.

Use Conventions: Correctly use sentence elements, punctuation, and spelling to produce clear writing.

Publish: Correctly use, format, and cite textual evidence to support your argument.

NOTE

These skills and habits are also listed on the *Student EBA Literacy Skills and Academic Habits Checklist*, which you can use to assess your work and the work of other students.

DELINEATING ARGUMENTS TOOL

Name _ _ _ _ _ _ _ _ _ _ _ **Topic** _ _ _ _ _ _ _ _ _ _ _ _ _ _ _ _

ISSUE

PERSPECTIVE

POSITION

PREMISE/CLAIM 1

Supporting evidence:

PREMISE/CLAIM 2

Supporting evidence:

PREMISE/CLAIM 3

Supporting evidence:

EVALUATING ARGUMENTS TOOL

As you read and delineate the argument, think about each of the **elements** and their **guiding evaluation questions.** Rate each element as

– a **questionable** part or weakness of the argument   ✔ a reasonable or **acceptable** part of the argument   + a **strength** of the argument

ELEMENTS	EVALUATING AN ARGUMENT: GUIDING QUESTIONS	?	✔	+	TEXT-BASED OBSERVATIONS
Issue	• How clearly is the issue presented and explained? • How accurate and current is the explanation of the issue?				
Perspective	• What is the author's relationship to the issue? What is the purpose for the argument? • What is the author's viewpoint or attitude about the issue? How reasonable is this perspective?				
Credibility and Bias	• What are the author's background and credentials relative to the issue? • Does the author have a bias that affect the argument's perspective or interferes with its reasoning? • Does the author use inflammatory language or make highly biased claims?				
Position/ Thesis	• How clearly is the author's position presented and explained? • How well is the position or thesis connected to the claims and evidence of the argument?				
Claims	• How clearly are the argument's claims explained and connected to the position? • Are the claims supported with evidence? • How well are the claims linked together as the premises of the argument?				
Evidence	• Does the supporting evidence come from a range of credible sources? Is it believable? • Is there enough evidence to make the argument convincing?				
Reasoning and Logic	• Are the claims and premises clearly and consistently connected to the position? • Are the connections among the position, premises, evidence, and conclusions of the argument clear and logical?				
Conclusions	• How logical and reasonable are the conclusions drawn by the author? • How well do the the argument's conclusions or suggestions address the issue and align with the position?				
Convincing Argument	• How do the author's overall perspective and position on the issue compare with others? With my own? • Does the argument make sense to me? Do I agree with its claims? Am I convinced?				
Comments:					

QUESTIONING PATH TOOL

Name: _____ **Text:** _____

APPROACHING: *I determine my reading purposes and take note of key information about the text. I identify the LIPS domain(s) that will guide my initial reading.*	Purpose: Key information: LIPS domain(s):

QUESTIONING: *I use Guiding Questions to help me investigate the text (from the **Guiding Questions Handout**).*

1.

2.

ANALYZING: *I question further to connect and analyze the details I find (from the **Guiding Questions Handout**).*

1.

2.

DEEPENING: *I consider the questions of others.*

1.

2.

3.

EXTENDING: *I pose my own questions.*

1.

2.

ODELL
EDUCATION

FORMING EVIDENCE-BASED CLAIMS TOOL (EBA)

Name _ _ _ _ _ _ _ _ _ _ _ _ _ _ _ _ _ Text _

A question I have about the text:

SEARCHING FOR DETAILS

I read the text closely and mark words and phrases that help me answer my question.

SELECTING DETAILS	Detail 1 (Ref.:)	Detail 2 (Ref.:)	Detail 3 (Ref.:)
I select words or phrases from my search that I think are the most important for answering my question. I write the reference next to each detail.			

ANALYZING DETAILS

	What I think about detail 1:	What I think about detail 2:	What I think about detail 3:
I reread parts of the texts and think about the meaning of the details and what they tell me about my question. Then I compare the details and explain the connections I see among them.			

CONNECTING DETAILS

	How I connect the details:
I compare the details and explain the connections I see among them.	

MAKING A CLAIM

	My claim about the text:
I state a conclusion I have come to and can support with evidence from the text after reading it closely.	

ORGANIZING EVIDENCE-BASED CLAIMS TOOL (2PT)

Name _ _ _ _ _ _ _ _ _ _ _ _ _ Text _

CLAIM:

Point 1

A Supporting Evidence	B Supporting Evidence
(Reference:)	(Reference:)
C Supporting Evidence	D Supporting Evidence
(Reference:)	(Reference:)

Point 2

A Supporting Evidence	B Supporting Evidence
(Reference:)	(Reference:)
C Supporting Evidence	D Supporting Evidence
(Reference:)	(Reference:)

ORGANIZING EVIDENCE-BASED CLAIMS TOOL (3PT)

Name _ _ _ _ _ _ _ _ _ _ _ _ _ _ _ _ **Text** _

CLAIM:

Point 1

A   Supporting Evidence

(Reference:)

B   Supporting Evidence

(Reference:)

C   Supporting Evidence

(Reference:)

Point 2

A   Supporting Evidence

(Reference:)

B   Supporting Evidence

(Reference:)

C   Supporting Evidence

(Reference:)

Point 3

A   Supporting Evidence

(Reference:)

B   Supporting Evidence

(Reference:)

C   Supporting Evidence

(Reference:)

ODELL
EDUCATION

DELINEATING ARGUMENTS: CASE STUDY

Friending a Teacher

ISSUE

Mr. Higgins is a twenty-three-year-old social studies teacher at Thunder Ridge Middle School. Over the weekend, he received a friend request on Facebook from Derek, who is one of his students. Derek is a B student who is generally quiet in class. Mr. Higgins has never had a problem with Derek, but he also hasn't interacted with Derek much, either inside or out of class. In order to keep his school life separate from his personal life, Mr. Higgins decided when he took the job at Thunder Ridge that he would not accept a friend request from any of his students. When Derek's parents hear that Mr. Higgins did not accept Derek's request, they scheduled a meeting with Mr. Higgins to demand that he accept the request. They are worried that Mr. Higgins will damage Derek's confidence in school if he continues to reject their son's request.

PERSPECTIVES

DEREK

Derek considers himself a technically savvy student. He thinks that social media are fascinating and he is an avid user of Facebook. One of the reasons he likes Facebook is that it gives teachers and students a way to get to know one another outside of class. Derek sent the request to Mr. Higgins in order to include Facebook as part of the learning environment at Thunder Ridge.

At the meeting, Derek explains why he thinks Mr. Higgins should accept his request:

Look, Mr. Higgins. Everyone is on Facebook these days. You should know this because you have a profile and even with your privacy settings I can tell you use it a lot. If you are using Facebook, you should be a good Facebook citizen and accept requests from people. It's just part of the deal. And it's not a big deal. There's no harm in being friends with students. If you post something, you're okay sharing it, so why not let me learn a bit more about you? I mean, I'll find out anyway when I Google you, so it's not like there are a lot of secrets to find. What really makes me mad about rejecting my friend request is that you aren't treating me fairly. I never do anything wrong in class, so there is no reason to reject my request.

MR. HIGGINS

Mr. Higgins is a popular teacher at Thunder Ridge. He is well known for creating new ways to bring technology to the classroom. Most of the students at Thunder Ridge follow him on Twitter. He doesn't hold Derek's request against him, but Mr. Higgins decided before he started his job that accepting friend requests from any student wouldn't be a good idea.

Mr. Higgins explains his decision to Derek:

Even though online platforms are changing the way students and teachers interact, there need to be boundaries. Facebook is a personal space and if I accept your request, I am worried that you'll forget that I am your teacher. There is a further problem to keep in mind. If I accept your request, I am obligated to accept a request from any student. Even if I had a guarantee that you would handle being friends on Facebook appropriately, I cannot be sure about this with everyone, so I don't want to be in a position in which others can accuse me of playing favorites based on what friend requests I accept. And I'd like to ask you, Derek, if you are friends with your parents on Facebook? I'm guessing that you are probably like most of your classmates who don't want to be friends with their parents because they want to keep their social lives private. My Facebook account is no different. It is a place for me to have a life that is separate from my job as your teacher.

OTHER PERSPECTIVES

Derek's parents, Derek's classmates, Mr. Higgins's colleagues

ODELL EDUCATION

DELINEATING ARGUMENTS: CASE STUDY

School Conflict

ISSUE

Recently, a student came to school wearing a T-shirt with a provocative graphic on it and what some people viewed as misogynistic lyrics from a song by a popular rap artist. A teacher who was offended by the shirt referred the student to the office, where the assistant principal told him to go home, change the shirt, and never wear it to school again. When the student refused to do so, he was suspended for insubordination. In protest, a large group of sympathetic students produced and wore T-shirts that read, "Life's a b . . . when you lose your right to free speech."

When asked to stop wearing the shirts, these students also refused to do so. Faced with the dilemma of what to do, the school administration is proposing changes to school policy and a dress code that prohibits clothing with any words, logos, graphics, or designer labels. Those opposed to the code claim that it essentially requires students to wear a school "uniform."

At a school board meeting, students and staff present arguments about the proposed policy change.

PERSPECTIVES

HIGH SCHOOL STUDENT

The junior class president, a male, has been one of the leaders of the T-shirt protest group. He sees the issue as a symbolic one and is opposed to policies and actions that deny students' rights. His parents, among the more affluent families in the school district, are active members of the American Civil Liberties Union (ACLU) and supported the production of the protesters' T-shirts.

He presents the following argument:

Any restriction on student dress violates students' basic rights. Once a student clothing choice is prohibited because it is considered "offensive," a precedent is set for limiting free speech in all areas of school life.

Americans, including American high school students, are guaranteed the right to free speech by the US Constitution. The First Amendment in the Bill of Rights states, "Congress shall make no law . . . abridging the freedom of speech. . . ."

Public schools are agencies of government, and therefore are expected to follow the law as established in the Constitution and Bill of Rights. The US Supreme Court has upheld the free speech rights of students. In a case similar to this one, Justice Abe Fortas wrote, "First Amendment rights, applied in light of the special characteristics of the school environment, are available to teachers and students. . ."

The school's argument to support banning the shirt was flawed. School officials said that the lyrics on the shirt were "offensive" and therefore "disruptive" to the school environment. As our protest T-shirts showed, however, there are many meanings for the word in question, most of which are not offensive to anyone. It is defined in the dictionary as meaning: "a female dog," "a difficult situation," or "a querulous, nagging complaint."

The protesters' T-shirts, which they were asked to remove, used the word to represent the "difficult situation" that will result if students' rights to free speech are not respected. The school administration has shown in a number of specific instances that it is more concerned with controlling student behavior than guaranteeing student rights. An example would be last spring in the student government elections, when posters making fun of some school rules were taken down.

In conclusion, restrictions on student dress violate students' basic rights. The school overstepped its bounds when it used an interpretation of the words on the shirt to argue that the shirt was offensive. The school's proposal of a more restrictive dress code will create a "difficult situation" in which students' rights may continue to be lost. Therefore, the wearing of such shirts should be allowed and the dress code should remain nonrestrictive so that we don't set a precedent that limits free speech in all areas of school life.

ODELL
EDUCATION

School Conflict (Continued)

HIGH SCHOOL PRINCIPAL

The high school principal, a woman, is concerned about disruptions in school resulting from the wearing of clothing that may be offensive to some students and staff members. Although she was personally offended by the words on the T-shirt, she has also tried to listen to and reason with the protesting students, to little avail. Regarding student dress in general, she is concerned that many of her students lack the money to afford the designer label clothing worn by some of her more affluent students and the class distinctions that result based mostly on student dress.

She presents the following argument:

The offensive T-shirt, and the student's refusal to remove it, put school administrators in a difficult, no-win situation. When the assistant principal asked the student to go home and change his shirt, he was making a "reasonable request," as defined in the school's Code of Conduct. When the student refused, the administrator had no choice but to suspend him for "insubordination."

The school has over 1,500 students and 100 staff members. Many staff members and a number of female students found the shirt's message and graphic to be offensive. In situations such as this one, the school administration must ensure that the school environment is not disrupted. Administrators often have to prioritize the "good of many" over the preferences of a few.

When the referring teacher and a group of students who accompanied her came to the office, they testified that they were "deeply offended" by how the shirt depicted women. They demanded that the student be sent home to change, and said they could not remain in class with him if he wore the shirt. In cases such as this, conflict often results. Our job is to prevent this sort of disruptive conflict.

Disruptive situations such as this incident can be prevented by a more uniform dress code. Shirts without any logos, graphics, or designer labels can not offend anyone and will not be seen as expressions of style, economic status (or free speech, for that matter). A more uniform dress code will help remove distinctions of class and lead to a more unified school community.

In conclusion, and because having to decide what is acceptable or offensive and what is not is a "slippery slope," the school administration therefore proposes a stricter dress code, clearly describing what is acceptable, uniform dress—with no words, logos, or graphics visible. In so doing, we can reduce the wearing of offensive clothing, disruptive interpersonal conflict, and class distinctions in our high school.

DELINEATING ARGUMENTS: CASE STUDY

Course Scheduling Conflict

ISSUE

It is spring and a eighth grader named Nicole is choosing classes for her ninth grade year. She is an excellent, well-rounded student with dreams of attending an Ivy League University. As they review the possible courses she can take next year, she and her parents discover that dance class and honors math will be given at the same time. Nicole has shown real talent in math and her teacher would like her to enroll in ninth grade honors math class. Nicole has been studying dance since she was 3 and wants to continue dancing in high school and perhaps beyond. The school's dance instructor used to be professional dancer and believes that if Nicole keeps studying, she may win a college scholarship for dance.

The guidance counselor has met with Nicole to explain the options. He always tries to allow students to select at least one course that they are really interested in taking. He has decided to hold a meeting with Nicole and her parents to make a decision. At the meeting, both Nicole and her parents present their positions.

PERSPECTIVES

NICOLE'S PARENTS

Nicole's parents have supported her participation in dance class since she was a young girl. They believe the extracurricular activities are important and want her to continue doing them. However, they believe the opportunity to take ninth grade honors math cannot be passed up because it will prepare her for upper level classes in high school and beyond. They consider taking this honors math class to be more important for providing her with those opportunities than taking the dance class.

They present the following argument:

We believe that being asked to take the honors math class presents an opportunity that cannot passed up-regardless of other courses that Nicole may want to take.

The honors math class will prepare Nicole to take upper level math classes like Calculus in high school. Taking Calculus in high school will allow her to earn college credit and start college in an advanced math course, thus, lowering the number of courses she has to take in college.

To get into a good college or university, students usually need to do well on the ACT or the SAT. There are other important components of college applications, but strong SAT/ACT match scores will show Nicole's academic talent.

Also, many high paying careers require a strong background in math and science. You need to be an innovator and have strong reasoning and problem-solving skills in today's job market. Nicole can develop these skills in higher-level math classes.

In conclusion, if Nicole wants to attend an Ivy League school and have the opportunity to get a good job, she needs to develop her abilities in the honors math class. It is difficult to give up on dance for a year but perhaps we can find another way to take dance class the following year. The opportunities the math class will provide her over the course of her life are limitless and are more important than one year of dance class.

NICOLE

Nicole wants to attend an Ivy League school and is committed to working hard to get good grades, participating in extracurricular activities, and volunteering to help boost her resume. She loves to dance because she has been doing it since she was very young, her best friends are all dancers, and she knows that to be considered for an Ivy League school, you have to have more than just good grades and test scores. She wants to take the honors math course, but not if it means giving up on her dance class which she believes is just as important.

She presents the following argument:

Dance is not easy. It takes a lot of training to do it well. Dancers practice steps thousands of times to become good at them. This type of dedication is something that dance has taught me and something I know will be required in Ivy League schools. I know it is not an academic course, but the skills of persistence, perfection, and passion I am learning through dance will be transferable to school.

Course Scheduling Conflict (Continued)

Participating in extra-curricular activities like dance is very important in the college applications. I know that schools expect you to be well rounded. This means participating in non-academic activities inside and outside of school. My dance career will look very nice on my resume when I am applying to school.

I am still a kid. I know I have ambitious goals and want to go to college and have a good career. But, I'm 12 years old and dance is who I am. Shouldn't I be able to still have fun, socialize with my friends, and follow my passions? Isn't that what most adults do? I already get straight As, volunteer, and have become an exceptional dancer. What is wrong with the path I'm on?

So, I would not be the person that I am without dance. I want to take the honors math course but not if it means missing a year of dance class with my dance teacher and friends. I do know the importance of developing my math skills and preparing for college admissions examinations, but I also cannot consider my life without dance in it right now.

OTHER PERSPECTIVES:

Guidance Counselor, Dance Instructor, Nicole's older sibling, Nicole's friend

DELINEATING ARGUMENTS: CASE STUDY

Tweeting about a Pop Quiz

ISSUE

Justin has Spanish class during first period. When the bell rings Monday morning, the teacher announces that there will be a pop quiz. Justin studied over the weekend, so he's confident he did well on the quiz. His friend Mark, however, told Justin on the ride to school that he didn't study at all. Mark has the same teacher during third period. Justin decides to Tweet a warning to Mark about the pop quiz so that Mark will have second period to study. Mark sees the Tweet and he studies during his history class.

His grade on the pop quiz is much higher than his average grade for the course, so the teacher becomes suspicious. The teacher eventually finds out that Justin Tweeted a warning to Mark about the quiz. The teacher calls a meeting with Justin and the school principal to inform Justin that the Tweet was cheating and he will be penalized as such. Justin argues that the Tweet isn't cheating and he shouldn't be punished for letting Mark know about the quiz.

PERSPECTIVES

THE TEACHER

The teacher has been at the school for more than twenty years. During that time, she has earned a reputation as a hard but fair grader. She has been nominated for teacher of the year several times. She has a policy in her class that cell phones are not allowed to be on.

The teacher explains why she considers the Tweet to be cheating:

When I decide to give a pop quiz, I want to evaluate whether my students are keeping up with the ideas and homework in my course. These quizzes need to be surprises in order to evaluate students' commitment to my course. I don't announce these quizzes ahead of time because this will just encourage students to study at the last minute. This doesn't provide the insight I want into students' performance. Because Justin sent that message to his friend, there was an opportunity for his friend and anyone else who heard about this message to prepare for the quiz. This is an unfair advantage and the grades for the third-period quizzes will almost certainly be higher. This isn't fair to my first-period students. In addition to undermining my quiz, Justin has also created extra work for me. I'll have to redo the quiz at another surprise point in the course. I am going to have to deal with complaints from students who did well on the quiz but will have to take a replacement.

JUSTIN

Justin is a good student. His GPA is a 3.7 and he takes a couple of AP courses. He is also involved in the speech and debate team and the chess club. He glazes hams for extra money on the weekend. He and Mark have been friends for five years, though they aren't best friends. Mark moved to Justin's street so they often see one another over the weekend. Justin knows that Mark struggles with school.

Justin defends his decision to Tweet with the following statement:

Sending a Tweet isn't cheating because I didn't tell Mark or anyone else who saw the Tweet what was on the quiz. I just said that we had a quiz so they might have a quiz. I had no idea if the teacher was going to have a quiz for the third-period class. I can't read her mind. What I did isn't different from the other students who told their friends about the quiz in person. Besides, couldn't Mark have thought there might be a quiz even if he hadn't seen the Tweet? At the end of the day, Mark studied and did well, so I don't see what the problem is. It doesn't matter what I Tweeted or what he thought. What matters is that he spent time preparing for the quiz and he earned his grade.

OTHER PERSPECTIVES

Other students, the principal, the teacher's colleagues

ODELL
EDUCATION

HABITS-BASED TEXT-CENTERED DISCUSSION CHECKLIST

DISCUSSION HABITS	DESCRIPTORS: *When—and how well—have I demonstrated these habits?*	EXAMPLES FROM *TEXT-CENTERED DISCUSSIONS*
PREPARING	Reads the text(s) closely and thinks about the questions to prepare for a text-centered discussion	
COLLABORATING	Pays attention to other participants while participating in and leading a text-centered discussion	
COMMUNICATING CLEARLY	Presents ideas and supporting evidence so others can understand them	

ODELL
EDUCATION

PEER REVIEW OF POSITIONS CHECKLIST

LITERACY SKILLS	DESCRIPTORS: *Find evidence of using the Literacy Skill in the draft.* *Does the writer's paragraph . . .*	NEEDS WORK	OKAY	VERY STRONG
FORMING CLAIMS	State a meaningful position that is well supported by evidence from the unit texts?			
EVALUATING INFORMATION	Assess the relevance, credibility, and logic of information encountered in the texts?			
USING EVIDENCE	Present a comprehensive view of the issue by providing textual evidence to support claims?			
RECOGNIZING PERSPECTIVE	Identify and explain an author's view of the text's topic?			

PLAN FOR WRITING AN ARGUMENT CHECKLIST

LITERACY SKILLS	DESCRIPTORS: *Find evidence of using the Literacy Skill in the draft.* *Does the writer's plan . . .*	NEEDS WORK	OKAY	VERY STRONG
FORMING CLAIMS	Establish a clear position that is supported by valid claims (premises)?			
USING EVIDENCE	Present comprehensive and well-chosen details from texts to explain and support claims?			
USING LOGIC	Support the position through a logical sequence of related claims, premises, and supporting evidence?			

ODELL
EDUCATION

BUILDING EVIDENCE-BASED ARGUMENTS TARGETED LITERACY SKILLS

TARGETED SKILLS	DESCRIPTORS
RECOGNIZING PERSPECTIVE	Uses textual details to recognize and establish a perspective on a topic
EVALUATING INFORMATION	Assesses the relevance and credibility of information, ideas, evidence, and logic presented in texts
DELINEATING ARGUMENTATION	Identifies and analyzes the components and accuracy of claims, evidence, and reasoning in explanations and arguments
FORMING CLAIMS	Establishes and presents a clear and defensible position that is supported by a series of valid premises and set in the context of the topic
USING EVIDENCE	Presents a comprehensive view of the issue by providing textual evidence to support claims and uses sufficient and accurate quotations, paraphrases, and references
USING LOGIC	Establishes and supports a position through a logical sequence of related premises and supporting evidence
ORGANIZING IDEAS	Sequences sentences, paragraphs, and parts of an essay to establish a coherent, logical, and unified argument
USING CONVENTIONS	Uses effective sentence structure, grammar, punctuation, and spelling to express ideas and achieve writing and speaking purposes
PUBLISHING	Uses effective formatting and citations to present ideas for specific audiences and purposes
REFLECTING CRITICALLY	Uses literacy terminology and concepts to reflect on, discuss, and evaluate personal and peer literacy development

BUILDING EVIDENCE-BASED ARGUMENTS
ACADEMIC HABITS DEVELOPED

HABITS DEVELOPED	DESCRIPTORS
REMAINING OPEN	Adopts a stance of inquiry—asking questions to learn more—rather than arguing for entrenched positions
QUALIFYING VIEWS	Modifies and further justifies ideas in response to thinking from others
REVISING	Rethinks and refines work based on teacher-, peer-, and self-review processes

ODELL
EDUCATION

BUILDING EVIDENCE-BASED ARGUMENTS LITERACY SKILLS AND ACADEMIC HABITS RUBRIC

Name _ _ _ _ _ _ _ _ _ _ _ _ _ _ _ _ _ **Text** _ _ _ _ _ _ _ _ _ _ _ _ _ _ _ _ _

NE: Not enough evidence to make a rating

1—**Emerging:** needs improvement

2—**Developing:** shows progress

3—**Becoming Proficient:** demonstrates skills

4—**Excelling:** exceeds expectations

+—**Growth:** evidence of growth within the unit or task

I. READING SKILLS CRITERIA	NE	1	2	3	4	+
1. **Recognizes Perspective:** Uses textual details to recognize authors' perspectives on a topic						
2. **Delineates Argumentation:** Identifies and analyzes the components and accuracy of claims, evidence, and reasoning in explanations and arguments						
3. **Evaluates Information:** Assesses the relevance and credibility of information, ideas, evidence, and logic presented in texts						
II. DEVELOPING AN EVIDENCE-BASED POSITION: SKILLS AND HABITS CRITERIA	NE	1	2	3	4	+
1. **Remains Open:** Adopts a stance of inquiry—asking questions to learn more—rather than arguing for entrenched positions						
2. **Qualifies Views:** Modifies and further justifies ideas in response to thinking from others						
3. **Revises:** Rethinks and refines work based on teacher-, peer-, and self-review processes						
4. **Reflects Critically:** Uses literacy terminology and concepts to reflect on, discuss, and evaluate personal and peer literacy development						
III. EVIDENCE-BASED WRITING CRITERIA	NE	1	2	3	4	+
1. **Forms Claims:** Establishes and presents a clear and defensible position that is supported by a series of valid premises and set in the context of the topic						
2. **Uses Evidence:** Presents a comprehensive view of the issue by providing textual evidence to support claims and using sufficient and accurate quotations, paraphrases, and references						
3. **Uses Language:** Selects and combines words that precisely communicate ideas, generate appropriate tone, and evoke intended responses from an audience						

EBA SKILLS AND HABITS RUBRIC (Continued)

	NE	1	2	3	4	+
4. **Uses Logic:** Establishes and supports a position through a logical sequence of related premises and supporting evidence						
5. **Organizes Ideas:** Sequences sentences and paragraphs to establish a coherent, logical, and unified argument						
6. **Uses Conventions:** Uses effective sentence structure, grammar, punctuation, and spelling to express ideas and achieve writing purposes						
7. **Publishes:** Uses effective formatting and citations to present ideas						
IV. FINAL ASSIGNMENT CRITERIA	**NE**	**1**	**2**	**3**	**4**	**+**
1. Presents a convincing argument that stems from an understanding of the issue, a reasoned perspective, and a clear, defensible position						
2. Organizes a set of evidence-based claims in a logical sequence that explains and supports the thesis of the argument						
3. Uses and cites relevant and credible (trustworthy) evidence to support all claims, counterarguments, and the overall position						
4. Revises essay based on teacher and peer feedback						
SUMMARY EVALUATION		**1**	**2**	**3**	**4**	

Comments:

1. Explanation of ratings—**evidence** found (or not found) in the work:

2. Strengths and **areas of growth** observed in the work:

3. Areas for improvement in future work:

ODELL
EDUCATION

BUILDING EVIDENCE-BASED ARGUMENTS LITERACY SKILLS AND ACADEMIC HABITS CHECKLIST

		EVIDENCE-BASED ARGUMENTATION LITERACY SKILLS AND ACADEMIC HABITS	✔	EVIDENCE Demonstrating the SKILLS AND HABITS
READING		1. **Recognizing Perspective:** Identifies and explains the author's view of the text's topic		
		2. **Evaluating Information:** Assesses the relevance and credibility of information in texts		
		3. **Delineating Argumentation:** Identifies and analyzes the claims, evidence, and reasoning in arguments		
ACADEMIC HABITS		4. **Remaining Open:** Asks questions of others rather than arguing for a personal idea or opinion		
		5. **Qualifying Views:** Explains and changes ideas in response to thinking from others		
		6. **Revising:** Rethinks ideas and refines work based on feedback from others		
		7. **Reflecting Critically:** Uses literacy concepts to discuss and evaluate personal and peer learning		
WRITING SKILLS		8. **Forming Claims:** States a meaningful position that is well supported by evidence from texts		
		9. **Using Evidence:** Uses well-chosen details from texts to explain and support claims; accurately paraphrases or quotes		
		10. **Using Logic:** Supports a position through a logical sequence of related claims, premises, and supporting evidence		
		11. **Organizing Ideas:** Organizes claims, supporting ideas, and evidence in a logical order		
		12. **Using Language:** Writes clearly so others can understand claims and ideas		
		13. **Using Conventions:** Correctly uses sentence elements, punctuation, and spelling to produce clear writing		
		14. **Publishing:** Correctly uses, formats, and cites textual evidence to support claims		
		General comments:		

ODELL EDUCATION

NOTES